MARQUEE SERIES

MICROSOFT®
OFFICE
2003

MW01121126

EMCParadigm
PUBLISHING

NITA RUTKOSKY
Pierce College at Puyallup – Puyallup, Washington

DENISE SEGUIN
Fanshawe College – London, Ontario

The Marquee Series Team: Desiree Faulkner, Developmental Editor; Leslie Anderson, Senior Designer; Jennifer Wreisner, Cover Designer; Leslie Anderson, Erica Tava, Desktop Production; Teri Linander, Tester; Sharon O'Donnell, Copyeditor; Lynn Reichel, Proofreader; and Nancy Fulton, Indexer.

Publishing Team: George Provol, Publisher; Janice Johnson, Director of Product Development; Tony Galvin, Acquisitions Editor; Lori Landwer, Marketing Manager; Shelley Clubb, Electronic Design and Production Manager.

Acknowledgment: The authors and publisher wish to thank the following reviewer for her technical and academic assistance in testing exercises and assessing instruction: Susan Lynn Bowen, Valdosta Technical College, Valdosta, GA.

Library of Congress Cataloging-in-Publication Data

Rutkosky, Nita Hewitt.
Microsoft Office 2003 / Nita Rutkosky, Denise Seguin.
p.cm. – (Marquee series)
Includes index.
ISBN 0-7638-2077-6 (text) – ISBN 0-7638-2074-1 (text & CD)
1. Microsoft Office. 2. Business—Computer programs. I. Seguin, Denise. II. Series

Text + CD: 0-7638-2074-1
Order Number: 05629

© 2004 by Paradigm Publishing Inc.
Published by **EMC**Paradigm
875 Montreal Way
St. Paul, MN 55102

(800) 535-6865
E-mail: educate@emcp.com
Web site: www.emcp.com

CONTENTS

Marquee MICROSOFT® WORD 2003

MICROSOFT OFFICE SPECIALIST SKILLS

Reference No.	Skill	Pages
WW03S-1	**Creating Content**	
WW03S-1-1	Insert and edit text, symbols and special characters	
	Insert and delete text	4-5, 8-9
	Insert special symbols and characters	48-49
	Insert hidden text	38-39
	Check spelling and grammar in a document	10-13
	Use Thesaurus to find synonyms for specific words	14-15
	Cut, copy, and paste text	78-79
	Use the Office Clipboard	80-81
	Use the Paste Special dialog box	78-79
WW03S-1-2	Insert frequently used and pre-defined text	
	Insert date and time	22-23
	Add words to and delete words from AutoCorrect	14-15
	Insert predefined AutoText	22-23
	Create and insert AutoText	62-63
WW03S-1-3	Navigate to specific content	
	Move insertion point within a document	4-5
	Scroll within a document	6-7
	Find and replace text	74-75
	Find and replace formatting	76-77
	Navigate in a document using Go To	6-7
	Navigate in document using Document Map	18-19
WW03S-1-4	Insert, position and size graphics	
	Insert, size, format, and move images	88-89
	Draw, size, format, and move shapes and text boxes	90-93
WW03S-1-5	Create and modify diagrams and charts	128-129
WW03S-1-6	Locate, select and insert supporting information	113-114
WW03S-2	**Organizing Content**	
WW03S-2-1	Insert and modify tables	
	Create and modify a table	106-107
	Customize and format a table	108-109
	Apply borders, shading, and autoformats to a table	110-111
	Convert text to a table	112-113
WW03S-2-2	Create bulleted lists, numbered lists and outlines	
	Insert bullets and numbering	46-47
	Create custom bullets	60-61
	Create an outline	122-123
WW03S-2-3	Format and modify hyperlinks	118-119
WW03S-3	**Formatting Content**	
WW03S-3-1	Format text	
	Change font, font style, font size	34-37
	Highlight text	16-17
	Apply text effects	38-39
	Adjust character spacing	36-37
	Apply styles to text and lists	58-59
	Apply a table style	112-113
	Clear style formatting	58-59
WW03S-3-2	Format paragraphs	
	Apply borders and shading	54-55
	Indent text	42-43
	Change line spacing and paragraph spacing	44-45
	Change alignment of text	40-41
	Set, modify, and remove tabs	50-53
WW03S-3-3	Apply and format columns	114-115
WW03S-3-4	Insert and modify content in headers and footers	14-15
	Insert and modify headers and footers	78-79
	Insert and format page numbering	80-81
WW03S-3-5	Modify document layout and page setup	
	Insert and delete a hard page break	78-79
	Insert and delete a hard section break	82-83
	Change margins and page orientation	82-83
WW03S-4	**Collaborating**	
WW03S-4-1	Circulate documents for review	114-115
WW03S-4-2	Compare and merge document versions	120-121
WW03S-4-3	Insert, view and edit comments	120-121
WW03S-4-4	Track, accept and reject proposed changes	124-127
WW03S-5	**Formatting and Managing Documents**	
WW03S-5-1	Create new documents using templates	24-25
WW03S-5-2	Review and modify document properties	
	Review and modify document properties	6-7
	Display word, paragraph, and character counts	10-13
WW03S-5-3	Organize documents using file folders	
	Create, rename, and delete folders; select documents	26-27
WW03S-5-4	Save documents in appropriate formats for different uses	
	Save a document in a different format	26-27
	Save a document as a Web page	118-119
WW03S-5-5	Print documents, envelopes and labels	
	Print documents	20-21
	Print envelopes	94-95
	Print labels	96-97
WW03S-5-6	Preview documents and Web pages	
	Preview a document	20-21
	Preview a document in Web Page Preview	118-119
WW03S-5-7	Change and organize document views and windows	
	Reveal formatting	76-77
	Reveal hidden text	38-39
	View and navigate in Reading layout, change document views and zoom, display full screen, and show/hide white space	18-19
	Split and arrange windows	84-85

Marquee MICROSOFT® EXCEL 2003

MICROSOFT OFFICE SPECIALIST SKILLS

Reference No.	Skill	Pages
XL03S-1	**Creating Data and Content**	
XL03S-1-1	Enter and Edit Cell Contents	
	Enter and edit data in cells	2-9, 28-31
	Fill series content using the fill handle	6-9, 28-31
	Clear data in cells	34-35
XL03S-1-2	Navigate to specific cell content	
	Finding and modifying or replacing cell content or formatting	54-55, 60
	Navigating to specific cell content (Go To)	24-25
XL03S-1-3	Locate, select, and insert supporting information	
	Research and request information	120-123
	Insert research information	120-123
XL03S-1-4	Insert, position, and size graphics	86-89, 93-95
XL03S-2	**Analyzing Data**	
XL03S-2-1	Filter lists using AutoFilter	116-117, 134
XL03S-2-2	Sort lists	116-117, 134
XL03S-2-3	Insert and modify formulas	
	Use AutoSum button to insert formula	12-13, 28
	Create and edit formulas including entering ranges by dragging	10-11, 28-31
	Insert formulas with the Insert Function button and edit formulas	72-73
	Use absolute and mixed cell references in formulas	14-15, 62
	Copy relative formulas	102-105,
	Create a formula that references other worksheets	130, 133
XL03S-2-4	Use statistical, date and time, financial, and logical functions	66-73,
XL03S-2-5	Create, modify, and position diagrams and charts based on worksheet data	91-94
	Create, edit, and position diagrams	118-119, 132
	Create, edit and position charts	80-85, 93-94
XL03S-3	**Formatting Data and Content**	
XL03S-3-1	Apply and modify cell formats	
	Apply and modify cell formats	50-53
	Format cells with AutoFormat	44-45
	Apply formatting using the Formatting toolbar	61-63
	Format data in cells; adjust decimal places	46-47, 61-63
	Apply borders and shading to cells	50-53, 61-63
	Align and indent text	48-49, 60-61
XL03S-3-2	Apply and modify cell styles	112-113, 132, 133
XL03S-3-3	Modify row and column formats	
	Change column width and row heights	42-43, 60, 63
	Insert, delete, hide, and unhide rows and columns	38-39, 46, 60, 62
XL03S-3-4	Format worksheets	
	Format worksheets	104-105, 130
	Format worksheet tabs	
	Hide and unhide a worksheet in a workbook	98-101
	Add a background image to a worksheet	105
XL03S-4	**Collaborating**	
XL03S-4-1	Insert, view, and edit comments	118-119, 132, 134
XL03S-5	**Managing Workbooks**	
XL03S-5-1	Create new workbooks from templates	110-111, 131, 135
XL03S-5-2	Insert, delete, and move cells	36-37, 60
	Insert and delete selected cells	40-41
	Cut, copy, and paste selected cells	
	Use Paste Special options when pasting copied cells	102-105
XL03S-5-3	Create and modify hyperlinks	114-115
XL03S-5-4	Organize Worksheets	
	Insert, delete, and rename worksheets	98-99, 130, 133
	Move and copy a worksheet	100-101, 130
XL03S-5-5	Preview data in other views	
	Preview a worksheet	22-23
	Preview page breaks in Page Break view	108-109
	Preview a worksheet in Web Page preview	114, 132-133
XL03S-5-6	Customize window layout	
	Split a worksheet into windows and freeze and unfreeze panes	56-57, 61
	Arrange, hide, and unhide workbooks	124-125
XL03S-5-7	Setup pages for printing	
	Print selected ranges and specify a print area	106-107
	Change worksheet orientation	23, 49, 53, 75
	Insert headers and footers in a worksheet	76-77, 91, 94
	Viewing and modifying page breaks	108-109
	Change worksheet margins, center horizontally and vertically	74-75, 94
	Print column and row titles on multiple pages, print gridlines	78-79, 91, 109
XL03S-5-8	Print data	
	Print data	106-107, 130
	Print selected ranges, worksheets, and workbooks	
XL03S-5-9	Organize workbooks using file folders	126-127
	Create, rename, and use folders for workbook storage	130
XL03S-5-10	Save data in appropriate formats for different uses	
	Convert a workbook to a different file format (csv)	126-127
	Save Excel data as a Web page	114-115, 132-133

Marquee MICROSOFT® ACCESS 2003

MICROSOFT OFFICE SPECIALIST SKILLS

Reference No.	Skill	Pages
AC03S-1	**Structuring Databases**	
AC03S-1-1	Create Access databases	
	Create a database using the Database Wizard	126-127
	Create blank databases	
AC03S-1-2	Create and modify tables	63-64, 96,136
	Create a table in design view	34-37, 59, 61
	Create a table using the Table Wizard	48-49, 60
	Modify table structure	38-41, 59, 62, 98-99, 130
AC03S-1-3	Define and modify field types	34-37, 59, 61
	Define, assign, and create field types	
	Create Lookup field	46-47, 61
AC03S-1-4	Modify field properties	42-45, 59, 62
	Create input masks	
	Change field properties in Table Design view	38-41, 59-60, 62, 64
AC03S-1-5	Create and modify one-to-many relationships	
	Create a one-to-many relationship between tables	52-53, 60, 62-63
AC03S-1-6	Enforce referential integrity	52-53, 60, 62-63
AC03S-1-7	Create and modify queries	66-67, 70-71, 94
	Create select queries in Design view	
	Create select queries using the Simple Query Wizard	68-69, 92
	Create a Crosstab query	102-103, 130
	Create a Find Duplicates query	108-109, 130
	Create an Unmatched query	104-107, 130
AC03S-1-8	Create forms	76-79, 93, 95
	Create a form using the Form Wizard	76-77
	Create an AutoForm	
AC03S-1-9	Add and modify form controls and properties	80-83, 93, 95
	Add, move, resize, and format control objects	110-113, 132
	Add a calculated control, align and space controls	
AC03S-1-10	Create reports	84-87, 93-94, 133
	Create a report using the Report Wizard	88-89
AC03S-1-11	Add and modify report control properties including calculated controls	114-117, 131, 133
AC03S-1-12	Create a data access page using the Page Wizard	122-123, 132, 135
AC03S-2	**Entering Data**	
AC03S-2-1	Enter, edit and delete records	
	Enter data in a table	10-11,
	Add and delete records	29-30
AC03S-2-2	Find and move among records	12-15, 28, 30
	Find records with specific data and replace with other data	8-9
	Using navigation controls to move among records	6-7
AC03S-2-3	Import structured data to Access	144-145, 151
	Import data to a new table	151
	Link data to a new table	146-149, 151
AC03S-3	**Organizing Data**	
AC03S-3-1	Create and modify calculated fields and aggregate functions	
	Add calculated fields to a query in Query Design view	72-73, 92
	Use aggregate functions (e.g. AVG, COUNT)	74-75, 92
AC03S-3-2	Modify form layout	
	Aligning and spacing controls	80-81, 93, 95
	Showing and hiding headers and footers	82-83, 93, 95
AC03S-3-3	Modify report layout and page setup	
	Align, resize, and space controls	88-89, 93-94, 114-117
	Change margins and page orientation	18-19, 114-117
AC03S-3-4	Format datasheets	50-51, 60
AC03S-3-5	Sort records	
	Sort records in a table	16-17, 29-30
	Sort fields in a query	69, 92, 94
	Sort records in a form	113
	Sort records in a report	114-117
AC03S-3-6	Filter records	100-101, 134
	Filter by selection	
	Filter by form	100-101, 132
AC03S-4	**Managing Databases**	
AC03S-4-1	Identify object dependencies	124-125
AC03S-4-2	View objects and object data in other views	18-19
	Previewing for print	2-7
	Using Datasheet view	18-19
	Use PivotTable and PivotChart view	118-121, 131, 134
	View Web pages	123, 135
AC03S-4-3	Print database objects and data	18-19
AC03S-4-4	Export data from Access	138-143, 150
AC03S-4-5	Back up a database	24-25,
AC03S-4-6	Compact and repair databases	22-23, 29, 31

Marquee MICROSOFT® POWERPOINT 2003

MICROSOFT OFFICE SPECIALIST SKILLS

Reference No.	Skill	Pages
PP03S-1	**Creating Content**	
PP03S-1-1	Create new presentations from templates	
	Create a presentation using a design template	6-9
	Create a presentation using the AutoContent Wizard	2-5
PP03S-1-2	Insert and edit text-based content	
	Insert and edit text in slides	6-9, 14-15
	Insert slides	10-11
	Complete a spelling check and use Thesaurus	16-19
	Import text from Word	132-133
PP03S-1-3	Insert table, charts and diagrams	
	Insert a table	80-81
	Customize and format a table	102-103
	Insert an organizational chart and diagram	84-85
PP03S-1-4	Insert pictures, shapes and graphics	
	Insert, size, move, and modify a clip art image	52-55; 52-55; 70-71
	Insert a logo	74-75
	Insert and format WordArt	
	Draw and customize an autoshape, text box, and connector line	76-77
PP03S-1-5	Insert Objects	
	Link an Excel chart with a presentation and edit a linked chart	134-137
	Embed a Word table in a presentation and edit the table	138-141
PP03S-2	**Formatting Content**	
PP03S-2-1	Format text-based content	
	Change text font typeface, style, size and color	40-43
	Change the default font and replace fonts	44-45
	Format with Format Painter	46-47
	Change alignment and line and paragraph spacing	48-49
PP03S-2-2	Format pictures, shapes and graphics	
	Insert, size, and move an image and format images using buttons on the Picture toolbar	52-53
	Draw and customize an autoshape, text box, and connector line	54-55
	Copying and rotating shapes	76-77
PP03S-2-3	Format slides	
	Apply a design template	6-9
	Choose a slide layout	12-13
	Change the slide layout	14-15
	Change the slide design and color scheme	14-15
	Modify page setup	24-25
PP03S-2-4	Apply animation schemes	56-57
PP03S-2-5	Apply slide transitions	22-23
PP03S-2-6	Customize slide templates	118-119
PP03S-2-7	Work with masters	86-87
	Insert headers and footers	
	Format with a slide master and title master slide	70-73
	Manage multiple slide masters	98-99
	Arrange placeholders on slide	14-15
PP03S-3	**Collaborating**	
PP03S-3-1	Track, accept and reject changes in a presentation	106-111
PP03S-3-2	Add, edit and delete comments in a presentation	114-115
PP03S-3-3	Compare and merge presentations	110-111
PP03S-4	**Managing and Delivering Presentations**	
PP03S-4-1	Organize a presentation	6-11
	Insert a slide	34-35
	Rearrange and delete slides	12-13
	Change views	88-89
	Insert a hyperlink	78-79
	Display guide lines and the grid	
PP03S-4-2	Set up slide shows for delivery	100-101
	Create and edit a custom show	82-83
	Insert action buttons	34-35
	Hide and unhide slides	112-113
PP03S-4-3	Rehearse timings	18-19
PP03S-4-4	Deliver presentations	
	Run a slide show	
	Use the pen and highlighter when running a presentation	20-21
PP03S-4-5	Prepare presentations for remote delivery	116-117
PP03S-4-6	Save and publish presentations	116-117
	Save a presentation in a different format	118-119
	Create a folder for presentation storage	88-89;
	Publish a presentation to the Web	120-121
PP03S-4-7	Print slides, outlines, handouts, and speaker notes	24-25
PP03S-4-8	Export a presentation to another Microsoft Office program	130-131

WELCOME

EMC/Paradigm's Office 2003 Marquee Series presents Office 2003 program features in a visual, project-based manner. You are introduced to a topic, read a short paragraph or two about the topic, and then complete a hands-on computer project. The book includes several additional features to enhance your learning, including:

- *Application Openers*—Provides a showcase of model answers.
- *In Addition*—Provides related information about the task or topic.
- *In Brief*—Identifies the steps required to accomplish a task.
- *Features Summary*—Summary of features learned in a specific section.
- *Procedures Check*—A knowledge self-check.
- *Skills Review*—Additional hands-on computer exercises to enhance learning.
- *Performance Plus*—A third level of computer activities requiring you to demonstrate mastery of computer skills as well as decision-making skills.
- *Help Activity*—Computer activity requiring use of the Help feature.
- *Internet Activity*—Computer activity involving research on the Internet.

The CD that accompanies this textbook contains prekeyed documents and files required for completing projects and activities. A CD icon and folder name displayed on the opening page of a section indicates that you need to copy a folder of files from the CD to your disk before beginning the section projects and activities. *(See the inside back cover for instructions on copying a folder.)*

Microsoft Office Specialist Certification

The Microsoft Office Specialist program is the only Microsoft approved program in the world for certifying proficiency in Microsoft Office desktop applications. The display of the Microsoft Office Specialist logo on the cover and title page of the Marquee Series *Office 2003* text means that this text has been approved to prepare students for the Specialist certification exams in Word, Excel, Access, and PowerPoint.

Office 2003 Marquee Series Ancillaries

Office 2003 Marquee Series includes some important resources that will help you succeed in your computer application course, including:

Online Resource Center

Internet Resource Centers hosted by EMC/Paradigm provide additional material for students and teachers using the Office 2003 Marquee Series textbooks. Online you will find Web links, updates to textbooks, study tips, quizzes and assignments, and supplementary projects.

Snap: A Web-based Tutorial and Skills Assessment Program

Snap is a Web-based program designed to optimize skill-based learning for Microsoft Office 2003. Snap course work simulates all operations of Office 2003 and is comprised of a web-based learning management system, multimedia tutorials, performance skill items, concept test bank, and online grade book and course planning tools.

Class Connection

Available for both WebCT and Blackboard e-learning platforms, EMC/Paradigm's Class Connection is a course management tool for traditional and distance learning. The Class Connection allows students to access the course syllabus and assignment schedule online, provides self-quizzes and study aids, and facilitates communication among students and instructors via e-mail and e-discussion.

MARQUEE SERIES

MICROSOFT®

WINDOWS XP

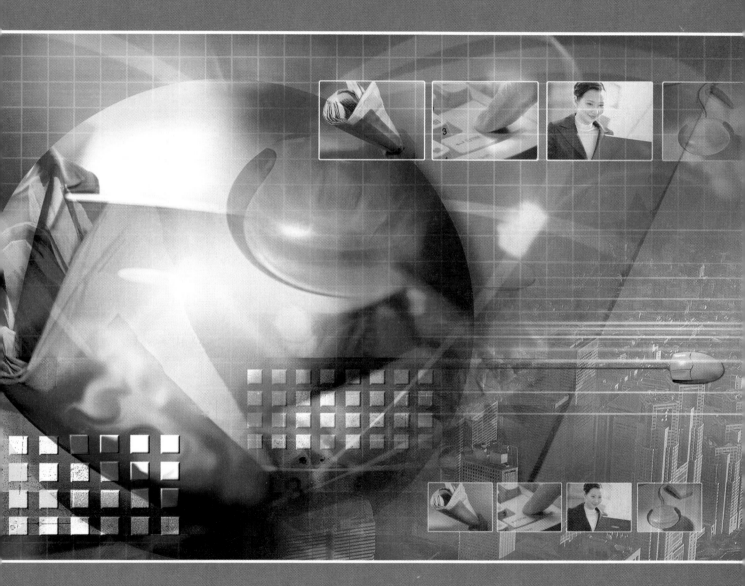

NITA RUTKOSKY
Pierce College at Puyallup – Puyallup, Washington

DENISE SEGUIN
Fanshawe College – London, Ontario

CONTENTS

The Marquee Series Team: Desiree Faulkner, Developmental Editor; Leslie Anderson, Senior Designer; Jennifer Wreisner, Cover Designer; Leslie Anderson, Erica Tava, Desktop Production.

Publishing Team: George Provol, Publisher; Janice Johnson, Director of Product Development; Tony Galvin, Acquisitions Editor; Lori Landwer, Marketing Manager; Shelley Clubb, Electronic Design and Production Manager.

Acknowledgment: The authors and publisher wish to thank the following reviewer for her technical and academic assistance in testing exercises and assessing instruction: Susan Lynn Bowen, Valdosta Technical College, Valdosta, GA.

© 2004 by Paradigm Publishing Inc.

Published by **EMC**Paradigm
875 Montreal Way
St. Paul, MN 55102

(800) 535-6865
E-mail: educate@emcp.com
Web site: www.emcp.com

Printed in the United States of America

10 9 8 7 6 5 4 3 2

Exploring Windows XP

A computer system consists of hardware and software. Hardware is the physical equipment while software is the instructions that tell the computer what to do. The main software, called the *operating system*, controls and manages the computer by translating instructions into a language the hardware can understand. In this section, you will learn about the Windows XP Professional operating system. Windows XP provides instructions on a multitude of processes, including loading programs, managing data, directing the flow of information to peripheral equipment, and displaying information. In this section, you will explore the Windows XP desktop and learn the skills and complete the project described here.

Skills

- Display the Windows XP desktop
- Perform the following actions using the mouse: point, click, double-click, and drag
- Start and close a program
- Open and close a window
- Shut down Windows XP
- Move a window
- Minimize, maximize, and restore a window
- Cascade and tile windows
- Display the Date and Time Properties dialog box
- Use components of a dialog box
- Display the Volume slider
- Display the Taskbar and Start Menu Properties dialog box

Project

Your department at Worldwide Enterprises has received new computers with the Windows XP operating system. You will explore the Windows XP desktop; open, close, and manipulate windows; open a program using the Start button; use options in the notification area of the Taskbar; and customize the Taskbar.

1.1 Exploring the Windows XP Desktop

The main portion of the screen that displays when Windows XP is loaded is called the *desktop*. This desktop can be compared to the top of a desk in an office. A business person places necessary tools—such as pencils, pens, paper, files, calculator—on his or her desktop to perform functions. Like those tools, the Windows XP desktop contains tools for operating the computer. These tools are logically grouped and placed in dialog boxes or windows that can be accessed using the icons located on the Windows XP desktop.

PROJECT: You work for Worldwide Enterprises and your department has just received new computers with the Windows XP operating system. You want to explore the Windows XP desktop to familiarize yourself with this new operating system.

STEPS

1 Complete the steps needed to display the Windows XP desktop.

Check with your instructor to determine the specific steps required to display Windows XP on your computer. This may be as simple as turning on the computer or may involve additional steps for logging on the computer system. When Windows XP is loaded, you will see a desktop similar to the one shown in Figure WIN1.1. Generally, the Windows XP desktop displays with one icon. Your desktop may contain additional icons.

FIGURE WIN1.1 Windows XP Desktop

Taskbar

Start Button

Icon

Recycle Bin

Notification Area

2 Move the mouse on the desk and notice how the corresponding pointer moves in the Windows desktop.

The mouse is a device that controls the pointer that identifies your location on the screen. Move the mouse on the desk (preferably on a mouse pad) and the pointer moves on the screen. For information on mouse terms, refer to Table WIN1.1 and for information on mouse icons, refer to Table WIN1.2.

TABLE WIN1.1 Mouse Terms

Term	Action
Point	Position the mouse pointer on the desired item.
Click	Quickly tap a button on the mouse once.
Double-click	Tap the left mouse button twice in quick succession.
Drag	Press and hold down the mouse button, move the mouse pointer to a specific location, and then release the mouse button.

TABLE WIN1.2 Mouse Icons

Icon	Description
I	The mouse appears as an I-beam pointer in a program screen where you enter text (such as Microsoft Word) and also in text boxes. You can use the I-beam pointer to move the insertion point or select text.
↖	The mouse pointer appears as an arrow pointing up and to the left (called the *arrow pointer*) on the Windows desktop and also in other program Title bars, Menu bars, and toolbars.
↗ ↖ ↔ ↕	The mouse pointer becomes a double-headed arrow (either pointing left and right, up and down, or diagonally) when performing certain functions such as changing the size of a window.
✥	Select an object in a program such as a picture or image and the mouse pointer becomes a four-headed arrow. Use this four-headed arrow pointer to move the object left, right, up, or down.
⧗	When a request is being processed or a program is being loaded, the mouse pointer may display with an hourglass beside it. The hourglass means "please wait." When the process is completed, the hourglass image is removed.
☝	When you position the mouse pointer on certain icons or hyperlinks, it turns into a hand with a pointing index finger. This image indicates that clicking the icon or hyperlink will display additional information.

(3) Move the mouse pointer to the current time that displays at the far right side of the Taskbar and after approximately one second, the current day and date will display in a yellow pop-up box.

> To identify the location of the Taskbar, refer to Figure WIN1.1.

Step 3

④ Position the mouse pointer on the Start button on the Taskbar and then click the left mouse button.

Clicking the Start button causes the Start menu to display. The Start menu contains a list of software programs, documents, and other options available on your computer. The menu is divided into two columns. Links to the most recently used programs display in the left column and links to folders, the Control Panel, online help, and the search feature display in the right column. The bottom of the Start menu contains options for logging off or turning off the computer.

⑤ At the Start menu, point to All Programs and then point to Microsoft Office.

To point to a menu option, simply position the mouse pointer on the option. Do not click a mouse button. Pointing to *All Programs* causes a side menu to display with a list of programs. A right-pointing triangle displays to the right of some options on the Start menu. This triangle indicates that a side menu will display when you point to the option.

⑥ Move the mouse pointer to *Microsoft Office Word 2003* in the side menu and then click the left mouse button.

Clicking *Microsoft Office Word 2003* causes the Word program to open and display on the screen.

⑦ Close Microsoft Word by clicking the Close button (contains a white X on a red background) that displays in the upper right corner of the program.

Step 7

Step 8

Recycle Bin

11:18 AM

⑧ At the Windows XP desktop, position the mouse pointer on the *Recycle Bin* icon and then double-click the left mouse button.

Icons provide an easy method for opening programs or documents. Double-clicking the *Recycle Bin* icon displays the Recycle Bin window. When you open a program, a defined work area, referred to as a *window*, appears on the screen.

⑨ Close the *Recycle Bin* window by clicking the Close button (contains a white X on a red background) that displays in the upper right corner of the window.

⑩ Shut down Windows XP by clicking the Start button and then clicking Turn Off Computer at the Start menu.

Check with your instructor before shutting down Windows XP. The steps you need to follow to shut down Windows may vary.

⑪ At the Turn off computer window, click the Turn Off option.

> With options at the Turn off computer window, you can shut down Windows, shut down and then immediately restart Windows, tell the computer to go to stand by, or tell the computer to hibernate. Do not turn off your computer until your screen goes blank. Important data is stored in memory while Windows XP is running and this data needs to be written to the hard disk before turning off the computer.

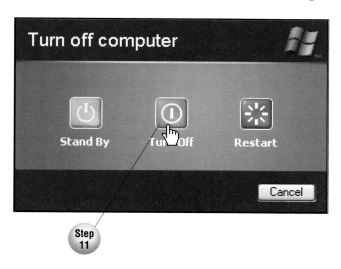

Step 11

In Addition

Putting the Computer on Stand By or Hibernate

When you shut down Windows, you can choose to shut down the computer completely, shut down and then restart, put the computer on stand by, or tell the computer to hibernate. Click the Stand By option at the Turn off computer window and the computer switches to a low power state causing some devices such as the monitor and hard disks to turn off. With these devices off, the computer uses less power. Stand by is particularly useful for saving battery power for portable computers. Tell the computer to "hibernate" by holding down the Shift key while clicking the Stand By option at the Turn off computer window. In hibernate mode, the computer saves everything in memory on disk, turns off the monitor and hard disk, and then turns off the computer. When you restart the computer, the desktop is restored exactly as you left it. You can generally restore your desktop from either stand by or hibernate by pressing once on the computer's power button. Bringing a computer out of hibernation takes a little longer than bringing a computer out of stand by.

IN BRIEF

Start a Program
1 Click Start button.
2 Point to All Programs.
3 Click desired program.

Shut Down Windows
1 Click Start button.
2 Click Turn Off Computer.
3 At Turn off computer window, click Turn Off.

1.2 Opening and Manipulating Windows

When you open a program, a defined work area, referred to as a *window*, appears on the screen. You can move a window on the desktop and change the size of a window. The top of a window is called the Title bar and generally contains buttons at the right side for closing the window and minimizing, maximizing, or restoring the size of the window.

More than one window can be open at a time and open windows can be cascaded or tiled.

PROJECT: You will continue your exploration of the Windows XP desktop by opening and manipulating windows.

STEPS

1 At the Windows XP desktop, double-click the *Recycle Bin* icon.

This opens the Recycle Bin window on the desktop. If the Recycle Bin window fills the entire desktop, click the Restore Down button, which is the second button from the right (immediately left of the Close button) located in the upper right corner of the window.

Step 1

2 Move the window on the desktop. To do this, position the mouse pointer on the window Title bar (the bar along the top of the window), hold down the left mouse button, drag the window to a different location on the desktop, and then release the mouse button.

3 Click the Start button on the Taskbar and then click My Computer at the Start menu.

The My Computer option is located in the right column of the Start menu. If the My Computer window fills the entire desktop, click the Restore Down button, which is the second button from the right (immediately left of the Close button) located in the upper right corner of the window. You now have two windows open on the desktop—My Computer and Recycle Bin.

Step 3

4 Make sure the Title bar of the Recycle Bin window is visible (if not, move the My Computer window) and then click the Recycle Bin Title bar.

Clicking the Recycle Bin Title bar makes the Recycle Bin window active, moving it in front of the My Computer window.

5 Minimize the Recycle Bin window to a task button on the Taskbar by clicking the Minimize button (contains an underscore symbol) located towards the right side of the Recycle Bin Title bar.

Step 5

6 Minimize the My Computer window to a task button on the Taskbar by clicking the Minimize button located at the right side of the Title bar.

7 Redisplay the Recycle Bin window by clicking the Recycle Bin task button on the Taskbar.

Step 7

8 Redisplay the My Computer window by clicking the My Computer task button on the Taskbar.

9 Click the Maximize button located at the right side of the My Computer window.

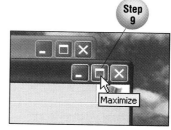

Step 9

> Clicking the Maximize button causes the window to expand to fill the entire desktop.

10 Click the Restore Down button located at the right side of the My Computer window.

Step 10

> Clicking the Restore Down button restores the window to the size it was before it was maximized.

11 Right-click on an empty section of the Taskbar and then click *Tile Windows Horizontally.*

> Tiled windows fill the desktop with the Title bar and a portion of each window visible.

12 Right-click on an empty section of the Taskbar and then click *Cascade Windows* at the pop-up menu.

Step 11

> Cascaded windows display in the upper left corner of the desktop with the Title bar of each open window visible.

13 Close the My Computer window by clicking the Close button (contains a white X on a red background) located at the right side of the Title bar.

14 Close the Recycle Bin window by clicking the Close button.

In Addition

Sizing a Window

Using the mouse, you can increase or decrease the size of a window. To increase the size vertically, position the mouse pointer on the border at the right or left side of the window until it turns into a left- and right-pointing arrow. Hold down the left mouse button, drag the border to the right or left, and then release the mouse button. Complete similar steps to increase or decrease the size of the window horizontally using the bottom border of the window. To change the size of the window both horizontally and vertically at the same time, position the mouse pointer at the left or right corner of the window until the pointer turns into a diagonally-pointed double-headed arrow, and then drag to change the size.

IN BRIEF

Move Window
1 Position mouse pointer on window Title bar.
2 Hold down left mouse button.
3 Drag window to desired position.
4 Release mouse button.

Tile Windows Horizontally
1 Right-click an empty section of the Taskbar.
2 Click *Tile Windows Horizontally* at pop-up menu.

Cascade Windows
1 Right-click an empty section of the Taskbar.
2 Click *Cascade Windows* at pop-up menu.

1.3 Exploring the Taskbar

The bar that displays at the bottom of the desktop is called the *Taskbar* and it is divided into three sections: the Start button, the task buttons area, and the notification area. Click the Start button to start a program, use the Help and Support feature, change settings, open files, or shut down the computer. Open programs display as task buttons in the task button area of the Taskbar. You can right-click an empty portion of the Taskbar to display a pop-up menu with options for customizing the Taskbar. The notification area displays at the right side of the Taskbar and contains a digital clock and specialized programs that run in the background.

PROJECT: As you continue exploring Windows XP, you want to learn more about the features available on the Taskbar.

STEPS

1 At the Windows XP desktop, double-click the current time that displays at the far right side of the Taskbar.

Figure WIN1.2 identifies the components of the Taskbar. Double-clicking the time causes the Date and Time Properties dialog box to display. Please refer to Table WIN1.3 for information on dialog box components.

FIGURE WIN1.2 Taskbar

Start Button | Task Button Area | Notification Area

TABLE WIN1.3 Dialog Box Components

Name	Image	Description
Tabs		Click a dialog box tab and the dialog box options change.
Text Box		Type or edit text in a text box. A text box may contain up-or-down-pointing arrows to allow you to choose a number or an option instead of typing it in.
Drop-down List Box		Click the down-pointing arrow at the right side of a drop-down list box and a list of choices displays.
List Box		A list of options displays in the list box.
Check Boxes		If a check box contains a check mark, the option is active; if the check box is empty, the option is inactive. Any number of check boxes can be active.
Option Buttons		The active option button contains a dark circle. Only one option button in a dialog box section can be selected at any time.

TABLE WIN1.3 Dialog Box Components *(continued)*

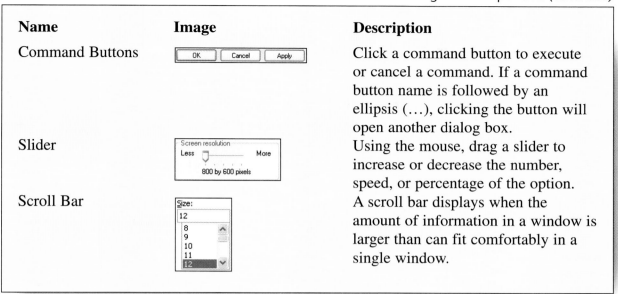

Name	Image	Description
Command Buttons		Click a command button to execute or cancel a command. If a command button name is followed by an ellipsis (…), clicking the button will open another dialog box.
Slider		Using the mouse, drag a slider to increase or decrease the number, speed, or percentage of the option.
Scroll Bar		A scroll bar displays when the amount of information in a window is larger than can fit comfortably in a single window.

2 Check to make sure the correct date and time display in the Date and Time Properties dialog box.

If the date is incorrect, click the down-pointing arrow at the right side of the Date list box (contains the month) and then click the correct month at the drop-down list. Click the up-or down-pointing arrows in the year text box to increase or decrease the year. To change the time, double-click either the hour, minute, or seconds and use the up-and-down-pointing arrows to adjust the time.

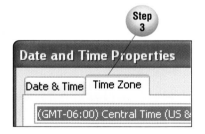

3 Click the Time Zone tab located towards the top of the Date and Time Properties dialog box.

Check to make sure the correct time zone displays. If it is not correct, click the down-pointing arrow at the right side of the list box and then click the desired time zone at the drop-down list.

4 Click OK to close the Date and Time Properties dialog box.

(continued)

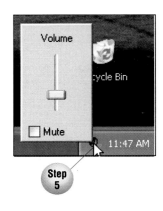

Step 5

5 Position the mouse pointer on the Volume button located towards the right side of the Taskbar and then click the left mouse button.

> If the Volume button is not visible in the notification area, click the left-pointing arrow located at the left side of the notification area. This expands the area to show all buttons. Clicking the Volume button causes a slider bar to display. Use this slider to increase or decrease the volume. Insert a check mark in the *Mute* check box if you want to turn off the sound.

6 After viewing the Volume slider, click on any empty location on the desktop to remove the slider.

7 Right-click on any empty location on the Taskbar and then click *Properties* at the pop-up menu that displays.

> This displays the Taskbar and Start Menu Properties dialog box with the Taskbar tab selected. Notice that the dialog box contains check boxes. A check mark in a check box indicates that the option is active. By default, the *Group similar taskbar buttons* option is active. With this option active, if the Taskbar becomes crowded with task buttons, task buttons for the same program are collapsed into a single button. Click a button representing collapsed files for the same program and a list of the files displays above the button.

8 Click the *Auto-hide the taskbar* option to insert a check mark in the check box.

9 Click the Apply command button located towards the bottom of the dialog box.

10 Click the OK button to close the Taskbar and Start Menu Properties dialog box.

> Notice that the Taskbar is no longer visible. To redisplay the Taskbar, move the mouse pointer to the bottom of the desktop.

Step 8

Step 10

Step 9

⑪ Display the Taskbar by moving the mouse pointer to the bottom of the desktop.

⑫ Right-click on any empty location on the Taskbar and then click *Properties* at the pop-up menu.

⑬ Click the *Auto-hide the taskbar* option to remove the check mark.

⑭ Click the Apply command button.

⑮ Click the OK button to close the Taskbar and Start Menu Properties dialog box.

In Addition

Using Natural Keyboard Shortcuts

If you are using a Microsoft Natural Keyboard or a compatible keyboard, you can use the Windows logo key 🖼 and the Application key 🖳 to access the following features:

Press	To Do This
🖼	Display the Start menu
🖼 + Break	Display the System Properties dialog box
🖼 + M	Minimize or restore all windows
🖼 + E	Open My Computer
🖼 + F	Search for a file or folder
🖼 + F1	Display Help and Support Center window
🖼 + R	Open the Run dialog box
🖼 + Tab	Switch between open items
🖳	Display the shortcut menu for selected item

IN BRIEF

Display Date/Time Properties Dialog Box
Double-click current time at right side of Taskbar.

Display Volume Slider
Click Volume button on Taskbar.

Display Taskbar and Start Menu Properties Dialog Box
1 Right-click an empty location on the Taskbar.
2 Click *Properties* at pop-up menu.

FEATURES SUMMARY

Feature	Button	Action
Close window	☒	Click Close button on Title bar
Data and Time Properties dialog box		Double-click time on Taskbar
Maximize window	☐	Click Maximize button on Title bar
Minimize window	▬	Click Minimize button on Title bar
Move window on desktop		Drag window Title bar
My Computer window		Click Start button, click My Computer
Restore window	❐	Click Restore Down button on Title bar
Shut down computer		Click Start button, click Turn Off Computer, click Turn Off at Turn off computer window
Start menu	start	Click Start button on the Taskbar
Taskbar pop-up menu		Right-click empty location on Taskbar
Taskbar and Start Menu Properties dialog box		Right-click empty location on Taskbar, click *Properties* at pop-up menu
Volume slider	🔊	Click Volume button on Taskbar

PROCEDURES CHECK

Completion: In the space provided at the right, indicate the correct term, symbol, button, or command.

1. This mouse term refers to positioning the mouse pointer on the desired item. _____

2. This mouse term refers to tapping the left mouse button twice in quick succession. _____

3. This symbol is attached to the mouse pointer when a request is being processed and means "please wait." _____

4. Click this button on a window Title bar to reduce the window to a task button on the Taskbar. _____

5. Click this button on a window Title bar to expand the window so it fills the entire screen. _____

6. Double-click the time located at the right side of the Taskbar and this dialog box displays. _____

7. This component of a dialog box generally contains a measurement or number and displays with an up- and down-pointing arrow. _____

8. Drag this component in a dialog box to increase or decrease the number, speed, or percentage of an option. _____

SKILLS REVIEW

Activity 1: OPENING AND MANIPULATING WINDOWS

1 At the Windows XP desktop, click the Start button on the Taskbar and then click My Documents. (If the My Documents window fills the desktop, click the Restore Down button located in the upper right corner of the window.)

2 Click the Start button on the Taskbar and then click My Computer. (If the My Computer window fills the desktop, click the Restore Down button.)

3 Position the mouse pointer on the My Computer title bar, hold down the left mouse button, and then drag the My Computer window so the My Documents Title bar is visible.

4 Click the My Documents Title bar to make it the active window.

5 Right-click on an empty location on the Taskbar and then click *Cascade Windows* at the pop-up menu.

6 Click the Minimize button (located towards the right side of the Title bar) on the My Documents window title bar to reduce the window to a task button on the Taskbar.

7 Click the Minimize button on the My Computer window to reduce the window to a task button on the Taskbar.

8 Click the My Computer task button to restore the My Computer window on the desktop.

9 Click the My Documents task button to restore the My Documents window on the desktop.

10 Click the Maximize button on the My Documents Title bar to expand the window to fill the screen.

11 Click the Restore Down button on the My Documents title bar to reduce the size of the My Documents window.

12 Close the My Documents window.

13 Close the My Computer window.

Activity 2: EXPLORING THE TASKBAR

1 At the Windows XP desktop, double-click the time that displays in the notification area at the right side of the Taskbar.

2 At the Date and Time Properties dialog box, click the down-pointing arrow at the right side of the month list box and then click the next month (from the current month) at the drop-down list.

3 Click the OK button.

4 Display the Date and Time Properties dialog box again, change the month back to the current month, and then click OK to close the dialog box.

5 Click the Start button, point to All Programs, point to Microsoft Office, and then click Microsoft Office Excel 2003.

6 Close Excel by clicking the Close button located at the right side of the Microsoft Office Excel title bar.

PERFORMANCE PLUS

Assessment 1: MANIPULATING WINDOWS

1 Click the Start button and then click My Pictures. (If the My Pictures window fills the entire desktop, click the Restore Down button.)
2 Click the Start button and then click My Music. (If the My Music window fills the entire desktop, click the Restore Down button.)
3 Cascade the two windows.
4 Make the My Pictures window the active window and then reduce it to a task button on the Taskbar.
5 Reduce the My Music window to a task button on the Taskbar.
6 Restore the My Pictures window.
7 Restore the My Music window.
8 Close the My Music window and then close the My Pictures window.

Assessment 2: EXPLORING THE TASKBAR

1 At the Windows XP desktop, display the Date and Time Properties dialog box.
2 Change the current hour one hour ahead and then close the dialog box.
3 Open the Date and Time Properties dialog box, change the hour back to the current hour, and then close the dialog box.
4 Display the Volume slider bar and then drag the slider to increase the volume.
5 Display the Volume slider bar and then drag the slider to the original position.
6 Display the Taskbar and Start Menu Properties dialog box, remove the check mark from the *Show the clock* option, and then close the dialog box. (Notice that the time no longer displays on the Taskbar.)
7 Display the Taskbar and Start Menu Properties dialog box, insert a check mark in the *Show the clock* option, and then close the dialog box.

WINDOWS XP

Maintaining Files and Customizing Windows

Use Windows XP features and accessory programs to get help with specific topics and features, manage and maintain files, search for files and/or folders, and customize the Windows desktop. An on-screen reference guide, called Help and Support, provides information, explanations, and interactive help on learning Windows features. Maintain files and folders with options at the My Computer window including creating folders and selecting, moving, copying, and/or pasting files and folders. Delete and/or restore files and folders with options at the Recycle Bin window. Additional accessories offered by Windows that you will explore in this section include the Control Panel, Search, WordPad, and Paint. In this section, you will explore Windows XP accessories and learn the skills and complete the project described here.

Note: Before beginning this section, copy to a disk the WindowsS2 folder on the CD that accompanies this textbook. Steps on copying a folder and deleting a folder are located on the inside back cover of your textbook.

Skills

- Use the Help and Support feature
- Create a folder
- Select, move, copy, and paste files
- Delete files/folders to and restore files/folders from the Recycle Bin
- Create and delete a shortcut
- Rename a file
- Explore the Control Panel
- Search for files and/or folders
- Use WordPad and Paint
- Customize the desktop

Project

You will use the Help feature to learn about new Windows XP features and then organize files for your department at Worldwide Enterprises. This organization includes creating a folder and moving, copying, and deleting files. You will also create a shortcut to a specific file you use when creating reports for your department, search for specific files for your supervisor, prepare a note to the manager of the IS Department, and customize your desktop.

2.1 Getting Help in Windows XP

Windows XP includes an on-screen reference guide, called Help and Support, that provides information, explanations, and interactive help on learning Windows features. The Help and Support feature contains complex files with hypertext used to access additional information by clicking a word or phrase. Display the Help and Support Center window by clicking the Start button on the Taskbar and then clicking Help and Support at the Start menu. At the Help and Support Center window, you can perform such actions as choosing a specific help topic, searching for a keyword or topic, and displaying an index of help topics.

PROJECT: You decide to use the Windows XP Help and Support feature to learn more about new Windows XP features. Your supervisor at Worldwide Enterprises has also asked you to learn how to copy files and create a folder and shortcut in Windows XP.

S T E P S

1 Display the Help and Support Center window by clicking the Start button on the Taskbar and then clicking Help and Support.

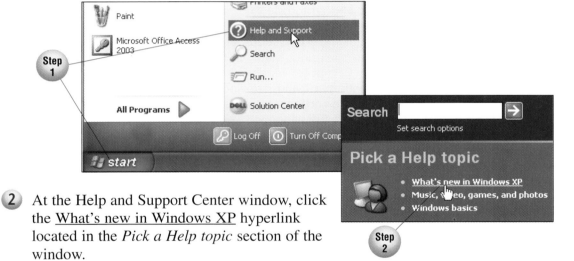

2 At the Help and Support Center window, click the What's new in Windows XP hyperlink located in the *Pick a Help topic* section of the window.

3 Click the What's new topics hyperlink located in the *What's new in Windows XP* section of the window.

This displays a list of Help options at the right side of the window.

4 Click the What's new in Windows XP hyperlink located at the right side of the window below the subheading *Overviews, Articles, and Tutorials.*

5 Read the information about Windows XP that displays at the right side of the window.

6 Print the information by clicking the Print button located on the toolbar above the information. At the Print dialog box that displays, click the Print button.

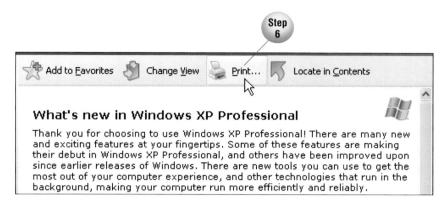

7 Return to the opening Help and Support Center window by clicking the Home button located on the Help and Support Center toolbar.

8 Click in the *Search* text box located towards the top of the Help and Support Center window, type **copying files** and then press Enter.

> After typing a search topic you can press Enter or click the Start searching button (white arrow on a green background) that displays at the right of the *Search* text box.

9 Click the <u>Copy a file or folder</u> hyperlink that displays in the *Search Results* section of the window (below the *Pick a task* subheading).

10 Read the information about copying a file or folder that displays at the right side of the window and then print the information by clicking the Print button on the toolbar and then clicking the Print button at the Print dialog box.

11 Click the Index button located on the Help and Support Center window toolbar.

12 With the insertion point positioned in the *Type in the keyword to find* text box, type **shortcuts**.

> The list of topics in the list box below the *Type in the keyword to find* text box will automatically scroll to related topics.

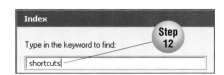

(continued)

⑬ Double-click the subheading *for specific programs* that displays below the *shortcuts* heading.

⑭ Read the information that displays at the right side of the window and then print the information.

⑮ Click the Home button located on the Help and Support Center toolbar.

⑯ Click in the *Search* text box located towards the top of the Help and Support Center window, type **create a folder**, and then press Enter.

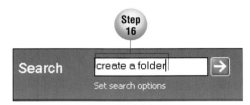

⑰ Click the Create a new folder hyperlink located in the *Pick a task* section of the Suggested Topics pane.

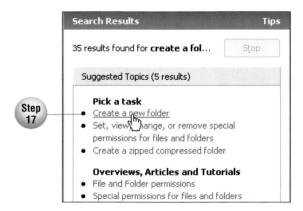

⑱ Read the information about creating a folder that displays at the right side of the window and then print the information by clicking the Print button on the toolbar and then clicking the Print button at the Print dialog box.

19 Click the Locate in Contents button on the toolbar located immediate above the information.

> Clicking this button locates the topic in the Help table of contents and displays the information in the Windows basic pane.

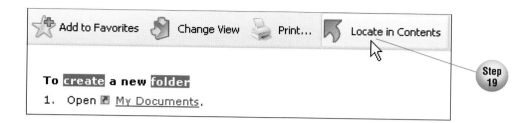

20 Click the Home button located on the Help and Support Center toolbar.

21 Close the Help and Support Center window by clicking the Close button located in the upper right corner of the window.

In Addition

Adding a Topic to the Favorites List

If you repeatedly use a help topic, you can add it to the Favorites list and then view the Favorites list by clicking the Favorites button on the Help and Support Center window toolbar. To add a help topic to the Favorites list, display the Help and Support Center window and then display the desired topic. Click the Add to Favorites button on the toolbar that displays above the topic information and then click OK at the message that displays. To view the Favorites list, click the Favorites button on the Help and Support Center window toolbar. To remove a topic from the Favorites list, display the Favorites list, click the topic, and then click the Remove button that displays towards the bottom of the list.

IN BRIEF

Display Help and Support Center Window
1 Click Start button on Taskbar.
2 Click Help and Support at Start menu.

2.2 Creating a Folder

As you begin working with programs in Windows XP, you will create files in which data (information) is saved. A file might contain a Word document, an Excel workbook, or a PowerPoint presentation. As you begin creating files, consider creating folders into which those files will be stored. File management tasks such as creating a folder and copying and moving files and folders can be completed at a variety of locations including the My Computer and My Documents windows.

PROJECT: You have decided you need to organize files for your department at Worldwide Enterprises. The first step is to create a folder at the My Computer window.

STEPS

① At the Windows XP desktop, click the Start button on the Taskbar and then click My Computer at the Start menu.

The My Computer window displays similar to the one shown in Figure WIN2.1.

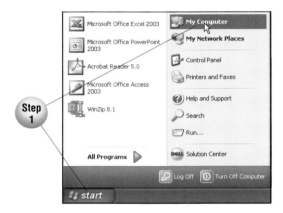

FIGURE WIN2.1 My Computer Window

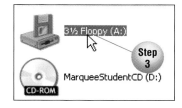

2 Insert into drive A the 3.5-inch disk on which you copied the WindowsS2 folder.

3 Double-click *3½ Floppy (A:)* in the contents pane.

This displays the contents of the disk in drive A in the contents pane and also changes the name in the My Computer window Title bar from *My Computer* to *3½ Floppy (A:)*. The active folder is reflected in the window Title bar.

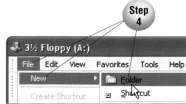

4 Click File on the Menu bar, point to New, and then click Folder.

5 Type **Revenue** and then press Enter.

This changes the name from *New Folder* to *Revenue*.

6 Close the window by clicking the Close button located in the upper right corner of the window.

In Addition

Displaying the Folders Pane

You can display a hierarchal list of folders and drives by displaying the My Computer window and then clicking the Folders button on the Standard Buttons toolbar. This displays the Folders pane at the left side of the window as shown in the image at the right. A plus symbol preceding a folder name indicates that the folder contains additional folders (or drives). Click the folder name in the Folders pane and the contents of the folder display in the Folders pane as well as the contents pane. Turn off the display of the Folders pane by clicking the Folders button.

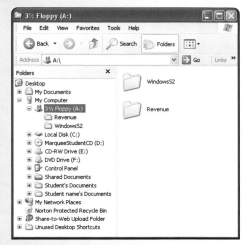

IN BRIEF

Display My Computer Window
1 Click Start button.
2 Click My Computer.

Create New Folder
1 Display My Computer window.
2 Click File, point to New, click Folder.
3 Type folder name and then press Enter.

2.3 Selecting and Copying Files

File and folder management activities might include selecting, moving, copying, or deleting files or folders. The My Computer window offers a variety of methods for completing file management activities. You can use options in the task pane, drop-down menu options, or shortcut menu options. More than one file or folder can be moved, copied, or deleted at one time. Select adjacent files/folders using the Shift key and select nonadjacent files/folders using the Ctrl key. When selecting multiple files or folders, you may want to change the view in the My Computer window. View choices include Thumbnails, Tiles, Icons, List, and Details. List and Details are good choices for selecting multiple files.

PROJECT: Continuing to organize files for your department, you will copy files to the *Revenue* folder you created.

S T E P S

1. At the Windows XP desktop, open the My Computer window by clicking the Start button and then clicking My Computer at the Start menu.

2. Make sure your disk containing the WindowsS2 and Revenue folders is inserted in drive A.

3. Double-click *3½ Floppy (A:)* in the contents pane.

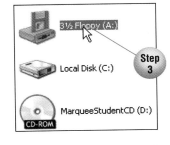

4. Double-click the WindowsS2 folder in the contents pane.

5. Change the view by clicking the Views button on the Standard Buttons toolbar and then clicking *List* at the drop-down list.

6. Click the file named **WEExcelRevenues** that displays in the contents pane.

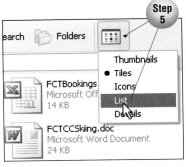

7. Hold down the Shift key, click the file named **WETable02** and then release the Shift key.

   Clicking **WETable02** while holding down the Shift key causes all files from **WEExcelRevenues** through **WETable02** to be selected.

8. Click the <u>Copy the selected items</u> hyperlink in the *File and Folder Tasks* section of the task pane.

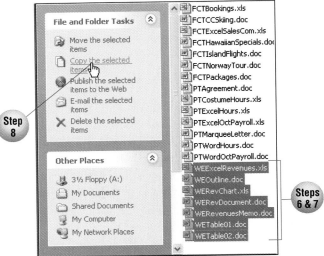

9 At the Copy Items dialog box, click *3½ Floppy (A:)* in the list box.

10 Click *Revenue* in the list box (below *3½ Floppy (A:)*).

11 Click the Copy button that displays towards the bottom of the dialog box.

> A message box with a progress bar appears as the files are copied. Copying the files may take a few moments.

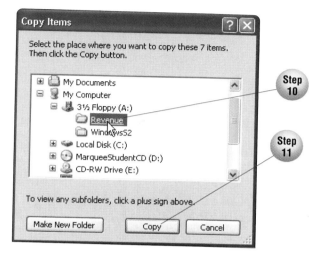

12 Click the *3½ Floppy (A:)* option that displays in the *Other Places* section of the task pane.

13 Display the files you just copied by double-clicking the *Revenue* folder in the contents pane.

14 Close the window by clicking the Close button located in the upper right corner of the window.

In Addition

Copying by Dragging

You can copy a file/folder to another location by dragging the file/folder. To copy by dragging, display the My Computer window and then click the Folders button on the Standard Buttons toolbar. (This displays the Folders pane at the left side of the window.) Display the desired file or folder in the contents pane of the My Computer window. Position the mouse pointer on the file or folder, hold down the *right* mouse button, drag to the desired drive or folder in the Folders pane, and then release the mouse button. At the shortcut menu that displays, click the Copy Here option.

IN BRIEF

Copy Adjacent Files to New Folder
1 Display My Computer window.
2 Click Views button on toolbar and then click *List*.
3 Click first file name.
4 Hold down Shift key and then click last file name.
5 Click the Copy the selected items hyperlink in the task pane.
6 At the Copy Items dialog box, specify destination folder, and then click Copy button.

2.4 Moving Files

Move files in the My Computer window in a manner similar to copying files. You can move a file or folder to a different folder or drive or you can select and then move multiple files or folders. Select the file/folder or files/folders you want to move and then click the appropriate move option in the *File and Folder Tasks* section of the task pane. This displays the Move Items dialog box. At this dialog box, specify where you want to move the file/folder and then click the Move button.

PROJECT: After looking at the files you copied into the Revenue folder, you decide to organize the files by creating another folder and moving some of the files from the Revenue folder into the new folder.

S T E P S

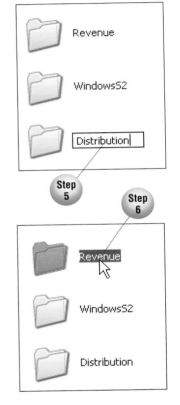

1. At the Windows XP desktop, display the My Computer window.

2. Make sure your disk containing the Revenue folder (and the copied files) is inserted in drive A.

3. Double-click *3½ Floppy (A:)* in the contents pane.

4. To create a new folder, click File on the Menu bar, point to New, and then click Folder.

5. Type **Distribution** and then press Enter.

   This changes the name from *New Folder* to *Distribution*.

6. Double-click the *Revenue* folder name in the contents pane.

7. Click the Views button on the Standard Buttons toolbar and then click *List* at the drop-down list.

8. Click once on the file named **WEOutline**.

   Clicking once on the file selects the file name.

9. Hold down the Ctrl key, click once on *WETable01*, click once on *WETable02*, and then release the Ctrl key.

   Using the Ctrl key, you can select nonadjacent files.

10. Click the Move the selected items hyperlink in the *File and Folder Tasks* task pane.

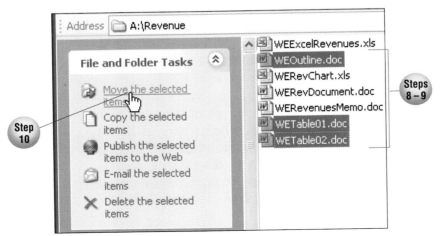

⑪ At the Move Items dialog box, click the folder named *Distribution* in the list box and then click the Move button.

⑫ Click the Up button on the Standard Buttons toolbar.

> This displays the contents of the folder that is up one folder from the current folder.

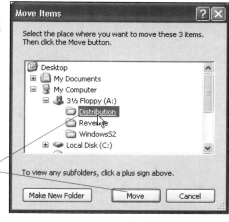

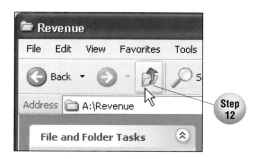

⑬ Double-click *Distribution* in the contents pane.

> The contents pane now displays the files you moved into the Distribution folder.

⑭ Close the window by clicking the Close button.

In Addition

Searching for Files/Folders at the My Computer Window

Click the Search button on the My Computer window Standard Buttons toolbar and a Search Companion pane displays at the left side of the window as shown in the image at the right. Specify the type of file for which you are searching and the options in the Search Companion pane. For example, if you are searching for a specific Word document, you would click the *Documents (word processing, spreadsheet, etc.)* option in the Search Companion pane. At the next step, you would specify the document name or a portion of the name and then click the Search button.

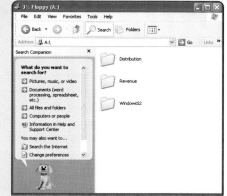

In Brief

Move Nonadjacent Files to New Folder
1 Display My Computer window.
2 Click Views button on toolbar and then click *List*.
3 Click first file name.
4 Hold down Ctrl key, click each additional file name, and then release Ctrl key.
5 Click the Move the selected items hyperlink in the task pane.
6 At the Move Items dialog box, specify destination folder, and then click Move button.

2.5 Deleting Files/Folders to the Recycle Bin

Deleting the wrong file can be a disaster, but Windows XP helps protect your work with the Recycle Bin. The Recycle Bin acts just like an office wastepaper basket; you can "throw away" (delete) unwanted files, but you can "reach in" to the Recycle Bin and take out (restore) a file if you threw it away by accident. Files or folders deleted from the hard drive are automatically sent to the Recycle Bin. Files or folders deleted from a disk are deleted permanently. (Recovery programs are available, however, that can help you recover deleted data.) To delete a file or folder, display the My Computer window and then display in the contents pane the file(s) and/or folder(s) you want deleted. Click the file or folder or selected multiple files or folders and then click the appropriate delete option in the task pane. At the message asking you to confirm the deletion, click the Yes button.

PROJECT: Continuing to organize your files, you will copy a file and a folder from your disk to the My Documents folder and then delete a file and folder to the Recycle Bin.

S T E P S

1. At the Windows XP desktop, display the My Computer window.

2. Make sure your disk containing the Revenue and Distribution folders is inserted in drive A.

3. At the My Computer window, double-click *3½ Floppy (A:)* in the contents pane.

4. Click once on the *Distribution* folder in the contents pane to select it.

5. Click the Copy this folder hyperlink in the *File and Folder Tasks* section of the task pane.

6. At the Copy Items dialog box, click *My Documents* in the list box and then click the Copy button.

7. Double-click the *Revenue* folder in the contents pane.

8. Click once on **WERevDocument** in the contents pane to select it.

9. Click the Copy this file hyperlink in the *File and Folder Tasks* section of the task pane.

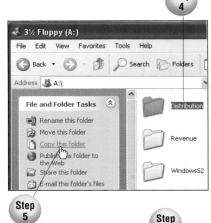

Step 4

Step 5

Step 6

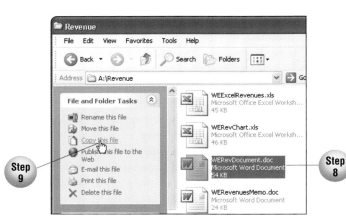

Step 9

Step 8

10 At the Copy Items dialog box, click *My Documents* in the list box and then click the Copy button.

11 Click <u>My Documents</u> in the *Other Places* section of the task pane.

12 Click once on the *Distribution* folder in the contents pane to select it.

13 Click the <u>Delete this folder</u> hyperlink in the *File and Folder Tasks* section of the task pane.

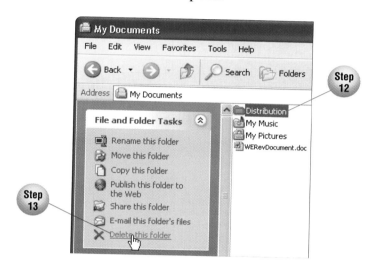

14 At the message asking you to confirm the deletion, click the Yes button.

15 Click once on ***WERevDocument*** in the contents pane to select it.

16 Click the <u>Delete this file</u> hyperlink in the *File and Folder Tasks* section of the task pane.

17 At the message asking you to confirm the deletion, click the Yes button.

18 Close the window.

In Addition

Dragging and Dropping Files/Folders

Another method for deleting a file or folder is to drag the file or folder to the *Recycle Bin* icon on the desktop. Drag a file icon to the *Recycle Bin* icon until the icon name *Recycle Bin* displays with a blue background, and then release the mouse button. This drops the file you are dragging into the Recycle Bin. You can also select multiple files or folders and then drag and drop the selected items in the Recycle Bin.

IN BRIEF

Delete a File/Folder
1 Display My Computer window.
2 Click file/folder to select it.
3 Click the <u>Delete this file</u> hyperlink (or the <u>Delete this folder</u> hyperlink) in the task pane.
4 At confirmation message, click Yes.

2.6 Restoring Files/Folders and Emptying Files from the Recycle Bin

A file or folder deleted to the Recycle Bin can be restored. Restore a file or folder with options at the Recycle Bin window. Display this window by double-clicking the Recycle Bin icon on the Windows desktop. A restored file or folder is removed from the Recycle Bin and returned to its original location. Just like a wastepaper basket, the Recycle Bin can get full. Emptying the Recycle Bin

deletes all files and folders. You can also delete a single file or folder from the Recycle Bin (rather than all files and folders).

PROJECT: You decide to experiment with the Recycle Bin and learn how to restore a file and then empty the Recycle Bin.

S T E P S

Step 1

1. At the Windows XP desktop, display the contents of the Recycle Bin by double-clicking the *Recycle Bin* icon.

    The Recycle Bin window displays similar to the one shown in Figure WIN2.2.

FIGURE WIN2.2 Recycle Bin Window

- Title Bar
- Menu Bar
- Standard Buttons Toolbar
- Address Bar
- Task Pane
- Contents Pane

2. At the Recycle Bin window, click the Views button on the Standard Buttons toolbar and then click *List* at the drop-down list.

3. Click once on **WERevDocument** in the contents pane to select it.

    Depending on the contents of the Recycle Bin, you may need to scroll down the Recycle Bin list to display this document.

Step 3

Step 4

4. Click the <u>Restore this item</u> hyperlink in the *Recycle Bin Tasks* section of the task pane.

5. Click once on the *Distribution* folder in the contents pane to select it.

6. Click the <u>Restore this item</u> hyperlink in the *Recycle Bin Tasks* section of the task pane.

    If you want to empty the entire contents of the Recycle Bin, you would click the <u>Empty the Recycle Bin</u> hyperlink in the *Recycle Bin Tasks* section of the task pane. At the message asking you to confirm the deletion, you would click the Yes button.

7. Close the Recycle Bin window by clicking the Close button that displays in the upper right corner of the window.

8. At the Windows XP desktop, display the My Computer window.

9. Click My Documents in the *Other Places* section of the task pane.

10. Delete the files you restored. To do this, click once on *Distribution* folder, hold down the Ctrl key, click once on the **WERevDocument** file, and then release the Ctrl key.

11. Click the Delete the selected items hyperlink in the *File and Folder Tasks* section of the task pane.

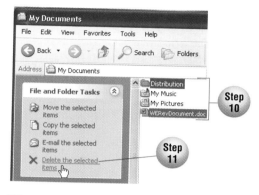

12. At the message asking you to confirm that you want the items deleted to the Recycle Bin, click the Yes button.

13. Close the window.

14. At the Windows XP desktop, double-click the *Recycle Bin* icon.

15. Click once on the *Distribution* folder, hold down the Ctrl key, click once on the **WERevDocument** file name, and then release the Ctrl key.

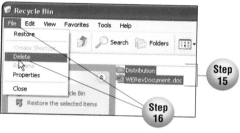

16. Click File on the Menu bar and then click Delete at the drop-down menu.

17. At the confirmation message, click the Yes button.

18. Close the Recycle Bin window.

In Addition

Arranging Icons in Recycle Bin Window

You can control the arrangement of file and folder icons in the Recycle Bin window with options from the View, Arrange Icons by side menu shown at the right. Display this side menu by clicking View on the Recycle Bin Menu bar, and then pointing to Arrange Icons by. Choose the option that best fits your needs. For example, choose Name if you want to see an alphabetic listing of your files and folders or click Date Deleted if you want to see files and folders listed by the date they were deleted.

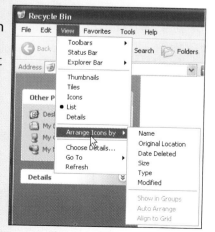

IN BRIEF

Restore File/Folder from Recycle Bin
1 At Windows desktop, double-click *Recycle Bin* icon.
2 At Recycle Bin window, click file/folder to select it (or select multiple files/folders).
3 Click the Restore this item hyperlink in the task pane.

Delete File/Folder from Recycle Bin
1 At Windows desktop, double-click *Recycle Bin* icon.
2 At Recycle Bin window, click file/folder to select it (or select multiple files/folders).
3 Click File on the Menu bar and then click Delete.
4 At the confirmation message, click Yes.

2.7 Creating and Deleting a Shortcut and Renaming a File

If you use a file or program on a consistent basis, consider creating a shortcut to the file or program. Shortcuts are specialized icons and are very small files that point the operating system to the actual item, whether it is a file, a folder, or a program. Double-click a shortcut icon and the file opens in the program in which it was created. Shortcuts provide quick and easy access to files or programs used every day without having to remember where the file is stored. Along with the file management tasks you have learned such as copying, moving, and deleting files/folders, you can also rename a file/folder. Rename a file/folder using an option from a drop-down menu or an option from a shortcut menu.

PROJECT: You use the WERevChart file when creating reports for your department so you decide to rename it and then create a shortcut to the file.

S T E P S

1. At the Windows XP desktop, display the My Computer window.

2. Make sure your disk containing the WindowsS2 and Revenue folders is inserted in drive A.

3. At the My Computer window, double-click *3½ Floppy (A:)* in the contents pane.

4. Double-click the *Revenue* folder.

5. Change the display of files to a list by clicking the Views button on the Standard Buttons toolbar and then click *List* at the drop-down list.

6. Right-click on the **WERevChart** file.

    Right-clicking on a file or folder causes a shortcut menu to display containing file management options.

7. At the shortcut menu that displays, click the Rename option.

    When you click Rename, the name of the file is selected.

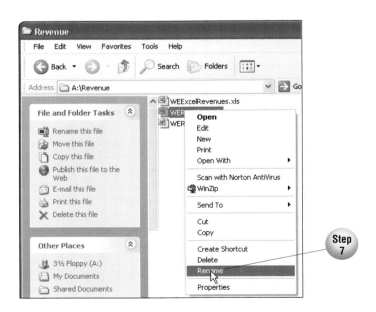

8. Type **RevenueChart.xls** and then press Enter.

   You can also rename a file by selecting the file, clicking File on the Menu bar, and then clicking Rename at the drop-down menu. Type the new name for the file and then press Enter.

Step 8

9. Create a shortcut to the file named *RevenueChart*. To do this, position the arrow pointer on *RevenueChart*. Hold down the *right* mouse button, drag the outline of the file to the desktop, and then release the mouse button.

   Click the Restore Down button on the Revenue window title bar if the window is currently maximized and you cannot see the desktop in which to drag the file.

10. At the pop-up menu that displays, click *Create Shortcuts Here*.

Step 10

11. Close the window.

12. Double-click the *Shortcut to RevenueChart* shortcut icon on the desktop.

    Double-clicking this icon opens Excel and the file named **RevenueChart**.

Step 12

13. After viewing the file in Excel, exit Excel by clicking the Close button (white X on a red background) that displays in the upper right corner of the window.

14. Delete the *Shortcut to RevenueChart.xls* shortcut icon. To do this, position the arrow pointer on the RevenueChart.xls shortcut icon. Hold down the left mouse button, drag the icon on top of the Recycle Bin icon, and then release the mouse button.

In Addition

Displaying Disk or Drive Properties

Information such as the amount of used space and free space on a disk or drive and the disk or drive hardware is available at the Properties dialog box. To display the Local Disk (C:) Properties dialog box, similar to the one shown at the right, display the My Computer window. At the My Computer window, right-click on *Local Disk (C:)* in the contents pane and then click *Properties* at the shortcut menu. With the General tab selected, information displays about used and free space on the drive. Click the Tools tab to display error-checking, backup, and defragmentation options. The dialog box with the Hardware tab selected displays the name and type of all disk drives as well as the device properties. Click the Sharing tab to display options for sharing folders and click the Quota tab to display disk quota management options.

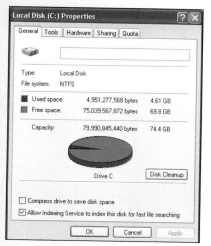

IN BRIEF

Rename a File
1 Display My Computer window.
2 Right-click file to be renamed.
3 At shortcut menu, click Rename.
4 Type new file name and then press Enter.

Create a Shortcut
1 Display My Computer window
2 Position mouse pointer on desired file.
3 Hold down *right* button, drag outline of file to the desktop, and then release the mouse button.
4 At pop-up menu, click *Create Shortcuts Here*.

2.8 Exploring the Control Panel

The Control Panel offers a variety of categories each containing icons you can use to customize the appearance and functionality of your computer. Display the Control Panel window by clicking the Start button and then clicking Control Panel at the Start menu. At the Control Panel window, available categories display in the contents pane. Click a category and a list of tasks, a list of icons, or a separate window displays.

PROJECT: You want to know how to customize your computer so you decide to explore the Control Panel window.

S T E P S

1 At the Windows XP desktop, click the Start button and then click Control Panel at the Start menu.

The Control Panel window displays similar to the one shown in Figure WIN2.3.

FIGURE WIN2.3 Control Panel Window

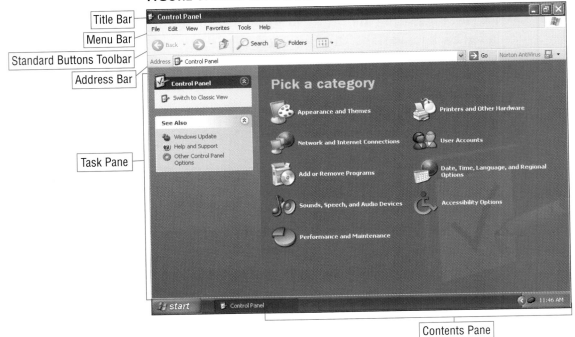

2 At the Control Panel window, click the <u>Appearance and Themes</u> hyperlink in the *Pick a Category* section.

3 After viewing the tasks and icons available in the Appearance and Themes category, click the Back button on the Standard Buttons toolbar.

This displays the opening Control Panel window, which was the previous window.

4 Click the <u>Printers and Other Hardware</u> hyperlink in the *Pick a Category* section.

(5) Click the <u>Mouse</u> hyperlink in the *or pick a Control Panel icon* section.

This displays the Mouse Properties dialog box.

(6) At the Mouse Properties dialog box, click each tab and notice the options available.

(7) Click the Cancel button to close the Mouse Properties dialog box.

(8) Click the Back button on the Standard Buttons toolbar.

(9) Click the <u>Add or Remove Programs</u> hyperlink in the *Pick a category* section.

(10) At the Add or Remove Programs window, scroll through the list of installed programs and then click the Close button.

(11) Click the <u>Performance and Maintenance</u> hyperlink in the *Pick a Category* section.

(12) Click the <u>System</u> hyperlink in the *or pick a Control Panel icon* section.

This displays the System Properties dialog box.

(13) At the System Properties dialog box, click each tab and notice the options available.

(14) Click the Cancel button to close the System Properties dialog box.

(15) Close the Control Panel window by clicking the Close button located in the upper right corner of the window.

In Addition

Changing the Control Panel View

By default, the Control Panel window displays categories of tasks in what is called the *Category View*. This view can be changed to the Classic View, which displays icons in a manner similar to that in previous Windows versions (Windows 95, 98, 2000, and Me). Change to the Classic View by clicking the <u>Switch to Classic View</u> hyperlink in the *Control Panel* section of the task pane. This displays the Control Panel window as shown above at the right. You can view a description of each icon by changing the view to Details. Changes made to options at the Control Panel window remain in effect each time Windows XP is opened.

IN BRIEF

Display Control Panel
1 Click Start button.
2 Click Control Panel.

2.9 Searching for a File or Folder

Windows XP includes a search feature you can use to search for files and/or folders that match specific criteria. To use the Search feature, click the Start button and then click Search at the Start menu. At the Search Results window, the Search Companion Wizard is automatically activated and walks you through the steps for completing a search.

PROJECT: Your supervisor has asked you to locate any files on your disk containing the Cinema House company name and any files containing the word *Revenues* in the file name.

STEPS

1. At the Windows XP desktop, click the Start button and then click *Search* at the Start menu.

2. Make sure your disk containing the WindowsS2 folder is inserted in drive A.

3. At the Search Results window, click the <u>All files and folders</u> hyperlink in the *What do you want to search for?* section.

4. Click in the *A word or phrase in the file* text box and then type **Cinema House**.

   This specifies that you want to find files containing the words *Cinema House*.

5. Click the down-pointing arrow at the right side of the *Look in* list box and then click *3½ Floppy (A:)* at the drop-down list.

6. Click the Search button.

   You can stop the search at any time by clicking the Stop button.

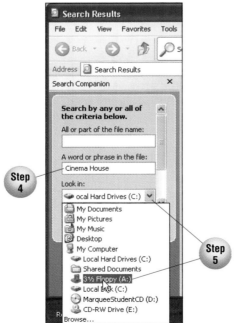

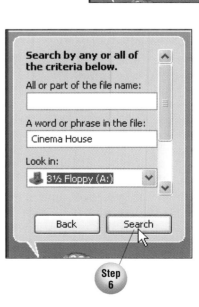

⑦ Click the Back button (located in the Search Companion Wizard section of the window).

⑧ With the insertion point positioned in the *All or part of the file name* text box, type **Revenues**.

⑨ Select and then delete the text *Cinema House* that displays in the *A word or phrase in the file* text box.

⑩ Make sure *3½ Floppy (A:)* displays in the *Look in* list box.

⑪ Click the Search button.

⑫ When the results display in the contents window, click the *Yes, finished searching* option.

Clicking this option turns off the Search Companion Wizard.

⑬ Close the Search Results window.

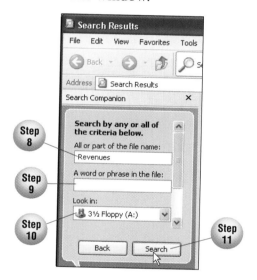

In Addition

Turning Off the Search Companion Wizard

The Windows XP Search feature provides the Search Companion Wizard to help you complete a search. You can turn off this wizard and complete a manual search. To turn off the Search Companion Wizard, display the Search Results window and then click the Change preferences hyperlink that displays at the end of the *What do you want to search for?* section. Click the Without an animated screen character hyperlink below the How do you want to use Search Companion? hyperlink. To turn on the Search Companion Wizard, display the Search Results window with the Search button active. Click the *Change preferences* option in the *What do you want to search for?* section and then click the With an animated screen character hyperlink.

IN BRIEF

Search for File Containing Specific Text
1 Click Start button.
2 Click *Search*.
3 Click the All files and folders hyperlink.
4 Click in *A word or phrase in the file* text box.
5 Type specific text.
6 Specify the location in the *Look in* list box.
7 Click Search button.

Search for File/Folder
1 Click Start button.
2 Click Search.
3 Click the All files and folders hyperlink.
4 Click in *All or part of the file name* text box.
5 Type specific file or folder name.
6 Specify the location in the *Look in* list box.
7 Click Search button.

2.10 Using WordPad and Paint

Windows XP offers accessory programs such as WordPad and Paint. WordPad is a word processing program with features for preparing, editing, and formatting text documents and documents with graphics. WordPad is a basic word processing program. If you need the features of a full-fledged word processing program consider using Microsoft Word. Another program offered by Windows XP is a drawing program named Paint. Use Paint to draw black-and-white or color images that can be saved as bitmap files.

PROJECT: You need to prepare a short note to the manager of the IS Department and decide to use the WordPad program. You also want to explore the Paint program and see if you can create a simple shape with an announcement inside.

STEPS

① At the Windows desktop, click the Start button, point to All Programs, point to Accessories, and then click WordPad.

The WordPad window opens and displays as shown in Figure WIN2.4.

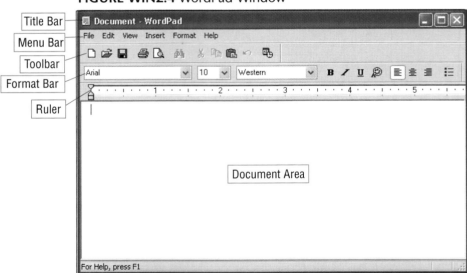

FIGURE WIN2.4 WordPad Window

② At the WordPad window, type the following paragraph. (Do not press the Enter key until you reach the end of the entire paragraph. WordPad contains a word wrap feature that will automatically wrap text to the next line.)

The Windows XP training is scheduled for Friday from 8:30 to 10:30 a.m. I would like to meet with you this afternoon to go over the details for this training.

③ Press the Enter key twice and then type your first and last names.

④ Print the document by clicking the Print button on the Toolbar.

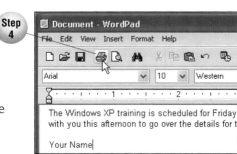

To save the document, you would click File and then Save. At the Save As dialog box, you would type a name for the document and then press Enter.

5 Close WordPad by clicking the Close button located in the upper right corner of the window. At the message asking if you want to save the document, click the No button.

6 At the Windows desktop, click the Start button, point to All Programs, point to Accessories, and then click Paint.

> The Paint window opens and displays as shown in Figure WIN2.5. Create an image in Paint by clicking the desired tool in the Toolbox and then using the mouse pointer to draw the image.

FIGURE WIN2.5 Paint Window

Title Bar · Menu Bar · Toolbox · Drawing Area · Color Box

7 Click the Rounded Rectangle tool in the Toolbox.

8 Position the pointer in the upper left corner of the drawing area, hold down the left mouse button, drag to the lower right corner of the drawing area, and then release the mouse button.

9 Click the Text tool in the Toolbox.

10 Drag to create a text box similar to the one shown at the right.

> When you release the mouse button after drawing the text box, the insertion point is positioned inside the text box.

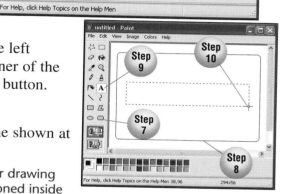

Step 9 · Step 10 · Step 7 · Step 8

11 Type **Windows XP Training**.

12 Click the down-pointing arrow at the right side of the size list box and then click *26* at the drop-down list.

> If the Text Toolbar (displays with Fonts at the left side of the toolbar) is not visible, click View and then Text Toolbar.

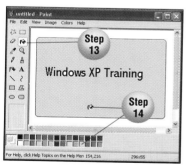

Step 13 · Windows XP Training · Step 14

13 Click the Fill With Color tool in the Toolbox.

14 Click a light turquoise color in the color palette and then click inside the rounded rectangle shape.

> This fills the rectangle with color. If you are not satisfied with the image, discard it by clicking File and then New. Click the No button when prompted to save the changes to the current image.

15 Print the image you created by clicking File on the Menu bar and then clicking Print. At the Print dialog box, click the Print button.

16 Close Paint by clicking File and then Exit. At the message asking if you want to save the changes, click the No button.

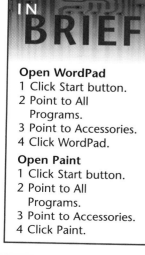

IN BRIEF

Open WordPad
1 Click Start button.
2 Point to All Programs.
3 Point to Accessories.
4 Click WordPad.

Open Paint
1 Click Start button.
2 Point to All Programs.
3 Point to Accessories.
4 Click Paint.

2.11 Customizing the Desktop

The Windows XP operating environment is very customizable. You can change background patterns and colors, specify a screen saver that will display when the screen sits idle for a specific period of time, or change the scheme for windows, menus, title bars, and system fonts. Make these types of changes at the Display Properties dialog box. This dialog box contains five tabs. Clicking each tab displays a different set of options for customizing the desktop.

PROJECT: You have been asked by your manager to determine how you want the Windows XP desktop to display on the computers in your department at Worldwide Enterprises. You decide to look at the customization options available for the desktop.

S T E P S

(Note: Before completing this exercise, check with your instructor to determine if you can customize the desktop.)

1 At the Windows XP desktop, position the arrow pointer on an empty location on the desktop, click the *right* mouse button, and then click *Properties* at the pop-up menu.

> This displays the Display Properties dialog box with the Themes tab selected.

2 At the Display Properties dialog box, click the Desktop tab.

> If a background is selected in the *Background* list box (other than the *(None)* option), make a note of this background name.

3 Click *Ascent* in the Background list box.

4 Click the Screen Saver tab.

> If a screen saver is already selected in the *Screen saver* list box, make a note of this screen saver name.

5 Click the down-pointing arrow at the right side of the *Screen saver* list box and then click *Beziers*.

> A preview of the screen saver displays in the screen located toward the top of the dialog box.

6 Click the down-pointing arrow in the *Wait* text box until *1* displays.

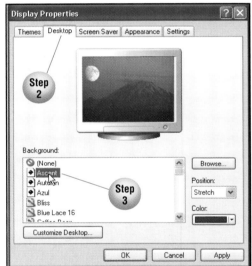

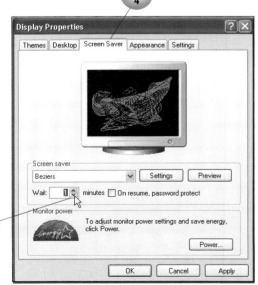

7. Click the Appearance tab.

8. Click the down-pointing arrow at the right side of the *Color scheme* list box and then click *Silver* at the drop-down list.

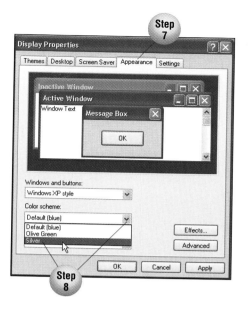

Step 7

Step 8

9. Click OK to close the Display Properties dialog box.

10. At the Windows XP desktop, notice the Ascent background. Let the screen remain idle for one minute and then notice the screen saver that displays.

11. Move the mouse to remove the screen saver and then double-click the *Recycle Bin* icon.

> Notice the color scheme that displays in the window.

12. Close the Recycle Bin window.

13. Return the settings back to the default. To do this, right-click an empty location on the desktop and then click *Properties* at the shortcut menu.

14. At the Display Properties dialog box, click the Desktop tab and then click the background in the *Background* list box that was originally selected.

15. Click the Screen Saver tab.

16. Click the down-pointing arrow at the right side of the *Screen Saver* list box and then click *(None).* (If a screen saver was selected before completing this exercise, return to that screen saver.)

17. Click the up-pointing arrow in the *Wait* text box until *15* displays (or the number that appeared before you changed it to *1*).

18. Click the Appearance tab.

19. Click the down-pointing arrow at the right side of the *Color scheme* list box and then click *Default (blue)* at the drop-down list (or the scheme that was selected before you changed it).

20. Click OK to close the Display Properties dialog box.

In Addition

Customizing Settings

Click the Settings tab at the Display Properties dialog box and options display for customizing the video display. You can increase or decrease the screen resolution by pixels and change the color quality. If you click the Troubleshoot button, the Help and Support Center window displays with information on troubleshooting the video display. Click the Advanced button to display a dialog box with a number of options for further customizing the display.

IN BRIEF

Open Display Properties Dialog Box
1 Click *right* mouse button on an empty location on the desktop.
2 Click *Properties* at the pop-up menu.

FEATURES SUMMARY

Feature	Button/Icon	Action
Control Panel window		Click Start button, click Control Panel
Copy selected files/folders		At My Computer window, select files to be copied, click the Copy the selected items hyperlink in the *File and Folder Tasks* section of the task pane, choose destination location in the Copy Items dialog box, click Copy
Create shortcut		At My Computer window, position mouse pointer on file, hold down right mouse button, drag to desktop, release button, click Create Shortcuts Here
Create new folder		At My Computer window, click File, point to New, click Folder
Delete files/folders		At My Computer window, select desired files/folders, click the Delete this file hyperlink or Delete this folder hyperlink in the *File and Folder Tasks* section of the task pane, click Yes
Delete shortcut icon		Drag shortcut icon to *Recycle Bin* icon
Display Properties dialog box		Right-click empty location on desktop, click Properties
Help and Support Center window		Click Start button, click Help and Support
Move selected files/folders		At My Computer window, select files to be moved, click the Move selected items hyperlink in the *File and Folder Tasks* task pane, choose destination location in the Move Items dialog box, click Move
My Computer window		Click Start button, click My Computer
Paint		Click Start button, point to All Programs, point to Accessories, click Paint
Recycle Bin window	Recycle Bin	Double-click *Recycle Bin* icon
Rename file/folder		At My Computer window, right-click file, click *Rename*, type new name, press Enter
Restore files/folders from Recycle Bin		At Recycle Bin window, select desired files/folders, click the Restore this item hyperlink in the Recycle Bin Tasks task pane
Search Results window		Click Start button, click Search
Select adjacent files/folders		Click first file/folder, hold down Shift key, click last file/folder
Select nonadjacent files/folders		Click first file/folder, hold down Ctrl key, click any other files/folders
WordPad		Click Start button, point to All Programs, point to Accessories, click WordPad

PROCEDURES CHECK

Completion: In the space provided at the right, indicate the correct term, symbol, button, or command.

1. Click this button on the Help and Support Center toolbar to find information on a topic by typing a keyword, browsing a list of related topics, and then double-clicking the desired topic in the left pane.

2. Click this button on the Help and Support Center toolbar to return to the opening Help and Support Center window. _____

3. Click this menu sequence to create a new folder in the My Computer window. _____

4. Change the display of files and folders in the My Computer window to Thumbnails, Tiles, Icons, List, or Details using this button on the Standard Buttons toolbar. _____

5. To select adjacent files, click the first file, hold down this key, and then click the last file. _____

6. To select nonadjacent files, click the first file, hold down this key, and then click any other desired files. _____

7. At the My Computer window, select a file, click the Copy this file hyperlink in the task pane, and this dialog box displays. _____

8. At the Move Items dialog box, choose the destination location in which to place the selected files or folders and then click this button to complete the action. _____

9. Files deleted from the hard drive are sent here. _____

10. Delete a shortcut icon by dragging the icon on top of this icon. _____

11. Open this window to display a list of categories in which you can customize the appearance and functionality of your computer. _____

12. This wizard is automatically activated in the Search window to walk you through the steps to complete a search. _____

13. This Windows accessory program contains features for preparing, editing, and formatting documents. _____

14. This Windows accessory program contains features for drawing black and white or color images that can be saved as bitmap files. _____

15. Customize the Windows XP desktop such as changing the theme, background, screen saver, color scheme, and so on, with options at this dialog box. _____

SKILLS REVIEW

Activity 1: USING HELP

1   At the Windows XP desktop, learn about keyboard shortcuts. To do this click the Start button on the Taskbar and then click Help and Support.
2   At the Help and Support Center window, make sure the insertion point is positioned in the *Search* text box, type **keyboard shortcuts**, and then press Enter.
3   Click <u>Windows keyboard shortcuts overview</u> in the *Overview, Articles, and Tutorials* section of the Suggested Topics list box.
4   Click <u>General keyboard shortcuts</u> in the contents pane below the heading Windows keyboard shortcuts overview.
5   Scroll through the list of keyboard shortcuts that displays in the contents pane below the heading General keyboard shortcuts.
6   Click the Index button on the Help and Support Center toolbar.
7   Type **keyboard shortcuts** in the *Type in the keyword to find* text box.
8   Double-click *for dialog boxes* in the left pane.
9   Click <u>Dialog box keyboard shortcuts</u> in the contents pane below the heading Windows keyboard shortcuts overview.
10 Read the list of keyboard shortcuts that displays in the contents pane.
11 Close the Help and Support Center window.

Activity 2: CREATING A FOLDER

1   At the Windows XP desktop, click the Start button and then click My Computer.
2   Insert your disk in drive A.
3   Double-click *3½ Floppy (A:)* in the contents pane.
4   Click File, point to New, and then click Folder.
5   Type **Worksheets** and then press Enter.
6   Close the window.

Activity 3: SELECTING, COPYING, MOVING, AND DELETING FILES

1   At the Windows XP desktop, open the My Computer window.
2   Make sure your disk is inserted in drive A.
3   Double-click *3½ Floppy (A:)* in the contents pane.
4   Double-click the *WindowsS2* folder name in the contents pane.
5   Click the Views button on the Standard Buttons toolbar and then click *List*.
6   Click once on ***FCTBookings*** to select it, hold down the Shift key, and then click ***FCTPackages***.
7   Click the <u>Copy the selected items</u> hyperlink in the *File and Folder Tasks* section of the task pane.
8   At the Copy Items dialog box, click *3½ Floppy (A:)* in the list box.
9   Click the folder name *Worksheets* in the list box.

10 Click the Copy button.

11 After the files are copied, deselect the files by clicking in any area in the contents pane outside of the selected files.

12 Click **WEExcelRevenues** in the contents pane, hold down the Ctrl key, and then click **WERevChart**.

13 Click the <u>Move the selected items</u> hyperlink in the *File and Folder Tasks* section of the task pane.

14 At the Move Items dialog box, click *Worksheets* in the list box and then click the Move button.

15 Click **FCTCCSkiing** in the contents pane, hold down the Ctrl key, and then click **FCTNorwayTour**.

16 Click the <u>Delete the selected items</u> hyperlink in the *File and Folder Tasks* section of the task pane.

17 At the confirmation message, click the Yes button.

18 Close the window.

Activity 4: RENAMING A FILE; CREATING AND DELETING A SHORTCUT

1 Make sure your disk is inserted in drive A.

2 Open the My Computer window.

3 Double-click *3½ Floppy (A:)* in the contents pane.

4 Double-click the *Worksheets* folder.

5 Right-click **FCTExcelSalesCom** and then click Rename.

6 Type FCTCommissions.xls and then press Enter.

7 Position the mouse pointer on **FCTCommissions**, hold down *right* mouse button, drag to the desktop, and then release the mouse button.

8 Click *Create Shortcuts Here* at the pop-up menu.

9 Close the window.

10 Double-click the *Shortcut to FCTCommissions* icon on the desktop.

11 After viewing the Excel worksheet, close the Excel window.

12 At the Windows XP desktop, drag the *Shortcut to FCTCommissions* shortcut icon on top of the *Recycle Bin* icon. (This deletes the shortcut.)

Activity 5: SEARCHING FOR FILES

1 Make sure your disk is inserted in drive A.

2 At the Windows XP desktop, click the Start button, and then click Search.

3 Click <u>All files and folders</u> in the *What do you want to search for?* section.

4 Click in the *A word or phrase in the file* text box and then type Sanderson.

5 Click the down-pointing arrow at the right side of the *Look in* list box and then click *3½ Floppy (A:)*.

6 Click the Search button. (Notice the file names that display in the Search Results pane.)

7 Click the Back button.

8 Type FCT in the *All or part of the file name* text box.

9   Select and then delete *Sanderson* in the *A word or phrase in the file* text box.
10 Make sure *3½ Floppy (A:)* displays in the *Look in* list box.
11 Click the Search button. (Notice the file names that display in the contents pane.)
12 Click the *Yes, finished searching* option.
13 Close the Search window.

Activity 6: USING WORDPAD

1   At the Windows XP desktop, click the Start button, point to All Programs, point to Accessories, and then click WordPad.
2   At the WordPad window, type the following:

Please reserve the conference room for next Thursday from 7 to 9 p.m. We anticipate approximately 25 participants for the "Vacationing on a Budget" workshop.

3   Click the Print button on the toolbar.
4   Click File on the Menu bar and then click Exit.
5   At the message asking if you want to save the changes, click the No button.

Activity 7: USING PAINT

1   At the Windows XP desktop, click the Start button, point to All Programs, point to Accessories, and then click Paint.
2   Click the Ellipse tool in the Toolbar.
3   Using the mouse, drag to create an oval shape in the Paint window that fills most of the window.
4   Click the Text tool and then, using the mouse, drag to draw a text box inside the oval.
5   Type Vacationing on a Budget.
6   Click the down-pointing arrow at the right side of the size list box and then click *18* at the drop-down list. (You may need to increase or decrease this number to ensure that the text fits on one line in the text box.)
7   Click the Fill With Color tool, click a color of your choice in the color palette, and then click inside the oval shape you drew.
8   Click File on the Menu bar and then click Print. At the Print dialog box, click the Print button.
9   Click File and then Exit. At the message asking if you want to save the changes, click the No button.

PERFORMANCE PLUS

Assessment 1: MANAGING FOLDERS AND FILES

1. Insert your disk in drive A.
2. Create a new folder on your disk in drive A named *PerformanceThreads*.
3. Display the contents of the WindowsS2 folder on your disk.
4. Change the view to *List*.
5. Copy all files beginning with *PT* to the PerformanceThreads folder.
6. Display the contents of the PerformanceThreads folder.
7. Change the view to *List*.
8. Create a new folder within PerformanceThreads named *Payroll*. (A folder created within a folder is referred to as a subfolder.)
9. Move **PTExcelOctPayroll** and **PTWordOctPayroll** from the PerformanceThreads folder into the Payroll subfolder.
10. Delete **PTMarqueeLetter** from the PerformanceThreads folder.
11. Rename the file named **PTAgreement** located in the PerformanceThreads folder to **CostumeAgreement.doc**.

Assessment 2: CREATING AND THEN DELETING A SHORTCUT

1. With the My Computer window open, create a shortcut icon to the file named **CostumeAgreement** located in the PerformanceThreads folder on your disk in drive A.
2. Close the My Computer window.
3. Double-click the shortcut icon. (This displays the **CostumeAgreement** file in Microsoft Word.)
4. Exit Microsoft Word.
5. Delete the *Shortcut to CostumeAgreement* shortcut icon.

Assessment 3: USING WORDPAD AND PAINT

1. Open WordPad and then type the following text:

   I have created a shortcut to the CostumeAgreement file. Print three copies of the agreement and then give one to the customer, one to the Accounting Department, and file the third in the Customer filing cabinet.

2. Print the text and then exit WordPad without saving the changes.
3. Open Paint.
4. Create a shape of your choosing with a text box inside. Type the following text in the text box: **Costume Research and Design**.
5. Increase or decrease the size of the text so it spans the text box and fits on one line.
6. Insert a fill color of your choosing in the shape.
7. Print the image.
8. Exit Paint without saving the changes.

Assessment 4: SEARCHING FOR INFORMATION ON MULTIPLE USER ACCOUNTS

1 You have been asked by your supervisor at First Choice Travel to learn about sharing your computer with other users. Your supervisor is considering adding an evening shift and wants to find out how existing computer equipment can be set up for other users who would be working evenings and weekends. Using the Windows XP Help and Support feature, learn how to share computers by creating user accounts. *(Hint: Display the Help and Support Center window, type* user accounts *in the* Search *text box, and then press Enter. Click* <u>What's new for user accounts and startup</u> *and then follow the links to read about sharing your computer.)*

2 When information on *Share your Computer* displays in the right pane, print the help topic.

3 Search for information on creating user accounts and then print the help topic.

4 Search for information on creating user passwords and then print the help topic.

5 Search for information on switching users and then print the help topic.

6 Close the Help and Support Center window.

MARQUEE SERIES

MICROSOFT®
INTERNET EXPLORER
6.0

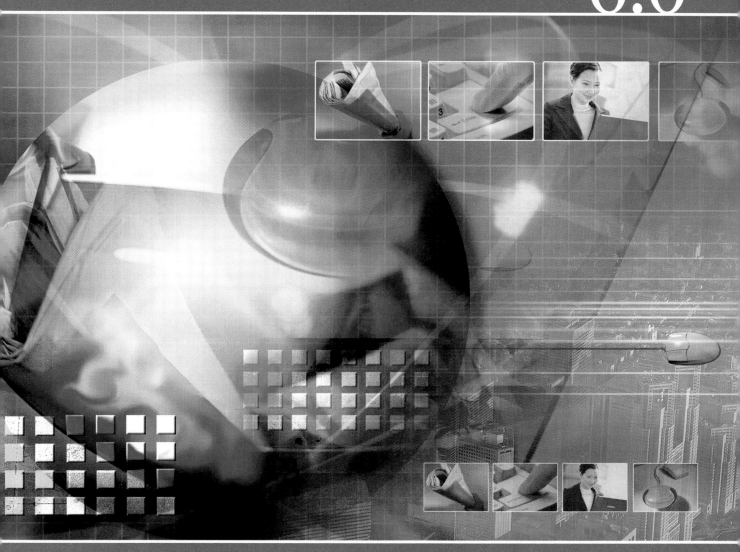

NITA RUTKOSKY
Pierce College at Puyallup – Puyallup, Washington

DENISE SEGUIN
Fanshawe College – London, Ontario

EMCParadigm
PUBLISHING

CONTENTS

The Marquee Series Team: Desiree Faulkner, Developmental Editor; Leslie Anderson, Senior Designer; Jennifer Wreisner, Cover Designer; Leslie Anderson, Erica Tava, Desktop Production.

Publishing Team: George Provol, Publisher; Janice Johnson, Director of Product Development; Tony Galvin, Acquisitions Editor; Lori Landwer, Marketing Manager; Shelley Clubb, Electronic Design and Production Manager.

Acknowledgment: The authors and publisher wish to thank the following reviewer for her technical and academic assistance in testing exercises and assessing instruction: Susan Lynn Bowen, Valdosta Technical College, Valdosta, GA.

© 2004 by Paradigm Publishing Inc.
        Published by **EMC**Paradigm   (800) 535-6865
        875 Montreal Way   E-mail: educate@emcp.com
        St. Paul, MN 55102   Web site: www.emcp.com

Printed in the United States of America   10 9 8 7 6 5 4 3 2

INTERNET EXPLORER

Browsing the Internet Using Internet Explorer 6.0

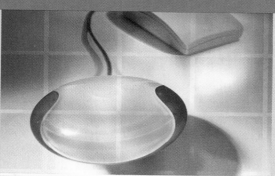

Microsoft Internet Explorer 6.0 is a Web browser program with options and features for displaying sites as well as navigating and searching for information on the Internet. The *Internet* is a network of computers connected around the world. Users access the Internet for several purposes: to communicate using e-mail, to subscribe to news groups, to transfer files, to socialize with other users around the globe in "chat" rooms, and largely to access virtually any kind of information imaginable. Using Microsoft Internet Explorer 6.0, you will learn the skills and complete the projects described here.

Skills

- Visit specific sites by using the site URL
- Click hyperlinks to navigate to specific sites and/or Web pages
- Search for sites containing specific information
- Narrow a search using advanced search options
- Use the Research pane to look up specific information and translate text
- Download a Web page to a separate file
- Download an image to a separate file

Projects

Visit Web sites for two national parks and print the Web site home pages. Search for Web sites pertaining to historical costume design. Use advanced search options to locate information on skydiving companies in the state of Oregon. Search for information on the Royal Ontario Museum and translate several English words into French. Locate a Web site for Banff National Park, save the Web page as a file, and save an image as a file.

Print the Web site home pages for the *New York Times* and *USA Today* online newspapers.

Search for and locate the Web page for the Theatre Department at York University and the Web page for the Department of Drama at New York University.

Locate a Web site for a snow skiing resort in Utah and then save the Web site home page as a file and save an image as a file.

1.1 Browsing the Internet Using Internet Explorer 6.0

Using the Internet, people can access a phenomenal amount of information for private or public use. To use the Internet, three things are generally required—an Internet Service Provider (ISP), a program to browse the Web (called a **Web browser**), and a **search engine**. In this section, you will use the Microsoft Internet Explorer Web browser to locate information on the Internet. **Uniform Resource Locators**, referred to as URLs, are the method used to identify locations on the Internet. The steps for browsing the Internet vary but generally include: opening Internet Explorer, typing the URL for the desired site, navigating the various pages of the site, printing Web pages, and then closing Internet Explorer.

PROJECT: Dennis Chun, the location director for Marquee Productions is gathering information for a new movie project. He has asked you to visit the Web sites for Yosemite National Park and Glacier National Park and print the Web site home page.

S T E P S

① Make sure you are connected to the Internet through an Internet Service Provider and that the Windows desktop displays.

> Check with your instructor to determine if you need to complete steps for accessing the Internet.

② Launch Microsoft Internet Explorer by double-clicking the Internet Explorer icon located on the Windows desktop.

FIGURE IE1.1 Internet Explorer Window

Title Bar
Menu Bar
Explorer Toolbar
Address Bar

Status Indicator

Vertical Scroll Bar

Status Bar

Depending on your system configuration, the steps you complete to open Internet Explorer may vary. Figure IE1.1 identifies the elements of the Internet Explorer, version 6.0, window. The Web page that displays in your Internet Explorer window may vary from what you see in Figure IE1.1.

③ At the Internet Explorer window, click in the Address bar (refer to Figure IE1.1), type **www.nps.gov/yose**, and then press Enter.

> For information on URL names, please refer to the *In Addition* section at the bottom of the next page.

Step 3

④ Scroll down the Web site home page for Yosemite National Park by clicking the down-pointing arrow on the vertical scroll bar located at the right side of the Internet Explorer window.

Step 4

⑤ Print the Web site home page by clicking the Print button located on the Internet Explorer toolbar.

Refer to Figure IE1.2 for the names of the buttons located on the Internet Explorer toolbar. (Your toolbar may not contain every button shown.)

FIGURE IE1.2 Internet Explorer Toolbar Buttons

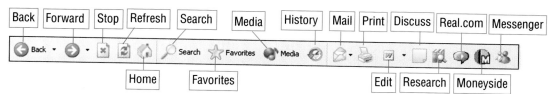

⑥ Display the Web site home page for Glacier National Park by clicking in the Address bar, typing **www.nps.gov/glac**, and then pressing Enter.

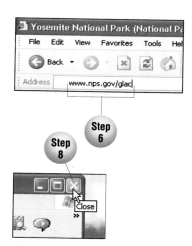

⑦ Print the Web site home page by clicking the Print button located on the Internet Explorer toolbar.

⑧ Close Internet Explorer by clicking the Close button (contains an X) located in the upper right corner of the Internet Explorer window.

You can also close Internet Explorer by clicking File on the Internet Explorer Menu bar and then clicking Close at the drop-down menu.

In Addition

Understanding URLs

URLs (Uniform Resource Locators) are the method used to identify locations on the Internet. The format of a URL is *http://server-name.path.* The first part of the URL, *http* stands for HyperText Transfer Protocol, which is the protocol or language used to transfer data within the World Wide Web. The colon and slashes separate the protocol from the server name. The server name is the second component of the URL. For example, in the URL http://www.microsoft.com, the server name is *microsoft.* The last part of the URL specifies the domain to which the server belongs. For example, *.com* refers to "commercial" and establishes that the URL is a commercial company. Other examples of domains include *.edu* for "educational," *.gov* for "government," and *.mil* for "military."

IN BRIEF

Display a Specific Web Site
1 At Windows desktop, double-click Internet Explorer icon.
2 Click in Address bar, type Web site URL, and then press Enter.

1.2 Navigating Using Hyperlinks; Searching for Specific Sites

Most Web pages contain *hyperlinks* that you click to connect to another page within the Web site or to another site on the Internet. Hyperlinks may display in a Web page as underlined text in a specific color or as images or icons. To use a hyperlink, position the mouse pointer on the desired hyperlink until the mouse pointer turns into a hand and then click the left mouse button. If you do not know the URL for a specific site or you want to find information on the Internet but do not know what site to visit, complete a search with a search engine. A variety of search engines are available on the Internet, each offering the opportunity to search for specific information. One method for searching for information is to click the Search button on the Internet Explorer toolbar. This displays a Search Companion pane with options for completing a search. Another method for completing a search is to visit the Web site home page for a search engine and use options at the site.

PROJECT: The research coordinator for Marquee Productions has asked you to locate sites on the Internet on Elizabethan and Renaissance costumes. Historical costumes are needed for the new movie project.

S T E P S

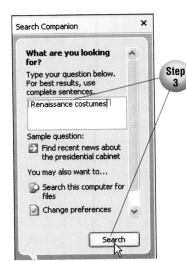

Step 3

① Make sure you are connected to the Internet and then double-click the Internet Explorer icon on the Windows desktop.

② At the Internet Explorer window, click the Search button on the Internet Explorer toolbar.

> When you click the Search button, the Search Companion pane displays at the left side of the Internet Explorer window.

③ Click in the search text box, type **Renaissance costumes,** and then click the Search button (or press Enter).

④ When a list of sites displays in the Search Companion pane, scroll down the list and then click a site hyperlink that interests you by positioning the mouse pointer on the hyperlink until the pointer turns into a hand and then clicking the left mouse button.

> If you position the mouse pointer on some hyperlinks a box displays next to the pointer containing information on the site. Use this feature to help you find the desired site.

⑤ When the Web site home page displays, click the Print button.

⑥ Click the Search button on the Internet Explorer toolbar to remove the Search Companion pane.

⑦ Use the Yahoo search engine to find sites on Renaissance costumes by clicking in the Address bar, typing **www.yahoo.com**, and then pressing Enter.

⑧ At the Yahoo Web site, type **Renaissance costumes** in the search text box and then press Enter.

Step 8

9 Click a hyperlink to a site that interests you.

10 When the site displays, click the Print button on the Internet Explorer toolbar.

11 Use the Google search engine to find sites on Elizabethan costumes by clicking in the Address bar, typing **www.google.com**, and then pressing Enter.

12 When the Google Web site home page displays, type **Elizabethan costumes** in the search text box and then press Enter.

13 Click a hyperlink to a site that interests you.

14 When the Web site home page displays, click the Print button on the Internet Explorer toolbar.

15 Close Internet Explorer.

In Addition

Adding Favorites to the Favorites List

If you find a site you want to visit on a regular basis, add the sight to the Favorites list. To do this, display the Favorites pane by clicking the Favorites button on the Internet Explorer toolbar. Click the Add button located at the top of the Favorites pane. At the Add Favorite dialog box that displays, make sure the information in the *Name* text box is correct (if not, select the text and then type your own information) and then click OK. The new site displays at the bottom of the list in the Favorites pane. Jump quickly to the site by clicking the Favorites button and then clicking the site name at the Favorites pane.

In BRIEF

Search for a Web Site
1 At the Internet Explorer window, click Search button.
2 Click in search text box, type text related to desired Web sites, and then click search button.

1.3 Completing Advanced Searches for Specific Sites

The Internet contains an extraordinary amount of information. Depending on what you are searching for on the Internet and the search engine you use, some searches can result in several thousand "hits" (sites). Wading through a large number of sites can be very time consuming and counterproductive. Narrowing a search to very specific criteria can greatly reduce the number of hits for a search. To narrow a search, use the advanced search options offered by the search engine.

PROJECT: The stunt coordinator at Marquee Productions has asked you to locate information on skydiving companies in the state of Oregon.

S T E P S

1. Make sure you are connected to the Internet and then double-click the Internet Explorer icon on the Windows desktop.

2. Click in the Address bar, type www.yahoo.com and then press Enter.

    If the Yahoo Web site home page does not display, choose another search engine Web site.

3. At the Yahoo Web site home page, click the advanced search hyperlink.

    The advanced search hyperlink will probably display at the right side of the search text box and display as _Advanced_. The location and name may vary.

4. At the advanced search page, click in the _the exact phrase_ text box (the name of this option may vary) and then type skydiving in Oregon.

    This limits the search to any Web sites that contain the exact phrase "skydiving in Oregon."

5. Scroll down the advanced search page and then click the _only .com domains_ option (the name of this option may vary).

    Clicking this option tells Yahoo to only display Web sites with a .com extension and to ignore any other extension. If this option is not available, choose another option that limits the display of Web sites.

6. Click the Search button.

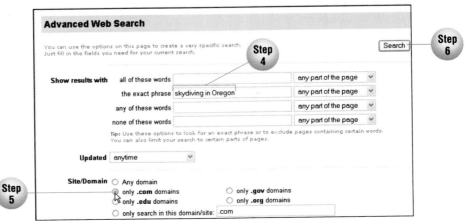

⑦ When the list of Web sites displays, click a hyperlink that interests you.

⑧ Click the Print button on the Internet Explorer toolbar to print the Web page.

⑨ Click the Back button on the Internet Explorer toolbar until the Yahoo advanced search page displays.

⑩ Select and then delete the text *skydiving in Oregon* located in the *the exact phrase* text box.

⑪ Click in the *all of these words* text box and then type skydiving Oregon tandem static line.

You want to focus on Web sites that offer tandem and static line skydiving in Oregon.

⑫ Click the *Any domain* option.

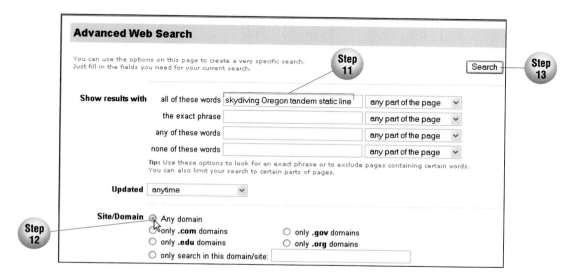

⑬ Click the Search button.

⑭ When the list of Web sites displays, click a hyperlink that interests you and then print the Web page.

⑮ Close Internet Explorer.

In Addition

Displaying a List of Sites Visited

As you visit different Web sites, Internet Explorer keeps track of the sites. Click the History button and a History pane displays. Click the desired hyperlink to display sites visited during the past two weeks, sites visited today, or sites visited on specific days of the week. When you click a specific date, a list of sites visited displays in the pane. This information can be useful for remembering Internet addresses previously visited and for monitoring Internet use.

IN BRIEF

Complete Advanced Search Using Yahoo
1 At Internet Explorer window, click in Address bar, type www.yahoo.com, and then press Enter.
2 Click the advanced search hyperlink.
3 Click in search text box, type specific text related to desired Web sites.
4 Select a search method and a search area.
5 Click the Search button.

1.4 Researching and Requesting Information

Click the Research button on the Internet Explorer toolbar and a Research pane displays at the left side of the window. Use options in this pane to search for and request specific information from online sources and to translate words to and from a variety of languages. The online resources available to you depend on the locale to which your system is set, authorization information indicating that you are allowed to download the information, and your internet service provider. Determine the resources available by clicking the down-pointing arrow at the right of the resources list box. The drop-down list contains lists of reference books, research sites, business and financial sites, and other services. If you want to use a specific reference in your search, click the desired reference at the drop-down list, type the desired word or topic in the *Search for* text box, and then press Enter. Items matching your word or topic display in the pane list box. Depending on the item, the list box may contain hyperlinks you can click to access additional information on the Internet.

PROJECT: Chris Greenbaum, production manager for the Toronto film project has asked for your assistance. She wants you to use the Research feature of Internet Explorer to search for information on the Royal Ontario Museum and to also use the translation tool to translate several English words into French.

STEPS

1. Open Internet Explorer.

2. Click the Research button on the Internet Explorer toolbar.

3. Type **Royal Ontario Museum** in the *Search for* text box in the Research pane.

4. Click the down-pointing arrow to the right of the resources list box (the down-pointing arrow immediately below the Start searching button) and then click *Encarta Encyclopedia: English (North America)* at the drop-down list.

   If this reference is not available, click any encyclopedia that is available.

5. Look at the information that displays in the Research pane and then click a hyperlink about the Royal Ontario Museum that interests you.

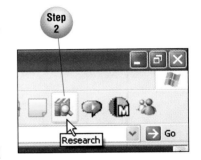

Step 2

Step 3

Step 4

6 Use the translation feature to translate *script* from English to French. To begin, select the text in the *Search for* text box and then type **script**.

7 Click the down-pointing arrow at the right of the resources list box and then click *Translation* at the drop-down list.

8 Make sure that *English (U.S.)* displays in the *From* option box.

> If it does not, click the down-pointing arrow at the right of the *From* option and then click *English (U.S.)* at the drop-down list.

9 Click the down-pointing arrow to the right of the *To* option and then click *French (France)* at the drop-down list.

10 Make a note of the translation of *script* into French.

11 Select *script* in the *Search for* text box, type **documentary**, and then press Enter.

12 When the translation of *documentary* displays in the Research pane, make a note of the translation.

13 Click the Research button on the Internet Explorer toolbar to turn off the Research pane.

14 Close Internet Explorer.

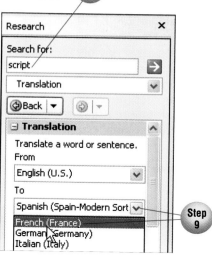

Step 6

Step 9

In Addition

Choosing Research Options

Determine the resources available by clicking the down-pointing arrow at the right of the resources list box (the list box located below the *Search for* text box). The drop-down list contains lists of reference books, research sites, business and financial sites, and other services. You can control the available research options by clicking the Research options hyperlink located at the bottom of the Research pane. This displays the Research Options dialog box shown at the right. At this dialog box, insert a check mark before those items you want available and remove the check mark from those items you do not want available.

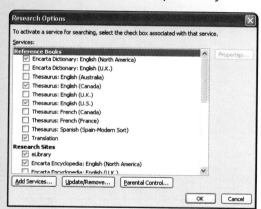

IN BRIEF

Use Research Pane
1. At the Internet Explorer window, click the Research button.
2. Click in the *Search for* text box and then type specific text.
3. Click the down-pointing arrow at right of the resources list box and then click the desired resource.

1.5 Downloading Images, Text, and Web Pages from the Internet

You can save as a separate file the image(s) and/or text that displays when you open a Web page. This separate file can be viewed, printed, or inserted in another file. The information you want to save in a separate file is downloaded from the Internet by Internet Explorer and saved in a folder of your choosing with the name you specify. Copyright laws protect much of the information on the Internet. Before using information downloaded from the Internet, check the site for restrictions. If you do use information, make sure you properly cite the source.

PROJECT: The production manager of the new movie project at Marquee Productions has asked you to locate a site on the Internet for Banff National Park. She wants you to save the Web page as a file and a picture of the park in another file. She needs these files for a presentation she is preparing for the next production meeting.

STEPS

1. Make sure you are connected to the Internet and then double-click the Internet Explorer icon on the Windows desktop.

2. Using the search engine of your choosing, search for sites on the Internet for Banff National Park.

3. From the list of sites that displays, choose a site that contains information about Banff National Park and at least one image of the park.

4. Insert a formatted disk in drive A.

   > Check with your instructor to determine if you should save the Web page on a disk or save it into a folder on the hard drive or network.

5. Save the Web page as a separate file by clicking File on the Internet Explorer Menu bar and then clicking Save As at the drop-down menu.

6. At the Save Web Page dialog box, click the down-pointing arrow at the right side of the *Save in* option and then click *3½ Floppy (A:)* at the drop-down list.

   > This step may vary depending on where your instructor wants you to save the Web page.

7. Select the text in the *File name* text box, type **BanffWebPage**, and then press Enter.

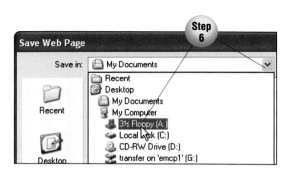

File name:	BanffWebPage
Save as type:	Web Page, complete (*.htm;*.html)
Encoding:	Western European (ISO)

8　Save the image as a separate file by right-clicking the image of the park.

> The image that displays may vary from what you see to the right.

9　At the shortcut menu that displays, click Save Picture As.

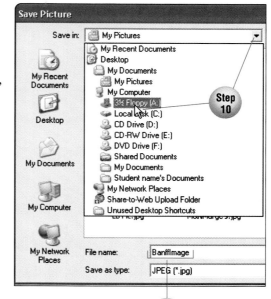

10　At the Save Picture dialog box, change the location to drive A (or the location specified by your instructor).

11　Select the text in the *File name* text box, type **BanffImage**, and then press Enter.

12　Close Internet Explorer.

Optional Steps

13　Open Microsoft Word by clicking the Start button on the Taskbar, pointing to All Programs, pointing to Microsoft Office, and then clicking Microsoft Office Word 2003.

14　With Microsoft Word open, click Insert on the Menu bar, point to Picture, and then click From File.

15　At the Insert Picture dialog box, change the *Look in* option to drive A (or the location where you saved the Banff image) and then double-click ***BanffImage***.

16　When the image displays in the Word document, print the document by clicking the Print button on the Word Standard toolbar.

17　Close the document by clicking File on the Menu bar and then clicking Close at the drop-down menu. At the message asking if you want to save the changes, click No.

18　Open the **BanffWebPage** file by clicking the Open button on the Word Standard toolbar.

19　At the Open dialog box, change the *Look in* option to drive A (or the location where you saved the Banff Web page), and then double-click ***BanffWebPage***.

20　Print the Web page by clicking the Print button on the Word Standard toolbar.

21　Close the **BanffWebPage** file by clicking File and then Close.

22　Close Word by clicking the Close button (contains an X) that displays in the upper right corner of the screen.

FEATURES SUMMARY

Feature	Button	Menu	Keyboard
Close Internet Explorer	✖	File, Close	
Display next Web page	➡	View, Go To, Forward	Alt + Right Arrow
Display previous Web page	⬅	View, Go To, Back	Alt + Left Arrow
Launch Internet Explorer	e		
Print a Web page	🖶	File, Print	Ctrl + P
Research pane	🔍	View, Explorer Bar, Research	
Save image as a separate file		Right-click image, click Save Picture As	
Save a Web page as separate file		File, Save As	
Search pane	🔍	View, Explorer Bar, Search	Ctrl + E

PROCEDURES CHECK

Completion: In the space provided at the right, indicate the correct term, symbol, button, or command.

1. Type a URL in this bar at the Internet Explorer window. _____
2. The letters *URL* stand for this. _____
3. Click this button on the Internet Explorer toolbar to display the previous Web page. _____
4. Clicking the Search button on the Internet Explorer toolbar causes this to display. _____
5. Use options in this pane to request specific information from online sources and to translate words to and from a variety of languages. _____
6. Save a Web page as a separate file by clicking File on the Internet Explorer Menu bar and then clicking this option at the drop-down menu. _____
7. Save an image as a separate file by right-clicking the image and then clicking this option at the shortcut menu. _____

SKILLS REVIEW

Activity 1: BROWSING THE INTERNET AND NAVIGATING WITH HYPERLINKS

1 Launch Internet Explorer.
2 Click in the Address bar, type **www.si.edu** and then press Enter. (This is the Web site home page for the Smithsonian Institution.)
3 Using hyperlinks navigate to a site in the Smithsonian that interests you and then print the Web page.
4 Click the Back button until the Smithsonian Institution Web site home page displays.

Activity 2: SEARCHING FOR SPECIFIC SITES

1 At the Internet Explorer window, click the Search button to display the Search Companion pane.
2 Use options in the Search Companion pane to look for Web sites on mountain climbing.
3 Visit a site that interests you and then print the Web site.
4 Display the Yahoo Web site and then use advanced options to search for Web sites on mountain climbing in British Columbia, Canada.
5 Visit a site that interests you and then print the Web site.
6 Turn off the display of the Search Companion pane.

Activity 3: REQUESTING INFORMATION AND TRANSLATING WORDS

1 At the Internet Explorer window, click the Research button to display the Research pane.
2 Use options in the Research pane to find information in an encyclopedia on the decade in the 1900s referred to as the "Roaring Twenties."
3 Click a hyperlink that interests you and then print the Web site.
4 Use options in the Research pane to translate the English word *history* into French.
5 Make a note of the French word and then click the Research button to turn off the display of the Research pane.

Activity 4: DOWNLOADING A WEB PAGE

1 Using a search engine of your choosing, search for Web sites on parasailing in Hawaii. Find a site that contains a parasailing image.
2 When the Web page displays, save it as a separate file by clicking File and then Save As.
3 At the Save Web Page dialog box, change the location to drive A (or the location specified by your instructor), type **ParasailWebPage** in the *File name* text box, and then press Enter.
4 Save the image by right-clicking the image and then clicking Save Picture As at the shortcut menu.
5 At the Save Picture dialog box, change the location to drive A (or the location specified by your instructor), type **ParasailImage** in the *File name* text box, and then press Enter.
6 Close Internet Explorer.

PERFORMANCE PLUS

Assessment 1: VISITING AND PRINTING WEB PAGES

1. Sam Vestering, a manager at Worldwide Enterprises, likes to keep up to date with current events by reading the daily headlines for various newspapers. He has asked you to print the Web site home pages for two online newspapers—the *New York Times* and *USA Today*. To begin, launch Internet Explorer.
2. Visit the Web site of the *New York Times* at www.nytimes.com and then print the Web site home page.
3. Visit the Web site of *USA Today* at www.usatoday.com and then print the Web site home page.

Assessment 2: NAVIGATING WEB SITES

1. Cal Rubine, the Chair of the Theatre Arts Division at Niagara Peninsula College has asked you to print the Web pages for the theater and/or drama departments at two universities. Visit the Web site home page for the York University, Toronto, Canada at www.yorku.ca.
2. Using hyperlinks navigate to the Web page for the Theatre Department and then print the Web page.
3. Visit the Web site home page for New York University at www.nyu.edu.
4. Using hyperlinks navigate to the Web page for the Department of Drama (undergraduate) and then print the Web page.

Assessment 3: RESEARCHING INFORMATION

1. You work for First Choice Travel and are preparing a brochure on snow skiing vacations. You need some information and images for the brochure. Using Internet Explorer, search for information on snow skiing resorts in Utah.
2. Visit a Web site that interests you and contains an image of the resort or mountains.
3. Save the Web page as a separate file.
4. Save an image as a separate file.
5. Close Internet Explorer.

OPTIONAL STEPS

6. Open Microsoft Word.
7. Insert the image into a Word document and then print the document.
8. Close the document without saving it.
9. Open the file containing the Web page and then print it.
10. Close the document and then close Word.
11. Close Internet Explorer.

MARQUEE SERIES

MICROSOFT®
WORD
2003

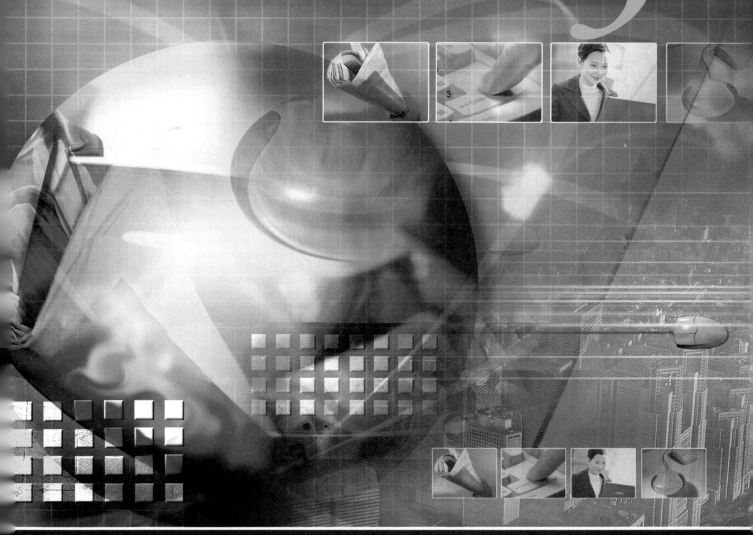

NITA RUTKOSKY
Pierce College at Puyallup – Puyallup, Washington

DENISE SEGUIN
Fanshawe College – London, Ontario

EMCParadigm
PUBLISHING

CONTENTS

The Marquee Series Team: Desiree Faulkner, Developmental Editor; Leslie Anderson, Senior Designer; Jennifer Wreisner, Cover Designer; Leslie Anderson Erica Tava, Desktop Production; Teri Linander, Tester; Sharon O'Donnell, Copyeditor; Lynn Reichel, Proofreader; and Nancy Fulton, Indexer.

Publishing Team: George Provol, Publisher; Janice Johnson, Director of Product Development; Tony Galvin, Acquisitions Editor; Lori Landwer, Marketing Manager; Shelley Clubb, Electronic Design and Production Manager.

Acknowledgment: The authors and publisher wish to thank the following reviewer for her technical and academic assistance in testing exercises and assess instruction: Susan Lynn Bowen, Valdosta Technical College, Valdosta, GA.

Library of Congress Cataloging-in-Publication Data
    Rutkosky, Nita Hewitt.
    Microsoft Word 2003 / Nita Rutkosky, Denise Seguin.
       p.cm. – (Marquee series)
    Includes index.
    ISBN 0-7638-2083-0 (text) – ISBN 0-7638-2082-2 (text & CD)
     1. Microsoft Word. 2. Word processing. I. Seguin, Denise. II. Title. III. Series

Text + CD: 0-7638-2082-2
Order Number: 05632

© 2004 by Paradigm Publishing Inc.
     Published by **EMC**Paradigm
     875 Montreal Way   (800) 535-6865
     St. Paul, MN 55102   E-mail: educate@emcp.com
                                  Web site: www.emcp.com

Printed in the United States of America   10 9 8 7 6 5 4

Introducing
WORD 2003

Microsoft Word 2003 is a word processing program used to create documents such as memos, letters, reports, research papers, brochures, announcements, newsletters, envelopes, labels, and much more. Word is a full-featured word processing program that provides a wide variety of editing and formatting features as well as sophisticated visual elements. Use the spelling, grammar, and Thesaurus features to prepare clear and accurate documents. Access the Help feature to look up information or learn more about a specific feature. Add visual appeal by applying formatting to text or inserting bullets, numbers, and special symbols. Design visually powerful documents by inserting clip art images, WordArt, diagrams, and drawn objects. Create interactive, dynamic documents by saving documents as Web pages and inserting hyperlinks linking to other documents or sites on the Internet.

While working in Word, you will produce business documents for the following six companies:

First Choice Travel is a travel center offering a full range of traveling services from booking flights, hotel reservations, and rental cars to offering traveling seminars.

Marquee Productions is involved in all aspects of creating movies from script writing and development to filming.

The Waterfront Bistro offers fine dining for lunch and dinner and also offers banquet facilities, a wine cellar, and catering services.

Performance Threads maintains an inventory of rental costumes and also researches, designs, and sews special-order and custom-made costumes.

Worldwide Enterprises is a national and international distributor of products for a variety of companies and is the exclusive movie distribution agent for Marquee Productions.

The mission of the Niagara Peninsula College Theatre Arts Division is to offer a curriculum designed to provide students with a thorough exposure to all aspects of the theatre arts.

Creating, Editing, and Formatting Documents Using Word 2003

Using Word, you can create, edit, and format a variety of business documents and use Word's powerful editing and formatting features to produce well-written and visually appealing documents. Word is a full-featured word processing application that provides many of features required to produce most business documents. Interesting Word features and elements that you will learn in each section are described below.

Section 1 Creating and Editing a Document

Start your Word experience by preparing and editing a document on vacation specials for First Choice Travel and then preparing a memo using a Word template.

Vacation Specials Document in Topics 1.2 – 1.10

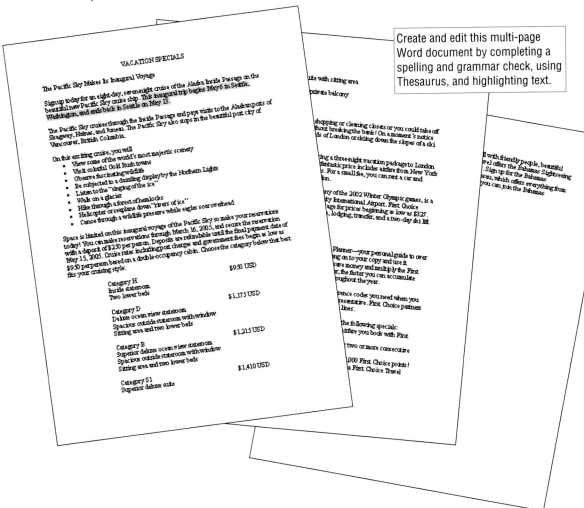

Create and edit this multi-page Word document by completing a spelling and grammar check, using Thesaurus, and highlighting text.

Memo Created Using Memo Template in Topic 1.11

Memorandum

Create this memo using Word's Contemporary Memo template.

To: Alex Torres, Manager, Toronto Office

CC: Terry Blessing, President

From: Melissa Gehring, Manager, Los Angeles Office

Date: 11/3/2005

Re: Marquee Productions Movie Site

Marquee Productions will be filming a movie in and around the Toronto area from July 8 through August 30. Robert Velarde, site coordinator for Marquee Productions, has requested scheduling and pricing information on flights from Los Angeles to Toronto and information on lodging.

Approximately 45 people from Marquee Productions will need flight reservations and hotel rooms. Please research this information and locate the best group rates. I would like the information by the end of next week.

Section 2

Formatting Characters and Paragraphs

Edit and format fact sheets for First Choice Travel by applying fonts and font effects and aligning and indenting text in paragraphs. Prepare a document on train travel and insert bullets, numbers, symbols, and special characters; type text in columns by setting tabs; and apply formatting using styles.

**Oslo, Norway Fact Sheet in
Topics 2.1 – 2.6**

Format this document by applying font and font effects, applying styles, and indenting text in paragraphs.

OSLO FACT SHEET

History

The founding of Oslo took place in the turbulent period between the Viking Age and Norway's Catholic Middle Ages. Many remnants and ruins can be found from Ancient Oslo in *Memorial Park*. The city has a fascinating, interesting, and dramatic history.

Oslo's population was substantially reduced during the time of the Black Death in 1348, which claimed over fifty percent of the inhabitants. This epidemic also had political consequences for Norway, which was reduced to a province of Denmark. During this period, Copenhagen was the actual capital of Norway. Oslo was also greatly affected by the Lutheran Protestant Reformation of 1537, with religious conflicts, political separation from the Catholic Church and the foundation of a Protestant National Church. Many ruins of churches and monasteries bear witness to this process.

Oslo was completely destroyed by fire in 1624. Following intense renewal and advanced city planning in the spirit of the Renaissance, a completely new city was created and named Christiania. In 1814 Norway was united with Sweden and Christiania experienced strong economic and political growth. In 1905 the union with Sweden was dissolved and Norway gained its independence. The original name of Oslo was reinstated in 1924.

Population

Oslo is the capital of Norway and has in excess of 500,000 inhabitants. Approximately 900,000 people live in the Greater Oslo area representing twenty percent of the total population of Norway.

Commerce and Industry

The working population of Oslo distributed according to occupation includes: Industry, 16%; building and construction, 6%; transport, 9%; and trade, services, and tourism, 69%.

Climate

Oslo's climate is temperate in the autumn and warm in spring and summer. Snow falls three to five months in the winter. Skiing conditions are good in the hills around Oslo between December and April. From May to July, the weather can be quite warm with long periods of sunshine. Drought can also occur from time to time. Statistically speaking, Oslo is Scandinavia's sunniest capital.

Holiday, Sport, and Leisure

Oslo is surrounded by forest and fjord. Preserving the fjord and area surrounding the city for leisure and outdoor pursuits is an important part of Oslo's political tradition. Some of the major sports events in Oslo include the Grete Waitz Race, Holmenkollen Relay, Oslo Marathon, and the Holmenkollen Ski Festival. Oslo includes over 2,000 kilometers of prepared ski tracks for cross-country skiing and a number of ski lifts for Alpine skiing.

Seeing Tours

Tour 1: Mini Cruise
Fifty-minute cruise that departs on the hour

Tour 2: Fjord Cruise
Two-hour cruise that departs on the half hour

Tour 3: Fjord Cruise with Dinner
Two-hour cruise followed by dinner at Restaurant Lanternen

Tour 4: Selected Oslo Sightseeing
Three-hour tour of Vigeland Sculpture Park, the Holmenkollen Ski Jump, the Viking Ships, and the Kon-Tiki Raft

BOAT AND COACH DEPART FROM PIER 3 IN FRONT OF THE OSLO CITY HALL.

Student Name
Date: 11/3/2005

Europe Train Travel Document in Topics 2.7–2.15

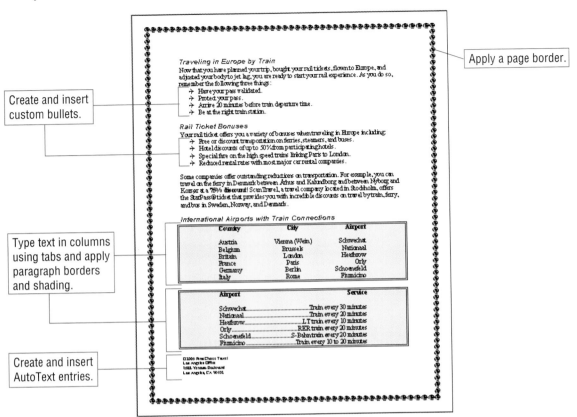

Apply a page border.

Create and insert custom bullets.

Type text in columns using tabs and apply paragraph borders and shading.

Create and insert AutoText entries.

Section 3
Formatting and Enhancing a Document

Prepare an announcement with center-and right-aligned text and insert a clip art image and logo to add visual appeal to the announcement. Create and print an envelope and mailing labels.

Travel Announcement in Topics 3.7 – 3.8

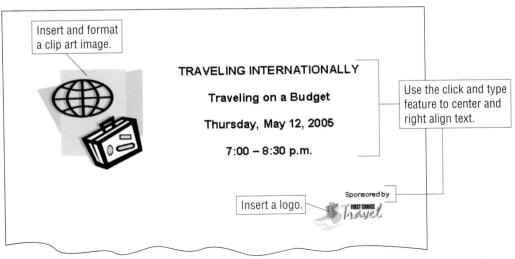

Insert and format a clip art image.

Use the click and type feature to center and right align text.

Insert a logo.

Envelope Created in Topic 3.11

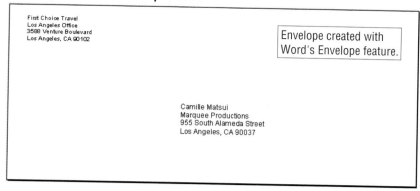

First Choice Travel
Los Angeles Office
3588 Venture Boulevard
Los Angeles, CA 90102

Camille Matsui
Marquee Productions
955 South Alameda Street
Los Angeles, CA 90037

> Envelope created with Word's Envelope feature.

Labels Created in Topic 3.12

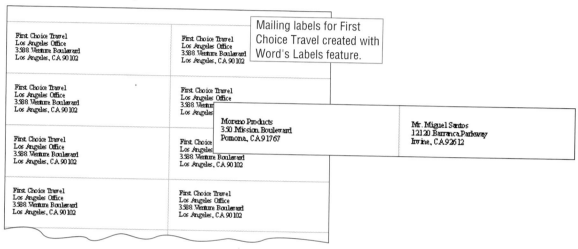

> Mailing labels for First Choice Travel created with Word's Labels feature.

First Choice Travel
Los Angeles Office
3588 Venture Boulevard
Los Angeles, CA 90102

Moreno Products
350 Mission Boulevard
Pomona, CA 91767

Mr. Miguel Santos
12120 Barranca Parkway
Irvine, CA 92612

Section 4

Formatting with Special Features

Create and modify a table for First Choice Travel containing information on Hawaiian vacation specials. Prepare a fact sheet and format the text in columns, insert a header and footer, save the fact sheet as a Web page, and insert a hyperlink to a Web site and Word document. Prepare a document containing an organizational chart and diagram for First Choice Travel.

Table Created in Topics 4.1 – 4.3

ISLAND SIGHTSEEING FLIGHTS

First Choice Travel has contracted with Tropic Airlines to offer First Choice Travel customers a fantastic deal on adventurous, sightseeing flights over the spectacular and breathtaking Hawaiian Islands. During your visit to any of the beautiful islands, take advantage of these Tropic Airlines flights to provide memories that will last a lifetime!

MAUI

MAUI FLIGHTS			
Adventure	Destination	Price	FCT
Special West Maui	Waterfalls, lush tropical valleys	$49	$35
West Maui Tropical	West Maui mountains, Hawaii's highest waterfalls	$79	$65
Haleakala-Keane	Haleakala crater, tropical rain forest, waterfalls	$89	$75
Molokai-West Maui	West Maui mountains, waterfalls, sea cliffs, Kalaupapa colony	$189	$175

> Create and format this table by inserting and deleting rows, merging cells, inserting a column, changing the font, and applying a border and shading to the table.

Petersburg, Alaska, Fact Sheet in Topics 4.5 – 4.8

Document containing text set in two columns with a line between.

Use comments to add notes, suggestions, or explanations.

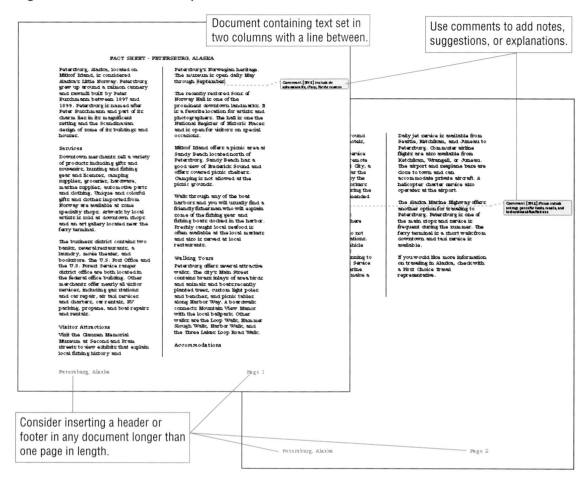

Consider inserting a header or footer in any document longer than one page in length.

First Choice Travel Document in Topic 4.11

Create organizational charts and diagrams using options from the Diagram Gallery.

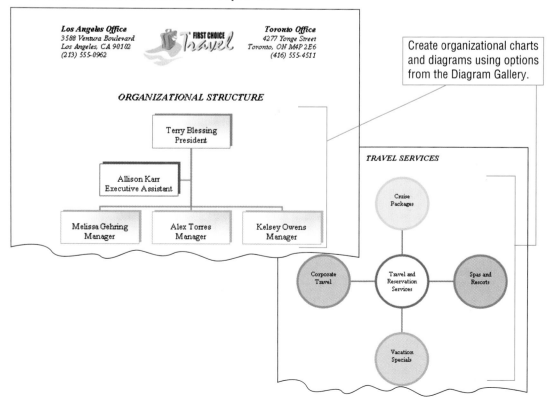

WORD SECTION 1

Creating and Editing a Document

Microsoft Word 2003 is a word processing program you can use to create documents such as letters, reports, research papers, brochures, newsletters, and much more. Word is a full-featured word processing program that provides a wide variety of editing and formatting features as well as sophisticated visual features. In this section, you will learn the skills and complete the projects described here.

 Note: Before beginning this section, copy to a disk or other location the WordS1 subfolder from the Word folder on the CD that accompanies this textbook and then make WordS1 the active folder. Steps on copying a folder, deleting a folder, and making a folder active are located on the inside back cover of this textbook.

Skills

- Complete the word processing cycle
- Move the insertion point
- Insert, replace, and delete text
- Scroll and navigate in a document
- Select and delete text
- Use Undo and Redo
- Check the spelling and grammar in a document
- Use AutoCorrect
- Use Thesaurus
- Use the Help feature
- Highlight text
- Change document views
- Preview a document
- Print a document
- Insert the date and time in a document
- Insert AutoText in a document
- Close a document
- Create a document using a template
- Create and rename a folder
- Save a document in a different format

Projects

 Prepare a document describing a special vacation package and edit and format three documents describing various vacation specials offered by First Choice Travel.

 Prepare a memo regarding a movie site using a memo template; edit an internal memo; prepare a memo regarding catering and costuming for a film; prepare a letter to the manager of The Waterfront Bistro requesting catering information.

 Prepare a memo regarding the distribution schedule.

 Edit a letter to Marquee Productions regarding costuming for a film.

1.1 Completing the Word Processing Cycle

The process of creating a document in Microsoft Word generally follows a word processing cycle. The steps in the cycle vary but typically include: opening Word; creating and editing the document; saving, printing, and closing the document; and then closing Word.

PROJECT: As an employee of First Choice Travel, you have been asked to create a short document containing information on a travel package offered by First Choice Travel.

STEPS

1. At the Windows desktop, click the Start button **🏁 start** on the Taskbar.

    Clicking the Start button causes a pop-up menu to display.

2. At the Start menu, point to All Programs and then point to Microsoft Office.

    A side menu displays when you point to an option on the Start menu that displays with a right-pointing arrow after it.

3. Click Microsoft Office Word 2003 on the Microsoft Office side menu.

    Depending on your system configuration, the steps you complete to open Word may vary.

4. At the Word document screen, identify the various features by comparing your screen with the one shown in Figure W1.1.

    Refer to Table W1.1 for a description of the screen features. Figure W1.1 shows the Standard and Formatting toolbars on two rows. Your screen may show the toolbars on one row.

FIGURE W1.1 Word Document Screen

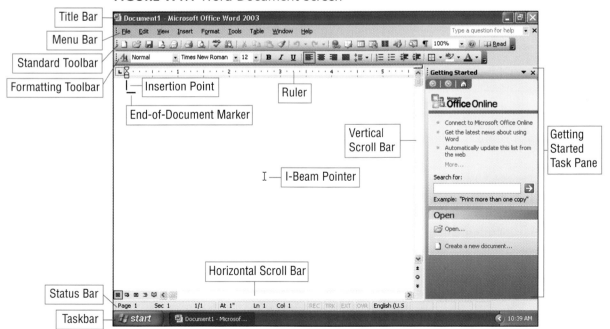

5. At the Word document screen, type the text shown in Figure W1.2.

    Type the text as shown. When you type *adn* and then press the spacebar, the AutoCorrect feature will automatically correct it to *and*. When you type *teh* and then press the spacebar, AutoCorrect corrects it to *the*. Do not press the Enter key to end a line of text. Word will automatically wrap text to the next line.

FIGURE W1.2

Are you spontaneous adn enjoy doing something on a moment's notice? If this describes you, then you will be interested in First Choice Travel Moment's Notice Travel Package. For teh low price of $499 you can fly from New York to London for a four-day stay. The catch to this incredible deal is that you must make your reservations within the next week and complete your London stay within thirty days.

6 Save the document by clicking the Save button 💾 on the Standard toolbar.

7 At the Save As dialog box, make sure the WordS1 folder on your disk is the active folder, type **WordS1-01** in the *File name* text box, and then click the Save button.

The *Save in* option at the Save As dialog box displays the active folder. If you need to make the WordS1 folder on your disk in drive A the active folder, click the down-pointing arrow at the right of the *Save in* option and then click *3½ Floppy (A:)*. Double-click *WordS1* in the list box. After typing the document name, you can press the Enter key instead of clicking the Save button.

8 Print the document by clicking the Print button 🖨 on the Standard toolbar.

9 Close the document by clicking File on the Menu bar and then clicking Close at the drop-down menu.

TABLE W1.1 Document Screen Features

Feature	Description
Title Bar	Displays document name followed by program name
Menu Bar	Contains a list of options to manage and customize documents
Standard Toolbar	Contains buttons that are shortcuts for the most popular commands
Formatting Toolbar	Contains buttons that can quickly apply formatting to text
Ruler	Used to set margins, indents, and tabs
I-Beam Pointer	Used to move the insertion point or to select text
Task Pane	Presents features to help user identify and use more of the program
Insertion Point	Indicates the location of where the next character entered at the keyboard will appear
End-of-Document Marker	Indicates the end of the document
Scroll Bars	Used to view various parts of the document
Status Bar	Displays position of insertion point and working mode buttons
Taskbar	Used to select one of a number of active programs

In Addition

Correcting Errors

The AutoCorrect feature automatically corrects certain words as they are being typed. For example, type *teh* and press the spacebar, and AutoCorrect changes it to *the*. Word also contains a feature called Spell It that inserts a red wavy line below words that are not contained in the Spelling dictionary or not corrected by AutoCorrect. If the word containing a red wavy line is correct, you can leave it as written. The red wavy line does not print. If the word is incorrect, edit it.

1.2 Moving the Insertion Point; Inserting, Replacing, and Deleting Text

Many documents you create will need to have changes made to them. These changes may include adding text, called *inserting*, or removing text, called *deleting*. To insert or delete text, move the insertion point to certain locations without erasing the text through which it passes. To insert text, position the insertion point in the desired location and then type the text. If you want to type over something, switch to the Overtype mode by pressing the Insert key. Delete text in a document by pressing the Backspace key or Delete key.

PROJECT: First Choice Travel marketing staff members have reviewed your document on vacation specials and have recommended a few changes. You need to create a revised version.

STEPS

① At the Word document screen, click the Open button 🖆 on the Standard toolbar. At the Open dialog box, make sure the WordS1 folder on your disk is the active folder and then double-click **FCTVacationSpecials** in the list box.

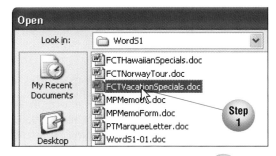

Your list of documents may vary from what you see above.

PROBLEM❓
> If the **FCTVacationSpecials** document does not display in the Open dialog box, check with your instructor.

② Click File and then Save As. At the Save As dialog box type **WordS1-02** in the *File name* text box and then press Enter.

> If you open an existing document, make changes to it, and then want to save it with the same name, click the Save button on the Standard toolbar. If you want to keep the original document and save the document with the changes with a new name, click File and then Save As.

③ Position the mouse pointer at the beginning of the second paragraph and then click the left mouse button. (This moves the insertion point to the location of the mouse pointer.)

④ Press the Up, Down, Left, and Right arrow keys located to the right of the regular keys on the keyboard.

> Use the information shown in Table W1.2 to practice moving the insertion point in the document.

⑤ Press Ctrl + Home, click at the beginning of the paragraph that begins *Sign up today for...*, and then type **Ocean Vista Cruise Lines announces the inaugural voyage of the Pacific Sky ocean liner.**

> By default, text you type in a document is inserted in the document and existing text is moved to the right.

⑥ Click at the beginning of the heading *Ocean Vista Cruise Lines*, press the Insert key on the keyboard, and then type **The Pacific Sky Makes Its Inaugural Voyage.**

> Pressing the Insert button turns on Overtype and anything you type will replace existing text. When Overtype is on, the letters *OVR* display in black on the Status bar.

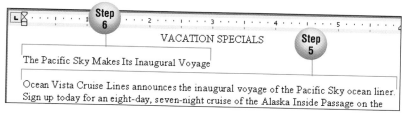

The Pacific Sky Makes Its Inaugural Voyage

VACATION SPECIALS

Ocean Vista Cruise Lines announces the inaugural voyage of the Pacific Sky ocean liner. Sign up today for an eight-day, seven-night cruise of the Alaska Inside Passage on the

7 Press the Insert key to turn off Overtype.

8 Press Ctrl + End (this moves the insertion point to the end of the document) and then click on any character in the last sentence in the document (the sentence that begins *Let First Choice Travel take…*).

9 Press the Backspace key until the insertion point is positioned at the left margin and then press the Delete key until you have deleted the remainder of the sentence.

> Pressing the Backspace key deletes any characters left of the insertion point. Press the Delete key to delete any characters to the right of the insertion point.

10 Click the Save button 🖫 on the Standard toolbar.

> Clicking the Save button saves the document with the same name (**WordS1-02**).

TABLE W1.2 Insertion Point Movements

Location	Press
End of a line	End key
Beginning of line	Home key
Up one screen	Pg Up key
Down one screen	Pg Down key
Beginning of document	Ctrl + Home
End of document	Ctrl + End

In Addition

Expanding Drop-Down Menus

When you click an option on the Menu bar, only the most popular options display (considered first-rank options). To expand the drop-down menu, click the down-pointing arrows that display at the bottom of the menu, or click an option on the Menu bar and then pause on the menu for a few seconds. Second-rank options display on the expanded drop-down menu with a lighter blue background in the color banner left of the option. If you choose a second-rank option, it becomes a first-rank option the next time you display the drop-down menu. If you want all menu options to display, click Tools and then Customize. At the Customize dialog box, click the Options tab. Click in the *Always show full menus* check box to insert a check mark and then click the Close button.

IN BRIEF

Open a Document
1 Click Open button.
2 Double-click document name.

Save a Document
1 Click Save button.
2 Type document name.
3 Click Save or press Enter.

1.3 Scrolling and Navigating in a Document

In addition to moving the insertion point to a specific location, you can use the mouse to move the display of text in the document screen. Use the mouse with the horizontal scroll bar and/or the vertical scroll bar to scroll through text in a document. The horizontal scroll bar displays toward the bottom of the Word screen and the vertical scroll bar displays toward the right side. Scrolling in a document changes the text displayed but does not move the insertion point. The Select Browse Object button located at the bottom of the vertical scroll bar contains options for browsing through a document. Scrolling in a document changes the text displayed while browsing in a document moves the insertion point.

PROJECT: To minimize the need for additional editing, you have decided to carefully review the First Choice Travel vacation specials document on screen.

S T E P S

1. With **WordS1-02** open, press Ctrl + Home to move the insertion point to the beginning of the document.

2. Position the mouse pointer on the down scroll arrow on the vertical scroll bar and then click the left mouse button several times.

   This scrolls down the lines of text in the document. Scrolling changes the display of text but does not move the insertion point.

3. Position the mouse pointer on the vertical scroll bar below the scroll box and then click the left mouse button a couple of times.

   The scroll box on the vertical scroll bar indicates the location of the text in the document screen in relation to the remainder of the document. Clicking on the vertical scroll bar below the scroll box scrolls down one screen of text at a time.

4. Position the mouse pointer on the scroll box on the vertical scroll bar, hold down the left mouse button, drag the scroll box to the top of the vertical scroll bar, and then release the mouse button.

   Dragging the scroll box to the top of the vertical scroll bar displays text at the beginning of the document.

5. Click the Select Browse Object button and then click the Go To option.

   The location of the Go To option may vary. It may be the first option from the left in the bottom row. Position the arrow pointer on the option and the name of the option displays at the bottom of the palette. Use other options at the palette to browse to document features such as a field, endnote, footnotes, comment, section, heading, and graphic.

   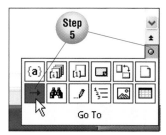

6) At the Find and Replace dialog box with the Go To tab selected, type **2** in the *Enter page number* text box, press the Enter key, and then click Close.

With options at the Find and Replace dialog box with the Go To tab selected, you can move the insertion point to various locations in a document such as a specific page, section, line, bookmark, and so on.

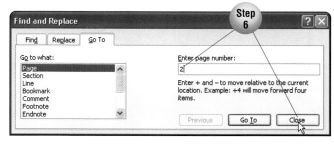

7) Click the Previous Page button located above the Select Browse Object button.

Clicking the Previous Page button moves the insertion point to the beginning of the previous page. The full names of and the tasks completed by the Previous and Next buttons vary depending on the last navigation completed.

8) Click the Next Page button located below the Select Browse Object button.

9) Press Ctrl + Home to move the insertion point to the beginning of the document.

10) Save the document by clicking the Save button on the Standard toolbar.

In Addition

Smart Tags and Option Buttons

Smart Tags: Using a smart tag, you can perform actions in Word that you would normally need to open another program to perform. For example, if you type a date, Word inserts a purple dotted line below the date, indicating a smart tag. Position the mouse pointer on the date and a smart tag icon displays. Click the icon and then choose an action from the pop-up menu such as scheduling a meeting in Outlook.

Option Buttons: As you insert and edit text in a document, you may notice an option button popping up in your text. The name and appearance of this option button varies depending on the action. If a word you type is corrected by AutoCorrect, if you create an automatic list, or if autoformatting is applied to text, the AutoCorrect Options button appears. Click this button to undo the specific automatic action. If you paste text in a document, the Paste Options button appears near the text. Click this button to display options for controlling how the pasted text is formatted.

IN BRIEF

Display Find and Replace Dialog Box
1 Click Select Browse Object button.
2 Click Go To option.

1.4 Selecting and Deleting Text; Using Undo and Redo

Previously, you learned to delete text by pressing the Backspace key or Delete key. You can also select text and then delete it, replace it with other text, or apply formatting to selected text. If you make a change to text, such as deleting selected text, and then change your mind, use the Undo and/or Redo buttons on the Standard toolbar.

PROJECT: You will continue editing the First Choice Travel vacation specials document and select, insert, and delete text.

S T E P S

1 With **WordS1-02** open, position the mouse pointer on the word *Behold* (located immediately after the first bullet) and then double-click the left mouse button.

> Selected text displays in white on a black background. You can also drag through text with the mouse to select the text.

PROBLEM?

> If you select the wrong text and want to deselect it, press the Esc key to turn off the Extend mode and then press any arrow key.

> **Step 1**
>
> On this exciting cruise, you will
> * Behold some of the world
> * Visit colorful Gold Rush t
> * Observe fascinating wildli
> * Be subjected to a dazzling

2 Type **View**.

> When you type *View*, it takes the place of *Behold*. If you select text and then decide you want to deselect it, click in the document window outside the selected text.

3 Move the insertion point to the beginning of the word *Glacier* (located in the second paragraph) and then press the F8 function key on the keyboard. Press the Right Arrow key until the words *Glacier Bay and* are selected.

> Pressing the F8 function key turns on the Extend mode and the *EXT* letters display in black on the Status bar. With the Extend mode on, use the insertion point movement keys to select text.

> **Step 3**
>
> The Pacific Sky cruises through Glacier Bay and the Alaskan ports of Skagway, Haines, and Juneau. The beautiful port city of Vancouver, British Columbia.

4 Press the Delete key.

> Pressing the Delete key deletes the selected text. If you want to cancel a selection, press the Esc key, and then press any arrow key.

5 Position the mouse pointer on any character in the first sentence that begins *Ocean Vista Cruise Lines announces...*, hold down the Ctrl key, click the mouse button, and then release the Ctrl key.

> Holding down the Ctrl key while clicking the mouse button selects the entire sentence.

6 Press the Delete key to delete the selected sentence.

7 Click the Undo button 🔄 on the Standard toolbar.

> When you click the Undo button, the deleted sentence reappears. Clicking the Undo button reverses the last command or deletes the last entry you typed. Click the down-pointing arrow at the right of the Undo button and a drop-down list displays containing changes made to the document since it was opened. Click an action and the action, along with any preceding actions, is undone.

8 Click the Redo button 🔄 on the Standard toolbar.

> Clicking the Redo button deletes the selected sentence. If you click the Undo button and then decide you do not want to reverse the original action, click the Redo button.

9 Position the mouse pointer between the left edge of the screen and the first line of text in the second paragraph until the pointer turns into an arrow pointing up and to the right (instead of the left) and then click the left mouse button.

> The space between the left edge of the screen and the text is referred to as the selection bar. Use the selection bar to select specific amounts of text. Refer to Table W1.3 for more information on selecting text.

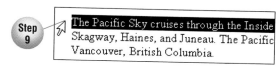

Step 9

10 Deselect the text by clicking in the document outside the selected area.

11 Save the document by clicking the Save button 💾 on the Standard toolbar.

TABLE W1.3 Selecting with the Mouse

To select	Complete these steps using the mouse
A word	Double-click the word
A line of text	Click in the selection bar to the left of the line
Multiple lines of text	Drag in the selection bar to the left of the lines
A sentence	Hold down the Ctrl key and then click anywhere in the sentence
A paragraph	Double-click in the selection bar next to the paragraph or triple-click anywhere in the paragraph
Multiple paragraphs	Drag in the selection bar
An entire document	Triple-click in the selection bar

In Addition

Undoing Multiple Actions

Word maintains actions in temporary memory. If you want to undo an action performed earlier, click the down-pointing arrow to the right of the Undo button. This causes a drop-down list to display. To make a selection from this drop-down list, click the desired action. Any actions preceding a chosen action are also undone. You can do the same with the actions in the Redo drop-down list. To display the Redo drop-down list, click the down-pointing arrow to the right of the Redo button. To redo an action, click the desired action. Any actions preceding the chosen action are also redone. Multiple actions must be undone or redone in sequence.

1.5 Checking the Spelling and Grammar in a Document

Use Word's spelling checker to find and correct misspelled words and find duplicated words (such as *and and*). The spelling checker compares words in your document with words in its dictionary. If a match is found, the word is passed over. If no match is found for the word, the spelling checker stops, selects the word, and offers replacements. The grammar checker will search a document for errors in grammar, style, punctuation, and word usage. The spelling checker and the grammar checker can help you create a well-written document but do not replace the need for proofreading. Use the Word Count feature to determine specific information about a document such as the number of characters, words, lines, paragraphs, and pages contained in the document.

PROJECT: Continuing with the editing process, you are ready to check the spelling and grammar in the First Choice Travel vacation specials document. To help determine production costs, the manager of the Marketing Department has asked you to determine the total number of characters (including spaces) in the vacation specials document.

STEPS

1. With **WordS1-02** open, press Ctrl + Home to move the insertion point to the beginning of the document, and then click the Spelling and Grammar button on the Standard toolbar.

2. When the word *inagural* is selected, make sure *inaugural* is selected in the *Suggestions* list box and then click the Change button in the Spelling and Grammar dialog box.

    Refer to Table W1.4 for an explanation of the buttons in the Spelling and Grammar dialog box.

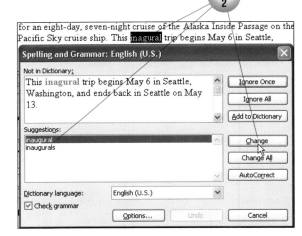

Step 2

TABLE W1.4 Spelling and Grammar Dialog Box Buttons

Button	Function
Ignore Once	During spell checking, skips that occurrence of the word; in grammar checking, leaves the currently selected text as written.
Ignore All	During spell checking, skips that occurrence of the word and all other occurrences of the word in the document.
Ignore Rule	During grammar checking, leaves the currently selected text as written and also ignores the current rule for the remainder of the grammar check in the document.
Add to Dictionary	Adds the selected word to the main spelling checker dictionary.
Change	Replaces the selected word in the sentence with the selected word in the *Suggestions* list box.
Change All	Replaces the selected word in the sentence with the selected word in the *Suggestions* list box and all other occurrences of the word in the document.
AutoCorrect	Inserts the selected word and the correct spelling of the word in the AutoCorrect dialog box.
Undo	Reverses the most recent spelling and grammar action.
Next Sentence	Accepts manual changes made to a sentence and then continues grammar checking.
Options	Displays a dialog box with options for customizing a spelling and grammar check.

3 When the sentence that begins *Space are limited...* is selected, click the Explain button, and then read the information on subject-verb agreement that displays in the yellow box above the Office Assistant.

Clicking the Explain button turns on the display of the Office Assistant. The yellow box above the Office Assistant provides information on the grammar rule.

4 Make sure *Space is* is selected in the *Suggestions* list box and then click the Change button.

PROBLEM

If you accidentally click outside the Spelling and Grammar dialog box, resume the checking by clicking the Resume button.

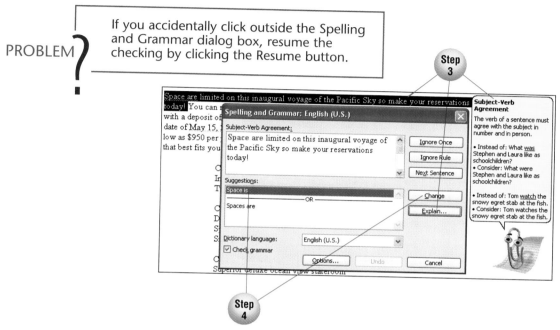

5 When the word *the* is selected (this word is repeated twice), click the Delete button in the Spelling and Grammar dialog box.

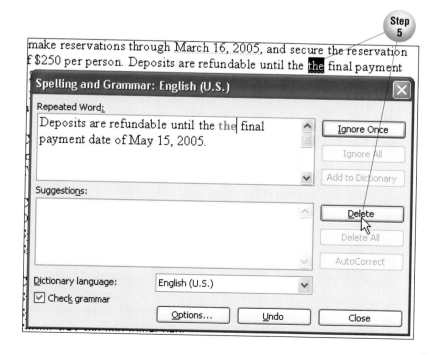

(continued)

6 When the sentence that begins *You could spent the weekend...* is selected, read the information on verb form that displays in the yellow box above the Office Assistant. Make sure *spend* is selected in the *Suggestions* list box and then click the Change button.

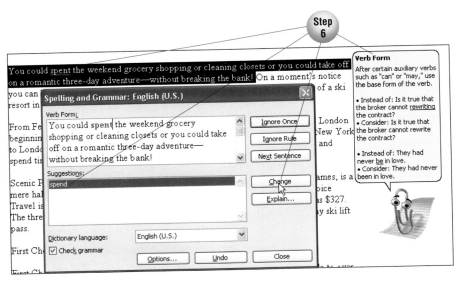

7 When the word *utah* is selected, click the Change button.

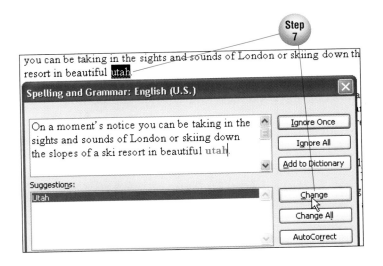

8 When the Readability Statistics dialog box displays, read the information, and then click the OK button.

The Readability Statistics dialog box displays a variety of information about the document such as word, character, paragraph, and sentence counts; and the average length of sentences, words, and characters. Readability percentages also display toward the bottom of the dialog box. Refer to Table W1.5 for a description of the percentages. (If the Readability Statistics dialog box does not display, turn on the feature by clicking Tools and then Options. At the Options dialog box, click the Spelling & Grammar tab. Insert a check mark in the *Show readability statistics* check box and then click OK.)

9 Determine additional information about the statistics of the document by clicking Tools and then Word Count. After viewing the document statistics, click the Close button.

10 Click the Save button  on the Standard toolbar to save the changes made to the document.

TABLE W1.5 Reading Statistics

Flesch Reading Ease	The Flesch reading ease is based on the average number of syllables per word and the average number of words per sentence. The higher the score, the greater the number of people who will be able to understand the text in the document. Standard writing generally scores in the 60–70 range.
Flesch-Kincaid Grade Level	This is based on the average number of syllables per word and the average number of words per sentence. The score indicates a grade level. Standard writing is generally written at the seventh- or eighth-grade level.

In Addition

Editing while Checking Spelling and Grammar

When checking a document, you can temporarily leave the Spelling and Grammar dialog box, make corrections in the document, and then resume checking. For example, suppose while spell checking you notice a sentence that you want to change. To correct the sentence, move the I-beam pointer to the location in the sentence where the change is to occur, click the left mouse button, and then make the changes to the sentence. To resume checking, click the Resume button, which was formerly the Ignore button.

Changing Spelling Options

Control spelling and grammar checking options at the Spelling & Grammar dialog box shown at the right. Display this dialog box by clicking the Options button at the Spelling & Grammar dialog box. You can also display this dialog box by clicking Tools and then Options. At the Options dialog box, click the Spelling & Grammar tab.

1.6 Using AutoCorrect and Thesaurus

The AutoCorrect feature automatically detects and corrects some typographical errors, misspelled words, and incorrect capitalizations. In addition to correcting errors, you can use AutoCorrect to insert frequently used text. Use the Thesaurus program to find synonyms, antonyms, and related words for a particular word. Synonyms are words that have the same or nearly the same meaning and antonyms are words with opposite meanings.

PROJECT: You need to insert additional text in the First Choice Travel vacation specials document. To speed up the process, you will add an entry to AutoCorrect. You will also use Thesaurus to find synonyms for specific words in the document.

STEPS

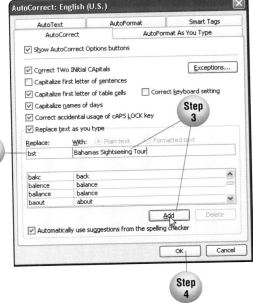

1. With **WordS1-02** open, click Tools and then AutoCorrect Options.

2. At the AutoCorrect dialog box with the AutoCorrect tab selected, type **bst** in the *Replace* text box and then press the Tab key.

3. Type **Bahamas Sightseeing Tour** in the *With* text box and then click the Add button.

4. Click OK to close the dialog box.

5. Press Ctrl + End to move the insertion point to the end of the document and then move the insertion point a double space below the last bulleted item.

6. Type the text shown in Figure W1.3. (Type the text exactly as shown. AutoCorrect will correct *bst* to *Bahamas Sightseeing Tour.*)

FIGURE W1.3

> bst
>
> The Bahamas consist of over 700 islands and cays, all with friendly people, beautiful beaches, and magnificent dive spots. First Choice Travel offers the bst to explore these exciting and breathtaking islands. Sign up for the bst and experience the bustling city of Nassau, which offers everything from parasailing to casino gaming. Call us to discover how you can join the bst at an incredibly low price.

7. Click anywhere in the word *breathtaking* located in the second sentence in the paragraph you just typed.

8. Click Tools, point to Language, and then click Thesaurus.

9) At the Research task pane, position the mouse pointer on the word *spectacular* in the task pane list box, click the down-pointing arrow, and then click Insert at the drop-down list.

10) Close the Research task pane by clicking the Close button **×** located in the upper right corner of the task pane.

11) Position the mouse pointer on the word *bustling* located in the third sentence in the paragraph you just typed and then click the *right* mouse button.

12) At the shortcut menu that displays, point to Synonyms and then click *lively* at the side menu.

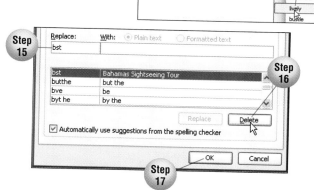

PROBLEM **?** If the shortcut menu does not display, check to make sure you clicked the *right* mouse button.

13) Click the Save button **🖫** to save the document with the same name.

14) Click Tools and then AutoCorrect Options.

15) At the AutoCorrect dialog box, type **bst** in the *Replace* text box.

> This inserts *Bahamas Sightseeing Tour* in the *With* text box and also selects the entry in the list box.

16) Click the Delete button.

17) Click OK to close the dialog box.

In Addition

Using the Research Task Pane

Depending on the word you are looking up, the words in the Research task pane list box may display followed by (n.) for *noun*, (adj.) for *adjective*, or (adv.) for *adverb*. Antonyms may display in the list of related synonyms, generally at the end of the list, and are followed by (Antonym). As you look up synonyms and antonyms for various words, you can display the list of synonyms and antonyms for the previous word by clicking the Previous search button (contains the word *Back* and a left arrow) or click the Next button to display the next search in the sequence. You can also click the down arrow at the right side of the Next search button to display a list of words for which you have looked up synonyms and antonyms.

IN BRIEF

Add an AutoCorrect Entry
1 Click Tools, AutoCorrect.
2 Type text in *Replace* text box.
3 Press Tab key.
4 Type text in *With* text box.
5 Click Add button.
6 Click OK to close dialog box.

1.7 Using the Help Feature; Highlighting Text

Microsoft Word includes a Help feature that contains information on Word features and commands. For example, you might want to find information on Word's highlighting feature. With the Help feature, you can find and print the information about the Highlight button on the Formatting toolbar. This button allows you to highlight important information electronically, similar to the way you might highlight with a marker or highlighter pen sentences in books, magazines, and papers.

PROJECT: You want to identify specific text in the First Choice Travel document for other marketing team members to evaluate. You will use the Help feature to search for and print information on highlighting text and then highlight specific text in the vacation specials document.

STEPS

1. With **WordS1-02** open, click the Microsoft Office Word Help button located at the right side of the Standard toolbar.

2. At the Word Help task pane, type **How do I highlight text?** in the *Search for* text box and then press Enter.

   This displays a list of topics in the Search Results task pane list box.

3. Click the Apply or remove highlighting hyperlink in the Search Results task pane list box.

4. Click the Show All hyperlink that displays in the upper right corner of the Microsoft Office Word Help window.

   This displays all information about the topic.

5. Read the information that displays in the Microsoft Office Word Help window and then click the Print button located toward the top of the window. At the Print dialog box, click the Print button.

6. Close the Microsoft Office Word Help window by clicking the Close button located in the upper right corner of the window and then close the Search Results task pane.

7. Press Ctrl + Home to move the insertion point to the beginning of the document.

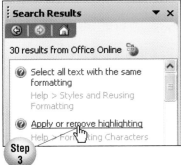

8 Click the Highlight button ⟨ab⟩ located toward the right side of the Formatting toolbar.

> If the Standard and Formatting toolbars display on one row, separate the toolbars by clicking Tools and then Customize. At the Customize dialog box with the Options tab selected, click the *Show Standard and Formatting toolbars on two rows* option to insert a check mark and then click the Close button.

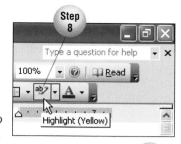

Step 8

Step 9

Step 10

9 Select the sentence *This inaugural trip begins May 6 in Seattle, Washington, and ends back in Seattle on May 13.* that displays in the first paragraph in the *The Pacific Sky Makes Its Inaugural Voyage* section.

> The Pacific Sky Makes Its Inaugural Voyage
>
> Sign up today for an eight-day, seven-night cruise of the Alaska Inside Passage on the beautiful new Pacific Sky cruise ship. This inaugural trip begins May 6 in Seattle, Washington, and ends back in Seattle on May 13.
>
> The Pacific Sky cruises through the Inside Passage and pays visits to the Alaskan ports of Skagway, Haines, and Juneau. The Pacific Sky also stops in the beautiful port city of Vancouver, British Columbia.

Step 12

10 Select the sentence *The Pacific Sky also stops in the beautiful port city of Vancouver, British Columbia.* that displays in the second paragraph in the *The Pacific Sky Makes Its Inaugural Voyage* section.

11 Click the Highlight button ⟨ab⟩ on the Formatting toolbar to turn off highlighting.

12 Click the down-pointing arrow at the right side of the Highlight button and then click *None* at the palette.

13 Select the sentence *The Pacific Sky also stops in the beautiful port city of Vancouver, British Columbia.*

> This removes the highlighting from the sentence.

14 Click the down-pointing arrow at the right side of the Highlight button and then click the yellow color (first color from the left in the top row).

15 Click the Highlight button ⟨ab⟩ to turn off highlighting.

16 Click the Save button 🖫 to save the document.

In Addition

Getting Help Using the *Ask a Question* Text Box

Click the text inside the *Ask a Question* text box located at the right side of the Menu bar (this removes the text), type a help question, and then press Enter. At the Search Results task pane, click the desired topic, and the Microsoft Office Word Help window displays with information about the topic.

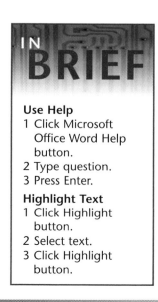

IN BRIEF

Use Help
1 Click Microsoft Office Word Help button.
2 Type question.
3 Press Enter.

Highlight Text
1 Click Highlight button.
2 Select text.
3 Click Highlight button.

1.8 Changing Document Views

By default, a document generally displays on the screen in Normal view. You can change this default to Print Layout, Full Screen, or Reading Layout views. You can also change the zoom percentage for viewing a document. In Print Layout view, a document displays on the screen in basically the same manner as it will appear when printed. In Print Layout view, you can show and/or hide white space. Choose the Full Screen view to expand the workspace on your screen. With the Zoom button on the Standard toolbar and options at the Zoom dialog box, you can change the percentage of display. Reading Layout view displays a document in a format for easy viewing and reading.

PROJECT: Several people will be reviewing the First Choice Travel document on screen so you decide to experiment with various views to determine the best view for reviewing on screen.

STEPS

1. With **WordS1-02** open, change to Print Layout view by clicking View and then Print Layout.

   You can also change to Print Layout view by clicking the Print Layout View button located to the left of the horizontal scroll bar.

2. Change the zoom by clicking the down-pointing arrow at the right of the Zoom button on the Standard toolbar and then clicking *Whole Page* at the drop-down list.

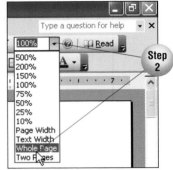

3. Click the down-pointing arrow at the right of the Zoom button and then click *50%* at the drop-down list.

4. Click View and then Zoom. At the Zoom dialog box, click *100%* and then click OK.

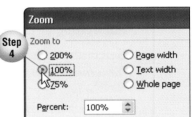

5. Expand the viewing area on the screen by clicking View and then Full Screen.

6. Return to Print Layout view by clicking the Close Full Screen button.

   You can also return to Print Layout view by pressing the Esc key.

7. To save space on the screen in Print Layout view, you decide to remove the white and gray space at the top and bottom of each page. To do this, press Ctrl + Home to move the insertion point to the beginning of the document, position the mouse pointer on the gray space at the top of the page until the pointer turns into the Hide White Space button, and then click the left mouse button.

8. Scroll through the document and then redisplay the beginning of the document. Redisplay white and gray spaces by positioning the mouse pointer on the thin gray line at the top of the page until the pointer turns into the Show White Space button and then clicking the left mouse button.

⑨ Click the Read button located at the right side of the Standard toolbar.

> This displays the document in Reading Layout view. You can also click View and then Reading Layout or press Alt + R to display a document in Reading Layout view.

⑩ Navigate in the document using the commands shown in Table W1.6.

Table W1.6 Navigating in Reading Layout View

Press this key	To complete this action
Page Down key or spacebar	Move to next page or section
Page Up key or Backspace key	Move to previous page or section
Right Arrow key	Move to next page
Left Arrow key	Move to previous page
Home	Move to first page in document
End	Move to last page in document
Esc	Return to previous view

⑪ Click the Document Map button on the Reading Layout toolbar to display the Document Map pane at the left side of the screen and then click the *First Choice Planner* heading.

Step 11

> This displays the page containing the heading.

⑫ Click the Document Map button to turn off the display of the Document Map pane.

⑬ Click the Thumbnails button to display miniatures of each page in the document and then click the Page 2 thumbnail.

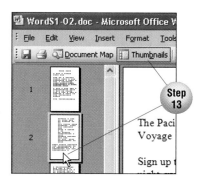

Step 13

⑭ Click the Thumbnails button to turn off the display of the miniatures.

⑮ Close Reading Layout view by clicking the Close button on the Reading Layout toolbar.

> You can also close the view by pressing Alt + C or pressing the Esc key.

⑯ Return to Normal view by clicking View and then Normal.

In Addition

Customizing the Reading Layout View

With some of the buttons on the Reading Layout toolbar, you can customize the Reading Layout view. Click the Increase Text Size button to increase the size of text in the viewing page or click the Decrease Text Size button to reduce the size of text. Click the Actual Page button to display the page as it will appear when printed. In this view, you may not be able to read the text on the page. Click the Allow Multiple Pages button on the Reading Layout toolbar to turn off two-page view and display only one viewing page. To exit Reading Layout view, click the Close button located at the right side of the Reading Layout toolbar.

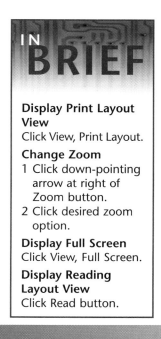

IN BRIEF

Display Print Layout View
Click View, Print Layout.

Change Zoom
1 Click down-pointing arrow at right of Zoom button.
2 Click desired zoom option.

Display Full Screen
Click View, Full Screen.

Display Reading Layout View
Click Read button.

1.9 Previewing and Printing a Document

Before printing a document, previewing a document may be useful. Word's Print Preview feature displays the document on the screen as it will appear when printed. With this feature, you can view a partial page, single page, multiple pages, or zoom in on a particular area of a page. With options at the Print dialog box, you can specify the number of copies to print and also specific pages for printing.

PROJECT: You are ready to print certain sections of the First Choice Travel vacation specials document. But first you will preview the document on screen.

S T E P S

1. With **WordS1-02** open, press Ctrl + Home to move the insertion point to the beginning of the document.

2. Click the Print Preview button on the Standard toolbar.

   This displays the **WordS1-02** document in Print Preview.

3. Click the Multiple Pages button on the Print Preview toolbar. This causes a grid to appear immediately below the button.

   Refer to Figure W1.4 for the names of the buttons on the Print Preview toolbar.

4. At the grid that displays, drag the mouse down and to the right until the message at the bottom of the grid displays as *2 x 2 Pages* and then click the left mouse button.

FIGURE W1.4 Print Preview Toolbar

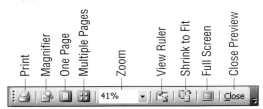

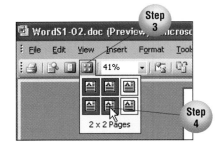

5. Click the One Page button on the Print Preview toolbar.

6. Click the down-pointing arrow at the right of the Zoom button 41% and then click *75%* at the drop-down list.

7. Click the One Page button on the Print Preview toolbar.

8. Click the Close button to close Print Preview.

9. Print only page 2 of the document by clicking File and then Print.

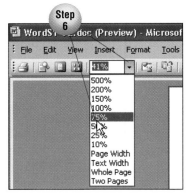

⑩ At the Print dialog box, click in the *Pages* text box in the *Page range* section and then type 2.

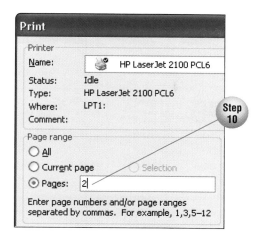

⑪ Click OK.

⑫ Move the insertion point to any character in page 3 and then print page 3 by clicking File and then Print.

⑬ At the Print dialog box, click the *Current page* option in the *Page range* section.

⑭ Click OK.

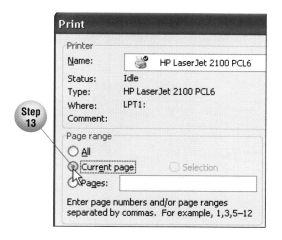

In Addition

Printing a Range of Pages

With the *Pages* option in the *Page range* section of the Print dialog box, you can identify a specific page, multiple pages, and/or a range of pages for printing. If you want specific multiple pages printed, use a comma to indicate *and* and use a hyphen to indicate *through*. For example, to print pages 2 and 5, you would type 2,5 in the *Pages* text box. To print pages 6 through 10, you would type 6-10.

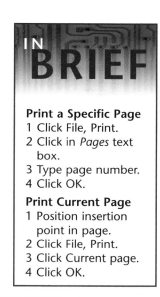

IN BRIEF

Print a Specific Page
1 Click File, Print.
2 Click in *Pages* text box.
3 Type page number.
4 Click OK.

Print Current Page
1 Position insertion point in page.
2 Click File, Print.
3 Click Current page.
4 Click OK.

1.10 Inserting the Date, Time, and AutoText; Closing a Document

Insert the current date and/or time with options at the Date and Time dialog box. The Date and Time dialog box contains a list of date and time options in the *Available formats* list box. If the *Update automatically* option at the Date and Time dialog box does not contain a check mark, the date and/or time are inserted in the document as normal text that can be edited in the normal manner. You can also insert the date and/or time as a field in a document. The advantage to inserting the date or time as a field is that you can update the field with the Update Field key, F9. Insert the date and/or time as a field by inserting a check mark in the *Update automatically*

check box. Word contains some built-in AutoText entries you can insert in a document. To display a list of built-in AutoText categories, click Insert and then AutoText. At the side menu that displays, position the mouse pointer on an AutoText category and then click the desired AutoText entry.

PROJECT: Your team is satisfied with the recent revisions to the First Choice Travel vacation specials document. You need to identify the document as confidential, track document versions by inserting the date, and then close the document.

S T E P S

1. With **WordS1-02** open, press Ctrl + End to move the insertion point to the end of the document.

2. Press the Enter key twice, type your name, and then press Enter.

3. Insert the word *CONFIDENTIAL* (in all capital letters) by clicking Insert, pointing to AutoText, pointing to Mailing Instructions, and then clicking CONFIDENTIAL.

    Mailing Instructions is only one of several AutoText categories containing built-in AutoText entries you can insert in a document.

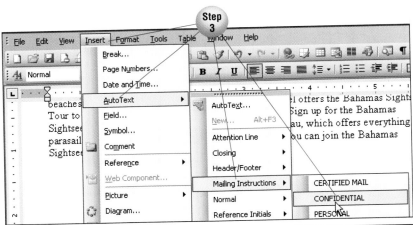

4. Press the Enter key, type **Date:**, and then press the spacebar once.

5. Click Insert and then Date and Time.

6. At the Date and Time dialog box, click the third option from the top in the *Available formats* list box.

    Your date will vary from what you see in the Date and Time dialog box at the right.

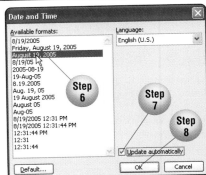

7. Click in the *Update automatically* check box to insert a check mark.

8. Click OK to close the dialog box.

⑨ Press the Enter key once, type **Time:**, and then press the spacebar once.

⑩ Click Insert and then Date and Time.

⑪ At the Date and Time dialog box, click the third option from the bottom in the *Available formats* list box.

⑫ Make sure the *Update automatically* check box contains a check mark and then click OK to close the dialog box.

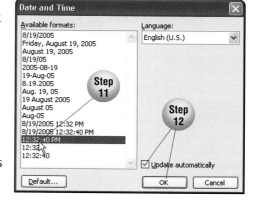

⑬ Print the entire document by clicking the Print button on the Standard toolbar.

⑭ Update the time by clicking the time and then pressing the F9 key.

> Pressing F9, the Update Field key, updates the time.

⑮ Print only page 3 of the document.

⑯ Click the Save button 🖫 to save the document.

⑰ Close the document by clicking File and then Close.

In Addition

Closing Multiple Documents

If you have more than one document open, you can close all open documents at the same time. To do this, hold down the Shift key, and then click File on the Menu bar. This causes the File drop-down menu to display with the Close All option instead of the Close option. Click Close All to close all open documents.

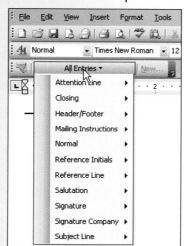

Inserting a Built-In AutoText Entry Using the AutoText Toolbar

You can display built-in AutoText entries with a button on the AutoText toolbar. Display this toolbar by clicking View, pointing to Toolbars, and then clicking AutoText. Click the All Entries button on the AutoText toolbar and a drop-down list displays with AutoText categories as shown at the right.

IN BRIEF

Display Date and Time Dialog Box
Click Insert, Date and Time.

Close a Document
Click File, Close.

1.11 Creating a Document Using a Template

Word includes a number of template documents that are formatted for specific uses. Each Word document is based on a template document with the Normal template the default. With Word templates, you can easily create a variety of documents such as letters, memos, and awards with specialized formatting. Templates are available at the Templates dialog box. This dialog box contains several tabs for displaying a variety of templates. Double-click the desired template and a template document is opened with certain formatting already applied.

PROJECT: Marquee Productions, a client of First Choice Travel, is planning to film a movie in Toronto. As Melissa Gehring, manager of the Los Angeles office of First Choice Travel, you are sending a memo to the manager of the Toronto office regarding flight and hotel information.

S T E P S

1. At a blank document screen, click File and then New.

    This displays the New Document task pane at the right side of the screen.

2. Click the <u>On my computer</u> hyperlink in the New Document task pane.

    This displays the Templates dialog box.

    Step 2

3. At the Templates dialog box, click the Memos tab.

    View the various templates available by clicking each of the tabs at the Templates dialog box.

    Step 3

4. Double-click *Contemporary Memo*.

5. At the contemporary memo template document, position the mouse pointer on the word *here* in the bracketed text *[Click **here** and type name]* after *To:* and then click the left mouse button.

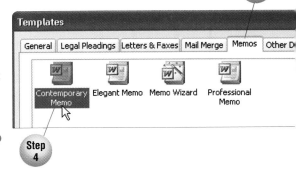

    Step 4

6. Type **Alex Torres, Manager, Toronto Office**.

7. Click the word *here* in the bracketed text *[Click **here** and type name]* after *CC:* and then type **Terry Blessing, President**.

8. Click the word *here* in the bracketed text *[Click **here** and type name]* after *From:* and then type **Melissa Gehring, Manager, Los Angeles Office**.

9. Click the word *here* in the bracketed text *[Click **here** and type subject]* after *Re:* and then type **Marquee Productions Movie Site**.

10. Select the text in the memo from ***How to Use This Memo Template*** to just past the period at the end of the last paragraph of text and then press the Delete key.

11. Type the text shown in Figure W1.5.

FIGURE W1.5

Marquee Productions will be filming a movie in and around the Toronto area from July 8 through August 30. Robert Velarde, site coordinator for Marquee Productions, has requested scheduling and pricing information on flights from Los Angeles to Toronto and information on lodging.

Approximately 45 people from Marquee Productions will need flight reservations and hotel rooms. Please research this information and locate the best group rates. I would like the information by the end of next week.

Memorandum

To:	Alex Torres, Manager, Toronto Office
CC:	Terry Blessing, President
From:	Melissa Gehring, Manager, Los Angeles Office
Date:	(current date)
Re:	Marquee Productions Movie Site

Step 11

Marquee Productions will be filming a movie in and around the Toronto area from July 8 through August 30. Robert Velarde, site coordinator for Marquee Productions, has requested scheduling and pricing information on flights from Los Angeles to Toronto and information on lodging.

Approximately 45 people from Marquee Productions will need flight reservations and hotel rooms. Please research this information and locate the best group rates. I would like the information by the end of next week.

12 Click the Save button on the Standard toolbar.

13 At the Save As dialog box, type **WordS1-03** and then press Enter.

14 Click the Print button on the Standard toolbar.

15 Close the document by clicking File and then Close.

In Addition

Displaying a New Blank Document Screen

By default, a Word document is based on the Normal template. You can choose a different template at the Templates dialog box or use the default template. If you close a document and then want to create another document based on the Normal template, click the New Blank Document button on the Standard toolbar or press the shortcut key, Ctrl + N.

In Brief

Create a Document Using a Template
1 Click File, New.
2 Click On my computer hyperlink.
3 Click desired tab.
4 Double-click desired template icon.

1.12 Managing Documents

As you continue working with documents, consider document management tasks such as creating a folder and copying, moving, and deleting documents. You can complete many document management tasks at the Open dialog box. You can perform document management tasks on one document or selected documents. By default, Word saves a file as a Word document and adds the extension *.doc* to the name. This extension identifies the file as a Word document. With the *Save as type* option at the Save As dialog box, you can save a document in a different format such as a Web page, a plain text file, a WordPerfect or Works file, or an earlier version of Word.

PROJECT: Since First Choice Travel will be communicating with Marquee Productions, you decide to create a folder into which you will insert Marquee Productions documents. You will also save a document as plain text to send to a colleague.

S T E P S

1. Click the Open button 📂 on the Standard toolbar.

2. At the Open dialog box with WordS1 the active folder, click the Create New Folder button 📁 on the dialog box toolbar.

3. At the New Folder dialog box, type **Marquee** and then press Enter.

   The new folder becomes the active folder.

4. Click the Up One Level button 📤 on the Open dialog box toolbar to return to the previous folder.

5. Click the document *MPMemo01* in the Open dialog box list box. Hold down the Ctrl key, click *MPMemoForm*, click *WordS1-02*, click *WordS1-03,* and then release the Ctrl key.

   Use the Ctrl key to select nonadjacent documents. Use the Shift key to select adjacent documents.

6. Right-click on any selected document and then click Copy at the shortcut menu.

7. Double-click the Marquee file folder.

   File folders display in the Open dialog box list box before documents. File folders display preceded by a file folder icon 📁 and documents display preceded by a document icon 📄 .

8. Position the mouse pointer in a white portion of the Open dialog box list box, click the *right* mouse button, and then click Paste at the shortcut menu.

   The copied documents are inserted in the Marquee folder.

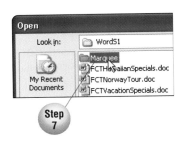

⑨ You need to send the **WordS1-02** document to a colleague that does not use Microsoft Word, so you decide to save it as a plain text document. At the Open dialog box with the Marquee folder active, double-click *WordS1-02.*

⑩ Click File and then Save As. At the Save As dialog box, type WordS1-02PlainText in the *File name* text box.

⑪ Click the down-pointing arrow at the right side of the *Save as type* list box, scroll down the drop-down list until *Plain Text (*.txt)* displays, click *Plain Text (*.txt)*, and then click the Save button.

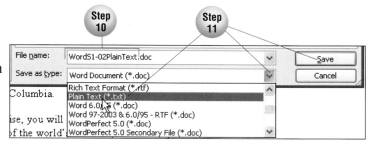

Saving a document as plain text removes most of the formatting.

⑫ At the File Conversion dialog box, click OK.

The first time you save a document as plain text, you may need to install conversion files.

⑬ Click File and then Close to close the document.

⑭ Open **WordS1-02PlainText,** click the Print button on the Standard toolbar, and then close the document.

When you open **WordS1-02PlainText**, notice how most of the formatting has been removed from the text.

⑮ Display the Open dialog box and then click the Up One Level button on the dialog box toolbar.

⑯ Rename the Marquee folder. To do this, right-click on the folder name and then click Rename at the shortcut menu. Type **MarqueeProductions** and then press Enter.

The new folder name replaces the original folder name. You can also rename a folder by clicking the Tools button, clicking Rename, and then typing the new folder name.

⑰ Delete the MarqueeProductions folder by clicking once on the folder to select it and then clicking the Delete button on the dialog box toolbar. At the message asking if you are sure you want to delete the folder and all of its contents, click the Yes button.

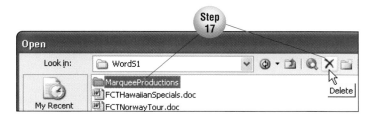

⑱ Close the Open dialog box.

⑲ Exit Word by clicking File and then Exit.

Create a Folder
1 Click Open button.
2 Click Create New Folder button.
3 Type folder name, press Enter.

Save Document in Different Format
1 Open document.
2 Display Save As dialog box.
3 Type document name.
4 Change *Save as type* option to desired format.
5 Click Save button.

FEATURES SUMMARY

Feature	Button	Menu	Keyboard
AutoCorrect dialog box		Tools, AutoCorrect Options	
Close a document	✕	File, Close	Ctrl + W
Date and Time dialog box		Insert, Date and Time	
Exit Word	✕	File, Exit	
Full Screen view		View, Full Screen	
Highlighting	ab✓		
Normal view	☰	View, Normal	
Preview a document	🔍	File, Print Preview	Ctrl + F2
Print a document	🖨	File, Print	Ctrl + P
Print Layout view	▣	View, Print Layout	
Reading Layout view	📖 Read	View, Reading Layout	Alt + R
Redo the last command or entry	↻	Edit, Redo	Ctrl + Y
Research task pane with list of synonyms		Tools, Language, Thesaurus	Shift + F7
Save a document	💾	File, Save	Ctrl + S
Save As dialog box		File, Save As	F12
Spelling and grammar check	ABC✓	Tools, Spelling and Grammar	F7
Undo the last command or entry	↺	Edit, Undo	Ctrl + Z
Zoom dialog box		View, Zoom	

PROCEDURES CHECK

Completion: In the space provided at the right, indicate the correct term, command, or option.

1. This toolbar contains buttons for working with documents such as the Open and Save buttons. _____
2. Click this option at the File drop-down menu to save a previously named document with a new name. _____
3. Use this keyboard command to move the insertion point to the beginning of the document. _____
4. Click this button to check the spelling in a document. _____
5. This feature detects and corrects some typographical errors, misspelled words, and incorrect capitalizations. _____
6. For easy viewing and reading, display a document in this view. _____

7. Expand the viewing area on the screen by changing to this view. _____

8. This dialog box displays a list of synonyms for a word. _____

9. Click these options on the Menu bar to display the Date and Time dialog box. _____

10. Click this hyperlink at the New Document task pane to display the Templates dialog box. _____

11. Click this button on the Open dialog box toolbar to display the New Folder dialog box. _____

12. Select nonadjacent documents at the Open dialog box by holding down this key while clicking each document. _____

SKILLS REVIEW

Activity 1: MOVING THE INSERTION POINT; SCROLLING; INSERTING TEXT

1 Open **FCTHawaiianSpecials**.
2 Save the document with Save As and name it **WordS1-R1**.
3 Practice moving the insertion point to the following locations:
   a Move the insertion point to the end of the document.
   b Move the insertion point back to the beginning of the document.
   c Scroll to the end of the document.
   d Scroll back to the beginning of the document.
   e Move the insertion point to the beginning of the second page.
   f Move the insertion point to the beginning of the document.
4 Move the insertion point between the words *the* and *Pacific* in the first sentence below the White Sands Charters heading and then type **spectacular**.
5 Move the insertion point to the beginning of the paragraph below the *Air Adventures* heading and then type the sentence **Experience beautiful coastlines, magnificent waterfalls, and fly inside an active volcano.**
6 Save **WordS1-R1**.

Activity 2: SELECTING AND DELETING TEXT; USING UNDO AND REDO

1 With **WordS1-R1** open, select and then delete the words *Depending on weather, marine conditions, and access, your* located in the third sentence in the paragraph below the *White Sands Charters* heading.
2 Capitalize the *g* in *guides*. (This word now begins the sentence.)
3 Select and then delete the last sentence in the *Air Adventures* section (the sentence that reads *Chart untouched areas from the moonscapes of volcanic craters to thundering waterfalls and rugged coastlines.*).
4 Undo the deletion.
5 Redo the deletion.
6 Select and then delete the fourth bulleted item in the *Bicycle Safari* section (the text that reads *Vista dining*).
7 Undo the deletion.
8 Deselect the text.
9 Save **WordS1-R1**.

Activity 3: CHECKING THE SPELLING AND GRAMMAR IN A DOCUMENT

1 With **WordS1-R1** open, move the insertion point to the beginning of the document.
2 Complete a spelling and grammar check on the document (*Molokini* is spelled correctly).
3 Save **WordS1-R1**.

Activity 4: CREATING AN AUTOCORRECT ENTRY; USING THESAURUS; INSERTING THE DATE AND TIME

1 With **WordS1-R1** open, add the following to the AutoCorrect dialog box: insert *HA* in the *Replace* text box and *Hawaiian* in the *With* text box.
2 Move the insertion point to the end of the document and then type the text shown in Figure W1.6.
3 After typing the text, use Thesaurus and make the following changes:
   a Change *lavish* to *sumptuous*.
   b Change *exceptional* to *extraordinary*.
4 Insert the current date and time by completing the following steps:
   a Move the insertion point to the end of the document.
   b Press the Enter key twice.
   c Insert the current date (you choose the format).
   d Press the Enter key.
   e Insert the current time (you choose the format).
5 Save, print, and then close **WordS1-R1**.

FIGURE W1.6 Activity 4

> Luau Legends
>
> Enjoy a spectacular HA dinner show featuring lavish prime rib and authentic HA buffet. This uniquely HA experience includes a traditional lei greeting, exceptional food and beverages, magical music of the islands, and Hawaii's finest performers. Join us each night beginning at 7:30 p.m. for an evening of delicious HA food and spectacular performances.

Activity 5: CREATING A MEMO USING A TEMPLATE

1 Use the Contemporary Memo template and create a memo with the following information:
   a The memo is to Hanh Postma, Manager, European Distribution.
   b Send a copy of the memo to Roman Deptulski, Manager, Overseas Distribution.
   c The memo is from Sam Vestering, Manager, North American Distribution.
   d The subject (Re:) of the memo is Distribution Schedule.
   e Type the text in Figure W1.7 as the body of the memo.
2 Save the completed memo and name it **WordS1-R2**.
3 Print and then close **WordS1-R2**.

I am preparing the quarterly distribution report and would like you to send your schedule to me as soon as possible. Please use the Excel worksheet provided by the Distribution Department and then e-mail the completed worksheet to me. I will send you the master schedule by the end of next month.

PERFORMANCE PLUS

Assessment 1: INSERTING TEXT IN A MEMO

1 Open **MPMemo01**.
2 Save the document with Save As and name it **WordS1-P1**.
3 Insert the words *or Buffalo* between *Toronto* and *area* in the second sentence in the body of the memo.
4 Move the insertion point to the end of the paragraph in the body of the memo and then add the following sentence: **We are anticipating having lunches and snacks catered on the set**.
5 Press the Enter key twice and then type the two paragraphs of text shown in Figure W1.8.
6 Save, print, and then close **WordS1-P1**.

FIGURE W1.8 Assessment 1

Since the film is a period piece, we need to locate a company that can research, locate, and/or design costumes for the movie. When you locate a costume company, please request information on time needed to research, locate, or sew costumes.

Please have the information on catering and costuming available for the production meeting on Thursday, May 5.

Assessment 2: PREPARING A MEMO

1 Open **MPMemoForm**.
2 Save the document with Save As and name it **WordS1-P2**.
3 Insert the following information after the specified heading:

To:	**Robert Velarde, Site Coordinator**
From:	**Camille Matsui, Production Assistant**
Date:	(Insert current date)
Re:	**Catering and Costuming Businesses**

4 Move the insertion point a triple space below the *Re:* heading and then write the body of the memo using the following information (write the information in paragraph form—do not use bullets):
   • You contacted the Chamber of Commerce in Buffalo and Toronto and determined that King Street Eatery in downtown Toronto and The Waterfront Bistro in Buffalo were the best choices.

- You have sent a letter to each catering business requesting menus and a pricing guide.
- The only costuming company you could find was Performance Threads in Niagara Falls, Canada. You sent a letter to that company requesting information on research, costume design, and pricing.
- You hope to have the information available before the production meeting.

5 Complete a spelling and grammar check on the memo (proper names are spelled correctly).
6 Save, print, and then close **WordS1-P2**.

Assessment 3: ADDING A PARAGRAPH TO A LETTER

1 Open **PTMarqueeLetter**.
2 Save the document with Save As and name it **WordS1-P3**.
3 Move the insertion a double space below the paragraph of text in the letter and then add the following information (write the information in paragraph form—do not use bullets):
- Costume research takes approximately two to three weeks.
- If appropriate costumes cannot be found, costumes are sewn.
- Anticipate five working days for a costume to be sewn.
- Include the number of costumes and approximate sizes.
- A price estimate will be provided before costumes are purchased or sewn.

4 Use Thesaurus to replace *regarding* in the first sentence in the letter to an appropriate synonym.
5 Complete a spelling and grammar check on the letter.
6 Save, print, and then close **WordS1-P3**.

Assessment 4: FINDING INFORMATION ON CHANGING GRAMMAR CHECKING OPTIONS

1 Use the Word Help feature to learn how to set grammar preferences. After learning about the preferences, click Tools and then Options to display the Options dialog box. Click the Spelling & Grammar tab and then explore the options at the dialog box. Change the *Writing style* option to *Grammar & Style*.
2 Open **FCTNorwayTour**.
3 Save the document with Save As and name it **WordS1-P4**.
4 Complete a spelling and grammar check on the document (*Myrdal* is spelled correctly).
5 Display the Options dialog box, change the *Writing style* option back to *Grammar Only*, and then close the dialog box.
6 Save, print, and then close **WordS1-P4**.

Assessment 5: LOCATING ONLINE TECHNICAL RESOURCES

1 Display the Word Help task pane and then click the Connect to Microsoft Office Online hyperlink.
2 Look at the Microsoft Office Online Web page and learn about the available online resources.
3 Using the information you learn, prepare a memo to your instructor describing at least three interesting or helpful features available at the Microsoft Office Online Web page.
4 Save the memo and name it **WordS1-P5**.
5 Print and then close **WordS1-P5**.

WORD SECTION 2

Formatting Characters and Paragraphs

As you work with Word, you will learn a number of commands and procedures that affect how the document appears when printed. The appearance of a document in the document screen and how it looks when printed is called the *format*. Formatting can include such tasks as changing the font, aligning and indenting text, changing line and paragraph spacing, setting tabs, and inserting elements such as bullets and numbers. In this section, you will learn the skills to complete the projects described here.

Note: Before beginning this section, delete the WordS1 folder on your disk. Next, copy to your disk or other location the WordS2 subfolder from the CD that accompanies this textbook and then make WordS2 the active folder.

Skills

- Apply fonts and font effects
- Adjust character spacing
- Use Format Painter
- Repeat a command
- Align text in paragraphs
- Indent text
- Change line and paragraph spacing
- Insert bullets and numbering
- Insert symbols and special characters
- Set tabs and tabs with leaders
- Add borders and shading to text
- Apply styles
- Create custom bullets
- Create an AutoText entry

Projects

Edit and format fact sheets on Oslo, Norway, and Petersburg, Alaska; format a document on traveling by train in Europe; format documents on vacation packages in Oregon and Nevada and cross-country skiing vacation packages; use the Internet to find information on museums and galleries in Toronto and then use that information to prepare a letter to Marquee Productions.

Prepare a letter to the chair of the Theatre Arts Division at Niagara Peninsula College requesting 20 theatre interns.

Prepare a movie distribution schedule.

2.1 Applying Fonts and Font Effects Using the Formatting Toolbar

The Formatting toolbar contains several buttons for applying font and font effects to text. Click the Bold button to apply bold formatting, click the Italic button to apply italic formatting, or click the Underline button to underline selected text. The default font used by Word is Times New Roman. Change this default with the Font button and change text size with the Font Size button. The default font color is black. Change this default color with the Font Color button. To view all buttons on the Formatting toolbar at once, display the Formatting toolbar on a line separate from the Standard toolbar.

PROJECT: You are working on a series of fact sheets that First Choice Travel is creating about the cities included in its special tours. The first fact sheet is about Oslo, Norway. You have been asked to improve the appearance of the document by applying different kinds of fonts and effects to the text.

STEPS

1. Open the **FCTOslo** document. Save the document with Save As and name it **WordS2-01**.

2. Select *OSLO FACT SHEET* and then click the Bold button **B** on the Formatting toolbar.

   > If the Standard and Formatting toolbars display on one row, separate the toolbars. To do this, click Tools and then Customize. At the Customize dialog box, click the Options tab, click the *Show Standard and Formatting toolbars on two rows* option to insert a check mark, and then click the Close button.

3. Select *History* and then click the Underline button **U** on the Formatting toolbar.

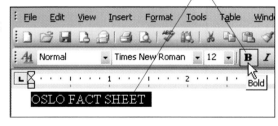

Step 2

4. Select and then underline the remaining headings including *Population*; *Commerce and Industry*; *Climate*; *Holiday, Sport, and Leisure*; and *Sightseeing Tours*.

5. Select the words *Memorial Park* located in the first paragraph below the *History* heading and then click the Italic button **I** on the Formatting toolbar.

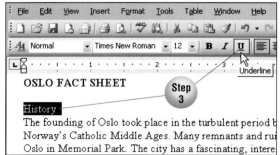

Step 3

6. Click Edit and then Select All to select the entire document.

7. Click the down-pointing arrow at the right side of the Font button [Times New Roman] on the Formatting toolbar. Click the down-pointing arrow at the bottom of the list scroll bar to scroll down the list until *Bookman Old Style* is visible and then click it. (If this font is not available, choose another font.)

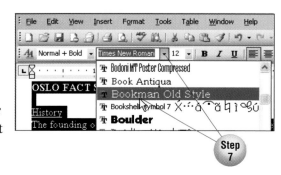

Step 7

⑧ Click the down-pointing arrow at the right side of the Font Size button [12 ▾] on the Formatting toolbar and then click *11* at the drop-down list.

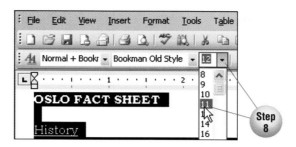

⑨ Click the down-pointing arrow at the right side of the Font Color button [A ▾] on the Formatting toolbar and then click the Dark Blue color at the color palette (sixth color from the left in the top row).

⑩ Deselect the text by clicking outside the selected text.

⑪ Save and then print **WordS2-01**.

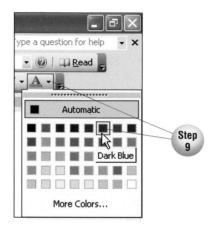

In Addition

Using Typefaces

A typeface is a set of characters with a common design and shape. Word refers to typeface as *font*. Typefaces can be decorative or plain and are either monospaced or proportional. A monospaced typeface allots the same amount of horizontal space for each character while a proportional typeface allots a varying amount of space for each character. Proportional typefaces are divided into two main categories: *serif* and *sans serif*. A serif is a small line at the end of a character stroke. Consider using a serif typeface for text-intensive documents because the serifs help move the reader's eyes across the page. Use a sans serif typeface for headings, headlines, and advertisements that are not text intensive.

In BRIEF

Display Toolbars on Separate Lines
1 Click Tools, Customize.
2 Click Options tab.
3 Insert check mark in *Show Standard and Formatting toolbars on two rows* option.
4 Click Close button.

2.2 Changing the Font at the Font Dialog Box; Adjusting Character Spacing; Using Format Painter

In addition to buttons on the Formatting toolbar, you can apply font formatting with options at the Font dialog box. With options at this dialog box, you can change the font, font size, and font style; change the font color; choose an underlining style; and apply formatting effects. Each typeface is designed with a specific amount of space between characters. You can change this character spacing with options at the Font dialog box with the Character Spacing tab selected. You can also turn on kerning, which refers to the adjustment of

spacing between certain character combinations. Kerning provides text with a more evenly spaced look and works only with TrueType or Adobe Type fonts. Once you apply character formatting to text, you can copy that formatting to different locations in the document using the Format Painter.

PROJECT: The changes you made to the Oslo fact sheet have enhanced the readability and visual appeal of the text. Now you will turn your attention to the headings.

S T E P S

1. With **WordS2-01** open, select the entire document by pressing Ctrl + A.

   Ctrl + A is the shortcut key to select the entire document.

2. Click Format and then Font.

3. At the Font dialog box, click *Times New Roman* in the *Font* list box (you will need to scroll down the list box to display this option) and click *12* in the *Size* list box.

4. Click the down-pointing arrow at the right of the *Font color* option and then click *Black* (first choice from the left in the top row).

5. Click OK to close the dialog box.

6. Select the heading *History*, click Format, and then click Font.

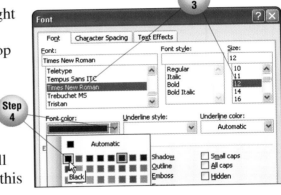

7. Click *Arial* in the *Font* list box (you will need to scroll up the list box to display this option), click *Bold* in the *Font style* list box, and then click *16* in the *Size* list box (you will need to scroll down this list box to display *16*).

8. Click the down-pointing arrow at the right of the *Underline style* option and then click *(none)* at the drop-down list.

9. Click the Character Spacing tab.

   At the Font dialog box with the Character Spacing tab selected, choose the *Scale* option to stretch or compress text horizontally as a percentage of the current size and expand or condense the spacing between characters with the *Spacing* option.

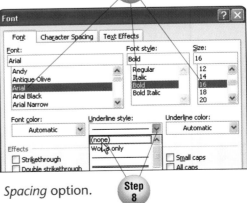

⑩ Click the down-pointing arrow at the right of the *Spacing* option and then click *Condensed* at the drop-down list.

⑪ Click in the *Kerning for fonts* check box to insert a check mark. Click the down-pointing arrow in the *Points and above* text box until *12* displays.

⑫ Click OK to close the dialog box.

⑬ Deselect the heading.

⑭ Click once on any character in the heading *History* and then double-click the Format Painter button 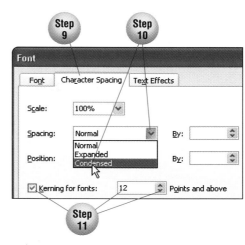 on the Standard toolbar.

> When Format Painter is active, the mouse pointer displays with a paintbrush attached.

⑮ Select the heading *Population*. (You will need to scroll down the document to display this heading.)

⑯ Select individually the remaining headings (*Commerce and Industry*; *Climate*; *Holiday, Sport, and Leisure*; and *Sightseeing Tours*).

PROBLEM ?

> If the pointer displays without a paintbrush attached, you clicked the Format Painter button only once. To format text in more than one location, you must double-click the Format Painter button.

⑰ Click once on the Format Painter button on the Standard toolbar to turn off the Format Painter feature.

⑱ Select the heading *OSLO FACT SHEET* and then change the font to Arial and the size to 16.

⑲ Save **WordS2-01**.

In Addition

Changing the Default Font

Microsoft Word uses a default font for text (usually 12-point Times New Roman). You can change this default font by choosing the desired font, font style, and font size at the Font dialog box and then clicking the Default button. At the message telling you that the change will affect all new documents based on the Normal template, click the Yes button. Once the default font is changed, the new font is in effect each time you open Word.

IN BRIEF

Change Font at Font Dialog Box
1 Click Format, Font.
2 Choose desired font.
3 Click OK.

Adjust Character Spacing
1 Click Format, Font.
2 Click Character Spacing tab.
3 Choose desired options.
4 Click OK.

Apply Formatting with Format Painter
1 Apply formatting.
2 Double-click Format Painter button.
3 Select text.
4 Click Format Painter button.

2.3 Applying Effects Using the Font Dialog Box; Repeating a Command

Use options in the *Effects* section of the Font dialog box to apply a variety of effects to documents. For example, you can create superscript and subscript text, change selected text to small caps or all caps, strikethrough selected text, hide text, and apply a shadow, outline, emboss, or engraving style to text. Display hidden text in a document by clicking the Show/Hide ¶ button on the Standard toolbar, which turns on the display of nonprinting characters. Add animation effects such as a blinking background, a shimmer or sparkle with options at the Font dialog box with the Text Effects tab

selected. Animation effects added to text display on the screen but do not print. If you apply formatting to text in a document and then want to apply the same formatting to other text, use the Repeat command. Repeat a command by pressing the F4 function key.

PROJECT: Continuing with your design work on the First Choice Travel fact sheet, you will apply small caps and shadow effects, hide specific text, and add animation effects to selected text in the document.

S T E P S

1. With **WordS2-01** open, press Ctrl + End to move the insertion point to the end of the document and then select the sentence *All tours by boat and coach depart from Pier 3 in front of the Oslo City Hall.*

2. Click Format and then Font.

3. At the Font dialog box with the Font tab selected, click *Small caps* in the *Effects* section.

   > Inserting a check mark in the check box activates the feature. The *Preview* section of the Font dialog box displays how the effect(s) chosen affect the text.

   Step 3

   Effects
   - [ ] Strikethrough
   - [ ] Double strikethrough
   - [ ] Superscript
   - [ ] Subscript
   - [ ] Shadow
   - [ ] Outline
   - [ ] Emboss
   - [ ] Engrave
   - [✓] Small caps
   - [ ] All caps
   - [ ] Hidden

   Preview

   ALL TOURS BY BOAT AND COACH DEPART FROM PIER 3 IN FRONT OF THE OSLO

   This is a TrueType font. This font will be used on both printer and screen.

4. Click OK to close the dialog box.

5. Select the text *Tour 1: Mini Cruise*, click Format, and then click Font.

6. At the Font dialog box, click *Shadow* in the *Effects* section and then click OK to close the dialog box.

   Effects
   - [ ] Strikethrough
   - [ ] Double strikethrough
   - [ ] Superscript
   - [ ] Subscript
   - [✓] Shadow
   - [ ] Outline
   - [ ] Emboss
   - [ ] Engrave
   - [ ] Small caps
   - [ ] All caps
   - [ ] Hidden

   Preview

   Step 6

   Tour 1: Mini Cruise

   This is a TrueType font. This font will be used on both printer and screen.

7. Select the text *Tour 2: Fjord Cruise* and then press F4.

   > Pressing F4 repeats the previous command and applies the Shadow effect to the selected text.

8. Select the text *Tour 3: Fjord Cruise with Dinner* and then press F4.

9. Select the text *Tour 4: Selected Oslo Sightseeing* and then press F4.

10. The fourth tour is not always available so you decide to hide the text. To begin, select the heading *Tour 4: Selected Oslo Sightseeing* and the two lines of text below the heading, click Format, and then Font.

11 At the Font dialog box with the Font tab selected, click the *Hidden* option in the *Effects* section and then click OK.

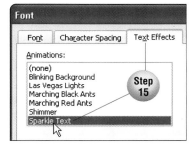

12 To display the hidden text, click the Show/Hide ¶ button ¶ on the Standard toolbar.

> Clicking the Show/Hide ¶ button turns on the display of nonprinting characters. A small circle between words indicates that the spacebar has been pressed, a paragraph symbol (¶) indicates that the Enter key has been pressed, and a right-pointing arrow indicates that the Tab key has been pressed.

13 Turn off the display of nonprinting characters and hidden text by clicking the Show/Hide ¶ button on the Standard toolbar.

14 Select the title *OLSO FACT SHEET* and then display the Font dialog box by clicking Format and then Font.

15 Click the Text Effects tab, click *Sparkle Text* in the *Animations* list box, and then click OK.

> Animation effects such as Sparkle Text do not print and are used primarily for documents that are viewed in a Web browser.

16 Unhide the text on the fourth tour. To do this, click the Show/Hide ¶ button on the Standard toolbar, and then select the heading *Tour 4: Selected Oslo Sightseeing* and the two lines of text below the heading.

17 Click Format and then Font. At the Font dialog box with the Font tab selected, click the *Hidden* option to remove the check mark and then click OK to close the dialog box.

18 Click the Show/Hide ¶ button on the Standard toolbar to turn off the display of nonprinting characters.

19 Save **WordS2-01**.

In Addition

Applying a Superscript and Subscript Effect

Use the *Superscript* option in the *Effects* section of the Font dialog box to create text that is raised slightly above the text line and create subscript text that is lowered slightly below the text line. Use the superscript effect to create a mathematical equation such as four to the second power (written as 4^2). Use the subscript effect to create a chemical formula such as H_2O. The shortcut key to create superscript text is Ctrl + Shift + = and the shortcut key to create subscript text is Ctrl + =.

In BRIEF

Apply Font Effects
1 Select text.
2 Click Format, Font.
3 Click desired effect check box.
4 Click OK.

Apply Animation Effect
1 Select text.
2 Click Format, Font.
3 Click Text Effects tab.
4 Click desired animation effect in *Animations* list box.
5 Click OK.

2.4 Aligning Text in Paragraphs

Paragraphs of text in a document are aligned at the left margin by default. This default alignment can be changed to center alignment (used for titles, headings, or other text you want centered), right aligned (used for addresses, date, time, or other text you want aligned at the right margin), and justified (used for text you want aligned at both the left and right margins such as text in a report or book). Change paragraph alignment with buttons on the Formatting toolbar, the Alignment option at the Paragraph dialog box, or with shortcut keys.

PROJECT: You will improve the appearance of the First Choice Travel fact sheet by changing text alignment.

S T E P S

1. With **WordS2-01** open, select the title *OSLO FACT SHEET* and then remove the Sparkle Text effect (do this at the Font dialog box with the Text Effects tab selected).

2. Center the title *OSLO FACT SHEET* by positioning the insertion point on any character in the title and then clicking the Center button on the Formatting toolbar.

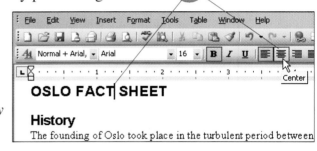

3. Select from the middle of the first paragraph of text below the *History* heading to somewhere in the middle of the third paragraph of text.

   The entire paragraphs do not have to be selected, only a portion of each paragraph.

4. Click the Justify button on the Formatting toolbar.

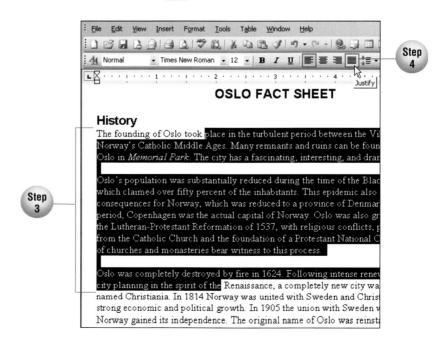

⑤ Click outside the selected text to deselect it.

⑥ Click anywhere in the paragraph below the *Population* heading and then press F4.

Pressing F4 repeats the justification command.

PROBLEM ?

If the paragraph alignment does not change, you may have executed a command after the Justify command. If this happens, click anywhere in the paragraph and then click the Justify button on the Formatting toolbar.

⑦ Click anywhere in the paragraph below the *Commerce and Industry* heading and then press F4.

⑧ Click anywhere in the paragraph below the *Climate* heading and then press F4.

⑨ Click anywhere in the paragraph below the *Holiday, Sport, and Leisure* heading and then press F4.

⑩ Press Ctrl + End to move the insertion point to the end of the document and then press the Enter key.

⑪ Click the Align Right button ▤ on the Formatting toolbar.

⑫ Type your first and last name and then press the Enter key.

⑬ Type **Date:**, press the spacebar once, and then press Alt + Shift + D.

Alt + Shift + D is the shortcut key to insert the current date.

⑭ Press the Enter key and then click the Align Left button ▤ on the Formatting toolbar.

This step returns the paragraph alignment back to left.

⑮ Save **Word S2-01**.

In Addition

Options for Changing Alignment

You can change paragraph alignment with the *Alignment* option at the Paragraph dialog box shown at the right. Display the Paragraph dialog box by clicking Format and then Paragraph. At the Paragraph dialog box, click the down-pointing arrow at the right side of the *Alignment* option and then click the desired alignment at the drop-down list. You can also change alignment with the following shortcut keys:

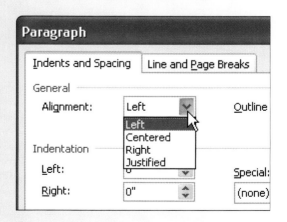

Alignment	Shortcut Key
Left	Ctrl + L
Center	Ctrl + E
Right	Ctrl + R
Justified	Ctrl + J

2.5 Indenting Text

To draw attention to specific text in a document, consider indenting the text. Indenting might include indenting the first line of text in a paragraph, indenting all lines of text in a paragraph, and indenting the second and subsequent lines of a paragraph (called a hanging indent). Several methods are available for indenting text including buttons on the Formatting toolbar, markers on the Ruler, options at the Paragraph dialog box with the Indents and Spacing tab selected, and shortcut keys.

PROJECT: You have decided to visually highlight certain paragraphs of information in the First Choice Travel fact sheet document. Indenting seems preferable to other formatting choices such as changing the font.

S T E P S

1. With **WordS2-01** open, select the three paragraphs below the *History* heading.

2. Position the mouse pointer on the Left Indent marker on the Ruler, shown in Figure W2.1, hold down the left mouse button, drag the marker to the 0.5-inch mark on the Ruler, and then release the mouse button.

   > When you position the mouse pointer on the Left Indent marker, a ScreenTip displays with *Left Indent* in a yellow box. To precisely position a marker on the Ruler, hold down the Alt key while dragging the marker.

3. Position the mouse pointer on the First Line Indent marker on the Ruler, hold down the left mouse button, drag the marker to the 1-inch mark on the Ruler, and then release the mouse button.

4. Position the mouse pointer on the Right Indent marker on the Ruler, hold down the left mouse button, drag the marker to the 5.5-inch mark on the Ruler, and then release the mouse button.

5. Deselect the text.

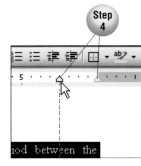

FIGURE W2.1 Ruler Indent Markers

First Line Indent

Left Indent | Hanging Indent | Right Indent

6. Click anywhere in the paragraph below the *Population* heading. Drag the Left Indent marker on the Ruler to the 0.5-inch mark and drag the Right Indent marker on the Ruler to the 5.5-inch mark. Follow the same procedures to indent the paragraphs below the headings *Commerce and Industry*; *Climate*; and *Holiday, Sport, and Leisure*.

7. Select from the line of text beginning *Tour 1: Mini Cruise* through the three lines of text pertaining to *Tour 4: Selected Oslo Sightseeing*.

8. Click twice on the Increase Indent button 🟰 on the Formatting toolbar and then deselect the text.

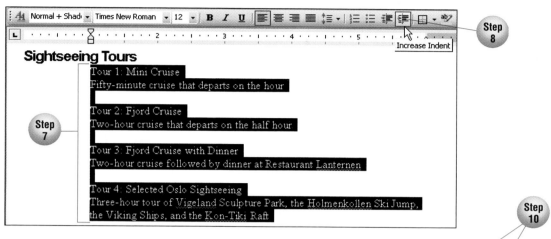

9. Select the three paragraphs below the *History* heading.

10. Drag the First Line Indent marker to the 0.5-inch mark on the Ruler and drag the Hanging Indent marker to the 1-inch mark on the Ruler.

   This creates hanging indent paragraphs.

11. Deselect the paragraph.

12. You decide that you do not like the size or condensed look of the headings. To change these, select the heading *History*, display the Font dialog box with the Font tab selected, and then click *14* in the *Size* list box. Click the Character Spacing tab, click the down-pointing arrow at the right of the *Spacing* option, click *Normal* at the drop-down list, and then click OK to close the dialog box.

13. Select each of the remaining headings (individually) and press the Repeat key, F4.

14. Save **WordS2-01**.

In Addition

Indenting Text at the Paragraph Dialog Box

Another method for indenting text is to use options at the Paragraph dialog box with the Indents and Spacing tab selected. Indent text from the left margin with the *Left* option and indent text from the right with the *Right* option. Create a hanging paragraph by choosing *Hanging* at the *Special* drop-down list. Specify the amount of indent for second and subsequent lines in the paragraph with the *By* option. You can also indent text with the following shortcut keys:

Action	Shortcut Key
Indent text from left margin	Ctrl + M
Decrease indent from left margin	Ctrl + Shift + M
Create a hanging indent	Ctrl + T
Remove hanging indent	Ctrl + Shift + T

2.6 Changing Line and Paragraph Spacing

By default, the word wrap feature single-spaces text. This default line spacing can be changed with the Line Spacing button on the Formatting toolbar, shortcut keys, or with the *Line spacing* and *At* options at the Paragraph dialog box. Control spacing above and below paragraphs with the *Before* and/or *After* options at the Paragraph dialog box with the Indents and Spacing tab selected.

PROJECT: The Oslo fact sheet project deadline is at hand. However, you have time to make a few spacing changes in the document before printing the final version.

STEPS

1. With **WordS2-01** open, select the entire document by pressing Ctrl + A.

2. Click Format and then Paragraph.

3. At the Paragraph dialog box with the Indents and Spacing tab selected, click in the *At* text box located in the *Spacing* section of the dialog box and then type **1.2**.

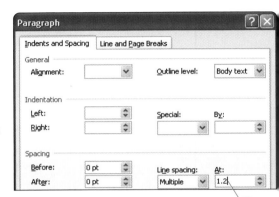

   The Paragraph dialog box also contains a *Line spacing* option. Click the down-pointing arrow at the right side of the option and a drop-down list displays with spacing choices.

4. Click OK to close the dialog box and then deselect the text.

PROBLEM

> If line spacing seems too spread out, make sure you typed the period in *1.2* in the *At* text box at the Paragraph dialog box.

5. Select from the line of text beginning *Tour 1: Mini Cruise* through the three lines of text pertaining to *Tour 4: Selected Oslo Sightseeing*.

6. Click the down-pointing arrow at the right side of the Line Spacing button and then click *1.0* at the drop-down list.

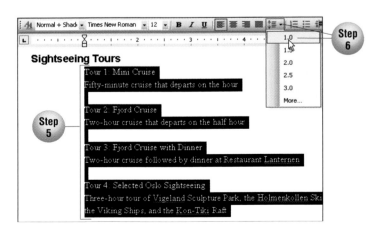

Choosing this option changes the line spacing to single for the selected paragraphs of text. You can also change line spacing with shortcut keys. Press Ctrl + 1 to change to single spacing, Ctrl + 2 to change to double spacing, and Ctrl + 5 to change to 1.5-line spacing.

7 Click anywhere in the *History* heading, click Format, and then click Paragraph.

8 At the Paragraph dialog box with the Indents and Spacing tab selected, click once on the up-pointing arrow at the right side of the *After* text box and then click OK to close the dialog box.

> Clicking the up-pointing arrow at the right side of the *After* text box inserts *6 pt* in the text box.

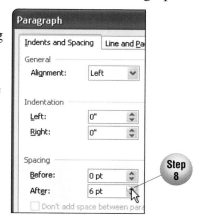

9 Click anywhere in the *Population* heading and then press F4. (You will need to scroll down the document to display the *Population* heading.)

> Pressing F4 repeats the paragraph spacing command.

10 Click individually anywhere in each of the remaining headings (*Commerce and Industry*; *Climate*; *Holiday, Sport, and Leisure*; and *Sightseeing Tours*) and then press F4.

11 You decide that you do not like the look of the justified paragraphs and want to change them to left alignment. To do this, select from the heading *History* through the paragraph of text below the heading *Holiday, Sport, and Leisure* and then click the Align Left button on the Formatting toolbar.

12 You also decide that you want to remove the hanging indent on the paragraphs in the *History* section. To do this, select the three paragraphs of text below the *History* heading and then press Ctrl + Shift + T.

13 Save and then print **WordS2-01**.

14 Close **WordS2-01**.

In Addition

Spacing Above or Below Paragraphs

Spacing above or below paragraphs is added in points. For example, to add 9 points of spacing below selected paragraphs, display the Paragraph dialog box with the Indents and Spacing tab selected, select the current measurement in the *After* text box, and then type 9. You can also click the up-pointing or down-pointing arrows to increase or decrease the amount of spacing before or after paragraphs.

IN BRIEF

Change Line Spacing
1 Click down-pointing arrow at right of Line Spacing button on Formatting toolbar.
2 Click desired line spacing at drop-down list.

OR
1 Display Paragraph dialog box.
2 Type desired line spacing in *At* text box.
3 Click OK.

2.7 Inserting Bullets and Numbering

If you want to draw the reader's attention to a list of items, consider inserting a bullet before each item. Insert a bullet before items in a list using the Bullets button on the Formatting toolbar or with options at the Bullets and Numbering dialog box. If a list of items is in a sequence, consider inserting numbers before each item. Insert a number before sequenced items using the Numbering button on the Formatting toolbar or with options at the Bullets and Numbering dialog box.

PROJECT: First Choice Travel has a new document on traveling in Europe by train. After reviewing the document, you decide to insert numbers and bullets before selected paragraphs to make the information easier to read.

S T E P S

1. Open **FCTRailTravel**.

2. Save the document with Save As and name it **WordS2-02**.

3. Select text from the paragraph *Have your pass validated.* through the paragraph *Be at the right train station.* and then click the Numbering button 📋 on the Formatting toolbar.

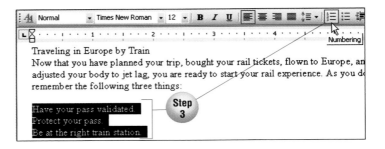

PROBLEM?
If you click the wrong button, immediately click the Undo button.

4. Position the insertion at the end of the second numbered paragraph (the paragraph that displays as *2. Protect your pass.*) and then press the Enter key once.

    Pressing the Enter key automatically inserts the number *3.* and renumbers the third paragraph to *4*.

5. Type **Arrive 20 minutes before train departure time.**

    Numbering before paragraphs is changed automatically when paragraphs of text are inserted and/or deleted.

> 1. Have your pass validated.
> 2. Protect your pass.
> 3. Arrive 20 minutes before train departure time.
> 4. Be at the right train station.
>
> Step 5

6 Select text from the paragraph that begins *Free or discount transportation…* through the paragraph that begins *Reduced rental rates with…* and then click the Bullets button on the Formatting toolbar.

Clicking the Bullets button on the Formatting toolbar inserts a round bullet before each paragraph. A variety of other bullets are available at the Bullets and Numbering dialog box.

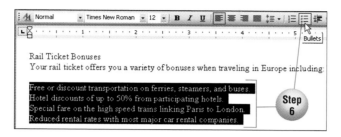

Rail Ticket Bonuses
Your rail ticket offers you a variety of bonuses when traveling in Europe including:

Free or discount transportation on ferries, steamers, and buses.
Hotel discounts of up to 50% from participating hotels.
Special fare on the high speed trains linking Paris to London.
Reduced rental rates with most major car rental companies.

Step 6

7 With the paragraphs still selected, click Format and then Bullets and Numbering.

8 At the Bullets and Numbering dialog box, make sure the Bulleted tab is selected and then click a bullet option similar to the arrow bullet shown at the right. If this bullet is not available, click a similar bullet.

Bullet choices at the Bullet and Numbering dialog box vary depending on the most recent bullets selected.

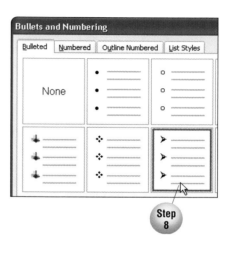

9 Click OK to close the Bullets and Numbering dialog box.

10 Deselect the text.

11 Save **WordS2-02**.

Step 8

In Addition

Inserting a Picture Bullet

Customize bullets by choosing a bullet option at the Bullets and Numbering dialog box and then clicking the Customize button. This displays the Customize Bulleted List dialog box shown at the right. At this dialog box, you can choose a different bullet character and change the bullet and text positions. Click the Picture button and the Picture Bullet dialog box displays with picture options for bullets.

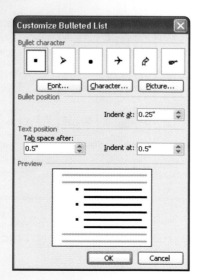

2.8 Inserting Symbols and Special Characters

Many of the fonts include special symbols such as bullets, publishing symbols, and letters with special punctuation (such as é, ö, and Ā). To insert a symbol, click Insert and then Symbol to display the Symbol dialog box. Click the desired symbol at the dialog box, click the Insert button, and then click the Close button. At the Symbol dialog box with the Symbols tab selected, you can change the font and display different symbols. Change the font by clicking the down-pointing arrow at the right of the Font list box and then clicking the desired font at the drop-down list. Click the Special Characters tab at the Symbol dialog box and a list displays containing special characters and the shortcut keys to insert the characters.

PROJECT: You have identified a few city names in the train travel document that need special letters in their spellings as well as a special character you need to insert in the document.

STEPS

1. With **WordS2-02** open, move the insertion point to the end of the document.

2. Type the text shown in Figure W2.2 up to the Å in *Århus*. To insert the Å symbol, click Insert and then Symbol.

3. At the Symbol dialog box with the Symbols tab selected, click the down-pointing arrow at the right side of the *Font* list box and then click *(normal text)* at the drop-down list. (You may need to scroll up to see this option. Skip this step if *(normal text)* is already selected.)

4. Scroll down the list box until the ninth row is visible and then click the Å symbol (approximately the fifth symbol from the left in the ninth row).

PROBLEM **?**

> If you do not see the Å symbol, make sure *(normal text)* is selected at the *Font* text box.

5. Click the Insert button and then click the Close button.

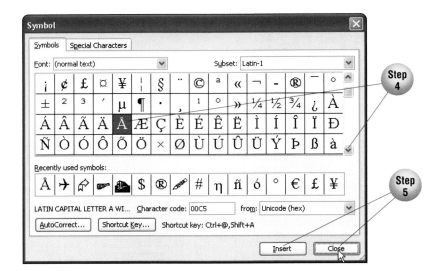

6. Type text up to the ø symbol. To insert the ø symbol, click Insert and then Symbol.

(7) At the Symbol dialog box, click the ø symbol (approximately the eighth symbol from the left in the twelfth row).

(8) Click the Insert button and then click the Close button.

(9) Type the text up to the ® character. To insert the character, click Insert and then Symbol. At the Symbol dialog box, click the Special Characters tab.

(10) Click the ® symbol in the *Character* list box.

(11) Click the Insert button and then click the Close button.

(12) Type the remaining text in Figure W2.2.

(13) Save **WordS2-02**.

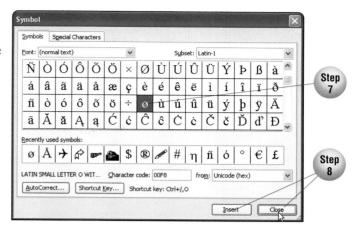

Step 7

Step 8

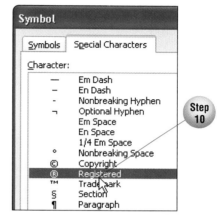

Step 10

FIGURE W2.2

Some companies offer outstanding reductions on transportation. For example, you can travel on the ferry in Denmark between Århus and Kalundborg and between Nyborg and Korsør at a 75% discount! ScanTravel, a travel company located in Stockholm, offers the StarPass® ticket that provides you with incredible discounts on travel by train, ferry, and bus in Sweden, Norway, and Denmark.

In Addition

Inserting a Symbol with a Shortcut Key

Another method for inserting symbols in a document is to use a shortcut key. The shortcut key for a symbol displays at the Symbol dialog box. Click a symbol at the Symbol dialog box and the shortcut keys display toward the bottom of the dialog box. For example, click the ø symbol and the shortcut key *Ctrl+/,O* displays toward the bottom of the dialog box. To insert the ø symbol in a document using the shortcut key, hold down the Ctrl key and then press the / key. Release the Ctrl key and then press the o key. Not all symbols contain a shortcut key.

In BRIEF

Insert a Symbol
1 Click Insert, Symbol.
2 Click desired symbol.
3 Click Insert button.
4 Click Close button.

Insert a Special Character
1 Click Insert, Symbol.
2 Click Special Characters tab.
3 Click desired character.
4 Click Insert button.
5 Click Close button.

2.9 Setting Tabs

Word offers a variety of default settings including left tabs set every 0.5 inch. You can set your own tabs using the Ruler or at the Tabs dialog box. Use the Ruler to set, move, and delete tabs. The default tabs display as tiny vertical lines along the bottom of the Ruler. With a left tab, text aligns at the left edge of the tab. The other types of tabs that can be set on the Ruler are center, right, decimal, and bar. The small button at the left side of the Ruler is called the Alignment button. Each time you click the Alignment button, a different tab or paragraph alignment symbol displays. To set a tab, display the desired alignment button on the Ruler and then click on the Ruler at the desired position.

PROJECT: You have done some additional research on train travel in Europe with train connections and decide to add airport names to the train travel document.

S T E P S

1. With **WordS2-02** open, move the insertion point to the end of the document and then press the Enter key twice.

2. Type **International Airports with Train Connections** and then press the Enter key once.

3. Make sure the left tab symbol ⌊**L**⌋ displays in the Alignment button at the left side of the Ruler.

   If the Ruler is not displayed, turn it on by clicking View and then Ruler.

4. Position the arrow pointer below the 1-inch mark on the Ruler and then click the left mouse button.

5. Click once on the Alignment button located at the left side of the Ruler to display the center tab symbol ⌊⊥⌋ .

6. Position the arrow pointer below the 3-inch mark on the Ruler and then click the left mouse button.

7. Click once on the Alignment button located at the left side of the Ruler to display the right tab symbol ⌊⌟⌋ .

8. Position the arrow pointer below the 5-inch marker on the Ruler and then click the left mouse button.

⑨ Type the text shown in Figure W2.3 pressing the Tab key before typing each tabbed entry. Make sure you press the Tab key before typing the entry in the first column.

PROBLEM **?**

> If your columns of text do not look similar to those in Figure W2.3, check to make sure you inserted the tab symbols at the correct locations on the Ruler and that you pressed Tab before typing each entry in the first column.

⑩ After typing the last entry in the third column (*Fiumicino*), press the Enter key twice, and then press Ctrl + Q, the shortcut key to remove paragraph formatting.

Pressing Ctrl + Q removes the tabs you set from the Ruler.

⑪ Save **WordS2-02**.

FIGURE W2.3

Country	City	Airport
Austria	Vienna (Wein)	Schwechat
Belgium	Brussels	Nationaal
Britain	London	Heathrow
France	Paris	Orly
Germany	Berlin	Schoenefeld
Italy	Rome	Fiumicino

In Addition

Moving a Tab

Move a tab on the Ruler by positioning the mouse pointer on the tab symbol on the Ruler. Hold down the left mouse button, drag the symbol to the new location on the Ruler, and then release the mouse button.

Deleting a Tab

Delete a tab from the Ruler by positioning the arrow pointer on the tab symbol, holding down the left mouse button, dragging the symbol down into the document screen, and then releasing the mouse button.

Setting a Decimal Tab

Set a decimal tab for column entries you want aligned at the decimal point. To set a decimal tab, click the Alignment button located at the left side of the Ruler until the decimal tab symbol  displays, and then click on the desired position on the Ruler.

In BRIEF

Set a Tab on the Ruler
1 Display desired alignment symbol on Alignment button.
2 Click on Ruler at desired position.

2.10 Setting Tabs with Leaders

The four types of tabs can be set with leaders. Leaders are useful for material where you want to direct the reader's eyes across the page. Leaders can be periods, hyphens, or underlines. Tabs with leaders are set with options at the Tab dialog box. To display this dialog box, click Format and then Tabs. At the Tabs dialog box, choose the type of tab, the type of leader, and then enter a tab position measurement.

PROJECT: The information you found listing airports with train connections also includes schedule times. You will add this data to the train travel document.

STEPS

1. With **WordS2-02** open, move the insertion point to the end of the document.

2. Click the Alignment button at the left side of the Ruler until the left tab symbol ⌞L⌟ displays.

3. Position the arrow pointer below the 1-inch mark on the Ruler and then click the left mouse button.

4. Click the Alignment button at the left side of the Ruler until the right tab symbol displays.

5. Position the arrow pointer below the 5-inch mark on the Ruler and then click the left mouse button.

6. To type the headings shown in Figure W2.4, press the Tab key, click the Bold button on the Formatting toolbar, and then type **Airport**.

7. Press the Tab key, type **Service**, and then click the Bold button to turn off Bold.

8. Press the Enter key twice and then press Ctrl + Q to remove the paragraph tab formatting.

9. Set a left tab and a right tab with leaders by clicking Format and then Tabs.

10. At the Tabs dialog box, make sure *Left* is selected in the *Alignment* section of the dialog box. (If it is not, click *Left*.) With the insertion point positioned in the *Tab stop position* text box, type **1**, and then click the Set button.

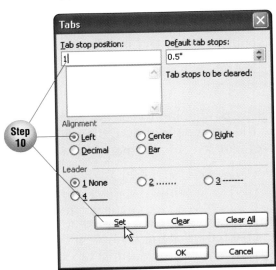

⑪ Type **5** in the *Tab stop position* text box, click *Right* in the *Alignment* section of the dialog box, and click *2.....* in the *Leader* section of the dialog box. Click the Set button and then click OK to close the dialog box.

⑫ Type the remaining text shown in Figure W2.4 making sure you press the Tab key before typing the first text entry.

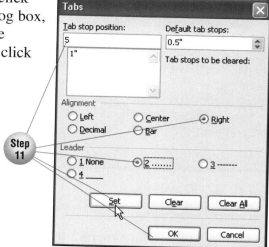

Step 11

PROBLEM ?

If your columns of text do not look similar to those in Figure W2.4, check to make sure you inserted the tab symbols at the correct measurements and that you pressed Tab before typing each entry in the first column.

⑬ Save **WordS2-02**.

FIGURE W2.4

Airport	**Service**
Schwechat	Train every 30 minutes
Nationaal	Train every 20 minutes
Heathrow	LT train every 10 minutes
Orly	RER train every 20 minutes
Schoenefeld	S-Bahn train every 20 minutes
Fiumicino	Train every 10 to 20 minutes

In Addition

Clearing Tabs at the Tabs Dialog Box

At the Tabs dialog box, you can clear an individual tab or all tabs. To clear all tabs, click the Clear All button. To clear an individual tab, specify the tab position, and then click the Clear button.

IN BRIEF

Set a Tab with Leaders
1 Click Format, Tabs.
2 Type tab measurement.
3 Click desired alignment.
4 Click desired leader.
5 Click Set.
6 Click OK.

2.11 Adding Borders and Shading

Insert a border around text in a paragraph or selected text with the Border button on the Formatting toolbar or with options at the Borders and Shading dialog box. To display this dialog box, click Format and then Borders and Shading. At the Borders and Shading dialog box with the Borders tab selected, you can specify the border type, style, color, and width. Click the Shading tab and the dialog box contains options for choosing a fill color and pattern style.

PROJECT: To highlight certain information in First Choice Travel's train travel document, you will apply a border to selected text. You will also apply border and shading formatting to the column text.

S T E P S

1. With **WordS2-02** open, select the numbered paragraphs.

2. Click the Outside Border button 🔲 ▾ on the Formatting toolbar.

   The name of the button changes depending on the border choice that was previously selected at the button drop-down palette. When Word is first opened, the button displays as Outside Border. Clicking this button inserts a border around the numbered paragraphs.

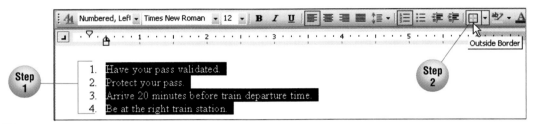

3. Select the bulleted paragraphs and then click the Outside Border button on the Formatting toolbar.

4. Select from the line of text containing the column headings *Country*, *City*, *Airport* through the line of text containing the column entries *Italy*, *Rome*, and *Fiumicino*.

5. Click Format and then Borders and Shading. At the Borders and Shading dialog box, make sure the Borders tab is selected.

6. Click the down-pointing arrow at the right side of the *Style* list box until the first double-line option displays and then click the double-line option.

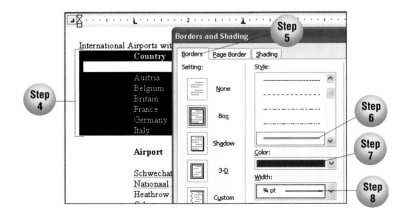

7 Click the down-pointing triangle at the right side of the *Color* list box and then click the Dark Blue option (sixth color from the left in the top row).

8 Click the down-pointing triangle at the right side of the *Width* list box and then click ¾ *pt* at the pop-up list.

9 Click the Shading tab and then click the fifth color (Light Turquoise) from the left in the bottom row of the Fill palette.

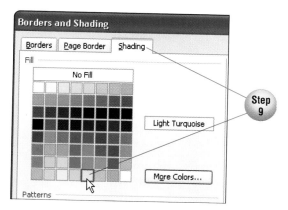

10 Click OK to close the dialog box.

PROBLEM?

If the border does not appear around all sides of the column text, display the Borders and Shading dialog box with the Borders tab selected and then click the *Box* option in the *Setting* section.

11 Add the same border and shading to the other columns of text by selecting from the line of text containing the column headings *Airport* and *Service* through the line of text containing the column entries *Fiumicino* and *Train every 10 to 20 minutes* and then pressing F4.

12 Save **WordS2-02**.

In Addition

Inserting Borders with the Border Button

Click the Border button on the Formatting toolbar and a border is inserted around the paragraph of text where the insertion point is positioned. Click the down-pointing arrow at the right side of the button and a palette of border choices displays as shown at the right. Click the option at the palette that will insert the desired border. Position the arrow pointer on an option at the palette and a ScreenTip displays with the name of the option.

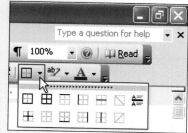

IN BRIEF

Insert Borders and Shading
1 Select text.
2 Click Format, Borders and Shading.
3 Choose desired border(s).
4 Click Shading tab.
5 Choose desired shading and/or pattern.
6 Click OK.

2.12 Inserting a Page Border

To improve the visual appeal of a document, consider inserting a page border. To insert a page border in a document, click Format and then Paragraph. At the Borders and Shading dialog box, click the Page Border tab. With options at the dialog box, you can specify the border style, color, and width. The Borders and Shading dialog box with the Page Border tab selected offers an option for inserting a page border containing an image. To display the images available, click the down-pointing arrow at the right side of the *Art* text box. Scroll down the list and then click the desired image.

PROJECT: After applying borders to selected text, you decide to continue adding visual appeal to the train travel document by inserting a page border. After reviewing and experimenting with the page border choices available, you decide to insert an art image border.

STEPS

① With **WordS2-02** open, display the Borders and Shading dialog box by clicking Format and then Borders and Shading.

② At the Borders and Shading dialog box, click the Page Border tab.

③ Click the *Shadow* option in the *Setting* section.

④ Click the down-pointing arrow at the right of the *Color* option and then click the Indigo color (second color option from the *right* in the top row).

⑤ Click the down-pointing arrow at the right of the *Width* option and then click *2 ¼ pt* at the drop-down list.

⑥ Click OK to close the Borders and Shading dialog box.

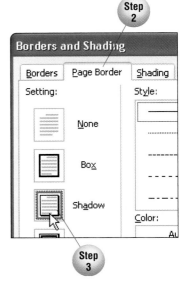

Step 2

Step 3

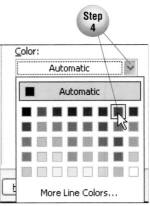

Step 4

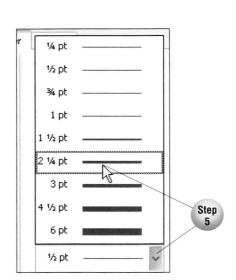

Step 5

(7) Click the down-pointing arrow at the right of the Zoom button on the Standard toolbar and then click *Whole Page* at the drop-down list.

> This displays the entire page on the screen so you can see how the page border appears on the page.

(8) After looking at the display of the page border, click the down-pointing arrow at the right of the Zoom button on the Standard toolbar and then click *100%* at the drop-down list.

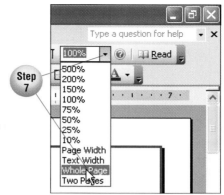

Step 7

(9) Change the page border to art images. To begin, click Format and then Borders and Shading to display the Borders and Shading dialog box. Make sure that the Page Border tab is selected.

(10) Click the *Box* option in the *Setting* section.

(11) Click the down-pointing arrow at the right side of the *Art* option box.

(12) Scroll down the list until the second globe art image displays (see figure at the right) and then click the globe images.

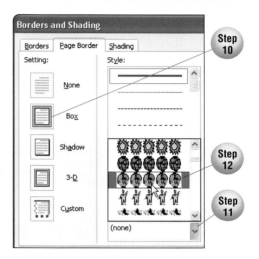

Step 10

Step 12

Step 11

(13) Click the down scroll arrow at the right side of the *Width* text box until *12 pt* displays.

(14) Click OK to close the dialog box.

(15) Save **WordS2-02**.

In Addition

Inserting Horizontal Lines

Word includes a horizontal line feature that inserts a graphic horizontal line in a document. To display the Horizontal Line dialog box shown at the right, display the Borders and Shading dialog box with any tab selected, and then click the Horizontal Line button located at the bottom of the dialog box. Insert a horizontal line into a document by clicking the desired line option and then clicking the OK button.

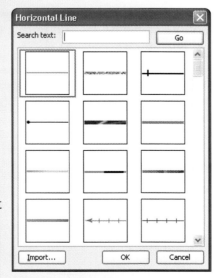

In Brief

Insert Page Border
1 Click Format, Borders and Shading.
2 Click Page Border tab.
3 Choose desired options.
4 Click OK.

2.13 Applying Styles

A Word document, by default, contains a number of styles that apply specific formatting. To display the available styles, click the down-pointing arrow at the right side of the Style button on the Formatting toolbar or click the Styles and Formatting button to display the Styles and Formatting task pane. This task pane contains a list of styles available with the current document and you can also display all available styles.

PROJECT: To further enhance the train travel document, you decide to apply paragraph and character styles to specific text.

S T E P S

1 With **WordS2-02** open, position the insertion point on any character in the heading *Traveling in Europe by Train*.

2 Apply a style by clicking the down-pointing arrow at the right side of the Style button `Normal ▾` on the Formatting toolbar and then clicking *Heading 2* at the drop-down list.

> The Heading 2 style applies 14-point Arial bold italic with 12 points of space above the heading and 3 points of space below the heading.

3 Click anywhere in the heading *Rail Ticket Bonuses* and then apply the Heading 2 style by completing directions similar to those in Step 2.

4 Click anywhere in the heading *International Airports with Train Connections* and then apply the Heading 2 style.

5 Click the Styles and Formatting button 🔠 on the Formatting toolbar.

> Clicking this button displays the Styles and Formatting task pane at the right side of the screen. This task pane contains styles available with the current document including styles for applying the bullet and borders and shading formatting you applied to text in the document.

6 Display all available styles by clicking the down-pointing arrow at the right of the *Show* option located toward the bottom of the Styles and Formatting task pane and then clicking *All styles* at the drop-down list.

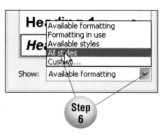

> Paragraph styles display in the Styles and Formatting task pane followed by a paragraph symbol (¶) and character styles display followed by a character symbol (**a**). To apply a paragraph style, position the insertion point anywhere in the paragraph and then click the style. To apply a character style, select the text first, and then click the desired style.

7 Select the words *75% discount* located in the last paragraph in the *Rail Ticket Bonuses* section and then click the *Strong* style in the *Pick formatting to apply* list box (you will need to scroll down the list box to display this style).

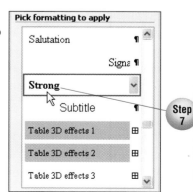

> Styles are alphabetized in the task pane. The Strong style is a character style.

8 Select the four numbered items that begin with *Have your pass validated.* and then click the *List Bullet 2* style in the *Pick formatting to apply* list box.

9 Click the down-pointing arrow at the right of the *Show* option in the Styles and Formatting task pane and then click *Available formatting* at the drop-down list. Turn off the display of the task pane by clicking the Close button located in the upper right corner of the task pane.

10 Remove the border around the second bulleted list by selecting the four items that begin *Free or discount transportation...*, clicking the down-pointing arrow at the right of the Outside Border button, and then clicking the No Border option.

11 Clear style formatting from the other bulleted list. To do this, select the four bulleted items (beginning with *Have your pass validated.*), click the down-pointing arrow at the right of the Style button on the Formatting toolbar, and then click *Clear Formatting*.

12 Deselect the text and then save **WordS2-02**.

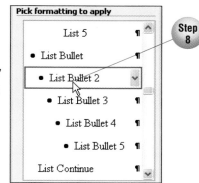

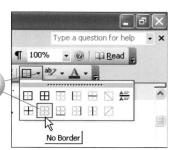

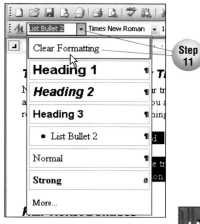

In Addition

Formatting Text with the Style Gallery

Each document is based on a template, with the Normal template document the default. You can use the Style Gallery dialog box to apply styles from other templates to the current document. This provides you with a large number of predesigned styles for formatting text. To display the Style Gallery dialog box, click Format and then Theme. At the Theme dialog box, click the Style Gallery button (located at the bottom of the dialog box). At the Style Gallery dialog box, the template documents display in the *Template* list box. The open document displays in the *Preview of* section of the dialog box. With this section, you can choose templates from the *Template* list box and see how the formatting is applied to the open document.

In BRIEF

Apply a Style Using Style Button
1 Click down-pointing arrow at right of Style button on Formatting toolbar.
2 Click desired style at drop-down list.

Apply a Style Using Styles and Formatting Task Pane
1 Click Styles and Formatting button on Formatting toolbar.
2 Click desired style in *Pick formatting to apply* list box.

2.14 Creating Custom Bullets

You can apply bullets to selected text with options at the Bullets and Numbering dialog box. You can also create and apply custom bullets with options at the Customize Bulleted List dialog box. Display this dialog box by clicking the Customize button at the Bullets and Numbering dialog box. You can create picture and character custom bullets.

PROJECT: To enhance the visual appeal of the document, you decide to create a custom airplane bullet and then apply it to the list items in the document.

S T E P S

1. With **WordS2-02** open, select the four items from *Have your pass validated.* through *Be at the right train station.*

2. Create a custom bullet by clicking Format and then Bullets and Numbering.

3. At the Bullets and Numbering dialog box with the Bulleted tab selected, click the first option in the bottom row and then click the Customize button.

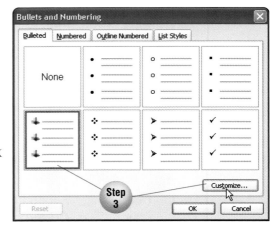

4. At the Customize Bulleted List dialog box, click the Character button.

5. In the *Font* list box at the Symbol dialog box, select *Wingdings* and then click the airplane symbol (approximately the second symbol from the left in the fourth row from the beginning of the list).

6. Click OK to close the Symbol dialog box and then click OK to close the Customize Bulleted List dialog box.

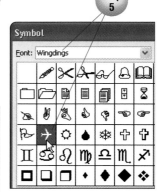

7. Select the four bulleted items (beginning with *Free or discount transportation...*), click Format, and then click Bullets and Numbering.

8. At the Bullets and Numbering dialog box with the Bulleted tab selected, click the airplane bullet item (first item from the left in the bottom row) and then click OK.

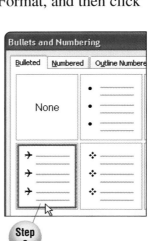

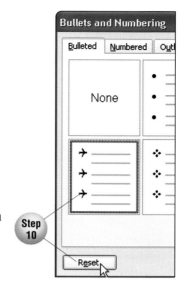

9. Press Ctrl + Home and then reset the bullets back to the original settings by clicking Format and then Bullets and Numbering.

10. At the Bullets and Numbering dialog box with the Bulleted tab selected, click the airplane bullet option (first option from the left in the bottom row) and then click the Reset button.

11. At the message asking if you are sure you want to reset to the default settings, click the Yes button.

12. Click the Close button located in the lower right corner of the dialog box. (Do not click the OK button because that would insert a bullet in the document.)

13. Save and then close **WordS2-02**.

In Addition

Creating an Outline Style Numbered List

Certain options at the Bullets and Numbering dialog box with the Outline Numbered tab selected as shown below are available only when heading styles have been applied to text. To create an outline style numbered list, apply heading styles to the titles and/or headings in the document, display the Bullets and Numbering dialog box with the Outline Numbered tab selected, and then click the desired numbering format.

In BRIEF

Create Custom Bullets
1 Click Format, Bullets and Numbering.
2 Click Bulleted tab.
3 Click Customize button.
4 Click Character button.
5 Click desired symbol.
6 Click OK.

2.15 Creating an AutoText Entry

Use the AutoText feature to insert predefined entries or create your own entries. The AutoText feature is useful for items such as addresses, company logos, lists, standard text, letter closings, or any other text that you use on a frequent basis. Use options at the Create AutoText dialog box to create an AutoText entry. Insert an AutoText entry in a document by typing the name of the AutoText and then pressing the Enter key or the shortcut key, F3; with an option from the AutoText side menu; or at the AutoCorrect dialog box with the AutoText tab selected. An AutoText entry name must be at least four characters in length to display the AutoText with the Enter key. Use the shortcut key,

F3, on an AutoText entry name of any length. To insert an AutoText entry with the Enter key, type the name given (at least four characters) to the AutoText entry (the full entry displays as a yellow box above the insertion point), and then press the Enter key.

PROJECT: The manager of First Choice Travel, Melissa Gehring, has asked you to include copyright information on any fact sheets produced by the company. You decide to create an AutoText with the information since you will be inserting it in a number of documents.

S T E P S

1. At a clear document screen, type at the left margin the text shown in Figure W2.5. (To create the copyright symbol, click Insert and then Symbol. At the Symbol dialog box, click the Special Characters tab. Click the copyright symbol, click the Insert button, and then click the Close button.)

FIGURE W2.5

©2005 First Choice Travel

Los Angeles Office
3588 Ventura Boulevard
Los Angeles, CA 90102

2. Select the entire document and then change the font size to 8.

3. Select ©2005 First Choice Travel.

   When you save selected text as an AutoText entry, the formatting applied to the text is also saved. If you are saving a paragraph or paragraphs of text that have paragraph formatting applied, make sure you include the paragraph mark with the selected text.

4. Click Insert, point to AutoText, and then click New.

5. At the Create AutoText dialog box, type **CR** and then click OK.

   An AutoText entry name can contain a maximum of 32 characters and can include spaces. Try to name the AutoText something that is short but also gives you an idea of the contents of the entry.

Step 5

6. Select *Los Angeles Office* and the two lines of text below.

⑦ Click Insert, point to AutoText, and then click New.

⑧ At the Create AutoText dialog box, type **FCTLA** and then click OK.

Create AutoText

Word will create an AutoText entry from the current selection.

Please name your AutoText entry:

FCTLA

[OK]   [Cancel]

Step 8

⑨ Close the document without saving it.

⑩ Open **WordS2-02**. Delete the following blank lines: blank line above and blank line below the first bulleted list, blank line above the second bulleted list, and the blank line immediately below the last paragraph in the *Rail Ticket Bonuses* section.

⑪ Press Ctrl + End to move the insertion point to the end of the document and then press the Enter key once. (This inserts a new line within the paragraph border.) Press Ctrl + Q to remove the paragraph border and shading formatting and then press the Enter key once.

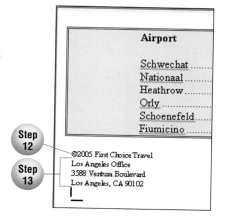

Airport

Schwechat ....
Nationaal ....
Heathrow ....
Orly ....
Schoenefeld ......
Fiumicino ....

©2005 First Choice Travel
Los Angeles Office
3588 Ventura Boulevard
Los Angeles, CA 90102

⑫ Type **CR** and then press the F3 function key.

This inserts the copyright information in the document.

Step 12

Step 13

⑬ Move the insertion point to the line below the copyright information, type **FCTLA**, and then press the Enter key.

⑭ Save, print, and then close **WordS2-02**.

In Addition

Editing/Deleting an AutoText Entry

Edit an AutoText entry by inserting the entry in a document, making any necessary changes, and then saving it again with the same AutoText entry name. At the message asking if you want to redefine the AutoText entry, click Yes. Remove an AutoText entry from the AutoCorrect dialog box with the AutoText tab selected. To do this, display the AutoCorrect dialog box with the AutoText tab selected, select the entry to be deleted, and then click the Delete button.

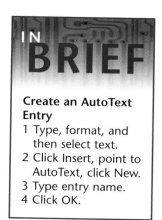

In BRIEF

Create an AutoText Entry
1 Type, format, and then select text.
2 Click Insert, point to AutoText, click New.
3 Type entry name.
4 Click OK.

FEATURES SUMMARY

Feature	Button	Menu	Keyboard
Apply style	Normal		
Bold	**B**		Ctrl + B
Borders and Shading dialog box		Format, Borders and Shading	
Bullets		Format, Bullets and Numbering	
Center align			Ctrl + E
Create AutoText dialog box		Insert, AutoText, New	Alt + F3
Decrease text indent from left margin			Ctrl + Shift + M
Double spacing			Ctrl + 2
Font Color palette	**A**		
Font dialog box		Format, Font	Ctrl + D
Font drop-down list	Times New Roman		
Font Size drop-down list	12		
Format Painter			
Hanging indent			Ctrl + T
Indent text from left margin			Ctrl + M
Insert AutoText entry			Enter or F3
Insert border			
Italics	*I*		Ctrl + I
Justify			Ctrl + J
Left align			Ctrl + L
Numbers		Format, Bullets and Numbering	
1.5-line spacing			Ctrl + 5
Remove a hanging indent			Ctrl + Shift + T
Remove paragraph formatting			Ctrl + Q
Repeat command		Edit, Repeat	F4 or Ctrl + Y
Right align			Ctrl + R
Select entire document		Edit, Select All	Ctrl + A
Single spacing			Ctrl + 1
Styles and Formatting Task Pane			
Symbol dialog box		Insert, Symbol	
Tabs dialog box		Format, Tabs	
Underline	<u>U</u>		Ctrl + U

PROCEDURES CHECK

Completion: In the space provided at the right, indicate the correct term, command, or option.

1. Press these keys on the keyboard to italicize selected text.
2. Click these options to display the Paragraph dialog box.
3. Click this button to indent text from the left margin.
4. Click these options to select the entire document.
5. Press this function key to repeat a command.
6. Press these keys on the keyboard to underline selected text.
7. Click this button on the Formatting toolbar to display a palette of font colors.
8. Click this button on the Formatting toolbar to right align text.
9. Click this button on the Formatting toolbar to number selected paragraphs.
10. Change line spacing with this button on the Formatting toolbar.
11. Click these options to display the Bullets and Numbering dialog box.
12. Set tabs at the Tabs dialog box or by using this.
13. Click these options to display the Borders and Shading dialog box.
14. Display all available styles by clicking the down-pointing arrow at the right of this option in the Styles and Formatting task pane and then clicking *All styles*.
15. This is the shortcut key command to insert an AutoText entry.

SKILLS REVIEW

Activity 1: APPLYING FONTS; USING THE FORMAT PAINTER

1 Open **FCTPetersburg**.
2 Save the document with Save As and name it **WordS2-R1**.
3 Select the entire document and then make the following changes:
   a Change the font to Bookman Old Style. (If this font is not available, choose a similar font such as Garamond or Century.)
   b Change the font size to 11 points.
4 Select the title *FACT SHEET – PETERSBURG, ALASKA*, change the font to 16-point Arial bold, and then deselect the text.
5 Select the heading *Services*, change the font to 14-point Arial bold, and then deselect the heading.

6 Using Format Painter, change the font to 14-point Arial bold for the remaining headings (*Visitor Attractions*, *Walking Tours*, *Accommodations*, and *Transportation*).

7 Save **WordS2-R1**.

Activity 2: APPLYING FONT EFFECTS; USING THE REPEAT COMMAND

1 With **WordS2-R1** open, select the last sentence in the document *(If you would like more information on traveling in Alaska, check with a First Choice Travel representative.)* and then apply a small caps effect.

2 Select the title *FACT SHEET – PETERSBURG, ALASKA* and then apply a shadow effect.

3 Select the heading *Services* and then apply a shadow effect.

4 Use the Repeat command to apply the shadow effect to the remaining headings in the document (*Visitor Attractions*, *Walking Tours*, *Accommodations*, and *Transportation*).

5 Save **WordS2-R1**.

Activity 3: ALIGNING AND INDENTING TEXT

1 With **WordS2-R1** open, position the insertion point anywhere in the paragraph below the title *FACT SHEET – PETERSBURG, ALASKA* and then change the paragraph alignment to Justify.

2 Position the insertion point anywhere in the last sentence of the document *(If you would like more information on traveling in Alaska, check with a First Choice Travel representative.)* and then change the paragraph alignment to center.

3 Select the two paragraphs below the *Services* heading and then make the following changes:
   • Change the paragraph alignment to Justify.
   • Indent the paragraphs 0.5 inch from the left margin using the Increase Indent button.
   • Deselect the paragraphs.

4 Change the paragraph alignment to Justify and indent paragraphs 0.5 inch from the left margin using the Increase Indent button for the following paragraphs:
   • Four paragraphs below the *Visitor Attractions* heading
   • One paragraph below the *Walking Tours* heading
   • Two paragraphs below *Accommodations* heading
   • Two paragraphs below the *Transportation* heading

5 Move the insertion point to the end of the document and then make the following changes:
   a Press the Enter key twice.
   b Change the alignment to Left and then insert the current date.
   c Press the Enter key once and then insert the current time.
   d Press the Enter key twice, type **CR**, and then press F3.
   e Press the Enter key once, type **FCTLA**, and then press the Enter key.

6 Save **WordS2-R1**.

Activity 4: CHANGING LINE AND PARAGRAPH SPACING

1 With **WordS2-R1** open, select the entire document, change the line spacing to 1.1, and then deselect the document.
2 Click anywhere in the heading *Services* and then change the paragraph spacing after to 6 points.
3 Use the Repeat command to insert 6 points of spacing after the remaining headings (*Visitor Attractions*, *Walking Tours*, *Accommodations*, and *Transportation*).
4 Save, print, and then close **WordS2-R1**.

Activity 5: INSERTING BULLETS AND SYMBOLS

1 Open **FCTPackages**.
2 Save the document with Save As and name it **WordS2-R2**.
3 Select the five lines of text below *Fast Facts* in the *OREGON* section of the document and then insert bullets.
4 Select the six lines of text below *Fast Facts* in the *NEVADA* section of the document and then insert bullets.
5 Deselect the text.
6 Move the insertion point to the end of the document, press the Enter key twice, and then type the text shown in Figure W2.6. Insert the é, è, and ñ symbols using the Symbol dialog box.
7 Move the insertion point to the end of the document, press the Enter key, and then insert the copyright AutoText (the AutoText named CR).
8 Save **WordS2-R2**.

FIGURE W2.6 Activity 5

Additional accommodations are available at the Ste. Thérèse Chateau and Silver Creek Resort. For information, please contact Carlos Nuñez.

Activity 6: SETTING TABS

1 With **WordS2-R2** open, move the insertion point a double space below the heading *Rates and Packages* in the *OREGON* section and then create the tabbed text shown in Figure W2.7 with the following specifications (type the text as shown in the figure):
a Set a left tab at the 1-inch mark on the Ruler.
b Set a center tab at the 3.25-inch mark on the Ruler.
c Set a right tab at the 5-inch mark on the Ruler.
2 Move the insertion point a double space below the heading *Rates and Packages* in the *NEVADA* section and then create the tabbed text shown in Figure W2.8. Use the same tab settings you set for the text in the *OREGON* section.
3 Save **WordS2-R2**.

FIGURE W2.7 Activity 6

Accommodation	No. Persons	Daily Price
Studio/one bedroom	2-4	$75-125
Two bedrooms	4-6	$95-225
Three bedrooms	6-8	$135-300
Four bedrooms	8-12	$160-400
Five/six bedrooms	10-16	$250-500

FIGURE W2.8 Activity 6

Package	Length	Price
Tuck 'n' Roll	3 days/2 nights	$269
Ski Sneak	4 days/3 nights	$409
Take a Break	6 days/5 nights	$649
Ultimate	8 days/7 nights	$1,009

Activity 7: ADDING BORDERS AND SHADING; APPLYING STYLES

1 With **WordS2-R2** open, select the tabbed text below the *Rates and Packages* heading in the *OREGON* section, insert a border and shading of your choosing, and then deselect the text.
2 Select the tabbed text below the *Rates and Packages* heading in the *NEVADA* section, insert a border and shading of your choosing, and then deselect the text.
3 Apply the Heading 1 style to the headings *OREGON* and *NEVADA*.
4 Apply the Heading 2 style to the *Fast Facts* and *Rates and Packages* headings in the *OREGON* and *NEVADA* sections.
5 Apply a page border of your choosing to the document. (Consider applying an art image border.)
6 Save and then close **WordS2-R2**.

Activity 8: CREATING AN AUTOTEXT ENTRY

1 At a clear document screen, type the following text at the left margin:
   Toronto Office
   4277 Yonge Street
   Toronto, ON M4P 2E6
2 Select the entire document and then change the font size to 8.
3 Select the text and then create an AutoText entry named FCTT.

4 Close the document without saving it.

5 Open **WordS2-R2**.

6 Move the insertion point to the blank line below the copyright information (at the end of the document) and then insert the FCTT AutoText entry.

7 Save, print, and then close **WordS2-R2**.

PERFORMANCE PLUS

Assessment 1: CHANGING FONTS; ALIGNING AND INDENTING TEXT; CHANGING PARAGRAPH SPACING

1 Open **FCTCCSkiing**.

2 Save the document with Save As and name it **WordS2-P1**.

3 Make the following changes to the document:

   a Set the entire document in Century Schoolbook. (If this typeface is not available, choose a similar typeface such as Bookman Old Style or Garamond.)

   b Set the title in 14-point Tahoma bold. (If Tahoma is not available, choose Arial.)

   c Set the names of the cross-country resorts in 12-point Tahoma bold and add a shadow effect.

   d Change the line spacing for the entire document to 1.3.

   e Insert 6 points of space after each of the names of the cross-country resorts.

   f Center align the title.

   g Indent the paragraph of text below each cross-country resort name 0.5 inch from the left margin and change the alignment to Justify.

   h Move the insertion point to the end of the document and then insert the CR AutoText entry.

4 Save, print, and then close **WordS2-P1**.

Assessment 2: PREPARING AND FORMATTING A LETTER

1 Open **MPLetterhead**.

2 Save the letterhead document with Save As and name it **WordS2-P2**.

3 You are Neva Smith-Wilder, Educational Liaison for Marquee Productions. Write a letter using the date April 18, 2005, to Cal Rubine, Chair, Theatre Arts Division, Niagara Peninsula College, 2199 Victoria Street, Niagara-on-the-Lake, ON L0S 1J0 and include the following information:

- Marquee Productions will be filming in and around the city of Toronto during the summer of 2005.
- Marquee Productions would like to use approximately 20 theatre interns to assist in the filming.

- Interns will perform a variety of tasks including acting as extras, assisting the camera crew, working with set designers on set construction, and providing support to the production team.
- Interns can work approximately 15 to 30 hours per week and will be compensated at minimum wage.
- Close your letter by asking Mr. Rubine to screen interested students and then send approximately 20 names to you.
- If Mr. Rubine has any questions, he may contact you at (612) 555-2005, or send the names to you by e-mail at NevaSW@emcp.net.

4 After typing the letter, apply the following formatting:
  a Select the letter text (do not select the letterhead image or text) and then change to a font other than Times New Roman.
  b Change the paragraph alignment to Justify for the paragraph(s) in the body of the letter.
5 Save, print, and then close **WordS2-P2**.

Assessment 3: SETTING LEADER TABS

1 At a clear document screen, type the text shown in Figure W2.9 with the following specifications:
  a Center, bold, and italicize the text as shown in the figure.
  b Set the tabbed text as shown using a left tab for the first column and a right tab with leaders for the second column.
  c After typing the text, select the entire document and then change to a typeface of your choosing (other than Times New Roman).
2 Save the document and name it **WordS2-P3**.
3 Print and then close **WordS2-P3**.

FIGURE W2.9 Assessment 3

WORLDWIDE ENTERPRISES
Distribution Schedule
Two by Two

United States...May 10
Canada ....June 7
Japan..July 26
Australia/New Zealand...August 2
Mexico ....September 20

Assessment 4: FINDING INFORMATION ON THE WIDOW/ORPHAN FEATURE; KEEPING TEXT TOGETHER

1 Use Word's Help feature to learn about the widow/orphan feature and how to keep paragraphs of text together on the same page.
2 Create a document containing information on these two features with the following specifications:
   a Create a title for the document that is centered and bolded.
   b Write a paragraph discussing the widow/orphan feature.
   c Write a paragraph discussing how to keep paragraphs of text together on the same page.
3 Save the completed document and name it **WordS2-P4A**.
4 Print and then close **WordS2-P4A**.
5 Open **FCTVacationSpecials**.
6 Save the document with Save As and name it **WordS2-P4B**.
7 Select all of the lines of indented text containing information on various categories (begins with *Category H* and continues through all lines pertaining to *Category S1*).
8 Insert a command to keep all lines of text together with the next line. *(Hint: Make sure you check the* **Keep with next** *option.)*
9 Save the document and then print only page 2 of **WordS2-P4B**.
10 Close **WordS2-P4B**.

Assessment 5: HYPHENATING WORDS IN A DOCUMENT

1 In some Word documents, the right margin may appear ragged. If the paragraph alignment is changed to Justify, the right margin will appear even, but extra spaces are added throughout the line. In these situations, hyphenating long words that fall at the end of the text line provides the document with a more balanced look. Use Word's Help feature to learn how to automatically hyphenate words in a document.
2 Open **FCTPetersburg**.
3 Save the document with Save As and name it **WordS2-P5**.
4 Automatically hyphenate words in the document, limiting the consecutive hyphens to 2. *(Hint: Specify the number of consecutive hyphens at the Hyphenation dialog box.)*
5 Save, print, and then close **WordS2-P5**.

Assessment 6: LOCATING INFORMATION AND WRITING A LETTER

1 You are a travel consultant for First Choice Travel and Camille Matsui, production assistant for Marquee Productions, has asked you to find information on art galleries and museums in Toronto, Ontario, Canada. Connect to the Internet and search for information on at least three art galleries and/or museums in the Toronto area.

2 Using the information you find on the Internet, write a letter to Camille Matsui, Production Assistant, Marquee Productions, 955 South Alameda Street, Los Angeles, CA 90037, and tell her about three galleries and/or museums providing a brief description of each one.

3 Use your name in the complimentary close and include the title Travel Consultant.

4 Save the completed letter and name it **WordS2-P6**.

5 Print and then close **WordS2-P6**.

WORD SECTION 3

Formatting and Enhancing a Document

Use formatting features to rearrange text in a document, add special elements, or change the appearance of text. With the find and replace feature you can find specific text and replace with other text. Use buttons on the Standard toolbar to move, copy, and paste text in a document or use the Clipboard task pane to collect up to 24 different items and then paste them in various locations in the document. Additional document formatting includes inserting page numbering; changing margins, orientation, and views; and changing vertical alignment. Add visual appeal to documents by inserting images, WordArt, and drawing and customizing shapes and text boxes. Use the Envelopes and Labels feature to easily create and format envelopes and labels. In this section, you will learn the skills and complete the projects described here.

Note: Before beginning this section, delete the WordS2 folder on your disk. Next, copy to your disk or other location the WordS3 subfolder from the CD that accompanies this textbook and then make WordS3 the active folder.

Skills

- Find and replace text
- Reveal formatting
- Find and replace formatting
- Cut, copy, and paste text
- Use the Paste Special feature
- Use the Clipboard task pane to copy and paste items
- Insert a page break
- Insert and modify page numbers
- Change margins
- Change page orientation
- Arrange windows
- Review and modify document properties
- Change views
- Use the click and type feature
- Vertically align text
- Insert, size, and move images
- Insert, size, and move WordArt
- Use buttons on the Drawing toolbar
- Prepare an envelope
- Prepare labels

Projects

Edit and format fact sheets on Petersburg and Juneau, Alaska; prepare an announcement about a workshop on traveling on a budget; prepare a document on special vacation activities in Hawaii; prepare envelopes and labels for mailing fact sheets and announcements.

Prepare an announcement about internship positions available at Marquee Productions; prepare an envelope and labels for the Theatre Arts Division.

Format a costume rental agreement.
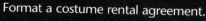

Prepare an announcement about a workshop on employment opportunities in the movie industry; prepare a banner with information on the Royal Ontario Museum.

Create an announcement for a stockholders' meeting; prepare an envelope.

3.1 Finding and Replacing Text

Use the find and replace feature to find specific text and replace with other text. For example, you can use abbreviations for common phrases when entering text and then replace the abbreviations with the actual text later, or you can set up standard documents with generic names and replace the names with other names to make a personalized document. You can also find and replace some formatting. These options are available at the Find and Replace dialog box with the Replace tab selected.

PROJECT: You are working on a First Choice Travel document containing information on Petersburg, Alaska. Your quick review identifies some spelling and capitalization errors that you will correct using the Find and Replace feature.

S T E P S

1. Open the **FCTPetersburg** document.

2. Save the document with Save As and name it **WordS3-01**.

3. After looking over the document, you realize that *Mitkoff* is spelled incorrectly. Display the Find and Replace dialog box by clicking Edit and then Replace.

4. At the Find and Replace dialog box with the Replace tab selected, type **Mitkoff** in the *Find what* text box and then press the Tab key.

   Pressing the Tab key moves the insertion point to the *Replace with* text box.

5. Type **Mitkof** in the *Replace with* text box and then click the Replace All button located toward the bottom of the dialog box.

   Clicking the Replace All button replaces all occurrences of the text in the document. If you want control over what is replaced in a document, click the Replace button to replace text or click the Find Next button to move to the next occurrence of the text.

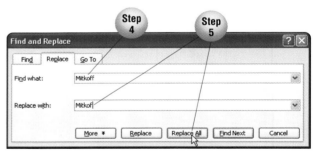

PROBLEM

If the *Replace with* text box does not display, click the Replace tab.

6. At the message telling you that two replacements were made, click the OK button.

7. Click the Close button to close the Find and Replace dialog box.

8. Looking at the document, you determine that *Alaska Marine Highway* is a proper name and should display in the document with the first letter of each word capitalized. Click Edit and then Replace.

9. At the Find and Replace dialog box with the Replace tab selected, type **Alaska marine highway**.

10. Press Tab, type Alaska Marine Highway in the *Replace with* text box, and then click the Replace All button.

11. At the message telling you that two replacements were made, click the OK button.

12. Click the Close button to close the Find and Replace dialog box.

13. Select the title *FACT SHEET – PETERSBURG, ALASKA* and then change the font to 16-point Arial bold and change the alignment to center.

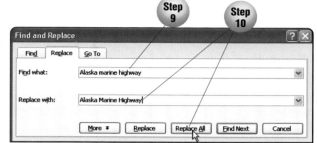

14. Select the heading *Services* and then change the font to 14-point Arial bold. Use Format Painter to format the remaining headings (*Visitor Attractions*, *Walking Tours*, *Accommodations*, and *Transportation)* with 14-point Arial bold.

15. Save **WordS3-01**.

In Addition

Options at the Expanded Find and Replace Dialog Box

The Find and Replace dialog box contains a variety of check boxes with options you can choose for completing a find and replace. To display these options, click the More button located at the bottom of the dialog box. This causes the Find and Replace dialog box to expand as shown at the right. The options are described below.

Option	Action
Match case	Exactly match the case of the search text. For example, if you search for *Book*, Word will stop at *Book* but not *book* or *BOOK*.
Find whole words only	Find a whole word, not a part of a word. For example, if you search for *her* and *did not* select Find whole words only, Word would stop at t*here*, *here*, *hers*, and so on.
Use wildcards	Search for wildcards, special characters, or special search operators.
Sounds like	Match words that sound alike but are spelled differently such as *know* and *no*.
Find all word forms	Find all forms of the word entered in the *Find what* text box. For example, if you enter *hold*, Word will stop at *held* and *holding*.

In Brief

Find and Replace Text
1 Click Edit, Replace.
2 Type find text.
3 Press the Tab key.
4 Type replace text.
5 Click Replace All button.

3.2 Revealing Formatting; Finding and Replacing Formatting

Display formatting applied to specific text in a document at the Reveal Formatting task pane. Display this task pane by clicking Format and then Reveal Formatting. The Reveal Formatting task pane displays font, paragraph, and section formatting applied to text where the insertion point is positioned or in selected text. With options at the Find and Replace dialog box with the Replace tab selected, you can search for specific formatting or characters containing specific formatting and replace it with other characters or formatting.

PROJECT: After reviewing the Petersburg document, you decide that the headings would look better set in a different font and font color. To display the formatting applied to specific text, you will use the Reveal Formatting task pane, and then find and replace the font formatting.

S T E P S

1 With **WordS3-01** open, press Ctrl + Home to move the insertion point to the beginning of the document, click Format, and then click Reveal Formatting.

> This displays the Reveal Formatting task pane with information on the formatting applied to the title. Generally, a minus symbol precedes *Font* and *Paragraph* and a plus symbol precedes *Section* in the *Formatting of selected text* section. Click the minus symbol to hide any items below a heading and click the plus symbol to reveal items. Some items in the Reveal Formatting task pane are hyperlinks. For example, click the Font hyperlink and the Font dialog box displays. Use these hyperlinks to make changes to the document formatting.

2 Click anywhere in the paragraph below the title and look at the Reveal Formatting task pane to determine the formatting.

3 Click anywhere in the heading *Services* and then notice the formatting applied to the text.

4 Close the Reveal Formatting task pane by clicking the Close button located in the upper right corner of the task pane.

5 Find text set in 14-point Arial bold and replace it with text set in 14-point Times New Roman bold italic and in Indigo color. To begin, position the insertion point at the beginning of the document, click Edit, and then click Replace.

6 At the Find and Replace dialog box, press the Delete key. (This deletes any text that displays in the *Find what* text box.)

7 Click the More button. (If a check mark displays in the *Find all word forms* check box, click the option to remove the mark.)

8 Click the Format button located at the bottom of the dialog box and then click *Font* at the drop-down menu.

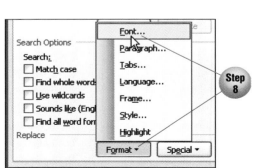

⑨ At the Find Font dialog box, change the font to Arial, the font style to Bold, and the size to 14, and then click OK to close the dialog box.

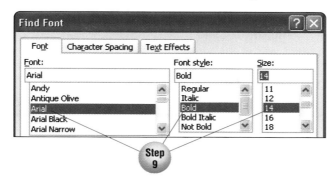

⑩ At the Find and Replace dialog box, select and then delete any text that displays in the *Replace with* text box.

⑪ With the insertion point positioned in the *Replace with* text box, click the Format button located at the bottom of the dialog box and then click *Font* at the drop-down menu.

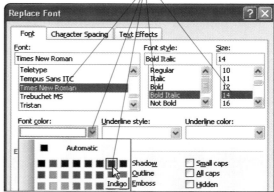

⑫ At the Replace Font dialog box, change the font to Times New Roman, the font style to Bold Italic, the size to 14, and the font color to Indigo, and then click OK to close the dialog box.

⑬ At the Find and Replace dialog box, click the Replace All button. At the message telling you that the search of the document is complete and five replacements were made, click OK.

⑭ Click the Less button to reduce the size of the Find and Replace dialog box and then close the dialog box.

⑮ Select the title *FACT SHEET – PETERSBURG, ALASKA* and then change the font to 14-point Times New Roman bold and the font color to Indigo.

⑯ Save **WordS3-01**.

In Addition

Comparing Formatting

Along with displaying formatting applied to text, you can use the Reveal Formatting task pane to compare formatting of two text selections to determine what formatting is different. To compare formatting, display the Reveal Formatting task pane and then select the first instance of formatting to be compared. Click the *Compare to another selection* check box to insert a check mark and then select the second instance of formatting to compare. Any differences between the two selections will display in the *Formatting differences* list box.

IN BRIEF

Reveal Formatting
1 Click in desired text.
2 Click Format, Reveal Formatting.

3.3 Cutting, Copying, and Pasting Text; Using Paste Special

With the Cut, Copy, and Paste buttons on the Standard toolbar, you can quickly move and/or copy words, sentences, or entire sections of text to other locations in a document. You can cut and paste text or copy and paste text within the same document or between documents. Specify the formatting of pasted text with options at the Paste Special dialog box. Use options at the dialog box to specify how you want text pasted in the document.

PROJECT: You decide that some of the text in the Petersburg fact sheet should be reorganized. You also decide to add more information to the document.

S T E P S

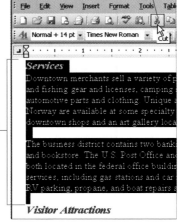

1. With **WordS3-01** open, move the *Services* section below the *Walking Tours* section by selecting the *Services* heading, the two paragraphs of text below it, and the blank line below the second paragraph.

2. Click the Cut button 🔪 on the Standard toolbar.

   This places the text in a special location within Word called the "clipboard."

PROBLEM ❓ If you click the wrong button, immediately click the Undo button.

3. Move the insertion point to the beginning of the *Accommodations* heading and then click the Paste button 📋 on the Standard toolbar.

   A Paste Options 📋 button displays below the pasted text. Click this button and options display for specifying the formatting of the pasted text. The default setting keeps source formatting for the pasted text. You can choose to match the destination formatting, keep only the text and not the formatting, or display the Styles and Formatting task pane where you can choose the desired formatting.

4. Copy text from another document and paste it in the Petersburg fact sheet. To begin, open **FCTPA01**.

5. Select the *Points of Interest* heading, the four lines of text below the heading and the blank line below the lines of text, and then click the Copy button 📋 on the Standard toolbar.

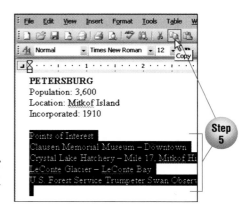

6. Click the button on the Taskbar representing **WordS3-01**.

7. Position the insertion point at the beginning of the sentence *If you would like more information...* located toward the end of the document and then click the Paste button 📋.

⑧ Click the button on the Taskbar representing **FCTPA01**.

⑨ Select the text *Resources:* and the three lines below it and then click the Copy button 🗎 .

⑩ Click the button on the Taskbar representing **WordS3-01**.

⑪ Move the insertion point to the end of the document (a double space below the last sentence) and then paste the copied text into the document without the formatting by clicking Edit and then Paste Special.

⑫ At the Paste Special dialog box, click *Unformatted Text* in the *As* list box and then click OK.

Step
12

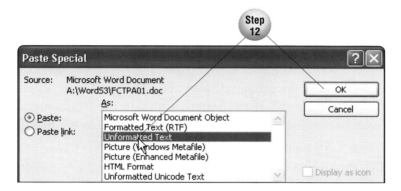

⑬ Save **WordS3-01**.

⑭ Click the button on the Taskbar representing the **FCTPA01** document and then close the document.

Closing the **FCTPA01** document displays the **WordS3-01** document.

In Addition

Moving and Copying Text with the Mouse

You can move selected text using the mouse. To do this, select the text with the mouse and then move the I-beam pointer inside the selected text until the I-beam pointer turns into an arrow pointer. Hold down the left mouse button, drag the arrow pointer (displays with a gray box attached) to the location where you want the selected text inserted, and then release the button. You can copy and move selected text by following similar steps. The difference is that you need to hold down the Ctrl key while dragging with the mouse. With the Ctrl key down, a box containing a plus symbol displays near the gray box by the arrow pointer.

IN BRIEF

Cut and Paste Text
1 Select text.
2 Click Cut button.
3 Move insertion point to desired position.
4 Click Paste button.

Copy and Paste Text
1 Select text.
2 Click Copy button.
3 Move insertion point to desired position.
4 Click Paste button.

Display Paste Special Dialog Box
1 Cut or copy text.
2 Click Edit, Paste Special.
3 Click desired format in *As* list box.
4 Click OK.

3.4 Using the Clipboard Task Pane

Using the Clipboard task pane, you can collect up to 24 different items and then paste them in various locations in a document. Display the Clipboard task pane by clicking Edit and then Office Clipboard or by pressing Ctrl + C twice. Cut or copy an item and the item displays in the Clipboard task pane. If the item is text, the first 50 characters display. Paste an item by positioning the insertion point at the desired location and then

clicking the item in the Clipboard task pane. When all desired items are inserted, click the Clear All button located in the upper right corner of the task pane.

PROJECT: You will open another fact sheet document, copy items in the document, and then paste the items into the Petersburg fact sheet document.

STEPS

1. Make sure **WordS3-01** is open and then open the **FCTPA02** document.

2. In the **FCTPA02** document, display the Clipboard task pane by clicking Edit and then Office Clipboard. If any items display in the Clipboard task pane, click the Clear All button located in the upper right corner of the task pane.

3. Select the *Sightseeing* heading, the two paragraphs of text below it and the blank line below the second paragraph and then click the Copy button 📄 .

   Notice how the copied item is represented in the Clipboard task pane.

4. Select the *Little Norway Festival* heading, the two paragraphs of text below it and the blank line below the second paragraph, and then click the Copy button 📄 .

5. Select the *Salmon Derby* heading, the paragraph of text below it and the blank line below the paragraph, and then click the Copy button 📄 .

6. Click the button on the Taskbar representing **WordS3-01**.

7. Press Ctrl + C twice to display the Clipboard task pane.

8. Move the insertion point to the beginning of the *Walking Tours* heading.

9. Click the item in the Clipboard task pane representing *Salmon Derby*.

10. Move the insertion point to the beginning of the *Points of Interest* heading.

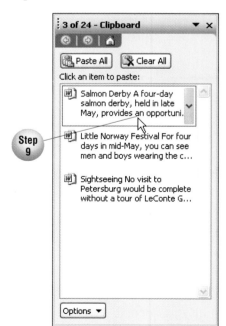

Step 9

11 Click the item in the Clipboard task pane representing *Sightseeing*.

12 Click the Clear All button located in the upper right corner of the Clipboard task pane.

13 Close the Clipboard task pane by clicking the Close button ☒ located in the upper right corner of the task pane.

14 Click the button on the Taskbar representing **FCTPA02** and then close the document.

> The **WordS3-01** document displays when you close **FCTPA02**.

15 Click anywhere in the heading *Visitor Attractions* and then double-click the Format Painter button on the Standard toolbar.

16 Select the headings *Salmon Derby*, *Sightseeing*, and *Points of Interest* and then click the Format Painter button to turn off the feature.

17 Save **WordS3-01**.

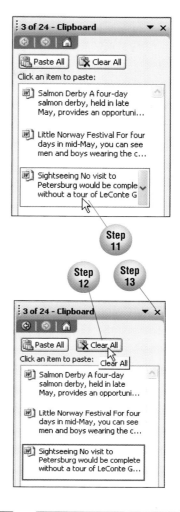

Step 11
Step 12
Step 13

In Addition

Clipboard Task Pane Options

Click the Options button located toward the bottom of the Clipboard task pane and a drop-down list displays with four options as shown at the right. Insert a check mark before those options that you want active. For example, you can choose

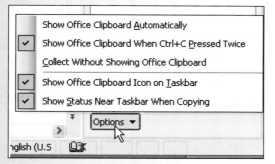

to display the Clipboard task pane automatically when you cut or copy text, cut and copy text without displaying the Clipboard task pane, display the *Office Clipboard* icon near the Taskbar when the clipboard is active, and display the item message when copying items to the Clipboard.

In Brief

Use the Clipboard Task Pane
1 Click Edit, Office Clipboard.
2 Select text.
3 Click Copy button.
4 Select and copy any additional items.
5 Move insertion point to desired position.
6 Click item in Clipboard task pane representing desired item.
7 Paste any other desired items from the Clipboard task pane.
8 Click Clear All button.

3.5 Inserting a Page Break and Page Numbers; Changing Margins and Page Orientation

By default, Word will insert a page break in a document at approximately 10 inches or approximately line 45 (this number may vary). If you want to control where a page breaks, insert your own page break by pressing Ctrl + Enter. Add page numbering to a document with options at the Page Numbers dialog box where you specify where page numbering appears on the page and the alignment of the numbering. Click the Format button at the Page Numbers dialog box and the Page Number Format dialog box displays. Use options at this dialog box to change numbering format and specify the beginning page number. A Word document, by default, contains 1-inch top and bottom margins and 1.25-inch left and right margins. You can change these default margins with options at the Page Setup dialog box. At this dialog box, you can also change the orientation of the page.

PROJECT: The Petersburg fact sheet is one of several fact sheets produced by First Choice Travel. You will insert a page break in the document, insert page numbering, and begin page numbering with page 12. You have also decided that the fact sheet will look better printed in landscape orientation and with different margins.

STEPS

1. With **WordS3-01** open, move the insertion point to the beginning of the heading *Points of Interest* (located toward the end of the document) and then insert a page break by pressing Ctrl + Enter.

   A page break appears in Normal view as a line of dots across the screen with the words *Page Break* displayed in the middle of the dots.

2. Press Ctrl + Home to move the insertion point to the beginning of the document, click Insert, and then click Page Numbers.

3. At the Page Numbers dialog box, click the down-pointing arrow at the right side of the *Position* text box and then click *Top of page (Header)*. Make sure the *Alignment* option displays as *Right*.

4. Click the *Show number on first page* option to remove the check mark.

   Removing the check mark from this option eliminates page numbering from the first page of the document.

5. Click the Format button that displays in the lower left corner of the dialog box.

6. At the Page Number Format dialog box, click *Start at* and then type **12**.

7. Click OK to close the Page Number Format dialog box and then click OK to close the Page Numbers dialog box.

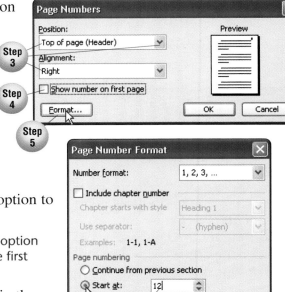

(8) Preview the document by clicking the Print Preview button 🔍 on the Standard toolbar. Scroll through the document to see how the page numbering appears (page numbering will not appear on the first page).

> If you cannot see the page number in Print Preview, increase the zoom size.

(9) Click the Close button on the Print Preview toolbar to close Print Preview.

(10) After looking at the pages in the document, you decide to delete the page break you inserted before the heading *Point of Interest*. To do this, make sure Normal view is selected, position the insertion point on the row of dots containing the words *Page Break*, and then press the Delete key.

(11) Click File and then Page Setup.

(12) At the Page Setup dialog box with the Margins tab selected, click the *Landscape* option.

(13) Click the up-pointing arrow at the right side of the *Top* option until *1.5"* displays.

> You can also change a margin measurement by selecting the measurement and then typing the new measurement.

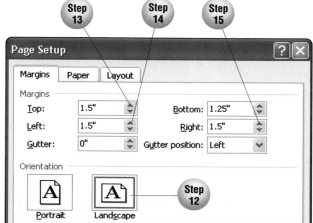

(14) Click the up-pointing arrow at the right side of the *Left* option until *1.5"* displays.

(15) Click the up-pointing arrow at the right side of the *Right* option until *1.5"* displays.

(16) Click OK to close the dialog box.

(17) Save, print, and then close **WordS3-01**.

In BRIEF

Insert Page Break
1 Move insertion point to desired position.
2 Press Ctrl + Enter.

Insert Page Numbering
1 Click Insert, Page Numbers.
2 Specify position and alignment of page numbering.
3 Click OK.

Change Margins
1 Click File, Page Setup.
2 Click Margins tab.
3 Specify margin measurements.
4 Click OK.

Change Page Orientation
1 Click File, Page Setup.
2 Click Margins tab.
3 Click desired orientation.
4 Click OK.

In Addition

Deleting Page Numbering

A page number is created in a document as a header or footer. To delete page numbering, click View and then Header and Footer. Display the header or footer pane containing the page numbering, select the page numbering, and then press the Delete key. Click the Close button on the Header and Footer toolbar.

3.6 Arranging Windows; Reviewing and Modifying Document Properties

In a multiple-page document, you may want to view different parts of the document at the same time. You can do this with the Split command from the Window drop-down menu or with the split bar. If you have more than one document open, you can use the Arrange All option from the Window drop-down menu to view a portion of all open documents. Use the Maximize and Minimize buttons at the right side of the Title bar in the active document window to change the size of the window. Word provides specific details about a document at the Properties dialog box. The Properties dialog box with the Summary tab selected contains fields such as title, subject, author, company, category, keywords, and comments. Select other tabs to view additional information about the document.

PROJECT: You want to make a final check of the Petersburg fact sheet to make sure it contains all of the desired formatting. You also decide to compare the formatted fact sheet with the original.

STEPS

1. Open **WordS3-01**.

2. Split the window by clicking Window and then Split. With the horizontal split line located approximately in the middle of the screen, click the left mouse button.

   You can also split the window with the split bar. To do this, position the arrow pointer on the split bar until it turns into a short double line with an up- and down-pointing arrow, drag the double-headed arrow into the document screen to the location where you want the window split, and then release the mouse button.

3. Scroll down the document that displays in the bottom window until the end of the document is visible.

   When a window is split, the insertion point is positioned in the bottom pane. To move the insertion point to the other pane with the mouse, position the I-beam pointer in the other pane, and then click the left mouse button. You can also press F6 to move to the next pane or Shift + F6 to move to the previous pane.

4. Remove the split line by clicking Window and then Remove Split.

   You can also remove the split by dragging the split line up to the top of the screen or down to the bottom of the screen.

5. Open **FCTPetersburg** and then arrange the two document windows by clicking Window and then Arrange All.

6. With **FCTPetersburg** the active document, scroll through the document and compare it with the **WordS3-01** document. Move back and forth between the two windows by pressing Ctrl + F6.

7. Make **FCTPetersburg** the active document and then close the document.

8. Click the Minimize button to reduce the **WordS3-01** document to a button on the Taskbar.

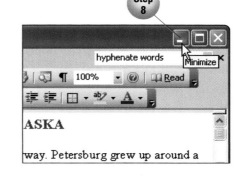

Step 8

(9) Click the **WordS3-01** button on the Taskbar to display the document.

Step 9

Step 10

(10) Click the Maximize button to expand the document so it fills the screen.

(11) Click File and then Properties. At the WordS3-01.doc Properties dialog box, click the Summary tab.

Click the General tab to display information about document type, size, and location; click the Statistics tab to view information such as the number of pages, paragraphs, lines, words, characters, and bytes in the document; click the Contents tab to view the document without bringing it to the document screen; and click the Custom tab to customize the document properties.

(12) Type the following in the specified text boxes:

Subject   = **Fact sheet**
Category   = **Travel documents**
Keywords = **Travel, Petersburg, Alaska**
Comments = **This document contains interesting facts about Petersburg, Alaska**

(13) Click OK to close the dialog box.

(14) Print only the document properties. To do this, first click File and then Print to display the Print dialog box.

(15) At the Print dialog box, click the down-pointing arrow at the right side of the *Print what* option, click *Document properties*, and then click OK.

(16) Save and then close **WordS3-01**.

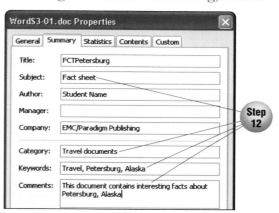

Step 12

In Addition

Changing Window Size

You can increase the size of arranged documents using the mouse. To do this, drag the border of the window until the window is the desired size. You can also move arranged documents. To do this, make active the desired document, position the mouse pointer on the Title bar, and then drag to the desired position.

IN BRIEF

Split Window
1 Click Window, Split.
2 Position split line in desired position.
3 Click left mouse button.

Arrange Windows
Click Window, Arrange All.

Display Properties Dialog Box
Click File, Properties.

3.7 Changing Views; Using Click and Type; Vertically Aligning Text

In a previous Word section, you learned to change paragraph alignment with buttons on the Formatting toolbar, shortcut commands, and options at the Paragraph dialog box. Another method for changing paragraph alignment is to use the *click and type* feature. Before using this feature, you must change to the Print Layout view. By default, text is aligned at the top of the page. This alignment can be changed to Center, Justified, or Bottom with the *Vertical alignment* option at the Page Setup dialog box with the Layout tab selected.

PROJECT: First Choice Travel is planning a workshop for people interested in traveling on a budget. You will create an announcement that contains center- and right-aligned text that is vertically centered on the page.

STEPS

1. Make sure a clear document screen displays (this is a screen with a white background). If a clear document screen is not displayed, click the New Blank Document button ⬚ on the Standard toolbar.

2. Change to Print Layout view by clicking View and then Print Layout.

    When you change to Print Layout view, a horizontal and vertical ruler display and the insertion point appears 1 inch from the top of the screen.

3. Position the I-beam pointer between the left and right margins at about the 3-inch mark on the horizontal ruler and the top of the vertical ruler. When the center alignment lines display below the I-beam pointer, double-click the left mouse button.

PROBLEM?
If the alignment lines are not displayed near the I-beam pointer when you double-click the left mouse button, a left tab is set at the position of the insertion point.

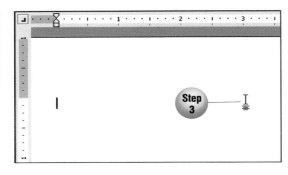

Step 3

4. Type the centered text shown in Figure W3.1, pressing the Enter key twice between each line of text.

5. Change to right alignment by positioning the I-beam pointer near the right margin at approximately the 2-inch mark on the vertical ruler until the right alignment lines display at the left side of the I-beam pointer and then double-clicking the left mouse button.

6. Type the right-aligned text shown in Figure W3.1.

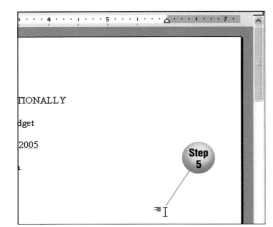

TIONALLY

dget

2005

Step 5

7 Select the centered text and then change the font to 14-point Arial bold.

8 Select the right-aligned text, change the font to 8-point Arial bold, and then deselect the text.

9 Vertically align the text by clicking File and then Page Setup.

10 At the Page Setup dialog box, click the Layout tab.

11 Click the down-pointing arrow at the right side of the *Vertical alignment* option and then click *Center* at the drop-down list.

12 Click OK to close the Page Setup dialog box.

13 Save the document and name it **WordS3-02**.

FIGURE W3.1

TRAVELING INTERNATIONALLY

Traveling on a Budget

Thursday, May 12, 2005

7:00 – 8:30 p.m.

Sponsored by
First Choice Travel

In Addition

Changing the View

Change the view by clicking View on the Menu bar and then clicking the desired view at the drop-down menu. Another method for changing the view is to click the desired button on the View toolbar shown below. For example, to change to Print Layout view, click the Print Layout View button.

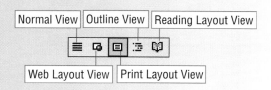

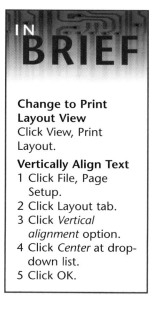

IN BRIEF

Change to Print Layout View
Click View, Print Layout.

Vertically Align Text
1 Click File, Page Setup.
2 Click Layout tab.
3 Click *Vertical alignment* option.
4 Click *Center* at drop-down list.
5 Click OK.

3.8 Inserting, Sizing, and Moving Images in a Document

Microsoft Office 2003 includes a gallery of media images you can insert in a document such as clip art, photographs, and movie images, as well as sound clips. Specify and insert images in a document with options at the Clip Art task pane. You can also insert a picture or image from a specific file location with options at the Insert Picture dialog box. You can move, size, and customize an inserted image or picture with buttons on the Picture toolbar. With options from the Zoom button on the Standard toolbar, you can increase or decrease the display of text and also display the whole page, which is useful for positioning images.

PROJECT: You have decided to insert a travel clip art image and the First Choice Travel logo to enhance the visual interest of the announcement.

STEPS

1. With **WordS3-02** open, return the vertical alignment to *Top*. To do this, click File and then Page Setup. At the Page Setup dialog box, click the Layout tab. Click the down-pointing arrow at the right side of the *Vertical alignment* option and then click *Top* at the drop-down list. Click OK to close the dialog box.

2. Press Ctrl + End to move the insertion point to the end of the document.

3. Display the Drawing toolbar by clicking the Drawing button on the Standard toolbar.

   The Drawing toolbar displays toward the bottom of the screen, above the Status bar. When you click the Drawing button, the view automatically changes to Print Layout.

4. Click the Insert Clip Art button on the Drawing toolbar.

   This displays the Clip Art task pane at the right of the screen.

5. Type **travel** in the *Search for* text box and then click the Go button.

6. When the clip art images display, click the image shown at the right. (If this image is not available, choose another image related to travel.)

7. Close the Clip Art task pane by clicking the Close button located in the upper right corner of the task pane.

8. Click the image in the document to select it.

   The selected image displays surrounded by black squares called *sizing handles* and the Picture toolbar displays. Refer to Figure W3.2 for the names of the Picture toolbar buttons. If the Picture toolbar is not displayed, right-click the image, and then click Show Picture Toolbar at the shortcut menu.

FIGURE W3.2 Picture Toolbar Buttons

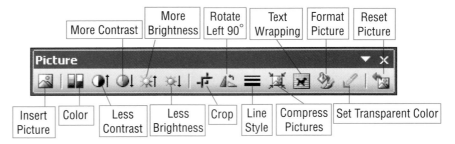

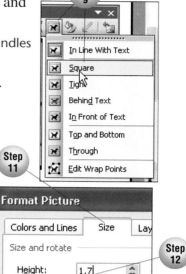

Step 9

In Line With Text
Square
Tight
Behind Text
In Front of Text
Top and Bottom
Through
Edit Wrap Points

Step 11

Format Picture

Colors and Lines | Size | Lay

Size and rotate

Height: 1.7
Rotation: 0°

Step 12

⑨ Click the Text Wrapping button 🖼 on the Picture toolbar and then click *Square* at the drop-down list.

> When you choose a text wrapping option, all the sizing handles change to white circles.

⑩ Click the Format Picture button 🖼 on the Picture toolbar.

⑪ At the Format Picture dialog box, click the Size tab.

⑫ Select the current measurement in the *Height* text box (in the *Size and rotate* section), type **1.7**, and then click OK.

> When you change the height measurement, the width measurement is automatically changed to maintain the proportions of the image.

⑬ Click the down-pointing arrow at the right side of the Zoom button on the Standard toolbar and then click *Whole Page* at the drop-down list.

⑭ Move the image by positioning the arrow pointer on the image until the pointer turns into a four-headed arrow, holding down the left mouse button, dragging the image up and to the left until it is positioned as shown in Figure W3.3, and then releasing the mouse button.

⑮ Click outside the image to deselect it.

⑯ Click the down-pointing arrow at the right side of the Zoom button on the Standard toolbar and then click *100%* at the drop-down list.

⑰ Select and then delete the text *First Choice Travel* that displays in small font size at the right side of the screen.

⑱ Press Ctrl + End to move the insertion point to the end of the document and then press the Enter key.

⑲ Insert the First Choice Travel logo below *Sponsored by*. To begin, click Insert, point to Picture, and then click From File.

⑳ At the Insert Picture dialog box, display the folder where your data documents are located and then double-click *FCTLogo*. Your document should display as shown in Figure W3.3.

㉑ Save, print, and then close **WordS3-02**.

FIGURE W3.3 Completed WordS3-02 Document

3.9 Inserting, Sizing, and Moving WordArt in a Document

Use the WordArt application to distort or modify text to conform to a variety of shapes. Consider using WordArt to create a company logo, letterhead, flier title, or heading. With WordArt, you can change the font, style, and alignment of text; use different fill patterns and colors; customize border lines, and add shadow and three-dimensional effects. Selected WordArt text can be sized and moved in the document.

PROJECT: You decide to add a WordArt heading to the document on Hawaiian specials to enhance the visual appeal of the document.

STEPS

1. Open **FCTHawaiianSpecials** and then save the document with Save As and name it **WordS3-03**.

2. Complete a spelling and grammar check on the document. You determine what to correct and what to ignore. (The name *Molokini* is spelled correctly in the document.)

3. Select and then delete the title *HAWAIIAN SPECIALS*.

4. Insert WordArt by clicking Insert, pointing to Picture, and then clicking WordArt.

   You can also display the WordArt Gallery by clicking the Insert WordArt button on the Drawing toolbar.

5. At the WordArt Gallery dialog box, double-click the fourth option from the left in the third row.

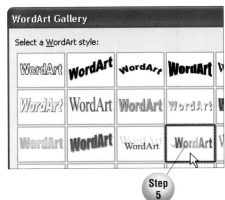

Step 5

6. At the Edit WordArt Text dialog box, type **Hawaiian Specials** and then click OK to close the dialog box.

   The text will wrap inside the text box.

7. Increase the height of the WordArt text by clicking the WordArt text to select it and then positioning the mouse pointer on the bottom, middle sizing handle until the pointer turns into an arrow pointing up and down. Hold down the left mouse button, drag down approximately 0.5 inch, and then release the mouse button.

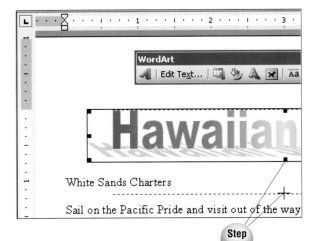

Step 7

PROBLEM?

If you do not like the size of the WordArt, click the Undo button and then size it again.

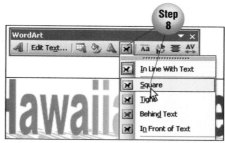

⑧ Click the Text Wrapping button 🖾 and then click Square at the drop-down list.

> Choosing a text wrapping style changes the black sizing handles to white sizing handles. Customize WordArt with buttons on the WordArt toolbar shown in Figure W3.4.

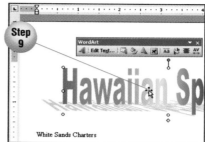

⑨ Drag the WordArt text so it is positioned centered between the left and right margins. To do this, position the mouse pointer on the WordArt text until the pointer displays with a four-headed arrow attached. Hold down the left mouse button, drag the WordArt text to the desired position, and then release the mouse button.

> Make sure that the heading *White Sands Charters* and the following text display below the WordArt text and not at the right side.

⑩ Click outside the WordArt text box to deselect it.

⑪ Apply the Heading 1 style to the following headings: *White Sands Charters*, *Air Adventures*, *Deep Sea Submarines*, *Snorkeling Fantasies*, and *Bicycle Safari*.

⑫ Press Ctrl + A to select the entire document and then change the font color to dark blue. To do this, click the down-pointing arrow at the right side of the Font Color button on the Formatting toolbar and then click *Dark Blue* (sixth color from the left in the top row).

⑬ Click outside the selected text to deselect it.

⑭ Save **WordS3-03**.

FIGURE W3.4 WordArt Toolbar Buttons

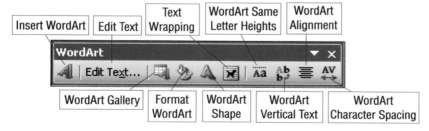

In Addition

Changing the Font and Font Size

The font for WordArt text will vary depending on the choice you make at the WordArt Gallery. You can change the font at the Edit WordArt text dialog box by clicking the down-pointing arrow at the right side of the *Font* option and then clicking the desired font at the drop-down list. Change the font size by clicking the down-pointing arrow at the right side of the *Size* text box. The Edit WordArt Text dialog box also contains a Bold button and an Italic button you can click to apply the specific formatting.

IN BRIEF

Insert WordArt
1 Click Insert, Picture, WordArt.
2 At WordArt Gallery, double-click desired option.
3 At Edit WordArt dialog box, type desired text.
4 Click OK.

3.10 Using the Drawing Toolbar

With buttons on the Drawing toolbar, you can draw a variety of shapes and lines and then customize the shapes or lines by changing line color, adding fill, adding a shadow, including a border, and so on. With options from the AutoShapes button, you can choose from a variety of predesigned shapes to draw shapes in a document. Use the Text Box button to draw a box and then type text inside the box. This box, like a shape, can be customized. A drawn object can be sized and moved in the same manner as an image or WordArt text.

PROJECT: You will add an autoshape containing text as a visual element to the end of the Hawaiian specials document.

S T E P S

① With **WordS3-03** open, press Ctrl + End to move the insertion point to the end of the document and then press the Enter key twice.

② Click the Drawing button on the Standard toolbar to turn on the display of the Drawing toolbar.

> Skip this step if the Drawing toolbar is already displayed. Refer to Figure W3.5 for the names of the Drawing toolbar buttons.

FIGURE W3.5 Drawing Toolbar Buttons

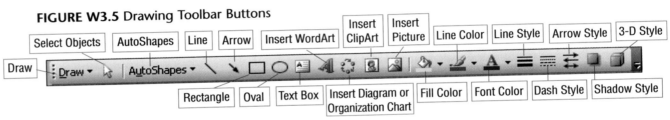

③ Draw the banner autoshape shown in Figure W3.6. To do this, click the AutoShapes button on the Drawing toolbar, point to Stars and Banners, and then click the second banner from the left in the bottom row (Horizontal Scroll).

> This displays a Drawing canvas in the document. Draw a shape in this canvas or delete the canvas and then draw the shape directly in the document.

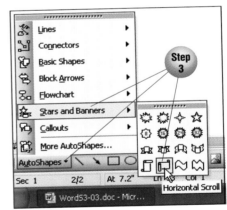

④ Press the Delete key to delete the drawing canvas.

⑤ Position the mouse pointer (displays as crosshairs) below the text at approximately the 1.5-inch mark on the horizontal ruler and the 7.5-inch mark on the vertical ruler. Hold down the left mouse button, drag down and to the right until the banner is approximately 3 inches wide and 1.25 inches high, and then release the mouse button.

FIGURE W3.6

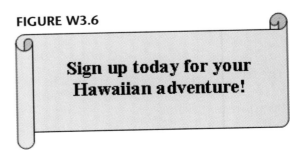

Sign up today for your Hawaiian adventure!

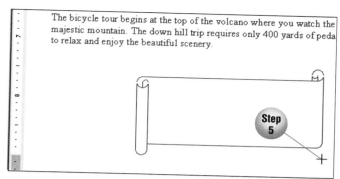

6. Fill the banner with light green color by clicking the down-pointing arrow at the right side of the Fill Color button 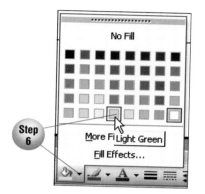 on the Drawing toolbar and then clicking Light Green (fourth color from the left in the bottom row) at the color palette.

7. Draw a text box inside the image by clicking the Text Box button on the Drawing toolbar.

8. Position the mouse pointer (displays as crosshairs) inside the banner, hold down the left mouse button, drag to create a text box similar to the one shown below, and then release the mouse button.

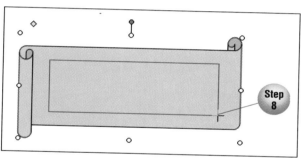

9. Change the font size to 14 points, click the Bold button, click the Center button, and then type **Sign up today for your Hawaiian adventure!**

10. Fill the text box with light green color by clicking the Fill Color button 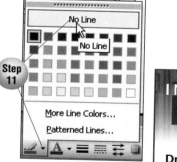 .

    The Fill Color button retains the color previously selected.

11. Remove the border around the text box by clicking the down-pointing arrow at the right side of the Line Color button on the Drawing toolbar and then clicking *No Line* that displays at the top of the color palette.

12. Deselect the text box by clicking outside the banner and text box.

13. Save, print, and then close **WordS3-03**.

IN BRIEF

Draw an AutoShape
1 Click AutoShapes button on Drawing toolbar.
2 Point to desired category and then click desired shape.
3 Drag with mouse to draw shape.

Draw a Text Box
1 Click Text Box button on Drawing toolbar.
2 Drag with mouse to draw text box.

3.11 Preparing an Envelope

Word automates the creation of envelopes with options at the Envelopes and Labels dialog box with the Envelopes tab selected. At this dialog box, type a delivery address and a return address. If you open the Envelopes and Labels dialog box in a document containing a name and address, the name and address are automatically inserted as the delivery address. If you enter a return address, Word will ask you before printing if you want to save the new return address as the default return address. Answer yes if you want to use the return address for future envelopes, or answer no if you will use a different return address for future envelopes.

PROJECT: You will create an envelope for sending the Hawaiian specials document to Camille Matsui at Marquee Productions.

STEPS

1 At a clear document screen, click Tools, point to Letters and Mailings, and then click Envelopes and Labels.

2 At the Envelopes and Labels dialog box, make sure the Envelopes tab is selected. (If not, click the Envelopes tab.)

3 With the insertion point positioned inside the *Delivery address* text box, type the following name and address:

> **Camille Matsui**
> **Marquee Productions**
> **955 South Alameda Street**
> **Los Angeles, CA 90037**

> When typing the name and address, press the Enter key to end each line *except* the last line (containing the city, state, and Zip Code).

4 Click in the *Return address* text box. If any text displays in the *Return address* text box, select it, and then delete it.

5 With the insertion point positioned in the *Return address* text box, type the following name and address:

> **First Choice Travel**
> **Los Angeles Office**
> **3588 Ventura Boulevard**
> **Los Angeles, CA 90102**

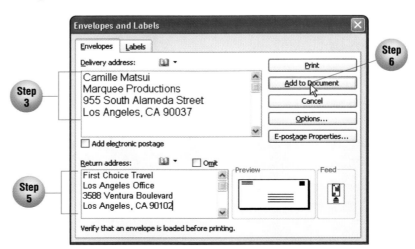

6 Click the Add to Document button.

> The envelope is inserted in the clear document screen when you click the Add to Document button. You can also send the envelope directly to the printer by clicking the Print button.

7 At the message asking if you want to save the new return address as the default address, click the No button.

8 Save the document and name it **WordS3-04**.

9 Print **WordS3-04**. *(Note: Manual feed of the envelope may be required. Please check with your instructor.)*

10 Close **WordS3-04**.

In Addition

Customizing Envelopes

With options at the Envelope Options dialog box you can customize an envelope. Display this dialog box by clicking the Options button at the Envelopes and Labels dialog box. At the Envelope Options dialog box, you can change the envelope size, insert a delivery point barcode, change the font for the delivery and return addresses, and specify the positioning of the addresses in relation to the left and top of the envelope. Insert a check mark in the *Delivery point bar code* check box and Word prints a POSTNET (POSTal Numeric Encoding Technique) bar code. This barcode is a machine-readable representation of the U.S. Zip Code and delivery address.

In Brief

Prepare an Envelope
1 Click Tools, Letters and Mailings, Envelopes and Labels.
2 Click Envelopes tab.
3 Type delivery address.
4 Type return address.
5 Click either Add to Document button or Print button.

3.12 Preparing Labels

Use Word's labels feature to print text on mailing labels, file labels, disk labels, or other types of labels. You can create labels for printing on a variety of predefined labels that you can purchase at an office supply store. With the labels feature, you can create a sheet of mailing labels with the same name and address or enter a different name and address on each label. Create a label with

options at the Envelopes and Labels dialog box with the Labels tab selected.

PROJECT: You will create a sheet of mailing labels containing the First Choice Travel name and address and then create mailing labels for sending the Hawaiian specials document to several First Choice Travel customers.

STEPS

1. At a clear document screen, click Tools, point to Letters and Mailings, and then click Envelopes and Labels. At the Envelopes and Labels dialog box, click the Labels tab.

2. Type the following information in the *Address* text box. (Press Enter at the end of each line, except the last line containing the city name, state, and Zip Code.)

    First Choice Travel
    Los Angeles Office
    3588 Ventura Boulevard
    Los Angeles, CA 90102

3. Click the New Document button.

4. Save the mailing label document and name it **WordS3-05**.

5. Print and then close **WordS3-05**.

    The number of labels printed on the page varies depending on the label selected at the Envelopes and Labels dialog box.

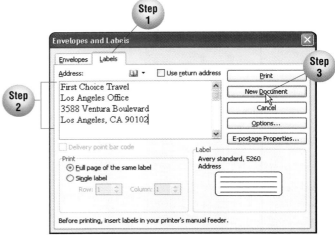

6. At a clear document screen, click Tools, point to Letters and Mailings, and then click Envelopes and Labels.

7. At the Envelopes and Labels dialog box with the Labels tab selected, click the Options button.

8. At the Label Options dialog box, make sure *Avery standard* displays in the *Label products* text box. Click the down-pointing arrow at the right side of the *Product number* list box until *5662 – Address* is visible and then click *5662 – Address*. Click OK to close the Label Options dialog box.

⑨ At the Envelopes and Labels dialog box, click the New Document button.

⑩ At the document screen, type the first name and address shown in Figure W3.7 in the first label. Press the Tab key to move the insertion point to the next label and then type the second name and address shown in Figure W3.7. Continue in this manner until you have typed all of the names and addresses in Figure W3.7.

⑪ Save the document and name it **WordS3-06**.

⑫ Print and then close **WordS3-06**.

⑬ Close the document screen.

FIGURE W3.7

Moreno Products
350 Mission Boulevard
Pomona, CA 91767

Mr. Miguel Santos
12120 Barranca Parkway
Irvine, CA 92612

Dr. Esther Riggins
9077 Walnut Street
Los Angeles, CA 90097

Automated Services, Inc.
4394 Seventh Street
Long Beach, CA 92602

In Addition

Customizing Labels

Click the Options button at the Envelopes and Labels dialog box with the Labels tab selected and the Label Options dialog box displays as shown below. At this dialog box, choose the type of printer, the desired label product, and the product number. This dialog box also displays information about the selected label such as type height, width, and paper size. When you select a label, Word automatically determines label margins. If, however, you want to customize these default settings, click the Details button at the Label Options dialog box.

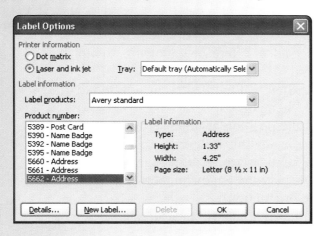

In BRIEF

Prepare Mailing Labels with Same Name and Address
1 Click Tools, Letters and Mailings, Envelopes and Labels.
2 Click Labels tab.
3 Type name and address in *Address* text box.
4 Click either New Document button or Print button.

Prepare Mailing Labels with Different Names and Addresses
1 Click Tools, Letters and Mailings, Envelopes and Labels.
2 Click Labels tab.
3 Click New Document button.
4 At document screen, type names and addresses.

FEATURES SUMMARY

Feature	Button	Menu	Keyboard
Arrange windows		Window, Arrange All	
Clipboard task pane		Edit, Office Clipboard	Ctrl + C, Ctrl + C
Copy selected text		Edit, Copy	Ctrl + C
Cut selected text		Edit, Cut	Ctrl + X
Envelopes and Labels dialog box		Tools, Letters and Mailings, Envelopes and Labels	
Find and Replace dialog box		Edit, Replace	Ctrl + H
Insert a page break		Insert, Break, Page Break	Ctrl + Enter
Insert Clip Art task pane		Insert, Picture, Clip Art	
Insert Picture dialog box		Insert, Picture, From File	
Normal view		View, Normal	
Page Numbers dialog box		Insert, Page Numbers	
Page Setup dialog box		File, Page Setup	
Paste selected text		Edit, Paste	Ctrl + V
Paste Special dialog box		Edit, Paste Special	
Print Layout view		View, Print Layout	
Properties dialog box		File, Properties	
Split windows		Window, Split	
WordArt Gallery		Insert, Picture, WordArt	

PROCEDURES CHECK

Completion: In the space provided at the right, indicate the correct term, symbol, or command.

1. Click this button at the Find and Replace dialog box to replace all occurrences of text. _____
2. Click this button on the Standard toolbar to cut selected text. _____
3. Click this button on the Standard toolbar to insert selected text in the document at the position of the insertion point. _____
4. Press Ctrl + C twice to display this task pane. _____
5. Press these keys on the keyboard to insert a page break. _____
6. Click these options to display the Page Numbers dialog box. _____
7. This is the default page orientation. _____
8. This is the default left and right margin measurement. _____

9. Click this option from the Window drop-down menu to arrange open documents. _____

10. Before using the click and type feature, change to this view. _____

11. One method for displaying the Clip Art task pane is to click the Insert Clip Art button on this toolbar. _____

12. Display the WordArt Gallery by clicking this option on the Menu bar, pointing to Picture, and then clicking WordArt. _____

13. Click this button on the Picture toolbar to choose a wrapping style. _____

14. Use options from this button on the Drawing toolbar to draw a variety of predesigned shapes. _____

15. To display the Envelopes and Labels dialog box, click Tools, point to this option, and then click Envelopes and Labels. _____

SKILLS REVIEW

Activity 1: FINDING AND REPLACING TEXT; CUTTING AND PASTING TEXT

1 Open **FCTJuneau**.
2 Save the document with Save As and name it **WordS3-R1**.
3 Find every occurrence of *Mendanhall* and replace it with *Mendenhall*.
4 Find every occurrence of *Treadwill* and replace it with *Treadwell*.
5 Select the heading *Visitor Centers*, the three paragraphs of text below it and the blank line below the three paragraphs, and then move the selected text before the heading *Visitor Attractions*.
6 Select the heading *Museums*, the three paragraphs of text below it and the blank line below the three paragraphs, and then move the selected text before the heading *Visitor Attractions*.
7 Save **WordS3-R1**.

Activity 2: COLLECTING AND PASTING TEXT

1 With **WordS3-R1** open, open the document named **FCTJA01**.
2 Press Ctrl + C twice to turn on the display of the Clipboard task pane. Make sure the Clipboard task pane is empty.
3 In the **FCTJA01** document, select and then copy from the heading *Visitor Services* through the two paragraphs of text below the heading and the blank line below the two paragraphs.
4 Select and then copy from the heading *Transportation* through the paragraph of text below the heading and the blank line below the paragraph.
5 Select and then copy from the heading *Points of Interest* through the columns of text below the heading and the blank line below the columns of text.
6 Make **WordS3-R1** the active document.
7 Turn on the display of the Clipboard task pane.
8 Move the insertion point to the end of the document and then paste the text that begins with the heading *Points of Interest*.
9 Move the insertion point to the beginning of the heading *Museums* and then paste the text that begins with the heading *Transportation*.

10   Move the insertion point to the beginning of the heading *Points of Interest* and then paste the text that begins with the heading *Visitor Services*.

11   Clear the contents of the Clipboard task pane and then close the task pane.

12   Save **WordS3-R1**.

13   Make **FCTJA01** the active document and then close it.

Activity 3: INSERTING PAGE NUMBERS; CHANGING MARGINS; CHANGING PAGE ORIENTATION

1   With **WordS3-R1** open, insert page numbers that print centered at the bottom of each page and change the starting page number to 7.

2   Change the left and right margins to 1 inch and the top and bottom margins to 1.5 inches.

3   Select the title *FACT SHEET – JUNEAU, ALASKA* and then change the font to 14-point Arial bold and center the title.

4   Set the headings in the document in 12-point Arial bold. (The headings include *History*, *Visitor Centers*, *Transportation*, *Museums*, *Visitor Attractions*, *Visitor Services*, and *Points of Interest*.)

5   Change the page orientation to landscape.

6   Save and then print **WordS3-R1**.

Activity 4: INSERTING WORDART AND DRAWING SHAPES

1   With **WordS3-R1** open, change the page orientation to portrait.

2   Select and then delete the title *FACT SHEET – JUNEAU, ALASKA*.

3   Insert a WordArt of your choosing at the beginning of the document that contains the words *Juneau, Alaska*.

4   Size and move the WordArt text so it spans the margins.

5   Move the insertion point to the end of the document and then press Enter twice.

6   Using the buttons on the Drawing toolbar, draw and format the shape and draw and format the text box as shown in Figure W3.8.

7   Save, print, and then close **WordS3-R1**.

FIGURE W3.8 Activity 4

Activity 5: CHANGING VIEWS; USING CLICK AND TYPE; VERTICALLY ALIGNING TEXT

1 At a clear document screen, change to the Print Layout view.
2 Using the click and type feature, type the text shown in Figure W3.9.
3 Select the centered text you just typed and then change the font to 14-point Arial bold.
4 Select the right-aligned text you just typed and then change the font to 10-point Arial bold.
5 Change the vertical alignment of the text on the page to *Center*.
6 Save the document and name it **WordS3-R2**.
7 Print **WordS3-R2**.

FIGURE W3.9 Activity 5

EMPLOYMENT OPPORTUNITIES

Working in the Movie Industry

Wednesday, March 16, 2005

7:00 – 8:30 p.m.

Sponsored by
Marquee Productions

Activity 6: INSERTING IMAGES

1 With **WordS3-R2** open, change the vertical alignment of the text on the page back to *Top*.
2 Insert a clip art image of your choosing related to the announcement. (You determine the clip art image as well as the size and position of the image.)
3 Delete the text *Marquee Productions* from the document and then insert below the Marquee Productions logo image named M_Prod.tif below the text *Sponsored by*. (**Hint: *Do this at the Insert Picture dialog box.*)**
4 Save, print, and then close **WordS3-R2**.

Activity 7: PREPARING AN ENVELOPE

1 At a clear document screen, prepare an envelope with the return and delivery addresses shown in Figure W3.10, and add the envelope to the document.
2 Save the document and name it **WordS3-R3**.
3 Print and then close **WordS3-R3**. (Manual feed may be required.)

FIGURE W3.10 Activity 7

First Choice Travel
Los Angeles Office
3588 Ventura Boulevard
Los Angeles, CA 90102

Chris Greenbaum
Marquee Productions
955 South Alameda Street
Los Angeles, CA 90037

Activity 8: PREPARING MAILING LABELS

1   At a clear document screen, prepare a sheet of mailing labels for the following name and address using the Avery standard 5662 – Address form.

First Choice Travel
Toronto Office
4277 Yonge Street
Toronto, ON M4P 2E6

2   Save the mailing label document and name it **WordS3-R4**.
3   Print and then close **WordS3-R4**.

PERFORMANCE PLUS

Assessment 1: FORMATTING A COSTUME RENTAL AGREEMENT

1   Open **PTAgreement**.
2   Save the agreement with Save As and name it **WordS3-P1**.
3   Search for all occurrences of *Customer* and replace with *Marquee Productions*.
4   Move the *4. Alterations* section above the *3. Marquee Productions* section. Renumber the two sections.
5   Select the entire document, change the font to 12-point Bookman Old Style, and then deselect the document. (If this typeface is not available, choose another typeface.)
6   Change the left and right margins to 1 inch.
7   Insert page numbering at the bottom right side of each page.
8   Save **WordS3-P1**.
9   Print and then close **WordS3-P1**.

Assessment 2: CREATING AN ANNOUNCEMENT

1 At a clear document screen, create an announcement for Niagara Peninsula College by typing the text shown in Figure W3.11.
2 After typing the text, change the horizontal alignment to center for the entire document.
3 Change the font for the entire document to a decorative font and size of your choosing and change the text color to dark blue.
4 Change the line spacing to double for the entire document.
5 Insert, size, and move a clip art image of your choosing in the document. Choose a clip art image related to the subject of the announcement.
6 Save the document and name it **WordS3-P2**.
7 Print and then close **WordS3-P2**.

FIGURE W3.11 Assessment 2

NIAGARA PENINSULA COLLEGE
Internship Opportunities
Marquee Productions, Toronto Office
June 16 through August 29, 2005
Contact Cal Rubine, Theatre Arts Division

Assessment 3: PREPARING AN ENVELOPE

1 Create an envelope to send the Niagara Peninsula College announcement to Camille Matsui, Marquee Productions, 955 South Alameda Street, Los Angeles, CA 90037. Include the following name and address as the return address: Niagara Peninsula College, Theatre Arts Division, 2199 Victoria Street, Niagara-on-the-Lake, ON L0S 1J0.
2 Save the envelope document and name it **WordS3-P3**.
3 Print and then close **WordS3-P3**.

Assessment 4: PREPARING MAILING LABELS

1 Prepare return mailing labels with the following information:

Niagara Peninsula College
Theatre Arts Division
2199 Victoria Street
Niagara-on-the-Lake, ON L0S 1J0

2 Save the labels document and name it **WordS3-P4**.
3 Print and then close **WordS3-P4**.

Assessment 5: FINDING INFORMATION ON FLIPPING AND COPYING OBJECTS

1 Use Word's Help feature to learn how to flip objects and copy objects.
2 At a clear document screen, create the document shown in Figure W3.12. Create the arrow at the left by clicking the AutoShapes button, pointing to Block Arrows, and then clicking Striped Right Arrow. Format the arrow with blue fill as shown. Copy and flip the arrow to create the arrow at the right side.

3 Save the completed document and name it **WordS3-P5**.
4 Print and then close **WordS3-P5**.

FIGURE W3.12 Assessment 5

Worldwide Enterprises
Stockholders' Meeting
January 6, 2005
7:30 p.m.

Assessment 6: CREATING AN ENVELOPE WITH A POSTNET BAR CODE AND FIM-A

1 Use Word's Help feature to learn how to create an envelope with a POSTNET bar code and a FIM-A.
2 Create an envelope with the return and delivery addresses shown in Figure W3.13. Include a POSTNET bar code and a FIM-A for the envelope.
3 Save the envelope document and name it **WordS3-P6**.
4 Print and then close **WordS3-P6**.

FIGURE W3.13 Assessment 6

Worldwide Enterprises
1112-1583 Broadway
New York, NY 10110

Marquee Productions
955 South Alameda Street
Los Angeles, CA 90037

Assessment 7: LOCATING INFORMATION AND CREATING A BANNER

1 You are Camille Matsui, production assistant for Marquee Productions. You have been asked by Chris Greenbaum, the production manager, to find information on the Royal Ontario Museum. Marquee Productions will need to do some interior shots and would like to contact the museum as a possible site. Connect to the Internet and search for information on the Royal Ontario Museum. Find the following information: the museum address, telephone number, and hours of operation.
2 Using the information you find on the museum, create a banner using an autoshape and insert the museum information inside the banner.
3 Save the banner document and name it **WordS3-P7**.
4 Print and then close **WordS3-P7**.

WORD SECTION 4

Formatting with Special Features

Word contains special formatting features you can apply in a document to enhance the display of text. For example, you can use the Tables feature to create, modify, and format data in columns and rows. Improve the ease with which a person can read and understand groups of words by setting text in columns. Create a header and/or footer with text you want to appear on each printed page. A Word document can be saved as a Web page and formatting can be applied to the page. Insert a hyperlink in a document to another document or a site on the Internet. Compare an edited document with the original document using the compare and merge feature and visually display text in an organizational chart and diagram. In this section, you will learn the skills and complete the projects described here.

Note: Before beginning this section, delete the WordS3 folder on your disk. Next, copy to your disk or other loacation the WordS4 subfolder from the CD that accompanies this textbook and then make WordS4 the active folder.

Skills

- Create, modify, customize, and format a table
- Apply a border and shading to a table
- Apply an autoformat to a table
- Convert text to a table
- Apply a table style
- Use the Research tool
- Insert a section break
- Create and modify columns
- Insert and modify a header and footer
- Save a document as a Web page
- Create a hyperlink
- Preview a Web page
- Compare and merge documents
- Insert and modify comments
- Create an outline
- Track, accept, or reject changes
- Send a document as an e-mail
- Create an organizational chart and a diagram

Projects

Create a table containing information on scenic flights on Maui; create and format newsletters with information on Petersburg, Alaska, and Hawaiian vacation specials; save the newsletters as Web pages and add hyperlinks; compare the edited newsletters with the original newsletters; accept or reject the edited changes on an Orcas Island fact sheet and e-mail the completed document; prepare an organizational chart and a diagram of services.

Create, modify, and format a table with information on classes offered by the Theatre Arts Division; create and format a newsletter about the Theatre Arts Division; compare the edited newsletter with the original newsletter.

The Waterfront Bistro

Create, modify, and format a table containing information about catered lunch options.

Create an organizational chart for the production department; create, modify, and format a table containing information on rental cars.

Create an organizational chart for the design department.

Insert a formula in a table that calculates total sales.

4.1 Creating and Modifying a Table

Word's Table feature is useful for displaying data in columns and rows. This data may be text, values, and/or formulas. You can create a table using the Insert Table button on the Standard toolbar or with options at the Insert Table dialog box. Once you specify the desired number of rows and columns, Word displays the table and you are ready to enter information into the cells. A *cell* is the "box" created by the intersection of a row and a column. Cells are designated with a letter-number label representing the column and row intersection.

Columns are lettered from left to right, beginning with A. Rows are numbered from top to bottom, beginning with 1. You can modify the structure of the table by inserting or deleting columns and/or rows and merging cells.

PROJECT: You are developing a new First Choice Travel information document about sightseeing flights around the island of Maui. You will create and then modify a table to display the data.

STEPS

1. Open **FCTIslandFlights**. Save the document with Save As and name it **WordS4-01**.

2. Press Ctrl + End to move the insertion point to the end of the document.

3. Position the mouse pointer on the Insert Table button on the Standard toolbar and then hold down the left mouse button. (This displays a grid below the button.) Drag the mouse pointer down and to the right until the number below the grid displays as *6 X 3* and then release the mouse button.

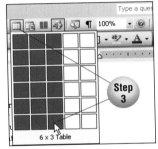

Step 3

4. Type the text in the cells as shown in Figure W4.1. Press the Tab key to move the insertion point to the next cell or press Shift + Tab to move the insertion point to the previous cell. When typing text in the cells in the second column, do not press the Enter key to end a line. Type the text and let the word wrap feature wrap the text within the cell. After typing text in the last cell do not press the Tab key. This will insert another row. If you press the Tab key accidentally, immediately click the Undo button.

> To move the insertion point to different cells within the table using the mouse, click in the desired cell. If you type the incorrect text in a cell, press Shift + Tab until the incorrect text is selected and then type the correct text.

FIGURE W4.1

Adventure	Destination	Price
Special West Maui	Waterfalls, lush tropical valleys	$49
West Maui Tropical	West Maui mountains, Hawaii's highest waterfalls	$79
Haleakala-Keane	Haleakala crater, tropical rain forest, waterfalls	$89
Special Circle Island	Hana, Haleakala, west Maui mountains, tropical rain forest, waterfalls	$169
Molokai-West Maui	West Maui mountains, waterfalls, sea cliffs, Kalaupapa colony	$189

⑤ You decide to add First Choice Travel discount prices to the table. Click in the cell containing the text *Price*, click Table, point to Insert, and then click Columns to the Right.

⑥ Click in the top cell of the new column, type **FCT**, and then press the Down Arrow key. Type the money amounts in the remaining cells as shown at the right. (Press the Down Arrow key to move to the next cell.)

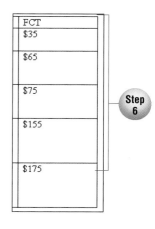

⑦ Click in the cell containing the text *Special Circle Island*. Click Table, point to Delete, and then click Rows.

> This deletes the entire row. You can delete a column in a similar manner. Click in any cell in the column, click Table, point to Delete, and then click Columns.

⑧ Click in the cell containing the text *Adventure*. Click Table, point to Insert, and then click Rows Above.

⑨ With the new top row selected, merge the cells by clicking Table and then Merge Cells.

⑩ Type **MAUI FLIGHTS** in the top row.

⑪ Click outside the table to deselect the cell.

⑫ Save **WordS4-01**.

In Addition

Other Methods for Creating a Table

Other methods for creating a table include using options from the Insert Table dialog box or using buttons on the Tables and Borders toolbar. Display the Insert Table dialog box by clicking Table, pointing to Insert, and then clicking Table. Specify the desired number of columns and rows and then click OK to close the dialog box. Another method for creating a table is to draw a table using buttons on the Tables and Borders toolbar. Display this toolbar, shown below, by clicking the Tables and Borders button 🔲 on the Standard toolbar. Using buttons on this toolbar, you can draw, format, and customize a table.

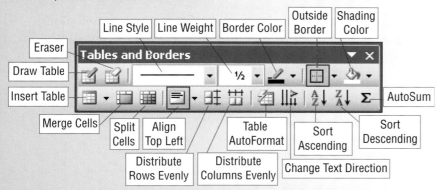

In Brief

Create a Table
1 Position mouse pointer on Insert Table button.
2 Hold down left mouse button.
3 Drag in grid to select desired number of columns and rows.
4 Release mouse button.

Insert Column/Row
Click Table, point to Insert, click desired option.

Delete Column/Row
Click Table, point to Delete, click desired option.

Merge Cells
1 Select cells.
2 Click Table, Merge Cells.

4.2 Customizing and Formatting a Table

When you create a table, columns are the same width and rows are the same height. The width of columns depends on the number of columns as well as the document margins. You can change column widths and row height using a variety of methods including dragging the gridlines. You can apply formatting to text in cells. Select text and then apply the formatting or select multiple cells and then apply formatting. Apply formatting with buttons on the Formatting toolbar or with options at the Table Properties dialog box. With options at the Table Properties dialog box, you can apply formatting to the entire table or a row, column, or cell.

PROJECT: The Maui Flights table needs adjustments to improve its appearance. You will increase and decrease column widths, increase the height of a row, and apply formatting to the entire table and to specific cells in the table.

STEPS

1. With **WordS4-01** open, click View and then Print Layout. (Skip this step if the view is already Print Layout.)

2. Position the mouse pointer on the gridline between the second and third columns until the pointer turns into a double-headed arrow pointing left and right with a short double line between. Hold down the left mouse button, drag to the right until the table column marker displays at the 3.5-inch mark on the horizontal Ruler, and then release the mouse button.

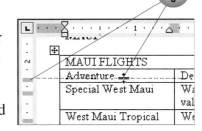

3. Following the same procedure, drag the gridline between the third and fourth columns to the left until the table column marker displays on the 4.25-inch marker on the horizontal Ruler.

4. Drag the gridline at the far right side of the table to the left until the table column marker displays on the 5-inch mark on the Ruler.

5. Position the mouse pointer on the gridline between the first and second row until the pointer turns into a double-headed arrow pointing up and down with a short double line between. Hold down the left mouse button, drag down approximately 0.25 inch on the vertical Ruler, and then release the mouse button.

6. Select the entire table by clicking Table, pointing to Select, and then clicking Table. With the table selected, change the font to Arial and font size to 11 points.

7. Click in the top cell containing the text *MAUI FLIGHTS*. Click Table, point to Select, and then click Cell. With the cell selected, change the font size to 16, click the Bold button, and then click the Center button.

8. With the cell still selected, click Table and then Table Properties.

(9) At the Table Properties dialog box, click the Cell tab and then click the *Center* option. Click OK to close the dialog box.

> This changes the vertical alignment to center for the text in the cell.

(10) Click in the cell containing the text *Adventure* and click Table, point to Select, and then click Row. With the row selected, click the Bold button and then the Center button on the Formatting toolbar.

(11) Position the mouse pointer in the cell containing the text *$49*, hold down the left mouse button, drag down and to the right to the cell containing the text *$175*, and then release the mouse button.

(12) With the cells selected, click the Center button on the Formatting toolbar.

(13) Click anywhere outside the table to deselect the cells.

(14) Save **WordS4-01**.

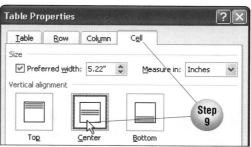

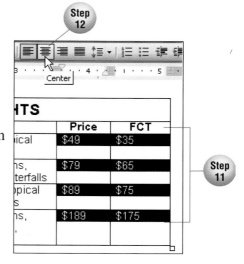

In Addition

Selecting Cells with the Keyboard

You have selected cells using the mouse and the Table drop-down menu. You can also select cells using the keyboard by completing the following steps:

To select	Press
The next cell's contents	Tab
The preceding cell's contents	Shift + Tab
The entire table	Alt + 5 (on the numeric keypad with Num Lock off)
Adjacent cells	Hold down the Shift key, then press an arrow key repeatedly
A column	Position insertion point in top cell of column, hold down Shift key, then press the Down Arrow key until column is selected

In Brief

Increase/Decrease Column/Row
1 Position mouse pointer on gridline until it turns into a double-headed arrow.
2 Hold down left mouse button, drag to desired position, then release the button.

Display Table Properties Dialog Box
1 Click in a cell in the table.
2 Click Table, Table Properties.

4.3 Applying Borders and Shading to a Table; Applying Autoformats

To enhance the visual appeal of a table, consider applying a border and/or shading to the entire table or cells within the table. Apply borders and/or shading to a table with options at the Borders and Shading dialog box. If you select specific cells in the table and then display the Borders and Shading dialog box, the choices made at the dialog box will apply only to the cells. If the insertion point is positioned in a table (with no cell selected) or if an entire table is selected, changes made to the

Borders and Shading dialog box will affect the entire table. You can easily format a table with autoformats provided by Word. These autoformats do all of the formatting work for you.

PROJECT: You will add final formatting touches to the Maui Flights table by creating a border and adding shading to specific cells and experiment with autoformats.

S T E P S

① With **WordS4-01** open, click in any cell in the table.

② Click Format and then Borders and Shading. At the Borders and Shading dialog box, make sure the Borders tab is selected.

③ Click the down-pointing arrow at the right side of the *Style* list box until the first thick/thin double-line option displays and then click the option.

④ Click the down-pointing arrow at the right side of the *Color* option box and then click the Indigo option (seventh color from the left in the top row).

⑤ Click the *Grid* option in the *Setting* section of the dialog box.

⑥ Click the Shading tab and then click the fifth color (Light Turquoise) from the left in the bottom row of the Fill palette.

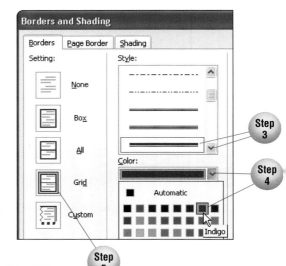

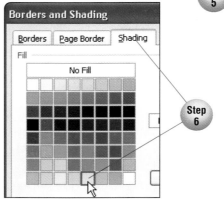

⑦ Click OK to close the dialog box.

⑧ Click in the cell containing the text *Adventure*, click Table, point to Select, and then click Row.

⑨ Click Format and then Borders and Shading.

10. At the Borders and Shading dialog box with the Shading tab selected, click the third color from the left in the top row (Gray-10%).

11. Click OK to close the dialog box.

12. Click anywhere outside the table to deselect the cells.

> Your table should look similar to the one shown in Figure W4.2.

13. Save and then print **WordS4-01**.

14. You decide to experiment with some of the autoformats provided by Word. To do this, click in any cell in the table, click Table, and then click Table AutoFormat.

15. At the Table AutoFormat dialog box, scroll up the *Table styles* list box and then double-click the *Table 3D effects 2* option.

> Notice the formatting applied to the table by the autoformat feature.

16. Click the Print button on the Standard toolbar.

17. Click the Undo button on the Standard toolbar (this removes the autoformat).

18. Click Table and then click Table AutoFormat.

19. At the Table AutoFormat dialog box, double-click *Table Contemporary*.

20. Click the Print button on the Standard toolbar.

21. Click the Undo button on the Standard toolbar to remove the autoformat.

22. Save and then close **WordS4-01**.

FIGURE W4.2

MAUI FLIGHTS			
Adventure	**Destination**	**Price**	**FCT**
Special West Maui	Waterfalls, lush tropical valleys	$49	$35
West Maui Tropical	West Maui mountains, Hawaii's highest waterfalls	$79	$65
Haleakala-Keane	Haleakala crater, tropical rain forest, waterfalls	$89	$75
Molokai-West Maui	West Maui mountains, waterfalls, sea cliffs, Kalaupapa colony	$189	$175

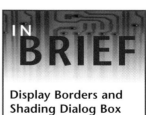

IN BRIEF

Display Borders and Shading Dialog Box
1 Click in a cell or select cells.
2 Click Format, Borders and Shading.

Display Table AutoFormat Dialog Box
1 Click in cell in the table.
2 Click Table, Table AutoFormat.

4.4 Converting Text to a Table; Applying a Table Style; Using the Research Tool

You can convert text in a document separated by a comma, tab, or other separator (such as a paragraph mark) to text in a table with options at the Convert Text to Table dialog box. You used the Research task pane to search for synonyms for specific words. You can also use options at this task pane to search for and request specific information from online sources and to translate words from and to a variety of languages. The online resources available to you depend on the locale to which your system is set, authorization information indicating that you are allowed to download the information, and your Internet Service Provider. Word offers a variety of table styles containing formatting that you can apply to a table.

PROJECT: You are preparing a travel document with Italian translations for cities and phrases. You want to improve the appearance of the document by setting some of the text in a table and then applying a style to the table. You also decide to use the translation tool to translate a city name and phrase.

STEPS

1. Open **FCTItalyTravel**. Save the document with Save As and name it **WordS4-02**.

2. Select the text in the two columns (from *English* through *Sicilia*). Click Table, point to Convert, and then click Text to Table.

3. At the Convert Text to Table dialog box, click *Tabs* in the *Separate text at* section (this changes the *Number of columns* option to *2*), click *AutoFit to contents* in the *AutoFit behavior* section, and then click OK.

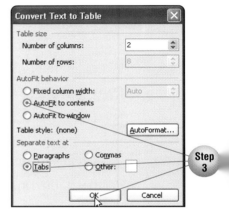

Step 3

4. With the table selected, display the Styles and Formatting task pane by clicking the Styles and Formatting button on the Formatting toolbar.

5. Click the down-pointing arrow at the right of the *Show* option (located toward the bottom of the task pane) and then click *All styles* at the drop-down list.

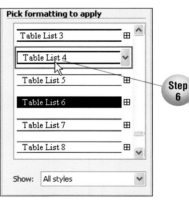

Step 6

6. Scroll down the *Pick formatting to apply* list box and then click the *Table List 4*.

7. Close the Styles and Formatting task pane and then click outside the table to deselect it.

8. Find the Italian name for the city of Florence. To do this, click the Research button on the Standard toolbar. At the Research task pane, type **Florence** in the *Search for* text box. Click the down-pointing arrow to the right of the resources list box (the down-pointing arrow immediately below the Start searching button) and then click *Translation* at the drop-down list.

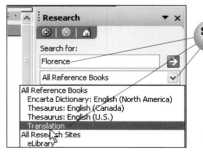

The drop-down list contains lists of reference books, research sites, business and financial sites, and other services. Depending on the item you select, the task pane list box may contain hyperlinks you can click to access additional information on the Internet.

⑨ Make sure that *English (U.S.)* displays in the *From* option box. (If it does not, click the down-pointing arrow at the right of the *From* option and then click *English (U.S.)* at the drop-down list.) Click the down-pointing arrow to the right of the *To* option and then click *Italian (Italy)* at the drop-down list.

⑩ Select *Firenze* that displays in the task pane list box, right-click the selected word, and then click Copy at the shortcut menu.

⑪ Click in the cell immediately right of the cell containing *Florence* and then click the Paste button on the Standard toolbar.

   This inserts *Firenze* in the cell.

⑫ Find a translation for the sentence *How much does this cost?* To do this, select *Florence* in the *Search for* list box and then press the Delete key. Type **How much does this cost?** and then press Enter.

⑬ When the Italian translation displays in the task pane list box, select the Italian sentence, right-click the selected sentence, and then click Copy at the shortcut menu.

⑭ Move the insertion point to the left margin of the line immediately below the sentence *How much does this cost?* and then click the Paste button.

⑮ **Optional**: If you have access to an online encyclopedia, select the text in the *Search for* text box and then type **Italy**. Click the down-pointing arrow to the right of the resources list box and then click *Encarta Encyclopedia: English (North America)*. (If this reference is not available, click any other encyclopedia that is available to you.) Click a hyperlink in the task pane list box that interests you. Search for general information about Italy. If you find general information, select a few paragraphs of text and then copy and paste it to the end of the **WordS4-02** document. Type an appropriate title for the text.

⑯ Close the Research task pane.

⑰ Save, print, and then close **WordS4-02**.

In Addition

Converting Text in a Table to Only Text

You can convert text in a table to only text. To do this, position the insertion point in any cell in the table, click Table, point to Convert, and then click Table to Text. At the Convert Table to Text dialog box, specify how you want the text separated in the document.

IN BRIEF

Convert Text to a Table
1 Select text.
2 Click Table, Convert, Text to Table.
3 Make desired changes at Convert Text to Table dialog box.
4 Click OK.

Apply a Table Style
1 Click Styles and Formatting button.
2 Click down-pointing arrow at right of *Show* option.
3 Click *All styles*.
4 Select table.
5 Click desired table style in task pane list box.

Display Research Task Pane
Click Research button on Standard toolbar.

4.5 Inserting a Section Break; Creating and Modifying Newspaper Columns

To increase the ease with which a person can read and understand groups of words (referred to as the *readability* of a document), consider setting text in the document in newspaper columns. Newspaper columns contain text that flows up and down on the page. Create newspaper columns with the Columns button on the Standard toolbar or with options at the Columns dialog box. If you want to apply column formatting to only a portion of a document, insert a section break in the document. Insert a section break in the document with options at the Break dialog box.

PROJECT: To improve the readability of the Petersburg fact sheet document, you will set the text in newspaper columns.

STEPS

1. Open **FCTPetersburg**. Save the document with Save As and name it **WordS4-03**.

2. Position the insertion point at the beginning of the first paragraph in the document (the paragraph that begins *Petersburg, Alaska, located on...*), click Insert, and then click Break.

3. At the Break dialog box, click *Continuous* in the *Section break types* section and then click OK to close the dialog box.

    In Normal view, the section break displays in the document as a double row of dots with the words *Section Break (Continuous)* in the middle. In Print Layout view, a continuous section break is not visible. A continuous section break separates the document into sections but does not insert a page break. Click one of the other three options in the *Section break types* section of the Break dialog box if you want to insert a section break that begins a new page.

4. With the insertion point positioned below the section break, format the text below the section break into three newspaper columns by clicking the Columns button ▥ on the Standard toolbar. At the Columns grid, drag the mouse pointer down and to the right until three columns display with a dark background on the grid, and then click the left mouse button.

    Formatting text into columns automatically changes the view to Print Layout.

    PROBLEM ❓ If the second and third columns of text align with the title, click the Undo button. Make sure the insertion point is positioned at the beginning of the first paragraph of text (not the beginning of the document) and then create the columns.

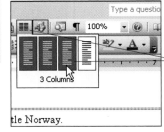

5. Find all occurrences of *Mitkoff* and replace with *Mitkof*. Find all occurrences of *Alaska marine highway* and replace with *Alaska Marine Highway*.

6. Select the title *FACT SHEET – PETERSBURG, ALASKA*, click the Bold button, and then click the Center button on the Formatting toolbar.

7. Select the heading *Services*, click the Bold button on the Formatting toolbar, and then add 6 points of space after the paragraph. (***Hint: Do this at the Paragraph dialog box with the Indents and Spacing tab selected.***) Using Format Painter, apply bold formatting and 6 points of space after the paragraph to each of the remaining headings (*Visitor Attractions*, *Walking Tours*, *Accommodations*, and *Transportation*).

8. As you view the document, you decide that the three columns are too narrow so you decide to set the text in two columns and also add a line between. To do this, click anywhere in the first paragraph of text that displays in a column. Display the Columns dialog box by clicking Format and then Columns.

9. At the Columns dialog box, click *Two* in the *Presets* section.

10. Increase the spacing between the two columns by clicking the up-pointing arrow at the right side of the *Spacing* option in the *Width and spacing* section until *0.7"* displays in the text box.

11. Make sure a check mark displays in the *Equal column width* check box. If not, click the option to insert the check mark.

> This option, when activated, makes the two columns the same width.

12. Click the *Line between* option to insert a check mark and then click OK to close the dialog box.

> Choosing the *Line between* option inserts a line between the two columns. The *Preview* section of the dialog box provides a visual representation of the columns.

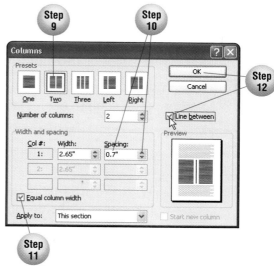

13. Press Ctrl + End to move the insertion point to the end of the document. Looking at the columns on the last (second) page, you decide to balance the two columns. To do this, click Insert and then Break. At the Break dialog box, click the *Continuous* option in the *Section break types* section of the dialog box, and then click OK.

14. Save **WordS4-03**.

In Addition

Changing Column Width

One method for changing column width in a document is to drag the column marker on the horizontal ruler. The horizontal ruler displays when the Print Layout view is selected. To change the width (and also the spacing) of columns of text, position the arrow pointer on the left or right edge of a column marker on the horizontal ruler until it turns into a double-headed arrow pointing left and right. Hold down the left mouse button, drag the column marker to the left or right to make the column of text wider or narrower, and then release the mouse button. Hold down the Alt key while dragging the column marker and measurements display on the horizontal ruler.

IN BRIEF

Insert a Continuous Section Break
1 Click Insert, Break.
2 Click Continuous.
3 Click OK.

Format Text into Columns
1 Click Columns button on Standard toolbar.
2 Drag to select desired number of columns in the Columns grid.
3 Release mouse button.

Display Columns Dialog Box
Click Format, Columns.

4.6 Inserting and Modifying a Header or Footer

Insert text that you want to appear at the top of each page in a header and text you want to appear at the bottom of each page in a footer. Headers and footers are common in manuscripts, textbooks, reports, and other publications. Create a header or footer by clicking View and then Header and Footer. Word automatically changes to Print Layout view, dims the text in the document, displays the Header and Footer toolbar, and inserts a pane where you enter the header or footer text. Header or footer text does not take on the character formatting of the document. If you want header or footer text character formatting to be the same as the document, format the header or footer in the header or footer pane. Delete a header or footer from a document by displaying the header or footer pane and then selecting and deleting the text.

PROJECT: To continue the formatting of the Petersburg fact sheet newsletter, you decide to add more information to the newsletter, including the page number and a footer. After reviewing the header and footer, you will decide if you need to make any modifications.

S T E P S

1. With **WordS4-03** open, press Ctrl + Home to move the insertion point to the beginning of the document, click View, and then click Header and Footer.

2. At the header pane, press the Tab key twice, type the word **Page**, press the spacebar, and then click the Insert Page Number button on the Header and Footer toolbar.

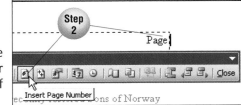

   The header pane contains tab stops at the center and the right side of the header pane. Refer to Figure W4.3 for the names of the Header and Footer toolbar buttons.

FIGURE W4.3 Header and Footer Toolbar Buttons

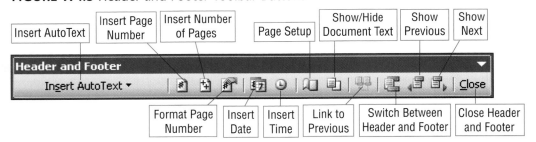

3. Click the Switch Between Header and Footer button on the Header and Footer toolbar.

   Clicking this button displays the footer pane.

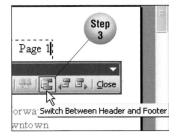

4. Press the Tab key once, click the Bold button, and then type **Petersburg, Alaska**.

5. Click the Close button located at the right side of the Header and Footer toolbar to close the toolbar.

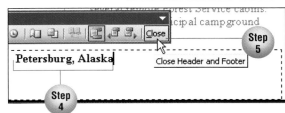

(6) Scroll through the document and notice the header and footer text that displays at the top and bottom of each page. (The header and footer text displays dimmed in Print Layout view.) After looking at the document, you decide to make some changes. First, select the entire document, change the font to 11-point Bookman Old Style (or a similar typeface), and then deselect the text.

(7) Make sure the insertion point is positioned at the beginning of the document, click View, and then click Header and Footer.

> This displays the header text in the header pane.

(8) At the Header pane, select the text *Page 1* and then press the Delete key on the keyboard.

> This deletes the header text from the document.

(9) Click the Switch Between Header and Footer button 🖻 on the Header and Footer toolbar.

> Clicking this button displays the footer text in the footer pane.

(10) Move the footer text back to the left margin by pressing the Delete key. Move the insertion point to the right side of the footer text and then press the Tab key twice.

(11) Type **Page**, press the spacebar, and then click the Insert Page Number button 🔢 on the Header and Footer toolbar.

(12) Select all of the footer text, change the font to 11-point Bookman Old Style bold (or the typeface you chose in Step 6), and then deselect the footer text.

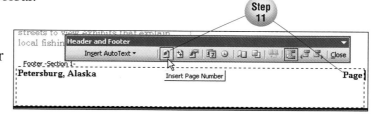

Step 11

(13) Click the Close button on the Header and Footer toolbar and then scroll through the document and view the footer text.

> In Print Layout, the footer text displays dimmed.

(14) Save, print, and then close **WordS4-03**.

In Addition

Inserting AutoText in a Header or Footer

Click the Insert AutoText button on the Header and Footer toolbar and the drop-down list shown at the right displays with a variety of options. Choose an option to automatically insert specific text. For example, choose the *Last printed* option and Word will insert the date the document was last printed; or, choose the *Filename and path* option and Word will insert the entire document name and path.

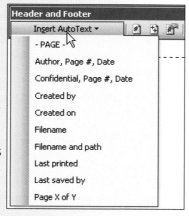

In Brief

Create a Header
1 Click View, Header and Footer.
2 Type desired text in header pane.
3 Click Close button.

Create a Footer
1 Click View, Header and Footer.
2 Click Switch Between Header and Footer button.
3 Type desired text in footer pane.
4 Click Close button.

You can save a Word document as a Web page and apply formatting to the Web page. When you save a document as a Web page, Word automatically changes to the Web Layout view. In this view, the page displays as it will appear when published to the Web or an intranet. Along with Web Layout view, you can also change to the Web Page Preview to view the page in the default Web browser and to view formatting supported by the browser. You can create a hyperlink in a document or Web page that connects to a site on the Internet or to another document.

PROJECT: Since many of First Choice Travel's clients have Internet access, you decide to save the Petersburg newsletter as a Web page, and then insert hyperlinks to another document containing information on Petersburg as well as the Alaska Division of Tourism.

S T E P S

1 Open **WordS4-03** and then save the document as a Web page by clicking File and then Save as Web Page. Type **PetersburgWebPage** in the *File name* text box and then press Enter.

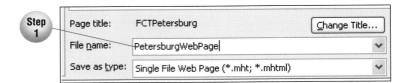

Step 1

Page title:	FCTPetersburg	Change Title...
File name:	PetersburgWebPage	
Save as type:	Single File Web Page (*.mht; *.mhtml)	

2 Apply a theme background to the Web page by clicking Format and then Theme. At the Theme dialog box, scroll to the end of the *Choose a Theme* list box and then double-click *Sumi Painting* in the list box.

> Depending on your system setup, this theme may need to be installed.

3 Press Ctrl + End to move the insertion point to the end of the document, press Enter twice, and then type **Additional Information**.

4 Insert a hyperlink to a Word document by selecting the text *Additional Information* and then clicking the Insert Hyperlink button on the Standard toolbar.

5 At the Insert Hyperlink dialog box, click the down-pointing arrow at the right side of the *Look in* option and then navigate to the WordS4 folder on your disk. Double-click **FCTPA01**.

> The Insert Hyperlink dialog box closes and *Additional Information* displays as hyperlink text.

Theme

Choose a Theme: | Sample of

Journal
Layers
Level
Network
Papyrus
Pixel
Profile
Quadrant
Radial
Refined
Rice Paper
Ripple
Romanesque
Satin
Sky
Slate
Sonora
Spring
Straight Edge
Studio
Sumi Painting
Water
Watermark

Step 2

6 Press Ctrl + End, press the Enter key once, and then type **Alaska Division of Tourism**.

7 Create a hyperlink to the tourism site by selecting *Alaska Division of Tourism* and then clicking the Insert Hyperlink button on the Standard toolbar.

8 At the Insert Hyperlink dialog box, type **www.dced.state.ak.us/tourism** in the *Address* text box and then click OK.

Word automatically adds *http://* to the beginning of the Web address.

9 Display the document containing additional information on Petersburg by holding down the Ctrl key and then clicking the <u>Additional Information</u> hyperlink.

10 After reading the information in the document, close the document.

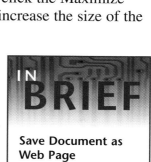

11 Make sure you are connected to the Internet and then connect to the Alaska tourism site by holding down the Ctrl key and then clicking the <u>Alaska Division of Tourism</u> hyperlink.

12 At the Alaska Division of Tourism page, click on any hyperlinks that interest you. When you are finished, click File and then Close.

13 Click File and then Web Page Preview. (You may need to click the Maximize button located in the upper right corner of the browser to increase the size of the Web page.)

14 After viewing the document in the Web browser, click File and then Close to close the browser.

15 Save, print, and then close **PetersburgWebPage**.

The document prints with the original formatting applied.

In Addition

Downloading and Saving Web Pages and Images

You can save the image(s) and/or text that displays when you open a Web page as well as the Web page itself. Copyright laws protect much of the information on the Internet so check the site for restrictions before copying or downloading. If you do use information, make sure you cite the source properly. To save a Web page as a file, display the desired page, click File on the Internet Explorer Menu bar, and then click Save As. At the Save Web Page dialog box, specify the folder where you want to save the Web page. Select the text in the *File name* text box, type a name for the page, and then click the Save button. Save a specific Web image by right-clicking the image and then clicking Save Picture As. At the Save Picture dialog box, type a name for the image in the *File name* text box and then press Enter.

IN BRIEF

Save Document as Web Page
1 Open document.
2 Click File, Save as Web Page.
3 Type name, press Enter.

Apply a Theme
1 Click Format, Theme.
2 Double-click desired theme.

Create a Hyperlink
1 Select text in document.
2 Click Insert Hyperlink button.
3 Type file name or Web site address.
4 Click OK.

Preview a Web Page
1 Open Web page document.
2 Click File, Web Page Preview.

4.8 Comparing and Merging Documents; Inserting and Modifying Comments

Use Word's Compare and Merge feature to compare two documents and display the differences between the documents. This might be useful in a setting where multiple individuals in a workgroup make changes to separate copies of the original document. Merge all of the changes made by each individual using the Compare and Merge feature. When you compare and merge documents, you can choose to display the results in the original document, in the currently open document, or in a new document. In Print Layout view, the results display in the document as well as in balloons in the right margin. If you want to make comments in a document, or if a reviewer wants to make comments in a document prepared by someone else, insert a comment. A comment is useful for providing specific instructions, identifying critical information, or for multiple individuals reviewing the same worksheet to insert comments.

PROJECT: You want to keep track of the changes you made to the Petersburg fact sheet document so you decide to use the merge and compare feature to compare the edited document with the original document. You then will read over the newsletter and make a few comments about additions that should be made to the newsletter.

STEPS

1. Open **WordS4-03** and then make sure the document displays in Print Layout view. (If not, click View and then Print Layout.)

2. Compare **WordS4-03** with the original document. To do this, click Tools and then Compare and Merge Documents.

3. At the Compare and Merge Documents dialog box, make sure WordS4 on your disk is the active folder and then click **FCTPetersburg** to select it.

4. Click the down-pointing arrow at the right side of the Merge button (located in the lower right corner of the dialog box) and then click *Merge into new document* at the drop-down list.

   Notice the marked changes that appear in the document.

PROBLEM ❓ If document text displays in red, make sure you click **FCTPetersburg** before clicking the down-pointing arrow at the right side of the Merge button.

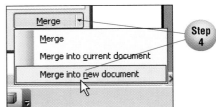

Step 4

5. Print the document with the marked changes by clicking File and then Print. At the Print dialog box, make sure *Document showing markup* displays in the *Print what* option, and then click OK.

   The *Document showing markup* is automatically selected at the Print dialog box when a document contains marked changes.

6. Save the document and name it **WordS4-04** and then close **WordS4-04**.

7. With **WordS4-03** open, move the insertion point to the end of the first paragraph of text, click Insert, and then click Comment.

   This inserts a Comment balloon at the right side of the margin.

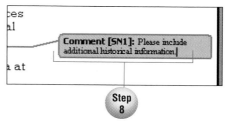

8. Type **Please include additional historical information.** in the Comment balloon.

9. Move the insertion point to the end of the first paragraph in the *Visitor Attractions* section, click Insert, and then click Comment.

Step 8

10. Type **Include the admissions fee, if any, for the museum.** in the Comment balloon.

11. Insert the comment *Please include average prices for hotels.* at the end of the first paragraph in the *Accommodations* section (located on the second page).

12. Print only the comments. To do this, click File and then Print. At the Print dialog box, click the down-pointing arrow at the right side of the *Print what* option, click *List of markup* at the drop-down list, and then click OK.

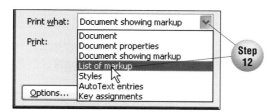

Step 12

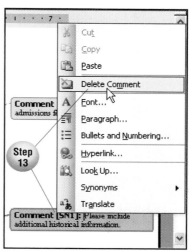

Step 13

13. Delete the comment located after the first paragraph. To do this, right-click the Comment balloon that contains the text *Please include additional historical information.*, and then click Delete Comment at the shortcut menu.

14. Click in the Comment balloon on the second page and then edit the comment so it reads *Please include average prices for hotels, motels, and bed-and-breakfast facilities.*

15. Print only the comments. (Refer to Step 12.)

16. Save and then close **WordS4-03**.

In Addition

Accepting and Rejecting Changes

After viewing the results of a compare and merge, you can choose to accept or reject individual changes with buttons on the Reviewing toolbar. Display this toolbar by clicking View, pointing to Toolbars, and then clicking Reviewing. To accept all of the changes in a document, click the down-pointing arrow at the right side of the Accept Change button on the Reviewing toolbar, and then click *Accept All Changes in Document*. To reject all changes, click the down-pointing arrow at the right side of the Reject Change/Delete Comment button, and then click *Reject All Changes in Document*.

IN BRIEF

Compare and Merge Documents
1 Open edited document.
2 Click Tools, Compare and Merge Documents.
3 Click original document.
4 Click down-pointing arrow at right of Merge button.
5 Click *Merge into new document*.

Insert Comment
1 Click Insert, Comment.
2 Type comment text.

4.9 Creating an Outline

Word includes the Outline view you can use to organize text in a document as well as manipulate outline headings and text. To create an outline, you identify particular headings and subheadings within a document as certain heading levels. Use the Outline view to assign particular heading levels to text. You can also enter text and edit text while working in Outline view. In Outline view, the Outlining toolbar displays below the Formatting toolbar containing buttons for assigning levels to headings and text.

PROJECT: You have prepared a fact sheet on Orcas Island and decide to format and organize it in Outline view.

STEPS

1. Open **FCTOrcasIsland** and then save the document with Save As and name it **WordS4-05**.

2. Change to the Outline view by clicking View and then Outline.

    You can also change to Outline view by clicking the Outline View button at the left side of the horizontal scroll bar.

3. Promote the title *San Juan Islands – Orcas Island* to Heading 1 by positioning the insertion point on any character in the title and then clicking the Promote to Heading 1 button ⟨⟩ on the Outlining toolbar.

    Refer to Figure W4.4 to determine the names of the buttons on the Outlining toolbar. Clicking the Promote to Heading 1 button applies the Heading 1 style to the title.

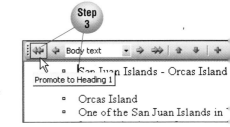

Figure W4.4 Outlining Toolbar Buttons

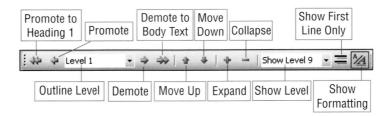

4. Position the insertion point on the heading *Orcas Island* and then click the Demote button ⟨⟩ on the Outlining toolbar.

    This applies the Heading 2 style to the heading.

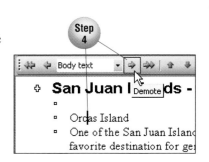

5. Position the insertion point on any character in the heading *Bicycle Safety* and then click the Promote button ⟨⟩ .

    This applies the Heading 2 style to the heading.

6. Click on any character in each of the remaining headings *Marine Parks*, *Directions to Orcas Island*, and *Activities on Orcas* and click the Promote button.

7. One of the major benefits of working in Outline view is the ability to see a condensed outline of your document without all of the text in between headings or subheadings. Collapse the document by moving the insertion point to any character in the title *San Juan Islands – Orcas Island* and then clicking the Collapse button ⊟ on the Outlining toolbar.

> This collapses the document so only the title and headings display. With the document collapsed, you can organize text in the document, move quickly from one portion of a document to another, and check headings to maintain consistency in the document.

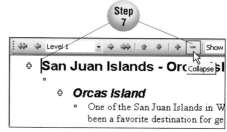

8. Move the *Directions to Orcas Island* section above the *Bicycling Safety* section by positioning the insertion point on any character in the heading *Directions to Orcas Island* and then clicking twice on the Move Up button ⬆ on the Outlining toolbar.

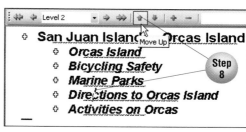

9. Move the *Bicycling Safety* section below the *Activities on Orcas* section by positioning the insertion point on any character in the heading *Bicycling Safety* and then clicking twice on the Move Down button ⬇ .

10. Expand the document by clicking on any character in the title *San Juan Islands – Orcas Island* and then clicking the Expand button ⬧ on the Outlining toolbar.

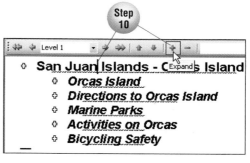

11. Change the view to Print Layout and then save **WordS4-05**.

In Addition

Assigning Levels

Applying a heading style applies formatting to the text. If you want to assign outline levels in a document without applying formatting, use the Outline Level button on the Outlining toolbar. You can assign an outline level in Normal view, Print Layout view, or Outline view. In Normal or Print Layout view, the Outlining toolbar displays with fewer buttons than the Outlining toolbar in Outline view. To assign a level, display the desired view, and then turn on the display of the Outlining toolbar. Position the insertion point on any character in the text to be assigned a level and then click the down-pointing arrow at the right side of the Outline Level button. At the drop-down list that displays, click the desired level. With levels assigned to text in a document, you can display the document in Outline view and then collapse, expand, and/or move level headings in a document.

IN BRIEF

Create an Outline
1 Click View, Outline.
2 Using buttons on Outlining toolbar, promote and/or demote headings as needed.

4.10 Tracking Changes; Accepting or Rejecting Changes; Sending a Document as E-mail

If you want to edit a document and keep track of the changes, turn on the tracking feature. With the tracking feature on, each deletion, insertion, or formatting change made to the document is tracked. For example, deleted text is not removed from the document but instead displays with a line through it and in a different color. As you review a document containing tracked changes, you can choose to accept or reject changes. In some situations, you may want to send a document to a colleague, customer, or client. In Word, you can send a document as an e-mail or as an e-mail attachment.

PROJECT: You have sent the Orcas Island fact sheet to Melissa Gehring for editing. She will use the Track Changes feature to make changes to the document and then you will review the document and accept or reject her changes. When the document is complete, Melissa has asked you to e-mail it to Alex Torres in the Toronto office.

STEPS

1 With **WordS4-05** open, make sure the document displays in Print Layout view, and then turn on tracking by clicking Tools and then Track Changes.

This turns on the display of the Reviewing toolbar as shown in Figure W4.5. Other methods for turning on tracking include clicking the Track Changes button on the Reviewing toolbar and pressing Ctrl + Shift + E. When tracking is on, the letters *TRK* display in black on the Status bar (located toward the bottom of the screen). With tracking on, Word displays some changes (such as insertion) in the text line and other changes appear in balloons in the margin of the document. Additionally, Word inserts a vertical line outside the left margin beside the line containing a change.

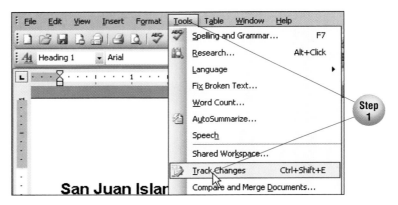

Figure W4.5 Reviewing Toolbar

2 With the insertion point positioned on the title *San Juan Islands – Orcas Island*, click the Center button on the Formatting toolbar.

This centers the title, inserts a vertical line at the left margin of the title, and inserts a balloon at the right margin with the text *Formatted: Centered* inside.

3 Select and then delete the sentence *To the north, on the mainland, is Vancouver, B.C.* located in the first paragraph in the *Orcas Island* section.

> This removes the sentence from the document and inserts a balloon at the right margin containing the word *Deleted:* followed by the sentence.

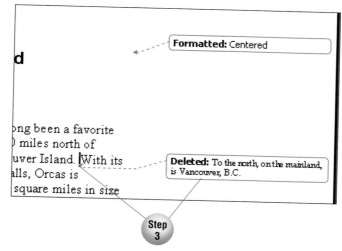

4 Move the insertion point immediately right of the period that ends the first bulleted item in the *Bicycling Safety* section, press the Enter key, and then type **Ride single file and keep to the right of the road.**

> The typed text is inserted in the document in a different color and a balloon displays at the right margins with the words *Formatting: Bullets and Numbering* inside.

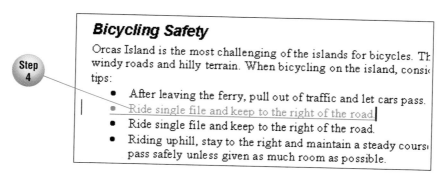

5 Turn off tracking by clicking the Track Changes button on the Reviewing toolbar.

6 Save, print, and then close **WordS4-05**.

7 Open **WordS4-05**. Make sure the document displays in Print Layout view and that the Reviewing toolbar is visible.

(continued)

⑧ Click the Next button ⟫ on the Reviewing toolbar and then click the Accept Change button 🖉 .

> When you click the Next button, the title is selected. When you click the Accept Change button, the balloon at the right margin of the title is removed.

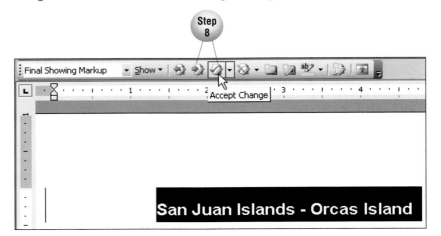

⑨ Click the Next button on the Reviewing toolbar and then click the Reject Change/Delete Comment button 🖉 .

> Clicking the Reject Change/Delete Comment button tells Word to insert the deleted sentence back into the document.

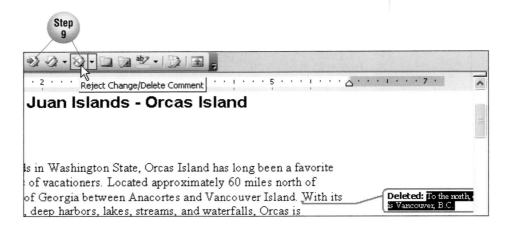

⑩ Click the Next button on the Reviewing toolbar and then click the Accept Change button.

> This accepts the change to add the bulleted item in the *Bicycling Safety* section.

⑪ Click the Next button and Word displays the message that the document does not change comments or tracked changes. At this message, click the OK button.

⑫ Turn off the display of the Reviewing toolbar.

⑬ Save and then print **WordS4-05**.

(14) Send the document as an e-mail to Alex Torres in the Toronto office. (You will not be able to actually send the document as an e-mail. Check with your instructor to determine if you should consider sending the document to him or her as an e-mail.) Click the E-mail button on the Standard toolbar.

Clicking the E-mail button inserts the e-mail header directly above the Ruler.

(15) Type your instructor's name in the *To* text box and then click the Send a Copy button. (Check with your instructor to determine if you should complete this step.)

(16) If necessary, click the E-mail button on the Standard toolbar to remove the e-mail header.

(17) Save and then close **WordS4-05**.

In Addition

Displaying Information on Tracked Changes

Display information on tracking changes by positioning the mouse pointer on a change. After approximately 1 second, a box displays above the change containing the author's name, date, time, and the type of change (for example, whether it was a deletion or insertion). You can also display information on tracking changes by displaying the Reviewing pane. To do this, click the Reviewing Pane button on the Reviewing toolbar or click the Show button and then click Reviewing Pane at the drop-down list. Each change is listed separately in the Reviewing pane. Use the arrow keys at the right side of the Reviewing pane to scroll through the pane and view each change. To remove the Reviewing pane, click the Reviewing Pane button on the Reviewing toolbar.

Sending a Document for Review

You can send a document in an e-mail to others for review, as an attachment to the e-mail, or as the body of the e-mail message. To send a document as an e-mail message for review, click File, point to Send To, and then click Mail Recipient (for Review). To send a document as an e-mail attachment, click File, point to Send To, and then click Mail Recipient (as Attachment). To send a document as an e-mail attachment, you must be using Microsoft Outlook, Microsoft Outlook Express, Microsoft Exchange, or an e-mail program compatible with the Messaging Application Programming Interface (MAPI). To send a document as the body of an e-mail message, click the E-mail button on the Standard toolbar or click File, point to Send To, and then click Mail Recipient. You must be using Outlook 2003 to complete this procedure.

In Brief

Track Changes
1 Click Tools, Track Changes.
2 Make desired changes.
3 Turn off tracking by clicking Track Changes button on Reviewing toolbar.

Accept Changes
1 Click Next button on Reviewing toolbar.
2 Click Accept Changes button on Reviewing toolbar.

Reject Changes
1 Click Next button on Reviewing toolbar.
2 Click Reject Change/Delete Comment button on Reviewing toolbar.

4.11 Creating Organizational Charts and Diagrams

If you need to visually illustrate hierarchical data, consider creating an organizational chart with options at the Diagram Gallery. At this gallery you can also create a diagram to illustrate a concept and enhance the visual appeal of a document. If you choose an organizational chart at the Diagram Gallery, chart boxes appear in the drawing canvas and the Organization Chart toolbar displays with buttons for customizing the chart. If you click a diagram option, the diagram is inserted in the drawing canvas and the Diagram toolbar displays with buttons for customizing the diagram.

PROJECT: Terry Blessing, president of First Choice Travel, has asked you to prepare a document containing information on the organizational structure of and services provided by First Choice Travel.

STEPS

1. Open **FCTStructure** and then save the document with Save As and name it **WordS4-06**.

2. Move the insertion point a double space below the heading *ORGANIZATIONAL STRUCTURE* and then create the organizational chart shown in Figure W4.6. To do this, click Insert and then Diagram.

3. At the Diagram Gallery, double-click the first option in the top row.

   > This inserts a drawing canvas in the document with an organizational chart inside.

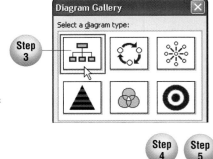

4. Add the assistant box to the chart by clicking the down-pointing arrow at the right side of the Insert Shape button on the Organization Chart toolbar and then clicking *Assistant* at the drop-down list.

5. Apply an autoformat to the chart by clicking the Autoformat button on the Organization Chart toolbar.

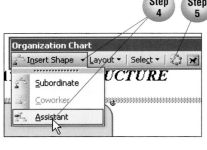

6. At the Organization Chart Style Gallery dialog box, double-click *Square Shadows* in the *Select a Diagram Style* list box.

7. Click inside the top box, press the Enter key once, and then type the text shown in Figure W4.6. Click in each of the remaining boxes and type the text as shown in Figure W4.6.

8. Press Ctrl + End to move the insertion point to the end of the document and then insert the diagram shown in Figure W4.7. To do this, click Insert and then Diagram.

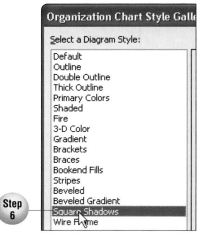

FIGURE W4.6 Organizational Chart

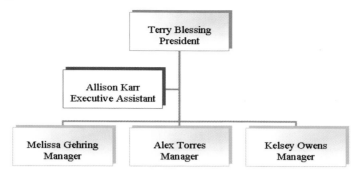

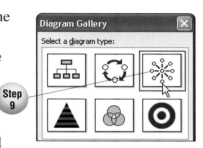

9. At the Diagram Gallery, double-click the last option in the top row.

   This inserts a radial diagram in the drawing canvas in the document.

10. Click the Insert Shape button on the Diagram toolbar.

    This inserts an additional circle in the radial diagram.

    Step 9

11. Click the AutoFormat button on the Diagram toolbar and then double-click *Thick Outline* in the *Select a Diagram Style* list box.

12. Click in the top circle in the drawing canvas, press Enter once, and then type **Cruise Packages** as shown in Figure W4.7. Click in each of the remaining circles and type the text as shown in Figure W4.7. (Press Enter before typing the text in each circle.)

    Step 11

13. Click outside the drawing canvas to deselect it and the chart.

14. Save, print, and then close **WordS4-06**.

FIGURE W4.7 Diagram

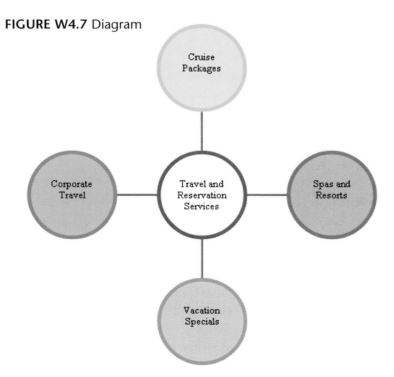

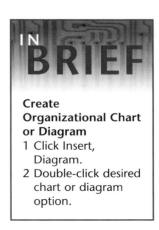

Create Organizational Chart or Diagram
1 Click Insert, Diagram.
2 Double-click desired chart or diagram option.

FEATURES SUMMARY

Feature	Button	Menu	Keyboard
Break dialog box		Insert, Break	
Columns dialog box		Format, Columns	
Compare and Merge dialog box		Tools, Compare and Merge Documents	
Convert Text to Table dialog box		Table, Convert, Text to Table	
Create columns	▦		
Diagram Gallery		Insert, Diagram	
Header pane		View, Header and Footer	
Insert a column	▦	Table, Insert, Columns to the Left or columns to the Right	
Insert a row	▦	Table, Insert, Rows Above or Rows Below	
Insert a comment		Insert, Comment	
Insert Hyperlink dialog box	▦	Insert, Hyperlink	Ctrl + K
Insert Table dialog box		Table, Insert, Table	
Outline view	▦	View, Outline	
Research task pane	▦	Tools, Research	Alt + Click
Save document as Web page		File, Save as Web Page	
Select a column		Table, Select, Column	
Select a row		Table, Select, Row	
Select the entire table		Table, Select, Table	
Table grid	▦		
Theme dialog box		Format, Theme	
Track changes	▦	Tools, Track Changes	Ctrl + Shift + E

PROCEDURES CHECK

Completion: In the space provided at the right, indicate the correct term, command, or option.

1. Use this button on the Standard toolbar to create a table. _____
2. Use this keyboard command to move the insertion point to the previous cell in a table. _____
3. To add shading to a cell or selected cells, display this dialog box. _____

4. To merge cells A1 and B1, select A1 and B1 and then click this option at the Table drop-down menu.

5. Choose predesigned table formats at this dialog box. _____

6. Click these options to display the Break dialog box. _____

7. Click this button on the Standard toolbar to create columns of equal width. _____

8. Insert a line between columns with the *Line between* option at this dialog box. _____

9. Display the header pane by clicking this option on the Menu bar and then clicking Header and Footer. _____

10. Switch to the footer pane by clicking this button on the Header and Footer toolbar. _____

11. Save a document as a Web page by clicking File and then this option. _____

12. Apply a predesigned background to a Web page with options at this dialog box. _____

13. Preview the Web page in the default browser at this view. _____

14. Click this button on the Reviewing toolbar to reject a change. _____

15. Click these options to display the Diagram Gallery. _____

SKILLS REVIEW

Activity 1: CREATING A TABLE

1 At a clear document screen, create a table with six rows and four columns.
2 Type the text in the cells as shown in Figure W4.8.
3 Save the table and name it **WordS4-R1**.

FIGURE W4.8 Activity 1

Course	Name	Days	Time
TR 101	Intro to Theatre	MTWRF	8:00 – 8:50 a.m.
TR 101	Intro to Theatre	MW	1:00 – 2:40 p.m.
TR 125	Beginning Acting	MTWR	9:00 – 9:50 a.m.
TR 211	Set Design	MTW	10:00 – 10:50 a.m.
TR 251	Costume Design	MW	3:00 – 4:20 p.m.

Activity 2: MODIFYING AND FORMATTING A TABLE

1 With **WordS4-R1** open, insert a new column at the right side of the table.
2 Type the following text in the new cells:
   Instructor
   Crowe
   Crowe
   Rubine
   McAllister
   Auve

3   Insert a row above the first row.
4   Select the new row and then merge the selected cells.
5   In the top row, type **THEATRE ARTS DIVISION – FALL SCHEDULE**.
6   Bold and center *THEATRE ARTS DIVISION – FALL SCHEDULE* in the cell.
7   Select the second row (contains the text *Course*, *Name*, *Days*, and so on) and then bold and center the text in the cells.
8   Decrease the width of the cells so the table appears as shown in Figure W4.9.
9   Save **WordS4-R1**.

FIGURE W4.9 Activity 2

THEATRE ARTS DIVISION - FALL SCHEDULE				
Course	**Name**	**Days**	**Time**	**Instructor**
TR 101	Intro to Theatre	MTWRF	8:00 – 8:50 a.m.	Crowe
TR 101	Intro to Theatre	MW	1:00 – 2:40 p.m.	Crowe
TR 125	Beginning Acting	MTWR	9:00 – 9:50 a.m.	Rubine
TR 211	Set Design	MTW	10:00 – 10:50 a.m.	McAllister
TR 251	Costume Design	MW	3:00 – 4:20 p.m.	Auve

Activity 3: APPLYING BORDERS AND SHADING TO A TABLE; APPLYING AN AUTOFORMAT

1   With **WordS4-R1** open, apply a thick/thin border to the table and add light green shading to all cells in the table.
2   Select the second row in the table (contains *Course*, *Name*, *Days*, and so on) and then add light gray shading to the row.
3   Save and then print **WordS4-R1**.
4   Apply the Table Colorful 1 autoformat to the table.
5   Save, print, and then close **WordS4-R1**.

Activity 4: INSERTING A SECTION BREAK; CREATING AND MODIFYING NEWSPAPER COLUMNS

1   Open **FCTHawaiianSpecials**.
2   Save the document with Save As and name it **WordS4-R2**.
3   Complete a spelling and grammar check on the document. (*Molokini* is spelled correctly.)
4   Position the insertion point at the beginning of the heading *White Sands Charters* and then insert a continuous section break.
5   With the insertion point positioned below the section break, format the text below the section break into two columns of equal width with .6 inch of space between the columns and a line between the columns.
6   Balance the two columns on the second (last) page in the document.
7   Save **WordS4-R2**.

Activity 5: INSERTING AND MODIFYING A FOOTER

1   With **WordS4-R2** open, select the entire document, and then change the font to a typeface (other than Times New Roman) of your choosing.

2 Bold the title *HAWAIIAN SPECIALS* and the headings (*White Sands Charters*, *Air Adventures*, *Deep Sea Submarines*, *Snorkeling Fantasies*, and *Bicycle Safari*).

3 Move the insertion point to the beginning of the document and then insert a footer that prints centered and bolded at the bottom of each page and reads *Hawaiian Specials - #* (where the page number is inserted in place of the # symbol).

4 Select the footer and change the font to the same typeface as chosen in Step 1. (Make sure the footer is bolded.)

5 Save **WordS4-R2**.

Activity 6: SAVING A DOCUMENT AS A WEB PAGE; CREATING A HYPERLINK; USING WEB PAGE PREVIEW

1 With **WordS4-R2** open, save the document as a Web page and name it **HawaiianNewsletter**.

2 Apply a theme background of your choosing to the Web page.

3 Move the insertion point toward the end of the document approximately a double space below the text.

4 Type **For more information on Hawaii, visit the Hawaii Tourism Authority Web site.**

5 Select the text *Hawaii Tourism Authority* and then insert a hyperlink to the Hawaii Tourism Authority at www.hawaii.gov/tourism.

6 Make sure you are connected to the Internet, hold down the Ctrl key, and then click the Hawaii Tourism Authority hyperlink.

7 At the Hawaii Tourism Authority site, click on any hyperlinks that interest you. When you are finished, click File and then Close.

8 Preview the Web page in Web Page Preview.

9 After viewing the page, click File and then Close to close the browser.

10 Save, print, and then close **HawaiianNewsletter**.

Activity 7: COMPARING AND MERGING DOCUMENTS

1 Open **WordS4-R2**.

2 Compare **WordS4-R2** with **FCTHawaiianSpecials** and merge the results to a new document.

3 Save the merged document and name it **WordS4-R3**.

4 Print and then close **WordS4-R3**. (Make sure the results print.)

5 With **WordS4-R2** open, move the insertion point to the end of the only paragraph in the *White Sands Charters* section and then insert the comment *These times have changed. Please call the charter company for the current times.*

6 Move the insertion point to the end of the heading *Air Adventures* and then insert the comment *Please include prices.*

7 Print only the comments.

8 Save and then close **WordS4-R2**.

Activity 8: CREATING AN ORGANIZATIONAL CHART

1 Open **MPProdDept**.

2 Save the document with Save As and name it **WordS4-R4**.

3 Press Ctrl + End to move the insertion point to the end of the document and then insert the organizational chart shown in Figure W4.10. Apply the Bookend Fills autoformat to the chart.

4 Save, print, and then close **WordS4-R4**.

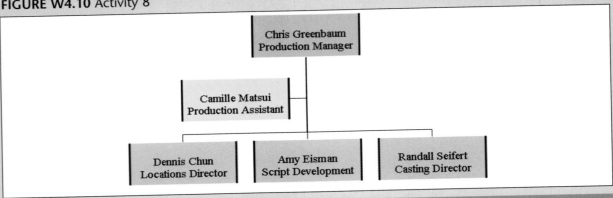

PERFORMANCE PLUS

Assessment 1: CREATING A TABLE FOR THE WATERFRONT BISTRO

1 At a clear document screen, create the table shown in Figure W4.11 for The Waterfront Bistro. Be sure to include the modifications and formatting as shown in the table. Set the title *CATERED LUNCH OPTIONS* in 16-point size.

2 Save the completed table and name it **WordS4-P1**.

3 Print and then close **WordS4-P1**.

FIGURE W4.11 Assessment 1

CATERED LUNCH OPTIONS			
Option	Contents	Cost Per Person	Discount Price
Option A: Hot	Vegetarian quiche, Caesar salad, vegetables, dressing, dessert, and beverages	$8.75	$7.95
Option B: Deli	Turkey or ham sandwiches, chips, vegetables, dressing, brownies, and beverages	$7.50	$6.55
Option C: Continental	Bagels, rolls, cream cheese, vegetables, dressing, cookies, and beverages	$6.75	$6.00

Assessment 2: FORMATTING A THEATRE ARTS DIVISION NEWSLETTER

1 Open **NPCTheatreNewsletter**.

2 Save the document with Save As and name it **WordS4-P2**.

3 Select the entire document and then change the font to a font of your choosing (other than Times New Roman).

4 Bold the title *THEATRE ARTS DIVISION* and the headings (*Division Description*, *Division Faculty*, and *Division Productions*).

5 Insert a continuous section break at the beginning of the heading *Division Description* and then format the document into newspaper columns (you determine the number of columns and the formatting of the columns).

6 Balance the columns on the last page in the document.

7 Insert a footer of your choosing in the newsletter. Format the footer in the same font as the document text.

8 Save, print, and then close **WordS4-P2**.

Assessment 3: COMPARING AND MERGING DOCUMENTS

1 Open **WordS4-P2**.
2 Compare **WordS4-P2** with **NPCTheatreNewsletter** and merge the results to a new document.
3 Save the new document and name it **WordS4-P3**.
4 Print and then close **WordS4-P3**.
5 Close **WordS4-P2**.

Assessment 4: CREATING AN ORGANIZATIONAL CHART

1 Open **PTDesignDept**.
2 Save the document with Save As and name it **WordS4-P4**.
3 Move the insertion point to the end of the document and then create an organizational chart (you determine the autoformat) with the following information:

Camilla Yong
Design Manager

Scott Bercini	Terri Cantrell	Paul Gottlieb
Designer	Designer/Sewer	Designer/Sewer

4 Save, print, and then close **WordS4-P4**.

Assessment 5: INSERTING FORMULAS IN A TABLE

1 Use Word's Help feature to learn how to perform calculations in a table and specifically how to total numbers in a row or column.
2 Open **WESales**. Save the document with Save As and name it **WordS4-P5**.
3 Using the information you learned about totaling numbers in a row or column, insert a formula in the cell immediately below *Total* that sums the amount in the cell immediately below *First Half* and the amount in the cell immediately below *Second Half*.
4 Insert a formula in each of the remaining cells in the *Total* column that sums the amount in the *First Half* column with the amount in the *Second Half* column.
5 Save, print, and then close **WordS4-P5**.

Assessment 6: CONVERTING A TABLE TO TEXT

1 Use Word's Help feature to learn how to convert a table to text.
2 Open **WordS4-R1**. Save the document with Save As and name it **WordS4-P6**.
3 Convert the table to text, separating text with tabs.
4 Save, print, and then close **WordS4-P6**.

Assessment 7: LOCATING INFORMATION AND WRITING A MEMO

1 You are Camille Matsui, production assistant for Marquee Productions. Chris Greenbaum, the production manager, has asked you to find information on renting a car in Toronto. Connect to the Internet and search for a car rental company in the Toronto area. Locate pricing information on economy and midsize cars and also minivans. Find out the daily rental fees for each as well as the weekly rental fee.
2 Using the information you find on the Internet, write a memo to Chris Greenbaum that includes a table containing the information you found on car rentals. Modify and format the table so the information in the table is attractive and easy to read.
3 Save the completed memo and name it **WordS4-P7**.
4 Print and then close **WordS4-P7**.

MARQUEE SERIES

MICROSOFT®
EXCEL
2003

EMCParadigm
PUBLISHING

NITA RUTKOSKY
Pierce College at Puyallup – Puyallup, Washington

DENISE SEGUIN
Fanshawe College – London, Ontario

CONTENTS

The Marquee Series Team: Desiree Faulkner, Developmental Editor; Leslie Anderson, Senior Designer; Jennifer Wreisner, Cover Designer; Leslie Anders Erica Tava, Desktop Production; Teri Linander, Tester; Sharon O'Donnell, Copyeditor; Lynn Reichel, Proofreader; and Nancy Fulton, Indexer.

Publishing Team: George Provol, Publisher; Janice Johnson, Director of Product Development; Tony Galvin, Acquisitions Editor; Lori Landwer, Marketin Manager; Shelley Clubb, Electronic Design and Production Manager.

Acknowledgment: The authors and publisher wish to thank the following reviewer for her technical and academic assistance in testing exercises and asses instruction: Susan Lynn Bowen, Valdosta Technical College, Valdosta, GA.

Library of Congress Cataloging-in-Publication Data
Rutkosky, Nita Hewitt.
Microsoft Excel 2003 / Nita Rutkosky, Denise Seguin.
p.cm. – (Marquee series)
Includes index.
ISBN 0-7638-2073-3 (text) – ISBN 0-7638-2072-5 (text & CD)
1. Microsoft Excel for Windows. 2. Business—Computer programs. 3. Electronic spreadsheets. I. Seguin, Denise. II. Title. III. Series

Text + CD: 0-7638-2072-5
Order Number: 05628

© 2004 by Paradigm Publishing Inc.
Published by **EMC**Paradigm
875 Montreal Way
St. Paul, MN 55102

(800) 535-6865
E-mail: educate@emcp.com
Web site: www.emcp.com

Printed in the United States of America   10 9 8 7 6 5 4

Introducing EXCEL 2003

Microsoft Excel 2003 is a popular choice among individuals and companies to organize, analyze, and present data organized in columns and rows in a document called a *worksheet*. A worksheet is the electronic version of an accountant's ledger—only with a lot more power and versatility. The potential uses for an application like Excel are only limited by your imagination—any type of document that can be set up in the column/row format is a candidate for an Excel worksheet.

Once a worksheet has been created you can perform *what-if* analysis. What if sales increase by 4 percent? What if spending on new equipment decreases? Changing a value in a worksheet causes Excel to automatically recalculate any other values that are dependent on the number you changed. In an instant you have your answer. This type of dynamic data analysis is one of the reasons working with Excel is a large part of the daily activity in today's workplace.

While working in Excel, you will produce business documents and manage business data for the following six companies:

 First Choice Travel is a travel center offering a full range of traveling services from booking flights, hotel reservations, and rental cars to offering traveling seminars.

 Marquee Productions is involved in all aspects of creating movies from script writing and development to filming.

 The Waterfront Bistro offers fine dining for lunch and dinner and also offers banquet facilities, a wine cellar, and catering services.

 Performance Threads maintains an inventory of rental costumes and also researches, designs, and sews special-order and custom-made costumes.

 Worldwide Enterprises is a national and international distributor of products for a variety of companies and is the exclusive movie distribution agent for Marquee Productions.

 The mission of the Niagara Peninsula College Theatre Arts Division is to offer a curriculum designed to provide students with a thorough exposure to all aspects of the theatre arts.

Preparing Workbooks and Analyzing Data Using Excel 2003

Excel 2003 is the application of choice to set up financial, statistical, or other types of information in columns and rows and then track, analyze, and chart the data. Create formulas to perform calculations and manipulate values to answer questions or create different scenarios. Excel's editing and formatting features as well as visual elements that can be added improve the presentation of data and help reader's understand complex information. Interesting Excel features and elements that you will learn in each section are described below.

Section 1
Analyzing Data Using Excel

Start your Excel experience by learning the basics of creating and editing an Excel worksheet that calculates a weekly payroll for The Waterfront Bistro.

Worksheet Created in Topics 1.2 – 1.8

	A	B	C	D	E	F	G	H	I	J	K
1						Payroll					
2					Week Ended: September 24, 2005						
3									Total	Pay	Gross
4	Name	Sun	Mon	Tue	Wed	Thu	Fri	Sat	Hours	Rate	Wage
5	Assante	8	5	6	8	7	0	6	40	7.35	$294.00
6	Corlliere	8	0	7	5	7	5	8	40	6.95	$278.00
7	Hill	8	0	0	8	8	8	8	40	8.25	$330.00
8	Knight	8	7	5	8	0	0	7	35	6.95	$243.25
9	Racine	8	6	5	5	0	8	8	40	6.95	$278.00
10	Su-Lin	8	0	5	0	8	8	5	34	6.95	$236.30
11											
12	Total	48	18	28	34	30	29	42	229		$1,659.55
13											
14	Hours Proof	229									
15	Gross Wage Proof	$294.00	$1,659.55								
16											
17	Worksheet prepared by: Student Name										

In Section 1, you will learn how to create labels, values, and formulas.

Section 2
Editing and Formatting Worksheets

Edit a quotation for catering services to be provided to Marquee Productions by copying and moving cells; performing a spell check; inserting, deleting, and hiding columns; and adjusting column widths and row heights. Apply formatting options to improve the worksheet's appearance. Learn to work with larger worksheets by freezing panes, splitting windows, and changing the zoom.

Quotation Created in Topics 2.1 – 2.8

The *Waterfront* Bistro

3104 Rivermist Drive
Buffalo, NY 14280
716-555-3166

Quotation

To:	Marquee Productions		Date:	21-Nov-05
	955 South Alameda Street			
	Los Angeles, CA 90037			
Attention:	Camille Matsui			
Re:	Toronto Location Filming			
	July 4 through August 31, 2005			

You can choose to hide columns or rows containing confidential information. By default, hidden columns do not print.

Item	No. of Persons	Price Per Person	No. of Days	Total		Our Cost	Gross Margin		GM Percent
Buffet Lunch	56	5.98	40	$	13,395.20	3.82	$	4,838.40	36.1%
Soup and salad									
Vegetable tray with dip									
Seafood hors d'oeuvres									
Hot entrée									
Deli tray and rolls									
Dessert									
Beverages	56	3.98	40		8,915.20	2.12		4,166.40	46.7%
Coffee and tea									
Assorted juice									
Mineral water									
Snacks	56	3.98	40		8,915.20	1.22		6,182.40	69.3%
Muffins									
Donuts									
Fruit tray									
Vegetable tray with dip									
Delivery		31	40		1,240.00	23.00		320.00	25.8%
Total				$	**32,465.60**		$	15,507.20	47.8%

Quotation is valid for 30 days
Note: All prices are tax included
Terms: Due upon receipt of invoice payable in US funds

Quotation Edited for Printing Customer Copy in Topics 2.9 – 2.11

The *Waterfront* Bistro

3104 Rivermist Drive
Buffalo, NY 14280
716-555-3166

Quotation

To:	Marquee Productions		Date:	21-Nov-05
	955 South Alameda Street			
	Los Angeles, CA 90037			
Attention:	Camille Matsui			
Re:	Toronto Location Filming			
	July 4 through August 31, 2005			

Quotation is edited before printing the customer's copy by hiding columns containing cost information and applying an autoformat to add color to the body of the quotation.

Item	No. of Persons	Price Per Person	No. of Days	Total	
Buffet Lunch	56	5.98	43	$	14,399.84
Soup and salad					
Vegetable tray with dip					
Seafood hors d'oeuvres					
Hot entrée					
Deli tray and rolls					
Dessert					
Beverages	56	3.98	43		9,583.84
Coffee and tea					
Assorted juice					
Mineral water					
Snacks	56	3.98	43		9,583.84
Muffins					
Donuts					
Fruit tray					
Vegetable tray with dip					
Delivery		31	43		1,333.00
Total				$	34,900.52

Quotation is valid for 30 days
Note: All prices are tax included
Terms: Due upon receipt of invoice payable in US funds

Using Functions, Setting Print Options, and Adding Visual Elements

Excel's statistical, date, financial, and logical functions are available to assist with creating formulas to analyze data. Add print options to control the printed copy of a worksheet. Create a chart, draw arrows, and add text boxes to further enhance a worksheet and draw a reader's attention to specific cells.

Inventory Units Purchased Worksheet with Statistical Functions Added in Topic 3.1

The Waterfront Bistro

Item	Unit	January	February
Cloves	case	1	0
Allspice	case	1	0
Seasoned Salt	case	1	0
Salt	case	1	1
Pepper	case	1	0
Total		101	65
Check Total	1033		
Average Units Purchased		2	1
Maximum Units Purchased		6	5
Minimum Units Purchased		0	0

AVERAGE, MAX, and MIN functions used to calculate statistics on inventory units purchased worksheet.

Using Date Functions in an Invoice in Topic 3.2

	A	B	C	D	E
1	The		3104 Rivermist Drive		
2			Buffalo, NY 14280		
3		Waterfront	(716) 555-3166		
4		Bistro	www.emcp.net/wfbistro		
5			Proudly serving you since		Jun-77
6			**Invoice**		
7	To:	Performance Threads		Date:	30-Aug-2005
8		4011 Bridgewater Street			
9		Niagara Falls, ON L2E 2T6		Due Date:	29-Sep-2005
10					
11	Attention:	Bobbie Sinclair			
12	Re:	Director's Meeting			
13	Item		No. of Persons	Price per Person	Total
14	1	Appetizer trays	15	4.15	62.25
15	2	Prime rib dinner	15	27.95	419.25
16	3	Dessert trays	15	6.55	98.25
17	4	Coffee and tea	15	1.35	20.25
18		Meeting room charge	15	3.50	52.50
19					
20		Total			652.50
21					
22	Note: All prices include tax and gratuity				
23	Terms: Due upon receipt of invoice payable in US funds				

The date in this c is enter using th DATE function and ther the cell i formatte to displa the date the form shown.

The NOW function in this cell causes the current date to appear when the invoice is opened or printed.

The due date for the invoice is calculated using a formula that adds 30 days to the invoice date.

Calculating Monthly Payments for a Loan in Topic 3.3

The Waterfront Bistro

Payments on expansion loan from Royal International Trust	
Interest Rate	10.25%
Amortization (years)	10
Loan Amount	$415,000
Monthly Payment	($5,541.87)

The PMT function is used here to calculate the monthly payments for a loan based on the above three values.

Visual Elements Added to Expenses Worksheet in Topics 3.8 – 3.11

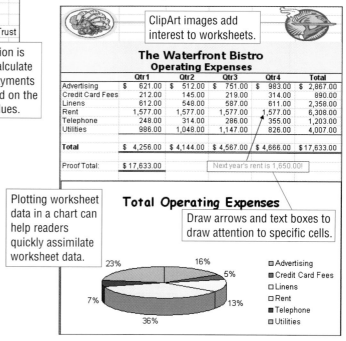

ClipArt images add interest to worksheets.

The Waterfront Bistro
Operating Expenses

	Qtr 1	Qtr 2	Qtr 3	Qtr 4	Total
Advertising	$ 621.00	$ 512.00	$ 751.00	$ 983.00	$ 2,867.00
Credit Card Fees	212.00	145.00	219.00	314.00	890.00
Linens	612.00	548.00	587.00	611.00	2,358.00
Rent	1,577.00	1,577.00	1,577.00	1,577.00	6,308.00
Telephone	248.00	314.00	286.00	355.00	1,203.00
Utilities	986.00	1,048.00	1,147.00	826.00	4,007.00
Total	$ 4,256.00	$ 4,144.00	$ 4,567.00	$ 4,666.00	$17,633.00
Proof Total:	$ 17,633.00		Next year's rent is 1,650.00!		

Plotting worksheet data in a chart can help readers quickly assimilate worksheet data.

Total Operating Expenses

Draw arrows and text boxes to draw attention to specific cells.

23%
16%
5%
7%
13%
36%

- ▫ Advertising
- ■ Credit Card Fees
- ▫ Linens
- ▫ Rent
- ■ Telephone
- ▫ Utilities

Section 4
Working with Multiple Worksheets and Workbooks and Managing Files

Organize large amounts of data using multiple worksheets and include formulas that reference cells in other worksheets within the same workbook. Other features you will learn include working in Page Break Preview, templates, styles, Web pages, filtering and sorting lists, adding comments and diagrams, using the Research task pane, viewing multiple open workbooks, and file management techniques.

Quarterly Sales Organized in Multiple Worksheets and Summarized in Topics 4.1 – 4.3

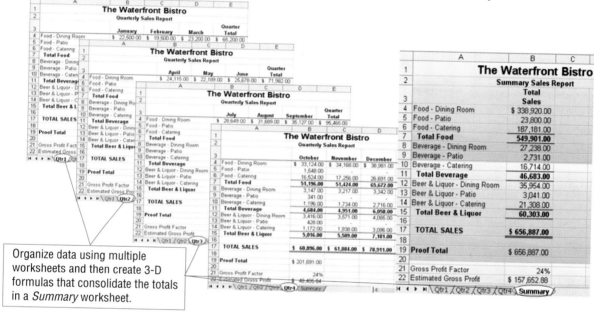

Organize data using multiple worksheets and then create 3-D formulas that consolidate the totals in a *Summary* worksheet.

Invoice to Performance Threads Created in Topic 4.6

Save time by using a template to create a sales invoice with preset formatting and formulas already built for calculations.

Formatting an Employee Schedule Using Styles, Inserting a Hyperlink, and Saving as a Web Page in Topics 4.7 – 4.8

Format using styles to maintain consistency and allow you to make changes quickly.

Employee Schedule
For the Week of February 6 - 12, 2005

Save a worksheet as a Web page for viewing in a browser.

Time	Sunday	Monday	Tuesday	Wednesday	Thursday	Friday	Saturday
7am - 3pm	Assante Hill	Assante Hill	Assante Hill	Assante Hill	Assante Hill	Corlliere Racine	Corlliere Racine
3pm - 11pm	Knight Su-Lin	Corlliere Knight	Corlliere Knight	Racine Su-Lin	Assante Racine	Knight Su-Lin	Knight Su-Lin
6pm - 2am						Knight Su-Lin	Knight Su-Lin

Next Week's Schedule

Add hyperlinks to allow users to navigate to a related worksheet or Web page.

Adding Comments and a Diagram to the Sales Worksheet in Topic 4.10

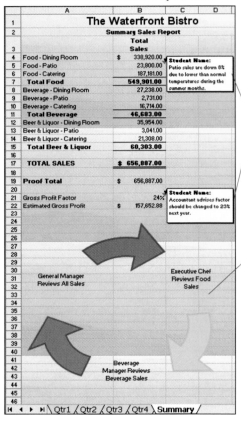

Comments provide instructions, identify significant information, or add other explanatory text to a cell.

Options in the Diagram Gallery can be used to add an organizational chart or depict relationships between steps or processes with a cycle, target, radial, venn, or pyramid diagram.

Finding Current Stock Prices Using the Research Task Pane in Topic 4.11

The *Waterfront* Bistro

Investment Scenario for Cash Surplus

Basic savings account interest rate	2.15%	per annum
Number of investment payments	10	years
Cash surplus available each year	$75,000	per annum
Future Value of Investment:	($826,883.39)	

Stock Watch

	Current Stock Price
International Business Machines (IBM)	US:IBM 83.59
Dell Computers (Dell)	US:DELL 31.92
General Electric (GE)	US:GE 28.63

		Market Value
International Business Machines (IBM)	83.59	$ 125,385
Dell Computers (Dell)	31.92	$ 47,880
General Electric (GE)	28.63	$ 42,945
Total Market Value of Stocks:		$ 216,210

Use the Research task pane to find and then insert current stock prices.

EXCEL

Analyzing Data Using Excel

Microsoft Excel is an application that is used to track, analyze, and chart numeric information such as financial data, statistical values, grades, or any other items that can be established in columns and rows. Once data has been entered in an Excel worksheet, you can create formulas to perform mathematical computations. Once these formulas are in place, you can manipulate the values to answer questions or create several scenarios. For example, if you are planning on buying a house, you could enter various house prices, down payment amounts, and interest rates, and use Excel to estimate mortgage payments. In this section you will learn the skills and complete the projects described here.

Note: Before beginning this section, copy to a disk or other location the ExcelS1 subfolder from the Excel folder on the CD that accompanies this textbook and then make ExcelS1 the active folder. Steps on copying a folder, deleting a folder, and making a folder active are located on the inside back cover of this textbook.

Skills

- Start Excel and identify features in the Excel window
- Enter labels and values
- Use the fill handle to enter a series
- Enter formulas
- Create a formula using AutoSum
- Copy a relative formula
- Test a worksheet for accuracy
- Apply the Currency format to values
- Right-align labels
- Use the Help feature
- Change the page orientation to landscape
- Preview and print a worksheet
- Save a workbook using Save and Save As
- Close a workbook and exit Excel
- Navigate a large worksheet using the mouse and the keyboard
- Jump to a specific cell using Go To

Projects

The Waterfront Bistro

Edit a weekly sales report, create a payroll worksheet, browse an inventory report, and create a condensed quarterly income statement.

MARQUEE PRODUCTIONS

Complete an estimated travel expenses worksheet.

Performance Threads
Theatrical Fabrics, Costumes and Supplies

Prepare a price estimate for costume design and rental.

WORLDWIDE Enterprises

Create a projected distribution revenue schedule for a new movie release.

1.1 Completing the Excel Worksheet Cycle

Information is created in Excel in a **_worksheet_** and is saved in a file called a **_workbook_**. A workbook can contain several worksheets. Imagine a worksheet as a page with horizontal and vertical lines drawn in a grid representing columns and rows. Data is entered into a **_cell,_** which is the intersection of a column with a row. Columns are lettered A to Z, AA to AZ, BA to BZ, and so on. The last column in the worksheet is labeled *IV*. Rows are numbered 1, 2, 3, and so on. A column letter and a row number identify each cell. For example, A1 is the cell address for the intersection of column A with row 1. Each worksheet in Excel contains 256 columns and 65,536 rows. In a default Excel 2003 installation, a workbook contains three worksheets labeled *Sheet1, Sheet2,* and *Sheet3.*

PROJECT: You have been asked to analyze data in a weekly sales report for The Waterfront Bistro by adding data and viewing the impact of changing a cell used to calculate gross margin.

STEPS

1. At the Windows XP desktop, click the Start button 🔊 *start* on the Taskbar.
2. Point to All Programs.
3. Point to Microsoft Office.
4. Click Microsoft Office Excel 2003.

   Depending on your operating system and/or system configuration, the steps you complete to open Excel may vary somewhat.

5. At the Excel screen, identify the various features by comparing your screen with the one shown in Figure E1.1. Depending on your system configuration, your screen may vary slightly. (See Table E1.1 for a description of the screen features.)

FIGURE E1.1 The Excel Screen

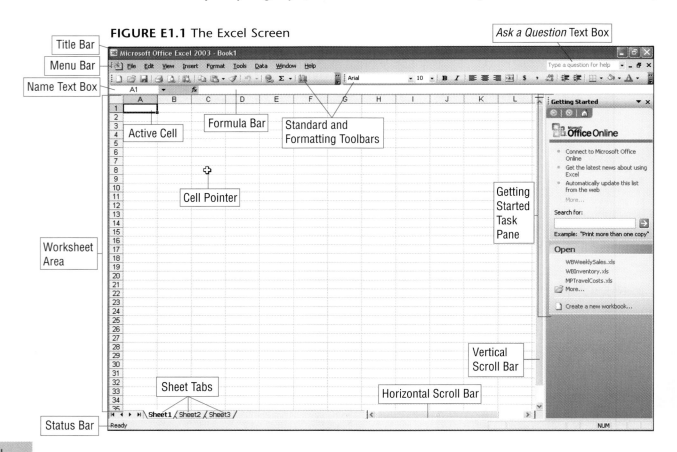

TABLE E1.1 Excel Screen Features

Feature	Description
Title Bar	Displays program name followed by workbook name
Menu Bar	Contains options used to manage and customize workbooks
Ask a Question Text Box	Used to access help
Standard and Formatting Toolbars	Contain buttons that are shortcuts for popular commands
Name Text Box	Displays the active cell address
Formula Bar	Displays the active cell entry
Active Cell	Location in the worksheet that will display keyed data or that will be affected by a command
Cell Pointer	Used to select cells
Scroll Bars	Used to navigate the worksheet
Sheet Tabs	Identifies the worksheets in the workbook
Worksheet Area	Contains cells used to create the worksheet
Status Bar	Displays information about a command or process
Task Pane	Contains options related to current task being performed

6 Click the Open button on the Standard toolbar or click the <u>More</u> hyperlink More... in the Getting Started task pane.

7 Make sure the ExcelS1 folder on your disk is the active folder.

> To change to a different drive, click the down-pointing arrow at the right of the *Look in* list box and then select the correct drive from the drop-down list. Double-clicking a folder name in the file list box changes the active folder.

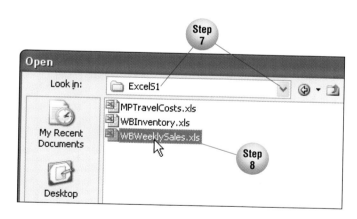

8 Double-click *WBWeeklySales.*

> This workbook contains one worksheet with sales for The Waterfront Bistro for the week ended September 24, 2005. The formulas to sum the sales have already been created. Notice some of the cells in the column labeled *Saturday* are empty. You will enter these values in Steps 11 through 14.

(continued)

9 Click File and then Save As.

> Use the Save option to save a file using the same name. If you want to keep the original workbook and save the workbook with the changes under a new name, use Save As.

10 At the Save As dialog box, make sure the ExcelS1 folder on your disk is the active folder, type **ExcelS1-01** in the *File name* text box, and then press Enter or click Save.

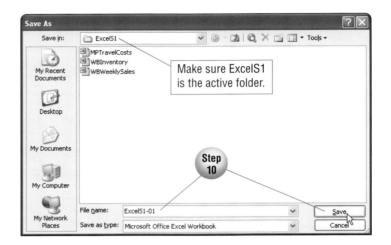

The *Save in* option at the Save As dialog box displays the active folder. If you need to make the ExcelS1 folder on your disk in drive A the active folder, click the down-pointing arrow at the right of the Save in option box and then click *3½ Floppy (A:)*. Double-click **ExcelS1** in the file list box. Excel automatically adds the file extension *.xls* to the end of a workbook name.

	G	H	I
	Friday	Saturday	Total
	1,455.00	1,948.00	9,994.00
	554.00	761.00	3,580.00
	3,175.00		8,213.00
	5,184.00	2,709.00	21,787.00
	198.00	235.00	1,510.00
	84.00	122.00	742.00
	394.00		1,511.00
	676.00	357.00	3,763.00

Step 11

11 Move the cell pointer over the intersection of column H with row 6 and click to make H6 the active cell.

12 Type **1750** and then press Enter.

> Notice that the entry in H7 has changed. This is because the formula created in H7 was dependent on H6. As soon as you enter a value in H6, any other dependent cells are automatically updated. Can you identify other cells that changed as a result of the new value in H6?

	G	H	I
	Friday	Saturday	Total
	1,455.00	1,948.00	9,994.00
	554.00	761.00	3,580.00
	3,175.00	1,750.00	9,963.00
	5,184.00	4,459.00	23,537.00
	198.00	235.00	1,510.00
	84.00	122.00	742.00
	394.00	371.00	1,882.00
	676.00	728.00	4,134.00
	487.00	624.00	4,040.00
	278.00	341.00	1,624.00
	1,267.00	837.00	4,628.00
	2,032.00	1,802.00	10,292.00
	7,892.00	6,989.00	37,963.00

Step 12

Step 13

Step 14

PROBLEM?

> Typing mistake? Press Backspace to delete the characters to the left of the insertion point and then type the correct text.

13 Make H10 the active cell and then type **371**.

14 Make H14 the active cell and then type **837**.

(15) Look at the entry in B19. This percentage is used to calculate the estimated gross profit in row 20 (Total Sales times the Gross Profit Factor). You will change the value in B19 to see the effect on the estimated gross profit values.

(16) Make B19 the active cell, type **24%**, and then press Enter.

Notice the new estimated gross profit values in cells B20 through I20.

Step 16

17	TOTAL SALES	9,567.00	1,674.00	2,353.00	4,351.00	5,137.00	7,892.00	6,989.00	37,963.00
18									
19	Gross Profit Factor	24%							
20	Estimated Gross Profit	2,296.08	401.76	564.72	1,044.24	1,232.88	1,894.08	1,677.36	9,111.12

New Estimated Gross Profit values as a result of changing B19.

(17) Click the Save button [icon] on the Standard toolbar.

(18) Click the Print button [icon] on the Standard toolbar.

The worksheet will print on two pages. Later in this section you will learn how to change the page orientation to landscape so that a wide worksheet will fit on one page.

(19) Click File and then Close.

Excel displays a blue-gray screen in the worksheet area when no workbooks are currently open.

(20) Click File and then Exit.

In Addition

AutoComplete

The AutoComplete feature in Excel will complete text entries for you as you start to type a new entry in a cell. If the first few letters that you type match another entry in the column, Excel automatically fills in the remaining text. Press Tab or Enter to accept the text Excel suggests, or continue typing the correct text. You can turn off AutoComplete by clicking Tools and then Options. Click the Edit tab in the Options dialog box, click the *Enable AutoComplete for cell values* check box to deselect it, and then click OK.

IN BRIEF

Start Excel
1 Click Start.
2 Point to All Programs.
3 Point to Microsoft Office.
4 Click Microsoft Office Excel 2003.

Open a Workbook
1 Click Open button.
2 Navigate to desired location and folder.
3 Double-click workbook name.

Save a Workbook with a New Name
1 Click File, Save As.
2 Type new workbook name.
3 Click Save or press Enter.

1.2 Entering Labels and Values; Using the Fill Handle

A *label* is an entry in a cell that helps the reader relate to the values in the corresponding column or row. Labels are generally entered first when creating a new worksheet since they define the layout of the data in the columns and rows. By default, Excel will align labels at the left edge of the column. A *value* is a number, formula, or function that can be used to perform calculations in the worksheet. By default, Excel will align values at the right edge of the column. Take a few moments to

plan or sketch out the layout of a new worksheet before entering labels and values. Decide what calculations you will need to perform and how to display the data so that it will be easily understood and interpreted.

PROJECT: You need to create a new payroll worksheet for The Waterfront Bistro. Begin by entering labels and values.

STEPS

① Start Excel.

② Type **Payroll** as the title for the new worksheet in A1.

> When you type a new entry in a cell, the entry appears in the Formula bar as well as within the active cell in the worksheet area. To end a cell entry, press Enter, move to another cell in the worksheet, or click the Enter button on the Formula bar.

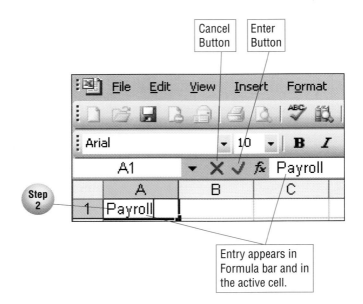

③ Press Enter.

PROBLEM **?**

If you catch a typing error after a cell has been completed, activate the cell and retype the entry.

4 With A2 the active cell, type **Week Ended: September 24, 2005** and then press Enter.

> Notice the entry in A2 is overflowing into columns B, C, and D. You can allow a label to spill over into adjacent columns as long as you do not plan to enter other data in the overflow cells. In a later section you will see how to adjust column widths.

5 Click the Close button ☒ at the top right corner of the Getting Started task pane.

> Closing the task pane will provide a larger viewing area for creating the payroll worksheet. Task panes are context-sensitive and will reappear when a command is being performed that has a task pane associated with it.

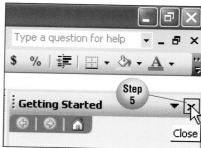

6 Enter the remaining labels as shown below. (Do not enter the labels for the days of the week except for *Sun*, as this will be done in the following steps.)

	A	B	C	D	E	F	G	H	I	J	K
1	Payroll										
2	Week Ended: September 24, 2005										
3											
4	Name	Sun							Total Hours	Pay Rate	Gross Wage
5	Assante										
6	Corlliere										
7	Hill										
8	Knight										
9	Racine										
10	Su-Lin										
11											
12	Total										
13											

Step 4 ... *Step 6*

7 Click B4 to make it the active cell.

> The active cell is displayed with a thick black border surrounding it. A small black square displays at the bottom right corner of the active cell. This black square is called the *fill handle*. The fill handle is used to fill adjacent cells with the same data or consecutive data. The entries that are automatically inserted in the adjacent cells are dependent on the contents of the active cell. You will use the fill handle in B4 to automatically enter the remaining days of the week in C4 through H4.

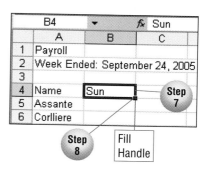

8 Point at the fill handle in B4. The cell pointer will change from the large white cross ⊹ to a thin black cross ✚.

(continued)

9 Hold down the left mouse button, drag the pointer to H4, and then release the mouse.

> The entries *Mon* through *Sat* appear in C4 to H4. As you drag the pointer to the right, a gray border surrounds the selected cells and a yellow box will appear below the pointer indicating the label or value that will be inserted. When you release the left mouse button, the cells remain selected and the Auto Fill Options button appears. Clicking the Auto Fill Options button will cause a drop-down list to appear with various alternatives for how to fill text or data in the cells.

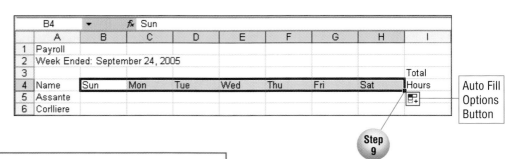

Step 9

PROBLEM

Mon–Sat do not appear? You probably dragged the mouse using the cell pointer instead of the fill handle. This selects cells instead of filling them. Go back to Step 7 and try again.

10 Click B5 to make it the active cell.

11 Type **8** and then press the Right Arrow key.

12 Type **5** in C5 and then press the Right Arrow key.

13 Type the following values in the cells indicated:

D5	=	6
E5	=	8
F5	=	7
G5	=	0
H5	=	6

14 Make B5 the active cell.

15 Point at the fill handle in B5 and then drag the pointer down to B10.

> This time the active cell contains a value. The value *8* is copied to the adjacent cells.

	A	B	C
1	Payroll		
2	Week Ended: September 24, 2005		
3			
4	Name	Sun	Mon	Tue
5	Assante	8	5
6	Corlliere	8	
7	Hill	8	
8	Knight	8	
9	Racine	8	
10	Su-Lin	8	
11			
12	Total		

Step 15

16 Enter the remaining values. Use the fill handle whenever possible to be more efficient.

	A	B	C	D	E	F	G	H	I	J	K
1	Payroll										
2	Week Ended: September 24, 2005										
3									Total	Pay	Gross
4	Name	Sun	Mon	Tue	Wed	Thu	Fri	Sat	Hours	Rate	Wage
5	Assante	8	5	6	8	7	0	6		7.35	
6	Corlliere	8	0	7	5	7	5	8		6.95	
7	Hill	8	0	0	8	8	8	8	Step 16	8.25	
8	Knight	8	7	5	8	0	0	7		6.95	
9	Racine	8	6	5	5	0	8	8		6.95	
10	Su-Lin	8	0	5	0	8	8	5		6.95	
11											
12	Total										

17 Click the Save button 🖫 on the Standard toolbar.

18 At the Save As dialog box, make sure the ExcelS1 folder on your disk is the active folder, type **ExcelS1-02** in the *File name* text box, and then press Enter.

In Addition

More about the Fill Command

In this topic you used the fill handle to continue the days of the week and copy a static value to adjacent cells. The fill handle is much more versatile and can be used to enter a series of values, dates, times, or other labels using a pattern. The pattern is established based on the cells you select before dragging the fill handle. In the worksheet shown below, the cells in columns C through F were all entered using the fill handle. In each row, the first two cells in columns A and B were selected and then the fill handle dragged right to column F. Notice the variety of patterns used to extend a series.

The Auto Fill Options button drop-down menu can be used to control how the series is entered. After dragging the fill handle, the Auto Fill Options button is displayed at the end of the series. Pointing at the button causes the button to expand and display a down arrow. Click the down-pointing arrow and then select the desired fill action from the options in the drop-down list. By default, Fill Series is active.

	A	B	C	D	E	F	G	H	I
1	Examples Using the Fill Handle to Continue a Series								
2	1	2	3	4	5	6			
3	10	20	30	40	50	60			
4	9:00	10:00	11:00	12:00	13:00	14:00			
5	2003	2004	2005	2006	2007	2008			
6	1st Qtr	2nd Qtr	3rd Qtr	4th Qtr	1st Qtr	2nd Qtr			
7	Period 1	Period 2	Period 3	Period 4	Period 5	Period 6			
8									
9							○ Copy Cells		
10							● Fill Series		
11							○ Fill Formatting Only		
12							○ Fill Without Formatting		
13									
14									

1.3 Performing Calculations Using Formulas

A *formula* is entered into a cell to perform mathematical calculations in a worksheet. All formulas in Excel begin with the equals sign (=) as the first character. After the equals sign, the cell addresses that contain the values you want to calculate are entered between mathematical operators. The mathematical operators are + (addition), - (subtraction), * (multiplication), / (division), and ^ (exponentiation). An example of a valid formula is =A3*B3. The value in A3 is multiplied by the value in B3 and the result is placed in the formula cell. By including the cell address in the formula rather than typing the actual value, you can utilize the powerful recalculation feature in Excel. If you change the contents of a cell that is included in a formula, the worksheet is automatically recalculated so that all values are current.

PROJECT: To calculate total hours and gross pay for the first two employees listed in the payroll worksheet for The Waterfront Bistro, you will use two methods to enter formulas.

S T E P S

1. With **ExcelS1-02** open, make I5 the active cell.

    Begin a formula by activating the cell in which you want the result placed.

2. Type **=b5+c5+d5+e5+f5+g5+h5** and then press Enter.

    The values in B5 through H5 are added and the result, *40*, is displayed in I5.

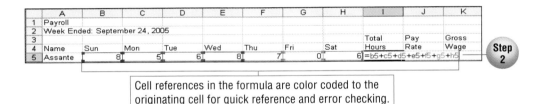

Cell references in the formula are color coded to the originating cell for quick reference and error checking.

3. Press the Up Arrow key to move the active cell back to I5.

    Notice that the result of the formula is displayed in the worksheet area and the formula used to calculate the result is shown in the Formula bar. Notice also that the column letters in cell addresses are automatically converted to uppercase.

4. Make I6 the active cell, type the formula **=b6+c6+d6+e6+f6+g6+h6**, and then press Enter.

    Seem like too much typing? A more efficient way to add a series of cells is available. This method will be introduced after you learn the pointing method for entering formulas.

5. Make K5 the active cell.

    To calculate gross wage you need to multiply the total hours times the pay rate. In Steps 6–10, you will enter this formula using the pointing method.

6. Type the equals sign (=).

7. Click I5.

    A moving dashed border (called a *marquee*) displays around I5, indicating it is the cell included in the formula, and the cell address is added to the formula cell (K5) with a blinking vertical bar (called the *insertion point*) after the reference. Notice also that the Status bar displays the action *Point*.

8 Type an asterisk (*).

The marquee surrounding cell I5 disappears and I5 is color coded with the cell reference I5 within the formula cell.

9 Click J5.

10 Click the Enter button ✓ on the Formula bar or press Enter.

11 Use the pointing method or type the formula **=I6*J6** to calculate the gross wage for Corlliere in K6.

12 Click the Save button 🖫 on the Standard toolbar.

I	J	K
Total Hours	Pay Rate	Gross Wage
40	7.35	=I5*J5
40	6.95	

Marquee displays around cell J5 in Step 9.

Steps 6–9

I	J	K
Total Hours	Pay Rate	Gross Wage
40	7.35	294
40	6.95	278

Step 11

In Addition

Order of Operations

If you include several operators in a formula, Excel calculates the result using the order of operations as follows: negations (e.g., -1) first, then percents (%), then exponentiations (^), then multiplication and division (* and /), and finally addition and subtraction (+ and -). If a formula contains more than one operator at the same level of precedence—for example, both an addition and subtraction operation—Excel calculates the equation from left to right. To change the order of operations, use parentheses around the part of the formula you want calculated first.

Examples:

=B5*C5/D5 — Both operators are at the same level of precedence—Excel would multiply the value in B5 times the value in C5 and then divide the result by the value in D5.

=(B5+B6+B7)*A10 — Excel would add the values in B5 through B7 before multiplying times the value in A10.

In BRIEF

Enter a Formula
1 Activate formula cell.
2 Type =.
3 Type first cell address.
4 Type operator.
5 Type second cell address.
6 Continue Steps 3–5 until finished.
7 Press Enter or click Enter button.

Enter a Formula Using the Pointing Method
1 Activate formula cell.
2 Type =.
3 Click first cell.
4 Type operator.
5 Click second cell.
6 Repeat Steps 3–5 until finished.
7 Press Enter or click Enter button.

1.4 Using AutoSum

The formulas to calculate the hours worked by the first two employees were rather lengthy. A more efficient way to calculate the total hours for Assante in I5 would be to enter the formula =SUM(B5:I5). This formula includes one of Excel's built-in functions called SUM. A function is a preprogrammed formula. The structure of a formula utilizing a function begins with the equals sign (=), followed by the name of the function, and then the *argument*. The argument is the term given to the values identified within parentheses. In the example provided, the argument B5:I5 contains the starting cell and the ending cell separated by a colon (:). This is called a *range* and is used when the cells to be added are located in a rectangular-shaped block of cells. Since the SUM function is used frequently, a button named *AutoSum* that will enter the SUM function is available on the Standard toolbar.

PROJECT: The management of The Waterfront Bistro wants you to find a more efficient method of payroll calculation, so you will use AutoSum to complete the hours worked for the payroll worksheet.

S T E P S

1 With **ExcelS1-02** open, make I5 the active cell and then press Delete.

> This deletes the formula in the cell. There was nothing wrong with the formula already entered in I5. You are deleting it so that the formulas in the completed worksheet will be consistent.

2 Click the AutoSum button **Σ** on the toolbar. (Do not click the down-pointing arrow to the right of AutoSum that is activated as the mouse is moved over the button.)

> A moving marquee surrounds cells B5 through H5 and a ScreenTip appears below the formula cell indicating the correct format for the SUM function. Excel enters the formula =SUM(B5:H5) in I5. The suggested range B5:H5 is selected within the formula so that you can highlight a different range with the mouse if the suggested range is not correct.

Step 2

	A	B	C	D	E	F	G	H	I	J	K
1	Payroll										
2	Week Ended: September 24, 2005										
3									Total	Pay	Gross
4	Name	Sun	Mon	Tue	Wed	Thu	Fri	Sat	Hours	Rate	Wage
5	Assante	8	5	6	8	7	0	6	=SUM(B5:H5)		0
6	Corlliere	8	0	7	5	7	5	8	SUM(**number1**, [number2], ...)		78

ScreenTip displays correct format for SUM function.

3 Press Enter.

> Since the range Excel suggests is the correct range, you can finish the formula by pressing Enter, clicking the AutoSum button again, or clicking the Enter button on the Formula bar.

4 With I6 the active cell, press Delete to delete the existing formula in the cell.

5 Click the AutoSum button. When Excel displays the formula =SUM(B6:H6), click the AutoSum button again.

6 Make I7 the active cell and then click the AutoSum button.

> Notice this time the range of cells Excel is suggesting to add (I5:I6) is the wrong range. When you click the AutoSum button, Excel looks for multiple values in the cells immediately above the active cell. If no more than one value exists above the active cell, Excel looks in the cells to the left. In this case there were multiple values above I7. You need to highlight the correct range of cells that you want to add.

7 Position the cell pointer over B7, hold down the left mouse button and drag the pointer to the right to H7, and then release the mouse button.

	B	C	D	E	F	G	H	I	J	K
	ed: September 24, 2005						Step 7			
	Sun	Mon	Tue	Wed	Thu	Fri	Sat	Total Hours	Pay Rate	Gross Wage
	8	5	6	8	7	0	6	40	7.35	294
	8	0	7	5	7	5	8	40	6.95	278
	8	0	0	8	8	8	8	=SUM(B7:H7)		
	8	7	5	8	0	0	7	SUM(number1, [number2], ...)		

8 Press Enter.

Now that you have seen how AutoSum operates, you already know that the suggested range for the next employee's total hours will be incorrect. In Step 9 you will select the range of cells *first* to avoid the incorrect suggestion.

9 Position the cell pointer over B8, hold down the left mouse button and drag the pointer to the right to I8, and then release the mouse button.

Notice you are including I8, the cell that will display the result, in the range of cells.

10 Click the AutoSum button.

The result, *35*, appears in cell I8.

	A	B	C	D	E	F	G	H	I	
1	Payroll									
2	Week Ended: September 24, 2005									
3										
4	Name	Sun	Mon	Tue	Wed	Thu	Fri	Sat	Total Hours	
5	Assante	8	5	6	8	7	0	6	40	Steps 9–10
6	Corlliere	8	0	7	5	7	5	8	40	
7	Hill	8	0	0	8	8	8	8	40	
8	Knight	8	7	5	8	0	0	7	35	

11 Click I8 and look in the Formula bar at the formula AutoSum created: =*SUM(B8:H8)*.

If Excel correctly enters the SUM formula from a range of selected cells, it should make sense that you can calculate total hours for more than one employee at the same time using the method employed in Steps 9 and 10.

12 Position the cell pointer over B9, hold down the left mouse button, drag the pointer down and to the right to I10, and then release the mouse button.

	B	C	D	E	F	G	H	I	
	ed: September 24, 2005								
	Sun	Mon	Tue	Wed	Thu	Fri	Sat	Total Hours	
	8	5	6	8	7	0	6	40	
	8	0	7	5	7	5	8	40	
	8	0	0	8	8	8	8	40	
	8	7	5	8	0	0	7	35	
	8	6	5	5	5	0	8	40	Steps 12–13
	8	0	5	0	8	8	5	34	

13 Click the AutoSum button.

14 Click cells I9 and I10 to confirm that the correct formulas appear in the Formula bar.

15 Click the Save button on the Standard toolbar.

1.5 Copying Relative Formulas

Many times you may create a worksheet in which several formulas are basically the same. For example, in the payroll worksheet, the formula to total the hours for Assante is *=SUM(B5:H5)*, for Corlliere *=SUM(B6:H6)*, and so on. The only difference is the row number. Whenever formulas are this similar, you can use the Copy and Paste feature in Excel to copy the formula from one cell to another. The cell containing the original formula is called the *source*, and the cell(s) to which the formula is copied is called the *destination*. When the formula is pasted, Excel automatically changes column letters or row numbers to reflect the destination location. This is referred to as *relative addressing*—the formula is changed relative to its destination.

PROJECT: To simplify your completion of the payroll worksheet for The Waterfront Bistro, you will copy formulas using two methods: Copy and Paste and the fill handle.

STEPS

1 With **ExcelS1-02** open, make K6 the active cell.

> This cell contains the formula *=I6*J6* to calculate the gross wage for Corlliere. You will copy this formula to the remaining cells in column K to finish the *Gross Pay* column.

2 Click the Copy button 📋 on the Standard toolbar, or click Edit on the Menu bar and then click Copy.

> A moving marquee surrounds the active cell indicating the source contents are copied to the Clipboard, which is a temporary storage location. What is being copied is the formula *=I6*J6*—not the value *278*.

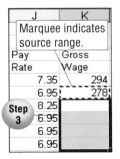

3 Select the range K7:K10. To do this, position the cell pointer over K7, hold down the left mouse button, drag the pointer down to K10, and then release the mouse button.

4 Click the Paste button 📋 on the Standard toolbar, or click Edit on the Menu bar and then click Paste.

> Excel copies the formula to the selected cells, displays the results, and the Paste Options button appears. Clicking the Paste Options button will display a drop-down list with various alternatives for pasting the data. The moving marquee remains around the source cell, and the destination cells remain highlighted. The moving marquee will disappear as soon as you start another activity. Press Esc to remove the marquee and the Paste Options button immediately.

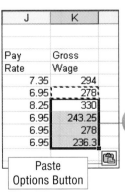

5 Make K7 the active cell and then look at the formula in the Formula bar: *=I7*J7*.

> The row number in the source formula was incremented by one to reflect the destination.

6 Use the Down Arrow key to check the formulas in K8, K9, and K10.

7 Make B12 the active cell.

8 Double-click the AutoSum button.

> Double-clicking the AutoSum button inserts the formula =*SUM(B5:B11)* into B12. Since you know that AutoSum looks for multiple values above the active cell for the suggested range, double-clicking is the fastest way to enter this formula. You will now copy the formula using the fill handle.

9 Drag the fill handle in B12 to the right to K12.

> When the active cell contains a formula, dragging the fill handle causes Excel to copy the formula and change cell references relative to the adjacent cells.

	A	B	C	D	E	F	G	H	I	J	K
1	Payroll										
2	Week Ended: September 24, 2005										
3									Total	Pay	Gross
4	Name	Sun	Mon	Tue	Wed	Thu	Fri	Sat	Hours	Rate	Wage
5	Assante	8	5	6	8	7	0	6	40	7.35	294
6	Corlliere	8	0	7	5	7	5	8	40	6.95	278
7	Hill	8	0	0	8	8	8	8	40	8.25	330
8	Knight	8	7	5	8	0	0	7	35	6.95	243.25
9	Racine	8	6	5	5	0	8	8	40	6.95	278
10	Su-Lin	8	0	5	0	8	8	5	34	6.95	236.3
11											
12	Total	48	18	28	34	30	29	42	229	43.4	1659.55

Step 9

PROBLEM?

> If the results do not appear in C12 through K12, you probably dragged the cell pointer instead of the fill handle. Click B12 and try again.

10 Make J12 the active cell and then press Delete.

> The sum of the *Pay Rate* column is not useful information.

11 Make C12 the active cell and look at the formula in the Formula bar: =*SUM(C5:C11)*.

> The column letter in the source formula was increased by one letter to reflect the destination.

12 Use the Right Arrow key to check the formulas in the remaining columns.

13 Click the Save button on the Standard toolbar.

In Addition

Copy and Paste versus Fill

What is the difference between Copy and Paste and the fill handle? When you use Copy, the contents of the source cell(s) are placed in the Clipboard. The data will remain in the Clipboard and can be pasted several times in the current worksheet or into any other worksheet that is open. Use Copy and Paste when the formula is to be inserted in more than one worksheet or into nonadjacent cells within the current worksheet. Using the fill handle is fast and should be used when the formula is only being copied to adjacent cells.

IN BRIEF

Copy a Formula
1 Activate source cell.
2 Click Edit, Copy.
3 Select destination cell(s).
4 Click Edit, Paste.

1.6 Testing the Worksheet; Improving the Appearance of Cells

When you have finished building the worksheet, it is a good idea to verify that the formulas you entered are accurate. The worksheet could contain formulas that are correct in structure but not mathematically correct for the situation. For example, the wrong range may be included in a SUM formula, or parentheses missing from a multioperator formula may cause an incorrect result. Various methods can be employed to verify a worksheet's accuracy. One method is to create a proof formula in a cell beside or below the

worksheet that will verify the totals. For example, in the payroll worksheet the *Total Hours* column can be verified by creating a formula that adds all of the hours for all of the employees.

PROJECT: To confirm the accuracy of your calculations in the payroll worksheet for The Waterfront Bistro, you will enter proof formulas to test the worksheet and then use two options for formatting the cells that will improve the worksheet's appearance.

STEPS

1 With **ExcelS1-02** open, make A14 the active cell.

2 Type **Hours**, press Alt + Enter, type **Proof**, and then press Enter.

> Alt + Enter is the command to insert a hard return in a cell. This command is used when you want multiple lines within the same cell. The height of the row is automatically expanded to accommodate the multiple lines.

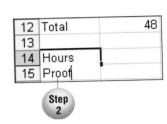

Step 2

3 Make B14 the active cell.

4 Click in the Formula bar, type **=sum(b5:h10)**, and then click the Enter button or press Enter. (Alternatively, you could click the AutoSum button and then drag the pointer across the range B5 through H10.)

> Excel displays the result, 229, which verifies that your total hours are correct. Can you think of another formula that would have accomplished the same objective? ***(Hint: Think of the direction you added to arrive at the total hours in I12.)***

PROBLEM **?**

> Didn't get 229? Then one of the cell entries is incorrect. Look through previous pages to see if the difference between 229 and your result equals a cell entry that you missed.

Step 4

Typed range is color coded for easy referencing and error checking.

PMT		✗ ✓ ƒ =sum(b5:h10)								
	A	B	C	D	E	F	G	H	I	J	K
1	Payroll										
2	Week Ended: September 24, 2005										
3									Total	Pay	Gross
4	Name	Sun	Mon	Tue	Wed	Thu	Fri	Sat	Hours	Rate	Wage
5	Assante	8	5	6	8	7	0	6	40	7.35	294
6	Corlliere	8	0	7	5	7	5	8	40	6.95	278
7	Hill	8	0	0	8	8	8	8	40	8.25	330
8	Knight	8	7	5	8	0	0	7	35	6.95	243.25
9	Racine	8	6	5	5	0	8	8	40	6.95	278
10	Su-Lin	8	0	5	0	8	8	5	34	6.95	236.3
11											
12	Total	48	18	28	34	30	29	42	229		1659.55
13											
14	Hours Proof	(b5:h10)									

5 Make A15 the active cell.

6 Type **Gross**, press Alt + Enter, type **Wage**, press Alt + Enter, type **Proof**, and then press Enter.

7 Make B15 the active cell.

Checking the *Gross Wage* column is not as straightforward as checking the *Total Hours*. For this example, you will calculate the first gross wage using the values instead of the cell addresses. Using the assumption that the formula was copied, it is safe to suppose that the remaining gross wage amounts are correct. As a final check, you will sum the *Gross Wage* column again. *(Note: In a small worksheet such as this one, it is feasible to quickly review each gross wage formula to ensure that the correct cells are being multiplied. The method described in Steps 6–9 is useful for larger worksheets.)*

8 Type **=40*7.35** and then press the Right Arrow key.

The result, *294*, confirms that the formula in K5 is correct. (Notice that in Step 8 Excel was used to calculate a value in a cell similar to how one might use an electronic calculator.)

12	Total		48
13			
14	Hours Proof		229
15	Gross Wage Proof		=40*7.35

Step 8

9 With C15 the active cell, type **=sum(k5:k10)** and then press Enter.

The result, *1659.55*, confirms that the total for the *Gross Wage* column is correct. The importance of testing a worksheet cannot be emphasized enough. Worksheets often contain financial or statistical data that is crucial for an organization. These worksheets can form the basis for strategic decisions by management. A worksheet containing incorrect formulas can lead to disastrous consequences.

	A	B	C	D	E	F	G	H	I	J	K
1	Payroll										
2	Week Ended: September 24, 2005										
3											
4	Name	Sun	Mon	Tue	Wed	Thu	Fri	Sat	Total Hours	Pay Rate	Gross Wage
5	Assante	8	5	6	8	7	0	6	40	7.35	294
6	Corlliere	8	0	7	5	7	5	8	40	6.95	278
7	Hill	8	0	0	8	8	8	8	40	8.25	330
8	Knight	8	7	5	8	0	0	7	35	6.95	243.25
9	Racine	8	6	5	5	0	8	8	40	6.95	278
10	Su-Lin	8	0	5	0	8	8	5	34	6.95	236.3
11											
12	Total	48	18	28	34	30	29	42	229		1659.55
13											
14	Hours Proof	229									
15	Gross Wage Proof	294	1659.55								

Formulas tested correctly.

Step 9

10 Select the range K5:K12.

These final steps in building a worksheet are meant to improve the appearance of cells. In the range K5 through K12 notice that some of the values show no decimals while others show 2 decimal places. Excel uses up to 15 decimal places for precision when calculating values. Since the *Gross Wage* column is representing a sum of money that would be paid to employees, you will format these cells to the Currency format.

11 Click Format and then Cells.

12 In the Format Cells dialog box with the Number tab selected, click *Currency* in the *Category* list box and then click OK.

> The Currency format adds a dollar sign, a comma in thousands, and two decimal places to each value in the selection.

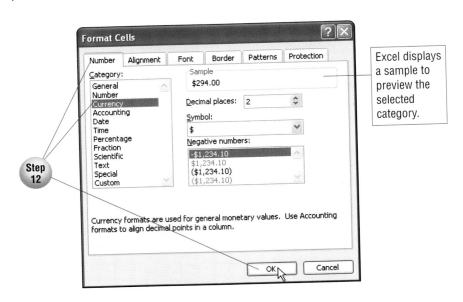

Excel displays a sample to preview the selected category.

Step 12

13 Select the range B15:C15, and then apply the Currency format. (If necessary, refer to Steps 10–12 for assistance.)

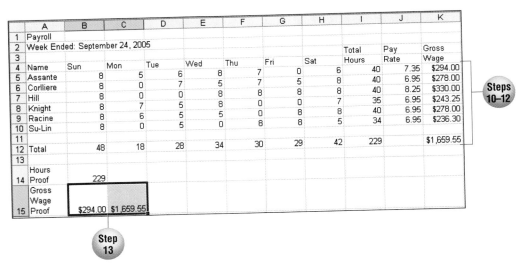

Steps 10–12

Step 13

14 Select the range B3:K4.

> As previously mentioned, labels are aligned at the left edge of a column while values are aligned at the right edge. In the next step you will align the labels at the right edge of the column so they appear directly over the values they represent.

15 Click Format and then Cells.

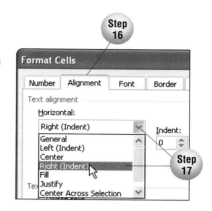

16. Click the Alignment tab in the Format Cells dialog box.

Step 16

17. Click the down-pointing arrow to the right of the *Horizontal* option box (currently displays *General*) and then click *Right (Indent)*.

18. Click OK.

19. Click in any cell outside the highlighted range to deselect the cells.

> Additional formatting options that can be used to enhance a worksheet's appearance will be covered in a later section.

20. Click the Save button on the Standard toolbar.

Steps 14–19

	A	B	C	D	E	F	G	H	I	J	K
1	Payroll										
2	Week Ended: September 24, 2005										
3											
4	Name	Sun	Mon	Tue	Wed	Thu	Fri	Sat	Total Hours	Pay Rate	Gross Wage
5	Assante	8	5	6	8	7	0	6	40	7.35	$294.00
6	Corlliere	8	0	7	5	7	5	8	40	6.95	$278.00
7	Hill	8	0	0	8	8	8	8	40	8.25	$330.00
8	Knight	8	7	5	8	0	0	7	35	6.95	$243.25
9	Racine	8	6	5	5	0	8	8	40	6.95	$278.00
10	Su-Lin	8	0	5	0	8	8	5	34	6.95	$236.30
11											
12	Total	48	18	28	34	30	29	42	229		$1,659.55
13											
14	Hours Proof	229									
15	Gross Wage Proof	$294.00	$1,659.55								

In Addition

Setting the Standard and Formatting Toolbars to Occupy Two Rows

When you install Microsoft Office 2003, the default setting is for the Standard and Formatting toolbars to share the same row. This means that several buttons from each toolbar are not visible. You can instruct Excel to use two rows to display the Standard and Formatting toolbars, thereby allowing you to see all of the available buttons on each toolbar. Click Tools, Customize, and then select the Options tab in the Customize dialog box. Click the *Show Standard and Formatting toolbars on two rows* check box to select the option and then click Close.

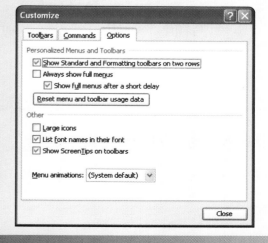

1.7 Using Help

An extensive help resource is available whenever you are working in Excel by clicking the text inside the *Ask a Question* text box located at the right side of the Menu bar, typing a term, phrase, or question, and then pressing Enter. This causes the Search Results task pane to open with a list of topics related to the text that you typed. Clicking a hyperlinked topic in the Search Results task pane opens a Microsoft Office Excel Help window from which you can further explore information on the topic. By default, the search feature will look for information in all Office resources at Microsoft Office Online as long as you are connected to the Internet. In the *Search* section at the bottom of the Search Results task pane you can change this setting to search only Offline Help resources.

PROJECT: After reviewing the payroll worksheet, the manager of The Waterfront Bistro thinks the first two title rows would look better if they were centered over the columns in the worksheet. You will use the *Ask a Question* text box to find out how to do this.

S T E P S

1 With **ExcelS1-02** open, make A1 the active cell.

2 Click the text inside the *Ask a Question* text box (currently reads *Type a question for help*) at the right end of the Menu bar.

> When you click inside the *Ask a Question* text box, an insertion point will appear and the text *Type a question for help* disappears. Once you have completed an initial search for help using the *Ask a Question* text box, the down-pointing arrow to the right of the text box will display a list of topics previously searched for in help.

3 Type **center over multiple columns** and then press Enter.

> The Search Results task pane opens with a list of help topics related to the term, phrase, or question typed in the *Ask a Question* text box.

Step 3

4 Click the Merge or split cells or data hyperlink.

> As you move the mouse pointer over a help topic, the pointer changes to a hand with the index finger pointing upward. When you click a topic, the help information displays in a separate Microsoft Office Excel Help window. You can continue clicking topics and reading the information in the Help window until you have found what you are looking for.

Your Search Results list of topics may vary if you are not connected to the Internet.

Step 4

5 Click the Spread the content of one cell over many cells hyperlink.

> The Help window expands below the selected topic to display information on the feature including the steps to complete the task.

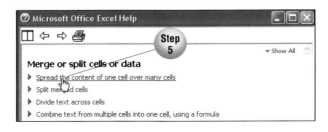

(6) Read the information in the *Spread the content of one cell over many cells* section.

(7) Click the Close button on the Microsoft Office Excel Help window title bar and then click the Close button in the Search Results task pane.

Step 6

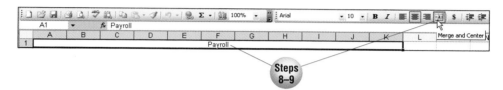

Merge or split cells or data

▼ Spread the content of one cell over many cells

   lorem ipsum

Text spread and centered over multiple cells

Warning Microsoft Excel places only the upper-leftmost data in the selected range into the resulting merged cell. If there is data in other cells, the data is deleted.

1. Copy the data you want into the upper-leftmost cell within the range.
2. Select the cells you want to merge.
3. To merge cells in a row or column and center the cell contents, click **Merge and Center** on the **Formatting** toolbar.

   ▷ Tip

(8) Select the range A1:K1.

(9) Click the Merge and Center button on the Formatting toolbar.

A1 is merged across columns A through K and the text *Payroll* is automatically centered within the merged cell.

Steps 8–9

(10) Select the range A2:K2 and then click the Merge and Center button.

The two titles in the payroll worksheet are now centered over the cells below them.

(11) Click the Save button on the Standard toolbar.

Step 10

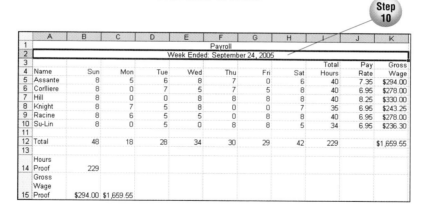

	A	B	C	D	E	F	G	H	I	J	K
1						Payroll					
2					Week Ended: September 24, 2005						
3									Total	Pay	Gross
4	Name	Sun	Mon	Tue	Wed	Thu	Fri	Sat	Hours	Rate	Wage
5	Assante	8	5	6	8	7	0	6	40	7.35	$294.00
6	Corlliere	8	0	7	5	7	5	8	40	6.95	$278.00
7	Hill	8	0	0	8	8	8	8	40	8.25	$330.00
8	Knight	8	7	5	8	0	0	7	35	6.95	$243.25
9	Racine	8	6	5	5	0	8	8	40	6.95	$278.00
10	Su-Lin	8	0	5	0	8	8	5	34	6.95	$236.30
11											
12	Total	48	18	28	34	30	29	42	229		$1,659.55
13											
14	Hours Proof	229									
15	Gross Wage Proof	$294.00	$1,659.55								

In Addition

The Excel Help Task Pane

Click Help on the Menu bar and then click Microsoft Office Excel Help to open the Excel Help task pane shown at the right. From this task pane you can access more extensive help resources such as online training courses for Excel features, Microsoft Office newsgroups, download updates to your Office programs, and more.

IN BRIEF

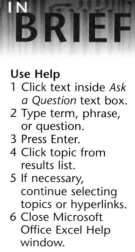

Use Help
1 Click text inside *Ask a Question* text box.
2 Type term, phrase, or question.
3 Press Enter.
4 Click topic from results list.
5 If necessary, continue selecting topics or hyperlinks.
6 Close Microsoft Office Excel Help window.

1.8 Previewing, Printing, and Closing a Workbook

Most of the time you will print a worksheet to have a paper copy, or **hard copy**, to file or to attach to a memo, letter, or report. Large, complex worksheets are often easier to proofread and check from a paper copy. The Print button on the Standard toolbar will print the active worksheet in the open workbook. If more than one worksheet exists in a workbook, open the Print dialog box by clicking File and Print, and then change the *Print what* option to *Entire workbook*. Use the Print Preview feature before printing to view how the page will appear when printed. This allows you to check whether the entire worksheet will fit on one page, and to view other page layout options.

PROJECT: The payroll worksheet for The Waterfront Bistro is finished, so you want to preview its appearance and then print it.

S T E P S

1. With **ExcelS1-02** open, make A17 the active cell, type **Worksheet prepared by: Student Name** (substitute your first and last name for *Student Name*), and then press Enter.

   Check with your instructor before proceeding to see if you should add other identifying information such as student number and class number.

2. Click the Print Preview button [🔍] on the Standard toolbar to display the worksheet in the Print Preview window shown in Figure E1.2.

FIGURE E1.2 Print Preview Window

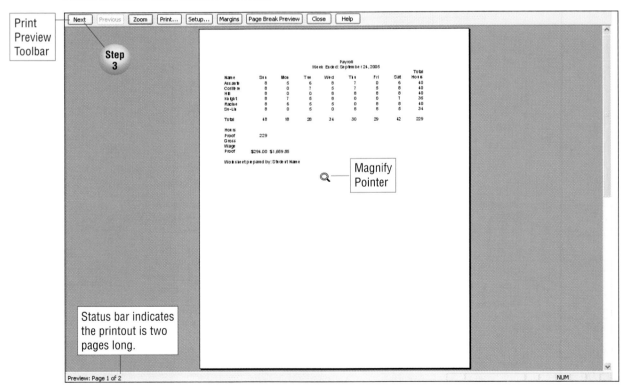

3. The Print Preview window displays a picture of what the printed page will look like. Notice the Status bar is indicating *Page 1 of 2*. Click the Next button on the Print Preview toolbar.

④ The second page of the printout appears showing the columns that could not fit on page 1. The mouse pointer displays as a magnifying glass [Q] in the Print Preview screen. Move the mouse pointer over the two columns and click the left mouse button.

This causes the display to enlarge so that you can read the data in the columns.

⑤ Click the mouse to return to the full-page view and then click the Previous button on the Print Preview toolbar.

⑥ Click the Setup button on the Print Preview toolbar.

One of the methods that can be used to reduce the printout to one page is to change the orientation of the paper from portrait to landscape. In *portrait* orientation, the page is printed on paper taller than it is wide. In *landscape* orientation, the data is rotated to print on paper that is wider than it is tall.

⑦ If necessary, click the Page tab in the Page Setup dialog box, click *Landscape* in the *Orientation* section, and then click OK.

The Print Preview screen will change to show how the worksheet will appear in landscape orientation. Notice that all of the columns now fit on one page.

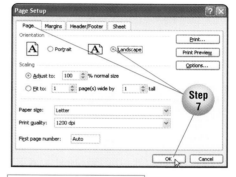

⑧ Click the Print button on the Print Preview toolbar.

The Print Preview window closes and the Print dialog box appears.

⑨ The default settings in the Print dialog box are to print one copy of all pages in the active sheet(s). Make any necessary changes to the settings in the Print dialog box and then click OK.

In a few seconds the worksheet will print on the printer.

Your printer name will vary.

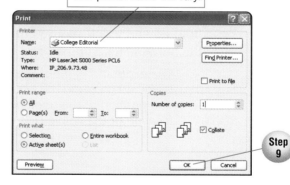

⑩ If necessary, click the right scroll arrow [>] a few times until you can see columns M and N.

The dotted vertical line between columns M and N is a page break. Page breaks appear after you have used Print Preview or Print and indicate how much information from the worksheet can fit on a page.

Dotted line is a page break.

⑪ Click the Save button on the Standard toolbar.

⑫ Click File and then Close.

Excel displays a blue-gray screen in the worksheet area when no workbooks are currently open.

1.9 Navigating a Worksheet

So far, you have been working with small worksheets that generally fit within the viewing area in the screen. Once worksheets become larger you will need to scroll to the right or scroll down to locate cells with which you need to work. The horizontal and vertical scroll bars are used to scroll with the mouse. Scrolling using the scroll bars does not move the position of the active cell. You can also scroll using the arrow keys or with keyboard commands. Scrolling using the keyboard moves the active cell.

PROJECT: To prepare for the creation of another report, you will open a workbook and practice various scrolling techniques using the mouse and the keyboard.

S T E P S

1. Click the Open button on the Standard toolbar.

2. At the Open dialog box with ExcelS1 the active folder, double-click the workbook *WBInventory*.

3. Position the mouse pointer on the down scroll arrow at the bottom of the vertical scroll bar and then click the left mouse button a few times to scroll down the worksheet.

4. Position the mouse pointer on the right scroll arrow at the right edge of the horizontal scroll bar and then click the left mouse button a few times to scroll to the right edge of the worksheet.

5. Position the mouse pointer on the scroll box in the horizontal scroll bar, hold down the left mouse button, drag the scroll box to the left edge of the horizontal scroll bar, and then release the mouse button.

   The width or height of the scroll box indicates the proportional amount of the used cells in the worksheet that are visible in the current window. The position of the scroll box within the scroll bar indicates the relative location of the visible cells within the remainder of the worksheet.

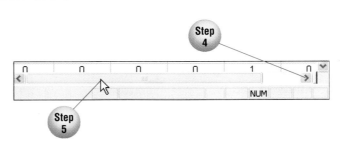

Step 4

Step 5

6. Position the mouse pointer on the scroll box in the vertical scroll bar, hold down the left mouse button, drag the scroll box to the top of the vertical scroll bar, and then release the mouse button.

   You are now back to viewing the beginning of the worksheet.

7. Click Edit and then Go To.

⑧ At the Go To dialog box, type **O54** in the *Reference* text box and then click OK or press Enter.

The active cell is positioned in O54, which is the total of all of the inventory units.

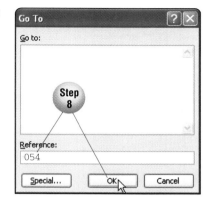

?ROBLEM If you receive the message *Reference is not valid* after you press Enter, you have probably typed zero *(0)* instead of the letter *O*. Click OK at the message box and try again.

⑨ Press Ctrl + Home.

Ctrl + Home moves the active cell to A1.

⑩ Press Page Down twice.

Each time you press Page Down you move down one screen.

⑪ Press the Right Arrow key four times.

Each time you press the Right Arrow key, you move the active cell one cell to the right.

⑫ Use the Up, Down, Left, and Right Arrow keys to practice moving around the worksheet.

Holding down a directional arrow key will cause the screen to scroll very quickly. Table E1.2 illustrates more keyboard scrolling techniques.

⑬ Close **WBInventory** and then exit Excel.

TABLE E1.2 Keyboard Movement Commands

Press	To move to
Arrow keys	One cell up, down, left, or right
Ctrl + Home	A1
Ctrl + End	Last cell in worksheet
Home	Beginning of row
Page Down	Down one screen
Page Up	Up one screen
Alt + Page Down	One screen to the right
Alt + Page Up	One screen to the left

In Addition

Smart Tags

Microsoft Office Excel 2003 has the ability to recognize certain types of data and present the user with a menu to perform actions on the data. The options on the Smart Tags Actions menu will depend on the data that has been recognized. For example, if you type in a cell the name of a person to whom you recently sent e-mail from Outlook, the Smart Tag Actions menu will display options such as Send Mail, Schedule a Meeting, and so on. A Smart Tag is indicated in Excel by a purple triangle at the bottom right corner of the cell. Point to the purple triangle and the Smart Tag Actions button will appear, as shown at the right. Smart Tags are turned on or off in the AutoCorrect Options dialog box. Click Tools and then AutoCorrect Options. Click the Smart Tags tab in the AutoCorrect Options dialog box and then select or deselect the *Label data with smart tags* check box.

In BRIEF

Go to a Specific Cell
1 Click Edit, Go To.
2 Type cell address.
3 Click OK.

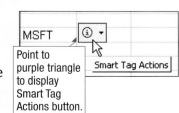

Point to purple triangle to display Smart Tag Actions button.

FEATURES SUMMARY

Feature	Button	Menu	Keyboard
Align Right	≡	Format, Cells, Alignment, Horizontal	
AutoSum	Σ		
Close a workbook		File, Close	Ctrl + F4
Copy		Edit, Copy	Ctrl + C
Currency Style Format	$	Format, Cells, Number	
Exit Excel	✕	File, Exit	Alt + F4
Fill Down		Edit, Fill, Down	Ctrl + D
Fill Left		Edit, Fill, Left	
Fill Right		Edit, Fill, Right	Ctrl + R
Fill Up		Edit, Fill, Up	
Go To		Edit, Go To	Ctrl + G
Help	Type a question for help	Help, Microsoft Office Excel Help	F1
Merge and Center		Format, Cells, Alignment, Merge cells	
Open		File, Open	Ctrl + O
Paste		Edit, Paste	Ctrl + V
Print		File, Print	Ctrl + P
Print Preview		File, Print Preview	
Save		File, Save	Ctrl + S
Save As		File, Save As	F12

PROCEDURES CHECK

Completion:

Look at the Excel screen shown in Figure E1.3. This screen contains numbers with lines pointing to specific items. Identify after the number below the item that corresponds with the number in the Excel screen.

1. _____   5. _____

2. _____   6. _____

3. _____   7. _____

4. _____   8. _____

FIGURE E1.3 Excel Screen

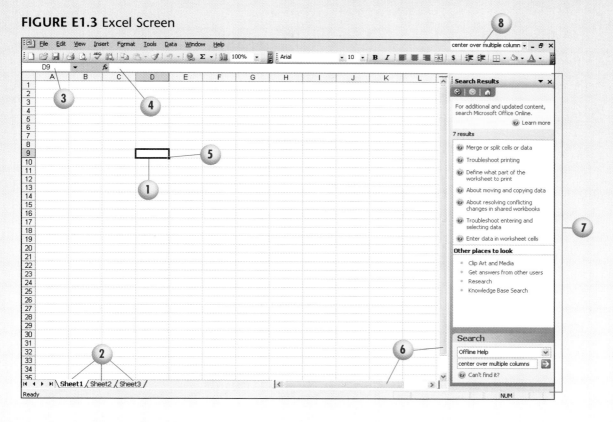

Identify the following buttons:

   9. _____

   10. _____

   11. _____

   12. _____

   13. _____

   14. _____

   15. _____

SKILLS REVIEW

Activity 1: ENTERING LABELS AND VALUES; FORMATTING CELLS

1 Start Excel and then close the Getting Started Task Pane.
2 Create the workbook shown in Figure E1.4. Use the fill handle whenever possible to facilitate data entry. In rows 8, 13, and 17 press the spacebar twice before typing the cell entry to indent the text.

FIGURE E1.4 Activity 1

	A	B	C	D	E	F	G	H
1	The Waterfront Bistro							
2	Condensed Quarterly Statement of Income							
3	For the Quarter Ended September 30, 2005							
4	In Thousands							
5					Jul	Aug	Sep	Total
6	Sales				49.5	42.8	39.7	
7	Cost of Goods Sold				33.1	31.6	27.2	
8	Gross Margin							
9								
10	Advertising Expense				1	1	1	
11	Wages and Benefits Expense				8.1	7.5	6.9	
12	Office and Miscellaneous Expense				1	1	1	
13	Total Expenses							
14								
15	Net Income Before Taxes							
16	Taxes							
17	Net Income After Taxes							

3 Select the range E6:H17 and then complete the following steps:
   a Display the Format Cells dialog box.
   b On the Number tab, choose *Currency* in the *Category* list box.
   c Click the down-pointing arrow at the right of the *Decimal places* text box to change the value from *2* to *1*.
   d Click OK.
   e Deselect the range.
4 Save the workbook and name it **ExcelS1-R1**.

Activity 2: ENTERING FORMULAS; USING AUTOSUM

1 With **ExcelS1-R1** open, create the following formulas by typing them in the Formula bar or the cell, using the pointing method, or by clicking the AutoSum button:
   a In cell E8, subtract Cost of Goods Sold from Sales by entering *=E6-E7*.
   b In cell E13, add the three expenses by entering *=SUM(E10:E12)*.
   c In cell E15, subtract Total Expenses from Gross Margin by entering *=E8-E13*.
   d In cell E16, multiply Net Income Before Taxes by 22% by entering *=E15*22%*.
   e In cell E17, subtract Taxes from Net Income Before Taxes by entering *=E15-E16*.

2 Copy and paste formulas in column E to columns F and G as follows:
  a Select E8 and then copy and paste the formula to the range F8:G8.
  b Select E13 and then copy and paste the formula to the range F13:G13. *(Note: Close the Clipboard task pane if it appears when you copy a second item. If a message displays saying the Clipboard task pane will not display again, click OK.)*
  c Select E15:E17 and then copy and paste the formulas to the range F15:G17.
3 Click in cell H6 and then click the AutoSum button to enter the formulas to add E6:G6. Using the AutoSum button, enter in the remaining cells in column H the formulas required to total columns E, F, and G.
4 Save **ExcelS1-R1**.

Activity 3: IMPROVING THE APPEARANCE OF THE WORKSHEET; PREVIEWING AND PRINTING

1 With **ExcelS1-R1** open, select the range A1:H1 and then click the Merge and Center button.
2 Merge and center A2, A3, and A4 by completing steps similar to that in Step 1.
3 Select the range E5:H5, display the Format Cells dialog box, click the Alignment tab, and then change the horizontal alignment to *Right (Indent)*. Click OK.
4 Deselect the range and then click the Print Preview button.
5 Close the Print Preview screen and then click the Print button.
6 Save **ExcelS1-R1**.

Activity 4: USING THE *ASK A QUESTION* TEXT BOX

1 With **ExcelS1-R1** open, click the text inside the *Ask a Question* text box, type **display fewer decimals**, and then press Enter.
2 Click the <u>Change the number of decimal places displayed</u> hyperlink in the Search Results task pane.
3 Read the information displayed under the heading *On a worksheet* in the Microsoft Office Excel Help window and then close the window.
4 Close the Search Results task pane.
5 Select the range E6:H17 and then decrease the number of decimal places to zero using the button on the Formatting toolbar that you learned about in the Help window.
6 Deselect E6:H17.
7 Save, print, and then close **ExcelS1-R1**.

PERFORMANCE PLUS

Assessment 1: ADDING LABELS, VALUES, AND FORMULAS TO A WORKSHEET

1 Open **MPTravelCosts**.
2 Save the workbook with Save As and name it **ExcelS1-P1**.
3 You have received a message from Melissa Gehring of First Choice Travel with quotations for return airfare, hotel, and airport transfers for the film crew to travel to Toronto for the location shoot July 4 to August 31, 2005. This information is summarized below.
   - Return airfare is $576.20 per person.
   - Melissa has negotiated a room rate of $7,250.00 per room for the entire duration with two persons per room.
   - Airport Transfer Limousine Service is a flat rate of $625.00 in Toronto and $495.00 in Los Angeles.
   - All of the above prices include taxes and are quoted in U.S. dollars.
4 Enter the appropriate labels, values, and formulas to complete the worksheet.
5 Make any formatting changes you think would improve the appearance of the worksheet.
6 Save, print, and then close **ExcelS1-P1**.

Assessment 2: CREATING A WORKBOOK

1 You are Bobbie Sinclair, business manager at Performance Threads. You are preparing a price estimate for costumes needed by Marquee Productions for its Toronto film shoot July 4 to August 31, 2005. Create a new workbook that will calculate the costume costs using the following information:
   a Click the New button on the Standard toolbar ⬜ to open a blank worksheet.
   b Five costumes must be researched, designed, and custom made at $3,250.00 per costume. Marquee Productions will own these costumes after the film shoot.
   c Seven costumes are in stock and can be rented at $212.50 per day. Marquee Productions has advised that it will need these costumes for 17 days.
   d Eighteen costumes require size and length adjustments. These costumes are subject to the same rental fee, but are required for only 11 days. A flat fee for alterations is $108.75 per costume.
2 Make any formatting changes you think would improve the appearance of the worksheet.
3 Save the workbook and name it **ExcelS1-P2**.
4 Print and then close **ExcelS1-P2**.

Assessment 3: CREATING A WORKBOOK

1 You are Sam Vestering, manager of North American Distribution for Worldwide Enterprises. You are preparing a projected distribution revenue schedule for Marquee Productions' latest film *Two By Two*, to be released February 11, 2005. Create a new workbook that will estimate Worldwide's projected revenue using the following information (see Figure E1.5):

a Preview cities receive the film on the Friday before the general release date and pay Worldwide Enterprises 1.15% of projected box office revenues.

b General release cities pay Worldwide Enterprises 1% of projected box office revenues.

c All projections are paid in U.S. dollars.

d Include a total of the projected revenue for Worldwide Enterprises. (*Hint: You may want to create this workbook by grouping the preview cities and the general release cities separately.*)

FIGURE E1.5 Assessment 3

City	Release Category	Projected Box Office Sales in Millions
New York	Preview	21.2
Tucson	General	12.5
Los Angeles	Preview	33.8
Denver	Preview	22.3
Orlando	General	32.1
Des Moines	General	11.2
Wichita	Preview	10.6
Boston	General	29.7

City	Release Category	Projected Box Office Sales in Millions
Philadelphia	General	20.6
Dallas	General	18.2
Milwaukee	General	17.8
Vancouver	General	14.6
Calgary	General	19.2
Toronto	Preview	27.9
Montreal	Preview	16.4

2 Make any formatting changes you think would improve the appearance of the workbook.
3 Save the workbook and name it **ExcelS1-P3**.
4 Print and then close **ExcelS1-P3**.

Assessment 4: FINDING INFORMATION ON HIDING ZERO VALUES

1 Using the *Ask a Question* text box, find out how to display or hide zero values on an entire worksheet.
2 Click the Print button on the Microsoft Office Excel Help window toolbar to print the help topic that you find and then close the Help window and the Search Results task pane.
3 Open **WBInventory**.
4 Save the workbook with Save As and name it **ExcelS1-P4**.
5 Hide the zero values.
6 Display the Print dialog box, change the Print range to print page 1 to 1, and then click OK.
7 Save and then close **ExcelS1-P4**.

Assessment 5: LOCATING TRAINING IN EXCEL HELP FROM OFFICE ONLINE

1 Display a new blank worksheet.
2 Click Help and then Microsoft Office Online.
3 Click the Training hyperlink.
4 Click the Excel hyperlink in the *BROWSE TRAINING COURSES* section.
5 Click a link to a training course for a topic that interests you.
6 Complete the training course.
7 Close Internet Explorer when you have completed the course.
8 Close the worksheet.

EXCEL

SECTION 2

Editing and Formatting Worksheets

Several techniques are available in Excel to change the content of cells or the layout of the worksheet. Formatting features are used to improve the appearance of the data and, when used strategically, can draw the reader's attention to a cell or series of cells deemed important. In this section you will learn the skills and complete the projects described here.

 Note: Before beginning this section, delete the ExcelS1 folder on your disk. Next, copy to your disk or other location the ExcelS2 subfolder from the CD that accompanies this textbook and then make ExcelS2 the active folder.

Projects

 Edit and format a quotation and invoice for catering services and format an inventory report.

 Edit and format a costume cost schedule and complete an invoice for costume production.

 Edit and format a revenue summary report for movie distribution.

Skills

- Edit the content of cells
- Clear cells and cell formats
- Perform a spell check
- Insert and delete cells, columns, and rows
- Use Undo and Redo
- Hide and unhide columns and rows
- Move and copy cells
- Use Paste Options to link cells
- Adjust column width and row height
- Change the font, size, style, and color of cells
- Apply numeric formats and adjust the number of decimal places
- Change cell alignment and indentation
- Add borders and shading
- Autoformat a worksheet
- Change options before applying an autoformat
- Find and replace cell entries and formats
- Freeze and unfreeze panes
- Split a worksheet into two windows
- Change the zoom percentage

2.1 Editing and Clearing Cells; Performing a Spell Check

The contents of a cell can be edited directly within the cell or in the Formula bar. Clearing a cell can involve removing the cell contents or format, or both. The spell check feature is a useful tool to assist with correcting typing errors within a worksheet. After completing a spell check you will still need to proofread the worksheet, since the spelling checker will not highlight all errors and cannot check the accuracy of values.

PROJECT: Dana Hirsch, manager of The Waterfront Bistro, has started a quotation for catering services to be provided to Marquee Productions. The quotation contains a few errors and notes. Dana has asked you to correct the errors and finish the quotation. You will be working on this quotation through most of this section.

STEPS

1 Open **WBQuotation**. *(Note: This worksheet contains intentional spelling errors that will be corrected in Steps 11–16.)*

2 Save the workbook with Save As and name it **ExcelS2-01**.

3 Double-click I21.

> Double-clicking a cell inserts a blinking insertion point in the cell indicating the Edit mode has been activated; *Edit* appears in the Status bar. The location of the insertion point within the cell will vary depending on where the cell pointer was positioned when Edit mode was activated.

4 Press the Right or Left Arrow key as needed to move the insertion point between the decimal point and *4,* and then press the Delete key.

5 Type **8** and then press Enter.

6 Make I27 the active cell.

7 Move the pointer after *8* in the Formula bar and then click the left mouse button.

> The cell pointer changes to an I-beam pointer ⬚ when positioned in the Formula bar.

8 Press Backspace to delete *8*, type **2**, and then click the Enter button on the Formula bar.

9 Make A9 the active cell and then press Delete.

> Pressing Delete or Backspace will clear the contents of the active cell. Any formats or comments applied to the cell remain active.

10 Select the range I17:I18, click Edit, point to Clear, and then click All.

> Use the Clear All feature to remove everything from a cell including formats or comments.

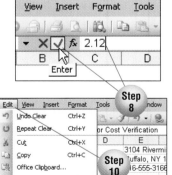

11 Press Ctrl + Home to move the active cell to A1.

12 Click Tools and then Spelling.

> A spell check begins at the active cell and compares words within the worksheet with words in the dictionary. Words that do not match are highlighted as potential errors. Buttons in the Spelling dialog box are used to skip the word (Ignore Once or Ignore All), replace the word with the highlighted word in the *Suggestions* list box (Change), or add the word to the dictionary (Add to Dictionary) if it is spelled correctly.

EXCEL

34

SECTION 2: EDITING AND FORMATTING WORKSHEETS

(13) Click the Ignore All button in the Spelling dialog box to instruct Excel to skip all occurrences of *Rivermist* in the worksheet since the street name is spelled correctly.

(14) Click the Change button in the Spelling dialog box to replace *Torontow* with *Toronto*.

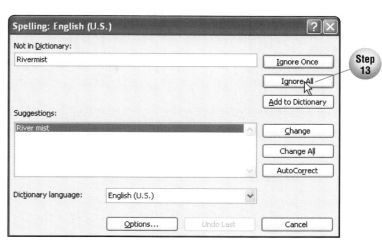

(15) Click the Change button in the Spelling dialog box to replace *Persns* with *Persons*.

(16) Complete the spell check, changing words as required. Click OK at the message that the spelling check is complete.

> If the correct word is not initially selected in the *Suggestions* list box, double-click to select the correct spelling. If the correct spelling does not appear in the *Suggestions* list box, click in the *Not in Dictionary* text box, insert and/or delete characters as required, and then click Change. Drag the Spelling dialog box out of the way if you need to see the selected word within the worksheet.

(17) Save the workbook using the same name **ExcelS2-01.**

In Addition

AutoCorrect

The AutoCorrect feature will automatically correct common typographical errors as you type. For example, if you type *teh* and press the spacebar, Excel will automatically change *teh* to *the*. Click Tools and then AutoCorrect Options to add your own frequently misspelled words to the AutoCorrect list, shown at the right. Type the word the way you misspell it in the *Replace* text box, type the correct spelling in the *With* text box, and then click Add.

In BRIEF

Edit a Cell
1 Double-click cell.
2 Insert and/or delete text.
3 Press Enter or click another cell.

Clear a Cell
1 Click Edit and point to Clear.
2 Click All, Formats, or Contents.

Spell Check
1 Click Tools, Spelling.
2 Click Ignore Once, Ignore All, Change, or Add to Dictionary as required.

2.2 Inserting and Deleting Cells; Using Undo and Redo

Insert cells if you need to add data to the worksheet. Existing cells can be shifted right or down in the worksheet. Previously you learned how to use the Delete key and the Clear command to remove the contents from cells. The existing cell was emptied and remained in the worksheet. Using the Delete command from the Edit menu will cause surrounding cells to shift to fill in the gap created by the deleted cells. Undo will reverse the last action or delete the last text typed. Click the down-pointing arrow next to the Undo button on the Standard toolbar to view a list of recent actions. Use the Redo feature if you change your mind after clicking Undo. Some actions (such as Save) cannot be reversed with Undo.

PROJECT: You will continue to edit the quotation for Marquee Productions by inserting and deleting cells.

STEPS

1 With **ExcelS2-01** open, select the range A24:A25.

In the next two steps you will insert cells to add two entries between *Soup and salad* and *Hot entrée.*

2 Click Insert and then Cells.

PROBLEM? Don't see the Cells command on the Insert menu? Click the double down-pointing arrows at the bottom of the menu, click Insert a second time, or simply wait a few seconds—the menu will expand to show additional options.

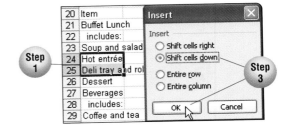

3 At the Insert dialog box, click *Shift cells down* and then click OK.

4 Click A24, type **Vegetable tray with dip**, and then press Enter.

5 Type **Seafood hors d'oeuvres** and then press Enter.

6 Make A32 the active cell.

7 Click Edit and then Delete.

8 At the Delete dialog box, make sure *Shift cells up* is selected and then click OK.

9 Look at C27:G27, C33:G33, C39:G39, and G41. The values for *Beverages, Snacks, Delivery,* and *Total* no longer appear beside the correct labels. This is because you did not insert or delete *entire rows.* You can correct the worksheet with Undo.

10 Click the Undo button 🔄 on the Standard toolbar.

The last action, deleting A32, is reversed. Notice *Milk* has been restored to cell A32 in the worksheet.

⑪ Click the down-pointing arrow to the right of the Undo button.

⑫ Point to *Insert Cells* and then click the left mouse button.

> The worksheet is now restored to its state when you started this topic. In the next topic you will add the new entries *Vegetable tray with dip* and *Seafood hors d'oeuvres*, and delete *Milk*, by inserting and deleting entire rows.

PROBLEM **?**

Your Undo list may not coincide with these steps if you have edited the worksheet beyond the steps in this topic. If necessary, you can preserve your editing by not using Undo—insert and delete cells as needed.

Step 11

Step 12

⑬ Make A43 the active cell.

⑭ Click Insert and then Cells.

⑮ At the Insert dialog box with *Shift cells down* selected, click OK.

> A new cell is inserted and the existing text in A43 and below is adjusted down by one row.

⑯ Type **Quotation is valid for 30 days** and then press Enter.

⑰ Click Undo.

⑱ Click Edit and then Redo Typing.

> Redo reverses the action of Undo.

⑲ Save **ExcelS2-01**.

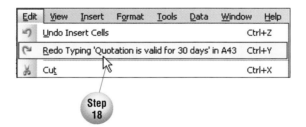

Step 18

In Addition

More about Undo

Some actions cannot be undone. For example, if you click the Save button on the Standard toolbar, Undo will not be available to reverse the save operation. If the action you have completed is not reversible, the Undo button on the toolbar is dimmed. If you click Edit, the option will read *Can't Undo* as shown.

Undo Button is dimmed.

IN BRIEF

Insert Cells
1 Select range of cells.
2 Click Insert, Cells.

Delete Cells
1 Select range of cells.
2 Click Edit, Delete.

Rows and columns can be inserted or deleted using options from the Insert and Edit menus, or from the shortcut menu. Context-sensitive shortcut menus display when you right-click the mouse over a selected area. A row or column can be hidden from the worksheet display. The data is removed from view but is not deleted. You might want to do this if the worksheet contains confidential information; hidden rows or columns do not print. Redisplay hidden data by unhiding the rows or columns.

PROJECT: You will add to and delete items from the quotation in the previous topic by inserting and deleting rows. The information in columns I through K is confidential profit data. You want to hide these columns so the printout of the quotation does not display them.

S T E P S

1. With **ExcelS2-01** open, position the cell pointer (displays as a right-pointing black arrow) over row indicator *24*, hold down the left mouse button, and then drag the mouse down over *25*.

   This selects rows 24 and 25. Inserted rows are placed *above* the selected rows and columns are inserted to the *left*.

2. Click Insert and then Rows.

   Two blank rows are inserted. All rows below the inserted rows are shifted down.

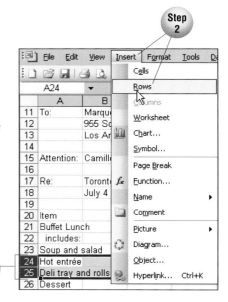

3. Click A24, type **Vegetable tray with dip**, and then press Enter.

4. Type **Seafood hors d'oeuvres** and then press Enter.

5. Select row 32.

6. Click Edit and then Delete.

   The data in row 32 is removed from the worksheet. All rows below the deleted row shift up to fill in the space.

7. Select row 22. Hold down Ctrl and then select rows 30 and 35.

   Hold down the Ctrl key to select multiple rows or columns that are not adjacent.

8. Position the pointer within any of the three selected rows, right-click to display the shortcut menu, and then click Delete.

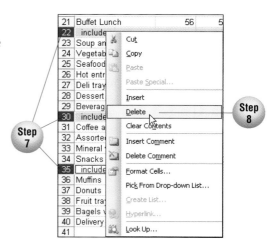

9 Select column F and display the shortcut menu by positioning the cell pointer over column indicator letter *F* and right-clicking the mouse.

10 At the shortcut menu, click Delete.

> Data in columns to the right of the deleted column are shifted left to fill in the space.

11 Position the cell pointer (displays as a down-pointing black arrow) over column indicator letter *H*, hold down the left mouse button, and drag the mouse right over *J*.

12 Click Format, point to Column, and then click Hide.

> Columns H, I, and J are now hidden. Notice the column letter indicators are now A through G, and then K and onward. Until you click the mouse in another location a thick black line also displays where the columns were hidden.

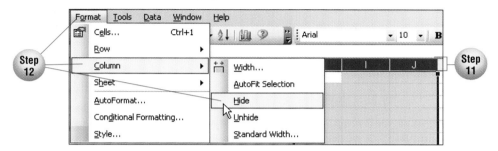

13 Make F11 the active cell, type **November 21, 2005**, and then press Enter.

> By default, Excel displays dates in the format *dd-mmm-yy* (21-Nov-05).

14 Save **ExcelS2-01**.

In Addition

Redisplaying Hidden Columns

To redisplay hidden data, select the column or row before and after the hidden data and then click Format, point to Row or Column, and click Unhide. For example, to redisplay the columns hidden in Step 12, you would select columns G and K.

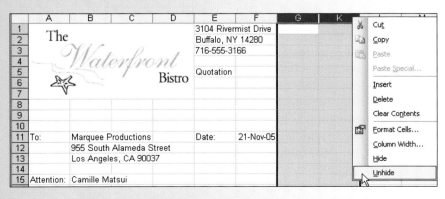

In Brief

Insert Rows or Columns
1 Select rows or columns required.
2 Click Insert.
3 Click Rows or Columns.

Delete Rows or Columns
1 Select rows or columns to be deleted.
2 Click Edit, Delete.

Hide Rows or Columns
1 Select rows or columns to be hidden.
2 Click Format.
3 Point to Row or Column.
4 Click Hide.

2.4 Moving and Copying Cells

You learned how to use copy and paste to copy formulas in the payroll worksheet for The Waterfront Bistro. You can also use cut and paste to move the contents of a cell or range of cells to another location in the worksheet. The selected cells being cut or copied are called the **source**. The cell or range of cells that is receiving the source data is called the **destination**. If data already exists in the destination cells, Excel will replace the contents in the destination location. Cells cut or copied to the Clipboard can be pasted more than once in the active workbook, in another workbook, or in another Office application.

PROJECT: In further changes to your catering quotation, you will move text in the quotation, duplicate the price per person from beverages to snacks by linking the cells containing the prices, and edit the snack items by copying a *Buffet Lunch* cell.

S T E P S

① With **ExcelS2-01** open, make E5 the active cell.

② Click the Cut button 🗴 on the Standard toolbar.

> A moving marquee surrounds the source after you use Cut or Copy, indicating the cell contents have been placed in the Clipboard.

PROBLEM ?
Can't find the Cut button? Click the Toolbar Options button in the middle of the toolbar (just left of the Font button) to display more Standard toolbar buttons in a drop-down palette.

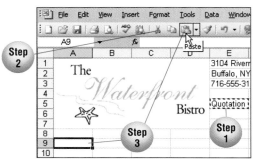

③ Make A9 the active cell and then click the Paste button 🗋 on the Standard toolbar.

> The text *Quotation* is removed from E5 and placed in A9. In the next step you will move a range of cells using a method called **drag and drop**.

④ Select the range A17:B18.

> You are only selecting to column B since the entries *Toronto Location Filming* and *July 4 through August 31, 2005* are stored in B17 and B18, respectively.

⑤ Point at any one of the four borders surrounding the selected range.

> When you point at a border, the pointer changes from the thick white cross to a white arrow with the move icon attached to it (four-headed arrow).

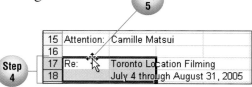

⑥ Hold down the left mouse button, drag the top left corner of the range to E15, and then release the mouse.

> A gray border will appear as you drag, indicating the placement of the range when you release the mouse. The destination range displays in a yellow ScreenTip below the gray border.

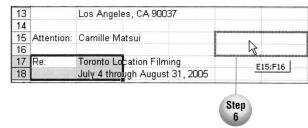

7 Make D28 the active cell.

8 Click the Copy button 🖺 on the Standard toolbar.

9 Make D32 the active cell, and then click the Paste button.

> The existing data in D32 is replaced with the value copied from D28 and the Paste Options button appears.

27	Dessert				
28	Beverages		56	4.1	40	9184
29	Coffee and tea				
30	Assorted juice				
31	Mineral water				
32	Snacks		56	4.1	40	9184
33	Muffins				
34	Donuts				
35	Fruit tray				
36	Bagels with cream cheese			
37	Delivery			31	
38					
39	Total				
40					
41	Quotation is valid for 30 days		
42	Note: All prices are tax included	
43	Terms: Due upon receipt of invoice payable in US funds	

Steps 7–8 / Step 9 / Step 10 / Step 11

10 Click the Paste Options button.

> A drop-down list appears with various options for controlling how the copied data is inserted into the destination cell. This list is useful when you are copying and pasting data to areas of a worksheet, or to a different workbook, in which the source and destination have different formats applied. You can control whether the format in the destination cell is the source cell's format or the destination cell's.

Paste Options list:
- Keep Source Formatting
- Match Destination Formatting
- Values and Number Formatting
- Keep Source Column Widths
- Formatting Only
- Link Cells

11 Click *Link Cells* at the drop-down list.

> Linking the source and destination cells means that any change made to one cell will automatically be applied to the other cell.

27	Dessert		
28	Beverages		56	3.98
29	Coffee and tea		
30	Assorted juice		
31	Mineral water		
32	Snacks		56	3.98

Step 13

D32 changes automatically since the two cells are linked.

12 Press Esc to remove the moving marquee from D28.

13 Make D28 the active cell and edit the value to *3.98*. Notice the value in D32 is also changed to *3.98* automatically.

14 Make A23 the active cell.

15 Point at any one of the four borders surrounding A23 until the pointer displays as a white arrow with the move icon attached to it, hold down Ctrl, and then drag the mouse to A36. Release the mouse button first, and then release the Ctrl key.

> A plus sign attached to the pointer indicates the source contents are being *copied*.

16 Save **ExcelS2-01**.

In Addition

Relative and Absolute Addressing

Previously, when you copied and pasted formulas in the payroll worksheet, the cell addresses in the destination cells were changed *relative* to the destination row or column. Sometimes you need a cell address to remain fixed when it is copied. This is referred to as **absolute addressing**. Make a cell address absolute by typing a dollar symbol ($) in front of the column letter or row number that cannot be changed. Following are some examples of ways to use absolute references in formulas that will be copied.

=$A$12*.01	Neither the column nor the row will change
=$A12*.01	The column will remain fixed but the row will change
=A$12*.01	The column will change but the row will remain fixed

IN BRIEF

Move Cells
1 Select source cells.
2 Click Cut.
3 Select starting destination cell.
4 Click Paste.

Copy Cells
1 Select source cells.
2 Click Copy.
3 Select starting destination cell.
4 Click Paste.

2.5 Adjusting Column Width and Row Height

By default, columns are all the same width and rows are all the same height. Columns are initially set to the average number of digits *0* through *9* that can fit in a cell in the standard font. In some cases you do not have to increase the width when the text is too wide for the column, since labels "spill over" into the next cell if it is empty. Some column headings in the quotation are truncated because an entry exists in the column immediately to the right. Excel automatically adjusts the height of rows to accommodate the size of the text within the cells. Manually increasing the row height adds more space between rows, which can be used as a design technique to draw attention to a series of cells.

PROJECT: To make sure Marquee Productions will understand all of the items in your quotation, you will adjust the column widths for columns in which the entire label is not currently visible and increase the height of the row containing the column headings.

STEPS

1 With **ExcelS2-01** open, make any cell in column C the active cell.

2 Click Format, point to Column, and then click Width.

3 At the Column Width dialog box, type **12** and then click OK or press Enter.

Step 1

Step 3

> In the next step you will adjust the width of column D using the mouse.

4 Position the mouse pointer on the boundary line in the column indicator row between columns D and E until the pointer changes to a vertical line with a left- and right-pointing arrow ⟷ .

5 Hold down the left mouse button, drag the boundary line to the right until *Width: 14.29 (105 pixels)* displays in the ScreenTip, and then release the mouse button.

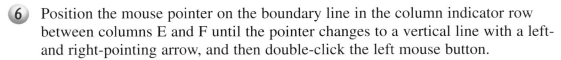

Step 5

> As you drag the boundary line to the right or left, a dotted line appears in the column in the worksheet area indicating the new width.

6 Position the mouse pointer on the boundary line in the column indicator row between columns E and F until the pointer changes to a vertical line with a left- and right-pointing arrow, and then double-click the left mouse button.

> Double-clicking the boundary line sets the width to fit the length of the longest entry within the column, referred to as *AutoFit*. If, after decreasing a column width, cells that previously had values in them now display as a series of pound symbols (########), the column is now too narrow. Widen the column to redisplay the values.

7 Increase the width of column B to *12 (89 pixels)* using either the Column Width dialog box or by dragging the column boundary.

> After reviewing the worksheet you decide all of the columns with numeric values should be the same width. In the next steps you will learn how to set the width of multiple columns in one operation.

8 Position the mouse pointer on column indicator letter *C*, hold down the left mouse button, and then drag the mouse right to column F.

> This selects columns C through F.

9 Position the mouse pointer on *any* of the right boundary lines within the selected range of columns until the pointer changes to a vertical line with a left- and right-pointing arrow.

> Any changes made to the width of one column boundary will affect all of the selected columns.

10 Drag the boundary line right until *Width: 15.00 (110 pixels)* displays in the ScreenTip and then release the mouse button.

11 Click in any cell to deselect the columns.

12 Move E15:F16 to A17:B18 and then click in any cell to deselect the range. Refer to Topic 2.4 if you need assistance with this step.

> In the next steps you will adjust row height using the mouse.

13 Position the mouse pointer on the boundary line below row 20 until the pointer changes to a horizontal line with an up- and down-pointing arrow.

14 Drag the boundary line down until *Height: 19.50 (26 pixels)* displays in the ScreenTip and then release the mouse button.

15 Save **ExcelS2-01**.

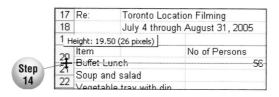

In Addition

Row Height Dialog Box

A similar sequence of steps that you used for adjusting column width using the Column Width dialog box can be used to increase or decrease the height of a row with the Row Height dialog box, shown at the right. Click any cell within the row, click Format, point to Row, and then click Height. Type the desired height and press Enter or click OK.

IN BRIEF

Increase or Decrease Column Width
1 Select column(s).
2 Click Format.
3 Point to Column.
4 Click Width.
5 Type desired width.
6 Click OK.

Increase or Decrease Row Height
1 Select row(s).
2 Click Format.
3 Point to Row.
4 Click Height.
5 Type desired height.
6 Click OK.

Adjust Width or Height Using Mouse
1 Select column(s) or row(s).
2 Drag boundary to right of column or below row.

2.6 Changing the Font, Size, Style, and Color of Cells

The *font* is the typeface used to display and print data. The default font in Excel is Arial, but several other fonts are available. The size of the font is measured in units called *points*. A point is approximately 1/72 of an inch measured vertically. The default font size used by Excel is 10-point. The larger the point size, the larger the type. Each font's style can be changed to display in **bold**, *italic*, or ***bold italic***. Text in cells displays in black with a white background. You can add emphasis or interest to the worksheet by changing the color of the text or the color of the background.

PROJECT: To add to the visual appeal of your quotation, you will change the font and font size, and apply attributes such as bold and color to the text *Quotation*.

STEPS

1 With **ExcelS2-01** open, click Tools and then Customize.

> Completing the remaining steps in this topic will be easier if you can see all of the buttons on the Formatting toolbar. In the next step, you will display the Standard and Formatting toolbars as two rows. Skip Steps 1 and 2 if your Standard and Formatting toolbars are already separated.

2 If necessary, click the Options tab in the Customize dialog box. Click the *Show Standard and Formatting toolbars on two rows* check box and then click Close.

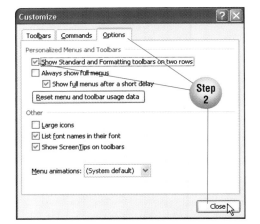

3 Make A9 the active cell.

4 Click the down-pointing arrow next to the Font button on the Formatting toolbar, scroll down the list of fonts, and then click *Times New Roman*.

Your list of fonts may vary.

5 Click the down-pointing arrow next to the Font Size button on the Formatting toolbar and then click *18* in the drop-down list.

> The row height is automatically increased to accommodate the larger type size.

6 Click the Bold button **B** on the Formatting toolbar.

7 With A9 still the active cell, click the down-pointing arrow next to the Font Color button on the Formatting toolbar and then click Dark Blue in the color palette.

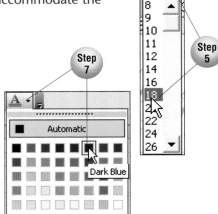

8 Select A9:F9 and then click the Merge and Center button 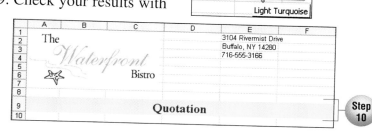 on the Formatting toolbar.

> The cells in the range A9:F9 have now been merged into one large cell that spans across the six columns. The text within A9, *Quotation*, is now centered within this large cell. Use the Merge and Center feature to center titles over multiple columns in a worksheet.

9 With A9:F9 still selected, click the down-pointing arrow next to the Fill Color button on the Formatting toolbar and then click Light Turquoise in the color palette.

> ***Fill*** is the color of the background in the cell. Changing the fill color is sometimes referred to as ***shading*** a cell.

10 Click in any cell to deselect A9. Check your results with row 9 in the worksheet shown at the right. If necessary, return to a previous step and redo the font, font size, bold, font color, merge and center, or fill color.

11 Make A39 the active cell.

12 Hold down Ctrl and then click F39.

> This selects both A39 and F39.

13 Click the Bold button **B** and the Italic button *I* on the Formatting toolbar.

> More than one attribute can be applied to a cell.

14 Click in any cell to deselect A39 and F39.

15 Save **ExcelS2-01**.

In Addition

Format Cells

The Format Cells dialog box with the Font tab selected (shown below) can be used to change the font, font size, font style, and color of text. Additional style options such as Underline are available, as well as special effects options such as Strikethrough, Superscript, and Subscript. Select the cells you want to change, click Format, and then click Cells. Click the Font tab in the Format Cells dialog box and then change the required options.

IN BRIEF

Change Font
1 Select cells.
2 Click down-pointing arrow next to Font button.
3 Click desired font.
4 Deselect cells.

Change Font Size
1 Select cells.
2 Click down-pointing arrow next to Font Size button.
3 Click desired size.
4 Deselect cells.

Change Font Attributes
1 Select cells.
2 Click desired attribute button.
3 Deselect cells.

2.7 Formatting Numeric Cells; Adjusting Decimal Places

In the payroll worksheet for The Waterfront Bistro, you learned how to format numeric cells to the Currency format which added a dollar symbol ($), comma in the thousands, and two decimal places to each value. Other numeric formats include Comma, Percent, and Accounting. By default, cells are initially set to the General format. The General format has no specific numeric style. The number of decimal places in a selected range of cells can be increased or decreased using the Increase Decimal and Decrease Decimal buttons on the Formatting toolbar.

PROJECT: Apply the Accounting, Comma, and Percent formats to the numeric cells within the quotation using buttons from the Formatting toolbar and the Format Cells dialog box. Begin by unhiding columns G through K so you can format the numbers within those columns along with the rest of the worksheet.

STEPS

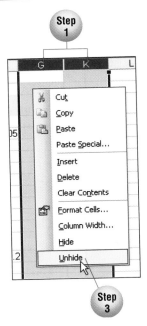

Step 1

Step 3

1 With **ExcelS2-01** open, position the mouse pointer on column indicator letter *G*, hold down the left mouse button, and drag right to column K.

> The ScreenTip indicates that five columns (5C) are selected (columns H through J are hidden).

2 Position the mouse pointer within the selected columns and right-click.

3 Click Unhide at the shortcut menu.

> Hidden columns H through J are now redisplayed.

4 Click in any cell to deselect the columns.

5 Make F21 the active cell.

6 Hold down Ctrl and then click I21, F39, and I39.

7 Click Format and then Cells.

8 If necessary, click the Number tab in the Format Cells dialog box, click *Accounting* in the *Category* list box, and then click OK.

> A preview of the selected cell with the format applied appears in the Sample box. Notice the options are available within the dialog box to change the number of decimal places and the currency symbol.

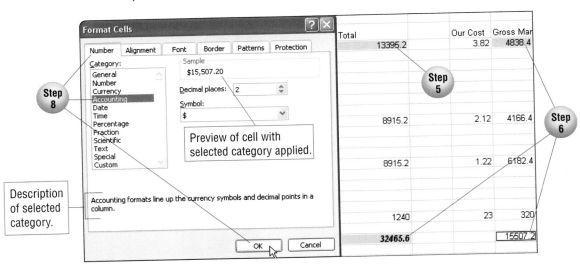

Step 8

Description of selected category.

Step 5

Step 6

(9) Click in any cell to deselect F21, I21, F39, and I39. Cells I21 and I39 display with pound symbols (#) since the column width is too narrow for the new format. Double-click the boundary line between columns I and J to AutoFit the column.

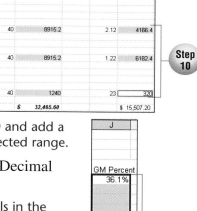

Step 10

(10) Select F28, I28, F32, I32, F37, and I37, and then click the Comma Style button 🔲 on the Formatting toolbar.

> Comma Style formats omits the currency symbol from the Accounting format.

Step 10

(11) Select J21:J39.

(12) Click the Percent Style button 🔲 on the Formatting toolbar.

> Percent Style causes Excel to multiply cell values by 100 and add a percent symbol (%) to the end of each result in the selected range.

(13) With the range J21:J39 still selected, click the Increase Decimal button 🔲 twice on the Formatting toolbar.

> One decimal place is added to or removed from the cells in the selected range each time you click Increase Decimal or Decrease Decimal.

(14) With the range J21:J39 still selected, click the Decrease Decimal button 🔲 once on the Formatting toolbar.

Steps 11–14

(15) Make H37 the active cell and then click the Increase Decimal button twice to display two decimal places.

> The value now displays as 23.00.

(16) Save **ExcelS2-01**.

In Addition

Styles

A *style* is a group of formats saved under a style name. Once a style has been defined, you can apply the group of formats by selecting the style name from a list of styles. A style is useful if you frequently apply a particular font, alignment, and numeric format to cells. By default, cells have the Normal style applied. Click Format and then Style to add, delete, or modify styles. The Style dialog box shown at the right displays the settings for the Normal style.

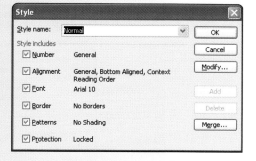

IN BRIEF

Change Numeric Format Using Toolbar
1 Select cells.
2 Click style button on Formatting toolbar.
3 Deselect cells.

Change Numeric Format Using Format Cells
1 Select cells.
2 Click Format, Cells.
3 Click Number tab.
4 Select desired format in *Category* list.
5 If necessary, change *Decimal places, Symbol,* or *Negative numbers* options.
6 Click OK.
7 Deselect cells.

2.8 Changing the Alignment and Indentation of Cells

Data in a cell can be left-aligned, right-aligned, or centered within the column. A heading or title that you want to position over several columns can be merged and then the text within the merged cell can be aligned at the left, center, or right. Data can be indented from the left edge of the cell or rotated to add visual interest.

PROJECT: Change the alignment of column headings and values, and indent labels from the left edge of column A to improve the appearance of the quotation.

S T E P S

1. With **ExcelS2-01** open, edit the column headings in C20 and E20 to include a period (.) after the abbreviation for *Number*. For example, the edited column heading in C20 will be *No. of Persons*.

2. Select C20:J20.

3. Click the Center button [icon] on the Formatting toolbar.

4. Select C21, C28, and C32 and then center them within the column.

5. Center the entries in column E.

Step 1

	A	B	C	D	E
19					
20	Item		No. of Persons	Price Per Person	No. of Days
21	Buffet Lunch		56	5.98	40
22	Soup and salad				
23	Vegetable tray with dip				
24	Seafood hors d'oeuvres				
25	Hot entrée				
26	Deli tray and rolls				
27	Dessert				
28	Beverages		56	3.98	40
29	Coffee and tea				
30	Assorted juice				
31	Mineral water				
32	Snacks		56	3.98	40
33	Muffins				
34	Donuts				
35	Fruit tray				
36	Vegetable tray with dip				
37	Delivery			31	40

Step 4

Step 5

6. Select A22:A27.

7. Click the Increase Indent button [icon] on the Formatting toolbar.

> Each time you click Increase Indent, the contents of the selected cells are indented by approximately one character width. If you click Increase Indent one too many times, click the Decrease Indent button [icon] to return the text to the previous indent position.

8. Select A29:A31 and then click Increase Indent.

9. Select A33:A36 and then click Increase Indent.

10. Select A20:J20 and then bold the cells.

	A	B
17	Re:	Toronto Locatic
18		July 4 through
19		
20	Item	
21	Buffet Lunch	
22	Soup and salad	
23	Vegetable tray with dip	
24	Seafood hors d'oeuvres	
25	Hot entree	
26	Deli tray and rolls	
27	Dessert	
28	Beverages	

Steps 6–7

⑪ AutoFit column J.

⑫ Make F11 the active cell and then click the Align Left button 📄 on the Formatting toolbar.

> By default, Excel aligns date entries at the right edge of a column since dates are converted to a serial number and treated in a similar manner to values. You will learn more about using dates in Excel in a later topic.

⑬ Click the Print Preview button on the Standard toolbar.

⑭ Click the Setup button on the Print Preview toolbar.

⑮ With the Page tab selected in the Page Setup dialog box, click *Landscape* in the *Orientation* section.

⑯ Click *Fit to [1] page(s) wide by [1] tall* in the *Scaling* section and then click OK.

> Use the *Fit to* option to instruct Excel to automatically calculate the scaling percentage needed to print a worksheet on a specified number of pages.

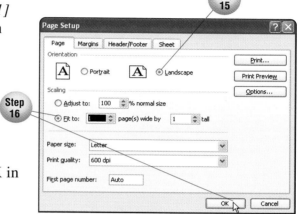

Step 15

Step 16

⑰ Click the Print button on the Print Preview toolbar and then click OK in the Print dialog box.

⑱ Save **ExcelS2-01**.

In Addition

Rotating, Vertical Alignment, and Text Controls

The Alignment tab in the Format Cells dialog box (shown at right) contains options not found on the Formatting toolbar to rotate text, align text vertically, control the length of labels within a cell, and designate the reading order for text. Use the *Wrap text* and *Shrink to fit* options in the *Text control* section to format long labels within a column.

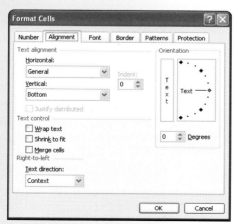

In Brief

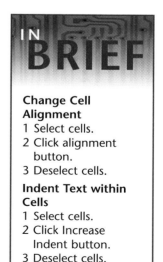

Change Cell Alignment
1 Select cells.
2 Click alignment button.
3 Deselect cells.

Indent Text within Cells
1 Select cells.
2 Click Increase Indent button.
3 Deselect cells.

2.9 Adding Borders and Shading; Autoformatting

Borders in various styles and colors can be applied to display and print in selected cells within the worksheet. Borders can be added to the top, left, bottom, or right edge of a cell. Use borders to underscore headings or totals, or to emphasize other cells. Shading adds color and/or a pattern to the background of a cell. Excel's AutoFormat feature includes several predefined worksheet format settings. In the AutoFormat dialog box you can scroll through samples of the predefined autoformats and select a style that suits your worksheet.

PROJECT: After reviewing the printout in the previous topic you decide to improve the presentation by adding borders, shading, and a pattern to cells. Finally, you will apply an autoformat to the body of the quotation.

STEPS

1. With **ExcelS2-01** open, use Save As and name the worksheet **ExcelS2-02**.

2. Hide columns H through J.

3. Select A20:F20.

    In the next steps you will add a border to the top and bottom of the column headings using the Borders button on the Formatting toolbar.

4. Click the down-pointing arrow to the right of the Borders button ⊞▼ on the Formatting toolbar.

    A palette of border style options displays. Click a border style to add the border to the selected cells. The most recently selected border style displays in the Borders button. To apply the same border style to another cell, select the cell and then click the Borders button.

5. Click the Top and Bottom Border button (third from left in second row).

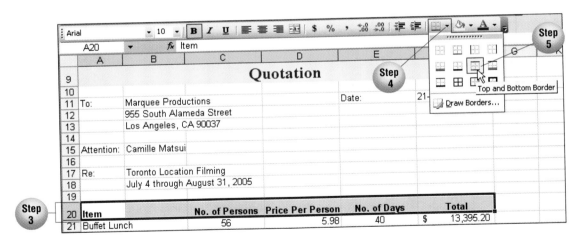

6. Click in any cell to deselect the range A20:F20 and view the border.

7. Make F39 the active cell.

    In the next steps you will add a double underline border to the bottom of F39 using options in the Format Cells dialog box. A Bottom Double Border button does exist on the Borders button; however, using the dialog box you will learn how to apply a custom border for future reference.

8. Click Format and then Cells.

9 Click the Border tab in the Format Cells dialog box.

10 Click the double line option in the *Style* list box (last option in second column), click the Bottom border button in the *Border* section, and then click OK.

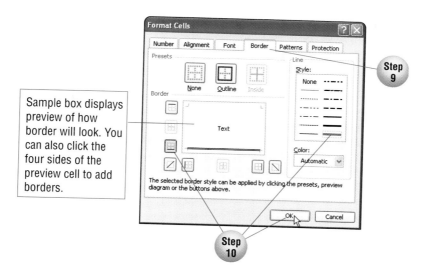

Sample box displays preview of how border will look. You can also click the four sides of the preview cell to add borders.

Step 9

Step 10

11 Click in another cell in the worksheet so you can view the double bottom border in F39.

12 Select A20:F20.

In the next steps you will use the Patterns tab in the Format Cells dialog box to add shading color to cells. The Format Cells dialog box provides more color choices than the Fill Color palette as well as including various patterns that can be placed in the background.

13 Click Format and then Cells.

14 Click the Patterns tab in the Format Cells dialog box.

15 Click the Pale Yellow color button (third from left in second row from bottom).

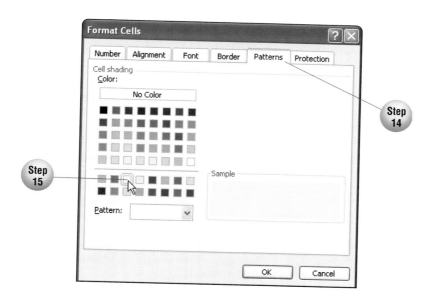

Step 14

Step 15

(continued)

16. Click the down-pointing arrow next to the *Pattern* option box.

> This displays the Pattern style and color palette.

17. Click 12.5% Gray (fifth from left in first row of patterns).

18. Click the down-pointing arrow next to the *Pattern* option box.

19. Click the Periwinkle color button (first from left in second row from bottom).

> Periwinkle is now the color of the patterned dots that will display in the foreground of the pale yellow shading in the selected cells. In Step 17 you instructed Excel to shade the pattern 12.5 percent of the periwinkle color.

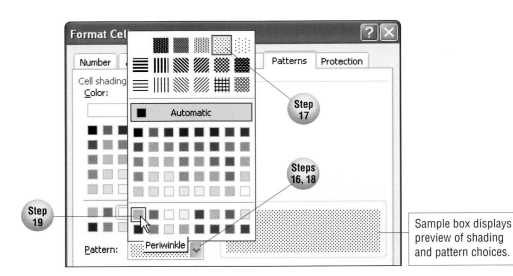

20. Click OK and then click in any cell to deselect the range and view the shading and pattern.

> After reviewing the border, shading, and pattern you have applied to cells in the quotation you decide to try one of Excel's predefined autoformat options to see if you prefer a different look.

21. Select A20:F39.

22. Click Format and then AutoFormat.

23. Scroll down the AutoFormat list box until you can see the Colorful 2 style.

24. Click *Colorful 2*.

25. Click the Options button in the AutoFormat dialog box.

> The AutoFormat dialog box expands to display a series of check boxes in the *Formats to apply* section at the bottom of the dialog box. Deselect the check boxes to customize the predefined format to suit your needs. For example, if you had applied a font to the selected cells that you want to retain, deselect the *Font* check box.

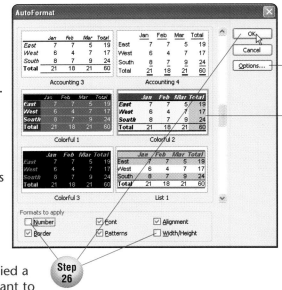

26 Click the *Number* and *Width/Height* check boxes in the *Formats to apply* section to deselect these options and then click OK.

> The Colorful 2 style is applied to the selected cells minus the number format and width/height options that you deselected. Any other formats that may have already been applied to the selected cells are overwritten with the Colorful 2 format settings.

27 Click in any cell to deselect the range.

28 Click the Print Preview button and then click the Setup button on the Print Preview toolbar.

29 Change the page orientation to *Portrait* and then click OK.

30 Click the Print button on the Print Preview toolbar and then click OK in the Print dialog box.

> If you are printing on a printer other than a color printer, the cells with color and shading applied to them are printed in shades of gray. Autoformats such as Colorful 2 may not be suitable for black and white printing.

31 Save **ExcelS2-02**.

In Addition

Copying Formats with Format Painter

The Format Painter button [icon] on the Standard toolbar can be used to copy formats from an existing cell to other cells in the worksheet. Activate the cell containing the desired formats and then click the Format Painter button. The cell pointer displays with a paintbrush attached to it. Select the cell or range of cells to which you want the formats copied. The formats are copied to the cells and Format Painter is automatically turned off. Double-clicking the Format Painter button will turn on Format Painter for consecutive copying until you turn off the feature by clicking the Format Painter button to deactivate it.

IN BRIEF

Add Borders
1 Select cells.
2 Click Format, Cells.
3 Click Border tab.
4 Select *Border* options.
5 Deselect cells.

Add Shading/Patterns
1 Select cells.
2 Click Format, Cells.
3 Click Patterns tab.
4 Select *Cell shading* options.
5 Deselect cells.

Autoformat a Worksheet
1 Select cells.
2 Click Format, AutoFormat.
3 Double-click desired autoformat style.
4 Deselect cells.

2.10 Using Find and Replace

Use the Find command to search for specific labels or values that you want to verify or edit. The Find command will move to each cell containing the text you specify. The Replace command will search for a label, value, or format and automatically replace it with another label, value, or format. The Find and Replace feature ensures that all occurrences of the specified text are included.

PROJECT: Use Find to review which items included a vegetable tray with dip. You have just received an e-mail from Camille Matsui of Marquee Productions advising you that the film crew will require catering services for three additional days. Use the Replace command to correct the number of days. Finally, you will use the Replace command to change all cells that are currently set in bold and italic to the regular font style.

STEPS

1 With **ExcelS2-02** open, press Ctrl + Home to move the active cell to A1.

2 Click Edit and then Find.

3 Type **vegetable tray with dip** in the *Find what* text box and then click Find Next.

The cell containing the first occurrence of *vegetable tray with dip* (A23) becomes active.

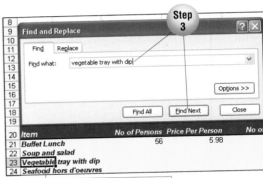

PROBLEM?

Can't see the active cell? Drag the Find and Replace dialog box out of the way if it is obscuring your view of the worksheet.

Active cell moves to the next occurrence each time you click Find Next.

4 Click Find Next.

The cell containing the next occurrence of *vegetable tray with dip* (A36) becomes active.

5 Click Find Next.

The cell containing the first occurrence of *vegetable tray with dip* becomes active since there are only two occurrences. You now know that this item is included in the Buffet Lunch and Snacks packages.

6 Click the Close button to close the Find and Replace dialog box.

In this example the Find command was used to find only two occurrences that were both visible within the current window. In a large worksheet with many rows and columns of data, the Find command is a very efficient method of moving to a specific cell.

7 Click Edit and then Replace.

Notice the previous entry that was searched for *(vegetable tray with dip)* appears in the *Find what* text box.

8 Drag to select *vegetable tray with dip* in the *Find what* text box and then type **40**.

9 Press Tab to move the insertion point to the *Replace with* text box and then type **43**.

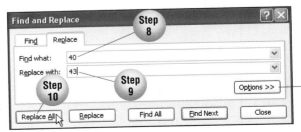

(10) Click Replace All.

> Excel will search through the entire worksheet and automatically change all occurrences of *40* to *43*.

(11) Click OK at the message that Excel has completed the search and has made 4 replacements.

(12) With the Find and Replace dialog box still open, click the Options button.

> In the next steps you will use the Replace feature to remove all bold and italic formatting.

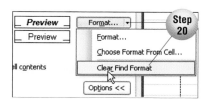

Preview of format that will be searched.

(13) Drag to select *40* in the *Find what* text box and then press Delete. Drag to select *43* in the *Replace with* text box and then press Delete.

(14) Click the Format button at the right of the *Find what* text box.

(15) If necessary, click the Font tab in the Find Format dialog box. Click *Bold Italic* in the *Font style* section and then click OK.

> A preview of the format that will be searched for displays between the *Find what* text box and the Format button.

(16) Click the Format button at the right of the *Replace with* text box.

(17) Click *Regular* in the *Font style* section and then click OK.

> A preview of the format that will be replaced for each occurrence of the found format displays between the *Replace with* text box and the Format button.

(18) Click Replace All.

(19) Click OK at the message that Excel has completed its search and has made the replacements.

(20) Click the down-pointing arrow next to the Format button at the right of *Find what* and then click Clear Find Format.

(21) Click the down-pointing arrow next to the Format button at the right of *Replace with* and then click Clear Replace Format.

(22) Click the Options button.

(23) Click the Close button in the Find and Replace dialog box.

(24) Use the Increase Indent button to indent the cells in the ranges A22:27, A29:A31, and A33:A36.

(25) Save **ExcelS2-02**.

Find a Label or Value
1 Click Edit, Find.
2 Type label or value in *Find what* text box.
3 Click Find Next.

Replace a Label or Value
1 Click Edit, Replace.
2 Type label or value in *Find what* text box.
3 Type replacement label or value in *Replace with* text box.
4 Click Find Next or Replace All.

2.11 Freezing Panes; Splitting the Window; Changing the Zoom

When you scroll to the right or down to view parts of a worksheet that do not fit in the current window, some column or row headings may scroll off the screen making it difficult for you to relate to the text or values. The Freeze Panes option from the Window menu will cause rows and columns to remain fixed when you scroll. As an alternative to freezing panes you can choose to split the worksheet into more than one window. Each window has its own set of scroll bars allowing you to scroll to different areas within the worksheet in the separate windows. Magnify or reduce the display by changing the settings in the Zoom dialog box.

PROJECT: You will freeze column and row headings in the quotation to facilitate scrolling; practice with splitting the window; and reduce the zoom percentage to view more cells at the same time.

STEPS

1. With **Excel S2-02** open, unhide columns H, I, and J.

2. Make A21 the active cell, click Window and then Freeze Panes.

   All rows above the active cell are frozen. A black line appears below row 20 to indicate which rows will remain fixed when scrolling.

3. Press the Page Down key several times to scroll down the worksheet.

   Notice rows 1 through 20 do not scroll off the screen.

4. Click Window and then Unfreeze Panes.

   The Freeze Panes option changes to Unfreeze Panes when rows or columns have been frozen.

5. Make C21 the active cell, click Window and then Freeze Panes.

   Rows 1 through 20 and columns A and B are frozen.

6. Scroll right several columns and down several rows.

   Black horizontal and vertical lines indicate which columns and rows are frozen, as shown in Figure E2.1.

7. Click Window and then Unfreeze Panes.

FIGURE E2.1 Lines Showing Frozen Rows and Columns

	A	B	F	G	H	I	J	K
15	Attention:	Camille Matsui						
16								
17	Re:	Toronto Locatio						
18		July 4 through						
19								
20	Item		Total		Our Cost	Gross Margin	GM Percent	
32	Snacks		9,583.84		1.22	6,646.08	69.3%	
33	Muffins							
34	Donuts							
35	Fruit tray							
36	Vegetable tray with dip							
37	Delivery		1,333.00		23.00	344.00	25.8%	
38								
39	**Total**		$ 34,900.52			$ 16,670.24	47.8%	
40								
41	Quotation is valid for 30 da							
42	Note: All prices are tax inc							
43	Terms: Due upon receipt							

Horizontal and Vertical lines indicate which rows and columns are frozen.

⑧ Make A21 the active cell, click Window and then Split.

> The worksheet is now split into two independent windows, each with its own scroll bar. Only one active cell exists in the split window.

17	Re:	Toronto Location Filming							
18		July 4 through August 31, 2005							
19									
20	Item	No of Persons	Price Per Person	No of Days	Total		Our Cost	Gross Margin	GM Percent
35	Fruit tray								
36	Vegetable tray with dip								
37	Delivery	31	43		1,333.00		23.00	344.00	25.8%
38									
39	Total				$ 34,900.52		$ 16,670.24	47.8%	
40									
41	Quotation is valid for 30 days								
42	Note: All prices are tax included								
43	Terms: Due upon receipt of invoice payable in US funds								
44									
45									
46									

Sheet1 / Sheet2 / Sheet3 /

Step 10

Step 9

⑨ Click the down scroll arrow in the lower window several times to scroll down the quotation. Notice the cells in the window at the top remain fixed.

⑩ Click the down scroll arrow in the upper window several times. Notice you are working with two copies of the worksheet—each in its own window.

⑪ Click Window and then Remove Split.

> Excel splits a window based on the location of the active cell when the Split command is invoked. Placing the active cell in row 1 of any column will cause a vertical split. If the active cell is placed within the worksheet in a column other than A and a row other than 1, the worksheet is split into four panes.

⑫ Click the down-pointing arrow on the Zoom button on the Standard toolbar (currently reads *100%*) and then click *75%* at the drop-down list.

> The worksheet is reduced to 75% magnification, allowing you to view more columns and rows. In addition to the options in the drop-down list you can type your own value in the *Zoom* text box.

⑬ Click inside the *Zoom* text box, type **80**, and then press Enter.

⑭ Hide columns H through J and then print the revised quotation.

⑮ Save and then close **Excel S2-02**.

In Addition

Splitting the Window Using the Split Box

A Split box (shown at the right) is located at the top of the vertical scroll bar and at the right edge of the horizontal scroll bar. You can also split the window by dragging the split box into the worksheet window. To remove the split, drag the split box back up to the top or left of the window. A window cannot be split if Freeze Panes is activated.

Split Box

IN BRIEF

Freeze Panes
1 Make cell active below and right of row or column headings you want to freeze.
2 Click Window, Freeze Panes.

Split Window
1 Make cell active below and right of cell where you want to split window.
2 Click Window, Split.

Change Zoom Setting
1 Click View, Zoom.
2 Choose magnification setting.
3 Click OK.

FEATURES SUMMARY

Feature	Button	Menu	Keyboard
Accounting Format		Format, Cells, Number	Ctrl + 1
AutoFormat		Format, AutoFormat	
Bold	**B**	Format, Cells, Font	Ctrl + B
Borders		Format, Cells, Border	Ctrl + 1
Center		Format, Cells, Alignment	Ctrl + 1
Clear Cell		Edit, Clear, All	
Clear Cell Contents		Edit, Clear, Contents	Delete
Clear Cell Formats		Edit, Clear, Formats	
Column Width		Format, Column, Width	
Comma Style	,	Format, Style, Style name	
Copy		Edit, Copy	Ctrl + C
Cut		Edit, Cut	Ctrl + X
Decrease Decimal	.00→.0	Format, Cells, Number	Ctrl + 1
Decrease Indent		Format, Cells, Alignment	Ctrl + 1
Delete Cells		Edit, Delete	
Delete Column or Row		Edit, Delete	
Fill Color/Shading		Format, Cells, Patterns	Ctrl + 1
Find		Edit, Find	Ctrl + F
Font	Arial	Format, Cells, Font	Ctrl + 1
Font Color	A	Format, Cells, Font	Ctrl + 1
Font Size	10	Format, Cells, Font	Ctrl + 1
Freeze Panes		Window, Freeze Panes	
Hide Column or Row		Format, Row or Column, Hide	
Increase Decimal	←.0.00	Format, Cells, Number	Ctrl + 1
Increase Indent		Format, Cells, Alignment	Ctrl + 1
Insert Cells		Insert, Cells	
Insert Column or Row		Insert, Columns or Rows	
Italic	*I*	Format, Cells, Font	Ctrl + 1
Left Align		Format, Cells, Alignment	Ctrl + 1
Paste		Edit, Paste	Ctrl + V

Feature	Button	Menu	Keyboard
Percent Style	%	Format, Style, Style name	
Redo	↻	Edit, Redo	Ctrl + Y
Replace		Edit, Replace	Ctrl + H
Right Align	≣	Format, Cells, Alignment	Ctrl + 1
Row Height		Format, Row, Height	
Spell Check	✓ABC	Tools, Spelling	F7
Split Window		Window, Split	
Undo		Edit, Undo	Ctrl + Z
Zoom		View, Zoom	

PROCEDURES CHECK

Matching: Identify the commands represented by the following buttons:

1. _____

2. _____

3. _____

4. _____

5. _____

6. _____

7. _____

8. _____

9. _____

10. _____

Completion: In the space provided at the right, indicate the correct term or command.

1. Make a cell active in this row to insert a new row between 11 and 12.

2. Make a cell active in this column to insert a new column between E and F. _____

3. Make a cell active here to freeze rows 1 through 9 and columns A and B. _____

4. Do this action with the mouse on a column boundary to adjust the width to the length of the longest entry. _____

5. Use this feature to automatically change all occurrences of a label, value, or format to another label, value, or format. _____

6. Use this feature if you change your mind after clicking Undo. _____

7. This is the term that refers to the unit of measurement for the font size. _____

8. By default, cells are initially set to this format. _____

9. This feature allows you to choose from predesigned formats to change the appearance of a worksheet. _____

10. Use this feature to view the worksheet in separate windows that can be scrolled independently of one another. _____

SKILLS REVIEW

Activity 1: EDITING, CLEARING, AND INSERTING CELLS; PERFORMING A SPELL CHECK; DELETING ROWS

1 Open **WBInvoice**.
2 Save the workbook with Save As and name it **ExcelS2-R1**.
3 Change the cost in I20 from *5.21* to *5.29*.
4 Clear the contents of I16:I17.
5 Change the label in A21 from *Soup* to *Seafood Chowder Soup*.
6 Insert cells above E10:F10 and then type the following data in the new cells:

E10 = **PO No.**
F10 = **TA-05-643**

7 Delete rows 7, 8, and 9.
8 Complete a spelling check of the worksheet. (All names are spelled correctly.)
9 Save **ExcelS2-R1**.

Activity 2: MOVING, COPYING, AND DELETING CELLS; INSERTING AND DELETING ROWS

1 With **ExcelS2-R1** open, move D5 to A15.
2 Move E7:F8 to E11:F12.
3 Copy A24 to A30.
4 Make cell F16 active, display the Delete dialog box, click *Shift cells up,* and then click OK.
5 Delete the entire row for those rows that contain the labels *Milk, Assorted juice,* and *Doughnuts.*
6 Insert a new row between *Prime Rib* and *Mixed Vegetables* and type **Seafood Pasta** in column A of the new row.
7 Save **ExcelS2-R1**.

Activity 3: ADJUSTING COLUMN WIDTH; REPLACING DATA; FORMATTING NUMBERS; INDENTING TEXT

1 With **ExcelS2-R1** open, select column C and then adjust the width to the length of the longest entry (AutoFit).
2 Change the width of column D to *15.00 (110 pixels)* and column E to *7.00 (54 pixels).*
3 Select columns I through K and then adjust the width to the length of the longest entry (AutoFit).

4 Use the Replace feature to replace the value *33* with *37*.
5 Format F17 and F32 to Accounting. *(Hint: Use Format Cells dialog box.)*
6 Format F27 and F30 to Comma Style.
7 Format K17 and K27 to Percent Style with one decimal place.
8 Indent once A18:A26 and A28:A29.
9 Save **ExcelS2-R1**.

Activity 4: CHANGING FONT, FONT ATTRIBUTES, AND ALIGNMENT; ADDING BORDERS AND SHADING; HIDING COLUMNS

1 With **ExcelS2-R1** open, change the font in A15 to 20-point Book Antiqua Bold. *(Note: If Book Antiqua is not available on your computer system, substitute another font such as Times New Roman.)*
2 Merge and center A15 across columns A through F.
3 Change the font color to red and the fill color to yellow in A15.
4 Center the values in columns C and D and in F16.
5 Add a top and bottom border to A16:F16 and turn on bold.
6 Add a bottom double border to F32 and turn on bold.
7 Display the worksheet in Print Preview, change the page orientation to *Landscape,* and then print the worksheet.
8 Hide columns I through K.
9 Display the worksheet in Print Preview, change the page orientation to *Portrait,* and then print the worksheet.
10 Save **ExcelS2-R1**.

Activity 5: FREEZING PANES, UNHIDING COLUMNS, SPLITTING THE WORKSHEET; CHANGING THE ZOOM

1 With **ExcelS2-R1** open, make active A17 and then freeze panes.
2 Scroll down the worksheet several rows.
3 Unfreeze the panes and then unhide columns I through K.
4 Make active C17 and then split the window.
5 Practice scrolling the worksheet in all four windows.
6 Remove the split windows.
7 Change the Zoom percentage to *85.*
8 Save and then close **ExcelS2-R1**.

PERFORMANCE PLUS

Assessment 1: FREEZING PANES AND CHANGING ZOOM, COLUMN WIDTH, FONT COLOR, AND FILL COLOR

1 Dana Hirsch, manager of The Waterfront Bistro, has asked you to review the *Inventory Units Purchased* report and modify it to make it more readable and to view as much data as possible in one window.
2 Open **WBInventory**.
3 Save the workbook with Save As and name it **ExcelS2-P1**.

4 Make the following changes:
  a Freeze panes so you can scroll the worksheet without losing the column and row headings.
  b Change the zoom so you can view as much of the worksheet as possible to minimize horizontal scrolling. Make sure the cells are still readable. (*Note: Depending on your monitor size and resolution setting, change the custom setting to a value between 50% and 80%.*)
  c Adjust all column widths to the length of the longest entry (AutoFit).
  d Change the color of the shading behind the title *Inventory Units Purchased*. You determine the color.
  e Change the font color and the shading color for A2:O2. You determine the colors.
5 Click the page orientation to landscape.
6 Print page 1 only. To do this, click *Page(s)* in the *Print range* section of the Print dialog box and then type 1 in the *From* and *To* text boxes.
7 Save and then close **ExcelS2-P1**.

Assessment 2: EDITING CELLS; INSERTING AND HIDING COLUMNS; COPYING A FORMULA; FORMATTING A WORKSHEET

1 Bobbie Sinclair of Performance Threads has started preparing a workbook that tracks the costs of costume research, design, and production for the Marquee Productions project. You have been asked to complete the workbook.
2 Open **PTCostumes**.
3 Save the workbook with Save As and name it **ExcelS2-P2**.
4 Complete the worksheet using the following information:
  a Design costs should be *29.50* instead of *27.50*.
  b Insert a new column between *Fabric* and *Total Cost* and type the column heading *Notions* in J9. Type the values in J10:J14 as follows:

Val Wingfield	110.00
Eunice Billings	78.43
Tony Salvatore	93.67
Celia Gopf	143.66
Jade Norwich	169.42

  c The formula to calculate total cost for each costume is incorrect. Enter the correct formula for the first costume (K10) and then copy the formula to K11:K14. (*Hint: The current formula does not include the* **Fabric** *and* **Notions** *costs.*)
  d Format the numeric cells in an appropriate style.
  e Change the alignment of any headings that could be improved in appearance.
  f Merge and center the titles in A6 and A7 over the columns.
  g Apply font, border, and color changes to enhance the appearance of the worksheet.
5 Print the worksheet in landscape orientation.
6 Hide the *Costume Fee* and *Profit* columns and then print the worksheet.
7 Save and then close **ExcelS2-P2**.

Assessment 3: COMPLETING AND FORMATTING A WORKSHEET

1 Camille Matsui, production assistant for Marquee Productions, has requested that Performance Threads send an invoice for the five custom-made costumes separate from the costume rentals. Bobbie Sinclair has started the invoice and has asked you to finish it.
2 Open **PTInvoice**.

3 Save the workbook with Save As and name it **ExcelS2-P3**.
4 Complete the invoice using the following information:
   a Type the current date in G6.
   b Each custom costume fee is $2,650.00. Enter this value in F15:F19.
   c Total the costume fees in F20.
   d A transportation and storage container for each of the five costumes is *$75.00.* Enter
      the appropriate formula in G22 that will calculate the fee for five containers.
   e Enter in F23 the delivery for all five costumes as *$142.75.*
   f Enter the formula in F24 that will add the total for the costume fees with the
      additional charges.
   g Enter the formula in F25 that will calculate 7% GST (Goods and Services Tax) on the
      total including additional charges.
   h Enter the formula to total the invoice in F26 as the sum of F24 and F25.
5 Format the worksheet to improve the appearance of the invoice.
6 Save **ExcelS2-P3**.
7 Print and then close **ExcelS2-P3**.

Assessment 4: PERFORMING SPELL CHECK; ADJUSTING COLUMN WIDTH; EDITING CELLS; USING FIND AND REPLACE; HIDING COLUMNS; FORMATTING WORKSHEETS

1 Sam Vestering, manager of North American Distribution for Worldwide Enterprises, has
  created a workbook to summarize revenues from distribution of Marquee Productions'
  film *Two By Two*. You have been asked to review the worksheet and make corrections
  and enhancements to the appearance.
2 Open **WERevenue**.
3 Save the workbook with Save As and name it **ExcelS2-P4**.
4 Make the following corrections:
   a Perform a spelling check.
   b Adjust column widths so all data is completely visible.
   c Check the *Projected Box Office Sales* in column H with the data in **ExcelS1-P3** and
      change any values that do not match. *(**Note: You can check these values on page 31 if
      you did not complete Performance Plus Assessment 3 in Section 1.**)*
   d Make active cell I8 and then enter the formula to calculate the Box Office Variance as
      Box Office Sales minus Projected Box Office Sales. Copy the formula to the
      remaining rows in the column.
   e Change all of the theaters named *Cinema House* to *Cinema Magic*.
   f Make active cell A3, type **Date:**, and then make active cell B3 and enter today's date.
   g Apply formatting enhancements to improve the appearance of the worksheet.
5 Print **ExcelS2-P4**.
6 Hide columns H and I.
7 Print **ExcelS2-P4**.
8 Save and then close **ExcelS2-P4**.

Assessment 5: FINDING THE SELECT ALL BUTTON

1 Use Excel's Help feature to find out where the Select All button is located in the Excel window.
2 Open **ExcelS2-P1**.
3 Save the workbook with Save As and name it **ExcelS2-P5**.
4 Click the Select All button.

5   Click the Align Right and Italic buttons on the Formatting toolbar.
6   Scroll the worksheet to view the new formats.
7   Change columns A and B to Align Left.
8   Save **ExcelS2-P5**.
9   Print page 1 only and then close **ExcelS2-P5**.

Assessment 6: FINDING INFORMATION ON DATES

1   Use Excel's Help feature to find information on how Excel stores dates and how they can be used in a formula.
2   Open **ExcelS2-P3**.
3   Save the workbook with Save As and name it **ExcelS2-P6**.
4   Add the label *Due Date:* to F12.
5   Create a formula in G12 that will add 30 days to the date of the invoice.
6   Save and print **ExcelS2-P6**.
7   Change the date of the invoice to *May 10, 2005*.
8   Save, print, and then close **ExcelS2-P6**.

Assessment 7: FINDING INFORMATION ON SPLITTING CELLS

1   Use Excel's Help feature to find information on how to split cells that have been merged and centered.
2   Open **ExcelS2-R1**.
3   Save the workbook with Save As and name it **ExcelS2-P7**.
4   Split the merged cells A15:F15 containing the label *Invoice*.
5   Hide columns I through K.
6   Preview and then print **ExcelS2-P7**.
7   Save and then close **ExcelS2-P7**.

Assessment 8: LOCATING INFORMATION ON THEATER ARTS PROGRAMS

1   You are considering enrolling in a drama/theater arts program at a college or university. Search the Internet for available programs in postsecondary schools in the United States and Canada. Choose five schools that interest you the most and find out as much as you can about the costs of attending these schools. Try to find information on costs beyond tuition and books, such as transportation and room and board.
2   Create a workbook that will summarize the information on the schools you have selected.
3   Apply formatting enhancements to the worksheet.
4   Save the workbook and name it **ExcelS2-P8**.
5   Print and then close **ExcelS2-P8**.

EXCEL

SECTION 3

Using Functions, Setting Print Options, and Adding Visual Elements

Functions in Excel are grouped into categories such as Statistical, Date, Financial, and Logical. The Insert Function dialog box can be used to find a preprogrammed function by searching based on a description or by browsing a list of functions within a category. The Page Setup dialog box is used to change options for printing worksheets such as changing margins, centering on a page, and repeating column or row labels on multiple sheets. Adding visual elements such as charts or drawn objects to a worksheet can assist the reader with interpreting numerical data. For example, a chart can illustrate variances in sales more dramatically than the numbers alone. Objects such as text boxes can be drawn to guide a reader's attention to a cell or range of cells. In this section you will learn the skills and complete the projects described here.

Note: Before beginning this section, delete the ExcelS2 folder on your disk. Next, copy to your disk or other location the ExcelS3 subfolder from the CD that accompanies this textbook and then make ExcelS3 the active folder.

Skills

- Use the AVERAGE, MAX, and MIN formulas to perform statistical analysis
- Create NOW and DATE formulas
- Determine loan payment amounts using the PMT function
- Create an IF formula to return a result based on a logical test
- Change margins
- Center a worksheet horizontally and vertically
- Insert headers and footers
- Print row headings, column headings, and gridlines
- Scale a worksheet to fit within a specified number of pages
- Create, edit, and format charts
- Insert, size, and move a picture
- Draw arrows and text boxes

Projects

Add function formulas and set print options for the *Inventory Units Purchased* and *Quarterly Expenses* reports; enter Date functions in an invoice and change the print options; calculate loan payment amounts for an expansion project; use an IF function to calculate bonuses; change print options; create and modify charts; insert pictures; draw an arrow and text box in an *Operating Expenses and Cost of Sales* worksheet.

Niagara Peninsula COLLEGE Set print options for the Theatre Arts Co-Op Work Term Placements report; add a formula based on a date; create and format charts for a grades analysis report.

Calculate commissions and analyze data in a Sales Agent Commission report; insert a picture and apply formatting enhancements to a European Destinations report.

WORLDWIDE Enterprises Calculate payments for a loan to construct a new building.

3.1 Using Statistical Functions AVERAGE, MAX, and MIN

You learned about functions when you used the AutoSum button, which assisted with entering the SUM function. Excel includes numerous built-in formulas that are grouped into function categories. The Statistical category contains several functions that can be used to perform statistical analysis on data, such as calculating medians, variances, frequencies, and so on. The structure of a function formula begins with the equals sign (=), followed by the name of the function, and then the *argument* within parentheses. The argument is the term given to the values to be included in the calculation. The structure of the argument is dependent on the function being used and can include a single range of cells, multiple ranges, single cell references, or a combination thereof.

PROJECT: You decide to include some basic statistical analysis in the *Inventory Units Purchased* report for The Waterfront Bistro such as the average quantity purchased, the maximum units purchased, and the minimum units purchased.

STEPS

1 Open **WBInventory**.

2 Save the workbook with Save As and name it **ExcelS3-01**.

3 Make C3 the active cell and then freeze the panes.

4 Type the following labels in the cells indicated:

A58 = **Average Units Purchased**
A59 = **Maximum Units Purchased**
A60 = **Minimum Units Purchased**

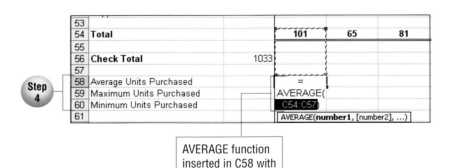

AVERAGE function inserted in C58 with suggested range highlighted (Step 7).

5 Make C58 the active cell.

In the next steps you will insert the AVERAGE function to determine the arithmetic mean of the cells in column C. If an empty cell or a cell containing text is included in the argument, Excel ignores the cell when determining the result. If, however, the cell contains a zero value, it is included in the average calculation.

6 Click the down-pointing arrow to the right of the AutoSum button on the Standard toolbar.

7 Click *Average* in the drop-down list.

Excel inserts the formula =*AVERAGE(C54:C57)* in the active cell with the suggested range highlighted. In the next step you will drag to select the correct range and then complete the formula.

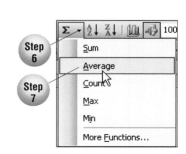

8 Scroll up the worksheet until you can see C3. Position the cell pointer over C3, hold down the left mouse button, drag down to C52, and then release the left mouse button.

> Excel inserts the range C3:C52 in the formula and the moving marquee expands to display the selected cells. Notice that Excel color codes the range entry in the formula with the expanded range border.

9 Press Enter or click the Enter button on the Formula bar.

> Excel returns the result *2.02* in C58.

10 Make C59 the active cell.

11 Click the down-pointing arrow to the right of the AutoSum button on the Standard toolbar and then click *Max* in the drop-down list.

> The MAX function returns the largest value in the argument.

12 Type **c3:c52** and then press Enter.

> Excel returns the result *6* in C59. Typing the range into the formula is sometimes faster if you are sure of the starting and ending cell references.

58	Average Units Purchased	2.02
59	Maximum Units Purchased	=MAX(c3:c52)
60	Minimum Units Purchased	
61		

MAX(**number1**, [number2], ...)

Step 12

13 With C60 the active cell, type the function **=min(c3:c52)** and then press Enter.

> The MIN function returns the smallest value in the argument. Type the entire function directly into the cell if you know the name of the function you want to use and the structure of the argument.

PROBLEM? Cell displays *#NAME?* A formula error generally causes this result to appear and a Trace Error button appears when the cell is activated. Click the Trace Error button to access error checking tools.

54	Total	101	65
55			
56	**Check Total**	1033	
57			
58	Average Units Purchased	2	
59	Maximum Units Purchased	6	
60	Minimum Units Purchased	0	
61			

Drag the fill handle right to column N.

Step 15

14 Format C58:C60 to the Number format with zero decimal places.

15 Select C58:C60 and then drag the fill handle right to column N.

> This copies the AVERAGE, MAX, and MIN formulas to columns D through N.

PROBLEM? Scrolling too fast? Don't let go of the mouse—drag in the opposite direction.

16 Click in any cell to deselect C58:N60.

17 Save and then close **ExcelS3-01**.

IN BRIEF

AVERAGE, MAX, MIN Functions
1 Make desired cell active.
2 Click down-pointing arrow on AutoSum button.
3 Click desired function.
4 Highlight argument range.
5 Press Enter or click Enter button.

3.2 Using Date Functions NOW and DATE

Excel stores dates as a serial number calculated from January 1, 1900, as serial number 1 and increased sequentially. Times are stored as decimal fractions representing portions of a day. This enables calculations to be performed on cells containing dates and times. The Date & Time category in the Insert Function dialog box contains functions that can be used to write formulas for cells containing dates. Cells containing dates and times can be formatted using the Format Cells dialog box to display the date or time in various formats.

PROJECT: You will open an invoice to Performance Threads and use the NOW function to enter the current date, and then calculate the due date by entering a formula to add 30 days to the invoice date. The DATE function will be used to enter the date The Waterfront Bistro opened.

STEPS

1. Open **WBInvoice2**.

2. Save the workbook with Save As and name it **ExcelS3-02**.

3. Make E7 the active cell, type **=now()**, and then press Enter.

   The current date and time is inserted in E7 and the column width automatically expands to accommodate the length of the entry. Excel includes another function *=TODAY()* that can be used to insert the current date without the time.

4. Make E9 the active cell, type **=e7+30**, and then press Enter to calculate the due date as 30 days from the invoice date.

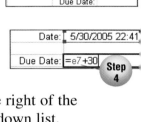

5. Make E5 the active cell, click the down-pointing arrow to the right of the AutoSum button, and then click *More Functions* in the drop-down list.

   The Insert Function dialog box opens. Search for a function by typing a phrase describing the type of formula you want in the *Search for a function* text box and then clicking the Go button, or by selecting a category name and then browsing a list of functions.

6. At the Insert Function dialog box, click the down-pointing arrow to the right of the *Or select a category* list box and then click *Date & Time* in the drop-down list.

   The *Select a function* list box displays an alphabetical list of date and time functions. Clicking a function name causes the formula with its argument structure and a description to appear below the list box. For more information on the selected function name, click the Help on this function hyperlink at the bottom left of the dialog box.

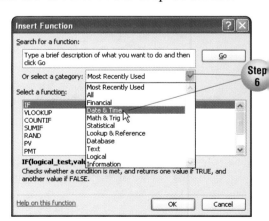

7. With the function name *DATE* already selected in the *Select a function* list box, read the description of the formula and then click OK.

   The Function Arguments dialog box opens with a text box for each section of the function argument.

8. Type **1977** in the *Year* text box.

⑨ Press Tab to move the insertion point to the *Month* text box and then type 06.

⑩ Press Tab to move the insertion point to the *Day* text box and then type 15.

⑪ Click OK to close the Function Arguments dialog box.

The Function Arguments dialog box displayed the serial number for June 15, 1977, as 28291; however, cell E5 displays the date. Notice the formula in the Formula bar is =DATE(1977,6,15).

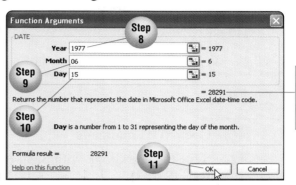

This is the serial number representing June 15, 1977.

⑫ With E5 the active cell, click Format and then Cells.

⑬ If necessary, click the Number tab in the Format Cells dialog box.

Since the active cell contained a date function, the Date category will be automatically selected in the Format Cells dialog box.

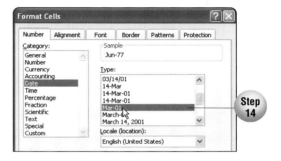

⑭ Scroll the list of formats in the *Type* list box, click the format that will display the date as *mmm-yy (Mar-01)*, and then click OK.

⑮ Format E5 to 9-point Arial Italic.

⑯ Select *E7:E9* and then display the Format Cells dialog box with the Number tab selected.

⑰ Click *Date* in the *Category* list box. Scroll down the *Type* list box, click the format that will display the date as *dd-mmm-yyyy (14-Mar-2001)*, and then click OK.

⑱ Click in any cell to deselect E7:E9.

⑲ Save and then close **ExcelS3-02**.

In Addition

TIME Function

Time values are stored as decimal numbers that represent the portion of a day starting at 0 (12:00:00 AM), and continuing up to 0.99999999 (representing 23:59:59 PM). The format of the TIME function is =TIME(hour,minute,second). In the time worksheet shown at the right, the formula =(C2-B2)*24 is used in D2 to calculate how many hours the employee worked.

The entry stored in C2 is =TIME(15,30,0).

3.3 Using Financial Function PMT

Excel's financial functions can be used to calculate depreciation, interest rates, payments, terms, present values, future values, and so on. The PMT function is used to calculate a payment for a loan based on constant payments, a constant interest rate, and a set period of time.

PROJECT: The Waterfront Bistro is planning a patio expansion next year. Dana Hirsch, manager, has asked you to calculate monthly payments for two construction loan scenarios.

STEPS

1. Open **WBFinancials**.

2. Save the workbook with Save As and name it **ExcelS3-03**.

3. Make B12 the active cell.

4. Click the Insert Function button 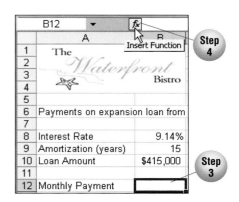 on the Formula bar.

   > Notice that Date & Time (the most recently displayed list of functions) is the category currently shown. In the next steps you will use the *Search for a function* feature to find the PMT function.

5. With the entry *Type a brief description of what you want to do and then click Go* already selected in the *Search for a function* text box, type **loan payments**, and then click the Go button.

   > A list of related functions display in the *Select a function* list box and the category name changes to *Recommended*.

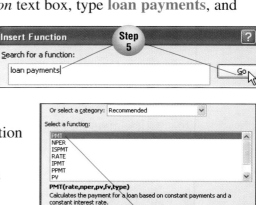

6. With *PMT* already selected in the *Select a function* list box, read the description below the list box and then click OK.

7. If necessary, drag the Function Arguments title bar to the right of column B.

8. With the insertion point positioned in the *Rate* text box, click in B8 and then type **/12**.

   > An explanation of each parameter in the function's argument displays near the bottom of the dialog box. The interest rate in the worksheet is stated per annum. Typing /12 divides the annual interest rate by 12 to obtain a monthly interest rate.

9. Click in the *Nper* text box, click B9, and then type ***12**.

   > The loan period, or **amortization**, is stated in years. Typing *12 multiplies the number of years times 12 to calculate the number of monthly payments that will be made on the loan.

10. Click in the *Pv* text box and then click B10.

    > Pv stands for *Present value* and represents the principal amount that is being borrowed.

11 Click OK.

Excel returns the payment amount *-$4,243.84* in B12. The result is displayed as a negative value. Consider loan payments as cash flowing outside your business or household, hence, a negative cash flow, or as money being subtracted from your cash balance. The PMT Function Arguments dialog box includes two parameters: *Fv* and *Type* not used in this example. *Fv*, or *future value*, represents the amount owing after the last payment is made. Leaving this blank means that the future value of the loan is zero; in other words, no balance exists after the last payment is made. *Type* is zero (payments are due at the end of the period) or one (payments due at the beginning of the period). The end of the period (zero) is assumed if this text box is left blank.

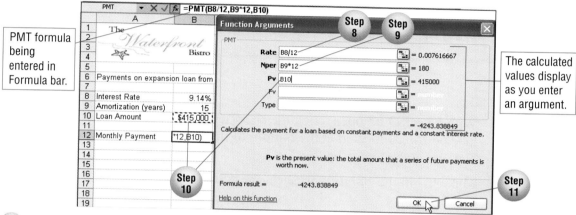

PMT formula being entered in Formula bar.

Step 8

Step 9

The calculated values display as you enter an argument.

Step 10

Step 11

12 Save **ExcelS3-03**.

Next, you will see what happens to the payment amount when you modify the amortization period and the interest rate.

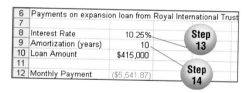

Step 13

Step 14

13 Make B8 the active cell and edit the interest rate amount from *9.14%* to *10.25%*.

14 Make B9 the active cell and edit the amortization period from *15* years to *10* years.

Excel recalculates the monthly payment with the new interest rate and term to *-$5,541.87*.

15 Save **ExcelS3-03**.

In Addition

Estimating Future Value

Use the *FV* function to calculate the future value of an investment based on periodic, constant payments and a constant interest rate (nonfluctuating terms). The FV function arguments in order are *Rate* (interest rate per period), *Nper* (number of payments made into the investment plan), and *Pmt* (amount invested each period).

Example: Assume a constant payment each year for 10 years of $5,000 into a retirement account that earns 7.75% interest per year. The formula =FV(7.75%,10,-5000) would return the result $71,578.53.

IN BRIEF

Financial Functions
1 Make desired cell active.
2 Click Insert Function button.
3 Click down-pointing arrow next to *Or select a category*.
4 Click *Financial* in drop-down list.
5 Click desired function name in *Select a function* list box.
6 Click OK.
7 Enter argument criteria in Function Arguments dialog box.
8 Click OK.

3.4 Using Logical Function IF

The IF function returns one of two values in a cell based on a true or false answer to a question called a *logical test*. For example, if the logical test is true, value *x* is placed in the cell. If the logical test is false, value *y* is placed in the cell. The format of an IF function is *=IF(logical_test,value_if_true,value_if_false)*. Logical functions allow you to use Excel to insert text or values based on a set of circumstances that you define. For example, a teacher could create an IF statement to insert the word *Pass* in a cell if a student's mark is greater than or equal to 50%, or the word *Fail* if the mark is less than 50%.

PROJECT: The dining room staff at The Waterfront Bistro receives a year-end bonus if profit targets are met. The bonus amount is based on the actual profit earned and the employee's years of service—0.50% for those with service of 4 years and more, and 0.25% for those with service less than 4 years. You will create the formula in the Bonus worksheet to calculate these bonuses.

STEPS

① With **ExcelS3-03** open, click the sheet tab labeled *Bonus* located at the bottom of the screen just above the Status bar.

Step 1

② Make C7 in the *Bonus* worksheet the active cell.

③ Type =if(b7>=4,f7*h7,f7*i7) and then press Enter.

Excel returns the value *762.48* in C7. The IF function entered in C7 is explained in Figure E3.1. The cell references in the true and false arguments contain dollar symbols to make them *absolute references*. Notice a dollar symbol is typed before both the column letter and the row number in the absolute cell references. The dollar symbol instructs Excel not to change the column or row relative to the destination when the formula is copied. Since the formula will be copied to rows 8–12, absolute references are required within the source formula for those cells that contain the actual profit and percentage values.

FIGURE E3.1
The IF Function

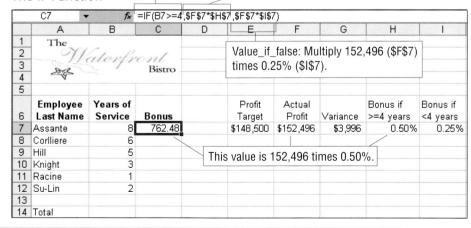

If you make a typing error, Excel displays a message and highlights the approximate area within the formula where the error occurred.

PROBLEM?

④ Press the Up Arrow key to move the active cell back to C7.

⑤ Drag the fill handle down to row 12.

> Excel copies the IF formula in row 7 to rows 8–12. The cell addresses containing the years of service are changed relative to each row (B7 is changed to B8, B9, and so on); however, the cell addresses containing the actual profit (F7) and bonus percentage values (H7 and I7) do not change. This is an example of a formula that uses *mixed addressing*—with some addresses relative and some addresses absolute.

⑥ With C7:C12 still selected, click the Currency Style button on the Formatting toolbar.

⑦ Make C14 the active cell and then use AutoSum to calculate the total.

⑧ Click each cell individually within the range C8 to C12 and review the formula in the Formula bar.

⑨ Save **ExcelS3-03**.

⑩ Close **ExcelS3-03**.

	A	B	C	D	E	F	G	H	I
1	The								
2		*Waterfront*							
3			Bistro						
4									
5									
6	Employee Last Name	Years of Service	Bonus		Profit Target	Actual Profit	Variance	Bonus if >=4 years	Bonus if <4 years
7	Assante	8	$ 762.48		$148,500	$152,496	$3,996	0.50%	0.25%
8	Corlliere	6	$ 762.48						
9	Hill	5	$ 762.48						
10	Knight	3	$ 381.24						
11	Racine	1	$ 381.24						
12	Su-Lin	2	$ 381.24						
13									
14	Total		$3,431.16						

Steps 5–6

Step 7

In Addition

Nested IF Function

If more than two actions are required when a logical test is performed, a nested IF function is used. For example, if three bonus rates were dependent on years of service for the dining room staff, the IF function entered in C7 would not have been sufficient. Assume the dining room staff receives 0.50% if they have 4 years of service or more, 0.25% for 2–4 years, and 0.1% for less than 2 years. The IF function required to calculate the bonus would be:

=IF(B7>=4,$F$7*0.50%,IF(B7>=2,$F$7*0.25%,$F$7*0.1%))

The two parentheses at the end of the argument are required to close both IF statements. Excel allows you to nest up to seven IF statements.

IN BRIEF

IF Function
1. Make desired cell active.
2. Click Insert Function button.
3. Click down-pointing arrow next to *Or select a category*.
4. Click *Logical* in drop-down list.
5. Click *IF* in *Select a function* list box.
6. Click OK.
7. Enter test condition in *Logical_test* text box.
8. Enter action required in *Value_if_true* text box.
9. Enter action required in *Value_if_false* text box.
10. Click OK.

3.5 Changing Margins; Centering a Worksheet on the Page

The margin on an Excel worksheet is the blank space at the top, bottom, left, and right edges of the page and the beginning of the printed text. Margin settings can be changed in the Page Setup dialog box or by dragging the margin handles on the Print Preview screen. The bottom section of the Margins tab in the Page Setup dialog box contains check boxes to center the worksheet on the page horizontally and/or vertically.

PROJECT: You will preview the invoice to Performance Threads, adjust the left margin to balance the worksheet on the page and then print. You will center the Bonus worksheet horizontally and vertically and print it in landscape orientation.

STEPS

1. Open **ExcelS3-02**.

2. Click the Print Preview button on the Standard toolbar, and then click the Zoom button on the Print Preview toolbar to enlarge the display.

   Notice the Invoice is unbalanced at the left edge of the page with a larger amount of white space on the right side. One method of correcting this is to change the left margin.

3. Click the Setup button on the Print Preview toolbar.

4. Click the Margins tab in the Page Setup dialog box.

5. Click the up-pointing arrow to the right of the *Left* text box until *1.5* displays and then click OK.

   Alternatively, you can drag the number in the *Left* text box to select the current value and then type the new margin setting. The worksheet now appears balanced between the left and right edges of the page.

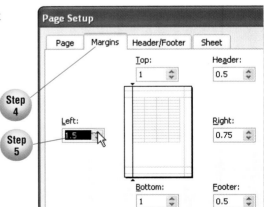

6. Click the Print button on the Print Preview toolbar.

   The Print Preview window closes and the Print dialog box appears.

7. At the Print dialog box, click OK.

8. Save and then close **ExcelS3-02**.

9. Open **ExcelS3-03** and make sure the *Bonus* worksheet is the active worksheet. *(Hint: Click the **Bonus** worksheet tab at the bottom of the worksheet area if it is not currently displayed.)*

10. Click File and then Page Setup.

11 Click the Page tab in the Page Setup dialog box.

12 Click *Landscape*.

13 Click the Margins tab.

14 Click the *Horizontally* check box in the *Center on page* section, and then click OK.

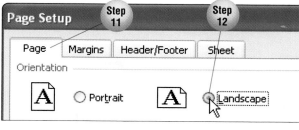

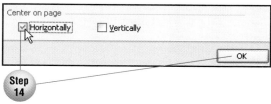

Centering the worksheet horizontally is another method that can be used to ensure the worksheet prints balanced between the left and right edges of the page. You can choose both the *Horizontally* and *Vertically* check boxes to print a worksheet that is centered between both the left and right edges (horizontally), and the top and bottom edges (vertically) of the page.

15 Click the Print Preview button on the Standard toolbar.

The Print Preview window displays the worksheet centered horizontally on the page.

16 Close the Print Preview window.

17 Click the Print button on the Standard toolbar.

18 Save **ExcelS3-03**.

In Addition

Changing Margins in Print Preview

Click the Margins button on the Print Preview toolbar to display column handles and horizontal and vertical guidelines. Drag the horizontal or vertical guidelines to adjust the left, right, top, bottom, and header and footer margins. Drag the column handles to adjust the column widths. Click Margins again to turn off the display of column handles and guidelines.

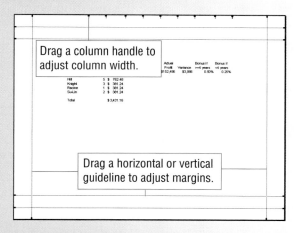

Drag a column handle to adjust column width.

Drag a horizontal or vertical guideline to adjust margins.

In BRIEF

Change Margins
1 Click File, Page Setup.
2 Click Margins tab.
3 Change required margin setting.
4 Click OK.

Center a Worksheet
1 Click File, Page Setup.
2 Click Margins tab.
3 Click *Horizontally* and/or *Vertically* check box.
4 Click OK.

3.6 Inserting Headers and Footers

A header is text that prints at the top of each worksheet and a footer is text that prints at the bottom of each worksheet. Headers and footers are created in the Page Setup dialog box. Excel includes predefined headers and footers that can be selected from a drop-down list, or you can create your own custom header or footer text. Header and footer text does not appear in the worksheet area—it is a function that affects printing.

PROJECT: To distinguish the Construction Loan worksheet, you will create a custom header that prints the current date aligned at the right margin and a custom footer that prints your name aligned at the left margin and the file name followed by the worksheet name aligned at the right margin.

STEPS

1. With **ExcelS3-03** open, click the sheet tab labeled *Construction Loan* located at the bottom of the screen just above the Status bar.

2. Click File, click Page Setup, and then click the Header/Footer tab in the Page Setup dialog box.

3. Click the Custom Header button.

    This displays the Header window as shown in Figure E3.2.

FIGURE E3.2
Header Window

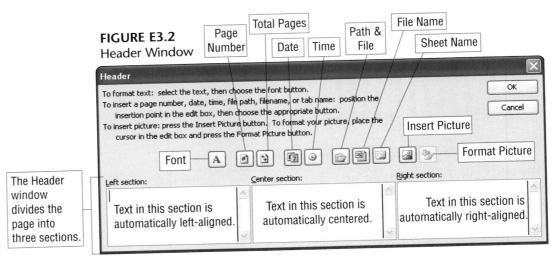

The Header window divides the page into three sections.

4. At the Header window, press Tab twice to move the insertion point to the *Right section* text box, or click the I-beam pointer in *Right section*.

5. Type **Date Printed:**, press the spacebar once, and then click the Date button 🗓 in the Header window.

    Excel inserts the code *&[Date]*, which will cause the current date to be inserted at the location of the code when the worksheet is printed.

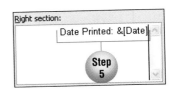

6. Click OK to close the Header window.

    The custom header now appears in the preview section of the Header/Footer tab in the Page Setup dialog box.

7 Click Custom Footer.

> The Footer window contains the same elements as the Header window.

8 At the Footer window, type your first and last name in the *Left section* text box.

9 Press Tab twice to move the insertion point to the *Right section* text box, or click the I-beam pointer in *Right section*.

10 Click the File Name button [icon], press the spacebar once, and then click the Sheet Name button [icon] in the Footer window.

> Excel inserts the codes *&[File] &[Tab]* which will cause the workbook file name followed by the worksheet name to be printed.

11 Click OK to close the Footer window.

> The custom header and custom footer display in the preview sections of the Page Setup dialog box with the Header/Footer tab selected, as shown in Figure E3.3.

12 Click OK to close the Page Setup dialog box.

13 Display the *Construction Loan* worksheet in Print Preview.

14 Change the left margin to 1.75 inches and then print the *Construction Loan* worksheet.

15 Save and then close **ExcelS3-03**.

FIGURE E3.3 Header/Footer Previews in Page Setup Dialog Box

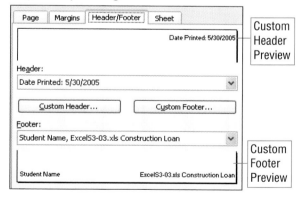

In Addition

Header and Footer Margins

By default, a header will print 0.5 inch from the top of the page and the footer will print 0.5 inch from the bottom of the page. Display the Page Setup dialog box and select the Margins tab to alter these settings.

IN BRIEF

Insert a Custom Header or Footer
1 Click File, Page Setup.
2 Click Header/Footer tab.
3 Click Custom Header or Custom Footer.
4 Insert desired codes and/or type text.
5 Click OK to close Header or Footer window.
6 Click OK to close Page Setup dialog box.

3.7 Printing Headings and Gridlines; Scaling a Worksheet

Column and row headings can be printed at the top and left edges of multiple pages when a large worksheet prints on more than one page. Turning on the gridlines will cause Excel to print the horizontal and vertical row and column boundary lines. A large worksheet can be reduced in size proportionately to fit within a specified number of pages.

PROJECT: Dana Hirsch has asked you to print the Inventory Units Purchased report. You will open the workbook and print two versions of the report—one at full size that includes the first two pages including headings and gridlines, and another that reduces the entire report to fit within one page.

STEPS

① Open **ExcelS3-01**.

② Click File and then Page Setup.

③ Click the Page tab in the Page Setup dialog box, click *Landscape*, and then click OK.

④ Display the worksheet in Print Preview, and view all of the pages in the preview window. *(Hint: Click the Next and Previous buttons on the Print Preview toolbar to view all of the pages.)*

⑤ Close the Print Preview window.

⑥ Click File, Page Setup, and then click the Sheet tab.

> The *Print titles* section in the Sheet tab contains two options: *Rows to repeat at top* and *Columns to repeat at left*. Use these options to print row or column labels at the top and left edges of each page in the printed worksheet.

⑦ Click the Collapse Dialog button to the right of the *Rows to repeat at top* text box.

> This reduces the size of the dialog box to the active option only. You can now enter the range by selecting cells within the worksheet.

⑧ Select rows 1 and 2.

⑨ Click the Expand Dialog button (the Collapse Dialog button changes to the Expand Dialog button when the dialog box is collapsed) to redisplay the entire Page Setup dialog box.

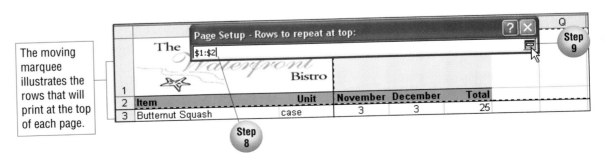

The moving marquee illustrates the rows that will print at the top of each page.

⑩ Click in the *Columns to repeat at left* text box and then click the Collapse Dialog button.

⑪ Select columns A and B and then click the Expand Dialog button.

ROBLEM ?

If necessary, drag the Title bar of the collapsed dialog box to move it out of the way so you can select columns A and B.

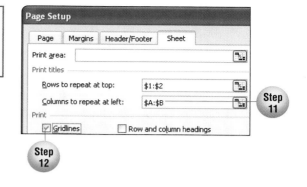

Step 11

⑫ Click the *Gridlines* check box in the *Print* section.

Step 12

⑬ Click OK to close the Page Setup dialog box.

⑭ Click File and then click Print.

⑮ At the Print dialog box, click *Page(s)* in the *Print range* section. With the insertion point positioned in the *From* text box, type **1**, press Tab or click in the *To* text box, type **2**, and then press Enter or click OK.

> Pages 1 and 2 only of the *Inventory Units Purchased* worksheet print. Notice on the second page that the first two rows are printed at the top of the page. Having these titles repeat help the reader to distinguish for which month each value is related. (To see the effect of repeating the first two columns, pages 3 and 4 of the worksheet would have to be printed.)

⑯ Click File, Page Setup, and then click the Page tab.

⑰ Click *Fit to [1] page(s) wide by [1] tall* in the *Scaling* section.

Step 17

⑱ Click the Margins tab, click the *Horizontally* and *Vertically* check boxes in the *Center on page* section, and then click OK to close the Page Setup dialog box.

⑲ Display the worksheet in the Print Preview window.

> Notice the automatic scaling has adjusted the print size so small that it is almost unreadable.

⑳ Click the Setup button on the Print Preview toolbar.

㉑ Click the Margins tab in the Page Setup dialog box and then change the *Top, Bottom, Left,* and *Right* margins to 0.5 inch.

㉒ Click the Page tab in the Page Setup dialog box and then click *Adjust to* in the *Scaling* section. With the current value in the *% normal size* text box already selected, type **68**, and then press Enter.

Step 22

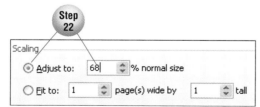

㉓ Close the Print Preview window.

㉔ Save and then print **ExcelS3-01**.

㉕ Close **ExcelS3-01**.

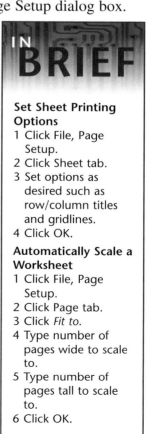

IN BRIEF

Set Sheet Printing Options
1 Click File, Page Setup.
2 Click Sheet tab.
3 Set options as desired such as row/column titles and gridlines.
4 Click OK.

Automatically Scale a Worksheet
1 Click File, Page Setup.
2 Click Page tab.
3 Click *Fit to*.
4 Type number of pages wide to scale to.
5 Type number of pages tall to scale to.
6 Click OK.

3.8 Creating a Chart

Numerical values in a worksheet can be represented visually by creating a chart. A chart is sometimes referred to as a graph. The chart can be placed in the same worksheet as the data or it can be inserted into its own sheet. The Chart Wizard guides you through the process of creating charts by means of four dialog boxes that are used to select the chart type, define the source data, select chart options, and specify the chart location.

PROJECT: Operating expenses by quarter for The Waterfront Bistro are stored in a workbook named WBExpenses. Dana Hirsch has requested that you create a chart to compare the expenses in each quarter and another chart to show each expense as a proportion of the total expenses.

STEPS

1 Open **WBExpenses**.

2 Save the workbook with Save As and name it **ExcelS3-04**.

3 Select A3:E9.

> The first step in creating a chart is to select the range of cells containing the data you want to chart. Notice in the range in Step 3 you are including the row labels in column A. Labels are included to provide the frame of reference for each bar, column, or other chart series.

4 Click the Chart Wizard button 📊 on the Standard toolbar.

5 The default choice in the *Chart type* list box is *Column*. Click the first chart in the second row of the *Chart sub-type* section (Clustered column with a 3-D visual effect) and then click Next.

> The first Chart Wizard dialog box is used to select a chart type and subtype. The *Chart type* list box includes 14 options for various types of charts that can be created. The options in the *Chart sub-type* section change dependent on the selected chart type.

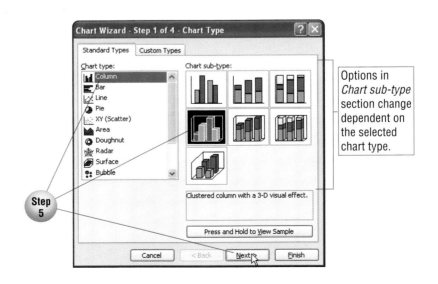

Options in *Chart sub-type* section change dependent on the selected chart type.

6 Make sure *Data range* displays as *=Sheet1!$A$3:$E$9* and then click Next.

The second Chart Wizard dialog box is used to define the source data that will be included to generate the chart. To assist you at this step, Excel includes a preview of the chart using the data range that was selected when the wizard was invoked.

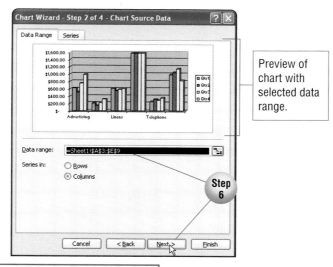

Preview of chart with selected data range.

Step 6

PROBLEM ? Data range is incorrect? Click the Data range Collapse Dialog button, drag to select the correct range, and then click the Collapse Dialog button again.

7 With the Titles tab selected in the Chart Options dialog box, click in the *Chart title* text box, type **Operating Expenses**, and then click Next.

Use these tabs to add and/or format chart options.

The third Chart Wizard dialog box is where chart options can be added to enhance the chart readability and appearance. In the next topic you will learn how to modify chart options after the chart has been created.

Step 7

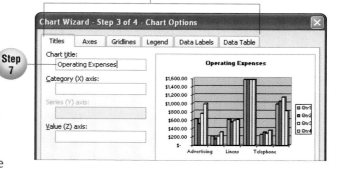

8 Click *As new sheet* in the Chart Location dialog box and then click Finish.

At the fourth Chart Wizard dialog box, the chart can be inserted in its own sheet or as an object in the active worksheet. Charts inserted in their own sheet are initially labeled *Chart1* and are automatically scaled to fill the entire page.

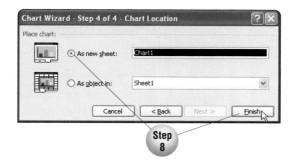

Step 8

(continued)

9 With *Chart1* the active sheet, click the Print Preview button to view how the chart will print.

10 Close the Print Preview window.

11 Click the *Sheet1* tab at the bottom of the window to return to the *Operating Expenses* worksheet.

12 Click in any blank cell in the worksheet to deselect the range A3:E9.

13 Select the range A3:A9, hold down the Ctrl key, and then select the range F3:F9.

14 Click the Chart Wizard button.

15 Click *Pie* in the *Chart type* list box, click the middle chart in the first row of the *Chart sub-type* section (Pie with a 3-D visual effect), and then click Next.

16 Make sure *Data range* displays as =Sheet1!$A$3:$A$9,Sheet1!$F$3:$F$9 and then click Next.

Step 15

Step 16

17 With the Titles tab selected in the Chart Options dialog box, click in the *Chart title* text box after the word *Total*, press the spacebar once, and then type **Operating Expenses**.

18 Click the Data Labels tab, click the *Percentage* check box in the *Label Contains* section, and then click Next.

Step 18

19 With *As object in Sheet 1* selected in the Chart Location dialog box, click Finish.

The chart is inserted as an object in the *Sheet1* worksheet and the Chart toolbar appears. Black sizing handles display around the perimeter of the chart. These handles indicate the chart is selected and can be moved or resized.

When chart is selected, the ranges used to generate the chart are color coded.

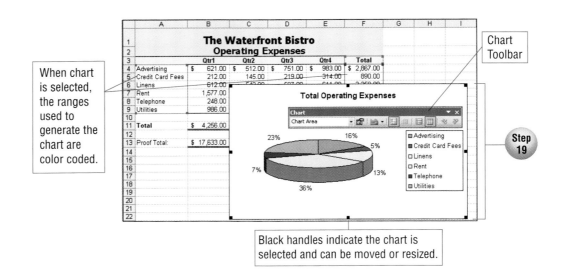

Chart Toolbar

Step 19

Black handles indicate the chart is selected and can be moved or resized.

20 Position the mouse pointer within a white area inside the chart, drag the mouse until the top left corner of the chart is positioned at the top left boundary of A15, and then release the mouse button.

> The pointer changes to a four-headed arrow move icon and a dotted box outline appears as you drag the chart to illustrate its placement when you release the mouse.

21 Position the mouse pointer on the black sizing handle at the bottom right corner of the chart until the pointer changes to a double-headed diagonal arrow. Drag the pointer down and right until the dashed border is positioned at the bottom right corner of F35 and then release the mouse button.

PROBLEM ?
> Having difficulty resizing the chart? First scroll down the window until you can see row 35.

22 Click in any cell within the worksheet to deselect the chart.

23 Click the Print Preview button to view the worksheet and the chart together on the same page.

24 Click the Setup button on the Print Preview toolbar.

25 At the Page Setup dialog box, click the Margins tab, click *Horizontally* in the *Center on page* section, and then click OK.

26 Click the Print button.

27 At the Print dialog box, click *Entire workbook* in the *Print what* section, and then click OK.

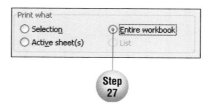

Step 27

28 Save **ExcelS3-04**.

In Addition

Printing Only the Chart

To print only the chart in a worksheet containing cells as well as a chart, click the chart to select it before clicking the Print button. The chart will automatically be scaled to fit the entire page.

IN BRIEF

Create a Chart
1 Select source cells.
2 Click Chart Wizard button.
3 Select chart type and subtype and click Next.
4 Verify data range/series and click Next.
5 Select chart options and click Next.
6 Select chart location and click Finish.

3.9 Modifying a Chart

Once a chart has been created, it can be edited by clicking the chart or a chart element to select it. When the black handles are displayed, the Chart command appears on the Menu bar with drop-down options to change the chart type, source data, chart options, and location. The Format menu changes to display options for formatting the chart or selected chart element.

PROJECT: You will modify the charts created for the Operating Expenses worksheet by formatting the legend, changing the font in the chart title, and changing the chart type.

STEPS

1 With **ExcelS3-04** open, click the mouse pointer inside the legend in the pie chart.

Black handles display around the legend indicating the legend element is selected. The Chart toolbar, if it is not already visible, will pop up when a chart or chart element is selected. Figure E3.4 shows some of the other elements that can be formatted in a chart.

2 Click Format and then Selected Legend.

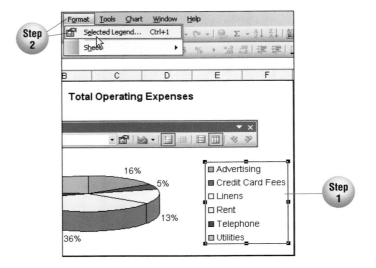

3 With the Patterns tab selected in the Format Legend dialog box, click *None* in the *Border* section and then click OK.

This will remove the border from around the legend.

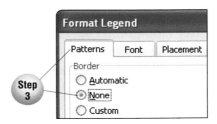

④ Right-click the chart title and then click Format Chart Title at the shortcut menu.

⑤ Click the Font tab in the Format Chart Title dialog box.

⑥ Change the font to 18-point Comic Sans MS Bold and then click OK.

> Choose another font such as Times New Roman if Comic Sans MS is not available on your system.

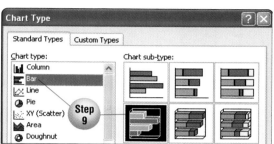

⑦ Click the *Chart1* tab to display the column chart.

⑧ Click Chart and then Chart Type.

⑨ Click *Bar* in the *Chart type* list box, click the first chart in the second row in the *Chart sub-type* section (Clustered bar with a 3-D visual effect), and then click OK.

⑩ Preview and print the bar chart.

⑪ Save **ExcelS3-04**.

FIGURE E3.4 Chart Element Formatting

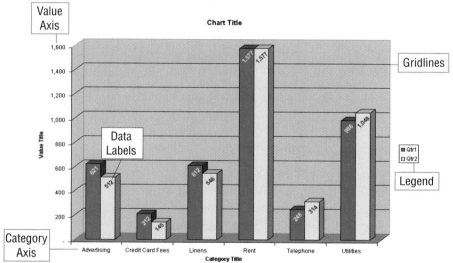

Chart Elements

The chart shown in Figure E3.4 illustrates some of the elements that can be added or formatted in a chart. Double-clicking a chart element will open a dialog box with formatting options available for the selected element.

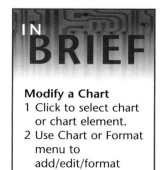

Modify a Chart
1 Click to select chart or chart element.
2 Use Chart or Format menu to add/edit/format options.

3.10 Inserting, Moving, and Resizing Pictures

Microsoft Office contains a clip art gallery containing pictures that can be inserted into worksheets. Once a picture has been inserted, it can be moved, resized, or deleted. The Clip Art task pane allows you to view images in the gallery and insert them into the worksheet with a single click. By default, Excel searches the Microsoft Office Online gallery if you are connected to the Internet.

This Web site is frequently updated and contains additional images that can be downloaded to your computer.

PROJECT: You will add two clip art images to the top of the worksheet to enhance its appearance. After inserting the images, you will resize and move them.

STEPS

1 With **ExcelS3-04** open, click the *Sheet1* tab to display the worksheet and chart.

2 Insert 4 rows above row 1 and then make A1 the active cell.

3 Click Insert, point to Picture, and then click Clip Art.

> The Clip Art task pane opens at the right side of the worksheet area.

4 Click in the *Search for* text box at the top of the Clip Art task pane, type **cafe**, and then click Go.

> Available images that have the keyword *cafe* associated with them display in the *Results* section of the Clip Art task pane. By default, Excel searches all media collections (clip art, photographs, movies, and sounds) in all categories of the Office gallery, in Microsoft Office Online, and in all favorites, unclassified clips, and downloaded clips that have been added to the computer you are using.

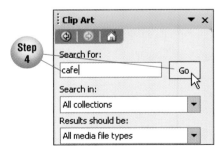

5 Scroll down the images in the *Results* section until you see the clip art shown below. Position the mouse pointer over the picture and then click the mouse once.

> The picture is inserted in the worksheet starting at A1 and the Picture toolbar appears.

PROBLEM

Select an alternate picture if the image shown is not available on your system.

6 Click the Close button ☒ in the right corner of the Picture toolbar.

7 Position the pointer on the white sizing handle at the bottom right corner of the image until the pointer changes to a double-headed diagonal arrow. Hold down the left mouse button and drag the pointer up and to the left until the picture fits within the first four rows above the worksheet title.

8 Drag the right middle sizing handle until the picture fits the width of column A.

9 Move the pointer over the image until the four-headed arrow move icon appears attached to the pointer. Hold down the left mouse button, drag the image until the right edge of the picture is aligned at the right edge of the worksheet, and then release the mouse button.

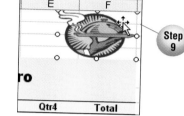

10 Click A1.

11 Drag the pointer across *cafe* in the *Search for* text box in the Clip Art task pane, type **seafood, dining**, and then click Go.

12 Insert and resize the image shown at the top left edge of the worksheet. Choose an alternate picture if the image shown is not available.

13 Click in any cell to deselect the clip art image.

14 Click the Close button in the upper right corner of the Clip Art task pane.

15 Save **ExcelS3-04**.

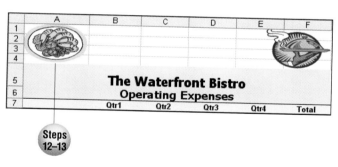

In Addition

Inserting Pictures from a File

Click Insert, point to Picture, and then click From File to insert a picture such as a company logo or other scanned image into a worksheet. Navigate to the location of the file in the Insert Picture dialog box and then double-click the picture file name.

3.11 Drawing Arrows and Text Boxes

The Drawing toolbar contains buttons that can be used to draw a variety of shapes such as circles, squares, rectangles, lines, arrows, and text boxes. Draw arrows or text boxes to add emphasis or insert explanatory notes in a worksheet. The AutoShapes button displays a pop-up menu in which palettes of shapes are grouped into categories such as Lines, Basic Shapes, and Block Arrows.

PROJECT: You will draw an arrow and text box to insert an explanatory note regarding the upcoming rent increase in the Operating Expenses worksheet.

STEPS

1 With **ExcelS3-04** open, click View, point to Toolbars, and then click Drawing to display the Drawing toolbar shown in Figure E3.5.

> Skip Step 1 if the Drawing toolbar is already visible. The Drawing toolbar generally docks at the bottom of the window just above the Status bar.

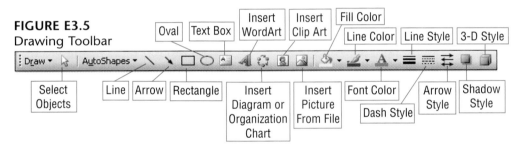

FIGURE E3.5
Drawing Toolbar

2 Click the Arrow button on the Drawing toolbar.

> When an object tool has been selected, the pointer changes to a crosshairs ⊞. To draw an object, position the crosshairs where you want the object to start, hold down the left mouse button, and then drag the crosshairs to the desired ending point.

3 Position the crosshairs near the bottom boundary of D16. Hold down the left mouse button and drag the crosshairs up toward the value *1,577.00* in E11, and then release the left mouse button.

PROBLEM **?**

> If you do not like the way the arrow turns out, press Delete to delete the arrow, then click the Arrow button and try again.

4 Click the Text Box button on the Drawing toolbar.

> When the Text Box tool has been selected, the pointer changes to a down-pointing arrow ↓.

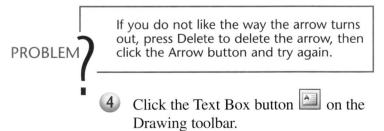

	Qtr3		Qtr4
$	751.00	$	983.00
	219.00		314.00
	587.00		611.00
	1,577.00		1,577.00
	286.00		355.00
	1,147.00		826.00
$	4,567.00	$	4,666.00

Step 3

Position crosshairs here, then drag up toward Ell.

(5) Position the pointer at the top left boundary of D17 and then drag the pointer down and to the right to draw the text box the approximate size shown in the illustration.

> An insertion point appears inside the box when you release the left mouse button indicating you can begin typing the text.

Qtr2	Qtr3	Qtr4	Total
512.00	$ 751.00	$ 983.00	$ 2,867.00
145.00	219.00	314.00	890.00
548.00	587.00	611.00	2,358.00
1,577.00	1,577.00	1,577.00	6,308.00
314.00	286.00	355.00	1,203.00
1,048.00	1,147.00	826.00	4,007.00
4,144.00	$ 4,567.00	$ 4,666.00	$17,633.00

Next year's rent is 1,650.00!

Steps 5–6

(6) Type **Next year's rent is 1,650.00!** inside the text box.

(7) Click outside the text box object to deselect it.

(8) Position the mouse pointer over the border of the text box until the pointer changes to display the four-headed arrow icon attached to it, and then click the left mouse button.

> This selects the text box object. White sizing handles display around the text box along with a thick gray border.

(9) Click the Font Color button [A] on the Drawing toolbar.

> This changes the color of the text inside the box to red.

-OBLEM ?
!

> Font Color button does not display red? Click the down-pointing arrow to the right of the button and select red from the color palette.

00	1,577.00	1,577.00	6,3
00	286.00	355.00	1,2
00	1,147.00	826.00	4,0
00	$ 4,567.00	$ 4,666.00	$17,6

Next year's rent is 1,650.00!

(10) Click the Line Color button on the Drawing toolbar.

> This changes the line color of the text box border to blue.

Steps 8–11

(11) Click the Center button on the Formatting toolbar to center the text inside the text box and then click outside the object to deselect the text box.

(12) Save **ExcelS3-04**.

(13) Print the worksheet and then close **ExcelS3-04**.

In Addition

AutoShapes

The AutoShapes button on the Drawing toolbar contains palettes of shapes grouped into the categories Lines, Connectors, Basic Shapes, Block Arrows, Flowchart, Stars and Banners, and Callouts. Point to a category to view a variety of objects that can be drawn. If space permits, use an AutoShape to add interest to a worksheet. The Stars and Banners palette is shown at the right.

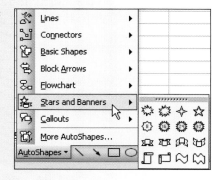

	Lines	▶
	Connectors	▶
	Basic Shapes	▶
	Block Arrows	▶
	Flowchart	▶
	Stars and Banners	▶
	Callouts	▶
	More AutoShapes...	

AutoShapes ▾

In BRIEF

Draw an Object
1 Display Drawing toolbar.
2 Click desired object button.
3 Drag to create shape.
4 Move, resize, or edit as required.

Delete an Object
1 Click object to select it.
2 Press Delete.

FEATURES SUMMARY

Feature	Button	Menu	Keyboard
Create a chart		Insert, Chart	F11
Draw an arrow			
Draw a text box			
Drawing toolbar		View, Toolbars, Drawing	
Insert clip art		Insert, Picture, Clip Art	
Insert function		Insert, Function	
Page Setup dialog box		File, Page Setup	
Print dialog box		File, Print	Ctrl + P
Print Preview		File, Print Preview	

PROCEDURES CHECK

Completion: In the space provided at the right, indicate the correct term or command.

1. AVERAGE, MAX, and MIN are some of the functions grouped in this category in the Insert Function dialog box. _____

2. The date January 1, 1900, is this serial number in Excel. _____

3. This Date & Time function inserts the current date and time in the active cell. _____

4. The financial function PMT returns a monthly payment based on constant payments, a set period of time, and this. _____

5. The IF function returns one of two values in a cell based on the result of this test. _____

6. To center a worksheet horizontally and vertically, click this tab in the Page Setup dialog box. _____

7. A header is text that prints here. _____

8. A worksheet can be scaled to print on a specific number of pages with this option in the Page Setup dialog box. _____

9. This is the first step in creating a chart before you click the Chart Wizard button. _____

10. Click *Percentage* in this tab in the Chart Options dialog box to display the percentage of 100 represented by each slice of a pie chart. _____

11. Display this dialog box to change the chart title after the chart has been created. _____

12. Do this action with the mouse over a chart to display the black handles.

13. By default, Excel will search all media categories in this gallery if you are connected to the Internet when searching for clip art. _____

14. Display this toolbar to create a text box in the worksheet. _____

15. Write the IF function to calculate a sales bonus given the following criteria:
    - sales bonuses are paid at the rate of 8% for sales over $1 million
    - sales bonuses are paid at the rate of 5% for sales less than or equal to $1 million
    - assume the sales amount is in B3

    _____

16. Write the PMT function to calculate a loan payment given the following criteria:
    - the interest rate *per annum* is in C5
    - the term of the loan *in years* is in C6
    - the amount of money borrowed is in C7

    _____

SKILLS REVIEW

Activity 1: INSERTING STATISTICAL FUNCTIONS

1. Open **WBExpenses**.
2. Save the workbook and name it **ExcelS3-R1**.
3. Make A15 the active cell.
4. Type Average Expense and then press Enter.
5. Type Maximum Expense and then press Enter.
6. Type Minimum Expense and then press Enter.
7. Increase the width of column A to *16.00 (117 pixels)*.
8. Make B15 the active cell and then create the formula that will calculate the average of the expense values in the range B4:B9.
9. Make B16 the active cell and then create the formula that will return the maximum expense value within the range B4:B9.
10. Make B17 the active cell and then create the formula that will return the minimum expense value within the range B4:B9.
11. Copy the formulas in B15:B17 to C15:F17.
12. Save **ExcelS3-R1**.

Activity 2: SETTING PRINT OPTIONS

1. With **ExcelS3-R1** open, display the Page Setup dialog box.
2. Change the top margin to 2 inches and the left margin to 1.5 inches.
3. Create a custom header that will print your first and last names at the left margin, and the current date and time at the right margin.
4. Create a custom footer that will print the word *Page* followed by the page number at the left margin and the file name at the right margin.
5. Turn on printing of the gridlines.

6 Display the worksheet in Print Preview.
7 Close the Print Preview window.
8 Save and then print **ExcelS3-R1**.

Activity 3: USING DATE FUNCTIONS

1 With **ExcelS3-R1** open, make A19 the active cell.
2 Type Date Created and then press the Right Arrow key.
3 With B19 the active cell, use the DATE function to insert the current date. (*Note: You do not want to use the NOW function, because the date will update each time you open the file.*)
4 Format B19 to display the date in the format *2005-03-14*.
5 Change the width of column B to *10.57 (79 pixels)*.
6 Make A20 the active cell.
7 Type Next Revision Date and then press the Right Arrow key.
8 With B20 the active cell, type the formula =b19+360 and then press Enter.
9 Save **ExcelS3-R1**.

Activity 4: USING THE IF FUNCTION

1 With **ExcelS3-R1** open, insert two rows above row 19.
2 Make A19 the active cell.
3 Type Expense Target, press Alt + Enter, type Variance, and then press Enter.
4 Dana Hirsch, manager of The Waterfront Bistro, has set a quarterly target of $4,250.00 for the total expenses. Dana wants you to create a formula to show the amount over target a quarter's total expenses are, if they have exceeded this target amount. Make B19 the active cell and then type the following IF function:
     =if(b11>4250,b11-4250,0)
5 Drag the fill handle from B19 to C19:E19.
6 In the space provided, write the values displayed as the results in the cells indicated.

     B19 _____
     C19 _____
     D19 _____
     E19 _____

7 In the space provided, write in your own words a brief explanation of the IF function entered in B19.

     _____

     _____

     _____

8 Assume that Dana Hirsch has changed the expense target to a different amount for each quarter. The revised targets are: *Qtr1–4250; Qtr2–4350; Qtr3–4600; Qtr 4–4650*. Revise the IF functions in B19:E19 to reflect these new targets.
9 Save, print, and then close **ExcelS3-R1**.

Activity 5: CREATING A CHART; DRAWING AN ARROW AND TEXT BOX; INSERTING A PICTURE

1 Open **WBCostofSales**.

2 Save the workbook with Save As and name it **ExcelS3-R2**.

3 Select the range A3:E6. Start the Chart Wizard and complete the dialog boxes using the following options.

   a Chart type: *Column*; Chart sub-type: *Clustered column with a 3-D visual effect.*

   b Make sure the Data range displays as *=Sheet1!$A$3:$E$6*.

   c Chart Title: *Cost of Sales*.

   d Choose *As new sheet* in the Chart Location dialog box.

4 With *Chart1* the active sheet, draw an arrow pointing to the column in the chart representing Food Purchases for the fourth quarter. Draw a text box anchored to the end of the arrow and then type the following text inside the box:

Includes 5% price increase from Lakeside Fishery

5 Click the *Sheet1* tab and make A12 the active cell. Search for a clip art image using the keyword *budgets*. Select an image from the *Results* section of the Clip Art task pane. Resize the image to an appropriate size.

6 Save **ExcelS3-R2**.

7 Print the entire workbook and then close **ExcelS3-R2**.

PERFORMANCE PLUS

Assessment 1: USING STATISTICAL AND IF FUNCTIONS

1 Alex Torres, manager of the Toronto office for First Choice Travel, has started a worksheet to calculate sales commission for the Toronto sales agents. First Choice Travel has implemented a new bonus commission based upon the number of cruises booked. Alex has asked for your help in writing the correct formulas to calculate the commission and analyze the results.

2 Open **FCTCommission**.

3 Save the workbook and name it **ExcelS3-P1**.

4 Create a formula to calculate the commission for T. Sanderson in D5 using the following criteria:

   • Sales agents are paid 1.75% of the total value of their travel bookings for zero to four cruise bookings.

   • A sales agent who has sold five or more cruises will receive 2.5%.

5 Copy the formula to the remaining rows in column D.

6 Calculate the total commissions.

7 Format the values as necessary.

8 Enter appropriate labels and create formulas to calculate the average, maximum, and minimum commissions below the total row.

9 Save **ExcelS3-P1**.

10 Print and then close **ExcelS3-P1**.

Assessment 2: CHANGING PRINT OPTIONS; USING DATE FORMULAS

1 You are the assistant to Cal Rubine, chair of the Theatre Arts Division at Niagara Peninsula College. The two co-op consultants have entered their grades for the work term placements into separate worksheets in the same workbook.
2 Open **NPCCo-op**.
3 Save the workbook and name it **ExcelS3-P2**.
4 Click the *Performance Threads* worksheet tab to display the work term placement information for the students who were placed there during the winter semester of 2005.
5 Type a formula in H4 that will add 12 days to the entry in the *Date Co-op Report Received* column.
6 Copy the formula to the remaining rows in column H.
7 Set the following print options:
   a Create a header that will print your name at the left margin and the current date at the right margin.
   b Change the top margin to *2.5* and center the worksheet horizontally.
   c Change the orientation to landscape.
8 Save **ExcelS3-P2**.
9 Print the *Performance Threads* worksheet.
10 Close **ExcelS3-P2**.

Assessment 3: APPLYING THE PMT FUNCTION

1 You are the assistant to Sam Vestering, manager of North American Distribution for Worldwide Enterprises. Sam has entered in a workbook details for a proposed building loan and has asked you to enter the formula to calculate the monthly loan payments.
2 Open **WELoan**.
3 Save the workbook and name it **ExcelS3-P3**.
4 Enter in B8 the PMT function formula to calculate the monthly payment in the *New Building Loan* worksheet.
5 Save **ExcelS3-P3**.
6 Print and then close **ExcelS3-P3**.

Assessment 4: CREATING AND FORMATTING CHARTS; DRAWING AN ARROW AND TEXT BOX

1 Cal Rubine, chair of the Theatre Arts Division at Niagara Peninsula College, has asked you to create charts from the grades analysis report to present at a divisional meeting. After reviewing the grades, you decide to create a line chart depicting the grades for all of the courses and a pie chart summarizing the total grades.
2 Open **NPCGrades**.
3 Save the workbook and name it **ExcelS3-P4**.
4 Create a line chart in its own sheet that will display the A+ through F grades for each course. Include an appropriate chart title. You determine any other chart elements to include that will make the chart easy to interpret.
5 Create a 3-D pie chart that will display the total of each grade as a percentage of 100. *(Hint: Select the ranges B4:G4 and B10:G10 before starting the Chart Wizard.)* Include an appropriate chart title and display percentages as the data labels. Place the pie chart at the bottom of the *Grades* worksheet starting in row 14.

6 Resize the chart so that its width extends to the right edge of column H and the height to the bottom boundary of row 31.

7 Draw an arrow pointing to the F slice in the pie chart. Create a text box at the end of the arrow containing the text *Lowest attrition since 1999!*

8 If necessary, resize the arrow and text box.

9 Change the font color of the text inside the text box to red.

10 Change the line color of the border of the text box to blue.

11 Save **ExcelS3-P4**.

12 Print the entire workbook.

13 Close **ExcelS3-P4**.

Assessment 5: INSERTING CLIP ART

1 Melissa Gehring, manager of the Los Angeles office for First Choice Travel, has prepared a worksheet listing European destinations and the current package pricing options. Melissa has requested that you enhance the worksheet with clip art and formatting before she presents it at the next staff meeting.

2 Open **FCTEurope**.

3 Save the workbook and name it **ExcelS3-P5**.

4 Insert an appropriate clip art image at the top right of the worksheet.

5 Increase the height of row 7 to *19.50 (26 pixels)* and row 8 to *27.00 (36 pixels)*.

6 Apply the following formatting attributes to the range A7:G8.
   • 11-point Times New Roman Bold
   • Pale blue fill color
   • Center align

7 Format the values in B9:G17 to Currency Style with zero decimals.

8 If necessary, adjust column widths.

9 Apply other formatting attributes that would enhance the appearance of the remainder of the worksheet.

10 Save **ExcelS3-P5**.

11 Print and then close **ExcelS3-P5**.

Assessment 6: FINDING INFORMATION ON CREATING WORDART

1 Use the Help feature to find information on how to create a WordArt object in a worksheet.

2 Open **FCTEurope**.

3 Save the workbook and name it **ExcelS3-P6**.

4 Create a WordArt object at the top right of the worksheet with the text *Europe this summer!*

5 Resize, move, and format the WordArt object as desired.

6 Save **ExcelS3-P6**.

7 Print and then close **ExcelS3-P6**.

Assessment 7: SEARCHING FOR VACATION DESTINATIONS

1   You are trying to choose among vacation alternatives. You decide to use the Internet to locate information on three cities that you would like to visit. Look for detailed travel information such as round-trip airfare, hotel, car rental, and currency exchange.

2   Create an Excel workbook that compares the travel costs for the three cities you researched.

3   Apply formatting enhancements to the worksheet.

4   Create a chart that graphs the total cost of each vacation destination as an object below the worksheet.

5   Add and format chart elements to make the chart easy to interpret.

6   Draw an arrow and text box to the total cost for the vacation destination that you have chosen. Type the text My Choice! in the text box.

7   Save the workbook and name it **ExcelS3-P7**.

8   Print and then close **ExcelS3-P7**.

EXCEL

SECTION 4

Working with Multiple Worksheets and Workbooks and Managing Files

Using multiple worksheets in a workbook is often the most logical way to organize large amounts of data. Formulas can be created that reference cells in other worksheets within the same workbook or within another workbook. Paste Special allows you to specify the attributes from the copied cell that you want pasted in the destination cell. One or more ranges can be defined as the print area when you do not require the entire worksheet printed. Working in Page Break Preview you can view and modify page breaks. Creating a workbook from a template, using styles, creating and previewing Web pages, filtering and sorting lists, attaching comments to cells, inserting a diagram, using the Research task pane, working with multiple open workbooks, and file management techniques are some of the other features you will explore. In this section you will learn the skills and complete the projects described here.

Note: Before beginning this section, delete the ExcelS3 folder on your disk. Next, copy to your disk or other location the ExcelS4 subfolder from the CD that accompanies this textbook and then make ExcelS4 the active folder.

Skills

- Insert, delete, rename, hide, and unhide a worksheet
- Move and copy a worksheet
- Link worksheets
- Create 3-D references in formulas
- Use Paste Special options
- Format sheet tabs
- Add a graphics file as a worksheet background
- Print multiple worksheets
- Set and clear a print area
- View and modify page breaks
- Create a new workbook using a template
- Define, apply, and remove a style
- Save and view a worksheet as a Web page
- Insert and edit a hyperlink
- Filter and sort a list
- Insert and edit comments
- Insert and format a diagram
- Research and insert information
- Arrange, hide, and unhide multiple workbooks
- Save a workbook in a different file format
- Create and rename a folder
- Move a file to a folder

Projects

Complete the quarterly sales report and the payroll report; create an invoice to Performance Threads and First Choice Travel; format using styles; save an employee schedule and a sales worksheet as a Web page and insert hyperlinks; filter and sort a list of inventory items; insert comments and a diagram to the weekly and quarterly sales reports; update investments by locating and inserting stock prices; convert the inventory file to the comma delimited file format.

Format a costume production schedule using styles and then save the schedule as a Web page; produce a list of costumes with a final delivery date of July 5; insert comments in the production schedule in preparation for the design team meeting.

Create a summary worksheet for the Theatre Arts Co-op Work Term Placements report.

4.1 Inserting, Deleting, Renaming, and Hiding a Worksheet

A new workbook initially contains three sheets named *Sheet1, Sheet2,* and *Sheet3.* Additional sheets can be added or deleted as needed. Organizing large amounts of data by grouping related topics in individual worksheets makes the task of creating, editing, and analyzing data more manageable. For example, you could keep track of your test grades in one worksheet and assignment grades in another. A summary sheet at the beginning or end of the workbook would be used to consolidate the test and assignment grades and calculate a final mark. By breaking down the data into smaller units, you are able to view, enter, and edit cells quickly. Worksheets that are not currently needed for editing or worksheets that contain confidential information can be hidden.

PROJECT: Dana Hirsch, manager of The Waterfront Bistro, has asked you to complete the Quarterly Sales report. To begin this project, you will insert, rename, delete, and hide a worksheet until it is needed at a later time.

S T E P S

① Open **WBQuarterlySales**.

② Save the workbook and name it **ExcelS4-01**.

③ Click the *Qtr2* tab and then view the worksheet.

④ Click the *Sheet3* tab and then view the worksheet.

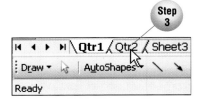

Step 3

> The quarterly sales report has been organized with each quarter's sales in a separate worksheet. In the next step you will insert a worksheet for the fourth quarter.

⑤ Click Insert and then Worksheet.

> New worksheets are inserted to the left of the active worksheet. In the next step you will insert at the beginning of the workbook a new worksheet that will be used to summarize the sales data from the four quarters.

⑥ Right-click the *Qtr1* tab.

> Right-clicking a worksheet tab activates the worksheet and displays the worksheet shortcut menu.

⑦ Click Insert at the shortcut menu.

⑧ With *Worksheet* already selected in the General tab in the Insert dialog box, click OK.

> Five worksheets now exist in **ExcelS4-01:** *Sheet2, Qtr1, Qtr2, Sheet1,* and *Sheet3.*

⑨ Right-click the *Sheet2* tab and then click Rename at the shortcut menu.

> This selects the current worksheet name in the sheet tab.

New worksheet inserted in Step 5.

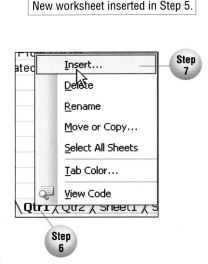

Step 7

Step 6

10 Type **Summary** and then press Enter.

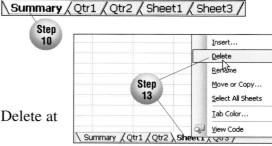

11 Double-click the *Sheet3* tab.

> You can also rename a worksheet by double-clicking the sheet tab.

12 Type **Qtr3** and then press Enter.

13 Right-click the *Sheet1* tab and then click Delete at the shortcut menu.

> You can also click Edit and then Delete Sheet to delete the active worksheet from the workbook. If the worksheet selected for deletion contains data, a message box will appear warning you that data may exist in the sheet. Click the Delete button in the Microsoft Office Excel message box to confirm the deletion. Be careful when deleting worksheets since Undo does not restore a deleted sheet.

14 Click the Summary tab to activate the *Summary* worksheet.

15 Click Format on the Menu bar, point to Sheet, and then click Hide.

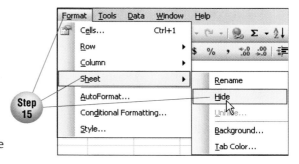

> The worksheet is hidden from view. The tab names at the bottom of the screen now display: *Qtr1, Qtr2,* and *Qtr3.* Hide worksheets containing sensitive or confidential information, or worksheets that are not currently needed. You will learn how to unhide a worksheet in Topic 4.2.

16 Save **ExcelS4-01**.

In Addition

Tab Scrolling Buttons

The tab scrolling buttons are located at the left edge of the horizontal scroll bar as shown below. Use these buttons to scroll the worksheet tabs if there are more tabs than currently displayed. Drag the tab split box to the right or left to increase or decrease the number of worksheet tabs displayed or to change the size of the horizontal scroll bar.

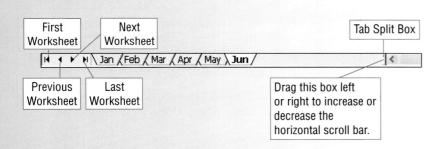

IN BRIEF

Insert a Worksheet
1 Activate worksheet that will follow new worksheet.
2 Click Insert, Worksheet.

Delete a Worksheet
1 Activate worksheet to be deleted.
2 Click Edit, Delete Sheet.

Rename a Worksheet
1 Double-click sheet tab.
2 Type new name.
3 Press Enter.

Hide a Worksheet
1 Activate worksheet to be hidden.
2 Click Format, Sheet, Hide.

4.2 Moving, Copying, and Unhiding a Worksheet

Drag a sheet tab to move a worksheet to a different position within the open workbook. Hold down Ctrl while dragging a worksheet tab to copy it. Worksheets can also be copied or moved from one workbook to another by opening the Move or Copy dialog box. Exercise caution when moving or copying a worksheet, since calculations may become inaccurate after the worksheet has been repositioned or copied. Open the Unhide dialog box to redisplay a hidden worksheet.

PROJECT: Continue your work on the Quarterly Sales report. You will copy the Qtr3 worksheet to create a worksheet for the fourth quarter, since copying will duplicate the labels and formatting. After copying Qtr3, you will rename the worksheet and delete the Qtr3 data. You unhide and then move the Summary worksheet to the end of the workbook after the four quarters. Finally, you will enter the data for the fourth quarter's sales.

STEPS

1 With **ExcelS4-01** open, and *Qtr3* the active worksheet, position the mouse pointer over the *Qtr3* tab, hold down Ctrl and drag the pointer right to the gray area in the scroll bar, release the mouse button, and then release the Ctrl key.

> As you drag the pointer to the right a black down-pointing arrow and a white page with a plus sign display with the pointer, indicating the position where the copied worksheet will be placed. The copied worksheet is labeled the same as the source worksheet with *(2)* added to the end of the name.

2 Double-click *Qtr3 (2)*, type **Qtr4**, and then press Enter.

3 With *Qtr4* the active worksheet, clear the contents only of the following ranges:

B4:D6
B8:D10
B12:D14

The black arrow indicates the position where the worksheet will be placed.

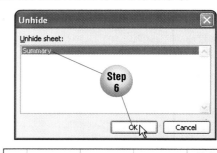

Step 1

4 Change B3 from *July* to *October;* C3 from *August* to *November;* and D3 from *September* to *December.*

> The worksheet is now cleared of the third quarter's data. All of the total cells have dashes displayed in them. As new data is typed, the totals will automatically update. First, you will unhide the *Summary* worksheet and move it to the end of the workbook after *Qtr4.*

5 Click Format, point to Sheet, and then click Unhide.

6 Click OK with *Summary* selected in the *Unhide sheet* list box in the Unhide dialog box.

> The *Summary* worksheet is redisplayed in the workbook.

7 Position the pointer over the *Summary* tab, hold down the left mouse button and drag the pointer right to the gray area in the scroll bar after *Qtr4*, and then release the mouse button.

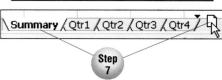

Step 7

> As you drag the pointer to the right a black down-pointing arrow and a white page display with the pointer, indicating the position where the worksheet will be repositioned.

⑧ Click *Qtr4* and enter the data for the fourth quarter as shown in Figure E4.1. You do not need to type the dollar symbols, commas, or zeros after decimals since the cells are already formatted. Type a zero in the cells displayed with a dash.

⑨ Save **ExcelS4-01**.

FIGURE E4.1 Data for Fourth Quarter

	A	B	C	D	E
1	**The Waterfront Bistro**				
2	**Quarterly Sales Report**				
3		October	November	December	Quarter Total
4	Food - Dining Room	$ 33,124.00	$ 34,168.00	$ 38,981.00	$ 106,273.00
5	Food - Patio	1,548.00	-	-	1,548.00
6	Food - Catering	16,524.00	17,256.00	26,691.00	60,471.00
7	**Total Food**	**51,196.00**	**51,424.00**	**65,672.00**	**168,292.00**
8	Beverage - Dining Room	3,147.00	3,217.00	3,342.00	9,706.00
9	Beverage - Patio	341.00	-	-	341.00
10	Beverage - Catering	1,196.00	1,734.00	2,716.00	5,646.00
11	**Total Beverage**	**4,684.00**	**4,951.00**	**6,058.00**	**15,693.00**
12	Beer & Liquor - Dining Room	3,416.00	3,571.00	4,085.00	11,072.00
13	Beer & Liquor - Patio	428.00	-	-	428.00
14	Beer & Liquor - Catering	1,172.00	1,938.00	3,096.00	6,206.00
15	**Total Beer & Liquor**	**5,016.00**	**5,509.00**	**7,181.00**	**17,706.00**

In Addition

Move or Copy Dialog Box

In Steps 1 and 7 you copied and moved a worksheet by dragging the sheet tab with the pointer. You can also use the Move or Copy dialog box (shown at the right) to move or copy worksheets within the active workbook or to another open workbook. Select the worksheet to be moved or copied, and then click Edit and Move or Copy Sheet. To move or copy to another open workbook, select the destination file name in the *To book* drop-down list. Click the worksheet in front of which you want to place the moved or copied worksheet in the *Before sheet* list box, and click OK to move, or click *Create a copy* and then click OK to copy.

IN BRIEF

Copy a Worksheet
1 Activate the source worksheet.
2 Hold down Ctrl key.
3 Drag sheet tab to position for copied sheet.

Move a Worksheet
1 Activate worksheet to be moved.
2 Drag sheet tab to new position.

Unhide a Worksheet
1 Click Format, Sheet, Unhide.
2 Click name of worksheet to restore.
3 Click OK.

4.3 Using 3-D References and Paste Special; Linking a Cell; Formatting Worksheets

A formula with **3-D references** is used to consolidate data from several worksheets into one worksheet. Open the Paste Special dialog box to choose the options you want pasted from the copied cell. Linking worksheets within the same workbook or between different workbooks involves entering a formula that references a cell containing the source data. If the source data changes, the cell that is linked to the source will automatically update to reflect the change. Apply a color to sheet tabs or insert a graphics file to the background of a worksheet to help visually organize related worksheets.

PROJECT: The Summary worksheet is the last worksheet to be completed in the Quarterly Sales report. You will copy labels from the Qtr4 worksheet to the Summary sheet, add labels, enter 3-D formulas that reference the total sales cells in the other worksheets, and link the Gross Profit cell to the Qtr1 worksheet. Finally, you will add color to the sheet tabs and a background to the Summary sheet cells.

STEPS

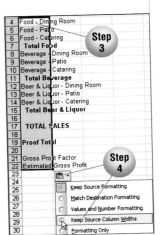

1. With **ExcelS4-01** open, click the *Qtr1* tab.

2. Select A4:A22 and then click the Copy button on the Standard toolbar.

3. Make *Summary* the active worksheet, click A4, and then click the Paste button on the Standard toolbar.

4. Click the Paste Options button and then click *Keep Source Column Widths* at the drop-down list that appears.

5. Make B3 the active cell, type **Total**, press Alt + Enter, type **Sales**, and then press Enter.

6. Bold and center B3.

7. Make *Qtr1* the active worksheet, copy A1, and then paste it to A1 in the *Summary* worksheet.

8. Create the subtitle **Summary Sales Report** in bold, merged and centered in A2:E2.

9. Change the width of column B to *12.00 (89 pixels)*.

10. Save **ExcelS4-01**.

    Saving the workbook before consolidating data using 3-D references is a good idea in case you encounter difficulties when performing the consolidation.

11. With *Summary* still the active worksheet, make B4 the active cell.

⑫ Type **=sum(qtr1:qtr4!e4)** and then click the Enter button on the Formula bar.

The result, *338920*, appears in B4 which is the total of the values in E4 in all four quarterly sales worksheets. The formula is called a *3-D Reference* since it references a cell spanning two or more worksheets. The argument in the SUM function begins with the range of worksheets *Qtr1:Qtr4* followed by the exclamation point to separate the worksheet range from the cell reference. The argument ends with the cell to be summed in the worksheet range.

PROBLEM

Cell displays *#NAME?* instead of *338920*? Be sure the formula does not include any spaces. Also confirm that you entered the correct symbols within the formula.

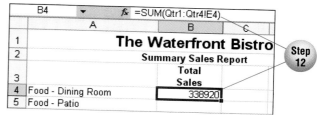

⑬ Make B5 the active cell.

In Steps 14–16 you will enter a 3-D formula using the point-and-click method.

⑭ Type **=sum(**.

⑮ Click the *Qtr1* tab, hold down Shift, and then click the *Qtr4* tab.

This selects the four quarterly sales worksheets and *Qtr1* is the worksheet now displayed. Notice the formula as it is being added to the Formula bar each time you click the mouse.

⑯ Click E5 and then press Enter.

⑰ Press the Up Arrow key to return the active cell back to B5 and then read the formula in the Formula bar, *=SUM(Qtr1:Qtr4!E5)*.

Notice Excel automatically included the closing bracket in the formula when you pressed Enter.

⑱ Drag the fill handle from B5 down through B15 to copy the 3-D formula to the remaining rows.

⑲ Make B17 the active cell and then type the formula **=b7+b11+b15**.

⑳ Apply the Comma Style format to B4:B15 and then deselect the range.

㉑ Make E7 in the *Qtr4* worksheet the active cell, and then click the Copy button on the Standard toolbar.

㉒ Click the *Summary* tab, click B7, hold down Ctrl, then click B11 and B15 to select all three cells.

㉓ Click Edit and then Paste Special.

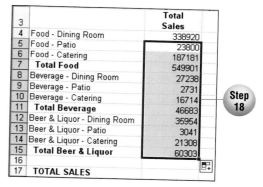

(continued)

(24) Click *Formats* in the *Paste* section of the Paste Special dialog box and then click OK.

> By default, Excel pastes all attributes from the copied cell to the destination range when you click the Paste button on the Standard toolbar. By opening the Paste Special dialog box you can control which attributes from the copied cell(s) are pasted. The *Operation* section of Paste Special provides options with which you can specify which mathematical operation you want to paste if the source contained a formula. Click the *Skip blanks* check box to prevent overwriting values in the destination cells when blank cells exist in the copied range. Click the *Transpose* check box to paste data copied in rows to columns and vice versa.

(25) Make E4 in the *Qtr4* worksheet the active cell, and then click the Format Painter button 🖌 on the Standard toolbar.

Total Sales
3🖌20.00
23,800.00

Step 26

(26) Click the *Summary* tab and then click B4.

> Format Painter is another method with which you can copy formats only from one cell to another. The cell pointer displays with a paintbrush when Format Painter has been activated. Double-clicking the Format Painter button turns on the feature so you can copy formats to multiple cells until you turn it off by clicking the button again.

(27) Use Copy and Paste Special or the Format Painter button to copy the formats from E17 in the *Qtr4* worksheet to B17 in the *Summary* worksheet.

(28) Make B21 in the *Summary* sheet the active cell.

(29) Type the equals sign (=).

(30) Click the *Qtr1* tab, click B21, and then press Enter.

> The value *24%* displays and the formula *=Qtr1!B21* is stored in B21 of the *Summary* worksheet. The contents of B21 in the *Summary* worksheet are now linked to the contents of B21 in the *Qtr1* worksheet. Any change made to B21 in *Qtr1* automatically causes B21 in *Summary* to update as well.

(31) With B22 the active cell, type **=b17*b21** and then press Enter.

> Estimated Gross Profit is calculated by multiplying Total Sales (B17) times the Gross Profit Factor (B21).

(32) Make B19 the active cell and then type a formula that will check the accuracy of the total sales in cell B17. (***Hint: Look at the proof total formulas in the Qtr1-Qtr4 worksheets as an example.***)

17	TOTAL SALES		$ 656,887.00
18			
19	Proof Total	Steps 28–30	$ 656,887.00
20			
21	Gross Profit Factor		24%
22	Estimated Gross Profit		$ 157,652.88

Step 32

Step 31

(33) Right-click the *Summary* tab and then click Tab Color at the shortcut menu.

> Changing the background color of the sheet tabs can help to identify related worksheets or the organizational structure of the workbook.

(34) Click the turquoise color button (fourth from left in last row) in the Format Tab Color palette and then click OK.

(35) Click the *Qtr1* tab, hold down Shift, and then click the *Qtr4* tab.

> Notice the entire background of the *Summary* tab is shaded turquoise when the sheet is not active.

(36) Click Format, point to Sheet, and then click Tab Color.

(37) Click the yellow color button (third from left in last row) and then click OK.

(38) Click the *Summary* tab.

(39) Click Format, point to Sheet, and then click Background.

> A graphics file can be inserted as a pattern that is tiled to fill the background of a worksheet. The background image does not print. Remove a background image by clicking File, pointing to Sheet, and then clicking Delete Background.

(40) If necessary, navigate to the drive and/or folder in which the student data files are stored and then double-click ***Background.gif*** in the Sheet Background file list box.

(41) Save **ExcelS4-01**.

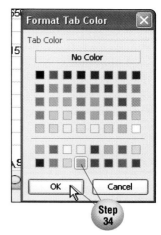

Step 34

Steps 35–37

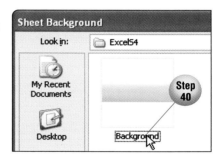

Step 40

In Addition

3-D References and Moving, Inserting, and Deleting Sheets

The following actions apply to a formula when worksheets are moved, added, or deleted within a 3-D range.

- **Move:** Values are removed from the calculation if a worksheet is moved to a location outside the 3-D range.
- **Insert new sheet:** 3-D formula is adjusted to include all values in the same range of cells in the new worksheet(s).
- **Delete:** Values are removed from the 3-D formula. If the worksheet that is deleted is the beginning or ending sheet in the 3-D range, the formula is automatically adjusted to the new range of worksheets.

IN BRIEF

Consolidate Data with 3-D References
1. Activate cell to contain consolidated data.
2. Type equals sign (=).
3. Click first worksheet to be included.
4. Hold down Shift and click last worksheet.
5. Click cell to be consolidated.
6. Press Enter.

Link Worksheets
1. Activate destination cell.
2. Type equals sign (=).
3. Click sheet tab for source data.
4. Click source cell.
5. Press Enter.

4.4 Printing Multiple Worksheets; Setting the Print Area

The Print button on the Standard toolbar prints the active worksheet or selected multiple worksheets. If multiple worksheets have not been selected, display the Print dialog box and change the *Print what* option to *Entire workbook*. To print a portion of a worksheet, select the cells and then change the *Print what* option to *Selection* in the Print dialog box. Setting a print area allows you to save one or more ranges of cells to print so that you do not need to define the selection range again the next time you print.

PROJECT: Now that the Quarterly Sales report is complete, you will experiment with various printing methods.

S T E P S

1 With **ExcelS4-01** open and the *Summary* sheet active, click the *Qtr1* tab, hold down Shift, and then click the *Qtr4* tab.

> This selects all of the worksheets from the first tab through the last tab *(Qtr1-Qtr4)*. To select multiple worksheets that are nonadjacent, hold down Ctrl while clicking each tab. Open the Print dialog box and click *Entire workbook* in the *Print what* section if you want to print all five worksheets in **ExcelS4-01** in one step.

2 Click the Print button.

> The four worksheets print and remain selected.

3 Click the *Summary* tab and then select the cells A3:B17.

> The *Print what* section of the Print dialog box also contains the option *Selection* that is used when you want to print only a portion of the active worksheet.

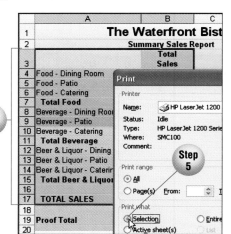

4 Click File and then Print to display the Print dialog box.

5 Click *Selection* in the *Print what* section and then click OK.

> Only the cells within A3:B17 print.

6 Click in any cell to deselect A3:B17.

> In the next steps you will define a print area that will be saved with the workbook.

7 Click the *Qtr1* tab, click View, and then click Page Break Preview.

PROBLEM

> Click OK if the Welcome to Page Break Preview message box displays.

8 Change the Zoom setting to *85%*.

> In Page Break Preview, page breaks are shown as dashed or solid blue lines. You can adjust a page break by dragging the blue line to the desired position. The worksheet can be edited in Page Break Preview.

⑨ Select A1:E17.

⑩ Position the mouse pointer within the selected range, right-click, and then click Set Print Area at the shortcut menu.

⑪ Click in any cell to deselect the range.

> The cells not included in the print area are shown outside the solid blue border in a shaded background.

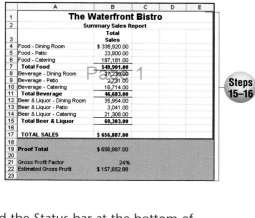

Step 9

Step 10

⑫ Click the Print button on the Standard toolbar.

> Only the cells within the print area are printed. In the next steps you will define another print area in a nonadjacent worksheet.

⑬ Click the *Summary* tab.

⑭ Click View, Page Break Preview, and then change the Zoom setting to *85%*.

⑮ Select A1:B17. Click File, point to Print Area, and then click Set Print Area.

⑯ Click in any cell to deselect the range.

⑰ Click the *Qtr1* tab, hold down Ctrl, and then click the *Summary* tab.

⑱ Click the Print Preview button on the Standard toolbar.

> The *Qtr1* worksheet displays in Print Preview and the Status bar at the bottom of the Preview window displays *Page 1 of 2*.

Steps 15–16

⑲ Click Next on the Print Preview toolbar to view the *Summary* worksheet.

⑳ Click the Close button on the Print Preview toolbar.

> You decide after viewing the worksheets in Print Preview to remove the print area from the *Qtr1* worksheet.

㉑ Click the *Qtr3* tab to deselect the two grouped worksheets.

㉒ Click the *Qtr1* tab, click File, point to Print Area, and then click Clear Print Area.

㉓ Click the *Summary* tab and then click the Print button to print the area defined in the worksheet.

㉔ Save and then close **Excel S4-01**.

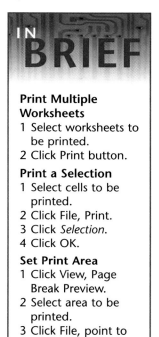

IN BRIEF

Print Multiple Worksheets
1 Select worksheets to be printed.
2 Click Print button.

Print a Selection
1 Select cells to be printed.
2 Click File, Print.
3 Click *Selection*.
4 Click OK.

Set Print Area
1 Click View, Page Break Preview.
2 Select area to be printed.
3 Click File, point to Print Area, click Set Print Area.

4.5 Adjusting Page Breaks in Page Break Preview; Removing a Page Break

In the previous topic you learned that page breaks are displayed as dashed or solid blue lines in Page Break Preview. A dashed line indicates the position of page breaks calculated automatically by Excel. If you do not like the position in which the page break has occurred, drag the blue line to a new location. Excel automatically adjusts the scaling percentage to a value less than 100 percent if you drag the page break further right or down. In Normal View you can insert your own page break by clicking Insert and then Page Break. Remove a

page break by positioning the active cell just below or right of the manual page break, click Insert, and then click Remove Page Break. Right-click any cell and then click Reset All Page Breaks to remove all manual page breaks.

PROJECT: The Inventory Units Purchased report for the current year needs to be printed. You will preview the page breaks in Page Break Preview, adjust the location of a horizontal and vertical page break, and then remove a manual page break.

STEPS

1. Open **WBInventory**.

2. Save the workbook and name it **ExcelS4-02**.

3. Click View and then click Page Break Preview.

4. Change the Zoom setting to *50%*.

5. Review the worksheet in Page Break Preview. The printout will require 4 pages as shown in Figure E4.2.

FIGURE E4.2 Inventory Units Purchased in Page Break Preview

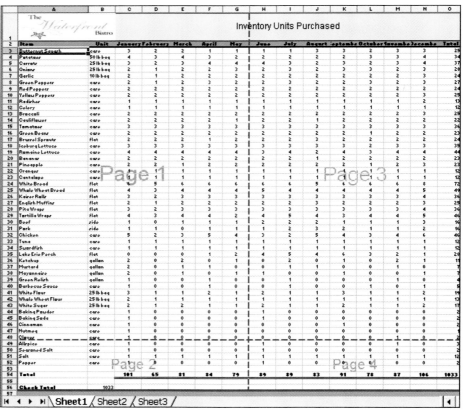

(6) Change the page orientation to *Landscape* in the Page Setup dialog box.

(7) Position the mouse pointer on the vertical dashed blue line between Page 1 and Page 3 until the pointer changes to a double-headed left- and right-pointing arrow, and then drag the page break to the right edge of the worksheet.

> The printout is reduced to two pages. Since the page break has been moved further right than its original location, Excel recalculates the scaling percentage less than 100 percent to fit the cells within the current margins.

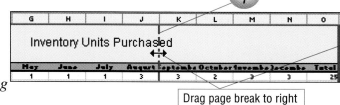

Drag page break to right edge of worksheet.

(8) Drag the horizontal dashed blue line up to position the page break between rows 43 (*White Sugar*) and 44 (*Baking Powder*).

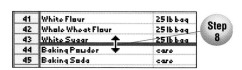

(9) Click File, click Page Setup, and then click the Sheet tab in the Page Setup dialog box.

(10) Click the Collapse Dialog button next to *Rows to repeat at top* in the *Print titles* section.

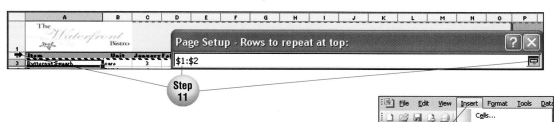

(11) Select rows 1 and 2 and then click the Expand Dialog button to redisplay the entire Page Setup dialog box.

(12) Click OK to close the Page Setup dialog box.

(13) Click the Print button.

(14) Click View and then click Normal.

(15) Scroll down the worksheet to row 44.

> The manual page break inserted at Step 8 displays as a dashed line between rows 43 and 44 in Normal view.

(16) Make A44 the active cell, click Insert, and then click Remove Page Break.

> The manual page break is removed. Excel recalculates the page break position and displays an automatic page break (short dashed line) between rows 48 and 49.

(17) Save and then close **ExcelS4-02**.

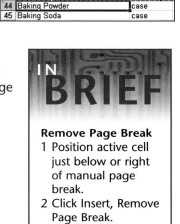

IN BRIEF

Remove Page Break
1 Position active cell just below or right of manual page break.
2 Click Insert, Remove Page Break.

4.6 Creating a Workbook from a Template

Excel includes worksheets that are formatted and have text and formulas created for specific uses such as creating sales invoices, expenses, timecards, and financial statements. These preformatted worksheets are called *templates*. Templates can be customized and saved with a new name to reflect individual company data. Additional templates can be downloaded from the Microsoft Office Online Web site. This Web site is frequently updated. Check back often if a template does not currently exist that meets your needs.

PROJECT: You will create an invoice to Performance Threads using the Sales Invoice template.

STEPS

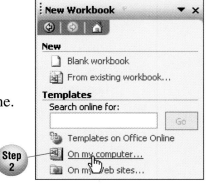

1 Click File and then New.

The New Workbook task pane opens.

2 Click the <u>On my computer</u> hyperlink in the *Templates* section in the New Workbook task pane.

3 Click the Spreadsheet Solutions tab in the Templates dialog box.

4 Double-click *Sales Invoice*.

PROBLEM?
A message will display indicating the component is being installed if this is the first time the template has been opened. Be patient for a few seconds until the template appears on the screen.

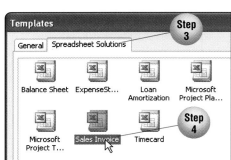

5 Click the Print Preview button to view the Sales Invoice layout.

6 Close the Print Preview window.

7 With the active cell positioned to the right of *Name*, type **Performance Threads** and then press Enter.

Pressing Enter moves the active cell next to *Address* (D14) in the template.

8 Type **4011 Bridgewater Street** and then click the cell pointer next to *City*.

9 Type **Niagara Falls** and then press Tab.

The active cell moves next to State and a comment cell displays with instructions.

10 Type **ON** and then press Tab.

11 With the active cell next to *ZIP*, type **L2E 2T6** and then press Enter.

12 With the active cell next to *Phone*, type **(905) 555-2971**.

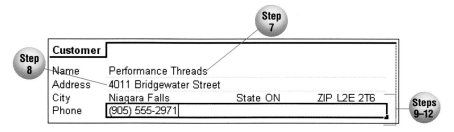

⑬ Type the remaining fields in the invoice as shown in Figure E4.3.

> Click the mouse pointer or press Tab or Enter to activate the desired cell before typing text. The cells in the yellow *TOTAL* column calculate automatically.

FIGURE E4.3 Invoice

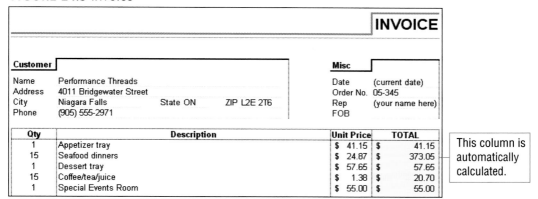

⑭ Scroll to the bottom of the invoice to view the remaining entries.

> In the next steps you will add information regarding terms of payment in the cell with the label *Insert Fine Print Here* and clear the contents of the bottom cell that displays *Insert Farewell Statement Here.*

⑮ Click over the text *Insert Fine Print Here.*

⑯ Type **Terms are net 10 days. Interest at the rate of 2% per month will be charged on overdue accounts**.

⑰ Click over the text *Insert Farewell Statement Here.*

⑱ Click Edit, point to Clear, and then click Contents.

⑲ Scroll to the top of the invoice.

⑳ Click over the text *Insert Company Information Here* and then type the following text:

The Waterfront Bistro (press Alt + Enter)
3104 Rivermist Drive (press Alt + Enter)
Buffalo, NY 14280 (press Enter)

㉑ Click next to *Invoice No.*, type **2462**, and then press Enter.

㉒ Click the Save button.

㉓ Type **ExcelS4-03** and then press Enter.

㉔ Print the invoice.

㉕ Close **ExcelS4-03**.

4.7 Using Styles

A *style* is a set of predefined formatting attributes that can be applied to a cell. The formatting attributes of a style can include such items as the font, font size, font color, alignment, borders, and numeric format. Using styles to format cells ensures consistent formatting in a workbook. Another advantage to formatting with styles is that all cells will automatically update if the contents of a style have been changed.

PROJECT: You will define, apply, and remove styles in an employee schedule.

STEPS

1. Open **WBSchedule**.

2. Save the workbook and name it **ExcelS4-04**.

3. Make A4 the active cell.

    In Steps 4–6 you will define a style by applying formats to an existing cell.

4. Apply the following formatting attributes to A4:

    Font – Comic Sans MS (choose an alternative font if Comic Sans MS is not available on your system)

    Center alignment
    Light Turquoise fill color
    Dark Blue font color

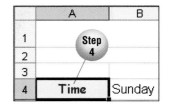

5. With A4 the active cell, click Format and then Style.

6. Type **EmpSchedule** in the *Style name* text box and then click OK.

7. Select B4:H4.

    In Steps 7–8 you will apply the EmpSchedule style to days of the week.

8. Click Format and then Style.

9. Click the down-pointing arrow at the right of the *Style name* text box, click *EmpSchedule* in the drop-down list, and then click OK.

The formats that will be stored in the style name are shown here.

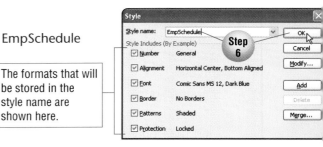

10. Select A5:A7 and then apply the EmpSchedule style.

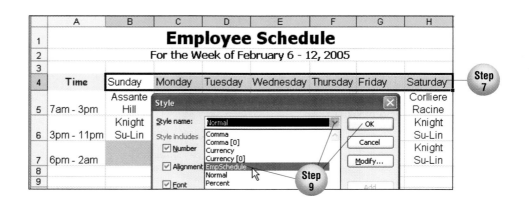

⑪ With A5:A7 still selected, click Format and then Style.

⑫ Click the down-pointing arrow at the right of the *Style name* text box, click *Normal* in the drop-down list, and then click OK.

> This removes the EmpSchedule style from the selected cells by restoring the default settings.

⑬ Click the Undo button to reapply the EmpSchedule style back to A5:A7.

⑭ Click on any cell that has the EmpSchedule style applied.

> In the next steps you will modify the EmpSchedule style and see the immediate effect on the worksheet.

⑮ Click Format and then Style,

⑯ Click the Modify button with *EmpSchedule* already selected in the *Style name* list box.

⑰ Click the Patterns tab in the Format Cells dialog box.

⑱ Click the pale green color square (fourth from left in the fifth row) and then click OK.

⑲ Click OK to close the Style dialog box.

> The cells with the EmpSchedule style applied to them immediately update to reflect the new color setting.

⑳ Save **ExcelS4-04**.

Time	Sunday	Monday	Tuesday	Wednesday	Thursday	Friday	Saturday
7am - 3pm	Assante Hill	Assante Hill	Assante Hill	Assante Hill	Assante Hill	Corlliere Racine	Corlliere Racine
3pm - 11pm	Knight Su-Lin	Corlliere Knight	Corlliere Knight	Racine Su-Lin	Assante Racine	Knight Su-Lin	Knight Su-Lin
6pm - 2am						Knight Su-Lin	Knight Su-Lin

Steps 14–19

In *Addition*

Copying Styles to Another Workbook

Styles you create are saved in the workbook in which they were created. To copy a style from an existing workbook to another workbook, make sure both workbooks are open and activate the workbook into which you want to copy the styles. Display the Style dialog box and then click Merge. In the Merge Styles dialog box, double-click the name of the workbook that contains the styles you want to copy.

IN BRIEF

Define a Style
1 Apply desired formatting to cell.
2 Activate cell containing formats.
3 Click Format, Style.
4 Type name for style.
5 Click OK.

Apply a Style
1 Select cells you want to format.
2 Click Format, Style.
3 Click down-pointing arrow next to *Style name* text box.
4 Click desired style name.
5 Click OK.

4.8 Creating a Web Page from a Worksheet; Inserting and Editing Hyperlinks

A worksheet can be saved as a Web page for publishing to a Web server. Excel worksheets or entire workbooks may be published on a company intranet as a method of distributing the data to employees. Use hyperlinks in a Web page to jump to another file or location on the Internet when the hyperlinked text is clicked.

PROJECT: You will save the employee schedule as a Web page, insert a hyperlink to another worksheet, edit a URL in an existing hyperlink, and preview the worksheets in the browser window.

STEPS

(Note: You will need an Internet connection to complete Step 18 in this topic.)

1. With **ExcelS4-04** open, click File and then Save as Web Page.

   This displays the Save As dialog box with the *Save as type* option automatically changed to *Web Page (*.htm; *.html)*. The extension *.htm* will automatically be added to the name typed in the *File name* text box.

2. Type **EmployeeSchedule-Feb12** in the *File name* text box and then click the Save button.

   The option *Entire Workbook* is selected by default. In a workbook with multiple worksheets, the Web page will contain sheet tabs in a manner similar to the Excel window. To save an individual worksheet only or a group of worksheets within the workbook, select the worksheets before opening the Save As dialog box and then click *Selection: Sheet*.

   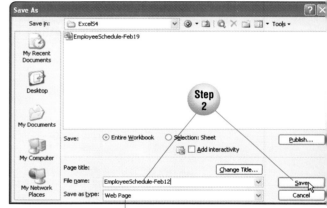

   Save as type is automatically set to *Web Page*.

3. Click File and then Web Page Preview.

   The worksheet is displayed in the default Web browser window as shown in Figure E4.4.

4. Close the browser window.

FIGURE E4.4 Employee Schedule in Web Browser Window

Your address will vary.

(5) Make B9 the active cell.

(6) Type **Next Week's Schedule** and then click the Enter button in the Formula bar.

In Steps 7–8 you will insert a hyperlink to the employee schedule file for the following week.

(7) With B9 the active cell, click the Insert Hyperlink button ![icon] on the Standard toolbar.

(8) With *Existing File or Web Page* selected in the Links bar and *Current Folder* selected in the Places bar, click **EmployeeSchedule-Feb19.htm** in the file list box and then click OK.

To hyperlink to a location on the Internet, type the URL for the location in the *Address* text box.

(9) Display the worksheet in Web Page Preview.

(10) Click the hyperlinked text *Next Week's Schedule* to display the linked file.

(11) Close the browser window.

(12) Save, print, and then close **EmployeeSchedule-Feb12.htm**.

In the next steps you will open a worksheet that has links already created and edit one of the links that has an error in it.

(13) Open **WBLinks**.

(14) Save the workbook and name it **ExcelS4-05**.

The Waterfront Bistro created this workbook for their customers to view areas of interest around Buffalo. A customer has reported the first link to the Web site for Buffalo.com Everything Buffalo! does not work.

(15) Position the cell pointer over A9, right-click, and then click Edit Hyperlink at the shortcut menu.

The Edit Hyperlink dialog box opens with the insertion point positioned in the *Address* text box. Notice the word *buffalo* is misspelled in the URL.

(16) Click the insertion point within the word *bufaloe*, insert and delete text as required correcting the spelling, and then click OK.

(17) Change the font size to *12* if the cell reverts to the default 10-point font size.

(18) Make sure you are connected to the Internet and then click the link in A9 to open the default Web browser and view the Web page.

(19) Close the browser window to return to the worksheet.

(20) Save, print, and then close **ExcelS4-05**.

Save as Web Page
1 Click File, Save as Web Page.
2 Type name for Web page.
3 Click Save.

Insert a Hyperlink
1 Select cell.
2 Click Insert, Hyperlink.
3 Type file name or URL.
4 Click OK.

4.9 Filtering Lists Using AutoFilter; Sorting a List

In Excel, a list is a worksheet with information set up in rows in which each column represents one unit of similar data called a *field*, and each row is called a *record*. The first row of the list contains labels, which describe the contents in each field (column). The data entered in each cell is called a field value. A record (row) contains all of the fields for one unit in the list. No blank rows should exist within the list. For example, a worksheet containing employee names, employee numbers, departments, and salaries would be considered a list. One row, or record, in the list would contain all of the information for one employee. A *filter* is used to display only certain records within the list that meet specified criteria. A list can be sorted by up to three sort keys.

PROJECT: Dana Hirsch has asked you for a list of inventory items showing unit purchases of 1 or 2 in the month of April.

STEPS

1 Open **WBInventory**.

2 Save the workbook and name it **ExcelS4-06**.

3 Make A3 the active cell.

> For Excel to recognize the list, the active cell must be positioned within the list range.

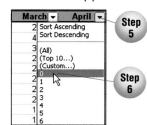

4 Click Data, point to Filter, and then click AutoFilter.

> The *AutoFilter* feature allows you to filter a list by selecting the criteria from a drop-down list. For each column (field) in the list, a button with a filter arrow appears.

5 Click the filter arrow next to *April* in F2.

> Excel looks in the active column and includes in the drop-down list each unique field value that exists within the column. In addition, the entries *Sort Ascending, Sort Descending, (All), (Top 10),* and *(Custom)* appear at the top of the list.

6 Click *0* in the drop-down list.

> Excel hides any records that have a value other than zero (0) in the column as shown in Figure E4.5. The row numbers of the matching items and the filter arrow in the column that was used to filter by are displayed in blue. The Status bar shows the message *Filter Mode*. A filtered worksheet can be edited, formatted, charted, or printed.

7 Click the filter arrow next to *April* in F2 and then click *(All)* in the drop-down list.

> All of the records are redisplayed in the worksheet. In the next steps you will filter by more than one criterion and then sort a list.

8 Click the filter arrow next to *April* in F2 and then click *(Custom)* in the drop-down list.

> The Custom AutoFilter dialog box appears. This dialog box is used when you want to filter by two criteria.

FIGURE E4.5 Filtered Worksheet

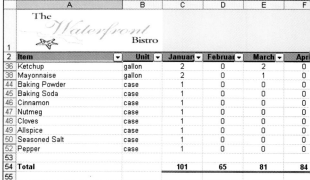

⑨ With the insertion point positioned in the text box next to *equals* in the *Show rows where* section, type 1.

⑩ Click *Or*.

⑪ Click the down-pointing arrow next to the list box below the *And* and *Or* option buttons and then click *equals* in the drop-down list.

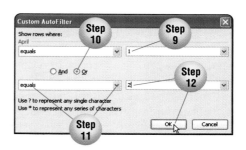

⑫ Click in the text box below *1*, type 2, and then click OK.

> Only those records with a value of either 1 or 2 in column F are displayed. In the next steps you will sort the filtered list and then print a selection of cells.

⑬ Click Data and then click Sort.

> The Sort dialog box opens and all cells within the list range are automatically selected. Use the Sort dialog box to sort a list by more than one column. To sort by a single column, click the active cell in the column by which you want to sort and then click the Sort Ascending ⬇ or Sort Descending ⬇ button on the Standard toolbar.

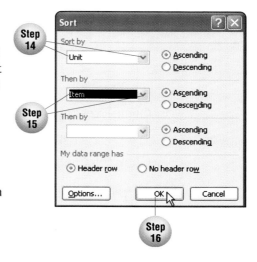

⑭ Click the down-pointing arrow at the right of the *Sort by* option box in the Sort dialog box and then click *Unit* at the drop-down list.

> By default the sort order is set to *Ascending*.

⑮ Click the down-pointing arrow at the right of the first *Then by* option box and then click *Item* in the drop-down list.

⑯ Click OK.

> Excel sorts the filtered records first in ascending order by the field values in the *Unit* field and then in ascending order by the field values in the *Item* field. In an alphanumeric sort, field values that begin with numbers are sorted and placed first in the list.

⑰ Select A2:F51 and then print the selected cells.

⑱ Click in any cell to deselect A2:F51.

⑲ Click Data, point to Filter, and then click AutoFilter.

> All records are automatically redisplayed and the buttons with the filter arrows are removed from each column.

⑳ Save and then close **ExcelS4-06**.

IN BRIEF

Filter List Using AutoFilter
1 Make active a cell within list range.
2 Click Data, point to Filter, click AutoFilter.
3 Click filter arrow in field by which to filter records.
4 Click criteria field value by which to filter.

Sort a List
1 Make active a cell within list range.
2 Click Data, Sort.
3 Select sort fields and sort order.
4 Click OK.

4.10 Inserting and Editing Comments; Inserting a Diagram

A *comment* is a yellow pop-up box with text inserted that displays when the cell pointer is positioned over a cell with an attached comment. A red triangle in the upper right corner of the cell alerts the reader that a comment exists. Use comments to provide instructions, identify significant information, or add other explanatory text to a cell.

Open the Diagram Gallery to add a visual element to a worksheet that illustrates a hierarchy with an organizational chart, or depicts relationships between steps or processes with a cycle, target, radial, venn, or pyramid diagram.

PROJECT: Dana Hirsch has asked for the updated quarterly sales summary report. You will insert and edit comments in the Summary tab and add a cycle diagram for Dana's review.

STEPS

1. Open **ExcelS4-01** and then save the workbook as **ExcelS4-07**.

2. With *Summary* the active worksheet, click View and then click Normal.

3. Click File, point to Print Area, and then click Clear Print Area.

4. Make B21 the active cell.

5. Click Insert and then Comment.

   A yellow comment box displays anchored to the active cell with the user's name inserted in bold text at the top of the box and a blinking insertion point.

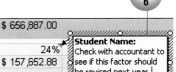

6. Type **Check with accountant to see if this factor should be revised next year.**

7. Click in the worksheet outside the comment box.

   The comment box closes and a diagonal red triangle appears in the upper right corner of B21 indicating a comment exists for the cell.

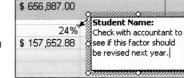

8. Position the cell pointer over B5 and then right-click the mouse.

9. Click Insert Comment at the shortcut menu.

10. Type **Patio sales are down 8% due to lower than normal temperatures during the summer months.**

11. Click in the worksheet outside the comment box.

12. Hover the cell pointer over B21.

    When you hover the cell pointer over a cell that contains a comment, the comment box appears.

13. Hover the cell pointer over B5.

    In the next steps you will edit the comment in cell B21.

14. Right-click over cell B21 and then click Edit Comment at the shortcut menu.

    The comment box appears with the insertion point positioned at the end of the existing text.

15 Move the cursor and insert and delete text as necessary to change the comment text to *Accountant advises factor should be changed to 23% next year* and then click outside the comment box.

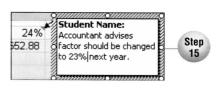

> In the next steps you will insert a cycle diagram to illustrate the continuous sales review process that the managers of The Waterfront Bistro perform.

16 Click Insert and then click Diagram.

17 At the Diagram Gallery, double-click the *Cycle Diagram* (middle diagram in first row).

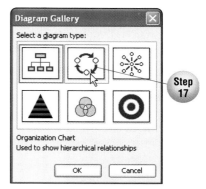

> A cycle diagram is used to visually present the steps or processes in a continuous loop.

18 Click the AutoFormat button [icon] on the Diagram toolbar.

> Use buttons on the Diagram toolbar to insert additional shapes; move shapes backward or forward or reverse the diagram; expand, scale, or fit the contents of the diagram; apply an autoformat to the diagram; or change the type of diagram.

19 At the Diagram Style Gallery dialog box, click *Primary Colors* in the *Select a Diagram Style* list box and then click OK.

20 Click the text *Click to add text* that displays at the top right of the diagram and then type **Executive Chef Reviews Food Sales**.

21 Click the text *Click to add text* that displays at the bottom of the diagram and then type **Beverage Manager Reviews Beverage Sales**.

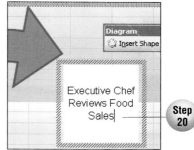

22 Click the text *Click to add text* that displays at the top left of the diagram, type **General Manager Reviews All Sales**, and then click outside the text box.

23 Resize and move the diagram so that it spans the width of columns A–D and the height of rows 25–45.

24 Click View and then click Comments.

> All comments in the worksheet are now displayed.

25 Click File, Page Setup, and then click the Sheet tab in the Page Setup dialog box.

26 Click the *Comments* list arrow in the *Print* section and then click *As displayed on sheet*.

> By default, comments do not print with the worksheet. Comments can be printed as they are displayed in the worksheet or at the end of the worksheet on a separate page.

27 Click the Margins tab, click the *Horizontally* check box in the *Center on page* section, and then click OK to close the Page Setup dialog box.

28 Print the *Summary* worksheet.

29 Save and then close **ExcelS4-07**.

IN BRIEF

Insert a Comment
1 Make active the cell in which to attach a comment.
2 Click Insert, Comment.
3 Type comment text.
4 Click outside comment box.

Insert a Diagram
1 Click Insert, Diagram.
2 Double-click diagram type.
3 Add text as required.
4 Click outside diagram box.

4.11 Using the Research Task Pane

Open the Research task pane to search for and request information from online sources or other resources on your computer without leaving your worksheet in Excel. From the task pane you can look up definitions and translations and conduct an Internet search. Determine the resources available to you by clicking the down-pointing arrow at the right of the resources list box (the list box located below the *Search for* text box). The drop-down list contains lists of reference books, research sites, business and financial sites, and other services. Use the Research options link at the bottom of the Research task pane to add and remove resources that you want the ability to search.

You can insert into your worksheet information that displays in the Research task pane or use the standard copy and paste feature for Internet searches.

PROJECT: Dana Hirsch is reviewing the value of the bistro investments before securing financing for an expansion loan and has asked for your assistance. Using the Research task pane, you will search for and insert current stock prices for stocks that Dana has put in the *Stock Watch* section of the Investment worksheet and then use this information to calculate market value.

S T E P S

(Note: Make sure that you are connected to the Internet before completing this topic.)

1. Open **WBInvestments** and then save the workbook as **ExcelS4-08**.

2. Click the Research button 🔍 on the Standard toolbar.

   The Research task pane opens. The online resources available to you depend on the locale to which your system is set, authorization information indicating that you are allowed to download information, and your Internet Service Provider.

3. If necessary, make active cell B15.

4. Click in the *Search for* text box in the Research task pane and then type **IBM**.

5. Click the down-pointing arrow at the right of the resources list box (below *Search for* text box), and then click *MSN Money Stock Quotes*.

   The current stock price quote and trading information for International Business Machines displays in the task pane.

6. Click the Insert Price button in the Research task pane.

   The current stock price is inserted in the active cell.

PROBLEM **?**

Insert Price button not visible? Scroll down the Research task pane until you can see the button.

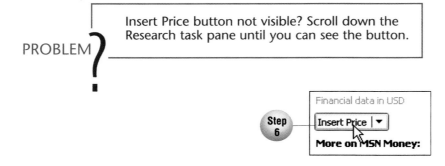

7. Make B16 the active cell.

8. Select *IBM* in the *Search for* text box, type **Dell**, and then press Enter.

9. Click the Insert Price button in the Research task pane.

10. Make B17 the active cell.

11. Select *Dell* in the *Search for* text box, type **GE**, and then press Enter.

12. Click the Insert Price button in the Research task pane.

> In the next steps you will use the Research task pane to look up a definition of the stock term *stop order*.

13. Select *GE* in the *Search for* text box, and then type **stop order**.

14. Click the down-pointing arrow at the right of the resources list box, and then click *Encarta Dictionary: English (North America)*. If this reference is not in the drop-down list, click any other dictionary reference available to you.

15. Read the definition that displays in the task pane.

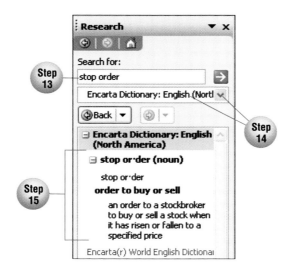

16. Select *stop order* in the *Search for* text box and then type **investment strategies**.

17. Click the down-pointing arrow at the right of the resources list box and then click *All Research Sites*.

(continued)

18. Scroll down the results listed in the Research task pane and then click a hyperlink to an article that interests you.

19. After reading the information that displays in your Web browser, close the browser window.

20. Close the Research task pane.

> Dana Hirsch has just told you a trustee has purchased 1,500 shares of each company in the *Stock Watch* section on behalf of The Waterfront Bistro. In the next steps, you will calculate the current market value of those shares based on this new information.

21. Select A15:A17 and then copy the range to the Clipboard.

22. Make A19 the active cell and then paste the range from the Clipboard.

23. Make B19 the active cell and then type the stock price that you inserted from MSN in B15 without the text US:IBM. For example, type *83.59*. **(*Note: Your value will vary from the example given since stock prices fluctuate.*)**

24. Make B20 the active cell and then type the stock price that you inserted from MSN in B16 without the text *US:Dell*.

25. Make B21 the active cell and then type the stock price that you inserted from MSN in B17 without the text *US:GE*.

Stock Watch		
	Current Stock Price	
International Business Machines (IBM)	US:IBM 83.59	
Dell Computers (Dell)	US:DELL 31.92	
General Electric (GE)	US:GE 28.63	
International Business Machines (IBM)	83.59	
Dell Computers (Dell)	31.92	
General Electric (GE)	28.63	

Step 23

Step 24

Step 22

Step 25

26. Make C18 the active cell, click the Bold button and the Align Right button, and then type Market Value.

27. Make C19 the active cell, type the formula =b19*1500, and then press Enter.

Current Stock Price		
US:IBM 83.59		
US:DELL 31.92		
US:GE 28.63		
	Market Value	
83.59	=b19*1500	
31.92		
28.63		

Step 27

28 Make C19 the active cell and then drag the fill handle to C20:C21.

29 With C19:C21 selected, format the range to Currency Style with zero decimals.

30 Make A23 the active cell, turn on bold, and then type Total Market Value of Stocks:.

31 Make C23 the active cell and then use the AutoSum button to total the values in C19:C21.

18			Market Value	
19	International Business Machines (IBM)	83.59	$	125,385
20	Dell Computers (Dell)	31.92	$	47,880
21	General Electric (GE)	28.63	$	42,945
22				
23	**Total Market Value of Stocks:**		$	216,210

Your values will vary.

Step 30

Step 31

32 Format C23 to bold, light turquoise fill color, and add a top and bottom border.

33 Click File, Page Setup, click the Margins tab, click the *Horizontally* check box in the *Center on page* section, and then click OK.

34 Save, print, and then close **ExcelS4-08**.

In Addition

Using the Research Task Pane for Translation

The Research task pane can be used to perform translation from English to a variety of other languages or vice versa. Type the word or phrase that you want to translate in the *Search for* text box. Click the down-pointing arrow at the right of the resources list box (below *Search for* text box) and then click *Translation*. Upon first use, the feature may need to be installed. In the Translation section of the Research task pane a *From* and a *To* drop-down list appear. If necessary, change the language from *English (U.S.)* in the From list box to the source language. Choose the language you wish to translate the word or phrase into in the To list box. Excel searches the requested language dictionary and displays the translation results. In the example shown, the word *investment* is shown translated from English to Spanish.

Research

Search for:

investment

Translation

Back

☐ **Translation**

Translate a word or sentence.
From

English (U.S.)

To

Spanish (Spain-Modern Sort)

Translation options...

☐ **Bilingual Dictionary**

☐ **investment**

inversión *femenino*

IN BRIEF

Research Information
1 Click Research button.
2 Type keyword in *Search for* text box.
3 Choose resources in which to search.
4 Browse results in task pane.

4.12 Arranging Multiple Workbooks; Hiding and Unhiding a Workbook

The Window menu in Excel provides options with which you can switch the active workbook or customize the layout of the Excel window by arranging multiple open workbooks to display within the same screen space. Use the *Compare Side by Side* option to display two workbooks at the same time and with synchronous scrolling turned on you can scroll both worksheets simultaneously. By viewing more than one workbook at the same time you can easily compare information in two files, copy and paste data from one file to another, or link data from one file to another. The *Hide* option on the Window menu allows you to remove from view an open workbook containing confidential or sensitive information that you do not want others to see.

PROJECT: You will experiment with the various options on the Window menu for arranging multiple workbooks, and then hide and unhide the workbook with the investment information for The Waterfront Bistro.

STEPS

1. Click the Open button on the Standard toolbar.

2. Click *ExcelS4-08* in the file list box, hold down Ctrl, click *WBLoan,* and then click the Open button.

   Both workbooks are now open. Use the Ctrl key when clicking file names that are not adjacent in the file list box. To select adjacent files, click the first file name, hold down Shift, and then click the last file name.

3. With **ExcelS4-08** the active workbook, click Window on the Menu bar and then click Compare Side by Side with WBLoan.xls.

   The two workbooks are arranged horizontally in separate windows. By default, synchronous scrolling is turned on and one scroll bar appears in the active workbook only. By viewing these two workbooks at the same time you can see the financial impact on The Waterfront Bistro of both the investment and loan scenarios at the same time.

4. Click the down scroll arrow a few times in the **ExcelS4-08** window. Notice the worksheet in the **WBLoan** workbook also scrolls down as you click the mouse.

5. Click the title bar for the **WBLoan** window.

   The workbook becomes the active workbook and the vertical scroll bar moves to the **WBLoan** window.

6. Click the up scroll arrow a few times to scroll back to the top of the worksheet.

7. Click the Close Side by Side button on the Compare Side by Side toolbar.

8. With **WBLoan** the active workbook, click File and then click Close.

   The **WBLoan** workbook closes and **ExcelS4-08** becomes the active workbook.

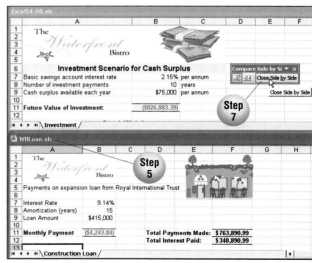

⑨ With **ExcelS4-08** the active workbook, click Window and then click Hide.

It appears that the Excel window is now empty; however, **ExcelS4-08** is still open—it is temporarily hidden from view until you choose to unhide it.

⑩ Click the Open button on the Standard toolbar.

⑪ Click *ExcelS4-03,* hold down Ctrl, click *ExcelS4-07,* and then click the Open button.

⑫ Click Window and then click Arrange.

⑬ At the Arrange Windows dialog box, click *Tiled,* and then click OK.

The two workbooks are displayed in a tile arrangement in the Excel window. Choose *Horizontal* or *Vertical* in the Arrange Windows dialog box to divide the open workbooks in the Excel window into equally sized horizontal or vertical windows. Click *Cascade* to divide the workspace into overlapping workbooks with the Title bar of each window visible.

⑭ Click Window and then click Unhide.

⑮ At the Unhide dialog box, with *ExcelS4-08.xls* selected in the *Unhide workbook* list box, click OK.

ExcelS4-08 is redisplayed overlapping the tiled windows below it.

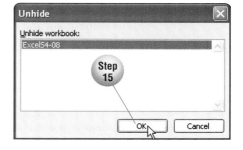

⑯ Click Window, Arrange, and then click OK with *Tiled* already selected in the Arrange Windows dialog box.

The tiled windows display as shown in Figure E4.6. Navigate within each window by clicking the window's title bar to make the workbook active and then using the horizontal and vertical scroll bars to scroll the worksheet.

⑰ Hold down the Shift key, click File, and then click Close All. Click No if prompted to save changes to any of the files.

The Close option on the File menu changes to Close All when multiple windows are open and the Shift key is used.

FIGURE E4.6 Tiled Window Arrangement

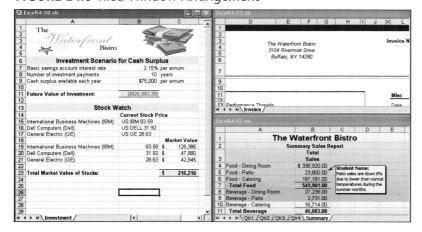

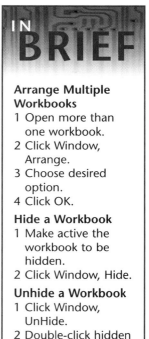

IN BRIEF

Arrange Multiple Workbooks
1 Open more than one workbook.
2 Click Window, Arrange.
3 Choose desired option.
4 Click OK.

Hide a Workbook
1 Make active the workbook to be hidden.
2 Click Window, Hide.

Unhide a Workbook
1 Click Window, UnHide.
2 Double-click hidden workbook file name.

4.13 Creating and Renaming a Folder; Moving Files to a Folder; Converting a Workbook to a Different File Format

Organizing your workbooks by creating folders for similar types of files will make the task of finding files faster and easier. Folders can be created or renamed and files can be moved to a folder within Excel using either the Open or Save As dialog box. An Excel workbook can be converted to a variety of different file formats for transportability of data to other applications. Use the *Save as type* option in the Save As dialog box to save a workbook in another format.

PROJECT: Begin organizing your Excel files by creating a new folder and then moving files into the folder. The inventory workbook needs to be converted to a comma delimited file format.

STEPS

1. Click the Open button on the Standard toolbar to display the Open dialog box.

2. Click the Create New Folder button 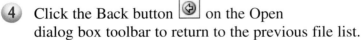 on the Open dialog box toolbar.

3. Type **Sales** in the *Name* text box in the New Folder dialog box and then press Enter or click OK.

    The new folder automatically becomes the active folder.

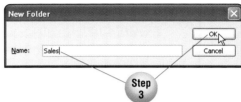

Step 3

4. Click the Back button on the Open dialog box toolbar to return to the previous file list.

5. Click **ExcelS4-01** in the file list, hold down Ctrl, click **ExcelS4-07**, and then release the Ctrl key.

6. Move the arrow pointer over either selected file name, hold down the left mouse button, drag the mouse to the folder named *Sales*, and then release the mouse.

    As you drag the mouse, dimmed file names move with the mouse indicating you are moving the files to a new location.

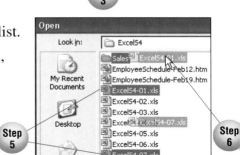

Step 5   **Step 6**

7. Double-click the *Sales* folder name.

8. Click the Back button on the Open dialog box toolbar to return to the previous file list.

    You decide the Sales folder should also contain invoices. In the next steps you will rename the Sales folder and then move an invoice to the folder.

9. Right-click the *Sales* folder name and then click Rename at the shortcut menu.

10. With the text *Sales* selected in the current folder name, press the Right Arrow key to move the insertion point to the end of the current name, type **andInvoices**, and then press Enter.

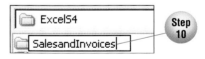

Step 10

⑪ Click *ExcelS4-03* in the file list and then drag the file name to the folder named *SalesandInvoices*.

⑫ Double-click *ExcelS4-02* in the file list box to open the workbook.

The executive chef uses an inventory program that doesn't recognize Excel workbooks however the program can import data stored in a **comma delimited (csv)** file format. The csv file format saves the data with a comma separating data between columns and a carriage return at the end of each row. Formulas are converted to text and all formatting within the worksheet is stripped from the file.

⑬ Click File and then click Save As.

File name:	ExcelS4-02.xls		Save
Save as type:	Microsoft Office Excel Workbook (*.xls)		Cancel

Microsoft Excel 5.0/95 Workbook (*.xls)
Microsoft Excel 97- Excel 2003 & 5.0/95 Workbook (*.xls)
CSV (Comma delimited) (*.csv)
Microsoft Excel 4.0 Worksheet (*.xls)
Microsoft Excel 3.0 Worksheet (*.xls)
Microsoft Excel 2.1 Worksheet (*.xls)

Step 14

⑭ Click the *Save as type* list arrow, scroll down the list box, and then click *CSV (Comma delimited) (*.csv)*.

⑮ With the file named changed to *ExcelS4-02.csv* in the *File name* text box, click the Save button.

⑯ Click OK at the Microsoft Office Excel message box that says the selected file type does not support workbooks that contain multiple sheets and that clicking OK will save only the active worksheet.

⑰ Click Yes to save the workbook at the Microsoft Office Excel message box that says *ExcelS4-02.csv* may contain features that are not compatible with CSV (Comma delimited).

⑱ Close **ExcelS4-02.csv**. Click No when prompted to save changes since the file has already been converted.

In Addition

Converting Multiple Worksheets

The list of file formats shown in the *Save as type* list box varies depending on the active worksheet. Excel can convert only the active worksheet in most file formats. If a workbook contains multiple sheets you will need to convert each sheet separately.

IN BRIEF

Create a Folder
1 Display the Open or Save As dialog box.
2 Click the Create New Folder button on the dialog box toolbar.
3 Type folder name and press Enter.

Convert Workbook to Different File Format
1 Open workbook to be converted.
2 Click File, Save As.
3 Change *Save as type* to file format desired.
4 Click Save.

FEATURES SUMMARY

Feature	Button	Menu	Keyboard
Arrange workbooks		Window, Arrange	
AutoFilter		Data, Filter, AutoFilter	
Background		Format, Sheet, Background	
Clear Print Area		File, Print Area, Clear Print Area	
Compare Side by Side		Window, Compare Side by Side	
Create a folder	📁	File, Open or File, Save As	
Delete a worksheet		Edit, Delete Sheet	
Format a sheet tab		Format, Sheet, Tab Color	
Hide a workbook		Window, Hide	
Hide a worksheet		Format, Sheet, Hide	
Insert a comment		Insert, Comment	
Insert a diagram	🔁	Insert, Diagram	
Insert a hyperlink	🌐	Insert, Hyperlink	Ctrl + K
Insert a worksheet		Insert, Worksheet	
Move or copy a worksheet		Edit, Move or Copy Sheet	
Page Break		Insert, Page Break	
Page Break Preview		View, Page Break Preview	
Paste Special		Edit, Paste Special	
Rename a worksheet		Format, Sheet, Rename	
Research	🔍	Tools, Research	Alt + click
Save As		File, Save As	F12
Save as Web Page		File, Save as Web Page	
Set Print Area		File, Print Area, Set Print Area	
Sort Ascending	A↓	Data, Sort	
Sort Descending	Z↓	Data, Sort	
Styles		Format, Style	
Templates		File, New	
Unhide a workbook		Window, Unhide	
Unhide a worksheet		Format, Sheet, Unhide	
Web Page Preview		File, Web Page Preview	

PROCEDURES CHECK

Completion: In the space provided at the right, indicate the correct term or command.

1. A new workbook initially contains this many sheets. _____
2. Click this menu sequence to hide the active worksheet. _____
3. Hold down this key while dragging a sheet tab to copy the sheet. _____
4. The formula =*SUM(Expense1:Expense4!G4)* includes this type of reference. _____
5. A worksheet is linked to another worksheet within the same workbook by creating this. _____
6. Change to this view to define a print area that will save one or more ranges to print in a worksheet. _____
7. Worksheets that are preformatted for specific uses, such as creating sales invoices or expenses, are called this. _____
8. Consider storing formatting attributes in this to ensure consistent formatting in a worksheet. _____
9. Worksheets saved as a Web page have this file extension added to the file name. _____
10. Use this preview feature to view a Web page in the default browser window. _____
11. Display this dialog box to enter a file name or URL to jump to when the selected text is clicked in the browser window. _____
12. This mode is active when only certain records that meet a criteria are displayed in the worksheet. _____
13. A list can be sorted by up to this many sort key fields. _____
14. Additional information about a cell that appears in a yellow pop-up box when the cell pointer is positioned over the cell is called this. _____
15. Open this task pane to search for a definition in an online resource. _____
16. Click this menu sequence to display two open workbooks at the same time in a horizontal arrangement with synchronous scrolling.

_____

_____

17. List the steps you would complete to insert a cycle diagram in the active worksheet with the following three processes to be labeled clockwise: *Prebudget Planning, Budget Approval, Budget Review.*

_____

_____

18. List the steps you would complete to set a print area to be saved with the workbook.

_____

_____

19. List the steps you would complete to create a new folder named Budgets within the default folder.

_____

_____

20. List the steps you would complete to save the active worksheet in a comma delimited (csv) file.

_____

_____

SKILLS REVIEW

Activity 1: CREATING A FOLDER; INSERTING, DELETING, COPYING, AND RENAMING A WORKSHEET; FORMATTING SHEETS

1 Open **WBPayroll**.
2 Display the Save As dialog box and create a new folder named ExcelS4Review.
3 Save the workbook and name it **ExcelS4-R1** in the ExcelS4Review folder.
4 Copy the *Week2* worksheet, positioning the new sheet after *Week3*.
5 Rename the *Week2 (2)* worksheet as *Week4*.
6 Delete the Week3 worksheet.
7 Copy the *Week2* worksheet, positioning the new sheet between *Week2* and *Week4*.
8 Rename the *Week2 (2)* worksheet as *Week3*.
9 Insert a new worksheet positioned before *Week1* and then rename the worksheet *Summary*.
10 Make *Week3* the active worksheet and then edit the following cells:
      Change E9 from *0* to *5*.
      Change I6 from *6* to *0*.
11 Make *Week4* the active worksheet and then edit the following cells:
      Change C11 from *0* to *8*.
      Change G11 from *9* to *0*.
12 Apply a dark purple color to the *Week1* through *Week4* sheet tabs.
13 Apply a dark blue color to the *Summary* tab.
14 Save **ExcelS4-R1**.

Activity 2: USING 3-D REFERENCES; LINKING WORKSHEETS; PRINTING MULTIPLE WORKSHEETS

1 With **ExcelS4-R1** open, copy A1:A2 from any worksheet to A1:A2 in the *Summary* worksheet keeping the source column widths.
2 Copy A5:A15 from any worksheet to A5:A15 in the *Summary* worksheet.
3 Copy J5:L5 from any worksheet to C5:E5 in the *Summary* worksheet keeping the source column widths.
4 With *Summary* the active worksheet, create a SUM formula with a 3-D reference in C6 that will total the hours for Assante for all four weeks.
5 Make C6 the active cell and then drag the fill handle down to row 11.
6 Make B15 the active cell and then enter a formula that will link B15 in the *Summary* worksheet to B15 in the *Week1* worksheet.
7 Make cell C3 in *Week1* the active cell and then use the DATE function to enter the date *May 7, 2005*.
8 Type a formula in C4 that will add three days to the date in C3 and then increase the width of column C as needed to display the dates.

9   Complete steps similar to those in Steps 7 and 8 to enter the week ended and payment dates in the remaining worksheets as follows:
    C3 in *Week2*   **May 14, 2005**
    C3 in *Week3*   **May 21, 2005**
    C3 in *Week4*   **May 28, 2005**

10 Make K6 in *Week1* the active cell and then type the formula =if(j6>40,j6-40,0).

11 Drag the fill handle from K6 down to K11 and then use the AutoSum button to calculate the total overtime hours in D13.

12 Make L6 the active cell and then type the formula =(j6*b15)+(k6*(b15*.5)). In your own words, describe what this formula is calculating and why the reference to B15 must be an absolute reference.

_____

_____

_____

13 Drag the fill handle from L6 down to L11 and then use the AutoSum button to calculate the total gross pay in L13.

14 Complete the overtime hours and gross pay for *Week2-Week4*. (**Hint: Use the Copy command to copy the IF and Gross Pay formulas from** *Week1*.)

15 Make *Summary* the active worksheet and then enter the 3-D reference formulas in D6 and E6 to consolidate the overtime hours and gross pay for Assante from all four worksheets.

16 Copy the 3-D formulas in D6:E6 to D7:E11.

17 Calculate the totals in C13:E13.

18 Format the *Gross Pay* column to Currency Style.

19 Select A1:A2 and then click the Merge and Center button on the Formatting toolbar. *This splits the merged cells.*

20 Select A1:E1 and then click the Merge and Center button. Repeat this step for A2:E2.

21 Display the Page Setup dialog box and center the worksheet horizontally on the page.

22 Select the *Week1-Week4* sheets. Display the Page Setup dialog box and then choose *Fit to 1 page(s) wide by 1 tall* in the *Scaling* section of the Page tab.

23 Print the entire workbook.

24 Save and then close **ExcelS4-R1**.

Activity 3: CREATING A WORKBOOK USING A TEMPLATE

1   Start a new workbook using the Sales Invoice template.

2   Complete the customer invoice using today's date and invoice number *2463* as follows:
    • First Choice Travel; 4277 Yonge Street; Toronto, ON M4P 2E6; 416-555-9834
    • Order No. – 05-421
    • Rep – Alex Torres
    • 16 Lunches @15.77
    • 16 Desserts @4.87
    • 16 Beverages @1.50
    • 1 Delivery and Setup @55.00

3   Change *Insert Company Information Here* to the following company name and address:
    The Waterfront Bistro
    3104 Rivermist Drive
    Buffalo, NY 14280

4   Change *Insert Fine Print Here* to *Terms are net 10 days. Interest at the rate of 2% per month will be charged on overdue accounts.*
5   Delete *Insert Farewell Statement Here*.
6   Save the invoice in the SalesandInvoices folder and name it **ExcelS4-R2**.
7   Print and then close **ExcelS4-R2**.

Activity 4: CREATING AND APPLYING STYLES

1   Open **WBSales-Feb19**.
2   Save the workbook in the SalesandInvoices folder and name it **ExcelS4-R3**.
3   Make B6 the active cell and then apply the following format attributes:
    • Light yellow fill color
    • Plum font color
    • Italic
4   Create a style named Totals using the formatting in B6.
5   Apply the Totals style to the following ranges:
    • C6:I6
    • B9:I9
    • B12:I12
    • B17:I17
6   Make B14 the active cell and then apply the following format attributes:
    • Light turquoise fill color
    • Dark blue font color
    • Italic
7   Create a style named Final_Totals using the formatting in B14.
8   Apply the Final_Totals style to C14:I14.
9   Save **ExcelS4-R3**.

Activity 5: SAVING A WORKSHEET AS A WEB PAGE; VIEWING A WORKSHEET IN WEB PAGE PREVIEW; INSERTING COMMENTS; INSERTING A DIAGRAM

1   With **ExcelS4-R3** open, save the worksheet in the SalesandInvoices folder as a Web page named **Sales-Feb19**.
2   View the Web page in the default browser window and then close the browser window.
3   Insert a comment in I17 that contains the following text:
    Compare with last year's GP total for same week to make sure GP is not declining.
4   Make sure Comments on the View menu is turned on.
5   Insert a Cycle Diagram using the following information:
    a   Add the following text labels clockwise:
        Input Weekly Sales in Worksheet
        Send to Dana Hirsch for Review
        Distribute Copies to Executive Chef and Beverage Manager
    b   Change the *Diagram Style* to *3-D Color*.
    c   Resize and move the diagram to span the widths of columns B–G and the height of rows 19–42.

6 Change the page orientation to *Landscape*, fit the printout to 1 page wide by 1 page tall, center the worksheet horizontally, and turn on printing of comments *As displayed on sheet*.

7 Save, print, and then close **Sales-Feb15**.

PERFORMANCE PLUS

Assessment 1: INSERTING, DELETING, AND RENAMING A WORKSHEET; LINKING WORKSHEETS

1 You are the assistant to Cal Rubine, chair of the Theatre Arts Division at Niagara Peninsula College. The two co-op consultants have entered their grades for the work term placements into separate worksheets in the same workbook. You need to create a worksheet to summarize the data.

2 Open **NPCCo-op**.

3 Save the workbook in the ExcelS4Review folder and name it **ExcelS4-P1**.

4 Insert a new worksheet and position it before the *Marquee Productions* worksheet.

5 Rename *Sheet1* as *Grade Summary*.

6 Complete the *Grade Summary* worksheet by completing the following tasks:

  a Copy A3:B7 in the *Marquee Productions* worksheet to A3:B7 in the *Grade Summary* keeping the source column widths.

  b Copy A4:B8 in the *Performance Threads* worksheet to A8:B12 in the *Grade Summary* worksheet.

  c Copy G3:H3 in the *Marquee Productions* worksheet to C3:D3 in the *Grade Summary* worksheet keeping the source column widths.

  d Link the data in columns C and D of the *Grade Summary* worksheet to the corresponding grades and dates in the *Marquee Productions* and *Performance Threads* worksheets. (*Note: The last five entries in the* **Date Co-op Grade Entered** *column will display as zero after linking since there is no data in the source cells.*)

  e Copy the title and subtitle in rows 1 and 2 from the *Marquee Productions* worksheet to the *Grade Summary* worksheet and adjust the format as necessary.

  f Make any other formatting changes you see fit to the *Grade Summary* worksheet.

7 Save **ExcelS4-P1**.

8 Select all three worksheets and then change the page orientation to landscape.

9 Change the left margin for the *Grade Summary* sheet only to 2.75 inches.

10 Print all three worksheets and then close **ExcelS4-P1**.

Assessment 2: CREATING AND APPLYING STYLES; SAVING A WORKSHEET AS A WEB PAGE; VIEWING A WORKSHEET IN WEB PAGE PREVIEW

1 Bobbie Sinclair, business manager at Performance Threads, needs a costume production schedule posted on the company intranet. You have reviewed the production schedule and have decided that using styles to format the schedule will ensure that consistent formatting attributes are applied to the worksheet before saving it as a Web page.

2 Open **PTCostumeSchedule**.

3 Save the workbook in the ExcelS4Review folder and name it **ExcelS4-P2**.

4 Make A11 the active cell and then create a style named Headings that will apply the following formatting attributes:
   - Center alignment
   - 11-point Lucida Sans Bold
   - Light yellow fill color
5 Apply the Headings style to the remaining column headings in the worksheet.
6 Create another style named Costumes that will apply the following formatting attributes:
   - 11-point Century Gothic
   - Light green fill color
7 Apply the Costumes style to the costume labels in A12:A16.
8 Adjust any column widths as necessary.
9 Apply Tan fill color to the range B12:H16.
10 Change the font and font size for the text in rows 8 and 9. You determine the font and size.
11 Save **ExcelS4-P2**.
12 Save **ExcelS4-P2** as a Web page and name it **CostumeSchedule**.
13 View the Web page in the default browser.
14 Print in landscape orientation from your Web browser and then close the window.
15 Close **CostumeSchedule**.

Assessment 3: USING AUTOFILTER; SORTING A LIST

1 Bobbie Sinclair, business manager at Performance Threads, needs a list of costumes for Marquee Productions that have a final delivery date of July 5. You decide to create the list using AutoFilter.
2 Open **PTCostumeSchedule**.
3 Save the workbook in the ExcelS4Review folder and name it **ExcelS4-P3**.
4 Select A11:H16.
5 Turn on the AutoFilter feature and then deselect the range.
6 Use the AutoFilter button in column H to list only those costumes with a delivery date of July 5.
7 Sort the filtered list in ascending order by *Costume*.
8 Change the page orientation to landscape and then print the filtered list.
9 Redisplay all of the data in the worksheet.
10 Turn off AutoFilter.
11 Save and then close **ExcelS4-P3**.

Assessment 4: INSERTING COMMENTS

1 The design team for the Marquee Productions costumes is meeting at the end of the week to discuss the production schedule. In preparation for this meeting, Bobbie Sinclair, business manager at Performance Threads, has asked you to review the schedule and send a revised worksheet with your comments inserted.
2 Open **PTCostumeSchedule**.
3 Save the workbook in the ExcelS4Review folder and name it **ExcelS4-P4**.
4 Make D12 the active cell and then create the following comment:
   Sue is not yet done with the research for this costume. Design may not be able to start June 10.

5 Make D16 the active cell and then create the following comment:
   This costume is the most complex in this project. These dates may need adjustment.
6 Make sure Comments on the View menu is turned on.
7 Change the page orientation to landscape.
8 Turn on printing of comments *As displayed on sheet*.
9 Print **ExcelS4-P4**.
10 Save and then close **ExcelS4-P4**.

Assessment 5: FINDING INFORMATION ON CREATING A TEMPLATE

1 Use the Help feature to find information on creating your own template. Print the Help topic that you find with the steps displayed on saving a template.
2 Open **ExcelS4-R3** in the SalesandInvoices folder.
3 Clear the contents of the following ranges:
   B2
   B4:H5
   B7:H8
   B10:H11
4 Save the revised worksheet as a template in the SalesandInvoices folder and name it **WeeklySalesReport**.
5 Close **WeeklySalesReport**.
6 Open **WeeklySalesReport** and then type the following data:

B2	26/02/2005
B4	995.00
B5	566.00
B7	112.00
B8	109.00
B10	219.00
B11	134.00

7 Save the workbook in the SalesandInvoices folder and name it **ExcelS4-P5**. *(Note: Be sure to change the* **Save as type** *back to* **Microsoft Excel Workbook***.)*
8 Change the page orientation to landscape.
9 Print and then close **ExcelS4-P5** saving changes.

Assessment 6: FINDING FINANCIAL DATA FOR A CORPORATION

1 You are seeking employment with a large Canadian or U.S. corporation. Use the Research task pane in a blank workbook with the *MSN Search* resource to locate financial data on the Internet such as sales and profits for at least three corporations for which you would like to target your job search. (Most corporations that have stocks listed on the New York Stock Exchange, the Toronto Stock Exchange, or the Vancouver Stock Exchange will have recent financial data posted on their Web site.)
2 Create an Excel workbook that summarizes the financial data you were able to find, using a separate worksheet for each corporation. Include the dates that the data represents and a hyperlink to the Web addresses that you used.

3 Apply formatting enhancements to the worksheets.

4 Create a summary worksheet that lists each corporation you researched and links a cell in the summary worksheet to the sales value in the related worksheet.

5 Create a footer on all of the worksheets that prints your name at the bottom left margin and the current date at the right margin.

6 Save the workbook in the ExcelS4Review folder and name it **ExcelS4-P6**.

7 Print the entire workbook.

8 Close **ExcelS4-P6**.

INTEGRATED 1
Integrating Word and Excel

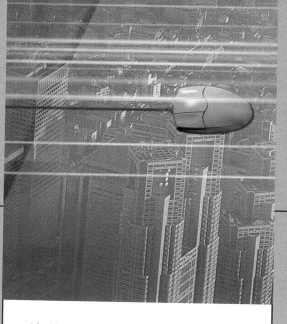

A variety of methods are available for copying and pasting data and objects between Office programs. An object can be a table, workbook, chart, picture, text, or any other type of information you create. You can copy an object in one program and paste it into another or you can copy and link an object or copy and embed an object. The program containing the object is called the *source* program and the program containing the pasted, linked, or embedded object is called the *destination* program. When an object is linked, the object exists in the source program but not as a separate object in the destination program. Changes made to the object in the source program are automatically reflected in the object in the destination program. An embedded object resides in both the source and destination programs. You can edit an embedded object in the destination program using the tools of the source program. Deciding whether to copy and paste, copy and link, or copy and embed depends on how the information in the object is used. In this section, you will learn the following skills and complete the projects described here.

Skills
- Copy and paste Word data into an Excel worksheet
- Link an Excel worksheet with a Word document
- Update linked data
- View linked data as an icon
- Link an Excel chart with a Word document
- Embed an Excel worksheet into a Word document
- Edit an embedded worksheet

 Note: Before beginning this section, copy to a disk or other location the Integrated01 subfolder from the Integrated folder on the CD that accompanies this textbook and then make Integrated01 the active folder.

Projects

Copy data in a Word document on costume research, design, and sewing hours for employees into an Excel worksheet; copy data in an Excel worksheet on employee payroll and then link the data to a Word document; update the payroll hours for the employees for the next week; copy employee payroll data in an Excel worksheet to a Word document and then update the data in Word.

Copy data in an Excel worksheet on theatre company revenues into a Word document and then update the data in Word.

Copy Word data on student scores into an Excel worksheet; copy an Excel chart containing data on student areas of emphasis in the Theatre Arts Division into a Word document and then update the chart in Excel.

Link a chart containing sales commissions for agents with a Word document and then update the sales commissions to reflect a higher percentage.

I-1.1 Copying and Pasting Word Data into an Excel Worksheet

Microsoft Office is a suite that allows integration, which is the combining of data from two or more programs into one document. Integration can occur by copying and pasting data between programs. The program containing the data to be copied is called the *source* program and the program where the data is pasted is called the *destination* program. For example, you can copy data from a Word document into an Excel worksheet. Copy and paste data between programs in the same manner as you would copy and paste data within a program.

PROJECT: Copy data on costume research, design, and sewing hours for Performance Threads and paste the data into an Excel worksheet.

STEPS

1 Open Word and then open the document named **PTWordHours**.

2 Open Excel and then open **PTExcelHours**.

3 Save the worksheet with Save As and name it **IntE1-01**.

4 Click the button on the Taskbar representing the Word document **PTWordHours**.

5 Select the five lines of text in columns as shown below.

6 Click the Copy button on the Standard toolbar.

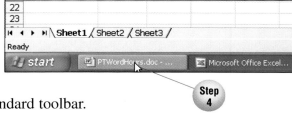

Step 4

Step 6

Hours for September 2002:

Employee	Research	Design	Sewing
Scott Bercini	3	8	14
Terri Cantrell	5	10	18
Paul Gottlieb	2	7	10
Tae Jeong	6	12	20

Step 5

7 Click the button on the Taskbar representing the Excel document **IntE1-01**.

8 Make sure cell A11 is the active cell and then click the Paste button on the Standard toolbar.

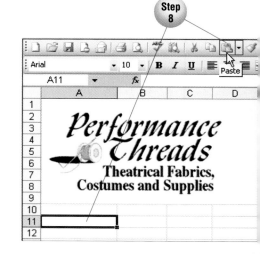

Step 8

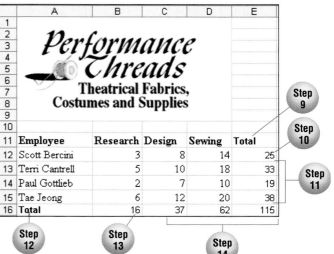

9. Make cell E11 the active cell, click the Bold button, and then type Total.

10. Make cell E12 the active cell, click the AutoSum button on the Standard toolbar, and then press Enter.

> This inserts a formula that calculates the total number of hours for Scott Bercini.

11. Copy the formula down to cells E13 through E15.

12. Make cell A16 the active cell, click the Bold button, and then type Total.

13. Make cell B16 the active cell, click the AutoSum button on the Standard toolbar, and then press Enter.

> This inserts a formula that calculates the total number of research hours.

14. Copy the formula in cell B16 to cells C16 through E16.

> If the results of your formula do not match what you see in the image, check your formula.

15. Select cells A11 through E16 and then apply an autoformat of your choosing.

16. Make any other changes needed to improve the visual display of the data in cells A11 through E16.

17. Save, print, and then close **IntE1-01**.

18. Click the button on the Taskbar representing the Word document **PTWordHours**.

19. Close **PTWordHours**.

In Addition

Cycling between Open Programs

Cycle through open programs by clicking the button on the Taskbar representing the desired program. You can also cycle through open programs by pressing Alt + Tab. Pressing Alt + Tab causes a menu to display. Continue holding down the Alt key and pressing the Tab key until the desired program icon is selected by a border in the menu and then release the Tab key and the Alt key.

In BRIEF

Copy Data from One Program to Another
1 Open desired programs and documents.
2 Select data in source program.
3 Click Copy button.
4 Click button on Taskbar representing destination program.
5 Click Paste button.

I-1.2 Linking an Excel Worksheet with a Word Document

In the previous section, you copied data from a Word document and pasted it into an Excel worksheet. If you continuously update the data in the Word document, you would need to copy and paste the data each time into the Excel worksheet. If you update data on a regular basis that is copied to other programs, consider copying and linking the data. When data is linked, the data exists in the source program but not as separate data in the destination program. The destination program contains only a code that identifies the name and location of the source program, document, and the location in the document. Since the data is located only in the source program, changes made to the data in the source program are reflected in the destination program. Office updates a link automatically whenever you open the destination program or you edit the linked data in the destination program.

PROJECT: Copy data in an Excel worksheet on employee payroll for Performance Threads and then link the data to a Word document.

STEPS

1. With Word open and the active program, open the document named **PTWordOctPayroll**.

2. Save the document with Save As and name it **IntW1-01**.

3. Make Excel the active program and then open the worksheet named **PTExcelOctPayroll**.

4. Save the worksheet with Save As and name it **IntE1-02**.

5. Link the data in cells A13 through D18 into the Word document by selecting cells A13 through D18.

6. With the cells selected, click the Copy button [icon] on the Standard toolbar.

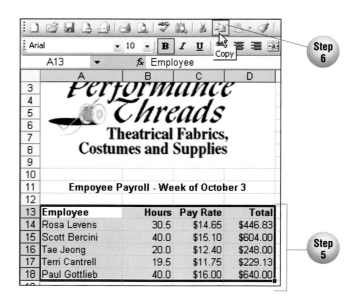

7. Click the button on the Taskbar representing the Word document **IntW1-01**.

8. Press Ctrl + End to move the insertion point to the end of the document (the insertion point is positioned a double space below *Week of October 3, 2005*).

9. Click Edit on the Menu bar and then click Paste Special.

10. At the Paste Special dialog box, click *Microsoft Office Excel Worksheet Object* in the *As* list box.

11. Click the *Paste link* option located at the left side of the dialog box.

12. Click OK to close the dialog box.

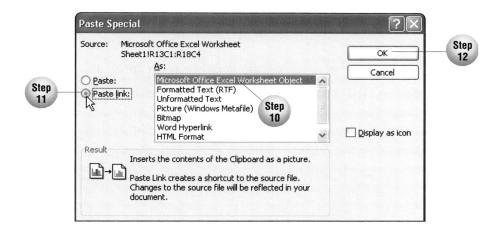

13. Save, print, and then close **IntW1-01**.

     The table gridlines do not print.

14. Click the button on the Taskbar representing the Excel worksheet **IntE1-02**.

15. Press the Esc key on the keyboard to remove the moving marquee around cells A13 through D18 and then click cell A10 to make it the active cell.

16. Save, print, and then close **IntE1-02**.

In Addition

Linking Data within a Program

Linking does not have to be between two different programs—you can link data between documents in the same program. For example, you can create an object in a Word document such as a table or chart, and then link the object with another Word document (or several Word documents). If you make a change to the object in the original document, the linked object in the other document (or documents) is automatically updated.

In BRIEF

Link Data between Programs
1 Open desired programs and documents.
2 Select data in source program.
3 Click Copy button.
4 Click button on Taskbar representing destination program.
5 Click Edit, Paste Special.
6 Click object in the *As* list box.
7 Click *Paste link*.
8 Click OK.

I-1.3 Updating Linked Data; Viewing a Link

The advantage of linking data over copying data is that editing the data in the source program will automatically update the data in the destination program. To edit linked data, open the document in the source program, make the desired edits, and then save the document. The next time you open the document in the destination program, the data is updated. The display of the linked data in the destination program can be changed to an icon. The icon represents the document and program to which the object is linked.

PROJECT: Update the payroll hours for the employees of Performance Threads in the Excel worksheet for the week of October 10.

STEPS

1. Make Excel the active program and then open **IntE1-02**.

2. Make cell B14 the active cell and then change the number to *20.0*.

   > Cells D14 through D18 contain a formula that multiplies the number in the cell in column B with the number in the cell in column C.

3. Make cell B16 the active cell and then change the number to *25.5*.

   > When you make cell B16 the active cell, the result of the formula in cell D14 is updated to reflect the change you made to the number in cell B14.

4. Make cell B17 the active cell and then change the number to *15.0*.

5. Make cell C17 the active cell and then change the pay rate to *12.00*.

6. Double-click cell A11 and then change the date from *October 3* to *October 10*.

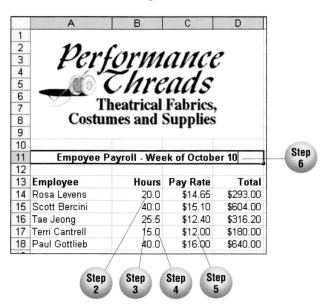

	A	B	C	D
11	Empoyee Payroll - Week of October 10				← Step 6
13	Employee	Hours	Pay Rate	Total
14	Rosa Levens	20.0	$14.65	$293.00
15	Scott Bercini	40.0	$15.10	$604.00
16	Tae Jeong	25.5	$12.40	$316.20
17	Terri Cantrell	15.0	$12.00	$180.00
18	Paul Gottlieb	40.0	$16.00	$640.00

Step 2   Step 3   Step 4   Step 5

7. Save **IntE1-02**.

8. Print and then close **IntE1-02**.

9. Make Word the active program and then open **IntW1-01**.

10. At the message asking if you want to update the document, click Yes.

> The document opens and is automatically updated to reflect the changes you made in **IntE1-02**.

11. Change the date above the table from *October 3* to *October 10*.

12. Save and then print **IntW1-01**.

13. Display the linked table as an icon by clicking once on the table to select it (black sizing handles display around the table). Click Edit, point to Linked Worksheet Object, and then click Convert.

14. At the Convert dialog box, click in the *Display as icon* check box to insert a check mark, and then click OK.

> Notice how the table changes to an icon representing the linked document.

15. Print **IntW1-01**.

16. Make sure the linked object icon is still selected and then redisplay the table by clicking Edit, pointing to Linked Worksheet Object, and then clicking Convert.

17. At the Convert dialog box, click the *Display as icon* check box to remove the check mark, and then click OK.

18. Save and then close **IntW1-01**.

Step 11

Employee Payroll

Week of October 10, 2005:

Employee	Hours	Pay Rate	Total
Rosa Levens	20.0	$14.65	$293.00
Scott Bercini	40.0	$15.10	$604.00
Tae Jeong	25.5	$12.40	$316.20
Terri Cantrell	15.0	$12.00	$180.00
Paul Gottlieb	40.0	$16.00	$640.00

Step 14

In Addition

Breaking a Link

The link between an object in the destination and source program can be broken. To break a link, select the object, click Edit, and then click Links. At the Links dialog box shown at the right, click the Break Link button. At the question asking if you are sure you want to break the link, click the Yes button.

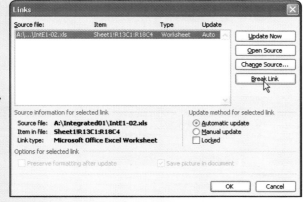

In Brief

Update Linked Data
1. Open document in source program.
2. Make desired edits.
3. Save and close document.
4. Open document in destination program.
5. Save and close document.

Display Linked Object as an Icon
1. Select object.
2. Click Edit, point to Linked Worksheet Object, click Convert.
3. At the Convert dialog box, click *Display as icon* check box.
4. Click OK.

I-1.4 Linking an Excel Chart with a Word Document

Although a worksheet does an adequate job of representing data, you can present some data more visually by charting the data. A chart is a visual representation of numeric data and, like a worksheet, can be linked to a document in another program. Link a chart in the same manner as you would link a worksheet.

PROJECT: Link a chart containing sales commissions for agents of First Choice Travel with a Word document. Change the sales commission in the worksheet chart from *3%* to *4%*.

STEPS

1. Make Word the active program and then open **FCTWordSalesCom**.

2. Save the document with Save As and name it **IntW1-02**.

3. Make Excel the active program and then open **FCTExcelSalesCom**.

4. Save the worksheet with Save As and name it **IntE1-03**.

5. Click once in the chart area to select it (black sizing handles display around the chart).

   Make sure you do not select a specific chart element.

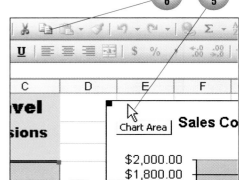

PROBLEM

If you select a chart element, click outside the chart to deselect the element and then try selecting the chart again.

6. Click the Copy button on the Standard toolbar.

7. Click the button on the Taskbar representing the Word document **IntW1-02**.

8. Press Ctrl + End to move the insertion point to the end of the document and then link the chart by clicking Edit and then Paste Special.

9. At the Paste Special dialog box, make sure *Microsoft Office Excel Chart Object* displays in the *As* list box, click *Paste link*, and then click OK.

10. Click outside the chart to deselect it.

11. Save, print, and then close **IntW1-02**.

12. Click the button on the Taskbar representing the Excel worksheet **IntE1-03**.

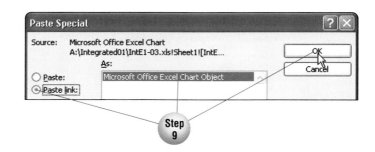

(13) The chart is based on a sales commission of 3 percent. Change the formula so it calculates a sales commission of 4 percent by double-clicking in cell C5 and then changing the *3* in the formula to a *4*.

(14) Press the Enter key.

> Pressing Enter displays the result of the formula calculating commissions at 4 percent.

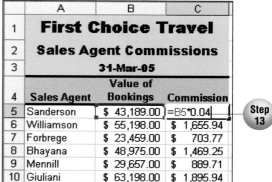

Step 13

(15) Make cell C5 the active cell and then copy the new formula down to cells C6 through C10.

(16) Save and then close **IntE1-03**.

(17) Click the button on the Taskbar representing Word and then open the **IntW1-02** document.

(18) At the message asking if you want to update the document, click Yes.

> Notice the change in the amounts in the chart.

(18) Save, print, and then close **IntW1-02**.

	A	B	C
1	**First Choice Travel**		
2	**Sales Agent Commissions**		
3	31-Mar-05		
4	**Sales Agent**	**Value of Bookings**	**Commission**
5	Sanderson	$ 43,189.00	$ 1,727.56
6	Williamson	$ 55,198.00	$ 2,207.92
7	Forbrege	$ 23,459.00	$ 938.36
8	Bhayana	$ 48,975.00	$ 1,959.00
9	Mennill	$ 29,657.00	$ 1,186.28
10	Giuliani	$ 63,198.00	$ 2,527.92
11			
12			

Step 15

In Addition

Customizing a Link

By default, a linked object is updated automatically and a linked object can be edited. You can change these defaults with options at the Links dialog box. If you want to control when to update linked data, click the *Manual* option located at the bottom of the Links dialog box. With the *Manual* option selected, update linked objects by clicking the Update Now button at the right side of the Links dialog box. If you do not want a linked object updated, click the *Locked* option at the Links dialog box.

I-1.5 Embedding an Excel Worksheet into a Word Document

An object can be copied between documents in a program, an object can be linked, and an object also can be embedded. A linked object resides in the source program but not as a separate object in the destination program. An embedded object resides in the document in the source program as well as the destination program. If a change is made to an embedded object at the source program, the change is not made to the object in the destination program. Since an embedded object is not automatically updated as is a linked object, the only advantage to embedding rather than simply copying and pasting is that you can edit an embedded object in the destination program using the tools of the source program.

PROJECT: Copy data in an Excel worksheet on employee payroll for Performance Threads and then embed the data in a Word document.

STEPS

1. With Word open and the active program, open the document named **PTWordOctPayroll**.

2. Save the document with Save As and name it **IntW1-03**.

3. Make Excel the active program and then open the worksheet named **PTExcelOctPayroll**.

4. Save the worksheet with Save As and name it **IntE1-04**.

5. Embed the data in cells A13 through D18 into the Word document by selecting cells A13 through D18.

6. With the cells selected, click the Copy button on the Standard toolbar.

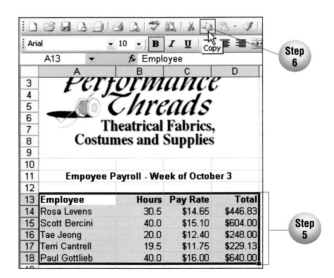

7 Click the button on the Taskbar representing the Word document **IntW1-03**.

8 Press Ctrl + End to move the insertion point to the end of the document (the insertion point is positioned a double space below *Week of October 3, 2005*).

9 Click Edit on the Menu bar and then click Paste Special.

10 At the Paste Special dialog box, click *Microsoft Office Excel Worksheet Object* in the *As* list box and then click OK.

Step 10

PROBLEM? Make sure you do not click the *Paste link* option.

Paste Special

Source: Microsoft Office Excel Worksheet
Sheet1!R13C1:R18C4

As:

○ Paste: Microsoft Office Excel Worksheet Object
○ Paste link: Formatted Text (RTF)
Unformatted Text
Picture (Windows Metafile)
Bitmap
Picture (Enhanced Metafile)
HTML Format

☐ Display as icon

Result

Inserts the contents of the Clipboard into your document so that you can edit it using Microsoft Office Excel Worksheet.

OK   Cancel

11 Click outside the table to deselect it.

12 Save, print, and then close **IntW1-03**.

13 Click the button on the Taskbar representing the Excel worksheet **IntE1-04**.

14 Press the Esc key to remove the moving marquee around cells A13 through D18.

15 Click in cell A10 to make it the active cell.

16 Save and then close **IntE1-04**.

In Addition

Inserting an Embedded Object from an Existing File

You embedded an Excel worksheet in a Word document using the Copy button and options at the Paste Special dialog box. Another method is available for embedding an object from an existing file. In the source program document, position the insertion point where you want the object embedded, click Insert, and then click Object. At the Object dialog box, click the Create from File tab. At the Object dialog box with the Create from File tab selected as shown, type the desired file name in the *File name* text box or click the Browse button and then select the desired file from the appropriate folder. At the Object dialog box, make sure the *Link to file* check box does not contain a check mark, and then click OK.

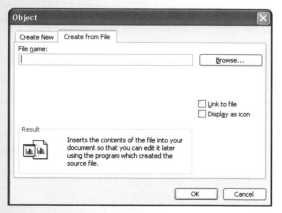

Object

Create New | Create from File

File name:

Browse...

☐ Link to file
☐ Display as icon

Result

Inserts the contents of the file into your document so that you can edit it later using the program which created the source file.

OK   Cancel

In Brief

Embed Data
1 Open desired programs and documents.
2 Select data in source program.
3 Click Copy button.
4 Click button on Taskbar representing destination program.
5 Click Edit, Paste Special.
6 Click object in the *As* list box.
7 Click OK.

I-1.6 Editing an Embedded Worksheet

An embedded object can be edited in the destination program using the tools of the source program. Double-click the object in the document in the destination program and the tools from the source program display. For example, if you double-click an Excel worksheet that is embedded in a Word document, the Excel Menu bar and Standard and Formatting toolbars display at the top of the screen.

PROJECT: Update the payroll hours for the employees of Performance Threads for the week of October 17 in the embedded Excel worksheet.

STEPS

1. With Word the active program, open **IntW1-03**.

2. Save the document with Save As and name it **IntW1-04**.

3. Change the date above the table from *October 3* to *October 17*.

4. Position the arrow pointer anywhere in the worksheet and then double-click the left mouse button.

   In a few moments, the worksheet displays surrounded by column and row designations and the Excel Menu bar, Standard toolbar, and Formatting toolbar display at the top of the screen.

5. To produce the ordered costumes on time, the part-time employees worked a full 40 hours for the week of October 17. Make cell B14 the active cell and then change the number to *40*.

6. Make cell B16 the active cell and then change the number to *40*.

7. Make cell B17 the active cell and then change the number to *40*.

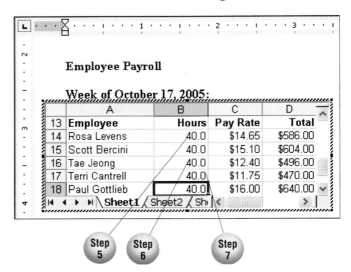

Step 5 Step 6 Step 7

8. Bobbie Sinclair, Business Manager, wants to know the payroll total for the week of October 17 to determine the impact it has on the monthly budget. Add a new row to the table by making cell A18 the active cell and then pressing the Enter key.

9. With cell A19 the active cell, type Total.

10 Make cell D19 the active cell and then click the AutoSum button **Σ** on the Standard toolbar.

11 Make sure *D14:D18* displays in cell D19 and then press the Enter key.

12 Increase the height of the worksheet by one row by positioning the arrow pointer on the bottom, middle black sizing square until the pointer turns into a double-headed arrow pointing up and down. Hold down the left mouse button, drag down one row, and then release the mouse button.

13 Using the arrow keys on the keyboard, make cell A13 the active cell and position cell A13 in the upper left corner of the worksheet. (This will display all cells in the worksheet containing data.)

14 Click outside the worksheet to deselect it.

15 Save, print, and then close **IntW1-04**.

The gridlines do not print.

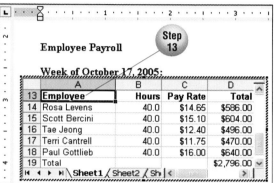

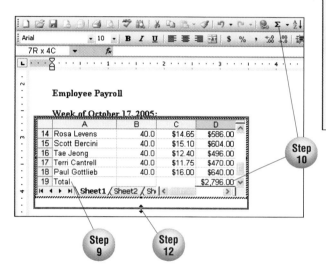

In Addition

Troubleshooting Linking and Embedding Problems

If you double-click a linked or embedded object and a message appears telling you that the source file or source program cannot be opened, consider the following troubleshooting options. Check to make sure that the source program is installed on your computer. If the source program is not installed, convert the object to the file format of a program that is installed. Try closing other programs to free memory and make sure you have enough memory to run the source program. Check to make sure the source program does not have any dialog boxes open and, if it is a linked object, check to make sure someone else is not working in the source file.

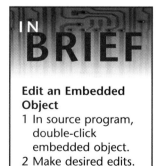

IN BRIEF

Edit an Embedded Object
1 In source program, double-click embedded object.
2 Make desired edits.
3 Click outside the object.

SKILLS REVIEW

Activity 1: COPYING AND PASTING DATA

1   With Word the active program, open the document named **NPCWordScores**.
2   Make Excel the active program and then open **NPCExcelScores**.
3   Save the worksheet with Save As and name it **IntE1-R1**.
4   Click the button on the Taskbar representing the Word document **NPCWordScores**.
5   Select the nine lines of text in columns (the line beginning *Student* through the line beginning *Yiu, Terry*) and then click the Copy button on the Standard toolbar.
6   Click the button on the Taskbar representing the Excel file **IntE1-R1**.
7   With cell A16 the active cell, paste the text into the worksheet.
8   Insert the text *Average* in cell E16.
9   Make cell E17 the active cell and then insert a formula that averages the numbers in cells B17 through D17.
10 Copy the formula in cell E17 down to cells E18 through E24.
11 With cells E17 through E24 selected, change the font to 12-point Tahoma and then click the Decrease Decimal button three times.
12 Select cells B17 through D24 and then click once on the Increase Decimal button on the Formatting toolbar. (This displays two numbers after the decimal point.)
13 Select cells B17 through E24, click the Center button on the Formatting toolbar, and then deselect the cells.
14 Save, print, and then close **IntE1-R1**.
15 Click the button on the Taskbar representing the Word document **NPCWordScores** and then close **NPCWordScores**.

Activity 2: LINKING AN OBJECT

1   With Word the active program, open the document named **NPCWordEnrollment**.
2   Save the document with Save As and name it **IntW1-R1**.
3   Make Excel the active program and then open the worksheet named **NPCExcelChart**.
4   Save the worksheet with Save As and name it **IntE1-R2**.
5   Link the chart to the Word document **IntW1-R1** a triple space below the *Student Enrollment* subtitle. (Make sure you use the Paste Special dialog box.)
6   Center the chart below the subtitle *Student Enrollment*.
7   Save, print, and close **IntW1-R1**.
8   Click the button on the Taskbar representing **IntE1-R2**.
9   Press the Esc key to remove the moving marquee and then click outside the chart to deselect it.
10 Save, print, and then close **IntE1-R2**.

Activity 3: EDITING A LINKED OBJECT

1 With Excel the active program, open **IntE1-R2**.
2 Make the following changes to the data in the specified cells:

A10	=	Change *Fall Term* to *Spring Term*
B12	=	Change *75* to *98*
B13	=	Change *30* to *25*
B14	=	Change *15* to *23*
B15	=	Change *38* to *52*
B16	=	Change *25* to *10*

3 Make cell A9 active.
4 Save, print, and then close **IntE1-R2**.
5 Make Word the active program and then open **IntW1-R1**. (At the message asking if you want to update the document, click Yes.)
6 Save, print, and then close **IntW1-R1**.

Activity 4: EMBEDDING AN OBJECT

1 With Word the active program, open the document named **WERevenuesMemo**.
2 Save the document with Save As and name it **IntW1-R2**.
3 Make Excel the active program and then open the worksheet named **WEExcelRevenues**.
4 Save the worksheet with Save As and name it **IntE1-R3**.
5 Embed the data in cells A13 through D19 to the Word document **IntW1-R2** a double space below the paragraph of text in the body of the memo.
6 Save, print, and then close **IntW1-R2**.
7 Click the button on the Taskbar representing **IntE1-R3**.
8 Press the Esc key to remove the moving marquee and then click outside the selected cells.
9 Save, print, and then close **IntE1-R3**.

Activity 5: EDITING AN EMBEDDED OBJECT

1 Make Word the active program and then open **IntW1-R2**.
2 Save the document with Save As and name it **IntW1-R3**.
3 Double-click the worksheet and then make the following changes to the data in the specified cells:

A13	=	Change *July Revenues* to *August Revenues*
B15	=	Change *1,356,000* to *1,575,000*
B16	=	Change *2,450,000* to *2,375,000*
B17	=	Change *1,635,000* to *1,750,000*
B18	=	Change *950,000* to *1,100,000*
B19	=	Change *1,050,000* to *1,255,000*

4 Click outside the worksheet to deselect it.
5 Save, print, and then close **IntW1-R3**.

MARQUEE SERIES

MICROSOFT®
ACCESS
2003

NITA RUTKOSKY
Pierce College at Puyallup – Puyallup, Washington

DENISE SEGUIN
Fanshawe College – London, Ontario

EMCParadigm
PUBLISHING

CONTENTS

The Marquee Series Team: Desiree Faulkner, Developmental Editor; Leslie Anderson, Senior Designer; Jennifer Wreisner, Cover Designer; Leslie Ander Erica Tava, Desktop Production; Teri Linander, Tester; Sharon O'Donnell, Copyeditor; Lynn Reichel, Proofreader; and Nancy Fulton, Indexer.

Publishing Team: George Provol, Publisher; Janice Johnson, Director of Product Development; Tony Galvin, Acquisitions Editor; Lori Landwer, Marketi Manager; Shelley Clubb, Electronic Design and Production Manager.

Acknowledgment: The authors and publisher wish to thank the following reviewer for her technical and academic assistance in testing exercises and asse instruction: Susan Lynn Bowen, Valdosta Technical College, Valdosta, GA.

Library of Congress Cataloging-in-Publication Data
> Rutkosky, Nita Hewitt.
> Microsoft Access 2003 / Nita Rutkosky, Denise Seguin.
>   p.cm. – (Marquee series)
> Includes index.
> ISBN 0-7638-2071-7 (text) – ISBN 0-7638-2070-9 (text & CD)
>   1. Microsoft Access. 2. Databse management. I. Seguin, Denise. II. Title. III. Series

Trademarks: Some of the product names and company names included in this book have been used for identification purposes only and may be trademar registered trademarks of their respective manufacturers and sellers. The authors, editor, and publisher disclaim any affiliation, association, or connection w or sponsorship or endorsement by, such owners.

Microsoft and the Microsoft Office Logo are trademarks or registered trademarks of Microsoft Corporation the United States and/or other countries, and th Microsoft Office Specialist Logo is used under license from owner.

EMC/Paradigm Publishing is independent from Microsoft Corporation, and not affiliated with Microsoft in any manner. This publication may be used in assisting students to prepare for a Microsoft Office Specialist Exam. Neither Microsoft, its designated program administrator or courseware reviewer, nor EMC/Paradigm Publishing warrants that use of this publication will ensure passing the relevant exam.

Text + CD: 0-7638-2070-9
Order Number: 05627

© 2004 by Paradigm Publishing Inc.
> Published by **EMC**Paradigm   (800) 535-6865
> 875 Montreal Way   E-mail: educate@emcp.com
> St. Paul, MN 55102   Web site: www.emcp.com

Printed in the United States of America   10 9 8 7 6 5 4

Introducing
ACCESS 2003

Interacting with a database occurs more often than we realize as we perform our daily routines. Consider the following activities that you might do today: use a bank machine to withdraw cash from your bank account; stop at the gas station and charge the purchase to your credit card; open a telephone book to look up a telephone number; browse an online catalog to comparison shop for something that you need to buy. In all of these activities you would be accessing and/or updating a database. Any time that you look for something by accessing an organized file system

you are probably using a database. Microsoft Access 2003 is the database management system included with Microsoft Office.

A ***database management system (DBMS)*** is used to design, create, input, maintain, manipulate, sort, and print data. Managing data effectively is a vital business activity since data forms the root of all business transactions. Access is a DBMS that includes a variety of powerful features for defining, editing, and formatting database tables, forms, reports, and queries.

While working in Access, you will produce business documents and manage business data for the following six companies:

First Choice Travel is a travel center offering a full range of traveling services from booking flights, hotel reservations, and rental cars to offering traveling seminars.

Marquee Productions is involved in all aspects of creating movies from script writing and development to filming.

The Waterfront Bistro offers fine dining for lunch and dinner and also offers banquet facilities, a wine cellar, and catering services.

Performance Threads maintains an inventory of rental costumes and also researches, designs, and sews special-order and custom-made costumes.

Worldwide Enterprises is a national and international distributor of products for a variety of companies and is the exclusive movie distribution agent for Marquee Productions.

The mission of the Niagara Peninsula College Theatre Arts Division is to offer a curriculum designed to provide students with a thorough exposure to all aspects of the theatre arts.

Managing Data Using Access 2003

Access is a database management system used to design, create, input, maintain, manipulate, sort, and print data. Managing data effectively is a vital business activity since data forms the root of all business transactions. Access is a powerful database management program that provides a range of features for defining, editing, and formatting database tables, forms, reports, and queries. Interesting Access features and elements that you will learn in each section are described below.

Section 1

Maintaining Data in Access Tables

Begin your Access journey by working with table data in Datasheet view. Learn to find and then edit data, add new records, and delete records. Change the appearance of a datasheet by adjusting column widths, moving columns, sorting, and formatting the datasheet. Compacting, repairing, and backing up databases are important Access tools you will also learn in Section 1.

US Distributors Table Datasheet in Topics 1.2 – 1.8

US Distributors   5/10/2003

State	City	Name	Street Address1	Street Address2	Zip Code	Telephone	Fax	E-Mail Address
AZ	Phoenix	LaVista Cinemas	111 Vista Road		86355-6014	602-555-6231	602-555-6233	lavista@emcp.net
CA	Los Angeles	Marquee Movies	1011 South Alameda Street		90045	612-555-2398	612-555-2377	marqueemovies@emcp.net
FL	Tampa	Sunfest Cinemas		341 South Fourth Avenue	33562	813-555-3185	813-555-3177	sunfest@emcp.net
GA	Atlanta	Liberty Cinemas	P. O. Box 998	12011 Ruston Way	73125	404-555-8113	404-555-2349	libertycinemas@emcp.net
IL	Oak Park	O'Shea Movies	59 Erie		60302	312-555-7719	312-555-7381	oshea@emcp.net
KS	Emporia	Midtown Moviehouse	1033 Commercial Street		66801	316-555-7013	316-555-7022	midtown@emcp.net
KY	Louisville	All Nite Cinemas	2188 3rd Street		40201	502-555-4238	502-555-4240	allnite@emcp.net
MA	Cambridge	Eastown Movie House	P. O. Box 429	1 Concourse Avenue	02142	413-555-0981	413-555-0226	eastown@emcp.net
MD	Baltimore	Dockside Movies	P. O. Box 224	155 S. Central Avenue	21203	301-555-7732	301-555-9836	dockside@emcp.net
MI	Detroit	Renaissance Cinemas	3599 Woodward Avenue		48211	313-555-1693	313-555-1699	renaissance-cinemas@emcp...
NJ	Baking Ridge	Hillman Cinemas	55 Kemble Avenue		07920	201-555-1147	201-555-1143	hillman@emcp.net
NY	Buffalo	Waterfront Cinemas	P. O. Box 3255		14288	716-555-3845	716-555-4860	waterfrontcinemas@emcp.ne
NY	New York	Cinema Festival	318 East 11th Street		10003	212-555-9715	212-555-9717	cinemafestival@emcp.net
NY	New York	Movie Emporium	203 West Houston Street		10014	212-555-7278	212-555-7280	movie-emporium@emcp.net
NY	New York	WestviewMovies	1112 Broadway		10119	212-555-4875	212-555-4877	westview@emcp.net
OH	Dublin	Mooretown Movies	P. O. Box 11	331 Metro Place	43107	614-555-8134	614-555-8339	mooretown@emcp.net
OR	Portland	Redwood Cinemas	P. O. Box 112F	336 Ninth Street	97466-3359	503-555-8641	503-555-8633	redwoodcinemas@emcp.net
PA	Philadelphia	Wellington 10	1203 Tenth Southwest		19178	215-555-9045	215-555-9048	wellington10@emcp.net
SC	Columbia	Danforth Cinemas	P. O. Box 22	18 Pickens Street	29201	803-555-3487	803-555-3421	danforth@emcp.net
TX	Arlington	Century Cinemas	3687 Avenue K		76013	817-555-2116	817-555-2119	centurycinemas@emcp.net
WA	Seattle	Mainstream Movies	P. O. Box 33	333 Evergreen Building	98220-2791	206-555-3269	206-555-3270	mainstream@emcp.net

Dashed line is used to show that the printout requires two pages.

US Distributors Table Datasheet in Topic 1.9

US Distributors   5/11/2003

State	City	Name	Street Address1	Street Address2	Zip Code	Telephone	Fax	E-Mail Address
AZ	Phoenix	LaVista Cinemas	111 Vista Road		86355-6014	602-555-6231	602-555-6233	lavista@emcp.net
CA	Los Angeles	Marquee Movies	1011 South Alameda Street		90045	612-555-2398	612-555-2377	marqueemovies@emcp.net
FL	Tampa	Sunfest Cinemas		341 South Fourth Avenue	33562	813-555-3185	813-555-3177	sunfest@emcp.net
GA	Atlanta	Liberty Cinemas	P. O. Box 998	12011 Ruston Way	73125	404-555-8113	404-555-2349	libertycinemas@emcp.net
IL	Oak Park	O'Shea Movies	59 Erie		60302	312-555-7719	312-555-7381	oshea@emcp.net
KS	Emporia	Midtown Moviehouse	1033 Commercial Street		66801	316-555-7013	316-555-7022	midtown@emcp.net
KY	Louisville	All Nite Cinemas	2188 3rd Street		40201	502-555-4238	502-555-4240	allnite@emcp.net
MA	Cambridge	Eastown Movie House	P. O. Box 429	1 Concourse Avenue	02142	413-555-0981	413-555-0226	eastown@emcp.net
MD	Baltimore	Dockside Movies	P. O. Box 224	155 S. Central Avenue	21203	301-555-7732	301-555-9836	dockside@emcp.net
MI	Detroit	Renaissance Cinemas	3599 Woodw...			313-555-1693	313-555-1699	renaissance-cinemas@emcp.net
NJ	Baking Ridge	Hillman Cinemas	55 Kemble A...			201-555-1147	201-555-1143	hillman@emcp.net
NY	Buffalo	Waterfront Cinemas	P. O. Box 325...			716-555-3845	716-555-4860	waterfrontcinemas@emcp.net
NY	New York	Cinema Festival	318 East 11th...			212-555-9715	212-555-9717	cinemafestival@emcp.net
NY	New York	Movie Emporium	203 West Ho...			212-555-7278	212-555-7280	movie-emporium@emcp.net
NY	New York	WestviewMovies	1112 Broadway		10119	212-555-4875	212-555-4877	westview@emcp.net
OH	Dublin	Mooretown Movies	P. O. Box 11	331 Metro Place	43107	614-555-8134	614-555-8339	mooretown@emcp.net
OR	Portland	Redwood Cinemas	P. O. Box 112F	336 Ninth Street	97466-3359	503-555-8641	503-555-8633	redwoodcinemas@emcp.net
PA	Philadelphia	Wellington 10	1203 Tenth Southwest		19178	215-555-9045	215-555-9048	wellington10@emcp.net
SC	Columbia	Danforth Cinemas	P. O. Box 22	18 Pickens Street	29201	803-555-3487	803-555-3421	danforth@emcp.net
TX	Arlington	Century Cinemas	3687 Avenue K		76013	817-555-2116	817-555-2119	centurycinemas@emcp.net
WA	Seattle	Mainstream Movies	P. O. Box 33	333 Evergreen Building	98220-2791	206-555-3269	206-555-3270	mainstream@emcp.net

An adjusted row height creates more space between records. Added space makes the printout easier to read.

Section 2
Creating Tables and Relationships

After you have mastered the basic terminology and navigated a table in datasheet view, you are ready to learn how to create tables. The ability to create a relationship between tables is one of the most powerful Access features, allowing the user to extract data from multiple tables as if they were one.

Employee Benefits Table Created in Topics 2.1 – 2.5

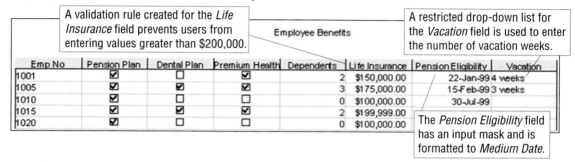

A validation rule created for the *Life Insurance* field prevents users from entering values greater than $200,000.

A restricted drop-down list for the *Vacation* field is used to enter the number of vacation weeks.

The *Pension Eligibility* field has an input mask and is formatted to *Medium Date*.

Employees Table Created in Topics 2.6 – 2.7

Employees   5/25/2003

Employee Number	First Name	Middle Name	Last Name	Address	City	State/Province	Postal Code
1001	Sam	Lawrence	Westering	287-1501 Broadway	New York	NY	10110

Employees table created using Table Wizard. The datasheet is formatted to add a background and gridline color and display in a different font and font size.

Relationships Report in Topic 2.8

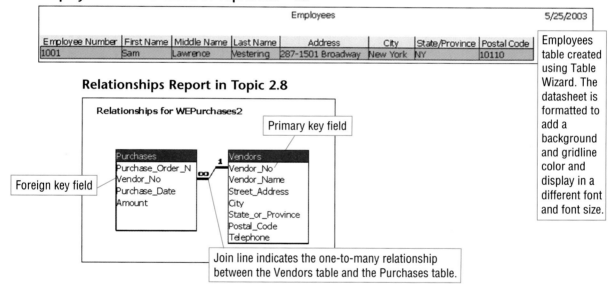

Primary key field

Foreign key field

Join line indicates the one-to-many relationship between the Vendors table and the Purchases table.

Relationships Report in Topic 2.9

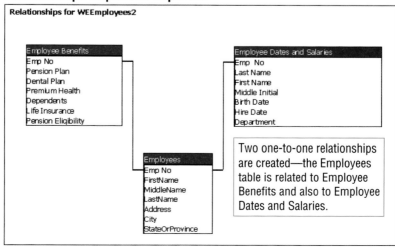

Two one-to-one relationships are created—the Employees table is related to Employee Benefits and also to Employee Dates and Salaries.

Section 3
Creating Queries, Forms, and Reports

In section 3 you learn how to extract specific information from tables using a query. Forms provide a more user-friendly interface for entering, editing, and deleting records. Create a report when you need to control the layout of data on the page and include rich text formatting options.

Query Showing Employees with Either 3 or 4 Weeks Vacation in Topic 3.3

Employees with 3 or 4 weeks vacation

Emp No	First Name	Last Name	Vacation
1015	Lyle	Besterd	4 weeks
1025	Jorge	Biliski	4 weeks
1005	Roman	Deptulski	3 weeks
1020	Angela	Doxtator	4 weeks
1010	Hanh	Postma	3 weeks
1001	Sam	Vestering	4 weeks

A criteria statement in the *Vacation* field instructs Access to extract from the table only those records in which the field value is *3 weeks* or *4 weeks*.

Performing Calculations in a Query in Topic 3.4

Employer Pension Contributions

Emp No	First Name	Last Name	Annual Salary	Pension Contribution
1001	Sam	Vestering	$69,725.00	$5,578.00
1005	Roman	Deptulski	$69,725.00	$5,578.00
1010	Hanh	Postma	$69,725.00	$5,578.00
1015	Lyle	Besterd	$44,651.00	$3,572.08
1020	Angela	Doxtator	$45,558.00	$3,644.64
1025	Jorge	Biliski	$44,892.00	$3,591.36
1030	Thom	Hicks	$42,824.00	$3,425.92
1035	Valerie	Fistouris	$44,694.00	$3,575.52
1040	Guy	Lafreniere	$45,395.00	$3,631.60
1045	Terry	Yiu	$42,238.00	$3,379.04
1050	Carl	Zakowski	$44,387.00	$3,550.96
1055	Edward	Thurston	$42,248.00	$3,379.84
1060	Donald	McKnight	$42,126.00	$3,370.08
1065	Norm	Liszniewski	$43,695.00	$3,495.60
1070	Balfor	Jhawar	$44,771.00	$3,581.68
1075	Mike	Fitchett	$42,857.00	$3,428.56
1080	Leo	Couture	$43,659.00	$3,492.72

The column *Pension Contribution* is a calculated field—this data does not exist in the table but is dynamically calculated each time the query is run.

Salary Statistics Calculated Using Aggregate Functions in Topic 3.5

Annual Salary Statistics

Total Annual Salaries	Average Annual Salary	Maximum Annual Salary	Minimum Annual Salary
$823,170.00	$48,421.76	$69,725.00	$42,126.00

Access includes aggregate functions that are used to calculate statistics on table data.

Salary Statistics Grouped by Department in Topic 3.5

Annual Salary Statistics by Department

Total Annual Salaries	Average Annual Salary	Maximum Annual Salary	Minimum Annual Salary	Department
$286,829.00	$47,804.83	$69,725.00	$42,126.00	European Distribution
$248,521.00	$49,704.20	$69,725.00	$43,695.00	North American Distribution
$287,820.00	$47,970.00	$69,725.00	$42,248.00	Overseas Distribution

Aggregate functions grouped by the *Department* field.

Employee Dates and Salaries Form Created in Topics 3.6 – 3.7

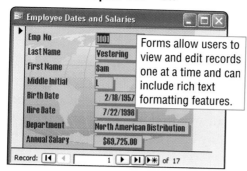

Forms allow users to view and edit records one at a time and can include rich text formatting features.

Employee Benefits and Employees Form with Label Objects Added in Topic 3.8

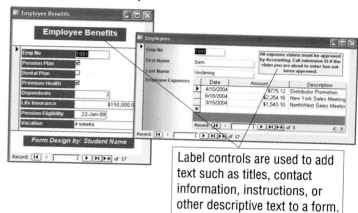

Label controls are used to add text such as titles, contact information, instructions, or other descriptive text to a form.

Employee Mailing Addresses Report Created in Topics 3.9 – 3.10

Create a report when you want to specify which fields to print and to have more control over the report layout and format.

Employee Mailing Addresses

Last Name	Besterd	City	New York
First Name	Lyle	State/Province	NY
Address	1258 Park Avenue	Postal Code	10110-
Last Name	Biliski	City	New York
First Name	Jorge	State/Province	NY
Address	439 7th Avenue	Postal Code	10111-
Last Name	Couture	City	New York
First Name	Leo	State/Province	NY
Address	908-1200 W 46th St.	Postal Code	10110-
Last Name	Deptulski	City	New York
First Name	Roman	State/Province	NY
Address	112-657 E 39th St.	Postal Code	10111-
Last Name	Doxtator	City	New York
First Name	Angela	State/Province	NY
Address	201-654 W 50th St.	Postal Code	10110-
Last Name	Fistouris	City	New York
First Name	Valerie	State/Province	NY
Address	210 York Avenue	Postal Code	10111-
Last Name	Fitchett	City	New York
First Name	Mike	State/Province	NY
Address	329-1009 W 23rd St.	Postal Code	10111-
Last Name	Hicks	City	New York
First Name	Thom	State/Province	NY
Address	329-5673 W 63rd St.	Postal Code	10111-

Section 4
Modifying Tables and Reports, Performing Calculations, and Viewing Data

The structure of a table is modified by inserting, deleting, and moving fields. Access provides many methods with which you can view data such as filtering; summarizing using a crosstab query, a PivotTable, or a PivotChart; finding duplicate or finding unmatched records; and data access pages for working in a database on the Web. Calculations are added to forms and reports by entering a formula in a text box control object.

Modified Employee Dates and Salaries Table in Topic 4.1

Employee Dates and Salaries : Table

	Emp	Birth Date	Annual Salary	Hire Date	Review Date	Department
+	1001	2/18/1957	$69,725.00	7/22/1998		North American Distribution
+	1005	3/12/1948	$69,725.00	8/15/1998		Overseas Distribution
+	1010	12/10/1952	$69,725.00	1/30/1999		European Distribution
+	1015	10/15/1959	$45,651.00	5/17/1999		North American Distribution
+	1020	5/22/1963	$45,558.00	8/3/		nerican Distribution
+	1025	6/18/1970	$44,892.00	12/1/		nerican Distribution
+	1030	7/27/1977	$42,824.00	1/22/		s Distribution
+	1035	2/4/1970	$44,694.00	3/15/		n Distribution
+	1040	9/14/1972	$45,395.00	3/10/		s Distribution
+	1045	6/18/1961	$42,238.00	4/12/		n Distribution
+	1050	5/9/1967	$44,387.00	2/9/		n Distribution
+	1055	1/3/1960	$42,248.00	6/22/2002		Overseas Distribution
+	1060	1/6/1964	$42,126.00	6/22/2003		European Distribution
+	1065	11/16/1970	$43,695.00	2/6/2003		North American Distribution
+	1070	9/3/1973	$44,771.00	11/22/2004		Overseas Distribution
+	1075	4/18/1966	$42,857.00	3/19/2004		Overseas Distribution
+	1080	1/8/1978	$43,659.00	1/17/2004		European Distribution
*			$0.00			

Modified table structure with new field *(Review Date)* inserted and moved *Annual Salary* field.

Modifying Forms and Reports in Topics 4.6 – 4.7

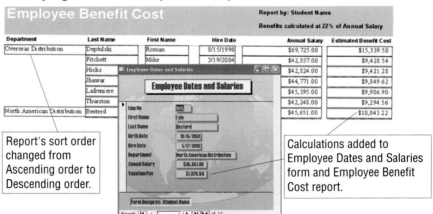

Report's sort order changed from Ascending order to Descending order.

Calculations added to Employee Dates and Salaries form and Employee Benefit Cost report.

Data Access Page Created in Topic 4.10

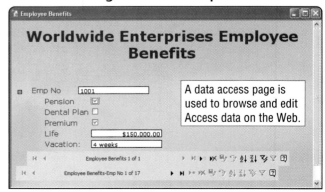

A data access page is used to browse and edit Access data on the Web.

ACCESS SECTION 1

Maintaining Data in Access Tables

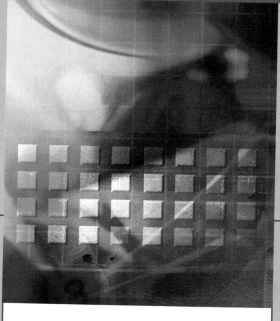

Managing business information effectively is a vital activity, since data forms the basis upon which transactions are conducted or strategic decisions are made. Microsoft Office Access 2003 is a database management system that is used to store, retrieve, and manage information. The type of information stored in an Access database can include such items as customer lists, inventory articles, human resources, and supplier lists. Activities that are routinely performed with a database include adding, editing, deleting, finding, sorting, querying, and reporting information. In this section you will learn the skills and complete the projects described here.

Note: The database files for this section are in the AccessS1 subfolder in the Access folder on the CD that accompanies this textbook. Because the database files are large and will increase in size as you work with them, do not copy the entire subfolder to a floppy disk. You will copy each database as it is used in the text and then remove the read-only attribute from the database file on your disk so that you can make changes to the database file. To remove the read-only attribute:

1. *Copy the database file from the CD to your disk.*
2. *In Access, display the Open dialog box with the drive active containing your disk.*
3. *Click once on the database file name.*
4. *Click the Tools button on the Open dialog box toolbar and then click Properties at the drop-down list.*
5. *At the Properties dialog box with the General tab selected, click Read-only in the Attributes section to remove the check mark.*
5. *Click OK to close the Properties dialog box.*
7. *Open the database file.*

Skills

- Define *field, record, table, datasheet,* and *database*
- Start and exit Access
- Identify features in the Access window
- Open and close a database
- Open and close tables
- Adjust column widths
- Navigate in Datasheet view
- Find and edit records
- Add records
- Delete records
- Sort records
- Move columns in Datasheet view
- Preview and print a table
- Change the page orientation
- Change the row height of records in a datasheet
- Use the Help feature
- Compact and repair a database
- Back up a database

Projects

Add, delete, find, and sort records; preview, change page orientation, margins, and print tables; increase row height; compact and back up the Distributors database; find, edit, add, delete, and sort records; preview, change page setup and print; compact and back up the Employees database.

Find student records and input grades into the Grades database; compact and back up the Grades database.

Maintain the Inventory database by adding and deleting records; compact the inventory database.

Delete records, sort, increase row height, and print two reports from the Costume Inventory database; compact the inventory database.

1.1 Exploring Database Objects

A *database* contains information logically organized into related units for easy retrieval. You access a database when you open a telephone book to look up a friend's telephone number, or browse the yellow pages looking for a restaurant. Microsoft Office Access 2003 is an application that is used to manage databases electronically. Information stored in an Access database is organized into *tables*. A table contains information for related items such as customers, suppliers, inventory, or human resources.

PROJECT: You will open and close two tables and a form in the Distributors database for Worldwide Enterprises to define and identify objects, fields, records, tables, datasheets, and forms.

STEPS

① At the Windows desktop, click the Start button ⟦⟧ start on the Taskbar.

② Point to All Programs.

③ Point to Microsoft Office.

④ Click Microsoft Office Access 2003.

> Depending on your operating system and/or system configuration, the steps you complete to open Access may vary.

⑤ Click the Open button 📂 on the Database toolbar or click the <u>More</u> hyperlink in the *Open* section of the Getting Started task pane.

> Refer to the Section 1 opening page for instructions on copying a database file from the CD that accompanies this textbook. These steps will have to be repeated for every database.

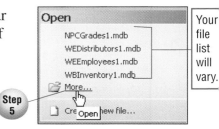

⑥ If necessary, change to the location where the student data files are located. To change to a different drive, click the down-pointing arrow to the right of the *Look in* option box and then select the correct drive from the drop-down list.

⑦ Double-click ***WEDistributors1.mdb***. *(Note: Click Yes and then click Open to confirm that you want to open the file if a Security warning message box appears stating that unsafe expressions are not blocked. This message may or may not appear depending on the security level setting on the computer you are using. If the message appears, expect that it will reappear each time you open a database file.)*

> Access databases end with the file name extension *mdb*.

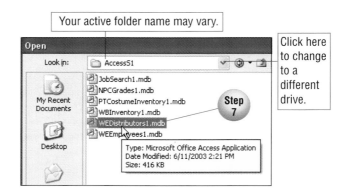

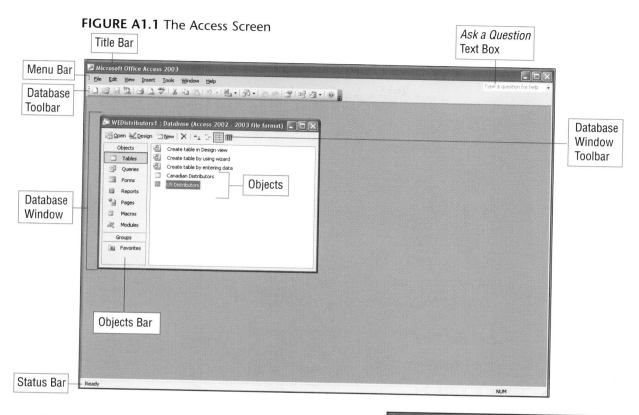

FIGURE A1.1 The Access Screen

Title Bar

Ask a Question Text Box

Menu Bar

Database Toolbar

Database Window Toolbar

Database Window

Objects

Objects Bar

Status Bar

8. At the Access screen, identify the various features by comparing your screen with the one shown in Figure A1.1.

Step 9

Unlike other Microsoft Office applications, only one database can be open at a time. A database is comprised of a series of objects. Descriptions of the seven types of objects that can be stored in a database are presented in Table A1.1 on page 5. An open database file displays in a Database window that contains the names of the various objects.

9. With Tables the default object selected on the Objects bar, double-click *Canadian Distributors*.

Canadian Distributors is one of two tables stored within the database. Double-clicking the object named *Canadian Distributors* opens the table in Datasheet view. Datasheets display the contents of a table in a column/row format.

10. Compare your screen with the one shown in Figure A1.2 on page 4 and examine the identified elements.

The identified elements are further described in Table A1.2 on page 5.

11. Identify the fields and the field names in the Canadian Distributors table. Notice each field contains only one unit of information.

The field names *Name, Street Address1, Street Address2,* and so on are displayed in the gray header row in Datasheet view.

12. Identify the records in the Canadian Distributors table. Each record is one row in the table.

The right-pointing arrow in the gray column (called the Record Selector bar) to the left of *EastCoast Cinemas* in Figure A1.2 illustrates the active record.

SECTION 1: MAINTAINING DATA IN ACCESS TABLES

(continued)

FIGURE A1.2 Canadian Distributors Datasheet

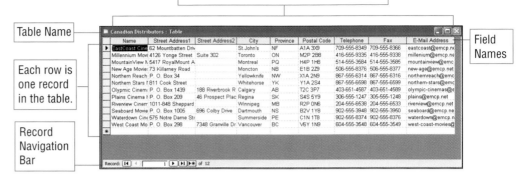

Each column represents a field in the table.

Table Name

Each row is one record in the table.

Record Navigation Bar

Field Names

13 Press the Down Arrow key four times to move the active record.

> The right-pointing arrow moves down the Record Selector bar as you move the insertion point and the record number at the bottom of the window changes to indicate you are viewing record 5 of a total of 12 records.

14 Click the Close button ⊠ at the right edge of the Canadian Distributors Table title bar.

> The Canadian Distributors table closes and you are returned to the WEDistributors1 : Database window.

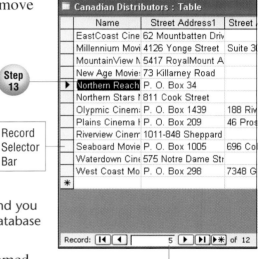

Step 13

Record Selector Bar

Record number changes as you move to a new record

15 Move the mouse pointer over the table named *US Distributors* and then click the mouse to select the object.

16 Click Open on the Database window toolbar.

> The US Distributors table opens in Datasheet view.

17 Review the fields and records in the US Distributors datasheet and then click the Close button on the US Distributors Table title bar.

18 Click the Forms button on the Objects bar.

19 Double-click *US Distributors*.

> The US Distributors form opens in Form view. A form is used to view and edit data in a table one record at a time. Use buttons on the Record Navigation bar to scroll the records.

Step 16

Step 18

Step 15

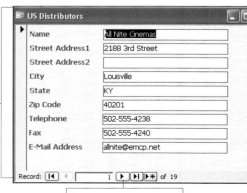

Step 19

Record Navigation Bar

20) Click the Close button on the US Distributors title bar.

21) Click File and then Exit.

TABLE A1.1 Database Objects

Object	Description
Tables	Organize data in fields (columns) and rows (records). A database must contain at least one table. The table is the base upon which other objects are created.
Queries	Used to display data from a table that meets a conditional statement and/or perform calculations. For example, display only those records in which the city is Toronto.
Forms	Allow fields and records to be presented in a different layout than the datasheet. Use to facilitate data entry and maintenance.
Reports	Print data from tables or queries. Calculations can be performed in a report.
Pages	Web pages designed for working with data within a Web browser.
Macros	Automate repetitive tasks.
Modules	Advanced automation through programming using Visual Basic for Applications.

TABLE A1.2 Elements of a Database

Element	Description
Field	A single component of information about a person, place, item, or object
Record	All of the fields for one unit such as a customer, supplier, or inventory item
Table	All of the records for one logical group
Datasheet view	Data for a table displayed in columns (fields) and rows (records)
Database	A file containing related tables

In Addition

Planning and Designing a Database

One of the first steps in designing a table for a new database is to look at the format from which the input will originate. For example, look at an existing file card for a customer to see how the information is currently organized. Determine how you will break down all of the information into fields. Discuss with others what the future needs of the company will be for both input and output. Include fields you anticipate will be used in the future. For example, add a field for a Web site address even if you do not currently have URLs for your customers. Refer to Performance Plus Assessment 5 at the end of this section for an exercise using the steps required to design a new database.

IN BRIEF

Start Access
1 Click Start.
2 Point to All Programs.
3 Point to Microsoft Office.
4 Click Microsoft Office Access 2003.

Open Objects
1 Open database file.
2 Select type of object from Objects bar.
3 Double-click object name.

1.2 Adjusting Column Width; Navigating in Datasheet View

A table opened in Datasheet view displays data in a manner similar to a spreadsheet, with a grid of columns and rows. Columns contain the field values, with the field names in the gray column headings row at the top of the datasheet. Records are represented in rows. A gray record selector bar is positioned at the left edge of the window. The Record Navigation bar displays along the bottom of the window with record selector buttons. Horizontal and/or vertical scroll bars appear if the entire table is not visible in the current window.

PROJECT: You will adjust column widths and practice scrolling and navigating through records using the US Distributors table.

STEPS

1. Start Access.

2. Click the WEDistributors1.mdb link in the *Open* section of the Getting Started task pane.

   By default, the last four database files opened are displayed in the *Open* section of the Getting Started task pane. The recently used file list option can be adjusted to include up to the last nine files opened. Display the Options dialog box using the Tools menu and then click the General tab to adjust this setting.

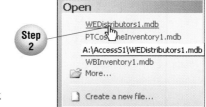

3. With the **WEDistributors1** database open, click Tables on the Objects bar and then double-click *US Distributors*.

   The US Distributors table opens in Datasheet view.

4. Click the Maximize button 🗖 on the US Distributors Table title bar.

   Notice that some columns contain data that is not entirely visible. In Steps 5–7, you will learn how to adjust the column widths using two methods.

PROBLEM❓
> If the table window is already maximized, the Maximize button is replaced with the Restore Down 🗗 button. Skip Step 4.

5. With the active record the first row in the table and the insertion point positioned at the left edge of the text in the *Name* field, click Format and then Column Width.

6. Click the Best Fit button in the Column Width dialog box.

   The column is automatically widened to accommodate the width of the longest entry. In the next step you will widen a column using the mouse in the column headings row.

⑦ Position the mouse pointer on the right column boundary line in the Field Name headings row between columns two and three (*Street Address1* and *Street Address2*) until the pointer changes to a vertical line with a left- and right-pointing arrow and then double-click the left mouse button.

> Double-clicking the column boundary performs the Best Fit command.

⑧ Best Fit the *Street Address2* column using either method learned in Steps 5–6 or Step 7.

⑨ Click the right-pointing horizontal scroll arrow as many times as necessary to scroll the datasheet to the right and view the remaining columns. (Scrolling can also be performed using keyboard commands, as shown in Table A1.3.)

⑩ Best Fit the *E-mail Address* column.

⑪ Drag the horizontal scroll box to the left edge of the horizontal scroll bar.

> This scrolls the screen to the left until the first column is visible.

⑫ Click the Save button 🖫 on the Database toolbar.

⑬ Click the Next Record button ▶ on the Record Navigation bar to move the active record down one row.

⑭ Click the Last Record button ▶I on the Record Navigation bar to move the active record to the last row in the table.

⑮ Click the Previous Record button ◀ on the Record Navigation bar to move the active record to the second last row in the table.

⑯ Click the First Record button I◀ on the Record Navigation bar to move the active record back to the first row in the table.

TABLE A1.3 Scrolling Techniques Using the Keyboard

Press	To Move to
Home	First field in the current record
End	Last field in the current record
Tab	Next field in the current record
Shift + Tab	Previous field in the current record
Ctrl + Home	First field in the first record
Ctrl + End	Last field in the last record

In Addition

Saving Data

Microsoft Access differs from other Office applications in that data is *automatically* saved as soon as you move to the next record or close the table. Database management systems are such a critical component of business activities that saving is not left to chance. The Save button was used in this topic to save the layout changes that were made when the column widths were enlarged.

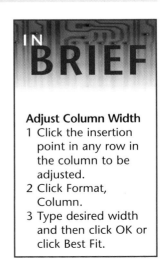

Adjust Column Width
1 Click the insertion point in any row in the column to be adjusted.
2 Click Format, Column.
3 Type desired width and then click OK or click Best Fit.

1.3 Finding and Editing Records

The Find command can be used to quickly move the insertion point to a specific record in a table. This is a time-saving feature when the table contains several records that are not all visible in one screen. Once a record has been located, click the insertion point within a field and insert or delete text as required to edit the record.

PROJECT: You have received a note from Sam Vestering that Waterfront Cinemas has changed its fax number and Eastown Movie House has a new P.O. Box number. You will use the Find feature to locate the records and make the changes.

S T E P S

① With the US Distributors table open and the insertion point positioned in the *Name* column, click the Find button 🔍 on the Database toolbar.

> This displays the Find and Replace dialog box.

② Type **Waterfront Cinemas** in the *Find What* text box and then click the Find Next button.

> The insertion point moves to record 17.

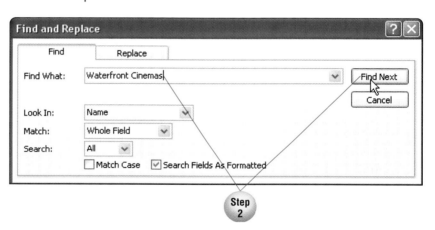

Step 2

③ Click the Close button on the Find and Replace dialog box title bar.

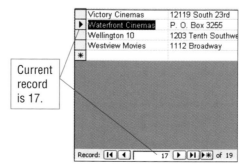

Current record is 17.

④ Press Tab or Enter seven times to move to the *Fax* column.

> The entire field value is selected when you move from column to column using Tab or Enter. If you need to edit only a few characters within the field you will want to use Edit mode. As an alternative, you could scroll and click the insertion point within the field to avoid having to turn on Edit mode.

⑤ Press F2 to turn on Edit mode.

⑥ Press the Left Arrow key four times, delete *3947*, and then type **4860**.

Step 6

619-555-8748	victory@emcp.net
716-555-4860	waterfrontcinemas@
215-555-9048	wellington10@emcp.
212-555-4877	westview@emcp.net

⑦ Look on the record selector bar for record 17 at the pencil icon that is displayed.

> The pencil icon indicates the current record is being edited and the changes have not yet been saved.

Pencil icon indicates record is being edited.

Step 7

	Victory Cinemas
∥	Waterfront Cinemas
	Wellington 10
	Westview Movies

⑧ Press Enter twice to move to the next record in the table.

> The pencil icon disappears, indicating the changes have now been saved.

⑨ Click in any record in the *Street Address1* column and then click the Find button.

⑩ Type **Box 722** in the *Find What* text box.

⑪ Click the down-pointing arrow next to the *Match* list box and then click *Any Part of Field* in the drop-down list.

> Using the options from the *Match* list box you can find records without specifying the entire field value. Specifically, you can instruct Access to stop at records where the entry typed in the *Find What* text box is the *Whole Field* entry; is *Any Part of Field;* or is the *Start of Field.*

⑫ Click Find Next.

> The insertion point moves to record 5. You were able to correctly locate the record for Eastown Movie House using only a portion of the field value for *Street Address1.* Notice Access has selected *Box 722* in the field—only the text specified in the *Find What* text box (not *P. O. Box 722* which is the entire field value).

Find and Replace

Find	Replace

Find What: Box 722 — **Step 10**

Look In: Street Address1

Match: Whole Field — **Step 11**

    Any Part of Field
    Whole Field
Search: Start of Field   arch Fields As Formatted

Find Next

Cancel

Step 12

⑬ Close the Find and Replace dialog box.

⑭ Press F2 to turn on Edit mode, press Backspace three times, type **429**, and then click in any other record to save the changes to record 5.

In Addition

Using the Replace Command

Use the Replace tab in the Find and Replace dialog box to automatically change a field entry to something else. For example, in Steps 9–12 you searched for *Box 722* and then edited the field to change the box number to *429*. The Replace command could have been used to change the text automatically. To do this, display the Find and Replace dialog box, click the Replace tab, type **Box 722** in the *Find What* text box, type **Box 429** in the Replace With text box, change the option in the *Match* option box to *Any Part of Field,* and then click the Find Next button. Click the Replace button when the record is found. Use the Replace All button in the dialog box to change multiple occurrences of a field.

In BRIEF

Find a Record
1 Click in any row in the field by which you want to search.
2 Click Edit, Find, or click Find button.
3 Type the search text.
4 Click Find Next.

1.4 Adding Records in Datasheet View

New records can be added to a table in either Datasheet view or Form view. To add a record in Datasheet view, open the table, click the New Record button on either the Table Datasheet toolbar or the Record Navigation bar, and then type the data. Press Tab or Enter to move from field to field. When you press Tab or Enter after typing the last field, the record is automatically saved. Initially, the new record will appear at the bottom of the datasheet until the table is closed. When the table is reopened, the records are rearranged to display alphabetically sorted by the field that has been defined as the primary key. In Addition at the end of this topic describes a primary key field.

PROJECT: Worldwide Enterprises has signed two new distributors in the United States. You will add the information in the US Distributors table.

S T E P S

1. With the US Distributors table open, click the New Record button 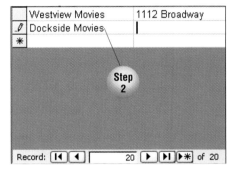 on the Table Datasheet toolbar.

    The insertion point moves to the first column in the blank row at the bottom of the datasheet and the record navigation box indicates you are editing record 20.

2. Type **Dockside Movies** and then press Tab.

3. Type **P. O. Box 224** and then press Tab.

4. Type **155 S. Central Avenue** and then press Tab.

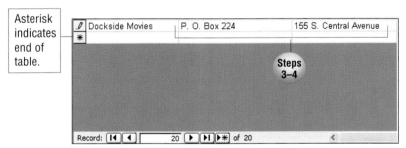

Asterisk indicates end of table.

5. Type **Baltimore** and then press Tab.

6. Type **MD** and then press Tab.

7. Type **21203** and then press Tab.

PROBLEM? Press Enter to move to the next field if you are using the numeric keypad to input numbers—it will be more comfortable.

8. Type **301-555-7732** and then press Tab.

9. Type **301-555-9836** and then press Tab.

10. Type **dockside@emcp.net** and then press Tab.

    The insertion point moves to a new row when you press Tab or Enter after the last field in a new record to allow you to continue typing the next new record in the table. The record just entered is automatically saved.

11. Type the following information in the next row:

Renaissance Cinemas
3599 Woodward
Avenue
Detroit, MI 48211
313-555-1693
313-555-1699
renaissance-
cinemas@emcp.net

State	Zip Code	Telephone	Fax	E-Mail Address
KY	40201	502-555-4238	502-555-4240	allnite@emcp.net
TX	76013	817-555-2116	817-555-2119	centurycinemas@emcp.net
VT	05201	802-555-1469	802-555-1470	countryside@emcp.net
SC	29201	803-555-3487	803-555-3421	danforth@emcp.net
MA	02142	413-555-0981	413-555-0226	eastown@emcp.net
NJ	07920	201-555-1147	201-555-1143	hillman@emcp.net
AZ	86355-6014	602-555-6231	602-555-6233	lavista@emcp.net
GA	73125	404-555-8113	404-555-2349	libertycinemas@emcp.net
WA	98220-2791	206-555-3269	206-555-3270	mainstream@emcp.net
CA	90045	612-555-2398	612-555-2377	marqueemovies@emcp.net
KS	66801	316-555-7013	316-555-7022	midtown@emcp.net
OH	43107	614-555-8134	614-555-8339	mooretown@emcp.net
IL	60302	312-555-7719	312-555-7381	oshea@emcp.net
OR	97466-3359	503-555-8641	503-555-8633	redwoodcinemas@emcp.net
FL	33562	813-555-3185	813-555-3177	sunfest@emcp.net
CA	97432-1567	619-555-8746	619-555-8748	victory@emcp.net
NY	14288	716-555-3845	716-555-4860	waterfrontcinemas@emcp.net
PA	19178	215-555-9045	215-555-9048	wellington10@emcp.net
NY	10119	212-555-4875	212-555-4877	westview@emcp.net
MD	21203	301-555-7732	301-555-9836	dockside@emcp.net
MI	48211	313-555-1693	313-555-1699	renaissance-cinemas@emcp.net

Step 12 / Step 11

New records initially appear at the bottom of the datasheet.

12. Increase the column width of the *E-Mail Address* column to view all of the data.

13. Close the US Distributors table. Click Yes when prompted to save changes to the layout of the table.

14. Reopen the US Distributors table to view where the new records are now positioned.

15. Close the US Distributors table.

New records have now been rearranged alphabetically by name.

Name	Street Address1
All Nite Cinemas	2188 3rd Street
Century Cinemas	3687 Avenue K
Countryside Cinemas	22 Hillside Street
Danforth Cinemas	P. O. Box 22
Dockside Movies	P. O. Box 224
Eastown Movie House	P. O. Box 429
Hillman Cinemas	55 Kemble Avenue
LaVista Cinemas	111 Vista Road
Liberty Cinemas	P. O. Box 998
Mainstream Movies	P. O. Box 33
Marquee Movies	1011 South Alameda Street
Midtown Moviehouse	1033 Commercial Street
Mooretown Movies	P. O. Box 11
O'Shea Movies	59 Erie
Redwood Cinemas	P. O. Box 112F
Renaissance Cinemas	3599 Woodward Avenue
Sunfest Cinemas	
Victory Cinemas	12119 South 23rd
Waterfront Cinemas	P. O. Box 3255
Wellington 10	1203 Tenth Southwest
Westview Movies	1112 Broadway

In Addition

Primary Key Field

When a table is created, usually one field is defined as the *primary key*. A primary key is the field by which the table is automatically sorted whenever the table is opened. The primary key field must contain unique data for each record. When a new record is being added to the table, Access checks to ensure there is no existing record with the same data in the primary key. If there is, Access will display an error message indicating there are duplicate values and will not allow the record to be saved. The primary key field cannot be left blank when a new record is being added, since it is the field that is used to sort and check for duplicates.

In BRIEF

Add a Record in Datasheet View
1 Open table.
2 Click New Record button.
3 Type data in fields.

1.5 Adding Records in Form View

Forms are used to enter, edit, view, and print data in tables. Forms are created to provide a user-friendly interface between the user and the underlying table of data. Adding records in a form is easier than using a datasheet since all of the fields in the table are presented in a different layout which usually allows all fields to be visible in the current window. Other records in the table do not distract the user since only one record displays at a time.

PROJECT: Worldwide Enterprises has just signed two new distributors in New York. You will add the information to the US Distributors table using a form.

STEPS

1. With the **WEDistributors1** database open, click the Forms button on the Objects bar.

2. Double-click *US Distributors*.

   The US Distributors form opens with the first record in the US Distributors table displayed in the form. A Record Navigation bar appears at the bottom of the form.

3. Click the New Record button on the Record Navigation bar.

   A blank form appears in Form view and the Record Navigation bar indicates you are editing record number 22. Notice the New Record and Next Record buttons on the Record Navigation bar are dimmed.

4. Type **Movie Emporium** and then press Tab or Enter.

5. Type **203 West Houston Street** and then press Tab or Enter.

   Records are added to a form using the same navigation methods as those learned in the previous topic on adding records to a datasheet.

6. Type the remaining fields as shown below.

   When you press Tab or Enter after the *E-Mail Address* field, a new form will appear in the window.

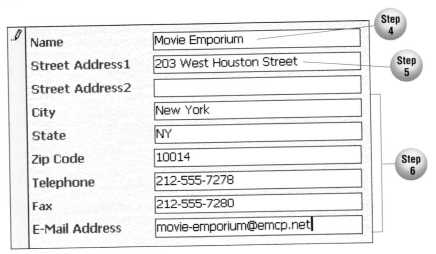

Name	Movie Emporium
Street Address1	203 West Houston Street
Street Address2	
City	New York
State	NY
Zip Code	10014
Telephone	212-555-7278
Fax	212-555-7280
E-Mail Address	movie-emporium@emcp.net

7 Type the following information in the new form for record 23:

Cinema Festival
318 East 11th Street
New York, NY 10003
212-555-9715
212-555-9717
cinemafestival@emcp.net

8 Click the First Record button 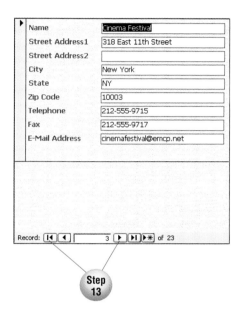 on the Record Navigation bar.

> This displays the information for All Nite Cinemas in Form view.

9 Click the Last Record button ▶I on the Record Navigation bar.

> This displays the information for Cinema Festival in Form view.

10 Close the US Distributors form.

11 Reopen the US Distributors form.

12 Click the Last Record button on the Record Navigation bar.

> Notice the last record displayed is the information for Westview Movies, not Cinema Festival. Access displays forms in the same manner as a datasheet—sorted by the primary key.

13 Click the First Record button on the Record Navigation bar, and then click the Next Record button two times to view the information for Cinema Festival.

> Cinema Festival is record number 3 of 23 when it is sorted alphabetically on the *Name* field.

14 Scroll through the remaining records in Form view.

15 Close the US Distributors form.

Step 13

In Addition

Scrolling in Form View Using the Keyboard

Records can be scrolled in Form view using the following keyboard techniques:
- Page Down displays the next record
- Page Up displays the previous record
- Ctrl + End moves to the last field in the last record
- Ctrl + Home moves to the first field in the first record
- Type a record value in the Specific Record box on the Record Navigation bar

IN BRIEF

Add a Record in Form View
1 Open form.
2 Click New Record button.
3 Type data in fields.

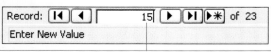

Type a record number here to move directly to a particular record if you know the record number value.

1.6 Deleting Records in Datasheet View

Records can be deleted in either Datasheet view or Form view. To delete a record, open the table in Datasheet view or Form view, activate any field in the record to be deleted, and then click the Delete Record button on the Table Datasheet toolbar or the Form View toolbar. Access will display a message indicating the selected record will be permanently removed from the table. Click Yes to confirm the record deletion.

PROJECT: The Countryside Cinemas and Victory Cinemas distributor agreements have lapsed and you have just been informed that they have signed agreements with another movie distributing company. You will delete their records in the US Distributors table.

STEPS

1. With the **WEDistributors1** database open, click Tables on the Objects bar.

2. Double-click *US Distributors*.

3. Click the insertion point in any field in the row for Countryside Cinemas.

    This selects record 4 as the active record.

4. Click the Delete Record button [×] on the Table Datasheet toolbar.

5. Access will display a message box indicating you are about to delete 1 record and that the undo operation is not available after this action. Click Yes to confirm the deletion.

PROBLEM?

Check that you are deleting the correct record before clicking Yes. Click No if you selected the wrong record by mistake.

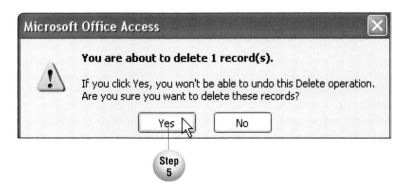

6. Position the mouse pointer in the record selector bar for Victory Cinemas until the pointer changes to a black right-pointing arrow ➡ and then right-click the mouse.

   This selects the entire row.

7. Click Delete Record at the shortcut menu.

8. Click Yes to confirm the deletion.

9. Close the US Distributors table.

10. Click Forms on the Objects bar and then double-click *US Distributors*.

11. With the insertion point positioned in the *Name* field in the first record, click the Find button on the Form View toolbar.

12. Type **LaVista Cinemas** in the *Find What* text box and then click Find Next.

    The active record moves to record 8.

13. Close the Find and Replace dialog box.

14. Click the Delete Record button on the Form View toolbar.

15. Click No when prompted to confirm the deletion.

    The LaVista Cinemas record is restored in the table.

16. Close the US Distributors form.

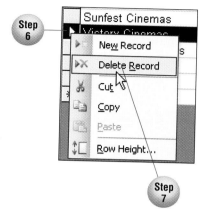

Step 6

Step 7

In Addition

More about Deleting Records

In a multiuser environment, deleting records is a procedure that should be performed only by authorized personnel; once the record is deleted, crucial data can be lost. It is a good idea to back up the database file before deleting records. Topic 1.11 on page 24 describes how to back up a database.

IN BRIEF

Delete a Record
1 Open table in Datasheet view or Form view.
2 Click in any field in the record to be deleted.
3 Click Delete Record button.
4 Click Yes.

1.7 Sorting Records

Records in a table are displayed alphabetically in ascending order by the primary key field. To rearrange the order of the records, click in any field in the column you want to sort by and then click the Sort Ascending or Sort Descending buttons on the Table Datasheet toolbar. To sort on more than one column, select the columns first and then click the Sort Ascending or Sort Descending button. Access will sort first by the leftmost column in the selection, then by the next column, and so on. Columns can be moved in the datasheet if necessary to facilitate a multiple-column sort. Access will save the sort order when the table is closed.

PROJECT: You will perform one sort routine using a single field and then perform a multiple-column sort. To do the multiple-column sort you will have to move columns in the datasheet.

STEPS

1 With the **WEDistributors1** database open, click Tables on the Objects bar and then double-click *US Distributors*.

2 Click in any row in the *City* column.

3 Click the Sort Ascending button [A↓] on the Table Datasheet toolbar.

> The records are rearranged to display the cities starting with *A* through *Z*.

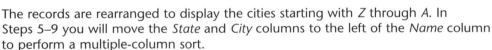

4 Click the Sort Descending button [Z↓] on the Table Datasheet toolbar.

> The records are rearranged to display the cities starting with *Z* through *A*. In Steps 5–9 you will move the *State* and *City* columns to the left of the *Name* column to perform a multiple-column sort.

5 Position the mouse pointer in the *State* column heading until the pointer changes to a downward-pointing black arrow and then click the left mouse button.

> The *State* column is now selected and can be moved by dragging the heading to another position in the datasheet.

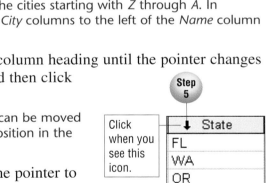

Click when you see this icon.

↓ State
FL
WA
OR
AZ

6 With the *State* column selected, move the pointer to the column heading *State* until the white arrow pointer appears.

City	State	Zip Code
Tampa	FL	33562
Seattle	WA	98220-2791
Portland	OR	97466-3359
Phoenix	AZ	86355-6014

(7) Hold down the left mouse button, drag to the left of the *Name* column, and then release the mouse. *State* is now the first column in the datasheet.

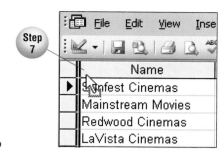

Step 7

> A thick black line appears between columns as you drag, indicating the position to which the column will be moved when you release the mouse. In addition, the mouse pointer displays with a gray box attached to it, indicating you are performing a move operation.

(8) Click in any field in the table to deselect the *State* column.

(9) Move the *City* column between *State* and *Name* by completing steps similar to those in Steps 5–8.

Step 10

State	City		Name
FL	Tampa		Sunfest Cinemas
WA	Seattle		Mainstream Movies
OR	Portland		Redwood Cinemas

(10) Position the mouse pointer in the *State* column heading until the pointer changes to a down-pointing black arrow, hold down the left mouse button, drag right until the *State, City,* and *Name* columns are selected, and then release the left mouse button.

(11) Click the Sort Ascending button.

> The records are sorted first by *State*, then by *City* within each state, and then by *Name* within each city.

(12) Look at the four records for the state of New York. Notice the order of the records is Waterfront Cinemas in Buffalo first, then Cinema Festival, Movie Emporium, and Westview Movies in New York City next.

(13) Close the US Distributors table. Click Yes when prompted to save the design changes.

In Addition

More about Sorting

When you are ready to conduct a sort in a table, consider the following:

• Records in which the selected field is empty are listed first.
• Numbers are sorted before letters.
• Numbers stored in fields that are not defined as numeric (i.e., social security number or telephone number) are sorted as characters (not numeric values). To sort them as if they were numbers, all field values must be the same length.

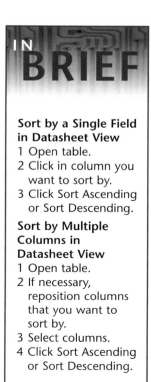

IN BRIEF

Sort by a Single Field in Datasheet View
1 Open table.
2 Click in column you want to sort by.
3 Click Sort Ascending or Sort Descending.

Sort by Multiple Columns in Datasheet View
1 Open table.
2 If necessary, reposition columns that you want to sort by.
3 Select columns.
4 Click Sort Ascending or Sort Descending.

1.8 Previewing and Printing; Changing Margins and Page Orientation

Click the Print button on the Table Datasheet toolbar to print the table in Datasheet view. To avoid wasting paper, use Print Preview to view how the datasheet will appear on the page before you print a table. By default, Access will print a datasheet on letter-size paper in portrait orientation with the top, bottom, left, and right margins at 1 inch. Change the margins and/or page orientation in the Page Setup dialog box.

PROJECT: Sam Vestering has requested a list of the US Distributors. You will open the table, preview the printout, change the page orientation, change the left and right margins, and then print the datasheet.

S T E P S

1. With the **WEDistributors1** database open, open the US Distributors table.

   Notice the datasheet is displayed sorted by *State* first, then by *City*, and then by *Name* since the design changes were saved in the last topic.

2. Click the Print Preview button on the Table Datasheet toolbar.

   The table is displayed in the Print Preview window as shown in Figure A1.3.

FIGURE A1.3 Print Preview Window

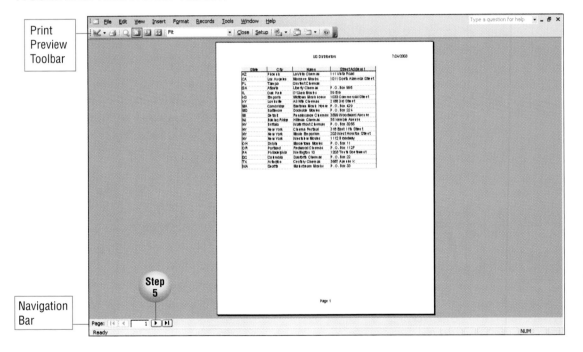

Print Preview Toolbar

Navigation Bar

Step 5

3. Move the mouse pointer (displays as a magnifying glass) over the top center of the table and click the left mouse button.

   The zoom changes to 100% magnification. Notice that Access prints the table name at the top center and the current date at the top right of the page. At the bottom center, Access prints the word *Page* followed by the current page number.

4. Click the left mouse button again.

   The zoom changes back to *Fit*.

⑤ Click the Next Page button ▶ on the Navigation bar two times.

> The US Distributors table requires three pages to print with the default margins and the orientation. In Steps 6–8 you will change the orientation to landscape to see if all of the columns will fit on one page.

⑥ Click File and then Page Setup.

⑦ Click the Page tab in the Page Setup dialog box.

⑧ Click *Landscape* in the *Orientation* section and then click OK.

> Landscape orientation rotates the printout to print wider than it is taller. Changing to landscape allows more columns to fit on a page.

⑨ Look at the page number in the Navigation bar at the bottom of the Print Preview window. Notice that the page number is now 2. In landscape orientation, the US Distributors table will still need two pages to print.

⑩ Click File and then Page Setup.

⑪ With the Margins tab in the Page Setup dialog box active, drag across *1* in the *Left* text box and then type **0.5**.

⑫ Press Tab, type **0.5** in the *Right* text box and then click OK.

> The Print Preview window still shows that the printout will require two pages.

⑬ Click the Print button 🖶 on the Print Preview toolbar.

> In a few seconds the table will print on the printer. Making the margins smaller than 0.5 inch would still not allow the entire datasheet to fit on one page. In Section 3 titled "Creating Queries, Forms, and Reports" you will learn how to create a report for a table. Use a report when you want control over which columns are printed and the data layout on the page.

⑭ Click Close on the Print Preview toolbar.

⑮ Close the US Distributors table.

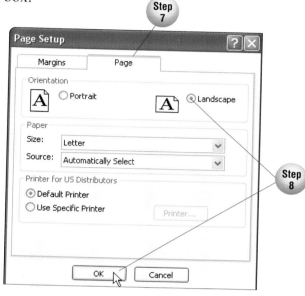

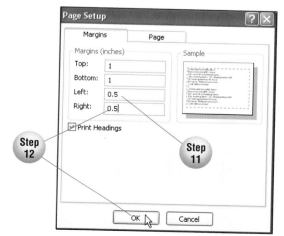

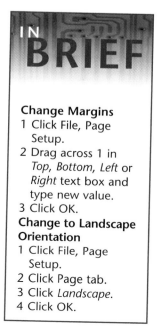

IN BRIEF

Change Margins
1 Click File, Page Setup.
2 Drag across 1 in *Top*, *Bottom*, *Left* or *Right* text box and type new value.
3 Click OK.

Change to Landscape Orientation
1 Click File, Page Setup.
2 Click Page tab.
3 Click *Landscape*.
4 Click OK.

1.9 Using Help

An extensive help resource is available whenever you are working in Access by clicking the text inside the *Ask a Question* text box located at the right side of the Menu bar, typing a term, phrase, or question, and then pressing Enter. This causes the Search Results task pane to open with a list of topics related to the text that you typed. Clicking a hyperlinked topic in the Search Results task pane opens a Microsoft Office Access Help window from which you can further explore information on the topic. By default, the search feature will look for information in all Office resources at Microsoft Office Online as long as you are connected to the Internet. In the *Search* list box at the bottom of the Search Results task pane you can change this setting to search only Offline Help resources.

PROJECT: After printing the US Distributors table, you decide it would look better if the height of the rows was increased to better space the records. You will use the Help feature to learn how to do this and then reprint the datasheet.

S T E P S

1. With the **WEDistributors1** database open, open the US Distributors table.

2. Click the text inside the *Ask a Question* text box (currently reads *Type a question for help*) at the right end of the Menu bar.

   When you click in the *Ask a Question* text box, an insertion point will appear and the text *Type a question for help* disappears. Once you have completed an initial search for help using the *Ask a Question* text box, the drop-down arrow will display a list of topics previously searched for in help.

3. Type **increase row height** and then press Enter.

   The Search Results task pane opens with a list of help topics related to the term, phrase, or question typed in the *Ask a Question* text box.

4. Click the <u>Resize a column or row</u> hyperlink.

   As you move the mouse pointer over a help topic, the pointer changes to a hand with the index finger pointing upward. When you click a topic, the help information displays in a separate Microsoft Office Access Help window. You can continue clicking topics and reading the information in the Help window until you have found what you are looking for.

5. Click the <u>Resize rows</u> hyperlink in the Microsoft Office Access Help window.

   The Help window expands below the selected topic to display information on the feature including the steps to complete the task.

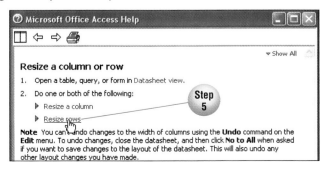

6 Read the information below *Resize rows* in the Microsoft Office Access Help window.

> If you would like a hard copy of the information, click the Print button on the Microsoft Office Access Help toolbar.

7 Click the Close button located on the Microsoft Office Access Help title bar.

8 Close the Search Results task pane.

9 Position the mouse pointer on the bottom row boundary for record 1 in the US Distributors table until the pointer changes to a horizontal line with an up- and down-pointing arrow attached (as shown in the Help window).

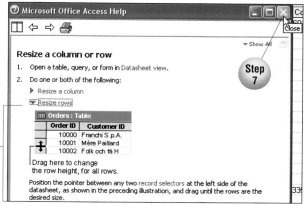

Step 7

Step 6

10 Drag the pointer down until the black line indicating the new row height is approximately at the position shown at the right and then release the mouse button.

State	City
AZ	Phoenix
CA	Los Angeles
FL	Tampa

Step 10

11 Click the Print Preview button to preview the datasheet.

12 Change the Page Setup to print the datasheet in *Landscape* orientation.

13 Print the US Distributors table.

14 Close the US Distributors table. Click Yes when prompted to save the layout changes.

In Addition

The Access Help Task Pane

Click Help on the Menu bar and then click Microsoft Office Access Help to open the Access Help task pane shown at the right. From this task pane you can access more extensive help resources such as online training courses for Access features, Microsoft Office newsgroups, download updates to your Office programs, and more.

IN BRIEF

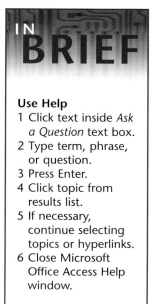

Use Help
1 Click text inside *Ask a Question* text box.
2 Type term, phrase, or question.
3 Press Enter.
4 Click topic from results list.
5 If necessary, continue selecting topics or hyperlinks.
6 Close Microsoft Office Access Help window.

1.10 Compacting and Repairing a Database

Once you have been working with a database file for a period of time, the data can become fragmented because of records and objects that have been deleted. The disk space that the database uses may be larger than is necessary. Compacting the database defragments the file and reduces the required disk space. Compacting and repairing a database also ensures optimal performance while using the file. The database can be set to automatically compact each time the file is closed.

PROJECT: You will run the compact and repair utility on the WEDistributors1 database and then turn on the Compact on Close option so that the database is automatically compacted each time the file is closed.

S T E P S

1. With the **WEDistributors1** database open, click the Minimize button ▬ on the Microsoft Office Access 2003 title bar to reduce Access to a button on the Taskbar.

   Step 2

2. Right-click the Start button on the Taskbar and then click Explore at the shortcut menu. If the Start Menu window is not currently maximized, click the Maximize button on the Start menu title bar.

3. If necessary, scroll up or down the Folders pane and then click the drive and/or folder name where the **WEDistributors1.mdb** file is stored.

   If your data files are stored in a subfolder, click the plus sign to the left of the drive or folder name in the Folders pane to expand the display. Click the subfolder name to display the contents in the file list pane at the right.

4. Click View and then Details.

   This displays the file names with the file size, date, and time.

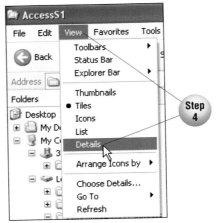

Step 4

5. Locate the file **WEDistributors1.mdb** and then write down the file size of the database.

   File size = _____

PROBLEM? Two files will appear in the file list: **WEDistributors1.ldb** and **WEDistributors1.mdb**. The *.ldb* file is used to lock records so that two users cannot request the same record at the same time.

6 Click the button on the Taskbar representing Access.

7 Click Tools, point to Database Utilities, and then click Compact and Repair Database.

> A message displays on the Status bar indicating the progress of the compact and repair process. In a multiuser environment, no other user can have the database open while the compact and repair procedure is running.

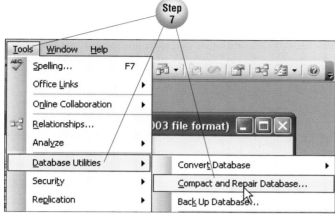

8 Click the button on the Taskbar representing the Explore window folder name or drive.

9 Write down the new file size of the **WEDistributors1.mdb** file. Notice that the amount of disk space is lower.

File size = _____

10 Click File and then Close to exit the Explore window.

11 With the **WEDistributors1** database open, click Tools and then Options.

12 Click the General tab in the Options dialog box.

13 Click the *Compact on Close* check box and then click OK.

> Turn on Compact on Close for each database so that the disk space the database uses is minimized.

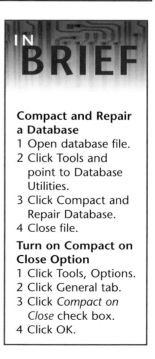

IN BRIEF

Compact and Repair a Database
1 Open database file.
2 Click Tools and point to Database Utilities.
3 Click Compact and Repair Database.
4 Close file.

Turn on Compact on Close Option
1 Click Tools, Options.
2 Click General tab.
3 Click *Compact on Close* check box.
4 Click OK.

1.11 Backing Up a Database

Regular backups of a database file should be maintained as part of the normal routine in a business setting for security and historical reasons. A loss of data as a result of theft, fire, breakdown in equipment, or other circumstance could have disastrous consequences. Damaged, lost, or stolen equipment can be replaced easily; however, it is the data stored on the computer that is the more valuable resource. Creating backups for historical reasons means that you have copies of a database before records are deleted, added, or edited. Access includes the Back Up Database command to facilitate the creation of a copy of the active database without having to leave Access. The Back Up Database feature automatically appends the current date to the end of the database file name to make the copy unique. The backup copy of the database is generally saved to an external media that can be stored away from the business operation for safekeeping.

PROJECT: You will create a backup copy of the WEDistributors1 database, using today's date for historical purposes, and then open the copy to check its content.

S T E P S

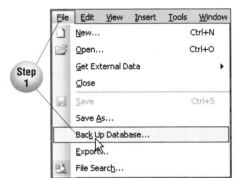

1. With the **WEDistributors1** database open, click File and then click Back Up Database.

   Step 1

   The Save Backup As dialog box opens. The default name in the *File name* text box is the current database file name followed by an underscore character (_) and then the current date. Appending the current date to the file name means that you can create several historical copies of the database at key time intervals for reference. The *Save in* list box shows the current drive or folder name from which the active database was opened.

2. Click the Save button in the Save Backup As dialog box with the default *Save in* and *File name* options.

   A message displays on the Status bar indicating the progress of the backup process. In a multiuser environment, no other user can have the database open while the backup procedure is running.

Your date will vary.

Step 2

3. When the backup is complete, click File and then Close to close the **WEDistributors1** database.

   Notice the Compact process starts automatically when the file is closed since the Compact on Close feature was turned on in the last topic.

4. Click the Open button on the Database toolbar.

⑤ Click *WEDistributors1_ current date.mdb* in the file list box where *current date* is today's date—the date at which the backup copy was made.

⑥ Click Open.

⑦ Open the US Distributors table.

> Notice the datasheet is the same as the US Distributors datasheet in **WEDistributors1** including the sort order and row height format.

⑧ Close the US Distributors table.

⑨ Click Tools and then Options.

⑩ If necessary, click the General tab in the Options dialog box.

> Notice the *Compact on Close* check box is not selected.

⑪ Click the *Compact on Close* check box and then click OK.

⑫ Close the **WEDistributors1_ current date.mdb** database.

⑬ Exit Access.

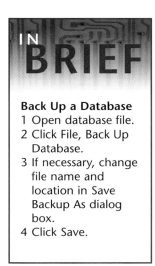

In Addition

Replicating a Database

A copy of a database can also be made by clicking Tools, pointing to Replication, and then clicking Create Replica. A *replica* is a copy of the database including all tables, queries, forms, reports, and so on. Replicas are generally created when you want to create a copy of a database for one or more remote users in cases where you cannot give access to the live data. For example, a sales representative who will be traveling with a laptop without network or dial-up access to the main database would need a replica. The database from which a replica is made is converted to a Design Master. Changes to the design of the database's objects can be made only in the Design Master. The difference between a replica of a database and a copy made with the Back Up Database command is that a replicated copy of a database can be synchronized with the Design Master. To continue with the previous example, the sales representative can enter orders from customers while on the road and then synchronize the replica copy with the Design Master when he or she returns to the office.

In BRIEF

Back Up a Database
1. Open database file.
2. Click File, Back Up Database.
3. If necessary, change file name and location in Save Backup As dialog box.
4. Click Save.

FEATURES SUMMARY

Feature	Button	Menu	Keyboard
Add records	▶	Insert, New Record	Ctrl + +
Back Up Database		File, Back Up Database; or, Tools, Database Utilities, Back Up Database	
Column width		Format, Column Width	
Compact and repair		Tools, Database Utilities, Compact and Repair Database	
Delete records	✗	Edit, Delete Record	
Find	🔍	Edit, Find	Ctrl + F
Help	Type a question for help	Help, Microsoft Office Access Help	F1
Page Setup		File, Page Setup	
Print	🖨	File, Print	Ctrl + P
Print Preview	🔍	File, Print Preview	
Sort Ascending	A↓Z	Records, Sort, Sort Ascending	
Sort Descending	Z↓A	Records, Sort, Sort Descending	

PROCEDURES CHECK

Completion: The Access screen in Figure A1.4 contains numbers pointing to elements of the Datasheet window. Identify the element that corresponds with the number in the screen.

Horizontal scroll box   Office Assistant   Record Selector bar
Maximize   Close   Table Title bar
Field names   Active Record   New Record
Record Navigation bar   Scroll arrow   Minimize

1. _____   5. _____

2. _____   6. _____

3. _____   7. _____

4. _____   8. _____

FIGURE A1.4 Access Table

	Name	Street Address1	Street Address2	City	Province	Postal Code	Telephone
▶	EastCoast Cine	62 Mountbatten Driv		St.John's	NF	A1A 3X9	709-555-8349
	Millennium Movi	4126 Yonge Street	Suite 302	Toronto	ON	M2P 2B8	416-555-9335
	MountainView M	5417 RoyalMount A		Montreal	PQ	H4P 1H8	514-555-3584
	New Age Movie:	73 Killarney Road		Moncton	NB	E1B 2Z9	506-555-8376
	Northern Reach	P. O. Box 34		Yellowknife	NW	X1A 2N9	867-555-6314
	Northern Stars I	811 Cook Street		Whitehorse	YK	Y1A 2S4	867-555-6598
	Olypmic Cinem:	P. O. Box 1439	188 Riverbrook R	Calgary	AB	T2C 3P7	403-651-4587
	Plains Cinema I	P. O. Box 209	46 Prospect Plac	Regina	SK	S4S 5Y9	306-555-1247
	Riverview Cinen	1011-848 Sheppard		Winnipeg	MB	R2P 0N6	204-555-6538
	Seaboard Movie	P. O. Box 1005	696 Colby Drive	Dartmouth	NS	B2V 1Y8	902-555-3948
	Waterdown Cine	575 Notre Dame Str		Summerside	PE	C1N 1T8	902-555-8374
	West Coast Mo	P. O. Box 298	7348 Granville Dr	Vancouver	BC	V6Y 1N9	604-555-3548
*							

Record: ◄◄ ◄ 1 ► ►◄ ►* of 12

Identify the following buttons:

9. _____

10. _____

11. _____

12. _____

13. _____

14. _____

15. _____

SKILLS REVIEW

Activity 1: ADJUSTING COLUMN WIDTHS; FINDING AND EDITING RECORDS

1 Start Access and open the **WEEmployees1** database.
2 Open the Employee Dates and Salaries table.
3 Maximize the table.
4 Adjust all columns to Best Fit.
5 Find the record for Carl Zakowski and then change the birth date from *5/9/1967* to *12/12/1977*.
6 Find the record for Roman Deptulski and then change the salary from *$69,725.00* to *$71,320.00*. **(*Note: You do not need to type the dollar symbol, comma, and decimal.*)**
7 Find the record for Terry Yiu and then change the hire date from *4/12/2001* to *8/11/2001*.
8 Close the Employee Dates and Salaries table. Click Yes when prompted to save changes to the layout.

Activity 2: ADDING AND DELETING RECORDS

1 Open the Employee Dates and Salaries table.
2 Delete the record for Valerie Fistouris.
3 Delete the record for Edward Thurston.
4 Add the following employees to the table using Datasheet view:

1085	1090
Yousef J Armine	Maria D Quinte
11/19/1974	4/16/1973
3/14/2005	11/29/2005
European Distribution	Overseas Distribution
$42,796	$42,796

5 Close the table and then add the following record using the Employee Dates and Salaries form:

1095
Patrick J Kilarney
2/27/1981
12/12/2005
North American Distribution
$42,796

6 Close the Employee Dates and Salaries form.

Activity 3: SORTING; PREVIEWING; CHANGING PAGE ORIENTATION; PRINTING A DATASHEET

1 Open the Employee Dates and Salaries table.
2 Sort the table in ascending order by *Last Name*.
3 Sort the table in descending order by *Annual Salary*.
4 Sort the table in ascending order first by *Department* and then by *Last Name*.
5 Preview the table in the Print Preview window.
6 Change the orientation to landscape and then print the datasheet.
7 Close the Employee Dates and Salaries table without saving the changes to the design.

Activity 4: COMPACTING AND REPAIRING A DATABASE; BACKING UP A DATABASE

1 With the **WEEmployees1** database open, run the compact and repair database utility.
2 Turn on the Compact on Close feature in the Options dialog box.
3 Use the Back Up Database feature to create a copy of the database in the active drive and/or folder using today's date in the copied database file name.
4 Close the **WEEmployees1** database.
5 Open the backup copy of the **WEEmployees1** database created in Step 3.
6 Open the Employee Dates and Salaries table, view the table, and then close the datasheet.
7 Turn on the Compact on Close feature in the Options dialog box.
8 Close the backup copy of the **WEEmployees1** database.

PERFORMANCE PLUS

Assessment 1: ADJUSTING COLUMN WIDTH; FINDING AND EDITING RECORDS; USING PRINT PREVIEW

1 Jai Prasad, instructor in the Theatre Arts Division of Niagara Peninsula College, has been called out of town to attend a family matter. The grades for SPE266 have to be entered into the database by the end of today. Jai has provided you with the following grades:

Student Number	Final Grade
138-456-749	A+
111-785-156	C
378-159-746	B
348-876-486	D
274-658-986	B
349-874-658	C
255-158-498	C
221-689-478	A
314-745-856	B
325-841-469	A
321-487-659	F

2 Open the **NPCGrades1** database.
3 Open the SPE266 Grades table.
4 Adjust column widths so that all data is entirely visible.
5 Enter the grades provided in Step 1 in the related records.
6 Preview and then print the table.
7 Close the SPE266 Grades table. Click Yes when prompted to save changes.
8 Turn on the Compact on Close feature.
9 Close the **NPCGrades1** database.

Assessment 2: FINDING, ADDING, AND DELETING RECORDS

1 Dana Hirsch, manager of The Waterfront Bistro, has ordered three new inventory items and decided to discontinue three others. Dana has asked you to update the inventory database.
2 Open the **WBInventory1** database.
3 Open the Inventory List table.
4 Locate and then delete the inventory items *Pita Wraps; Tuna;* and *Lake Erie Perch.*
5 Add the following new records to the Inventory List table.

Item No	Item	Unit	Supplier Code
051	Atlantic Scallops	case	9
052	Lake Trout	case	9
053	Panini Rolls	flat	1

6 Adjust column widths so that all data is entirely visible.
7 Preview the table.
8 Adjust the top and bottom margin settings until all of the records will print on one page and then print the table.
9 Close the Inventory List table. Click Yes when prompted to save changes.
10 Turn on the Compact on Close feature.
11 Close the **WBInventory1** database.

Assessment 3: FINDING, SORTING, AND DELETING RECORDS; CHANGING ROW HEIGHT

1 You are the assistant to Bobbie Sinclair, business manager of Performance Threads. You have just been informed that several costumes in the rental inventory have been destroyed in a fire at a site location. These costumes will have to be written off since the insurance policy does not cover them when they are out on rental. After updating the costume inventory, you will print two reports.
2 Open the **PTCostumeInventory1** database.
3 Open the Costume Inventory table.
4 Locate and then delete the records for the following costumes that were destroyed in a fire at a Shakespearean festival:

Macbeth   Lady Macbeth   Hamlet   Othello   King Lear   Richard III

5 Sort the table in ascending order by *Character.*

6 Preview and then print the table.
7 Sort the table in ascending order first by *Date Out*, then by *Date In*, and then by *Character*.
8 Increase the height of the rows by approximately one-half their current height.
9 Save the changes to the design of the table.
10 Preview and then print the table.
11 Close the Costume Inventory table.
12 Turn on the Compact on Close feature.
13 Close the **PTCostumeInventory1** database.

Assessment 4: BACKING UP A DATABASE

1 You have been reading articles on disaster recovery planning in a computer-related periodical. Cal Rubine, chair of the Theatre Arts Division of Niagara Peninsula College, has advised you that the department does not currently have an up-to-date recovery plan for the information systems and has asked you to begin researching best practices. In the meantime you decide that the grades database needs to be backed up immediately.
2 Open the **NPCGrades1** database.
3 Create a backup copy of the database in the current drive and/or folder with today's date appended to the end of the file name.
4 Close the **NPCGrades1** database.
5 Open the backup copy of the **NPCGrades1** database.
6 Open and view each table to ensure the data was copied.
7 Turn on the Compact on Close feature.
8 Close the backup copy of the **NPCGrades1** database.

Assessment 5: FINDING INFORMATION ON DESIGNING A DATABASE

1 Use Access's Help feature to find information on the steps involved in designing a database.
2 The Help window for *About designing a database* lists several basic steps that should be followed when designing a database. Read the information presented in the first four links.
3 Use Microsoft Word to create a memo to your instructor as follows:
   - Use one of the memo templates.
   - Include an opening paragraph describing the body of the memo.
   - List the basic steps to designing a database in a bulleted list.
   - Briefly describe the first four steps.
4 Save the memo in Word and name it **AccessS1-P1Memo**.
5 Print and close **AccessS1-P1Memo** and then exit Word.

Assessment 6: CREATING A JOB SEARCH COMPANY DATABASE

1 You are starting to plan ahead for your job search after graduation. You have decided to start maintaining a database of company information in Access.

2 Search the Internet for company names, addresses, telephone numbers, and fax numbers for at least eight companies in your field of study. Include at least four companies that are out of state or out of province.

3 Open the **JobSearch1** database.

4 Open the Company Information table.

5 Enter at least eight records for the companies you researched on the Internet.

6 Adjust column widths as necessary.

7 Sort the records in ascending order by the *Company Name* field.

8 Preview the table. Change Page Setup options so that the entire table will fit on one page and then print the table.

9 Close the Company Information table.

10 Turn on the Compact on Close feature.

11 Close the **JobSearch1** database.

Creating Tables and Relationships

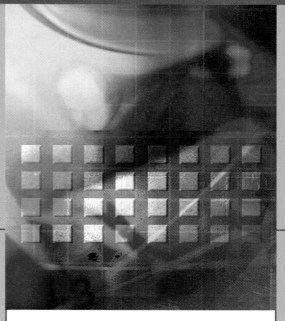

Tables in a database file are the basis upon which all other objects are built. A table can be created in three ways: using Design view, using the Table Wizard, or by entering data in a blank datasheet. When a common field exists in two or more tables, the tables can be joined to create a relationship. A relationship allows the user to extract data from multiple tables as if they were one. In this section you will learn the skills and complete the projects described here.

Note: Before beginning this section, delete any existing databases on your disk and copy each database as needed. Remember to remove the read-only attribute from each database after copying. If necessary, refer to page 1 for instructions on how to remove the read-only attribute. If necessary, check with your instructor before deleting any database files.

Skills

- Create a table in Design view
- Set the primary key for a table
- Limit the number of characters allowed in a field
- Enter a default value to display in a field
- Verify data entry using a Validation Rule property
- Restrict data entered into a field using an Input Mask property
- Set the Format property to control how data is displayed after it has been entered
- Confine data to a list of values using a *Lookup* field
- Enter data into a field by looking up data in another table
- Create a table using the Table Wizard
- Format a datasheet
- Create a one-to-many relationship between two tables
- Enforce referential integrity
- Create a one-to-one relationship between two tables
- Modify table structure by deleting fields
- Display records in a subdatasheet

Projects

Create and modify tables to store employee benefit information, employee addresses, employee review and training activities, and expenses; format a datasheet; create relationships between a Vendors and a Purchases table, an Employees and a Benefits table, an Employee and a Dates and Salaries table, and an Employees and an Expenses table; view records from a related table in a subdatasheet.

Create a table to store student grades for a course in the Theatre Arts Division.

Modify and correct field properties in the Costume Inventory table to improve the design.

Create a new database from scratch to track employee expense claims.

Create a Suppliers table in the Inventory database and create a relationship between the Suppliers table and the Inventory List table.

2.1 Creating a Table in Design View

Creating a new table in Design view involves the following steps: entering field names, assigning a data type to each field, entering field descriptions, modifying properties for the field, designating the primary key, and naming the table object. All of the preceding steps are part of a process referred to as "defining the table structure." Fields comprise the *structure* of a table. Once the structure has been created, records can be entered into the table in Datasheet view.

PROJECT: Rhonda Trask, human resources manager of Worldwide Enterprises, has asked you to review the employee benefit plan files and enter the information in a new table in the WEEmployees2 database.

STEPS

1 Open **WEEmployees2**.

2 With Tables already selected on the Objects bar, double-click *Create table in Design view*.

Tables is already selected on the Objects bar.

> This opens the Table1 : Table window, where the structure of the table is defined. Each row in the top section represents one field in the table.

3 With the insertion point already positioned in the *Field Name* column in the first row, type **Emp No** and then press Enter or Tab to move to the next column.

> The message at the right side of the *Field Properties* section changes at each column to provide information on the current option (see Figure A2.1).

PROBLEM

Do not type additional characters—field names can contain letters, numbers, and some symbols. Periods (.), commas (,), exclamation points (!), or square brackets ([]) are not accepted in a field name.

FIGURE A2.1 Field Properties Option Message

Field Properties

The data type determines the kind of values that users can store in the field. Press F1 for help on data types.

Message changes at each column to provide help on the current item.

4 With *Text* already entered in the *Data Type* column, press Enter or Tab to move to the next column.

> Table A2.1 on page 37 provides a list and brief description of the available data types. The *Emp No* field will contain numbers; however, leave the data type defined as Text since no calculations will be performed with employee numbers.

5 Type **Enter the four-digit employee number** in the *Description* column and then press Enter to move to the second row.

> Entering information in the *Description* column is optional. The *Description* text appears in the Status bar when the user is adding records in Datasheet view.

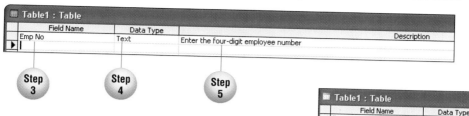

6 Type **Pension Plan** in the *Field Name* column in the second field row and then press Enter.

7 Click the down-pointing arrow at the right of the *Data Type* option box, click *Yes/No* in the drop-down list, and then press Enter.

> See Table A2.1 on page 37 for a description of the Yes/No data type.

8 Type **Click or press the spacebar for Yes; leave empty for No** and then press Enter.

9 Enter the remaining field names, data types, and descriptions as shown in Figure A2.2. Click the down-pointing arrow at the right of the *Data Type* option box to select data types other than Text.

FIGURE A2.2 Table Entries

Field Name	Data Type	Description
Emp No	Text	Enter the four-digit employee number
Pension Plan	Yes/No	Click or press the spacebar for Yes; leave empty for No
Dental Plan	Yes/No	Click or press the spacebar for Yes; leave empty for No
Premium Health	Yes/No	Click or press the spacebar for Yes; leave empty for No
Dependents	Number	Type the number of dependents related to this employee
Life Insurance	Currency	Type the amount of life insurance benefit for this employee

10 Click the insertion point in any character in the *Emp No* field row.

> This moves the field selector (right-pointing arrow) to the *Emp No* field. In Step 11, you will designate *Emp No* as the primary key field for the table.

11 Click the Primary Key button [icon] on the Table Design toolbar.

> A key icon will appear in the field selector bar to the left of *Emp No*, indicating the field is the primary key for the table. The primary key is the field that will contain unique data for each record in the table. In addition, Access automatically sorts the table data by the primary key field when the table is opened.

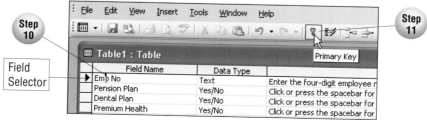

(continued)

(12) Click the Save button on the Table Design toolbar.

> The Save As dialog box opens.

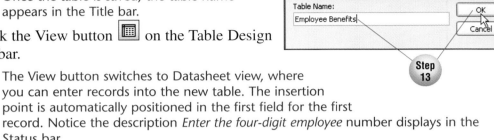

Key icon indicates the field has been defined as the primary key.

(13) Type **Employee Benefits** in the *Table Name* text box and then press Enter or click OK.

> Once the table is saved, the table name appears in the Title bar.

(14) Click the View button ▦ on the Table Design toolbar.

> The View button switches to Datasheet view, where you can enter records into the new table. The insertion point is automatically positioned in the first field for the first record. Notice the description *Enter the four-digit employee* number displays in the Status bar.

(15) Type **1001** and then press Enter.

(16) Press the spacebar or click the box in the *Pension Plan* column and then press Enter.

> A check mark in the box indicates Yes, True, or On in a *Yes/No* field.

(17) Press Enter to leave the *Dental Plan* box empty and move to the next column.

> An empty box indicates No, False, or Off in a *Yes/No* field.

(18) Press the spacebar or click the box in the *Premium Health* column and then press Enter.

(19) Type **2** in the *Dependents* column and then press Enter.

(20) Type **150000** in the *Life Insurance* column and then press Enter.

> The dollar symbol, comma in the thousands, decimal point, and two zeros are automatically inserted in the field since the data type was defined as Currency.

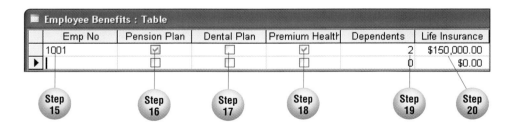

(21) Type the following two records in the datasheet:

Emp No	1005	*Emp No*	1010
Pension Plan	Yes	*Pension Plan*	Yes
Dental Plan	Yes	*Dental Plan*	No
Premium Health	Yes	*Premium Health*	No
Dependents	3	*Dependents*	0
Life Insurance	175000	*Life Insurance*	100000

(22) Close the Employee Benefits table.

Data Type	Description
Text	Alphanumeric data up to 255 characters in length, such as a name or address. Fields that will contain numbers that will not be used in calculations, such as a student number or telephone number, should be defined as Text.
Memo	Alphanumeric data up to 64,000 characters in length.
Number	Positive and/or negative values that can be used in mathematical operations. Do not use for values that will calculate monetary amounts (see Currency).
Date/Time	Stores dates and times. Use this format to ensure dates and times are sorted properly. Access displays an error message if an invalid date is entered in a Date/Time data field.
Currency	Values that involve money. Access will not round off during calculations.
AutoNumber	Access will automatically number each record sequentially (incrementing by 1) when you begin typing a new record. If you do not define a primary key and you respond Yes for Access to define one for you when you save the table, Access creates an AutoNumber field.
Yes/No	Data in the field will be either Yes or No, True or False, On or Off.
OLE Object	Used to embed or link objects created in other Office applications (such as Microsoft Word or Microsoft Excel) to an Access table.
Hyperlink	Field that will store a hyperlink such as a URL.
Lookup Wizard	Starts the Lookup Wizard, which creates a data type based on the values selected during the wizard steps. The Lookup Wizard can be used to enter data in the field from another existing table or display a list of values in a drop-down list for the user to choose from.

In Addition

Creating a Table by Adding Records

A new table can be created by typing directly into a blank datasheet. Double-click *Create table by entering data* in the Database window. Fields are initially named *Field1, Field2,* and so on. Access assigns data types and formats for each field based on the entry in each column when you save the datasheet. Rename a field by double-clicking the column header (e.g. *Field1*), typing a new name, and then pressing Enter. Open the table in Design view to edit the fields.

IN BRIEF

Create a Table in Design View
1 Open database or create a new database.
2 Click Tables on Objects bar.
3 Double-click *Create table in Design view.*
4 Type field names, descriptions, and assign data types in Table dialog box.
5 Assign primary key field.
6 Click Save button.
7 Type name for table and press Enter.

ACCESS

2.2 Modifying Field Size and Default Value Properties

Field properties are a set of characteristics used to control how the field displays or how the field interacts with data. For example, the **Field Size** property can be used to limit the number of characters that are allowed in a field entry. A field size of 6 for a customer number field would prevent customer numbers longer than 6 characters from being stored in a record. The **Default Value** property is useful if most records will contain the same value. The contents of the Default Value property appear in the field automatically when a new record is added to the table. The user has the option of accepting the default value by pressing Enter or Tab at the field, or of overwriting the default by typing a different value.

PROJECT: Worldwide Enterprises uses a four-digit employee number. You will modify the *Emp No* Field Size property to set the maximum number of characters to 4. Since most employees opt into the Pension Plan, you will set the default value for the *Pension Plan* field to *Yes*.

S T E P S

1. With **WEEmployees2** open, right-click the Employee Benefits table name in the WEEmployees2 : Database window and then click Design View at the shortcut menu.

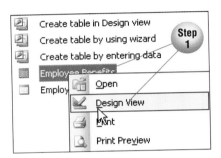

2. With *Emp No* already selected in the *Field Name* column, double-click the value *50* that appears in the *Field Size* property box in the *Field Properties* section and then type **4**.

   Alternatively, click in the *Field Size* property box to activate the insertion point, delete 50, and then type **4**.

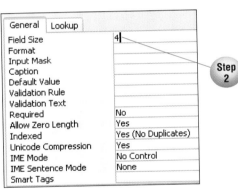

3. Click in the *Pension Plan* row in the *Field Name* column to display the Pension Plan properties in the *Field Properties* section.

   Notice the list of available properties has changed. The items displayed in the *Field Properties* section in Table Design View change to reflect the options for the active field's data type. Since *Pension Plan* is a Yes/No field, the list of properties shown is different than those for *Emp No*, which is a Text field.

4. Click in the *Default Value* property box and then type **Yes**.

5. Click the Save button on the Table Design toolbar.

   Since the field size for a field was changed *after* data has been entered into the table, Access displays a warning message that some data may be lost since the field size is now shorter.

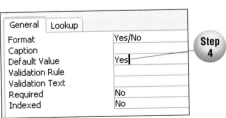

6 Click Yes to instruct Access to continue.

> If a large amount of data was entered into a table before the field size was changed, make a backup of the file before changing the Field Size property. Check for errors by comparing the field data in the backup copy with the data in the working copy after Access saves the table.

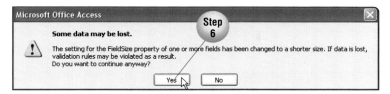

7 Click the View button 🔲 to switch to Datasheet view.

> Notice the *Pension Plan* column in the blank row at the bottom of the datasheet contains a check mark since the default value is now *Yes*.

8 Type 1020111 in the *Emp No* field in the blank row at the bottom of the datasheet and then press Enter.

> A beep will sound each time you type a character that extends beyond the field size of 4 and Access does not display any characters in the field after the fourth character typed.

9 Press Enter to move to the *Pension Plan* field and then press Enter again to accept the default value of Yes.

Emp No	Pension Plan	Dental Plan	Premium Health	Dependents	Life Insurance
1001	☑	☐	☑	2	$150,000.00
1005	☑	☑	☑	3	$175,000.00
1010	☑	☐	☐	0	$100,000.00
1020	☑	☐	☐	0	$100,000.00

Step 8   Step 9   Step 10

10 Enter the following data in the remaining fields:

Dental Plan	No	*Dependents*	0
Premium Health	No	*Life Insurance*	100000

11 Close the Employee Benefits table.

In Addition

Propagating Field Properties

The Property Update Options button appears whenever changes are made to an existing field. Click the button to automatically apply the same change to other objects within the database that are bound to the same field. Clicking the option to update the property everywhere the field is used displays a dialog box in which you can choose the objects that you want to inherit the change.

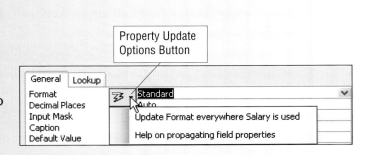

Property Update Options Button

2.3 Validating Field Entries

The **Validation Rule** property can be used to enter a statement containing a conditional test that is checked each time data is entered into a field. When data is entered that fails to satisfy the conditional test, Access does not accept the entry and displays an error message. For example, suppose a customer number must be within a certain range of values. By entering a conditional statement in the validation rule property that checks each entry against the acceptable range, you can reduce errors and ensure that only valid numbers are stored in the customer number field. Enter in the **Validation Text** property the content of the error message that you want the user to see.

PROJECT: Worldwide Enterprises offers life insurance benefits up to a maximum of $199,999. You will add a validation rule and enter an error message in the validation text for the *Life Insurance* field in the Employee Benefits table to ensure no benefit exceeds this maximum.

S T E P S

1 **WEEmployees2** open and the Employee Benefits table selected in the Database window, click the Design button on the Database window toolbar.

2 Click in the *Life Insurance* field row.

> The properties for the *Life Insurance* field display in the *Field Properties* section.

3 Click in the *Validation Rule* property box, type **<200000**, and then press Enter.

> Pressing Enter after typing the validation rule moves the insertion point to the *Validation Text* property box.

4 Type **Enter a value that is less that $200,000** and then press Enter.

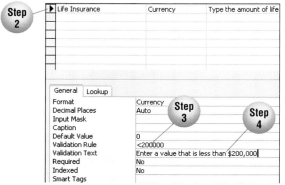

5 Click the Save button.

> Since a validation rule has been created *after* data has been entered into the table, Access displays a warning message that some data may not be valid.

6 Click Yes to instruct Access to test the data with the new rules.

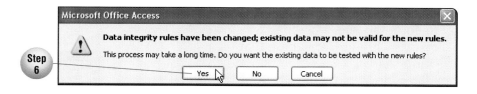

⑦ Click the View button to switch to Datasheet view.

⑧ Add the following record to the table:

Emp No	**1015**
Pension Plan	Yes
Dental Plan	Yes
Premium Health	Yes
Dependents	2
Life Insurance	**210000**

When you enter *210000* into the *Life Insurance field* and press Enter or Tab, Access displays an error message. The text in the error message is the text you entered in the *Validation Text* property box.

⑨ Click OK at the Microsoft Office Access error message.

⑩ Backspace to delete *210000*, type **199999**, and then press Enter.

⑪ Close the Employee Benefits table.

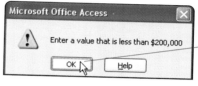

Step 9

Step 8

Step 10

Emp No	Pension Plan	Dental Plan	Premium Health	Dependents	Life Insurance
1001	☑	☐	☑	2	$150,000.00
1005	☑	☑	☑	3	$175,000.00
1010	☑	☐	☐	0	$100,000.00
1020	☑	☐	☐	0	$100,000.00
1015	☑	☑	☑	2	$199,999.00

In Addition

Other Validation Rule Examples

Validation rules should be created whenever possible to avoid data entry errors. The examples below illustrate various ways to use the validation rule to verify data.

Field Name	Validation Rule	Data Check
Customer No	>1000 And <1100	Limits customer numbers to 1001 through 1099
Credit Limit	<=5000	Restricts credit limits to values of 5000 or less
State	"CA"	Only the state of California is accepted
Country	"CA" Or "US"	Only the United States or Canada is accepted
Order Qty	>=25	Quantity ordered must be a minimum of 25

IN BRIEF

Create a Validation Rule

1 Open the table in Design view.
2 Click in field row to select field.
3 Click in *Validation Rule* property box.
4 Type conditional statement.
5 Click in *Validation Text* property box.
6 Type error message.
7 Click Save.

2.4 Creating Input Masks; Formatting Fields

An *input mask* displays a pattern in the datasheet or form indicating how data is to be entered into the field. For example, an input mask in a telephone number field that displays (___)___-____ indicates to the user that the three-digit area code is to be entered in front of all telephone numbers. Input masks ensure that data is entered consistently in tables. In addition to specifying the position and amount of characters in a field you can create masks that restrict the data entered to digits, letters, or characters, and whether or not each digit, letter, or character is required or optional. Access provides the Input Mask Wizard to assist with creating the entry

in the *Input Mask* property box.

The **Format** property controls how the data is *displayed* in the field *after* it has been entered.

PROJECT: You will create a new field in the Employee Benefits table for Pension Plan eligibility dates and include an input mask in the field indicating dates should be entered as *dd-mmm-yy*. To avoid confusion you will format the field to display the date in the same manner in which it was entered. Next, you will create an input mask for the *Emp No* field making all four characters required digits.

STEPS

1. With **WEEmployees2** open, open the Employee Benefits table in Design view.

2. Click in the *Field Name* column in the blank row below *Life Insurance*, type **Pension Eligibility**, and then press Enter.

3. Change the data type to *Date/Time* and then press Enter.

4. Type **Type date employee is eligible for pension plan in the format dd-mmm-yy (example: 12-Dec-05)**.

5. Click Save.

6. Click in the *Input Mask* property box in the *Field Properties* section and then click the Build button [...].

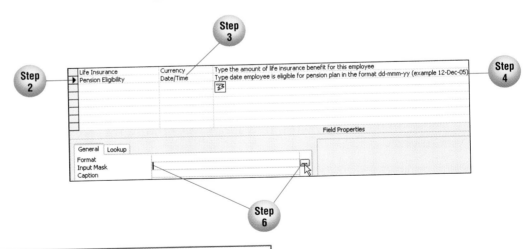

PROBLEM?

Click Yes if a message displays informing you the feature is not installed and asking if you want to install it now. If necessary, check with your instructor.

7 Click *Medium Date* in the first Input Mask Wizard dialog box and then click Next.

> The input masks that display in the list in the first dialog box are dependent on the data type for the field for which you are creating an input mask.

8 Click Next in the second Input Mask Wizard dialog box.

> This dialog box displays the input mask code in the *Input Mask* text box and sets the placeholder character that will display in the field. The default placeholder is the underscore character. Other available placeholder characters are #, @, and !. See In Addition on page 45 for an explanation of the symbols used in the *Input Mask* text box to create the medium date.

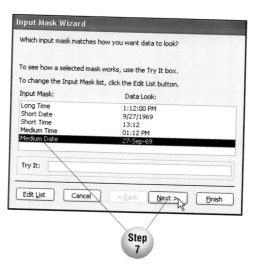

Step 7

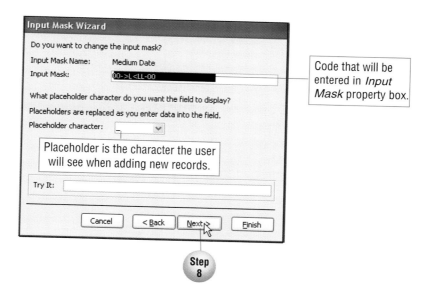

Code that will be entered in *Input Mask* property box.

Placeholder is the character the user will see when adding new records.

Step 8

9 Click Finish at the last Input Mask Wizard dialog box to complete the entry *00->L<LL-00;0;_* in the *Input Mask* property box.

10 Click the Save button and then click the View button to switch to Datasheet view.

11 Maximize the Employee Benefits table if it is not already maximized.

Step 9

(continued)

(12) Click in the *Pension Eligibility* column for the first row in the datasheet.

The input mask __-___-__ appears in the field.

PROBLEM **?**

Input mask not visible in the field? Start to type the date in Step 13. As soon as you type the first character in the field, the mask will appear.

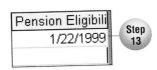

Pension Eligibili
1/22/1999

Step 13

(13) Type **22-jan-99** and then press the Down Arrow key.

The date *1/22/1999* displays in the field. By default, dates are displayed in the format *m/dd/yyyy*. To avoid confusion, in Steps 14–17 you will format the field to display the date in the same format that the input mask accepts the data.

(14) Click the View button 🔲 to switch to Design view.

The View button toggles between Datasheet view and Design view depending on which view is active.

(15) With *Pension Eligibility* as the selected field, click in the *Format* property box, click the down-pointing arrow that appears, and then click *Medium Date* in the drop-down list.

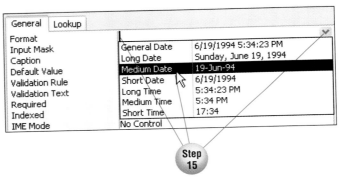

General	Lookup
Format	
Input Mask	General Date	6/19/1994 5:34:23 PM
Caption	Long Date	Sunday, June 19, 1994
Default Value	Medium Date	19-Jun-94
Validation Rule	Short Date	6/19/1994
Validation Text	Long Time	5:34:23 PM
Required	Medium Time	5:34 PM
Indexed	Short Time	17:34
IME Mode	No Control	

Step 15

(16) Click Save and then click View to switch to Datasheet view.

Notice the first Pension Eligibility date now displays as *22-Jan-99* instead of *1/22/1999*.

(17) Click in the *Pension Eligibility* column in the second row in the datasheet and type **15feb99** and then press the Down Arrow key.

Notice the hyphens are not required to enter the date. In the next step you try to enter a date that does not conform to the input mask to test how Access restricts the entry.

(18) Type **07/09/99** in the third row of the *Pension Eligibility* column.

A beep sounds as you type every character after *07*. The only characters Access has accepted in the field are *07* since the input mask requires that the next segment of the date be entered as letters in the format *mmm*. Notice the insertion point remains in the month section of the date.

(19) Press Backspace twice to delete *07*, type **30jul99**, and then press Enter.

The difference between the input mask and the Format properties is that the input mask *restricts* the data that is entered into the field, while the Format property controls the *display* of the data after it is accepted into the field.

20 Best Fit the column width of the *Pension Eligibility* column.

In the next steps you will add an input mask to the *Emp No* field by typing input mask code directly into the field property box.

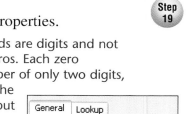

Life Insurance	Pension Eligibility
$150,000.00	22-Jan-99
$175,000.00	15-Feb-99
$100,000.00	30-Jul-99
$199,999.00	
$100,000.00	

Step 20
Step 17
Step 19

21 Click the View button to switch to Design view.

22 Click in the *Emp No* field row to display the related field properties.

To ensure that all employee numbers entered into the records are digits and not letters or symbols you will add the input mask using four zeros. Each zero represents a required digit. For example, an employee number of only two digits, such as *55*, would not be accepted. Refer to In Addition at the end of this topic for further explanation and examples of input mask code.

General	Lookup	
Field Size		4
Format	Step 23	
Input Mask		0000
Caption		

23 Click in the *Input Mask* property box and then type **0000**.

24 Click Save and then click View to switch to Datasheet view.

25 Click in the blank row at the bottom of the *Emp No* column and then type **abcd**.

A beep will sound as you type each letter since the input mask in the field requires that only digits zero through nine are allowed.

26 Press ESC twice to abort the new record and then close the Employee Benefits table.

In Addition

Input Mask Codes

The Input Mask Wizard is available only for fields with a data type set to Text or Date/Time. For fields such as Number or Currency you have to manually enter the mask. Following is a list of valid codes for an input mask and how each is used.

Use	To restrict data entry to
0	Digit, zero through nine, entry is required
9	Digit or space, entry is not required
L	Letter, A through Z, entry is required
?	Letter, A through Z, entry is not required
A	Letter or digit, entry is required
a	Letter or digit, entry is not required
&	Any character or space, entry is required
C	Any character or space, entry is not required
>	All characters following are converted to uppercase
<	All characters following are converted to lowercase

The mask created by the wizard in the *Pension Eligibility* field is broken down as *00-* (two required digits for the day) *>L<LL-* (three required letters for the month with the first letter uppercase and the remaining two letters lowercase) *00* (two required digits for the year). An input mask can have up to three sections separated by semicolons. In the second section *;0* zero instructs Access to store literal characters used in the field (hyphens between dates). The third section *;_* is the placeholder character.

IN BRIEF

Use Input Mask Wizard
1 Open table in Design view.
2 Enter field name, data type, and description.
3 Click Save.
4 Click in *Input Mask* property box.
5 Click Build button.
6 Click input mask you want to create.
7 Click Next.
8 Select placeholder character.
9 Click Next.
10 Click Next to store data without symbols.
11 Click Finish at last wizard dialog box.
12 Click Save.

2.5 Creating Lookup Fields

Create a *Lookup* field when you want to restrict the data entered into the field to a list of values from an existing table, or a list of values that you enter in the wizard dialog box. The Lookup tab in the *Field Properties* section in Table Design view contains the options used to create a *Lookup* field. Access includes the Lookup Wizard, which facilitates entering the option settings.

PROJECT: You will use the *Lookup* Wizard to create a new field in the Employee Benefits table that will display a drop-down list of vacation entitlements. Since the list will contain the only available vacation periods offered by Worldwide Enterprises you will further restrict the field by preventing items other than those in the list from being entered into the field.

S T E P S

1. With **WEEmployees2** open, open the Employee Benefits table in Design view.

2. Click in the *Field Name* column in the blank row below *Pension Eligibility*, type **Vacation**, and then press Enter.

3. Click the down-pointing arrow at the right of the *Data Type* option box and then click *Lookup Wizard* from the drop-down list.

4. Click *I will type in the values that I want* and then click Next.

5. Click in the blank row below *Col1*, type **1 week**, and then press Tab.

> **PROBLEM**
>
> If you press Enter by mistake and find yourself at the next step in the Lookup Wizard, click Back to return to the previous dialog box.

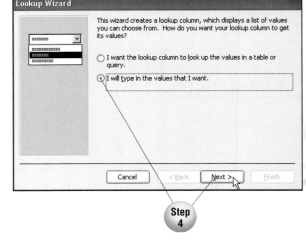

6. Type **2 weeks** and then press Tab.

7. Type **3 weeks** and then press Tab.

8. Type **4 weeks** and then click Next.

9. Click Finish in the last Lookup Wizard dialog box to accept the default label *Vacation*. No entry is required in the *Description* column.

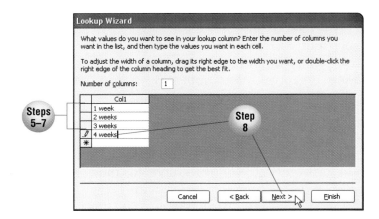

10 Click the Lookup tab in the *Field Properties* section and view the entries made to each option by the Lookup Wizard.

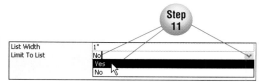

Changes made to Lookup options through Lookup Wizard.

General	Lookup
Display Control	Combo Box
Row Source Type	Value List
Row Source	"1 week";"2 weeks";"3 weeks";"4 weeks"
Bound Column	1
Column Count	1
Column Heads	No
Column Widths	1"
List Rows	8
List Width	1"
Limit To List	No

Step 10

11 Click in the *Limit To List* property box, click the down-pointing arrow that appears, and then click *Yes*.

By changing the *Limit To List* property to *Yes* you are further restricting the field to only those items in the drop-down list. If a user attempts to type an entry other than 1 week, 2 weeks, 3 weeks, or 4 weeks, Access will display an error message and not store the data.

Step 11

List Width	1"
Limit To List	No
	Yes
	No

12 Click Save and then click View to switch to Datasheet view.

13 Click in the *Vacation* column in the first row in the datasheet, click the down-pointing arrow that appears, and then click *4 weeks* from the drop-down list.

Pension Eligibility	Vacation
22-Jan-99	
15-Feb-99	1 week
30-Jul-99	2 weeks
	3 weeks
	4 weeks

Step 13

14 Press the Down Arrow key to move to the *Vacation* column in the second row, type **6 weeks**, and then press Enter.

15 Click OK at the message that displays informing you that the text entered is not an item in the list, and then click *3 weeks* from the drop-down list.

16 Display the datasheet in Print Preview. Change the page orientation to landscape and then print the datasheet.

17 Close the Print Preview window and then close the Employee Benefits table.

In Addition

Looking Up Data from Another Table

In this topic the items in the drop-down list were created by typing them in rows at the second Lookup Wizard dialog box. Items in the drop-down list can also be generated by specifying an existing field in another table or query. To do this, click Next at the first Lookup Wizard dialog box to accept the default setting *I want the lookup column to look up values in a table or query*. At the second Lookup Wizard dialog box, select the table or query name that contains the field you want to use. Specify the field to be used to generate the list in the third dialog box, and then set the column width at the preview of the list in the fourth dialog box. Creating field entries using this method ensures that data is consistent between tables and eliminates duplicate keying of information, which can lead to data errors.

IN BRIEF

Create a List of Values Using Lookup Wizard
1 Open table in Design view.
2 Type field name and press Enter.
3 Click *Data Type* arrow.
4 Click *Lookup Wizard*.
5 Click *I will type in the values that I want* and click Next.
6 Type field values in *Col1* column and click Next.
7 Click Finish in last wizard dialog box.
8 Click Save.

2.6 Creating a Table Using the Table Wizard

Creating a table using the Table Wizard involves choosing the type of table from a list of sample tables and then selecting fields from the sample field list. Access creates the field names and assigns data types based on the samples. Once created, the fields in the table can be edited in Design view.

PROJECT: You will use the Table Wizard to create a new table that will store employee addresses.

S T E P S

1. With **WEEmployees2** open, double-click *Create table by using wizard.*

2. Click *Employees* in the *Sample Tables* list box.

3. Click *EmployeeNumber* in the *Sample Fields* list box and then click the Add Field button **>** to the right of the *Sample Fields* list box.

    This inserts the *EmployeeNumber* field in the *Fields in my new table* list box and moves the selected field in the *Sample Fields* list box to the next field after *EmployeeNumber,* which is *NationalEmplNumber.*

4. Double-click *FirstName* in the *Sample Fields* list box.

    Double-clicking a field name in the *Sample Fields* list box is another method of adding the field in the *Fields in my new table* list box.

5. Double-click the following field names in the *Sample Fields* list box.

    MiddleName
    LastName
    Address
    City
    StateOrProvince
    PostalCode

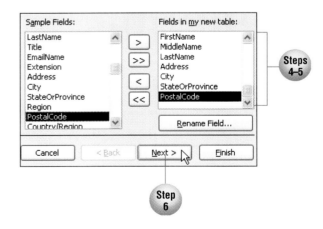

> **PROBLEM** ? Cannot locate some of the field names? You will need to scroll down the *Sample Fields* list box.

6. Click Next.

7. Click Next at the second Table Wizard dialog box to accept the table name *Employees* and *Yes, set a primary key for me.*

⑧ Click Next at the third Table Wizard dialog box to accept *not related to 'Employee Benefits'* in the *My new 'Employees' table is* list box since at this time we do not want to create a relationship between the new table and either of the two existing tables in the database.

⑨ Click *Modify the table design* at the fourth Table Wizard dialog box, and then click Finish.

> The new Employees table appears in the Design view window. When you elected to let Access set the primary key field, Access added the field *EmployeesID* to the table with the data type AutoNumber. An *AutoNumber* field automatically increments each field value by one each time a new record is added to the table. You decide this is a redundant field since each employee has a unique employee number. In Steps 10–13 you will delete the *EmployeesID* field and modify *EmployeeNumber* to make it the primary key field.

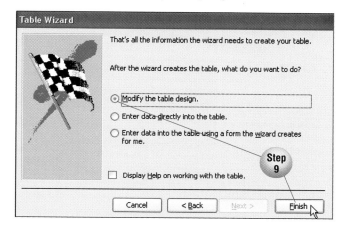

⑩ Click in the field selector bar next to *EmployeesID* and then click the Delete Rows button on the Table Design toolbar.

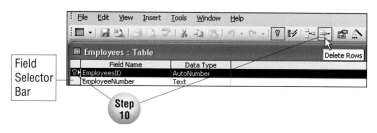

Field Selector Bar

⑪ Click Yes to confirm the deletion.

⑫ Make the following changes to the *EmployeeNumber* field:

Field Name	**Emp No**
Field Size	**4**
Input Mask	**0000**

⑬ Make *Emp No* the primary key field.

⑭ Click the Save button.

⑮ Close the Employees table.

IN **BRIEF**

Create a Table Using Wizard
1 Open database file.
2 Double-click *Create table by using wizard*.
3 Click type of table in *Sample Tables* list box.
4 Add fields from *Sample Fields* list box to *Fields in my new table* list box.
5 Click Next.
6 Choose table name and primary key and click Next.
7 Choose to enter data directly in table or edit table in Design view.
8 Click Finish.

2.7 Formatting the Datasheet

The appearance of the datasheet can be changed using options on the Format menu. The default font and color of text in Access tables is 10-point Arial black. The Datasheet Formatting dialog box contains options to change the cell effect from the default flat appearance to raised or sunken appearance and alter the colors of the datasheet background and gridlines. Gridlines can be set to display horizontal lines only, vertical lines only, or both horizontal and vertical. The border and line styles of the datasheet, gridlines, and column headers can be changed from solid lines to a variety of other line styles.

PROJECT: You will change the appearance of the Employees datasheet by changing the background color, gridline color, font, and by freezing the first four columns so that scrolling right will not cause the *Employee Number, FirstName, MiddleName,* and *LastName* columns to disappear.

STEPS

① With the **WEEmployees2** database open, open the Employees table.

② Add the following information into a new record for *Emp No* 1001 in the table:

> **Sam Lawrence Vestering**
> **287-1501 Broadway**
> **New York, NY 10110**

③ Adjust all of the column widths to Best Fit in the datasheet.

④ Click Format and then Datasheet.

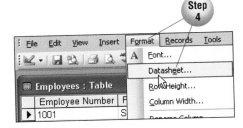

⑤ Click the down-pointing arrow at the right side of the *Background Color* option box and then click *Aqua* in the drop-down list.

⑥ Click the down-pointing arrow at the right of the *Gridline Color* option box, scroll up the list box, and then click *Dark Blue.*

> The *Sample* section of the Datasheet Formatting dialog box displays the datasheet with the new settings.

⑦ Click OK to close the Datasheet Formatting dialog box.

⑧ Click Format and then Font.

⑨ Scroll down the *Font* list box and then click *Tahoma.*

⑩ Click *12* in the *Size* list box and then click OK.

> Notice some columns have to be readjusted after increasing the font size to redisplay entire field values.

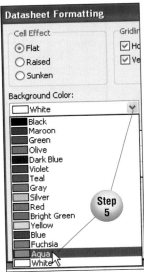

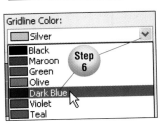

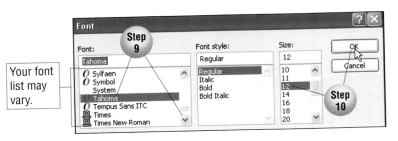

Your font list may vary.

⑪ Adjust all of the column widths to Best Fit.

⑫ Position the mouse pointer in the *Employee Number* column heading until the pointer changes to a downward-pointing black arrow, hold down the left mouse button, drag right until the *Employee Number, First Name, Middle Name,* and *Last Name* columns are selected, and then release the left mouse button.

⑬ Click Format and then Freeze Columns.

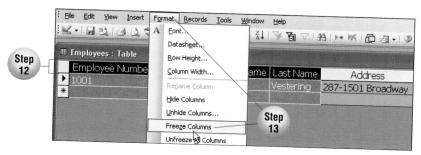

Step 12

Step 13

⑭ Click in any field to deselect the first four columns.

⑮ Select the *First Name, Middle Name,* and *Last Name* columns, click Format, click Column Width, type **20** in the *Column Width* text box, and then click OK.

⑯ Change the column width of the *Address* column to *30*.

⑰ Scroll right in the datasheet. Notice the first four columns remain fixed and do not disappear off the screen as you scroll.

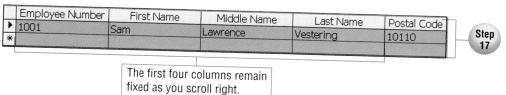

Step 17

The first four columns remain fixed as you scroll right.

⑱ Display the datasheet in Print Preview and then change the page orientation to landscape. *(**Note: Click Yes if you receive a message saying at least one column is too wide and data in the column will be cut off.**)*

⑲ Scroll the pages in Print Preview. Notice that the frozen columns, *Employee Number, First Name, Middle Name,* and *Last Name* repeat at the left edge of each page.

⑳ Close the Print Preview window, click Format and Unfreeze All Columns, and then change all column widths in the datasheet to Best Fit.

㉑ Display the datasheet in Print Preview. Change the left and right margins to 0.5 inch and then print the datasheet.

㉒ Close the Print Preview window and then close the Employees table. Click Yes when prompted to save changes to the layout of the table.

㉓ Close the **WEEmployees2** database.

IN BRIEF

Change Datasheet Formatting
1 Open table.
2 Click Format, Datasheet.
3 Change settings as desired.
4 Click OK.

Change Font
1 Open table.
2 Click Format, Font.
3 Change settings as desired.
4 Click OK.

Freeze Columns
1 Open table.
2 Select columns to remain fixed.
3 Click Format, Freeze Columns.

2.8 Creating a One-to-Many Relationship

Access is sometimes referred to as a *relational database management system*. A relational database is one in which relationships exist between tables, allowing two or more tables to be treated as if they were one when generating reports or looking up data. Joining one table to another using a field common to both tables creates a relationship. Access allows for three types of relationships: one-to-many, one-to-one, and many-to-many. In a relationship, one table is called the *primary* table and the other table in called the *related* table. In a one-to-many relationship, the common field value in the primary table is often the primary key field since only one record can exist for each unique entity. The related table can have more than one record for the corresponding field in the primary table.

PROJECT: You will create and print a one-to-many relationship between the Vendors table and the Purchases table in a database that is used to record purchase information.

S T E P S

1. Open **WEPurchases2**.

2. Open the Vendors table, look at the field names and data in the datasheet, and then close Vendors.

3. Open the Purchases table, look at the field names and data in the datasheet, and then close Purchases.

   Notice that the Purchases table has more than one record for the same vendor number since buying goods and services from the same vendor several times within a year is possible. You will create a *one-to-many* relationship between the Vendors table and the Purchases table. Vendors is the primary table in this relationship since only one record for each vendor will exist. Purchases is the related table—many records for the same vendor can exist.

4. Click the Relationships button 🖼 on the Database toolbar.

5. With *Purchases* already selected in the Show Table dialog box, click Add.

PROBLEM ❓

Show Table dialog box does not appear? Right-click in Relationships window and then click Show Table at the shortcut menu.

6. Click *Vendors* and then click Add.

7. Click Close to close the Show Table dialog box.

   A common field in two tables is the basis upon which the tables are joined. In the next step, you will drag the common field *Vendor_No* from the primary table (Vendors) to the related table (Purchases).

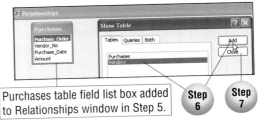

Purchases table field list box added to Relationships window in Step 5.

8. Position the mouse pointer over *Vendor_No* in the *Vendors* field list box, hold down the left mouse button, drag the pointer left to *Vendor_No* in the *Purchases* field list box, and then release the mouse button.

   The Edit Relationships dialog box appears when you release the mouse button.

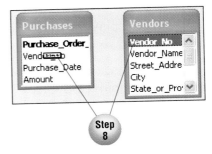

9 Notice *One-To-Many* displays in the *Relationship Type* box of the Edit Relationships dialog box.

> Access determined the relationship type based on the common field that was used to join the tables. In the primary table (Vendors), *Vendor_No* is the primary key while in the related table (Purchases) *Vendor_No* is not the primary key. In the Purchases table, the field *Vendor_No* is referred to as the **foreign key**. A foreign key is the field used to relate a table and refers to the primary key in the other table.

10 Click the *Enforce Referential Integrity* check box in the Edit Relationships dialog box and then click Create.

> **Referential integrity** means that Access will ensure that a record with the same vendor number already exists in the primary table (Vendors) when a new record is being added to the related table (Purchases). If no matching record exists, Access will display an error message.

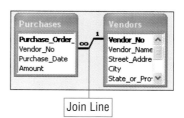

Join Line

11 Click the Save button.

> A black line (referred to as a **join line**) joins the two tables in the Relationships window. A *1* appears next to the primary table, Vendors, indicating the *one* side of the relationship and the infinity symbol ∞ appears next to the related table, Purchases, indicating the *many* side of the relationship.

12 Click File and then click Print Relationships.

13 Click the Print button on the Print Preview toolbar.

14 Click the Close button on the Relationships for WEPurchases2 title bar. Click No when prompted to save changes to the design of the report.

15 Click the Close button on the Relationships window title bar.

16 Open the Purchases table.

> In Steps 17–19 you will test referential integrity by attempting to add a record for a vendor that does not exist in the primary table.

17 Click the New Record button, type **6552** in the *Purchase_Order_No* column, and then press Enter.

18 Type **150** in the *Vendor_No* column and then press Enter.

19 Press Enter through the *Purchase_Date* and *Amount* fields to move to the next row.

> Access displays an error message indicating you cannot add or change a record because a related record is required in the Vendors table.

20 Click OK to close the message window.

21 Close the Purchases table. Click OK at the error message that appears for the second time. Click Yes at the second error message box to close the object and confirm that the data changes will be lost.

22 Close **WEPurchases2**.

2.9 Creating a One-to-One Relationship; Deleting Fields

A one-to-one relationship exists when both the primary table and the related table will contain only one record for the common field. For example, in the WEEmployees2 database that has been used throughout this section, the Employees table would contain only one record for each employee. The Employee Benefits table and the Employee Dates and Salaries table would also contain only one record for each employee. If two of these tables are joined on the common *Emp No* field, a one-to-one relationship would be created.

PROJECT: You will create two one-to-one relationships in the WEEmployees2 database and then delete fields in the Employee Dates and Salaries table that are duplicated in the Employees table.

STEPS

1 Open **WEEmployees2**.

2 Click Tools on the Menu bar and then click Relationships.

3 With *Employee Benefits* already selected in the Show Table dialog box, hold down Shift and then click *Employees*.

4 Click the Add button in the Show Table dialog box.

5 Click the Close button in the Show Table dialog box.

> A field list box for each table is added to the Relationships window. In the next steps you will move and resize the field list boxes to make it easier to create the relationships.

6 Position the mouse pointer on the Title bar for the *Employees* field list box, hold down the left mouse button, and then drag the field list box down below the first two tables as shown.

7 Position the mouse pointer on the right border of the field list box for the *Employee Dates and Salaries* table (top right) until the pointer changes to a left- and right-pointing arrow, and then drag the border right until the Title bar shows the entire table name.

8 Move and resize the top two field list boxes as shown.

9 Position the mouse pointer over *Emp No* in the *Employees* field list box, hold down the left mouse button, drag the pointer to *Emp No* in the *Employee Dates and Salaries* field list box, and then release the mouse button.

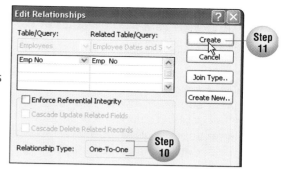

(10) Notice *One-To-One* displays in the *Relationship Type* box of the Edit Relationships dialog box.

> Access determined the relationship type as one-to-one since the common field that was used to join the two tables is the primary key field in each table. In both tables, only one record can exist for each unique employee number.

(11) Click Create.

> A black join line connecting the two *Emp No* fields appears between the two tables in the Relationships window. The join line does not show a *1* at each end similar to that shown in the previous topic because we have not turned on referential integrity. At this time we cannot turn on the referential integrity option since only one employee record exists in the Employees table while several employee records exist in the other two tables.

(12) Position the mouse pointer over *Emp No* in the *Employees* field list box and then drag to *Emp No* in the *Employee Benefits* field list box.

(13) Click Create in the Edit Relationships dialog box.

(14) Move the field list boxes in the Relationships window as shown to spread out the join lines so that they are easier to see.

(15) Print the Relationships. Refer to Steps 12–14 in the previous topic if you need assistance.

(16) Click the Save button and then close the Relationships window.

(17) Open the Employee Dates and Salaries table in Design view.

> Now that the Employee Dates and Salaries table is joined to the Employees table, you can delete the three fields relating to the employee names to avoid duplication of data. (In the next topic you will learn how to view data from two related tables in subdatasheets.)

(18) Move the pointer in the field selector bar next to *Last Name* until the pointer changes to a right-pointing black arrow, drag down to *Middle Initial*, and then release the mouse.

(19) Click the Delete Rows button on the Table Design toolbar.

(20) Click Yes to confirm the deletion.

(21) Click the Save button and then close the Employee Dates and Salaries table.

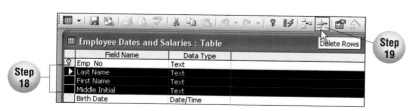

IN BRIEF

Delete Fields
1 Open table in Design View.
2 Select field(s) to be deleted.
3 Click Delete Rows button on Table Design toolbar.
4 Click Yes to confirm deletion.

2.10 Displaying Records in a Subdatasheet

When two tables are joined, you can view the related records from the two tables within one datasheet window by displaying a *subdatasheet*. To do this, open one of the tables in Datasheet view. Click Insert on the Menu bar and then click Subdatasheet. Select the related table name in the Insert Subdatasheet dialog box and then click OK. A column appears between the record selector bar and the first field in each row displaying a plus symbol. Click the plus symbol (referred to as the *expand indicator*) next to the record for which you want to view the record in the related table. A subdatasheet opens below the selected record. To

remove the subdatasheet, click the minus symbol (referred to as the *collapse indicator*) to collapse it (the plus symbol changes to a minus symbol after the record has been expanded).

PROJECT: You will open the Employees table in Datasheet view and then insert a subdatasheet to view the related benefits for Sam Vestering in the Employee Benefits table. While the subdatasheet is open you will update the benefit information to reflect the new life insurance for which Sam has subscribed, and then view the related dates and salary while in the same datasheet.

STEPS

1. With **WEEmployees2** open, open the Employees table in Datasheet view.

2. Click Insert and then click Subdatasheet.

3. With the Tables tab selected in the Insert Subdatasheet dialog box, click *Employee Benefits* in the table list box and then click OK.

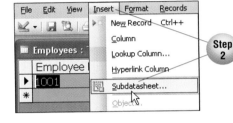

A new column containing a plus symbol (+) appears between the record selector bar and the first field in the datasheet *(Emp No)*. The plus symbol is called the *expand indicator*. Clicking the expand indicator next to a record displays the related record in a subdatasheet from the table you chose in the Insert Subdatasheet dialog box.

4. Click the plus symbol (expand indicator) between the record selector bar and *1001* in the first row in the datasheet.

The subdatasheet opens to display the record for the same employee (Emp No 1001) in the related table (Employee Benefits).

5. Drag across the value $150,000.00 in the *Life Insurance* field, and then type **190000**.

One of the advantages to displaying subdatasheets is the ability to edit in a table while viewing related information from another table. Since the Employee Benefits table does not store fields with the employee names, viewing the benefit record in a subdatasheet from the Employees table which does display employee names ensures you are editing the correct record.

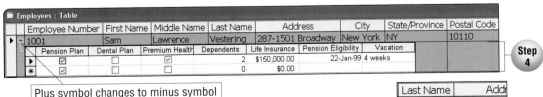

Plus symbol changes to minus symbol when record has been expanded.

(6) Press Enter to complete life insurance entry.

(7) With the Employee Benefits subdatasheet active, click Insert and then click Subdatasheet.

(8) Click *Employee Dates and Salaries* in the table list box.

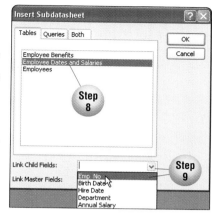

(9) Click the down-pointing arrow at the right of the *Link Child Fields* option box and then click *Emp No* at the drop-down list.

(10) Click the down-pointing arrow at the right of the *Link Master Fields* option box and then click *Emp No* at the drop-down list.

> Since the common field *Emp No* did not appear automatically in the *Link Child Fields* and *Link Master Fields* list boxes, you need to instruct Access on the field to which the two tables should be linked. Access could not determine the linked field automatically since a relationship does not currently exist between Employee Benefits and Employee Dates and Salaries.

(11) Click OK to close the Insert Subdatasheet dialog box. Click Yes at the message asking if you want Access to create a relationship for you.

> A new column containing an expand indicator appears between the record selector bar and the first field in the subdatasheet *(Pension Plan)*.

(12) Click the expand indicator between the record selector bar and the first row in the *Pension Plan* subdatasheet.

Step 12

	Employee Number	First Name	Middle Name	Last Name	Address	City	State/Province	Postal Code
1001	Sam	Lawrence	Vestering	287-1501 Broadway	New York	NY	10110

	Pension Plan	Dental Plan	Premium Health	Dependents	Life Insurance	Pension Eligibility	Vacation
	☑	☐	☑	2	$190,000.00	22-Jan-99	4 weeks

	Birth Date	Hire Date	Department	Annual Salary
	2/18/1957	7/22/1998	North American Distribution	$69,725.00
*				$0.00

| | ☑ | ☐ | ☐ | 0 | $0.00 | | |

> The subdatasheet opens to display the record for the same employee (Emp No 1001) in the related table (Employee Dates and Salaries). You are now viewing related information for one employee from all three tables in the database in one datasheet window.

(13) Close the Employees table. Click Yes to save changes to all objects.

> By saving the changes to all objects, expand indicators will now automatically appear in the datasheets alleviating the need to open the Insert Subdatasheet dialog box.

(14) Open the Relationships window. Notice the new join line between the Employee Benefits and the Employee Dates and Salaries tables as a result of the subdatasheet you added in Step 11.

(15) Close the Relationships window and then close **WEEmployees2**.

IN BRIEF

Display Records in Subdatasheet
1 Open table in Datasheet view.
2 Click Insert, Subdatasheet.
3 Click related table name.
4 Click OK.
5 Expand subdatasheet for desired record.
6 Edit and/or print as required.
7 Click minus symbol next to expanded record to collapse it.

FEATURES SUMMARY

Feature	Button	Menu	Keyboard
Datasheet view	🖽	View, Datasheet View	
Delete rows	➡	Edit, Delete Rows	
Design view	✎	View, Design View	
Font		Format Font	
Format datasheet		Format, Datasheet	
Freeze columns		Format, Freeze Columns	
Lookup Wizard		Insert, Lookup Field	
Primary key	🔑	Edit, Primary Key	
Relationships	⧉	Tools, Relationships	
Save table	💾	File, Save	Ctrl + S
Subdatasheet		Insert, Subdatasheet	
Table Wizard		Insert, Table, Table Wizard	

PROCEDURES CHECK

Completion: In the space provided at the right, indicate the correct term or command.

1. Display a table in this view to modify a field's properties. _____
2. Assign a field this data type if the field will contain dollar values that you do not want rounded off in calculations. _____
3. This is the term for the field in a table that must contain unique information for each record. _____
4. Enter a value in this field property if you want the value to appear automatically in the field whenever a new record is created. _____
5. Enter a conditional statement in this field property to prevent data that does not meet the criteria from being entered into the field. _____
6. An input mask that uses the character zero (0) means only this type of data is accepted into the field. _____
7. This is the name of the wizard used to create a drop-down list of entries that will appear when the user clicks in the field. _____
8. One table in a relationship is referred to as the primary table. The other table is referred to as this. _____
9. This type of relationship is created when the field used to join the two tables is the primary key in both tables. _____
10. The records in two related tables can be displayed in one datasheet window by clicking Insert and then this option. _____

11. Display this dialog box to change the appearance of the datasheet by modifying the background color and/or gridlines. _____

12. You can prevent columns from scrolling off the screen by selecting the columns you wish to remain fixed and then clicking this menu sequence. _____

SKILLS REVIEW

Activity 1: CREATING A TABLE IN DESIGN VIEW

1 Open the **WEEmployees2** database.
2 Create a table in Design view using the following field names and data types. You determine an appropriate description. Do not set any field properties since these will be changed in a later activity.

Field Name	Data Type	Field Name	Data Type
Emp No	Text	Review Date	Date/Time
Supervisor Last Name	Text	Increment Date	Date/Time
Supervisor First Name	Text	Training Days	Number

3 Define *Emp No* as the primary key field.
4 Save the table and name it *Review and Training*.
5 Switch to Datasheet view and then enter the following two records:

Emp No	1015	Emp No	1030
Supervisor Last Name	Vestering	Supervisor Last Name	Deptulski
Supervisor First Name	Sam	Supervisor First Name	Roman
Review Date	5/20/05	Review Date	1/24/05
Increment Date	7/01/05	Increment Date	3/03/05
Training Days	5	Training Days	10

6 Best Fit the column widths.
7 Close the Review and Training table. Click Yes when prompted to save layout changes.

Activity 2: CHANGING FIELD SIZE; VALIDATING ENTRIES; CREATING AN INPUT MASK; FORMATTING DATES

1 Open the Review and Training table in Design view.
2 Change the field size for the *Emp No* field to *4*.
3 Create a validation rule for the *Training Days* field to ensure that no number greater than 10 is entered into the field. Enter an appropriate validation text error message.
4 Save the table. Click Yes to test the data with the new rules.
5 Create the following input masks:
  a In *Emp No* create a mask that will ensure that four required digits only are entered into the field.
  b In *Review Date* and *Increment Date*, use the Input Mask Wizard to set the pattern for entering dates to *Medium Date*.
6 Change the format property for *Review Date* and *Increment Date* to display the date in the Medium Date format.
7 Save the table.

8 Switch to Datasheet view and add the following two records:

Emp No	1035	*Emp No*	1040
Supervisor Last Name	**Postma**	*Supervisor Last Name*	**Deptulski**
Supervisor First Name	**Hanh**	*Supervisor First Name*	**Roman**
Review Date	**14-Mar-05**	*Review Date*	**10-Mar-05**
Increment Date	**01-May-05**	*Increment Date*	**01-May-05**
Training Days	**8**	*Training Days*	6

9 Preview and then print the Review and Training table.

10 Close the Review and Training table.

Activity 3: CREATING A TABLE USING THE TABLE WIZARD; MODIFYING FIELD PROPERTIES; FORMATTING THE DATASHEET

1 Double-click *Create table by using wizard.*

2 Scroll down the *Sample Tables* list box and then click *Expenses*.

3 Add the following fields from the *Sample Fields* list box to *the Fields in my new table* list box and then click Finish:

EmployeeID	*AmountSpent*
ExpenseType	*DateSubmitted*

4 Switch to Design view to edit the table structure.

5 Make the following changes to the *EmployeeID* field:

    a Change the field name to *Emp No* and the data data type to *Text.*

    b Set the maximum number of characters allowed in the field to *4.*

    c Set an input mask that will accept four required digits only in the field.

6 Save the Expenses table and then switch to Datasheet view.

7 Add the following record to the Expenses table:

Employee ID	**1001**	*Amount Spent*	**1,543.10**
Expense Type	**Sales**	*Date Submitted*	**03/14/04**

8 Format the datasheet as follows:

    a Change the background color to silver.

    b Change the gridline color to maroon.

9 Change the font for the datasheet to 12-point Times New Roman.

10 Adjust any column widths that might be necessary after changing the font.

11 Preview and then print the Expenses table.

12 Close the Expenses table. Click Yes to save layout changes.

Activity 4: CREATING A ONE-TO-MANY RELATIONSHIP; DISPLAYING SUBDATASHEETS

1 Open the Expenses table in Design view.

2 With the *Emp No* field selected, click the Primary Key button to remove *Emp No* as a primary key field. *(Note: You are removing the primary key in the Expenses table so that the relationship that will be created in the following steps will be a one-to-many relationship. If Emp No remained as a primary key, Access would create a one-to-one relationship.)*

3 Click Save and then close the Expenses table.

4 Click the Relationships button on the Database toolbar.

5 Click the Show Table button 🗗, or click Relationships, Show Table to open the Show Table dialog box.

6 Add the Expenses table to the Relationships window and then close the Show Table dialog box.

7 Move the *Expenses* field list box to the right of the *Employees* field list box.

8   Create a one-to-many relationship by dragging the *Emp No* field name in the *Employees* field list box to the *Emp No* field name in the *Expenses* field list box.
9   Click *Enforce Referential Integrity* and then click Create in the Edit Relationships dialog box.
10 Print the Relationships.
11 Close the Relationships window. Click Yes to save changes to the report design and then click OK in the Save As dialog box to accept the default report name of *Relationships for WEEmployees2*.
12 Close the Relationships window.
13 Open the Employees table in Datasheet view.
14 Click Insert, click Subdatasheet, and then select the Expenses table in the Insert Subdatasheet dialog box.
15 Expand the subdatasheet for Emp No 1001.
16 Add the following record to the Expenses table using the subdatasheet:
Expense Type	**Shipping**
Amount Spent	**55.27**
Date Submitted	**04/22/04**
17 Close the Employees table. Click No when prompted to save the layout changes.
18 Close the **WEEmployees2** database.

PERFORMANCE PLUS

Assessment 1: CREATING A TABLE IN DESIGN VIEW; CREATING A LOOKUP FIELD

1   Gina Simmons, instructor in the Theatre Arts Division of Niagara Peninsula College, has asked you to create a new table to store the grades for the MKP245 course she teaches. Gina would like to be able to select the student grade from a drop-down list rather than type it in.
2   Open the **NPCGrades2** database.
3   Create a new table in Design view using the following field names: *Student No*; *Last Name*; *First Name*; *Grade*. You determine the appropriate data type and descriptions for each field with the exception of the *Grade* field.
4   Use the Lookup Wizard in the *Grade* field to create a drop-down list with the following grades: A+, A, B, C, D, F. Set the *Limit To List* property for the *Lookup* field to Yes.
5   Define the *Student No* field as the primary key.
6   Save the table and name it *MKP245*.
7   Enter the following four records in Datasheet view:

Student No	**111-785-156**	*Student No*	**118-487-578**
Last Name	**Bastow**	*Last Name*	**Andre**
First Name	**Maren**	*First Name*	**Ian**
Grade	**A+**	*Grade*	**C**
Student No	**137-845-746**	*Student No*	**138-456-749**
Last Name	**Knowlton**	*Last Name*	**Yiu**
First Name	**Sherri**	*First Name*	**Terry**
Grade	**B**	*Grade*	**D**

8   Best Fit the column widths.
9   Preview, print, and then close the MKP245 table.
10 Close the **NPCGrades2** database.

Assessment 2: CHANGING FIELD SIZE; VALIDATING ENTRIES; CREATING AN INPUT MASK; FORMATTING DATES

1 Bobbie Sinclair, business manager of Performance Threads, has asked you to look at the design of the Costume Inventory table and try to improve it with data restrictions and validation rules. While looking at the design, you discover an error was made in assigning the data type for the *Date In* field.
2 Open the **PTCostumeInventory2** database.
3 Open the Costume Inventory table in Design view.
4 Change the *Date In* field to a Date/Time data field.
5 Change the field size for the *Costume No* field to *5*.
6 Performance Threads has a minimum daily rental fee of $85.00. Create a validation rule and validation text property that will ensure no one enters a value less than $85.00 in the *Daily Rental Fee* field.
7 To ensure no one mixes the order of the month and day when entering the *Date Out* and *Date In* fields, create an input mask for these two fields to require that the date be entered in the Medium Date format.
8 Since Performance Threads is open seven days a week, format the *Date Out* and *Date In* fields to display the dates in the Long Date format. This will add the day of the week to the entry and spell the month in full.
9 Save the table and then switch to Datasheet view.
10 Best Fit the columns.
11 Preview the datasheet. Change the margins for the page as necessary so that the entire datasheet fits on one page.
12 Print and then close the Costume Inventory table.
13 Close the **PTCostumeInventory2** database.

Assessment 3: CREATING A TABLE USING THE TABLE WIZARD; ESTABLISHING RELATIONSHIPS

1 Dana Hirsch, manager of The Waterfront Bistro, has asked you to create a new table in the inventory database that will store the supplier information. Since the Table Wizard provides a sample Suppliers table, you decide the wizard would be the most expedient method to use.
2 Open **WBInventory2**.
3 Create a new table using the Table Wizard. Use the Suppliers sample table and add the following fields to the new table: *SupplierID*; *SupplierName*; *Address*; *City*; *StateOrProvince*; *PostalCode*; *PhoneNumber*; *FaxNumber*.
4 Choose the option to set the primary key yourself, select the *SupplierID* field as the primary key field, and set the type of data to *Numbers and/or letters I enter when I add new records*.
5 Accept all other default settings in the wizard dialog boxes.
6 Switch to Design view for the new table.
7 Change the field name for *SupplierID* to *Supplier Code*, change the field size to *50*, and delete the entry in the *Caption* property box.
8 Enter the following record in the new table:

Supplier Code	1	*State/Province*	NY
Supplier Name	**Danby's Bakery**	*Postal Code*	**14280**
Address	**3168 Rivermist Drive**	*Phone Number*	**(716) 555-4987**
City	**Buffalo**	*Fax Number*	**(716) 555-5101**

9 Best Fit the column widths.
10 Preview the datasheet, change the page orientation to landscape, print, and then close the Suppliers table. Save the layout changes.

11 Display the Relationships window.

12 Create a one-to-many relationship using the *Supplier Code* field with the Suppliers table as the primary table and the Inventory List table as the related table. Enforce referential integrity when you create the relationship.

13 Click the Save button.

14 Print the relationships and then close the Relationships window. Click No to save the changes to the design of the report.

15 Close the **WBInventory2** database.

Assessment 4: CREATING A NEW DATABASE

1 Alex Torres, manager of the Toronto office of First Choice Travel, has asked you to help the accounting staff by creating a database to track employee expense claims information. You will create the database from scratch.

2 At a blank Database window, click the New button  on the Database toolbar.

3 Click the <u>Blank database</u> hyperlink in the New File task pane.

4 Type **FCTExpenses** in the *File name* text box in the File New Database dialog box and then click the Create button.

5 Look at the sample expense form in Figure A2.3. On your own or with another student in the class, make a list of the fields that would be needed to store the information from this form in a table. For each field on your list determine the appropriate data type and field properties that could be used.

6 Create a new table named **Expense Claims** in Design view. Use the information from Step 5 to enter the field names, data types, descriptions, and field properties.

7 Set an appropriate primary key field for the table and then save the table.

8 Switch to Datasheet view and then enter the expense information shown in Figure A2.3 in a record in the table.

9 Preview, print, and then close the Expense Claims table.

10 Turn on the Compact on Close feature.

11 Close **FCTExpenses**.

FIGURE A2.3 Assessment 4

Assessment 5: FINDING INFORMATION ON DELETING RELATIONSHIPS

1 Use the Help feature to find information on how to delete a relationship.

2 Print the Help topic that you find.

3 Open the **WEEmployees2** database.

4 Display the Relationships window and then delete the one-to-many relationship between the Employees and the Expenses tables.

5 Click Yes to confirm that you want to delete the selected relationship and then save the relationships.

6   Print the relationships. Click Yes to save the changes to the report name and accept the default name provided.
7   Close the Relationships window.
8   Close the **WEEmployees2** database.

Assessment 6: FINDING INFORMATION ON REQUIRED ENTRIES

1   Use the Help feature to find information on requiring that data be entered into a field. For example, you want to specify that a field cannot be left blank. *(Hint: Type require data in a field in the Ask a Question text box.)*
2   Print the Help topic you find.
3   Open the **WEEmployees2** database.
4   Open the Employees table in Design view.
5   You want to make sure that all records in the table have an entry in the *PostalCode* field, since you will be using this table to print mailing labels. Using the information you learned in help, change the field property for the *PostalCode* field to ensure that the field will have data entered in it.
6   Save the table and switch to Datasheet view.
7   Add a new record to the table using Emp No 9999. Use your name and address as the *Employee* information. When you reach the *PostalCode* field, try to press Enter to move past the field without entering any data. When Access displays the error message, click OK. Enter your postal code in the *PostalCode* field.
8   Change the page setup to fit all fields on one page and then print the Employees table.
9   Close the Employees table and then close the **WEEmployees2** database.

Assessment 7: CAR SHOPPING ON THE INTERNET

1   After graduation, you plan to reward yourself by buying a new car. Identify at least three different makes and models of cars that you like.
2   Search the Internet for the manufacturer's suggested retail price (MSRP) for the cars you would like to own, including whatever options you would order with the vehicle. *(Hint: Try searching by the manufacturers' names to locate their Web sites.)*
3   Create a new database in Access to store the information you find.
    • Click the New button on the Database toolbar, and then click the Blank database hyperlink in the New File task pane.
    • Type NewCars in the *File name* text box in the File New Database dialog box and then click Create.
4   Create a table named *New Car Pricing* using Design view. Include the manufacturer's name, brand, model of the car, options, and MSRP. Include other fields that you might want to track, such as color choice.
5   Best Fit the column widths.
6   Preview and then print the New Car Pricing table.
7   Close the New Car Pricing table and then close the **NewCars** database.

ACCESS

Creating Queries, Forms, and Reports

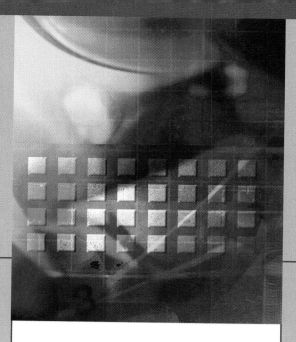

The ability to extract specific information from a table that can contain hundreds or thousands of records is an important feature in Access. Data is extracted from a table by performing a *query*. Creating a query is analogous to asking Access a question, such as *How many distributors are located in New York?* Forms are used to view, enter, and edit data. Generally, only one record at a time is displayed in a form. Forms can be designed to resemble existing forms used by the business, making the transition to an electronic database easier for employees. Reports are created to print the information in tables or queries in a variety of formats or styles. In this section you will learn the skills and complete the projects described here.

Note: Before beginning this section, delete any existing databases on your disk and copy each database as needed. Remember to remove the read-only attribute from each database after copying. If necessary, refer to page 1 for instructions on how to remove the read-only attribute. If necessary, check with your instructor before deleting any database files.

Skills

- Create, run, and print a select query in Design view
- Add multiple tables to a query
- Create and run a query using the Simple Query Wizard
- Sort the query results
- Add criteria statements to a query
- Delete fields from a query
- Perform calculations in a query
- Use aggregate functions in a query to calculate statistics
- Create an AutoForm
- Create a form using the Form Wizard
- Create a form with a subform
- Move and resize control objects in a form
- Modify properties of controls
- Add objects using the Control Toolbox
- Create and print a report using the Report Wizard
- Move and resize controls in a report

Projects

Create queries to extract fields from tables to print custom employee lists, add criteria, calculate pension contributions and monthly salaries, and perform statistical analysis on annual salaries and employee expenses; create and modify forms to facilitate data entry and viewing in the employees database; create and modify reports to produce custom printouts of employee and distributor data.

Create and print a query that will extract the records of students who achieved A+ in all of their courses.

Create a query, and create and print a report that lists all costumes rented in the month of August 2004; create and modify a form for browsing the costume inventory.

3.1 Creating a Query in Design View

A *query* is an Access object that is designed to extract specific data from a table. Queries can be created to serve a variety of purposes, from very simple field selection to complex conditional statements or calculations. When a table is viewed or printed in Datasheet view, all of the fields in the table are included. In its simplest form, a query selects only some of the fields from the table(s) to display or print. A criteria statement can be added to a query to display or print only certain records from the table(s). Queries can be saved for future use.

PROJECT: Rhonda Trask, human resources manager of Worldwide Enterprises, has asked for a list that includes employee number, employee name, date hired, department, and salary. This data is stored in two different tables. You will create a query to obtain the required fields from each table to generate the list.

STEPS

1 Open **WEEmployees3**.

2 Click the Queries button on the Objects bar.

3 Double-click *Create query in Design view*.

4 Double-click *Employees* in the Show Table dialog box with the Tables tab selected.

> A field list box for the Employees table is added to the top of the Query1 : Select Query window.

5 Double-click *Employee Dates and Salaries* in the Show Table dialog box.

Field list box for Employees table added in Step 4.

> A black join line with *1* at each end of the line between the Employees and the Employee Dates and Salaries tables appears illustrating the one-to-one relationship that has been defined between the two tables.

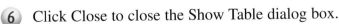
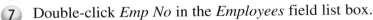

6 Click Close to close the Show Table dialog box.

7 Double-click *Emp No* in the *Employees* field list box.

> *Emp No* is added to the *Field* row in the first column of the design grid. In Steps 8 and 9 you will practice two other methods of adding fields to the design grid.

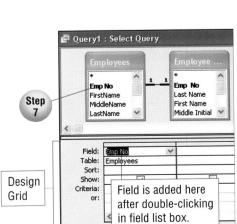
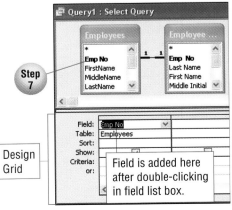

Design Grid

Field is added here after double-clicking in field list box.

8 Position the mouse pointer on the *FirstName* field in the *Employees* field list box, hold down the left mouse button, drag the field to the *Field* row in the second column of the design grid, and then release the mouse button.

9 Click in the *Field* row in the third column of the design grid, click the down-pointing arrow that appears, and then click *Employees.LastName* in the drop-down list.

10 Using any of the three methods learned in Steps 7–9, add the fields *Hire Date*, *Department*, and *Annual Salary* from the *Employee Dates and Salaries* field list box to the design grid. You may need to scroll down the field list box to see the required field names.

11 Click the Save button on the Query Design toolbar.

12 Type **Trask Employee List** in the *Query Name* text box in the Save As dialog box and then press Enter or click OK.

13 Click the Run button ⊞ on the Query Design toolbar.

> The query results are displayed in Datasheet view as shown in Figure A3.1. The query results datasheet can be sorted, edited, or formatted in a manner similar to a datasheet. Data displayed in query results is not stored as a separate entity—the query is simply another interface for viewing and editing data in the associated table(s). When a saved query is opened, the query results are dynamically updated each time by automatically running the query.

14 Close the Trask Employee List : Select Query window.

FIGURE A3.1 Query Results Datasheet

Trask Employee List : Select Query

Emp No	First Name	Last Name	Hire Date	Department	Annual Salary
1001	Sam	Vestering	7/22/1998	North American Distribution	$69,725.00
1005	Roman	Deptulski	8/15/1998	Overseas Distribution	$69,725.00
1010	Hanh	Postma	1/30/1999	European Distribution	$69,725.00
1015	Lyle	Besterd	5/17/1999	North American Distribution	$44,651.00
1020	Angela	Doxtator	8/3/2000	North American Distribution	$45,558.00
1025	Jorge	Biliski	12/1/1999	North American Distribution	$44,892.00
1030	Thom	Hicks	1/22/1999	Overseas Distribution	$42,824.00
1035	Valerie	Fistouris	3/15/2001	European Distribution	$44,694.00
1040	Guy	Lafreniere	3/10/2001	Overseas Distribution	$45,395.00
1045	Terry	Yiu	4/12/2001	European Distribution	$42,238.00
1050	Carl	Zakowski	2/9/2002	European Distribution	$44,387.00
1055	Edward	Thurston	6/22/2002	Overseas Distribution	$42,248.00
1060	Donald	McKnight	6/22/2003	European Distribution	$42,126.00
1065	Norm	Liszniewski	2/6/2003	North American Distribution	$43,695.00
1070	Balfor	Jhawar	11/22/2004	Overseas Distribution	$44,771.00
1075	Mike	Fitchett	3/19/2004	Overseas Distribution	$42,857.00
1080	Leo	Couture	1/17/2004	European Distribution	$43,659.00

Record: 1 of 17

IN BRIEF

Create a Query in Design View
1 Click Queries on Objects bar.
2 Double-click *Create query in Design view*.
3 Double-click required table(s) in Show Table dialog box.
4 Close Show Table dialog box.
5 Add required field names from field list box(es) to columns in design grid.
6 Click Save button.
7 Type query name and click OK.
8 Click Run button.

3.2 Using the Simple Query Wizard

Access includes the Simple Query Wizard to facilitate creating a query. At the first Simple Query Wizard dialog box, the table(s) and the fields within the table(s) are added to the query. Select a Detail or Summary query in the second dialog box. If you select Summary, click Summary Options to specify which field to group by and whether to calculate the sum, average, minimum, or maximum values in the group. Type the name for the query in the last dialog box.

PROJECT: Using the Simple Query Wizard, you will generate a list of each employee's name, number of dependents, life insurance, pension plan eligibility date, and vacation entitlement.

S T E P S

1. With **WEEmployees3** open and Queries selected on the Objects bar, double-click *Create query by using wizard*.

2. Click the down-pointing arrow at the right of the *Tables/Queries* text box and then click *Table: Employees* in the drop-down list.

3. With *Emp No* selected in the *Available Fields* list box, click the Add Field button `>` to move *Emp No* to the *Selected Fields* list box.

4. Click the Add Field button to move *FirstName* to the *Selected Fields* list box.

5. Click *LastName* in the *Available Fields* list box and then click the Add Field button.

6. Click the down-pointing arrow at the right of the *Tables/Queries* text box and then click *Table: Employee Benefits* in the drop-down list.

7. Double-click *Dependents* in the *Available Fields* list box.

   > Double-clicking a field name is another way to move a field to the *Selected Fields* list box.

8. Move the following fields from the *Available Fields* list box to the *Selected Fields* list box:

   Life Insurance
   Pension Eligibility
   Vacation

9. Click Next.

10. Click Next at the second Simple Query Wizard dialog box to accept the default *Detail* report.

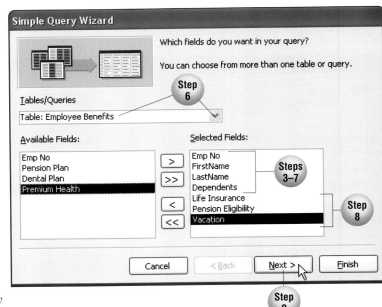

⑪ Type **Employee Non-Medical Benefits** in the *What title do you want for your query?* text box, and then click Finish.

⑫ View the query results in the datasheet and then click the View button ⊠ on the Query Datasheet toolbar to switch to Design view.

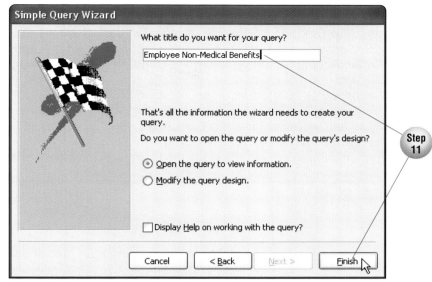

Step 11

In the next step you will modify the query design to sort the query results in ascending order by the employee's last name. In Query Design view notice that by using the wizard you added the tables and fields to the design grid through dialog boxes instead of using the techniques learned in the last topic.

Step 13

⑬ Click in the *Sort* row in the *LastName* column in the design grid, click the down-pointing arrow that appears, and then click *Ascending* in the drop-down list.

Field:	Emp No	FirstName	LastName
Table:	Employees	Employees	Employees
Sort:			
Show:	☑	☑	Ascending
Criteria:			Descending
or:			(not sorted)

⑭ Click the Save button on the Query Design toolbar and then click the Run button.

The query results datasheet appears with the records sorted by the *LastName* column.

⑮ Close the Employee Non-Medical Benefits : Select Query window.

In Addition

Action Queries

In the last topic and in this topic, you have created *select* queries that displayed specific fields from a table. An *action* query makes changes to records in one procedure. There are four types of action queries: delete, update, append, and make-table. A delete query will delete a group of records from one or more tables. An update query is used to make global changes to a group of records in one or more tables. An append query adds a group of records from one or more tables to the end of one or more other tables. A make-table query will create a new table from all or part of the data in existing tables.

IN BRIEF

Create a Query Using the Simple Query Wizard
1 Double-click *Create query by using wizard.*
2 Choose table(s) and field(s) to include in query.
3 Click Next.
4 Choose *Detail* or *Summary* query.
5 Click Next.
6 Type title for query.
7 Click Finish.

ACCESS

3.3 Extracting Records Using Criteria Statements

All of the records in the tables were displayed in the query results datasheet in the two queries you have done so far. Adding a criterion statement to the query design grid will cause Access to display only those records that meet the criterion. For example, you could generate a list of employees who are entitled to four weeks of vacation. Extracting specific records from the tables is where the true power in creating queries is found since you are able to separate out only those records that serve your purpose.

PROJECT: Rhonda Trask has requested a list of employees who receive either three or four weeks of vacation. Since you already have the employee names and vacation fields in an existing query, you will modify the existing query to add the criteria statement and then save it under a new name.

STEPS

① With **WEEmployees3** open and Queries selected on the Objects bar, right-click the *Employee Non-Medical Benefits* query name, and then click Design View at the shortcut menu.

② Maximize the query window if it is not already maximized.

③ Click in the *Criteria* row in the *Vacation* column in the design grid.

④ Type **4 weeks** and then press Enter.

> The insertion point moves to the *Criteria* row in the next column and Access inserts quotation marks around *4 weeks* in the *Vacation* column. Since quotation marks are required in criteria statements for text fields, Access automatically inserts them if they are not typed into the *Criteria* text box.

⑤ Click in the *or* row in the *Vacation* column in the design grid (blank row below *4 weeks*), type **3 weeks**, and then press Enter.

> Including a second criteria statement below the first one instructs Access to display records that meet either of the two criteria.

⑥ Click File and then Save As. Type **Employees with 3 or 4 weeks vacation** in the *Save Query 'Employee Non-Medical ...' To* text box in the Save As dialog box and then click OK.

⑦ Click the Run button on the Query Design toolbar.

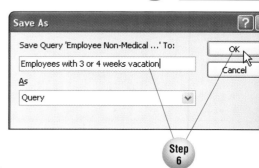

PROBLEM? Is the query results datasheet blank? Check the criteria statement in Design view. A typing error, such as *4 weks* instead of *4 weeks*, can cause a blank datasheet to appear.

⑧ View the query results in the datasheet and then click the View button on the Query Datasheet toolbar to switch to Design view.

> Since Rhonda Trask is interested only in the employee names and vacation weeks, you will instruct Access not to display the other fields in the query results datasheet.

⑨ Click the check box in the *Show* row in the *Dependents* column to remove the check mark.

> Deselecting the check box instructs Access to hide the column in the query results datasheet.

Step 9

⑩ Deselect the *Show* check boxes in the *Life Insurance* and *Pension Eligibility* columns in the design grid.

⑪ Run the query.

⑫ Click the Print button on the Query Datasheet toolbar.

⑬ Close the Employees with 3 or 4 weeks vacation : Select Query window. Click Yes to save changes to the design of the query.

> Examples of other criteria statements are listed in Table A3.1.

TABLE A3.1 Criteria Examples

Criteria Statement	Records That Would Be Extracted
"Finance Department"	Those with *Finance Department* in the field
Not "Finance Department"	All *except* those with *Finance Department* in the field
"Fan*"	Those that begin *Fan* and end with any other characters in the field
>15000	Those with a value greater than 15,000 in the field
>=15000 And <=20000	Those with a value from 15,000 to 20,000 in the field
#05/01/05#	Those that contain the date May 1, 2005 in the field
>#05/01/05#	Those that contain dates after May 1, 2005 in the field

In Addition

Extracting Based on Two or More Criteria Statements

A query can be created that extracts records based on meeting two or more criteria statements at the same time. In the query design grid shown below, Access will display the records of employees who work in the North American Distribution department *and* who earn over $40,000. Typing two criteria in the same row means the record will have to satisfy *both* criteria to be displayed in the query results datasheet.

IN BRIEF

Add a Criteria Statement to a Query
1 Open query in Design view.
2 Click in *Criteria* row in column to attach criteria to.
3 Type criteria statement.
4 Click Save button.
5 Click Run button.

Field:	FirstName	Address	Department	Annual Salary
Table:	Employees	Employees	Employee Dates and Salaries	Employee Dates an⸱
Sort:				
Show:	☑	☑	☑	☑
Criteria:			"North American Distribution"	>40000
or:				

3.4 Performing Calculations in a Query; Deleting Fields

Calculations such as adding or multiplying two fields can be included in a query. To do this, in a blank field text box in Query Design view type the text that you want to appear as the column heading followed by a colon and then the mathematical expression for the calculated values. Field names in the mathematical expression are encased in square brackets. For example, the entry *Total Salary:[Base Salary]+[Commission]* would add the value in the field named *Base Salary* to the value in the field named *Commission*. The result would be placed in a new column in the query datasheet with the column heading *Total Salary*. The *Total Salary* column does not exist in the table used to create the query; the values are dynamically calculated each time the query is run.

In the last topic you deselected the *Show* text box to prevent a field from being displayed in the query results. If the field is no longer required it can be removed from the query design grid by selecting the field and then choosing the Cut command on the Edit menu.

PROJECT: Worldwide Enterprises contributes 8% of each employee's annual salary to a registered pension plan. You will modify the Trask Employee List query to include a calculation for the employer pension contribution.

STEPS

1. With **WEEmployees3** open and Queries selected on the Objects bar, open the Trask Employee List query in Design view.

2. Click File and then Save As.

3. Type **Employer Pension Contributions** and then click OK in the Save As dialog box.

    In the next step you will delete the *Hire Date* and *Department* columns in the design grid, since they are not required in the new query.

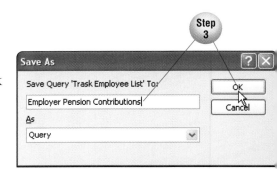

Step 3

4. Position the mouse pointer in the gray field selector bar above the *Hire Date* field in the design grid until the pointer changes to a downward-pointing black arrow, hold down the left mouse button, drag right to select both the *Hire Date* and *Department* columns, and then release the mouse button.

5. Click Edit and then Cut.

    The selected columns are deleted from the design grid.

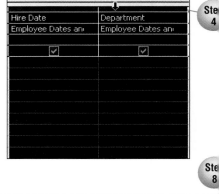

Step 8

6. Click in the blank *Field* row next to the *Annual Salary* column in the design grid.

Step 7

7. Type **Pension Contribution:[Annual Salary]*.08** and then press Enter.

> **PROBLEM?**
> Message appears stating expression has invalid syntax? Check that you have used the correct type of brackets, typed a colon, and that there are no other typing errors.

8 Position the mouse pointer on the right vertical boundary line in the gray field selector bar above the *Pension Contribution* column until the pointer changes to a black vertical line with a left- and right-pointing arrow, and then double-click the left mouse button.

> Double-clicking the right field boundary line adjusts the width of the column to the length of the text in the field row.

9 Click the Save button and then click the Run button.

PROBLEM**?**

Does an Enter Parameter Value dialog box appear? A mistake in typing of *[Annual Salary]* in the calculated field will cause Access to display this dialog box, since it does not recognize the field name.

Properties

Step 12

Pension Contribution: [Annual Salary]*0.8

10 In the query results datasheet, click in any record in the *Pension Contribution* column, click Format, click Column Width, and then click Best Fit in the Column Width dialog box.

> The values in the calculated column need to be formatted to display a consistent number of decimal places. You will correct this in the next steps by changing the format option in the Pension Contribution's Field Properties sheet.

Step 13   Step 14

Field Properties

| General | Lookup |

Description . . . .
Format . . . .
Decimal Places . . . .
Input Mask . . . .
Caption . . . .
Smart Tags . . . .

General Number	3456.78
Currency	$3,456.
Euro	€3,456.
Fixed	3456.79
Standard	3,456.79
Percent	123.00%
Scientific	3.46E+0

11 Switch to Design view.

12 Click the insertion point anywhere within the *Pension Contribution* field row in the design grid and then click the Properties button on the Query Design toolbar.

13 Click in the *Format* property box, click the down-pointing arrow that appears, and then click *Currency* in the drop-down list.

14 Click the Close button on the Field Properties title bar.

15 Click the Save button and then click the Run button.

16 In the query results datasheet, click Format and then Font.

17 Click *12* in the *Size* list box and then click OK.

18 Adjust column widths as necessary so that all column headings are entirely visible.

19 Preview and then print the query results datasheet.

20 Close the Employer Pension Contributions query. Click Yes when prompted to save changes to the layout of the query.

IN BRIEF

Create a Calculated Field in a Query
1 Open query in Design view.
2 Click in first available blank *Field* row in design grid.
3 Type column heading for calculated field.
4 Type a colon (:).
5 Type mathematical expression.
6 Press Enter or click in another field.
7 Click Save button.
8 Click Run button.

3.5 Calculating Statistics Using Aggregate Functions

Aggregate functions such as Sum, Avg, Min, Max, or Count can be included in a query to calculate statistics from numeric field values of all of the records in the table. When an aggregate function is used, Access displays one row in the query results datasheet with the formula result for the function used. To display the aggregate function list, click the Totals button on the Query Design toolbar. Access adds a *Total* row to the design grid with a drop-down list from which you select the desired function.

Using the *Group By* option in the *Total* drop-down list you can add a field to the query upon which you want Access to group records for statistical calculations.

PROJECT: Rhonda Trask has asked for statistics on the salaries currently paid to employees. You will create a new query in Design view and use aggregate functions to find the total of all salaries, the average salary, and the maximum and minimum salaries. In a second query you will calculate the same statistics by department.

STEPS

1. With **WEEmployees3** open and Queries selected on the Objects bar, double-click *Create query in design view*.

2. At the Show Table dialog box with the Tables tab selected, click *Employee Dates and Salaries,* click the Add button, and then click the Close button.

   The field upon which the statistics are to be calculated is added to the design grid once for each aggregate function you want to use.

   Step 3

Field:	Annual Salary	Annual Salary	Annual Salary	Annual Salary
Table:	Employee Dates an	Employee Dates an	Employee Dates an	Employee Dates an
Sort:				
Show:	☑	☑	☑	☑

3. Scroll down to the bottom of the *Employee Dates and Salaries* field list box and then double-click *Annual Salary* four times.

4. Click the Totals button **Σ** on the Query Design toolbar.

   A *Total* row is added to the design grid between *Table* and *Sort* with the default option *Group By*.

   Step 5

Field:	Annual Salary
Table:	Employee Dates an
Total:	Group By
Sort:	Group By
Show:	Sum
Criteria:	Avg
or:	Min
	Max
	Count
	StDev
	Var

5. Click in the *Total* row in the first *Annual Salary* column in the design grid, click the down-pointing arrow that appears, and then click *Sum* in the drop-down list.

6. Click in the *Total* row in the second *Annual Salary* column, click the down-pointing arrow that appears, and then click *Avg* in the drop-down list.

7. Change the *Total* option to *Max* for the third *Annual Salary* column.

8. Change the *Total* option to *Min* for the fourth *Annual Salary* column.

9. Click the Save button on the Query Design toolbar, type **Annual Salary Statistics** in the *Query Name* text box in the Save As dialog box, and then press Enter or click OK.

10. Click the Run button.

    Step 10

SumOfAnnual S	AvgOfAnnual Sa	MaxOfAnnual S	MinOfAnnual Sa
$823,170.00	$48,421.76	$69,725.00	$42,126.00

    Access calculates the Sum, Avg, Max, and Min functions for all annual salary values in the table and displays one row with the results. By default Access assigns column headings in the datasheet using the function name, the word *Of*, and the field name from which the function has been derived such as *SumOfAnnual Salary, AvgOfAnnual Salary, MaxOfAnnual Salary,* and *MinOfAnnual Salary.*

11) Switch to Design view.

12) Click in any row in the first column in the design grid and then click the Properties button on the Query Design toolbar.

13) Click in the *Caption* property box, type **Total Annual Salaries**, and then click the Close button on the Field Properties title bar.

Field Properties

General | Lookup

Description . . . .
Format . . . .
Decimal Places . . . .
Input Mask . . . .
Caption . . . . Total Annual Salaries
Smart Tags . . . .

Step 13

Close

14) Right-click over any row in the second column in the design grid, click Properties at the shortcut menu, click in the *Caption* property box, type **Average Annual Salary**, and then click the Close button on the Field Properties Title bar.

15) Repeat Step 14 to change the *Caption* field property for the third and fourth columns to **Maximum Annual Salary** and **Minimum Annual Salary**, respectively.

16) Click the Save button and then click the Run button.

17) In the query results datasheet, change the font size to *12*, Best Fit all column widths, change the page orientation to landscape, and then print the query results datasheet.

18) Switch to Design view.

Total Annual Salaries	Average Annual Salary	Maximum Annual Salary	Minimum Annual Salary
$823,170.00	$48,421.76	$69,725.00	$42,126.00

Steps 14–17

19) Double-click *Department* in the field list box for the Employee Dates and Salaries table.

> The *Department* field is added to the design grid with *Total* automatically set to *Group By*. Adding this field produces a row in the query results datasheet for each department in which Access calculates the total, average, maximum, and minimum salary.

20) Click File and then Save As. Click in the *Save Query 'Annual Salary Statistics' To* text box at the end of the current query name, press the spacebar once, type **by Department**, and then press Enter or click OK.

21) Click the Run button.

22) Best Fit the *Department* column in the query results datasheet, change the left and right margins to 0.5 inch, and then print the query results datasheet.

23) Close the Annual Salary Statistics by Department query. Click Yes when prompted to save changes to the layout of the query.

3.6 Creating Forms Using AutoForm and the Form Wizard

As you saw in Section 1, forms provide a more user-friendly interface than a datasheet for viewing, adding, editing, and deleting records since only one record is displayed at a time and generally all fields are visible in one screen. AutoForm creates a new form by automatically including all of the fields from the specified table. The layout and style are predefined based on the selection of AutoForm: Columnar; AutoForm: Tabular; AutoForm: Datasheet; AutoForm: PivotTable; or AutoForm: PivotChart in the New Form dialog box.

The Form Wizard provides more choices for the form design than AutoForm. In the Form Wizard

the user is guided through a series of dialog boxes to generate the form, including selecting the table and fields that will be used to make up the form; choosing a layout for the fields; selecting the form style from various colors and backgrounds; and entering a title for the form.

PROJECT: You will create an Autoform using the Employee Dates and Salaries table; another form for the Employee Benefits table using the Form Wizard; and a form with a subform for employees and expenses using the Form Wizard.

STEPS

1. With **WEEmployees3** open, click Forms on the Objects bar.

2. Click the New button on the Database window toolbar.

3. Click *AutoForm: Columnar* in the New Form dialog box list box.

4. Click the down-pointing arrow next to *Choose the table or query where the object's data comes from*, click *Employee Dates and Salaries* in the drop-down list, and then click OK.

> In a few seconds the Employee Dates and Salaries form appears, with the data from the first record in the table displayed in the form as shown in Figure A3.2.

FIGURE A3.2 Employee Dates and Salaries Form

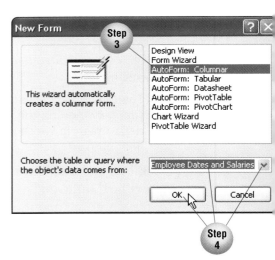

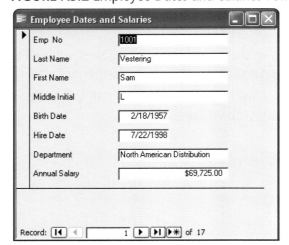

5 Click the Next Record button ▶ on the Record Navigation bar a few times to scroll the records in the table. When you are finished scrolling records, click the Close button on the Employee Dates and Salaries form Title bar.

6 Click Yes to save changes to the design of the form and then click OK in the Save As dialog box to accept the default form name *Employee Dates and Salaries*.

7 At the WEEmployees3 database window, with Forms still selected on the Objects bar, double-click *Create form by using wizard*.

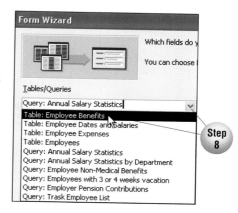

8 Click the down-pointing arrow at the right of the *Tables/Queries* text box and then click *Table: Employee Benefits* in the drop-down list.

> The list of fields in the *Available Fields* list box changes to the field names for the Employee Benefits table. In the next step you will choose which fields to include in the form.

9 Click the Add All Fields button >> to move all of the fields in the *Available Fields* list box to the *Selected Fields* list box and then click Next.

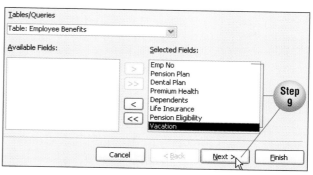

10 Click *Tabular* in the second Form Wizard dialog box to view the tabular layout in the preview window.

11 Click *Datasheet* to preview the datasheet layout.

12 Click *Justified* to preview the justified layout.

13 Click *Columnar* and then click Next.

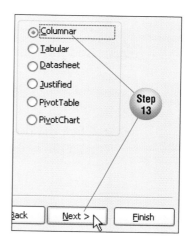

14 Click each of the styles in the list box in the third Form Wizard dialog box to preview each style's colors and backgrounds in the preview window.

15 Click *Industrial* and then click Next.

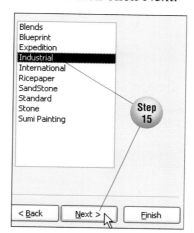

(continued)

16 Click Finish at the last Form Wizard dialog box to accept the default title of *Employee Benefits* and make sure *Open the form to view or enter information* is selected.

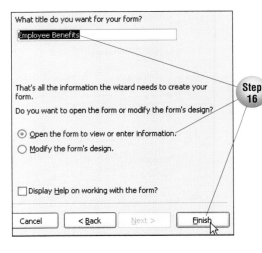

Step 16

> In a few seconds the Employee Benefits form appears with the data displayed for record 1 as shown in Figure A3.3.

17 Click the Next Record button to display record 2 in the form.

18 Continue clicking the Next Record button to view several records using the form.

19 Close the Employee Benefits form.

FIGURE A3.3 Employee Benefits Form

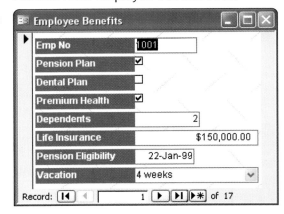

> When a relationship exists between two tables, a form can be created that includes fields from both tables. The related table is created as a **subform** of the primary table. In the next steps you will create a form and subform for the Employees and the Employee Expenses tables.

20 With Forms still selected on the Objects bar, double-click *Create form by using wizard*.

21 Click the down-pointing arrow at the right of the *Tables/Queries* text box and then click *Table: Employees* in the drop-down list.

22 Add the following fields to the *Selected Fields* list box:
> *Emp No*
> *FirstName*
> *LastName*

23 Click the down-pointing arrow at the right of the *Tables/Queries* text box and then click *Table: Employee Expenses* in the drop-down list.

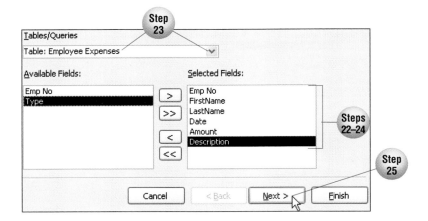

24 Add the following fields to the *Selected Fields* list box:
   Date
   Amount
   Description

25 Click Next.

26 Click Next at the second Form Wizard dialog box to accept the default options of viewing data *by Employees* and *Form with subform(s)*.

27 Complete the remaining steps in the Form Wizard as follows:
   • Accept the default layout of *Datasheet* for the subform.
   • Choose the *Blends* style.
   • Accept the default titles for the form and subform and open the form to view information.

   The form and subform appear as shown in Figure A3.4. Notice a separate Record Navigation bar exists for each form. The Record Navigation bar in the subform is used to scroll the records in the Employee Expenses table for the employee shown in the Employees form. The Record Navigation bar in the Employees form will move to the specified record in the Employees table and automatically display the related record(s) in the Employee Expenses table in the subform.

28 Click the Next Record button on the Record Navigation bar for the Employees form to view record 2. Notice the subform automatically changes to display the related record for Roman Deptulski in the Employee Expenses table.

FIGURE A3.4 Employees Form with Employee Expenses Subform

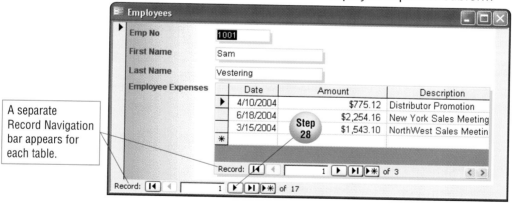

A separate Record Navigation bar appears for each table.

29 Continue clicking the Next Record button on the Record Navigation bar for the Employees form until you have viewed several employee names and related expense records.

30 Close the Employees form.

   Notice the two forms added to the Forms object list: *Employees* and *Employee Expenses Subform*. The subform is a separate object that can be viewed and/or edited separately from the Employees form; however, opening the Employees form will automatically open the Employee Expenses subform.

3.7 Modifying Controls in a Form

Once a form has been created using AutoForm or the Form Wizard, the form can be modified by opening it in Design view. A form is comprised of a series of objects referred to as *controls*. Each field from the table has a *label control* and a *text box control* placed side-by-side with the label control object placed first. The label control contains the field name and is used to describe the data that will be entered or viewed in the adjacent text box control. The text box control is the field placeholder where data is entered or edited. The controls can be moved, resized, formatted, or deleted from the form. A form's style which

includes the color theme and fonts can be changed after the form has been created by opening the AutoFormat dialog box and selecting a different AutoFormat.

PROJECT: Some of the controls in the Employee Dates and Salaries form are wider than necessary for the data that will be entered or viewed. You will open the form in Design view, resize these controls, apply an AutoFormat to the form to improve its appearance, and change the font size of the controls on the form.

S T E P S

FIGURE A3.5 Employee Dates and Salaries Form Design View

1. With **WEEmployees3** open and Forms still selected on the Objects bar, right-click *Employee Dates and Salaries,* and then click Design View at the shortcut menu. Maximize the window if it is not already maximized.

   A form contains three sections, as shown in Figure A3.5: Form Header, Detail, and Form Footer. The control objects for the fields in the table are displayed in the Detail section. A floating Toolbox displays in the window and a field list box may also appear. These can be dragged out of the way or closed.

2. Click the *Emp No* text box control. This is the control object with the white background, containing the text *Emp No*. Eight sizing handles display around the object.

3. Position the mouse pointer on the middle sizing handle at the right edge of the control object until the pointer changes to a left- and right-pointing double arrow, drag left until the right border is at position 2 on the horizontal ruler, and then release the left mouse button.

4. Resize the *Annual Salary* text box control to position 2 on the horizontal ruler by completing steps similar to those in Steps 2–3.

5. Resize the *Middle Initial* text box control to position 1.5 on the horizontal ruler by completing steps similar to those in Steps 2–3.

6 Click in a gray area outside the form to deselect the Middle Initial control.

> In the next step you will use the AutoFormat dialog box to change the form's style. Make sure no controls are selected before opening the AutoFormat dialog box or the new format will apply only to the selected control.

7 Click the AutoFormat button 🖺 on the Form Design toolbar.

8 Click *International* in the *Form AutoFormats* list box and then click OK.

9 Click Edit and then Select All.

> All of the controls in the form are selected. You can also use the Shift key and click control objects to select multiple controls.

10 Click the Properties button 🖺 on the Form Design toolbar.

> This opens the Multiple selection property sheet for the selected controls. Each control object in the form has a property sheet that can be used to change settings such as font, font size, color, and so on.

11 Click the Format tab in the Multiple selection property sheet. Scroll down the property sheet, click in the *Font Size* property box, click the down-pointing arrow that appears, and then click *12* in the drop-down list.

12 Close the Multiple selection property sheet.

13 Click in the gray shaded area within the Form window to deselect the objects and then click the Save button.

14 Click the View button 🖼 on the Form Design toolbar to switch to Form view.

15 With the first record in the table displayed in the form, click File, click Print, click *Selected Record(s)* in the *Print Range* section of the Print dialog box, and then click OK.

16 Close the Employee Dates and Salaries form.

AutoFormat

Form AutoFormats:
Blends
Blueprint
Expedition
Industrial
International
Ricepaper
SandStone
Standard
Stone
Sumi Painting

Step 8

In Addition

Moving Control Objects

To move a selected control, position the mouse pointer on the border of the selected object until the pointer changes to a black hand and then drag the object to the desired location. Both the label and text box control move together. To move a text box or label control independently, drag the large black handle that appears in the top left corner of the control object.

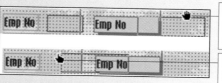

Point to border to move both controls simultaneously.

Point to large black handle at top left corner to move control independently.

3.8 Adding Controls to a Form

The **Toolbox** that displays when the form is opened in Design view contains a palette of control object buttons that are used to add controls to a form. To add a control to a form, click the control object button in the Toolbox for the type of control you want to add, and then drag the outline of the object in the design grid the approximate height and width you want the control to be. Depending on the control object created, type the text or expression for the object and modify properties as required.

PROJECT: You will add label control objects that add descriptive text to the Employee Benefits form in the *Form Header* and *Form Footer* sections.

S T E P S

1. With **WEEmployees3** open and Forms still selected on the Objects bar, open the Employee Benefits form in Design view.

2. Position the mouse pointer at the top of the gray *Detail* section border until the pointer changes to a black horizontal line with an up- and down-pointing arrow, drag the pointer down the approximate height shown at the right, and then release the mouse button.

PROBLEM **?** *Form Header/Form Footer* sections not visible? Click View and then click Form Header/Footer.

Step 2

3. Click the Label object button 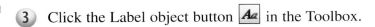 in the Toolbox.

PROBLEM **?** Toolbox not visible? Click the Toolbox button 🛠 on the Form Design toolbar.

4. Position the crosshairs pointer with the label icon attached to it at the top left edge of the *Form Header* section, drag down to the approximate height and width shown at the right, and then release the mouse button.

> Label objects are used to add descriptive text, such as a heading, to a form. When the mouse button is released, a label box will appear with the insertion point at the top left edge of the box.

5. Type **Employee Benefits** and then press Enter.

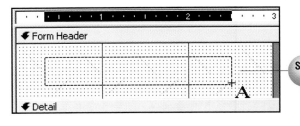

6. With the label control object selected, click the Center button ≣ on the Formatting (Form/Report) toolbar. Click View, point to Toolbars, and then click Fomatting (Form/Report) if the toolbar is not visible.

7 With the label control still selected, click the *Font Size* list arrow on the Formatting (Form/Report) toolbar and then click *14* at the drop-down list.

8 Position the mouse pointer on the bottom of the gray *Form Footer* section border line until the pointer changes to a black horizontal line with an up- and down-pointing arrow, drag down until the *Form Footer* section is the approximate height shown below, and then release the mouse button.

9 Add a label control object to the *Form Footer* section as shown using the following specifications. *(Hint: Review Steps 3–7 if you need assistance creating this object.)*

- Substitute your first and last name for *Student Name*.
- Change the font size to *11* and click the Italics button on the Formatting (Form/Report) toolbar.

10 Click the Save button and then switch to Form view.

11 Print the selected record only.

12 Close the Employee Benefits form.

13 Open the Employees form in Design view.

14 Add a label control object to the right of *Emp No, First Name,* and *Last Name* in the *Detail* section as shown using the following specifications:

- Change the font size to *8* and center the text.
- Click the down-pointing arrow at the right of the *Fill/Back Color* option box and then click a pale yellow color square.
- Click the down-pointing arrow at the right of the *Line/Border Color* option box and then click a dark blue color square.

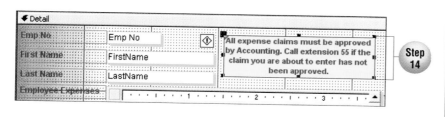

15 Click the Save button and then switch to Form view.

16 Print the selected record.

17 Close the Employees form.

Add Controls to a Form

1 Open form in Design view.
2 Click control object button in Toolbox.
3 Drag control in design grid the approximate height and width desired.
4 Type text or expression as required.
5 Click Save button.

3.9 Creating, Previewing, and Printing a Report

Information from the database can be printed while viewing tables in Datasheet view, while viewing a query results datasheet, or while browsing through forms by clicking the Print button on the toolbar. In these printouts all of the fields are printed in a tabular layout for datasheets or in the designed layout for forms. Create a report when you want to specify which fields to print and to have more control over the report layout and format. Access includes the Report Wizard, which generates the report based on selections made in a series of dialog boxes.

PROJECT: You will use the Report Wizard to create a report that will list the mailing addresses of the employees in a columnar format.

STEPS

1. With **WEEmployees3** open, click Reports on the Objects bar.

2. Double-click *Create report by using wizard*.

3. Click the down-pointing arrow at the right of the *Tables/Queries* text box and then click *Table: Employees* in the drop-down list.

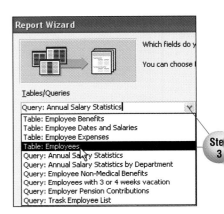

4. Click the Add All Fields button >> to move all of the fields in the Employees table from the *Available Fields* list box to the *Selected Fields* list box.

5. Click *Emp No* in the *Selected Fields* list box and then click the Remove Field button < to move *Emp No* back to the *Available Fields* list box.

6. Click *MiddleName* in the *Selected Fields* list box and then click the Remove Field button to move *MiddleName* back to the *Available Fields* list box.

7. Click Next.

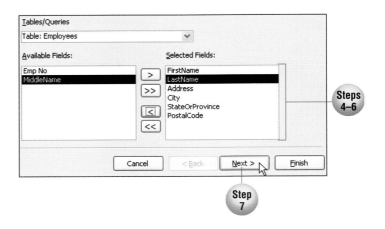

8 Click Next at the second Report Wizard dialog box to indicate that there is no grouping in the report.

> A grouping level in a report allows you to print records by sections within a table. For example, in an employee report you could print the employees grouped by city. In this example, you would double-click the *City* field to define the grouping level. The buttons with the up- and down-pointing arrows are used to modify the position of a field in the grouping level to increase or decrease its priority level if there is grouping by multiple fields.

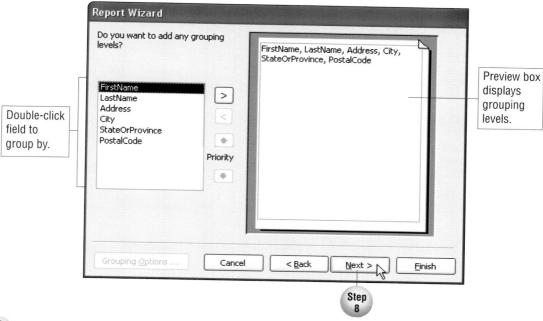

Double-click field to group by.

Preview box displays grouping levels.

Step 8

9 Click the down-pointing arrow next to the first text box in the third Report Wizard dialog box and then click *LastName* in the drop-down list.

> You can sort a report by up to four fields in the table.

Click here to change sort order from Ascending to Descending.

Step 9

10 Click Next.

11 Click *Columnar* in the *Layout* section in the fourth Report Wizard dialog box and then click Next.

> Use the preview box to view the selected layout before clicking the Next button.

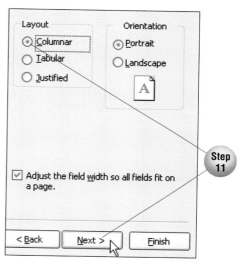

Step 11

(continued)

12 Click *Corporate* in the style list box in the fifth Report Wizard dialog box and then click Next.

13 With *Preview the report* selected in the sixth Report Wizard dialog box, type **Employee Mailing Addresses** in the title text box and then click Finish.

> In a few seconds the report will appear in the Print Preview window.

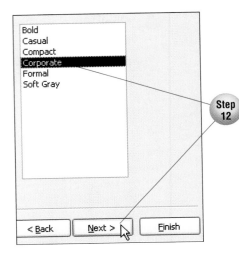

Step 12

What title do you want for your report?

Employee Mailing Addresses

That's all the information the wizard needs to create your report.

Do you want to preview the report or modify the report's design?

◉ Preview the report.

○ Modify the report's design.

Step 13

☐ Display Help on working with the report?

Cancel   < Back   Next >   Finish

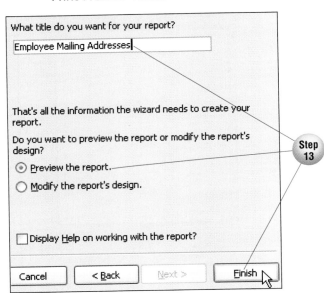

14 Move the pointer (displays as a magnifying glass) to the middle of the report and then click the left mouse button.

> The zoom changes to *Fit* and the entire page is displayed in the Print Preview window, as shown in Figure A3.6.

FIGURE A3.6 Report Page in Print Preview

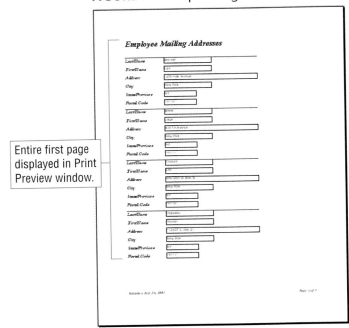

Entire first page displayed in Print Preview window.

(15) Click the Next Page button ▶ on the Page navigation bar to display page 2 of the report.

(16) Continue clicking the Next Page button until you have viewed all five pages in the report.

(17) Click File and then Print.

(18) Click *Pages* in the *Print Range* section.

(19) With the insertion point positioned in the *From* text box, type **1** and then press Tab.

(20) With the insertion point positioned in the *To* text box, type **1**.

(21) Click OK.

In a few seconds, the first page only of the five-page *Employee Mailing Addresses* report will print.

Step 20
Step 18
Step 19
Step 21

Print Range — All / Pages From: 1 To: 1 / Selected Record(s) — Setup...
Copies — Number of Copies: 1 — Collate — OK — Cancel

(22) Click the Close button on the Print Preview toolbar.

The Print Preview window closes and the report is displayed in Report Design view.

(23) Close the Employee Mailing Addresses report.

In Addition

Creating a Report in Design View

A report can be created in a blank Design view window as shown below. Initially, the field list box is blank until a table or query is associated with the report. Double-click the Report Selector button to display the Report property sheet. Click the Data tab and then click the down-pointing arrow in the *Record Source* property box to select a table or query name. To add fields to the design grid, drag the field name from the field list box to the position in the grid where you want the field to appear.

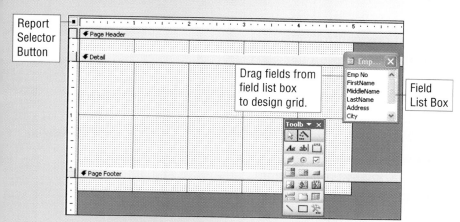

Report Selector Button

Drag fields from field list box to design grid.

Field List Box

IN BRIEF

Create a Report Using Report Wizard
1 Click Reports on Objects bar.
2 Double-click *Create report by using wizard.*
3 Choose table(s) and field(s) to include in report.
4 Click Next.
5 Choose grouping level(s) and click Next.
6 Choose field(s) to sort by and click Next.
7 Choose report layout and click Next.
8 Chose report style and click Next.
9 Type report title and click Finish.

3.10 Resizing and Moving Controls in a Report

Once a report has been created using the Report Wizard, the report can be modified by opening it in Design view. A report is similar to a form in that it is comprised of a series of objects referred to as controls. A report can be modified using similar techniques to those learned in Topics 3.7 and 3.8 on modifying and adding controls to a form.

PROJECT: After looking at the printout of the first page of the Employee Mailing Addresses report you decide that the space on the right side of the page is wasted. To reduce the number of pages required for the full report you will resize some controls, and move the *City, State/Province,* and *Postal Code* fields to the right side of the page.

S T E P S

(1) With **WEEmployees3** open and Reports selected on the Objects bar, open the Employee Mailing Addresses report in Design view.

> A report contains five sections, as shown in Figure A3.7: Report Header, Page Header, Detail, Page Footer, and Report Footer. The control objects for the fields in the table are displayed in the *Detail* section. In a tabular report layout, the *Page Header* section contains the label control objects for the fields placed in the report. In Addition at the end of this topic explains the purpose of each report section.

FIGURE A3.7 Employee Mailing Addresses Report Design View

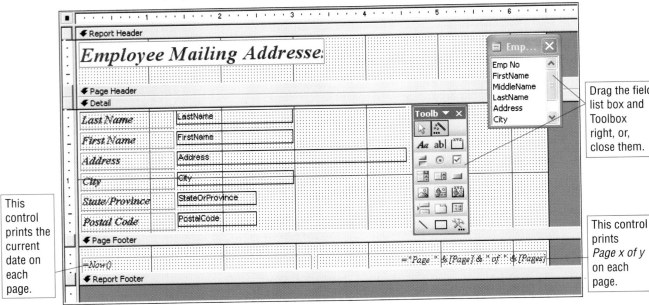

This control prints the current date on each page.

Drag the field list box and Toolbox right, or, close them.

This control prints *Page x of y* on each page.

(2) Click the *Address* text box control object to select it. This is the control with the black *Address* text.

(3) Position the mouse pointer on the right middle sizing handle until the pointer displays as a left- and right-pointing arrow, drag left until the control is resized to position 3 on the horizontal ruler, and then release the mouse button.

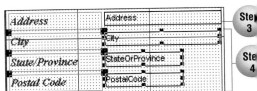

Step 3

Step 4

(4) Click the *City* text box control object. Hold down Shift and click the *StateOrProvince* text box control object. Hold down Shift and click the *PostalCode* text box control object.

All three objects are now selected. Any actions performed while the objects are selected affect all three.

5 Position the mouse pointer over the border of any of the selected objects until the pointer displays as a black hand, drag the selected objects to the right of the *LastName* text box control as shown, and then release the mouse button.

Step 5

6 Click in a gray area outside the report to deselect the objects.

Moving the last three fields beside the first three will reduce the pages required for printing the mailing addresses since you are now using the full width of the page. In the next step you will reduce the size of the *Detail* section so that the space below *Address* where the fields were originally placed is not left blank on the printout.

7 Position the mouse pointer on the top of the gray *Page Footer* section border until the pointer changes to a black horizontal line with an up- and down-pointing arrow, drag the pointer up just below *Address* as shown, and then release the mouse button.

8 Click the Save button and then click the Print Preview button.

9 Click the Next Page button on the Page navigation bar to display page 2.

Step 7

Notice the report now requires only two pages.

10 Print the first page only of the report.

11 Close the Print Preview window and then close the Employee Mailing Addresses report. Click Yes when prompted to save changes to the report design.

12 Close the **WEEmployees3** database.

In Addition

Report Sections

The five sections of a report are described below.

Report Header:	Controls in this section are printed once at the beginning of the report.
Page Header:	Controls in this section are printed at the top of each page in the report.
Detail:	Controls in this section make up the body of the report.
Page Footer:	Controls in this section are printed at the bottom of each page in the report.
Report Footer:	Controls in this section are printed once at the end of the report.

IN BRIEF

Resize Control Objects
1 Open report in Design view.
2 Click object to be resized.
3 Drag sizing handles to increase or decrease size of object.
4 Click Save button.

Move Control Objects
1 Open report in Design view.
2 Click to select control to be moved.
3 Position pointer over border of selected control until pointer changes to black hand.
4 Drag control to desired location.
5 Click Save button.

ACCESS

FEATURES SUMMARY

Feature	Button	Menu	Keyboard
Aggregate functions	Σ	View, Totals	
AutoForm		Insert, Form, AutoForm	
Design View		View, Design View	
Form Header/Footer		View, Form Header/Footer	
Form View		View, Form View	
Form Wizard		Insert, Form, Form Wizard	
Property sheet		View, Properties	Alt + Enter
Report Wizard		Insert, Report, Report Wizard	
Run a query	!	Query, Run	
Select all controls		Edit, Select All	Ctrl + A
Simple Query Wizard		Insert, Query, Simple Query Wizard	
Toolbox		View, Toolbox	

PROCEDURES CHECK

Completion: In the space provided at the right, indicate the correct term or command.

1. This is the name of the wizard used to facilitate creating a query to select records from a table. _____

2. Type this entry in the *Annual Salary* criteria row in Query Design view to extract records of employees who earn more than $40,000. _____

3. Click the check box in this row in the query design grid to prevent a column from being displayed in the query results. _____

4. Click this button on the Query Design toolbar to add a new row to the design grid in which you can select statistical functions. _____

5. Use this method of creating a form if you want to choose the layout and style of the form. _____

6. The label control object button is located in this palette. _____

7. Click this button on the Form Design toolbar to change the formats of a selected control object. _____

8. Click this option in the Print dialog box to print only the active form. _____

9. A report is comprised of a series of objects referred to as this. _____

10. Provide the entry you would type in a blank *Field* row in the Query Design grid to calculate the total cost of an item given the following information:

- The total cost is calculated by multiplying the units ordered by the unit price.
- The units ordered is stored in a field named *UnitsOnOrder.*
- The unit cost is stored in a field named *UnitCost.*
- The new column should have the column heading *Total Cost.*

_____

List the names of the five sections found in a report.

11. _____   14. _____

12. _____   15. _____

13. _____

FIGURE A3.8

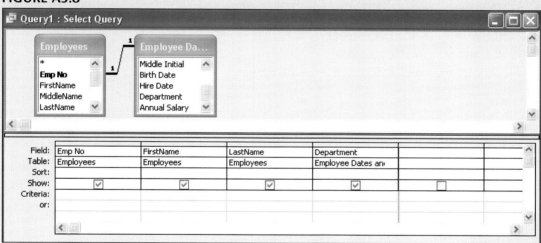

Use the Query Design window shown in Figure A3.8 to answer questions 16–18.

16. List the steps you would complete to sort the query results by the *LastName* field.

_____

_____

_____

17. List the steps you would complete to add the field named *Annual Salary* in the Employee Dates and Salaries table to the blank column after *Department* in the query design grid.

_____

_____

_____

18. List the steps you would complete to extract records of employees who work in the Overseas Distribution department.

_____

_____

_____

SKILLS REVIEW

Activity 1: CREATING A QUERY USING THE SIMPLE QUERY WIZARD

1. Open the **WEEmployees3** database.
2. Use the Simple Query Wizard to create a query that will display the fields from the Employees, Employee Dates and Salaries, and Employee Benefits tables as follows:

Employees	**Employee Dates and Salaries**	**Employee Benefits**
Emp No	*Hire Date*	*Life Insurance*
FirstName	*Annual Salary*	
LastName		

3. Accept the default Detail query and then type Salaries and Life Insurance as the title for the query.
4. View the query results datasheet.
5. Print the query results datasheet.
6. Close the Salaries and Life Insurance query.

Activity 2: SORTING A QUERY; ADDING A CRITERIA STATEMENT; CREATING A CALCULATED FIELD

1. With **WEEmployees3** open, open the Salaries and Life Insurance query in Design view.
2. Sort the query results by the *LastName* field in ascending order.
3. Add a criteria statement in the *Annual Salary* field that will extract the records of employees who earn more than $44,000. *(Hint: Numeric fields do not require quotation marks and should not include any currency symbols or commas.)*
4. Create a calculated field in the column after *Life Insurance* that will divide the *Annual Salary* column by 12 to display the monthly salary. Label the new column *Monthly Salary*.
5. Format the *Monthly Salary* column to display the calculated values in Currency format.
6. Use the Save As command to save the revised query as Employees Earning Over 44,000.
7. Run the query.
8. Preview and then print the query results datasheet.
9. Close the Employees Earning Over 44,000 query.

Activity 3: CALCULATING STATISTICS USING AGGREGATE FUNCTIONS

1. With **WEEmployees3** open, create a new query in Design view.
2. Add the Employee Expenses table to the design grid.
3. Add the *Amount* field to the design grid two times.
4. Display the *Total* row in the design grid.
5. Change the *Total* option in the first column to *Sum*.
6. Change the *Total* option in the second column to *Count*.
7. Change the caption property for the first column to *Total Expenses* and for the second column to *Number of Expense Claims*.
8. Save the query and name it Expense Statistics.
9. Run the query.

10 Best Fit the column widths in the query results datasheet.
11 Print and then close the Expense Statistics query, saving the changes.

Activity 4: CREATING A FORM USING THE FORM WIZARD; ENTERING RECORDS

1 With **WEEmployees3** open, create a new form for the Employee Expenses table using the following specifications:
   • Add all of the fields in the Employee Expenses table to the form.
   • Choose the *Columnar* layout.
   • Choose the *Sumi Painting* style.
   • Accept the default title for the form.
2 Add the following records to the Employee Expenses table using the form created in Step 1:

Emp No	1045	*Emp No*	1025
Date	5/13/05	*Date*	6/18/05
Amount	153.15	*Amount*	1127.88
Type	Sales	*Type*	Sales
Description	Tradeshow	*Description*	Sales Conference

3 Print all records in the table using the form.
4 Close the Employee Expenses form.

Activity 5: MODIFYING A FORM

1 With **WEEmployees3** open, open the Employee Expenses form created in Activity 4 in Design view.
2 Maximize the form window.
3 Expand the *Form Header* section approximately 1 inch and then insert the title *Expenses Form* in a label control object in the Form Header. Center the text in the label control object and then change the font size to 16 point.
4 Expand the *Form Footer* section approximately 1 inch and then insert the text *Form Design by: Student Name* in a label control object in the Form Footer. Substitute your first and last name for *Student Name*.
5 Decrease the width of the *Amount* text box control to position the right edge of the control at approximately 2.25 on the horizontal ruler.
6 Decrease the width of the *Type* text box control to position the right edge of the control at approximately 2.5 on the horizontal ruler.
7 Drag the right edge of the form (right edge of design grid) to approximately 3.5 on the horizontal ruler and then increase the width of the *Description* text box control to position the right edge of the control at approximately 3.25 on the horizontal ruler.
8 Switch to Form view.
9 Print the first record only in the form.
10 Close the Employee Expenses form, saving the changes.

Activity 6: CREATING A REPORT; RESIZING CONTROLS

1 With **WEEmployees3** open, use the Report Wizard to create a report based on the Salaries and Life Insurance query as follows:
   • Add all of the fields from the query to the report.
   • Do not include any grouping or sorting.

- Select the *Tabular* layout.
- Select the *Bold* style.
- Accept the default title for the report.

2 Preview and then print the report.
3 Display the report in Design view and then resize controls as follows:
- Drag the right edge of the *Last Name* label control object in the *Page Header* section to position 3 on the horizontal ruler.
- Drag the left edge of the *Hire Date* label control object in the *Page Header* section to approximately position 3.25 on the horizontal ruler.

4 Add your name in a label control object at the right side of the *Report Header* section.
5 Preview and then print the report.
6 Close the Salaries and Life Insurance report. Click Yes to save changes to the report design.
7 Close the **WEEmployees3** database.

PERFORMANCE PLUS

Assessment 1: CREATING A QUERY IN DESIGN VIEW; ADDING CRITERIA

1 The Bursary Selection Committee at Niagara Peninsula College would like you to provide them with the names of students who have achieved an A+ in all three of their courses.
2 Open **NPCGrades3**.
3 Create a query in Design view that will extract the records of those students who have an A+ in all three courses. Include student numbers, first names, last names, and grades. Sort the query in ascending order by student's last name. (*Hint: Type "A+" in the* **Criteria** *row to indicate the plus symbol is not part of an expression.*)
4 Save the query and name it A+ Students.
5 Run the query.
6 Best Fit the columns in the query results datasheet.
7 Print the query results datasheet in landscape orientation.
8 Close the A+ Students query.
9 Close **NPCGrades3**.

Assessment 2: CREATING A QUERY AND REPORT

1 Bobbie Sinclair, business manager of Performance Threads, would like a report that lists the costumes that were rented in August 2004.
2 Open **PTCostumeInventory3**.
3 Create a new query in Design view using the Costume Inventory table that will list the fields in the following order: *Costume No., Date Out, Date In, Character, Daily Rental Fee.*
4 Type the following criteria statement in the *Date Out* column that will extract the records for costumes that were rented in the month of August 2004:
   Between August 1, 2004 and August 31, 2004
5 Expand the column width of the *Date Out* column to view the entire criteria statement.
6 Notice Access converted the long dates to short dates and added pound symbols to the dates in the criteria statement. Dates in Access queries are encased in pound symbols (#).

7 Sort the query results first by *Date Out*, then by *Date In*, and then by *Character* in ascending order.
8 Save the query and name it August 2004 Rentals.
9 Run the query. Close the query after viewing the query results datasheet.
10 Create a report based on the August 2004 Rentals query. Add all of the fields to the report. You determine the layout, style, and title for the report.
11 Add your name in a label object control at the right side of the *Report Header* section.
12 Preview and then print the report.
13 Close **PTCostumeInventory3**.

Assessment 3: CREATING AND MODIFYING A FORM

1 Staff at Performance Threads have mentioned that looking up a costume in the costume inventory datasheet is difficult, since there are so many records in the table. You decide to create a form for the staff in which they see only one record on the screen at a time as they are browsing the inventory.
2 Open **PTCostumeInventory3**.
3 Create a new form using the Form Wizard for the Costume Inventory table. You determine the layout, style, and title of the form. Include all of the fields in the form.
4 Modify the form as follows:
   • Add the title *Costume Inventory* in a label control object in the *Form Header.* You determine font size, color, and so on.
   • Add the text *Check for damage/repairs upon return* in a label control object in the *Form Footer.* You determine font size, color, and so on.
   • Resize the *Daily Rental Fee* text box control so that the right edge of the control aligns with the right edge of the *Date Out* and *Date In* objects below it.
   • Move and/or resize any other controls to improve the appearance of the form.
5 Change the font and font size of all of the control objects in the *Detail* section of the form to a font and size of your choosing. Resize controls if necessary after changing the font size.
6 Display the form in Form view.
7 Print the first record only in the form.
8 Close the form. Choose Yes to save changes to the form design.
9 Close **PTCostumeInventory3**.

Assessment 4: FINDING INFORMATION ON ADDING A PICTURE TO A FORM

1 Use the Help feature to find out how to insert a picture that doesn't change from record to record in a form. **(*Hint: Start by typing* add a picture to a form *in the* Ask a Question *text box. Click the link* Add a picture or object *and then click the link in the Help window that describes how to use an image control to add an unbound picture.*)**
2 Print the Help topic that you find.
3 Open **WEEmployees3**.
4 Open the Employee Expenses form in Design view.
5 Decrease the size of the label control object in the *Form Header* section so that the title requires only one-half of the width of the form.

6   Insert the company logo to the other half of the *Form Header* section. The logo file name is **Worldwide.jpg**. After inserting the JPEG file within the control object open the property sheet and then change the *Size Mode* property box to *Zoom*. Adjust the sizes of the objects in the *Form Header* section as necessary.

7   Print the first record only in the form.

8   Close the Employee Expenses form. Choose Yes to save the changes to the form design.

9   Close **WEEmployees3**.

Assessment 5: RESEARCHING TRAVEL DESTINATIONS ON THE INTERNET

1   You are considering taking a one-week vacation at the end of the term. The destination is flexible and will depend on available flights, costs, and activities.

2   Search the Internet for flight information to at least four destinations to which you might like to travel. Determine departure times, arrival times, and airfares for the week following the end of the current term.

3   Search the Internet for additional travel costs that you might incur for the destinations you used in Step 2. Include hotel accommodations, car rentals, and any tours or other activities that you might like to purchase.

4   Create a new database and name it **TravelDestinations** to store your travel data. Design and create a table within the database that will include all of the data you collected. *(Hint: If necessary, refer to Section 2, Performance Plus Assessment 7 for the steps on how to start a new blank database.)*

5   Design and create a form to be used to enter the data into the tables.

6   Enter data using the form created in Step 5.

7   Print all of the records in the form.

8   Close the form.

9   Close **TravelDestinations**.

Modifying Tables and Reports, Performing Calculations, and Viewing Data

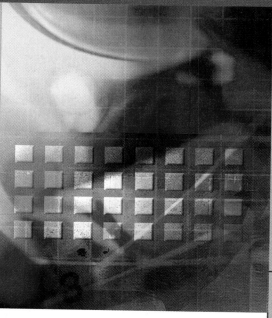

The structure of a table is modified by inserting, deleting, and moving fields. Filtering records allows the user to view a portion of the table data that meets a specific criterion. Access includes query wizards other than the Simple Query Wizard that assist with building queries for specific circumstances such as summarizing data, and finding duplicate or unmatched records in tables. Control objects can be created in which Access performs mathematical computations whenever a form or report is viewed or printed. Two views, PivotTable and PivotChart, are used to summarize and filter data. Tables and queries can be converted to a Web page to post on the Internet or a company's intranet by saving data in a data access page. Once a database contains several objects, it can be difficult to track the source from which objects are derived or are dependent. Display the Object Dependencies task pane to help with finding these associations. In this section you will learn the skills and complete the projects described here.

Note: Before beginning this section, delete any existing databases on your disk and copy each database as needed. Remember to remove the read-only attribute from each database after copying. If necessary, refer to page 1 for instructions on how to remove the read-only attribute. If necessary, check with your instructor before deleting any database files.

Skills

- Insert and delete fields in a table
- Move a field in a table
- Apply and remove filters to a table
- Create a crosstab query
- Create a find unmatched query
- Create a find duplicates query
- Create a calculated control object in a form and report
- Use align and spacing options in a form and report to improve the layout
- Move and resize control objects in a report
- Modify properties of form and report controls
- Summarize data in a PivotTable
- Summarize data in a PivotChart
- Save a table and a query as a Web page
- View a list of objects within a database
- View dependencies for an object
- Create a new database using a database wizard

Projects

Move, insert, and delete fields in tables; filter records; create queries to total field values grouped by two fields; create queries to find the records in a related table with no match in the primary table; use a query to find duplicate records; modify a form and report to include a calculated control; summarize and filter data in a PivotTable and PivotChart; save a table and query as a Web page; view a list of objects and associations between objects; create a new database in which to store contact information; create and modify a report.

Filter records of students who achieved A+ in a course.

Modify the structure of the Inventory List table; filter records by a supplier code; create a query and PivotChart; create a Web page.

Modify a form for browsing the costume inventory to include a calculation that will display the rental fee including tax.

4.1 Inserting, Deleting, and Moving Fields

Display a table in Design view to insert or delete fields or to reposition a field. In a previous section, you learned how to move columns in Datasheet view for sorting purposes. Although the column can be moved in the datasheet, the position of the field in the table structure will remain where it was originally created unless the field is moved in Design view. Exercise caution when making changes to the table structure after records have been entered. Data in deleted fields will be lost and existing records will have null values in new fields that have been added. As a precaution it is a good idea to make a backup of the database before making structural changes.

PROJECT: After consultation with Rhonda Trask, human resources manager of Worldwide Enterprises, you realize that the three name fields in the Employee Dates and Salaries table are redundant since the same fields also exist in the Employees table. You will delete these fields, add a new field for annual performance review dates, and reposition the *Annual Salary* field.

S T E P S

1. Open **WEEmployees4**.

2. Open the Employee Dates and Salaries table in Design view.

3. Click the insertion point in any text in the *Last Name* row.

4. Click the Delete Rows button on the Table Design toolbar.

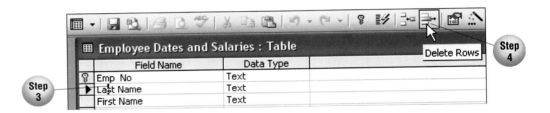

5. Click Yes at the Microsoft Office Access message asking you to confirm that you want to permanently delete the selected field(s) and all of the data in the field(s).

   Multiple fields can be deleted in one operation. In the next step, you will select both the *First Name* and *Middle Initial* fields, and in Step 7 you will delete both fields at the same time.

6. Position the mouse pointer in the field selector bar for the *First Name* field until the pointer changes to a right-pointing black arrow, and then drag the pointer down until both the *First Name* and *Middle Initial* fields are selected.

7. Click the Delete Rows button on the Table Design toolbar.

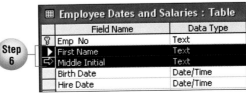

(8) Click Yes at the Microsoft Office Access message.

(9) Click the insertion point in any text in the *Department* row.

> New rows are inserted *above* the active field.

(10) Click the Insert Rows button [icon] on the Table Design toolbar.

> The new row is positioned between the *Hire Date* and *Department* fields.

Step 11

Employee Dates and Salaries : Table	
Field Name	Data Type
🔑 Emp No	Text
Birth Date	Date/Time
Hire Date	Date/Time
▶ Review Date	Date/Time ▾
Department	Text
Annual Salary	Currency

(11) Type **Review Date** in the *Field Name* column and then change the data type to *Date/Time*.

(12) Move the mouse pointer in the field selector bar beside *Annual Salary* until the pointer changes to a right-pointing black arrow and then click the left mouse button to select the field.

Step 13

Step 12

Employee Dates and Salaries : Table	
Field Name	Data Type
🔑 Emp No	Text
Birth Date	Date/Time
Hire Date	Date/Time
Review Date	Date/Time
Department	Text
▶ Annual Salary	Currency

(13) With the pointer still positioned in the field selector bar beside *Annual Salary* (pointer now displays as a white arrow), drag the pointer up between the *Birth Date* and *Hire Date* fields, and then release the left mouse button.

> As you drag the mouse, a black line appears between existing field names, indicating where the selected field will be repositioned when the mouse button is released and the white arrow pointer displays with a gray shaded box attached to it.

(14) Click in any field to deselect the *Annual Salary* row and then click the Save button.

(15) Switch to Datasheet view.

(16) Print and then close the Employee Dates and Salaries table.

In Addition

Adding Data in a New Field

Consider the following tips for entering data in the datasheet for a new field that has been inserted into a table after several records have already been created.

- Click in the new column (e.g., *Review Date*) in the first row of the table, type the data for the new field, and then press the Down Arrow key to remain in the same column for the next record.
- Press Ctrl + ' (apostrophe) if the data for the current record is the same field value as the data in the field immediately above the current record. Microsoft Access will automatically duplicate the entry that is above the active field.

IN BRIEF

Delete a Field
1 Open table in Design view.
2 Select field(s) to be deleted.
3 Click Delete Rows button on Table Design toolbar.
4 Click Yes.
5 Click Save button.

Insert a Field
1 Open table in Design view.
2 Click in field row immediately below where new field is to be located.
3 Click Insert Rows button on Table Design toolbar.
4 Type field name, assign data type, and modify properties as needed.
5 Click Save button.

Move a Field
1 Open table in Design view.
2 Select and then drag field to new location.
3 Click Save button.

4.2 Applying and Removing Filters

A *filter* is used to view only those records in a datasheet that meet specified criteria. For example, you might want to view only those records of employees who work in a specific department. Once the filter has been applied, you can view, edit, and print the filtered records. The records that do not meet the criteria are temporarily removed from the datasheet. Click the Remove Filter button on the Table Datasheet toolbar to redisplay all records in the table. Records can be filtered using two methods—*Filter By Selection*, and *Filter By*

Form. The difference between a filter and a query is that the query can be saved for future use, whereas the filter has to be redone each time.

PROJECT: You will use the Filter By Selection method in the Employee Dates and Salaries table to display and print records of employees who work in the European Distribution department. In the Employee Benefits table, you will use the Filter By Form method to print a list of employees who receive four weeks of vacation.

STEPS

1. With **WEEmployees4** open, open the Employee Dates and Salaries table in Datasheet view.

2. Select the text *European Distribution* in the *Department* column in the third row of the datasheet.

3. Click the Filter By Selection button 🍸 on the Table Datasheet toolbar.

Department
North American Distribution
Overseas Distribution
European Distribution
North American Distribution
North American Distribution

Step 2

Only records of employees in the European Distribution department are displayed, as shown in Figure A4.1. Notice the word *(Filtered)* appears after the number of records on the Record Navigation bar at the bottom of the datasheet.

FIGURE A4.1 Filtered Datasheet

⊞ Employee Dates and Salaries : Table						
	Emp	Birth Date	Annual Salary	Hire Date	Review Date	Department
▶ +	1010	12/10/1952	$69,725.00	1/30/1999		European Distribution
+	1035	2/4/1970	$44,694.00	3/15/2001		European Distribution
+	1045	6/18/1961	$42,238.00	4/12/2001		European Distribution
+	1050	5/9/1967	$44,387.00	2/9/2002		European Distribution
+	1060	1/6/1964	$42,126.00	6/22/2003		European Distribution
+	1080	1/8/1978	$43,659.00	1/17/2004		European Distribution
*			$0.00			

4. Print the table.

5. Click the Remove Filter button 🍸 on the Table Datasheet toolbar.

   All records in the table are redisplayed.

6. Close the Employee Dates and Salaries table. Click No if prompted to save changes.

7. Open the Employee Benefits table in Datasheet view.

8. Click the Filter By Form button 🗐 on the Table Datasheet toolbar.

   All records are temporarily removed from the datasheet and a blank row appears. Specify the field value in the field by which you want to filter by using the drop-down lists in the fields in the blank row. The Table Datasheet toolbar is replaced by the Filter/Sort toolbar.

⑨ Click in the *Vacation* column, click the down-pointing arrow that appears, and then click *4 weeks* in the drop-down list.

Step 9

Emp No	Pension Plan	Dental Plan	Premium Health	Dependents	Life Insurance	Pension Eligibility	Vacation
▶	☐	☐	☐				

Employee Benefits: Filter by Form

1 week
2 weeks
3 weeks
4 weeks

⑩ Click the Apply Filter button 🔽 on the Table Datasheet toolbar.

> The Apply Filter button changes to the Remove Filter button once a filter has been applied to a table.

Employee Benefits : Table

	Emp No	Pension Plan	Dental Plan	Premium Health	Dependents	Life Insurance	Pension Eligibility	Vacation
▶ +	1001	☑	☐	☑	2	$150,000.00	22-Jan-99	4 weeks
+	1015	☑	☑	☑	2	$199,999.00	17-Nov-99	4 weeks
+	1020	☑	☐	☐	0	$100,000.00	03-Feb-01	4 weeks
+	1025	☑	☑	☑	1	$150,000.00	01-Jun-01	4 weeks
*		☑	☐	☐	0	$0.00		

Step 10

⑪ Change the page orientation to landscape and then print the table.

⑫ Click the Remove Filter button on the Table Datasheet toolbar.

> All records in the table are redisplayed.

⑬ Close the Employee Benefits table. Click No if prompted to save changes.

In Addition

Filtering by Multiple Criteria

The Filter By Form window contains a tab labeled *Or* at the bottom of the window (shown at the right), just above the Status bar. Use this tab to filter by more than one criterion. For example, you could display records of employees who receive three weeks or four weeks of vacation. To do this, click the Filter By Form button and select *3 weeks* in the *Vacation* field, click the Or tab, and then select *4 weeks* in the *Vacation* field in the second form. Click the Apply Filter button. Records that meet either the three weeks or four weeks criterion will be displayed.

Use this tab to add a second criterion to filter by.

IN BRIEF

Filter By Selection
1 Open table in Datasheet view.
2 Select field value in field you want to filter by.
3 Click Filter By Selection button.
4 View, print, and/or edit data as required.
5 Click Remove Filter button.

Filter By Form
1 Open table in Datasheet view.
2 Click Filter By Form button.
3 Click in field you want to filter by.
4 Click down-pointing arrow and click value you want to filter by.
5 Click Apply Filter button.
6 View, print, and/or edit data as required.
7 Click Remove Filter button.

4.3 Summarizing Data Using a Crosstab Query

A *crosstab query* calculates aggregate functions such as sum and avg in which field values are grouped by two fields. A wizard is included that guides you through the steps to create the query. The first field selected causes one row to display in the query results datasheet for each group. The second field selected displays one column in the query results datasheet for each group. A third field is specified that is the numeric field to be summarized. The intersection of each row and column holds a value that is the result of the specified aggregate function for the designated row and column group. For example, suppose you want to find out the total sales achieved by each salesperson by state. Each row in the query results could be used to display a salesperson's name with the state names in columns. Access summarizes the total sales for each person for each state and shows the results in a spreadsheet-type format.

PROJECT: Worldwide Enterprises has been in an expansion phase in the last seven years and has been hiring aggressively to keep up with growth. Rhonda Trask wants to find out the salary cost that has been added to the payroll each year by department. You will use a crosstab query to calculate the total value of annual salaries for new hires in each year by each department.

STEPS

1 With **WEEmployees4** open, click Queries on the Objects bar and then click the New button on the Database window toolbar.

Step 1

2 Click *Crosstab Query Wizard* in the New Query list box and then click OK.

> The fields that you want to use for grouping must all exist in one table or query. In situations where the fields that you want to group by are in separate tables, you would first create a new query that contains the fields you need and then start the crosstab query wizard. In your project, all three fields that you need are in one table.

3 If necessary click *Tables* in the *View* section of the first Crosstab Query Wizard dialog box and then click *Table: Employee Dates and Salaries*.

Step 3

4 Click Next.

> In the second Crosstab Query Wizard dialog box you choose the field in which the field's values become the row headings in the query results datasheet.

5 Double-click *Department* in the *Available Fields* list box to move the field to the *Selected Fields* list box and then click Next.

> At the next dialog box you choose the field in which the field's values become the column headings in the query results datasheet.

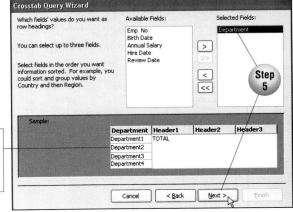

Step 5

Sample section previews the query results as you make each selection.

⑥ Click *Hire Date* in the field list box and then click Next.

> Whenever a date/time field is chosen for the column headings, Access displays a dialog box asking you to choose the time interval to summarize by with the default option set to *Quarter*.

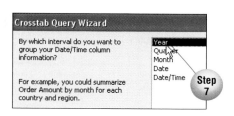

⑦ Click *Year* in the list box and then click Next.

> The final field to be selected is the numeric field to be summarized and the aggregate function to be used to calculate the values.

⑧ Click *Annual Salary* in the *Fields* list box and then click *Sum* in the *Functions* list box.

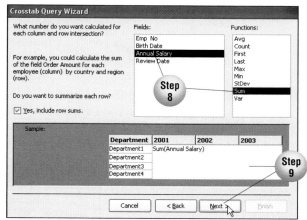

⑨ Look at the datasheet layout displayed in the *Sample* section of the Crosstab Query Wizard and then click Next.

⑩ Type **New Hire Payroll Costs by Department by Year** in the *What do you want to name your query?* text box and then click Finish.

> The query results datasheet displays as shown in Figure A4.2. Notice a total column is inserted next to each department name with the total broken down to show the amount for each year that makes up each department's payroll cost.

FIGURE A4.2 Crosstab Query Results Datasheet

Department	Total Of Annual	1998	1999	2000	2001	2002	2003	2004
European Distribution	$266,829.00		$69,725.00		$86,932.00	$44,387.00	$42,126.00	$43,659.00
North American Distribution	$249,521.00	$69,725.00	$90,543.00	$45,558.00			$43,695.00	
Overseas Distribution	$287,820.00	$69,725.00	$42,824.00		$45,395.00	$42,248.00		$87,628.00

⑪ Best Fit each column's width.

⑫ Display the Page Setup dialog box and change the left and right margins to 0.5 inch and the page orientation to landscape.

⑬ Print the query results datasheet.

⑭ Close the New Hire Payroll Costs by Department by Year query. Click Yes to save changes to the layout.

IN BRIEF

Create a Crosstab Query
1 Click Queries on Objects bar.
2 Click New button.
3 Click Crosstab Query Wizard and click OK.
4 Choose table or query name and click Next.
5 Choose field for row headings and click Next.
6 Choose field for column headings and click Next.
7 Choose numeric field to summarize and function to calculate and click Next.
8 Type query name and click Finish.

SECTION 4: MODIFYING TABLES AND REPORTS, PERFORMING CALCULATIONS, AND VIEWING DATA

4.4 Using a Query to Find Unmatched Records

A **find unmatched query** is used when you want Access to compare two tables and produce a list of the records in one table that have no matching record in the other related table. This type of query is useful to produce lists such as customers who have never placed an order or an invoice with no payment record. Access provides the Find Unmatched Query Wizard that builds the select query by guiding the user through a series of dialog boxes.

PROJECT: You will create a find unmatched query to make sure that you have entered a record in the Employee Benefits table for all employees at Worldwide Enterprises.

S T E P S

① With **WEEmployees4** open and Queries selected on the Objects bar, click the New button on the Database window toolbar.

② Click *Find Unmatched Query Wizard* in the New Query list box and then click OK.

> At the first dialog box in the Find Unmatched Query Wizard you choose the table or query in which you want to view records in the query results datasheet. If an employee is missing a record in the benefits table you will need the employee's number and name which is in the Employees table.

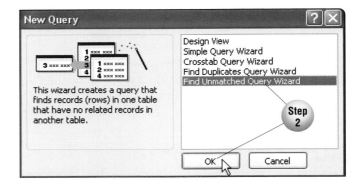

③ With *Tables* selected in the *View* section of the first Find Unmatched Query Wizard dialog box, click *Table: Employees* and then click Next.

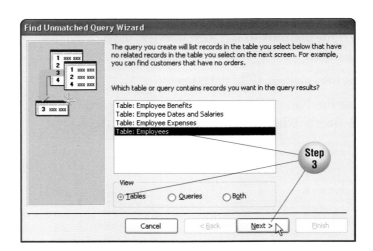

4. With *Table: Employee Benefits* already selected in the table list box, click Next.

> In order for Access to compare records you need to specify the field in each table that would have matching field values.

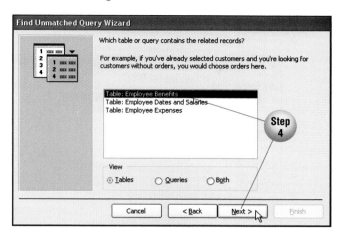

5. With *Emp No* already selected in the *Fields in 'Employees'* and *Fields in 'Employee Benefits'* list boxes, click Next.

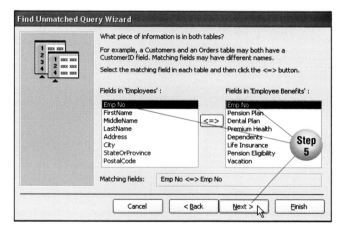

6. At the fourth Find Unmatched Query Wizard dialog box, double-click *Emp No, FirstName,* and *LastName* to move the fields from the *Available fields* list box to the *Selected fields* list box below *What fields do you want to see in the query results?* and then click Next.

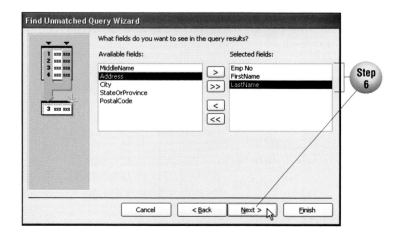

(continued)

7 Click Finish at the last Find Unmatched Query Wizard dialog box to accept the default name of *Employees Without Matching Employee Benefits* and *View the results* option.

> The query results datasheet opens with four records displayed showing the four employees that are missing a record in the benefits table.

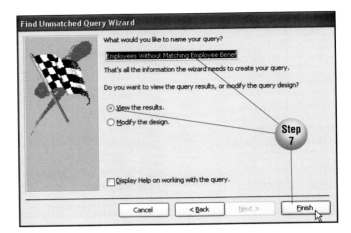

8 Look at the records displayed in the query results datasheet. Access has found four records in the Employees table for which no matching record exists in the Employee Benefits table.

9 Print the query results datasheet.

10 Close the Employees Without Matching Employee Benefits query.

11 Click Tables on the Objects bar and then open the Employee Benefits table in Datasheet view.

12 Add the following records to the Employee Benefits table.

> You are adding records for employee numbers 1045, 1070, and 1080 only. You suspect an error has occurred in the Carl Zakowski record which you will explore in the next topic.

Emp No	1045
Pension Plan	Yes
Dental Plan	No
Premium Health	Yes
Dependents	1
Life Insurance	100000
Pension Eligible	10-Oct-01
Vacation	2 weeks

Emp No	**1070**
Pension Plan	Yes
Dental Plan	Yes
Premium Health	Yes
Dependents	3
Life Insurance	195000
Pension Eligible	22-May-05
Vacation	1 week
Emp No	**1080**
Pension Plan	Yes
Dental Plan	No
Premium Health	No
Dependents	0
Life Insurance	50000
Pension Eligible	17-Jul-04
Vacation	1 week

13 Change the page orientation to landscape and then print the Employee Benefits datasheet.

14 Close the Employee Benefits table.

15 Click Queries on the Objects bar.

In Addition

Design View for a Find Unmatched Query

The dialog boxes in the Find Unmatched Query Wizard assist with creating a Select Query that searches the records in the related table for null field values in the field specified as common to both tables. *Null* is the term used for a field in which the field value is blank, or empty. The design view for the Employees Without Matching Employee Benefits is shown below. Notice the entry in the criteria row for the *Emp No* field from the Employee Benefits table is *Is Null*.

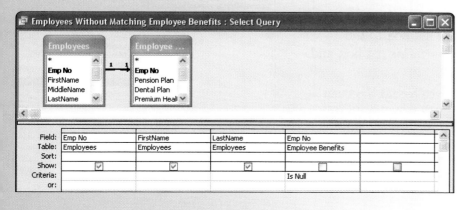

In BRIEF

Create a Find Unmatched Query
1 Click Queries on Objects bar.
2 Click New button.
3 Click Find Unmatched Query Wizard and click OK.
4 Choose table or query to display in query results and click Next.
5 Choose related table or query and click Next.
6 Choose matching field in each table field list and click Next.
7 Choose fields you want to view in query results and click Next.
8 Type query name and click Finish.

4.5 Using a Query to Find Duplicate Records

A ***find duplicates query*** searches a specified table or query for duplicate field values within a designated field or fields. Create this type of query if you suspect a record, such as a product record, has inadvertently been entered twice under two different product numbers. Other examples of applications for this type of query are included in the In Addition section following this topic. Access provides the Find Duplicates Query Wizard that builds the select query based on the selections made in a series of dialog boxes.

PROJECT: You suspect that someone who filled in for you last week while you were away at a conference added an employee record to the Employees table in error. You will use a find duplicates query to check for this occurrence in the Employees table.

S T E P S

1 With **WEEmployees4** open and Queries selected on the Objects bar, click the New button on the Database window toolbar.

2 Click *Find Duplicates Query Wizard* in the New Query list box and then click OK.

> At the first dialog box in the Find Duplicates Query Wizard you choose the table or query in which you want Access to look for duplicate field values.

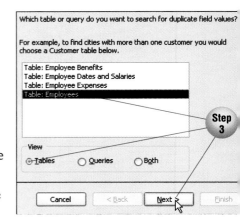

3 With *Tables* selected in the *View* section of the first Find Duplicates Query Wizard dialog box, click *Table: Employees* and then click Next.

> At the second Find Duplicates Query Wizard dialog box you choose the fields that may contain duplicate field values. Since *Emp No* is the primary key field in the Employees table you know that it is not possible for an employee record to be duplicated using the same employee number, therefore, you will use the name fields to check for duplicates.

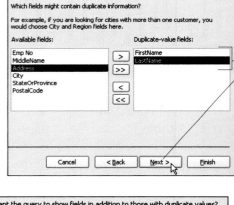

4 Double-click *FirstName* and *LastName* to move the fields from the *Available fields* list box to the *Duplicate-value fields* list box and then click Next.

5 Move all of the fields from the *Available fields* list box to the *Additional query fields* list box and then click Next.

> If an employee record has been duplicated you would want to see all of the fields to ensure that the information in both records is exactly the same. If not, you would need to check which record contains the accurate information before deleting the duplicate.

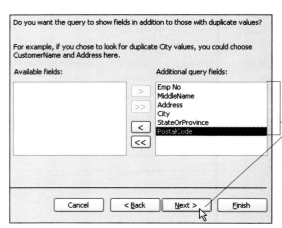

⑥ Click Finish at the last dialog box to accept the default name *Find duplicates for Employees* and *View the results* option.

The query results datasheet displays showing that Carl Zakowski has two records in the Employees table under two different employee numbers.

	First Name	Last Name	Emp No	Middle Name	Address	City	State/Province	Postal Code
Step 6 ▶	Carl	Zakowski	1077	Waylon	65 Dyer Avenue	New York	NY	10110-
	Carl	Zakowski	1050	Waylon	65 Dyer Avenue	New York	NY	10110-
*								

⑦ Change the page orientation to landscape and then print the query results datasheet.

⑧ Move the mouse pointer in the record selector bar next to the first record (with *Emp No 1077*) until the pointer changes to a right-pointing black arrow, right-click, and then click Delete Record at the shortcut menu.

Find duplicates for Employees : Select Query

	First Name	Last Name	Emp No	Middle
		Zakowski	1077	Waylon
New Record		akowski	1050	Waylon
Delete Record				
Cut				

Step 8

⑨ Click Yes to confirm the record deletion.

⑩ Close the Find duplicates for Employees query.

⑪ Double-click *Find duplicates for Employees* in the query list. The query result now displays a blank datasheet. Since you deleted the duplicate record for Carl Zakowski in Step 8, duplicate records no longer exist in the Employees table.

⑫ Close the Find Duplicates for Employees query.

In Addition

More Examples for Using a Find Duplicates Query

In this topic you used a find duplicates query to locate and then delete an employee record that was entered twice. A find duplicates has many other applications. Consider the following examples:

- Find the records in an Orders table with the same customer number so that you can identify who your loyal customers are.
- Find the records in a Customer table with the same last name and mailing address so that you send only one mailing to a household to save on printing and postage costs.
- Find the records in an Employee Expenses table with the same employee number so that you can see which employee is submitting the most claims.

IN BRIEF

Create a Find Duplicates Query
1 Click Queries on Objects bar.
2 Click New button.
3 Click Find Duplicates Query Wizard and click OK.
4 Choose table or query to search for duplicates and click Next.
5 Choose the field(s) that might contain duplicate field values and click Next.
6 Choose additional fields to display in query results and click Next.
7 Type query name and click Finish.

4.6 Adding a Calculated Control to a Form; Using Align and Spacing Controls

Add a text box control object to a form to perform calculations. Formulas are based on existing fields in the table similar to the method used to calculate in queries. A calculated control is not stored as a field—each time the form is opened, the results are dynamically calculated. The align options *Left, Right, Top,* and *Bottom* are used to arrange selected objects at the same horizontal or vertical position on a form or report. The spacing between controls can be adjusted using the Horizontal Spacing and Vertical Spacing options on the Format menu. The spacing can be increased, decreased, or made even.

PROJECT: Worldwide Enterprises pays its employees 4% of their annual salary as vacation pay each year. You will add a control object to the Employee Dates and Salaries form to calculate the vacation pay entitlement for each employee and use align and spacing options to improve the layout of the form.

STEPS

① With **WEEmployees4** open, click Forms on the Objects bar, and then open the Employee Dates and Salaries form in Design view.

② Maximize the form window if it is not already maximized.

③ Position the mouse pointer at the top of the gray *Form Footer* section border and then drag the *Form Footer* section down the approximate height shown.

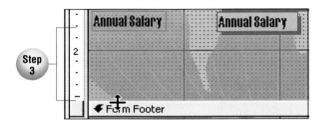

④ Click the Text Box object button ab in the Toolbox.

⑤ Position the crosshairs pointer with the text box icon attached to it below the *Annual Salary* text box control, drag to create the object the approximate height and width shown below, and then release the mouse button.

> A text box label control object and an unbound control object box appear. An **unbound control** contains data that is not stored anywhere. A control that displays a field value in a table is referred to as a **bound control** since the object contents are bound to the table.

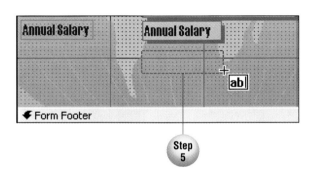

6 Click in the unbound text box control.

An insertion point appears so that you can type the formula. A mathematical expression in a text box control begins with the equals sign (=) and field names are encased in square brackets.

7 Type =[Annual Salary]*0.04 and then press Enter.

Do not be concerned if a portion of the formula is not visible within the control object. The entire formula is stored in the object's property sheet as the *Data Source.* In Form view, the object will be displaying the calculated values, not the formula.

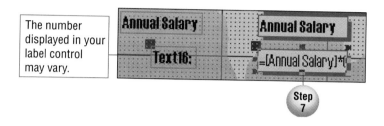

The number displayed in your label control may vary.

Step 7

8 Right-click over the calculated control object and then click Properties at the shortcut menu.

9 Click the Format tab in the Text Box property sheet. With the insertion point positioned in the *Format* property box, click the down-pointing arrow that appears, scroll down the drop-down list, and then click *Currency.*

10 Scroll down the Format property sheet, click in the *Font Size* property box, click the down-pointing arrow that appears, and then click *12* in the drop-down list.

11 Close the Text Box property sheet.

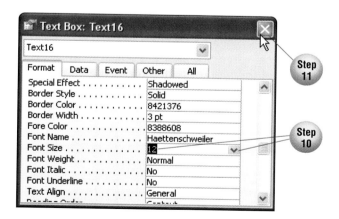

Step 11

Step 10

12 Click the label control object adjacent to the text box control (currently displays *Text##* [where ## is the number of the label object]) to select it.

(continued)

(13) Click a second time inside the selected label control object to display the insertion point, delete the current text, type **Vacation Pay**, and then press Enter.

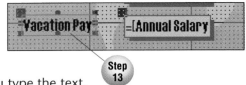

Step 13

The width of the box will increase as you type the text.

(14) With the *Vacation Pay* label control still selected, hold down the Shift key and then click the *Annual Salary* label control above *Vacation Pay*.

(15) Click Format, point to Align, and then click Left.

Align Left arranges the left edges of the controls with the left edge of the leftmost control in the selected group.

Steps 14–15

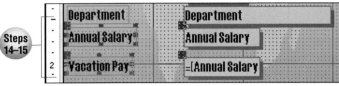

(16) Click in a gray area to deselect the *Annual Salary* and *Vacation Pay* label objects.

(17) Position the white arrow pointer at the top left of the *Detail* section (just below the *Detail* section border and not on an individual object) and then drag a selection rectangle around all of the control objects within the section.

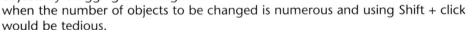

Ste 17

Use the mouse to select multiple objects by dragging a rectangle when the number of objects to be changed is numerous and using Shift + click would be tedious.

(18) With all objects in the *Detail* section selected, click Format, point to Vertical Spacing, and then click Make Equal.

The vertical space between the selected objects is now evenly distributed. The position of the highest control does not change.

Step 18

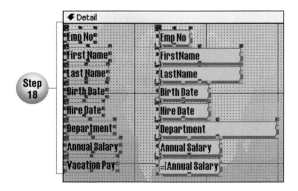

(19) Click in a gray area to deselect the objects.

20 Change the text in the label control object in the *Form Footer* section to insert your name in place of *Student Name*.

21 Click the Save button and then switch to Form view.

22 With the record for employee number 1001 displayed, click in the *Last Name* field, and then click the Sort Ascending button on the Form View toolbar.

> The record for employee number 1015, Lyle Besterd displays. You can now scroll the records alphabetically by employee last name.

23 Print the selected record only and then close the Employee Dates and Salaries form, saving changes.

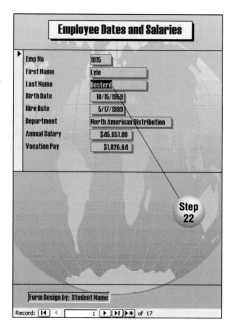

In Addition

Error Checking in Access

Automatic error checking for common types of errors in forms and reports is turned on by default in Access 2003. When Access determines that an error has occurred, a small green diagonal triangle appears in the upper left corner of the control. Click the control with an error indicator to display the Error Checking Options button. Pointing to the Error Checking Options button displays a ScreenTip indicating the type of error that has occurred. Click the Error Checking Options button to choose from a list of options with which you can correct the error. In the example shown below an equals sign is missing at the beginning of the mathematical expression in the calculated control. To correct the error, click *Edit the Control's Control Source Property* at the Error Checking Options drop-down menu. The property sheet for the calculated control opens with an insertion point active in the Control Source property box. Add the equals sign and close the property sheet. The Error Checking indicator will be removed once the error is corrected.

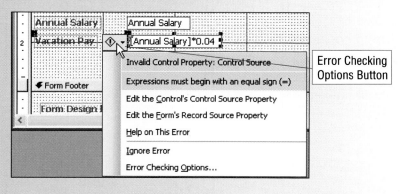

IN BRIEF

Add a Calculated Control Object to a Form
1 Open form in Design view.
2 Click Text Box object button in Toolbox.
3 Drag control in design grid the approximate height and width desired.
4 Click in Unbound control object and type formula.
5 Change format properties for unbound control as required.
6 Type desired label in text box label control.
7 Click the Save button.

4.7 Modifying a Report; Creating a Calculated Control

Modifying a report by resizing, moving, aligning, spacing, and formatting controls is often required to fine-tune the appearance after the Report Wizard creates the report. A calculated control object can be created in a report by completing steps similar to those learned in the previous topic. As in a form, the calculations are not stored in the table, but are dynamically calculated each time the report is previewed or printed.

PROJECT: Worldwide Enterprises estimates that it incurs benefit costs of an additional 22% of an employee's annual salary to pay for the benefit plans it offers to employees. You will create a report to print a list of employees based on a query, add a control to calculate the estimated benefit cost, and then modify the report.

S T E P S

1. With **WEEmployees4** open, click Reports on the Objects bar and then create a new report using the Report Wizard as follows.

   - Add all fields from the Trask Employee List query.
   - Double-click the *Department* field in the second Report Wizard dialog box to group the entries in the report by department.
   - Sort the report by *LastName* in ascending order.
   - Choose the block layout in landscape orientation.
   - Choose the soft gray style.
   - Type **Employee Benefit Cost** as the title of the report.

2. Click the Close button on the Print Preview toolbar after viewing the report to display the report in Design view.

   > This report contains an additional section named *Department Header* since the report is grouped by the *Department* field.

3. Maximize the report window if it is not already maximized.

4. Click the *Emp No* label control in the *Page Header* section.

5. Hold down the Shift key and then click *Emp No* in the *Detail* section.

   > Both controls are now selected.

6. Press Delete.

7. Click the *Last Name* label control in the *Page Header* section, Shift + click *LastName* in the *Detail* section, and then resize the right edge of either control to position 3 on the horizontal ruler.

   > With both controls selected, dragging the right sizing handle of one control will also resize the other control.

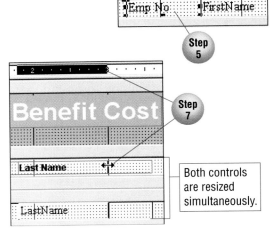

8 Select both *First Name* controls. Position the mouse pointer on the border of one of the selected controls until the pointer changes to a black hand, and then drag the controls left to align the left edge at position 3.25 on the horizontal ruler.

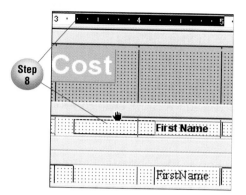

9 With both *First Name* controls still selected, resize the right edge of either control to position 4.25 on the horizontal ruler.

10 Select both *Hire Date* controls and then drag the border of either control left to align the left edge at position 4.5 on the horizontal ruler.

11 Select both *Annual Salary* controls and then drag the border of either control left to align the left edge at position 5.5 on the horizontal ruler.

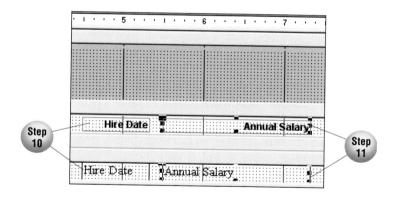

12 If necessary, scroll right until you can see the right edge of the report.

13 Click the Label object button **Aa** in the Toolbox.

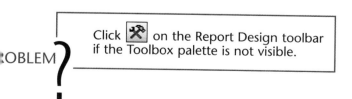

Click 🔨 on the Report Design toolbar if the Toolbox palette is not visible.

ROBLEM❓❗

(continued)

14 Position the crosshairs with the label icon attached in the *Page Header* section to the right of *Annual Salary*, drag to create the outline the approximate height and width shown, and then release the mouse button.

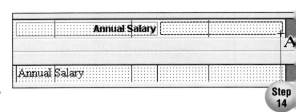

Step 14

15 Type **Estimated Benefit Cost** and then press Enter.

16 Click the *Annual Salary* control in the *Page Header* section, click the Format Painter button ✍ on the Report Design toolbar, and then click the *Estimated Benefit Cost* label control. Widen the control if necessary to display the entire label contents.

> Format Painter copies the formatting attributes for the *Annual Salary* label to the *Estimated Benefit Cost* label.

17 Click the Text Box object button `ab|` in the Toolbox.

18 Position the crosshairs with the text box icon attached in the *Detail* section below the *Estimated Benefit Cost* label, drag to create an object the same height and width as the label, and then release the mouse button.

19 Click in the text box control (displays *Unbound*), type **=[Annual Salary]*0.22**, and then press Enter.

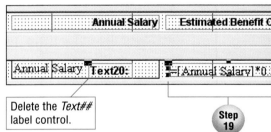

Delete the *Text##* label control.

Step 19

20 Click the label control to the left of the text box control (displays *Text##* [where ## is the text box label number]) and press Delete.

21 Click the Print Preview button to preview the report. If necessary, scroll right to view the right edge of the report where the calculated values display.

> Notice that the calculated values are aligned at the left edge of the column, do not display a consistent number of decimal places, and the border lines are not surrounding the values as in the remainder of the report.

22 Close the Print Preview window.

23 Click the *Annual Salary* control in the *Detail* section, click the Format Painter button, and then click the control object containing the mathematical expression.

> The border attributes are copied to the calculated control object.

24 Right-click the calculated control object, and then click Properties at the shortcut menu.

25 Change the following properties on the Format tab in the property sheet and then close the property sheet.

- Format property to *Currency*
- Text Align property to *Right*

26 Preview the Employee Benefit Cost report. Close the Print Preview window and if necessary, adjust controls by moving and/or resizing objects to improve the report's appearance. Make sure all text is entirely visible within the report.

PROBLEM? Click Format and then Snap to Grid to turn off the snapping feature if you are having difficulty resizing or moving an object a small distance. Snapping means the control will jump to the nearest grid point when you release the mouse.

27 Click the Save button.

28 Click the Sorting and Grouping button ▣ on the Report Design toolbar.

Display the Sorting and Grouping dialog box to make changes to the report's grouping and sort order after the report has been created. In this report, *Department* is shown first with the grouping icon ▣ in the field selector bar since the report is grouped and sorted first by the department name and then sorted by the *LastName* field.

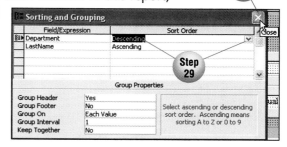

Step 30

Step 29

29 Click in the *Sort Order* column next to *Department*, click the down-pointing arrow that appears, and then click *Descending*.

30 Close the Sorting and Grouping dialog box.

31 Create a label object at the right side of the *Report Header* section with the text *Report by: Student Name*. Substitute your name for *Student Name*.

32 Create another label object below your name in the *Report Header* section with the text *Benefits calculated at 22% of Annual Salary*. Resize the control if necessary so that the text does not wrap to a second line.

33 Select both label controls created in Steps 31 and 32.

Your vertical spacing may vary depending on where the two label controls were originally situated.

Steps 31–35

34 Click Format, point to Align, and then click Left.

35 With both label controls still selected, click Format, point to Vertical Spacing, and then click Increase.

36 Click the Save button and then preview the report in the Print Preview window.

37 Print and then close the Print Preview window.

38 Close the Employee Benefit Cost report.

In Addition

Form, Report, and Section Properties

A property sheet is available for each form, report, and for each section within a form or report. Open the property sheets to change formats, control page breaks, and so on. To display the property sheet for a form or report, double-click the Form or Report Selector button ▣ at the top left corner of the horizontal and vertical rulers in Design view. Double-click the gray section bar to display the property sheet for a section.

In BRIEF

Modify Report Control Properties
1 Display report in Design view.
2 Click control object to be modified.
3 Change properties as required.
4 Save changes.
5 Preview report.

4.8 Summarizing Data Using PivotTable View

A PivotTable is an interactive table that organizes and summarizes data based on the fields you designate for row headings, column headings, and source record filtering. Aggregate functions such as sum, avg, and count are easily added to the table using the AutoCalc button on the PivotTable toolbar. A PivotTable provides more options for viewing data than a crosstab query because you can easily change the results by filtering data by an item in a row, a column, or for all source records. This interactivity allows you to analyze the data for numerous scenarios. PivotTables are easily created using a drag-and-drop technique in PivotTable view.

PROJECT: The accountant for Worldwide Enterprises wants a report that illustrates the expenses by type submitted by employees in the North American Distribution department. You will begin by creating a query since the required information is in more than one table and then use a PivotTable to summarize the data.

STEPS

1 With **WEEmployees4** open, click Queries on the Objects bar and then create a new query in Design view as follows.
- Add the Employees, Employee Dates and Salaries, and Employee Expenses tables to the design grid.
- Add the following fields in order: *FirstName, LastName, Department, Date, Type,* and *Amount.*
- Save the query and name it Expenses for PivotTable.

2 Run the query to view the query results datasheet.

3 Click View and then click PivotTable View.

> The datasheet changes to PivotTable layout with four sections and a PivotTable Field List box. Dimmed text in each section describes the type of fields that should be dragged and dropped.

4 Click LastName in the PivotTable Field List box, drag the field to the section labeled *Drop Row Fields Here* until a blue border outlines the section, and then release the mouse.

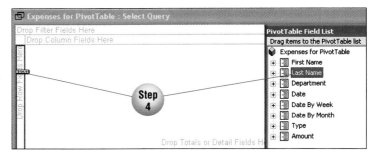

> When you release the mouse, a row for each field value in the *LastName* field appears with the caption *Last Name* and a filter arrow at the top of the list.

5 Click *Type* in the PivotTable Field List box, drag the field to the section labeled *Drop Column Fields Here* until a blue border outlines the section, and then release the mouse.

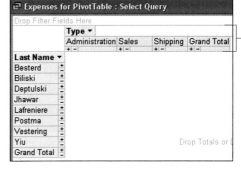

> A column for each field value in the field named *Type* appears with the caption **Type** and filter arrow above the list.

6 Click *Department* in the PivotTable Field List box and then drag the field to the section labeled *Drop Filter Fields Here*.

Step 6

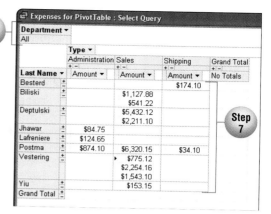

7 Click *Amount* in the PivotTable Field List box and then drag the field to the section labeled *Drop Totals or Detail Fields Here*.

Step 7

Access summarizes and arranges the data within the columns and rows.

8 Click one of the *Amount* column headings.

All cells in the table containing values from the *Amount* field are selected as indicated by the light blue color.

9 Click the AutoCalc button Σ on the PivotTable toolbar and then click *Sum* at the drop-down list.

Step 9

Step 8

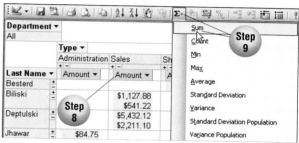

Each employee's expenses are subtotaled and the Grand Totals are now calculated. A *Totals* field showing the *Sum of Amount* function is added to the PivotTable Field List box.

10 Click the filter arrow (black down-pointing arrow) to the right of *Department*.

Step 10

11 Click the *(All)* check box to deselect all department names, click the *North American Distribution* check box, and then click OK.

Step 11

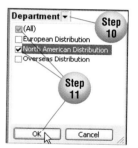

The PivotTable hides all data except those employees in the North American Distribution department.

12 Right-click over the *Sum of Amount* column heading and then click Properties at the shortcut menu.

13 Click the Captions tab in the Properties sheet, click in the *Caption* text box, delete *Sum of Amount,* and then type **Total Expenses**.

Step 13

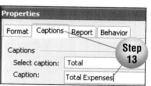

14 Click the Format tab, click the Bold button, click the *Fill Color* arrow next to *Background color,* click a light blue color square, and then close the Properties sheet.

15 Right-click over the *Grand Total* row heading, click Properties at the shortcut menu, click the Format tab, click the Red Font Color button in the *Text format* section, and then close the Properties sheet.

Step 16

Step 15

16 Change the font color of the values in the *Grand Total* column by completing steps similar to those in Step 15.

17 Click the Save button. Change the left margin to 1.5 inches and then print the PivotTable.

18 Close the Expenses for PivotTable query.

4.9 Summarizing Data Using PivotChart View

A PivotChart performs the same function as a PivotTable with the exception that the source data is displayed in a graph instead of a table. A chart is created by dragging fields from the Chart Field List box to the *Filter, Data, Category,* and *Series* sections of the chart. By default, the Sum function is used to total the summarized data. To change to a different function, click the Sum of [Field name] button, click the AutoCalc button on the PivotChart toolbar, and then click the desired function in the drop-down

list. As with a PivotTable, the PivotChart can be easily altered using the filter arrows.

PROJECT: After reviewing the table prepared in Topic 4.8, the accountant has asked for two more reports in chart form. You will display the Expenses for PivotTable query in a PivotChart, modify the filter and chart settings, and then print the PivotCharts.

S T E P S

1. With **WEEmployees4** open and Queries selected on the Objects bar, open the Expenses for PivotTable query in Datasheet view.

2. Click View and then click PivotChart View.

   The information created in the PivotTable in the last topic is automatically graphed in a column chart with filter buttons for *Department, Last Name,* and *Type.*

3. Click the Field List button 🔲 on the PivotTable toolbar to close the Chart Field List box.

4. Click the *Department* filter arrow (blue down-pointing arrow), click the *(All)* check box, and then click OK.

   The chart is updated to reflect expense claims in all departments.

5. Click the *Type* filter arrow, click the *(All)* check box to deselect all types, click the *Sales* check box, and then click OK.

   The chart is updated to reflect only sales expense claims for all departments.

6. Right-click *Axis Title* at the bottom of the chart and then click Properties at the shortcut menu.

7. Click the Format tab in the Properties sheet, click in the *Caption* text box, delete the existing text, type **Employee Last Name**, and then close the Properties sheet.

8. Change the vertical *Axis Title* at the left side of the chart to *Sales Expenses* by completing steps similar to those in Steps 6–7.

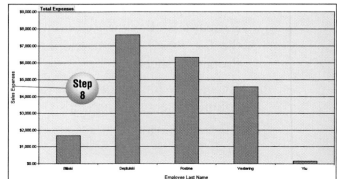

(9) Click the Save button.

(10) Change the page orientation to landscape and then print the PivotChart.

(11) Click View and then click PivotTable View.

> Notice the PivotTable is dynamically linked to the PivotChart. Changes made to the filter settings in Chart view are also updated in Table view.

(12) Click the *Department* filter arrow, click the *North American Distribution* check box to deselect the department, and then click OK.

> The PivotTable updates to reflect expenses for all departments except North American Distribution.

(13) Click View and then click PivotChart.

(14) Print the revised PivotChart.

(15) Click the Save button and then close the Expenses for PivotTable query.

Department ▾				
All				
		Type ▾		
		Sales	Grand Total	
		+ −	+ −	
Last Name ▾		Amount ▾	Total Expenses	
Biliski	±	$1,127.88	$1,669.10	
		$541.22		
		$1,669.10		
Deptulski	±	$5,432.12	$7,643.22	
		$2,211.10		
		$7,643.22		
Postma	±	$6,320.15	$6,320.15	
		$6,320.15		
Vestering	± ▸	$775.12	$4,572.38	
		$2,254.16		
		$1,543.10		
		$4,572.38		
Yiu	±	$153.15	$153.15	
		$153.15		
Grand Total	±	$20,358.00	$20,358.00	

Step 11

In Addition

Creating a PivotChart from Scratch

In this topic, a PivotChart was automatically created when you selected PivotChart View because an existing PivotTable was saved with the query. When you open a table or query without an existing PivotTable and choose PivotChart View, the screen looks like the one shown below. Drag the fields from the PivotChart Field List box to the appropriate sections in the chart. You will create a PivotChart from scratch in a Performance Plus assessment at the end of this section.

IN BRIEF

Create a PivotChart
1. Open desired table or query in datasheet view.
2. Click View, PivotChart View.
3. Drag field for X-axis categories from Chart Field List to *Drop Category Fields Here*.
4. Drag field to use for filtering data from Chart Field List to *Drop Filter Fields Here*.
5. Drag field(s) with data to be graphed to *Drop Data Fields Here*.
6. Change axis titles as required.
7. Filter data as required.
8. Click Save.

4.10 Creating Data Access Pages

Data access pages are Web pages created from tables or queries that are used for interacting with Microsoft Access databases on the Internet or on a company's intranet. Data access pages are stored outside the database file. Designing and modifying a data access page is similar to designing forms and reports. Access includes a Page Wizard that can be used to create a data access page.

PROJECT: You will create a Web page that will enable employees to view their benefits through a Web browser.

STEPS

1. With **WEEmployees4** open, click Pages on the Objects bar.

2. Double-click *Create data access page by using wizard.*

3. With *Table: Employee Benefits* already selected in the *Tables/Queries* list box in the first Page Wizard dialog box, double-click *Emp No* in the *Available Fields* list box to move the field to the *Selected Fields* list box.

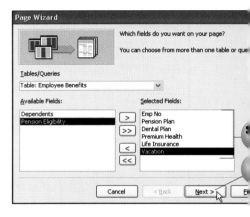

4. Double-click *Pension Plan, Dental Plan, Premium Health, Life Insurance,* and *Vacation* to move the fields from the *Available Fields* list box to the *Selected Fields* list box.

5. Click Next.

6. Click Next at the second Page Wizard dialog box to continue without adding a grouping level to the page.

7. Click Next at the third Page Wizard dialog box to continue without specifying a field to sort the records by.

8. Click Finish at the last Page Wizard dialog box to accept the default title *Employee Benefits* and *Modify the page's design.*

   In a few seconds the data access page is displayed in Design view, as shown in Figure A4.3.

FIGURE A4.3 Data Access Page Design View

9. Close the Field List task pane and the Toolbox and then maximize the Data Access Page window.

10. Click over the text *Click here and type title text* and then type **Worldwide Enterprises Employee Benefits**.

   As soon as you click over *Click here and type title text*, the text will disappear and will be replaced with the text you type.

11. Click Format and then Theme.

   A *theme* is a group of predefined formats and color schemes for bullets, fonts, horizontal lines, background images, and other data access page elements.

⑫ Scroll down the *Choose a Theme* list box and then click *Sky*.

> The selected theme's colors, bullet style, line style, text and hyperlinked text style, button style, and text box formats display in the *Sample of the theme Sky* section.

⑬ Click OK.

⑭ Click the Save button on the Page Design toolbar.

⑮ Type **WEEmployeeBenefits** in the *File name* text box and then click Save. (If a message appears stating that the connection string of this page specifies an absolute path and might not be able to connect to data through the network, click OK.)

⑯ Click File and then Web Page Preview.

> The data access page displays in the default Web browser window.

⑰ Click the plus symbol next to employee number *1001* in the Web browser window.

> The record expands to display the benefits associated with employee number 1001.

⑱ Click File on the Web browser Menu bar and then click Print.

⑲ Scroll through a few of the records in the data access page in the Web browser window by clicking the Next Record button on the lower navigation bar and then expanding the record by clicking the plus symbol.

⑳ Close the Web browser window.

㉑ Close the WEEmployeeBenefits Data Access Page window.

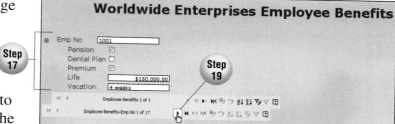

In Addition

More about Data Access Pages

When a data access page is created, Access creates a folder in which to store the Web page files. Although the Web pages are not stored directly within the database, the data access page is directly connected to the source database. When a user displays the data access page in the browser, she or he is viewing a copy of the page. Any filtering or sorting that is done to affect the way the data is *displayed* affects only this copy of the page. Changes made to the *content* of the data, however, such as inserting, editing, or deleting field values, are updated immediately in the source database so that everyone viewing the data access page is working with the same information.

IN BRIEF

Create a Data Access Page
1 Click Pages on Objects bar.
2 Double-click *Create data access page by using wizard*.
3 Choose table or query and field(s) to include in Web page.
4 Click Next.
5 Choose a grouping level and click Next.
6 Choose a field to sort by and click Next.
7 Type page title and click Finish.
8 Modify page in Design view as required.
9 Click Save.
10 Type Web page file name, click Save.

4.11 Viewing Objects and Object Dependencies

As you have learned throughout this book, the structure of a database is comprised of table, query, form, and report objects. Tables are related to other table(s) by creating one-to-one, one-to-many, or many-to-many relationships. Queries, forms, and reports draw the source data from records in the tables to which they have been associated and forms and reports can include subforms and subreports, which further expand the associations between objects. A database with a large number of interdependent objects is more complex to work with. Viewing a list of the objects within a database and viewing the dependencies between objects can be beneficial to ensure an object is not deleted or otherwise modified causing an unforeseen affect on another object. Access provides two features that provide information on objects: Database Properties and the Object Dependencies task pane.

PROJECT: You will view a list of objects in the WEEmployees4 database and then view the other objects dependent on a table in the Object Dependencies task pane.

S T E P S

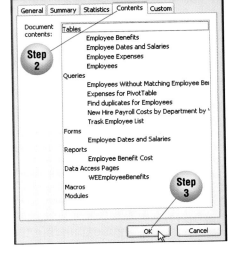

1. With **WEEmployees4** open, click File and then click Database Properties.

2. Click the Contents tab in the WEEmployees4.mdb Properties dialog box.

3. Review the list of objects within the *Document contents* list box and then click OK.

4. Click Tables on the Objects bar and then click *Employee Dates and Salaries*.

5. Click View and then click Object Dependencies to open the Object Dependencies task pane.

   > By default, *Objects that depend on me* is selected and the task pane lists the names of objects for which the Employee Dates and Salaries table is the source. Next to each object in the task pane list is an expand button (plus symbol). Clicking the expand button will show objects dependent at the next level. For example, if a query is based upon the Employee Dates and Salaries table and the query is used to generate a report, clicking the expand button next to the query name would show the report name.

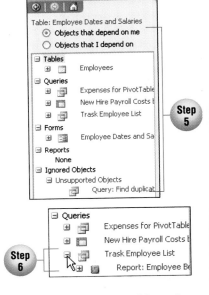

6. Click the expand button (plus symbol) next to the Trask Employee List link in the *Queries* list in the Object Dependencies task pane.

   > The object expands to show that the Trask Employee List is used to generate the report named Employee Benefit Cost.

7. Click *Objects that I depend on* at the top of the Object Dependencies task pane.

   > The objects in the task pane list change to illustrate the names of other objects in the database for which Employee Dates and Salaries is dependent upon.

⑧ Position the mouse pointer over the table named Employees in the Object Dependencies task pane until the name displays as a hyperlink and then click the left mouse button.

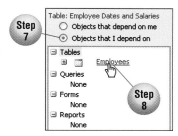

Step 7

Step 8

> Clicking an object name in the Object Dependencies task pane opens the object in Design view. Tables which have a relationship defined are shown as dependent objects in the expanded Tables list. Deleting a relationship in the Relationships window removes the dependency between tables. See In Addition at the end of this topic for information on deleting relationships.

⑨ Close the Employees : Table window.

⑩ Close the Object Dependencies task pane.

⑪ Click Reports on the Objects bar and then click the Employee Benefit Cost report.

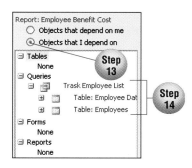

Step 13

Step 14

⑫ Click View and then click Object Dependencies.

⑬ Click *Objects that I depend on* at the top of the Object Dependencies task pane.

⑭ If necessary, expand the Trask Employee List query name.

> The expanded list shows that the Trask Employee List is derived from two tables: Employee Dates and Salaries and Employees.

⑮ Close the Object Dependencies task pane.

⑯ Close the **WEEmployees4** database.

In Addition

Deleting Relationships between Tables

To delete a relationship between tables, open the Relationships window, right-click the black join line between the table names, and then click Delete at the shortcut menu. A dialog box will appear asking you to confirm that you want to permanently delete the relationship from the database.

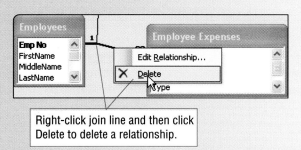

Right-click join line and then click Delete to delete a relationship.

View Database Objects
1 Click File, Database Properties.
2 Click Contents tab.
3 Review list of objects in list box.
4 Click OK.

View Object Dependencies
1 Click to select object name for which you want to view dependencies.
2 Click View, Object Dependencies.
3 Choose either *Objects that depend on me* or *Objects that I depend on.*
4 Expand items in list as desired.
5 Close Object Dependencies task pane.

4.12 Creating a New Database Using a Wizard

Access provides database wizards that can be used to create new database files. The wizards include a series of dialog boxes that guide you through the steps of creating the database by selecting from predefined tables, fields, screen layouts, and report layouts. When the database is created, a Main Switchboard window displays on the Access screen in place of the Database window. The Main Switchboard is a special type of form that contains options used to access the various objects generated by Access. The Main Switchboard form is automatically displayed each time the database is opened.

PROJECT: You will create a new database to store contact information for Worldwide Enterprises using the Contact Management Wizard.

STEPS

1. Click the New button ☐ on the Database toolbar.

2. Click the <u>On my computer</u> link in the *Templates* section of the New File task pane.

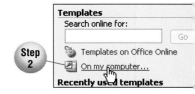

Step 2

3. Click the Databases tab in the Templates dialog box and then double-click *Contact Management* in the *Databases* list box.

Step 3

4. Type **WEContacts** in the *File name* text box in the File New Database dialog box and then click Create.

5. Click Next at the first Database Wizard dialog box that contains information about the type of data the database will store.

6. Click Next at the second Database Wizard dialog box to accept the default fields in the tables.

> Access displays the predefined tables in the *Tables in the database* list box. For each table, a set of predefined fields are displayed in the *Fields in the table* list box. Fields displayed in italics are not created by default but can be included by clicking the check box next to the field name.

Step 6

7. Click *Industrial* as the screen display style in the third Database Wizard dialog box and then click Next.

8. Click *Bold* for the report style in the fourth Database Wizard dialog box and then click Next.

9. Click Finish at the last Database Wizard dialog box to accept the default title of *Contact Management* for the database.

> The Database Wizard creates the tables, forms, and reports for the new database. A progress box displays indicating the tasks Access is completing. When the database is complete, Access opens the Main Switchboard window that is used to access the various components of the new database.

10. Click *Enter/View Contacts* in the Main Switchboard window.

11. Type the data in the first record as shown in Figure A4.4.

12. Click the button for Page 2 at the bottom of the record.

13. Type **sgrey@emcp.net** in the *Email Name* field.

14. Close the Contacts form.

15. Click *Preview Reports* in the Main Switchboard window.

16. Click *Preview the Alphabetical Contact Listing Report*.

17. Click the Print button on the Print Preview toolbar and then click the Close button.

18. Click *Return to Main Switchboard* in the Reports Switchboard window.

19. Click Tools, Options, and then click the General tab in the Options dialog box.

20. Click the *Compact on Close* check box and then click OK.

21. Click *Exit this database* in the Main Switchboard window.

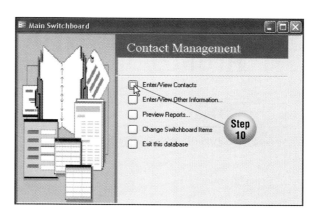

Step 10

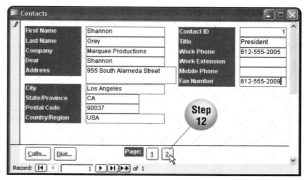

FIGURE A4.4 Data for First Record

Step 12

In Addition

Closing the Main Switchboard

Click the Close button on the Main Switchboard title bar if you need to work with the objects in the Database window. A minimized title bar with the name of the database will be positioned just above the Status bar. Click the Maximize or Restore button on the Database title bar to restore the Database window. Tables or other objects can be customized by opening them in Design view and making the required changes. To return to the Main Switchboard after closing it, click Forms on the Objects bar, and then double-click *Switchboard*.

IN BRIEF

Create a New Database Using a Wizard
1 Click New button.
2 Click <u>On my computer</u> link in New File task pane.
3 Click Databases tab in Templates dialog box and double-click desired database wizard.
4 Type database file name and click Create.
5 Click Next.
6 Select fields to include in each table and click Next.
7 Select screen layout and click Next.
8 Select report style and click Next.
9 Type title for database and click Finish.

FEATURES SUMMARY

Feature	Button	Menu	Keyboard
Align controls on form or report		Format, Align, Left, Right, Top, or Bottom	
Crosstab query		Insert, Query, Crosstab Query Wizard	
Database Wizard	🗋	File, New	Ctrl + N
Delete rows	⇥	Edit, Delete Rows	
Filter by form	📇	Records, Filter, Filter By Form	
Filter by selection	🈺	Records, Filter, Filter By Selection	
Find Duplicates Query Wizard		Insert, Query, Find Duplicates Query Wizard	
Find Unmatched Query Wizard		Insert, Query, Find Unmatched Query Wizard	
Horizontal spacing in form or report		Format, Horizontal Spacing	
Insert rows	⧉	Insert, Rows	
Object dependencies		View, Object Dependencies	
Page Wizard		Insert, Page, Page Wizard	
PivotChart view		View, PivotChart View	
PivotTable view		View, PivotTable View	
Property sheet	📇	View, Properties	Alt + Enter
Theme		Format, Theme	
Toolbox	🛠	View, Toolbox	
Vertical spacing in form or report		Format, Vertical Spacing	

PROCEDURES CHECK

Completion: In the space provided at the right, indicate the correct term or command.

1. To move, insert, or delete a field in a table, open the table in this view. _____

2. Click this button on the Datasheet toolbar to temporarily remove all records from the display and then select a criterion from a drop-down list of field values in a field. _____

3. Start this query wizard to sum data in a field that is grouped by two fields. _____

4. Use this query wizard to produce a datasheet showing names and telephone numbers from the Customer table for those customers who have no record in the Order table. _____

5. Click this button in the Toolbox to create a calculated field in a form or report. _____

6. Use this option to position multiple controls at the leftmost edge of the selected group in Design view for a form or report. _____

7. This is the name of the view in which you can create an interactive table that organizes and summarizes data based on fields you drag and drop for row and column headings. _____

8. This is the name of the wizard used to facilitate creating a Web page for a table or query. _____

9. This is the name given to a group of predefined formats and color schemes that can be applied to Web pages. _____

10. Open this task pane to find out which other objects are based upon the selected object. _____

Identify the following features represented by the buttons:

11. _____

12. _____

13. _____

14. _____

15. _____

16. _____

SKILLS REVIEW

Activity 1: MOVING AND DELETING FIELDS; FILTERING RECORDS

1 Open the **WEEmployees4** database.
2 Open the Employee Expenses table in Design view.
3 Move the *Amount* field between the *Emp No* and *Date* fields.
4 Delete the *Type* field.
5 Save the table.
6 Switch to Datasheet view.
7 Print the datasheet.
8 Select the word *Sales* in the *Description* column of any record and then use Filter by Selection to view sales-related expenses.
9 Print the filtered datasheet.
10 Remove the filter and then close the Employee Expenses table. Click No to save changes.

Activity 2: CREATING A CROSSTAB QUERY; FINDING UNMATCHED AND DUPLICATE RECORDS

1 With **WEEmployees4** open, create a crosstab query that will summarize expenses by employee by quarter using the following information:
  a Use the Employee Expenses table to generate the crosstab query.
  b Display the employee numbers in rows.
  c Display the date in quarter intervals in columns.
  d Sum the expense amounts.
  e Name the query Expenses by Employee by Quarter.
2 Adjust column widths as necessary and then print the query results datasheet.
3 Close the Expenses by Employee by Quarter query, saving changes.
4 Use the Find Unmatched Query Wizard to compare the Employees table with the Employee Expenses table and produce a list of employees who have not submitted an expense claim. Display the fields *Emp No, FirstName,* and *LastName* in the query results. Accept the default name for the query.
5 Print the query results datasheet.
6 Close the Employees Without Matching Employee Expenses query.
7 Use the Find Duplicates Query Wizard to analyze the *Emp No* field in the Employee Expenses table and produce a list of employees who have submitted more than one expense claim. Display the remaining three fields in the query results. Accept the default name for the query.
8 Print the query results datasheet.
9 Close the Find Duplicates for Employee Expenses query.

Activity 3: CREATING AND MODIFYING A REPORT; CREATING A CALCULATED CONTROL

1 With **WEEmployees4** open, create a new report using the Report Wizard based on the Trask Employee List query as follows:
   a Add all of the fields from the query to the report.
   b Do not include any grouping or sorting.
   c Select the *Columnar* layout.
   d Select the *Corporate* style.
   e Accept the default title for the report.
2 Display the Trask Employee List in Design view and then modify the report as follows:
   a Insert a label control in the *Report Header* section that will print the text *Report Design by: Student Name*. Substitute your first and last names for *Student Name*. Position the control near the right edge of the *Report Header* section and change the font size to 12-point. If necessary, resize the control after changing the font size. Select the report title and label control in the Report Header section and then use the Align Bottom option to position the bottom edges of both controls at the same horizontal position on the report.
   b Create a calculated control object to the right of the *Annual Salary* text box control that will calculate the monthly salary by dividing the Annual Salary by 12. Type the label Monthly Salary for the calculated control object.
   c Change the Format property for the calculated control object to *Currency*.
   d Use the Format Painter to copy the border style from the *Annual Salary* control object to the *Monthly Salary* control object.
   e Select the *Annual Salary* label and text box controls and the *Monthly Salary* label and text box controls. Use the Align Top option to make sure the controls are all at the same vertical position.
3 Save and then print the first page only of the report.
4 Close the Trask Employee List report.

Activity 4: CREATING A PIVOTTABLE

1 With **WEEmployees4** open, open the Trask Employee List query in Datasheet view.
2 Switch to PivotTable view.
3 Create a PivotTable that will summarize the annual salaries of employees by hire dates using the following information:
   a Drag the *Department* field to *Drop Filter Fields Here*.
   b Drag the *Last Name* field to *Drop Row Fields Here*.
   c Drag the *Hire Date By Month* field to *Drop Column Fields Here*.
   d Drag the *Annual Salary* field to *Drop Totals or Detail Fields Here*.
4 Close the PivotTable Field List box.
5 Filter the PivotTable on the Department field to display only those employees in the European Distribution and Overseas Distribution departments.
6 Filter the PivotTable on the Years field to display only those employees hired in the year 2000 and beyond.
7 Click any of the *Annual Salary* column headings. Turn on bold, change the font color to dark green, and choose a light green fill color.
8 Click the Save button and then print the PivotTable.
9 Close the Trask Employee List query.

Activity 5: CREATING A WEB PAGE; USING WEB PAGE PREVIEW

1 With **WEEmployees4** open, use the Page Wizard to create a Web page based on the Employee Dates and Salaries table as follows:
   • Add all of the fields except *Review Date* from the table to the Web page.
   • Do not include any grouping or sorting.
   • Accept the default title for the Web page.
2 Apply the *Compass* theme to the Web page.
3 Type Worldwide Enterprises Dates and Salaries as the title text in the Web page.
4 Save the Web page and name it **WEDatesAndSalaries**.
5 Display the Web page in the default browser window, and then view two or three records.
6 Print the Web page with the record expanded for employee number 1010.
7 Close the browser window.
8 Close the **WEDatesAndSalaries** Web page.
9 Close **WEEmployees4**.

PERFORMANCE PLUS

Assessment 1: MODIFYING A TABLE; APPLYING AND REMOVING A FILTER

1 After reviewing the inventory list with Dana Hirsch, manager of The Waterfront Bistro, you realize some adjustments need to be made to the structure of the table. Dana has also asked for a list of items that are purchased from supplier code 4.
2 Open **WBInventory4**.
3 Open the Inventory List table in Design view.
4 Make the following changes to the table:
   a Move the *Unit* field between the *Item No* and *Item* fields.
   b Move the *Supplier Code* field between the *Item No* and *Unit* fields.
5 Save the table and then switch to Datasheet view.
6 Turn on Filter By Form and then filter the records by *Supplier Code 4*.
7 Print the filtered datasheet and then remove the filter.
8 Close the Inventory List table. Click No to save changes.
9 Close the **WBInventory4** database.

Assessment 2: ADDING A CALCULATED CONTROL TO A FORM

1 Staff at Performance Threads have commented positively on the usefulness of the form created for browsing the inventory table. They have asked for a modification to the form that will allow them to tell customers what the daily rental fee is with the tax included.
2 Open **PTCostumeInventory4**.
3 Open the Costume Inventory form in Form view and review the current form layout and design.
4 Switch to Design view and then make the following changes:
   a Create a calculated control object to the right of the *Daily Rental Fee* object that will calculate the Daily Rental Fee with 7% GST included. (GST is the goods and services tax levied on all purchases by the government of Canada.)

   b Type **Rental fee tax included** as the label for the calculated control.

   c Format the calculated control object to *Currency*.

   d Use the Align Top option to make sure the calculated object is aligned horizontally with the top edge of the *Daily Rental Fee* object.

   e If necessary, resize the label and text box control to ensure the text and values are entirely visible.

   f Make sure the new object is the same font and font size as the other objects on the form.

   g Select all control objects within the *Detail* section of the form and increase vertical spacing twice. If necessary, drag the *Form Footer* section down to make more room in the *Detail* section.

5 Save the revised form and then switch to Form view.

6 Print the first record only in the form.

7 Close the form.

8 Close **PTCostumeInventory4**.

Assessment 3: CREATING AND MODIFYING A REPORT

1 Heidi Pasqual, financial officer of Worldwide Enterprises, requires a report that will print the names and addresses of the Canadian distributors. Since Heidi is not familiar with Access, she has asked you to create the report for her.

2 Open **WEDistributors4**.

3 Create a new report using the Report Wizard as follows:
   - Select the *Name, Street Address1, Street Address2, City, Province,* and *Postal Code* fields from the Canadian Distributors table.
   - Do not include any grouping or sorting.
   - Choose the *Tabular* layout in *Portrait* orientation.
   - Choose the *Corporate* style.
   - Accept the default title of *Canadian Distributors*.

4 Preview the report at 100% magnification. Notice that some of the names and street addresses are truncated on the report.

5 Switch to Design view.

6 Resize and move the *City, Province,* and *Postal Code* controls in the *Page Header* and *Detail* sections to make enough room on the page to widen the name and address columns.

7 Widen the *Name, Street Address1,* and *Street Address2* controls in the *Page Header* and *Detail* sections.

8 View the report in Print Preview.

9 If necessary, switch to Design view and make further adjustments to the size and placement of the controls.

10 Select all of the control objects in the *Page Header* section and then use Align Top or Align Bottom to make sure all objects are at the same horizontal position.

11 Select all of the control objects in the *Detail* section and then use Align Top or Align Bottom to make sure all objects are at the same horizontal position.

12 Add a label object at the left side of the report in the *Report Footer* that includes the text *Report Design by: Student Name.* Substitute your first and last names for *Student Name*.

13 Save, print, and then close the Canadian Distributors Addresses report.

14 Close **WEDistributors4**.

Assessment 4: APPLYING AND REMOVING FILTERS

1 Niagara Peninsula College has received two student grants from Performance Threads to be awarded to the top two students in the Theatre Arts Division. Cal Rubine, chair of the Theatre Arts Division of Niagara Peninsula College, has requested a list of students who achieved A+ in a course for review by a selection committee.
2 Open **NPCGrades4**.
3 Open the ACT104 Grades table.
4 Filter the table to display only those records with an A+ in the *Grade* field.
5 Print and then close the table. Click No to save changes.
6 Open the PRD112 Grades table.
7 Filter the table to display only those records with an A+ in the *Grade* field.
8 Print and then close the table. Click No to save changes.
9 Open the SPE266 Grades table.
10 Filter the table to display only those records with an A+ in the *Grade* field.
11 Print and then close the table. Click No to save changes.
12 Close **NPCGrades4**.

Assessment 5: CREATING A PIVOTCHART

1 Dana Hirsch, manager of The Waterfront Bistro, is reviewing the recent purchases made by the executive chef and has requested a chart showing the dollar value of inventory purchases by item.
2 Open **WBInventory4**.
3 Create a new query in Design view as follows:
   • Add the Inventory List and Purchases tables to the design grid.
   • Add the fields in order: *Item No, Item, Unit, Supplier Code, Purchase Date, Amount*.
   • Name the query *Inventory Purchases*.
4 Run the query.
5 Switch to PivotChart view.
6 Create a PivotChart as follows:
   • Drag the *Supplier Code* field to *Drop Filter Fields Here*.
   • Drag the *Item* field to *Drop Category Fields Here*.
   • Drag the *Amount* field to *Drop Data Fields Here*.
7 Close the Chart Field List box.
8 Change the page orientation to landscape and then print the chart.
9 Filter the chart to display only those items purchased from Supplier Code 1.
10 Print the chart.
11 Redisplay all items in the chart.
12 Save and then close the Inventory Purchases query.

Assessment 6: CREATING AND MODIFYING A WEB PAGE

1 Dana Hirsch, manager of The Waterfront Bistro, has been considering posting the inventory purchases information on the company intranet for the executive chef, who is more familiar with Web browser navigation methods than Access. Dana has asked you to create a Web page from the Purchases table.

2 With **WBInventory4** open, create a Web page using the Page Wizard adding all fields from the Purchases table. Accept all other default settings in the Page Wizard dialog boxes.

3 Apply a theme of your choosing to the Web page.

4 Type The Waterfront Bistro Inventory Purchases as the title of the page.

5 Save the Web page and name it *InventoryPurchases*.

6 View the Web page in the Web browser window.

7 Scroll through and expand a few records in the Web browser window.

8 Switch back to Design view and move and resize controls as necessary so that all labels and field values are entirely visible.

9 Save the revised Web page and display Web Page Preview.

10 Scroll to record 5, expand the record, and then print the Web page from the browser window.

11 Close the Web browser window.

12 Close the **InventoryPurchases** Web page.

13 Close **WBInventory4**.

Assessment 7: FINDING INFORMATION ON ADDING FIELDS TO AN EXISTING REPORT

1 Use the Help feature to find out how to add a field to an existing report in Design view. *(Hint: A control that displays data from the associated table is considered a bound control.)*

2 Print the Help topic that you find.

3 Open **WEDistributors4**.

4 Open the Canadian Distributors Addresses report in Design view.

5 Change the page orientation to landscape and then drag the right edge of the design grid to position 8 on the horizontal ruler.

6 Add the *Telephone* field to the report. *(Hint: Cut and paste the label control for the Telephone field from the Detail section to the Page Header section after you have added the field. You may have to edit the control after it is pasted.)*

7 Adjust the length of the lines below the *Page Header* and above the *Page Footer* objects. Drag the page numbering control in the *Page Footer* section to the right edge of the report.

8 Preview the report.

9 Save, print, and then close the Canadian Distributors report.

10 Close **WEDistributors4**.

Assessment 8: RESEARCHING MOVIES ON THE INTERNET

1 Choose four movies that are currently playing in your vicinity that you have seen or would like to see, and then find their Web sites on the Internet. Look for the information listed in Step 3 that you will be entering into a new database.

2 Create a new database named **Movies**.

3 Create a table named Movie Facts that will store the following information:

Movie title
Director's name
Producer's name
Lead actor—male
Supporting actor—male

Lead actor—female
Supporting actor—female
Movie category—drama, action, thriller, and so on
Web site address

4 Design and create a form to enter the records for the movies you researched.

5 Enter the records using the form created in Step 4.

6 Print the last form only.

7 Design and create a report for the Movie Facts table. Add your name to the *Report Header* or *Report Footer* section in a label control object.

8 Print the Movie Facts report.

9 Close the **Movies** database.

INTEGRATED 2

Integrating Word, Excel, and Access

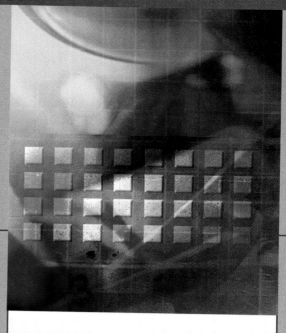

Data in one program within the Microsoft Office suite can be imported and/or exported to another program. For example, you can export data in an Access table to an Excel worksheet or a Word document. One of the advantages of exporting data to Excel or Word is that formatting can be applied using Excel or Word formatting features. You can also import data into an Access database file. If you know that you will update data in a program other than Access, link the data. Changes made to linked data are reflected in both the source and destination programs. In this section, you will learn the following skills and complete the projects described here.

 Note: The database files for this section are in the Integrated02 subfolder in the Integrated folder on the CD that accompanies this textbook. Before beginning this section, delete any existing databases on your disk and copy each database as needed. Remember to remove the read-only attribute from each database after copying. If necessary, refer to page 1 for instructions on how to remove the read-only attribute. If necessary, check with your instructor before deleting any database files.

Skills

- Export Access data in a table to Excel
- Export Access data in a table to Word
- Export Access data in a report to Word
- Import Excel data to a new Access table
- Link data between an Excel worksheet and an Access table
- Edit linked data

Projects

 Export grades for PRD112 from an Access table to an Excel worksheet. Import grades for a Beginning Theatre class from an Excel worksheet into an Access database table. Link grades for TRA220 between an Excel worksheet and an Access database table.

 Export data on costume inventory from an Access table to an Excel worksheet. Export data on costume inventory from an Access report to a Word document. Import data on costume design hours from an Excel worksheet into an Access table.

 Export data on overseas distributors from an Access table to a Word document. Export data on Canadian distributors from an Access report to a Word document.

 Export data on inventory from an Access table to a Word document.

 Link data on booking commissions between an Excel worksheet and an Access table and then update the data.

I-2.1 Exporting Access Data to Excel

One of the advantages of a suite program like Microsoft Office is the ability to exchange data from one program to another. Access, like the other programs in the suite, offers a feature to export data from Access into Excel and/or Word. Export data using the OfficeLinks button on the Database toolbar. You can export Access data saved in a table, form, or report to Excel. The data is saved as an Excel file in the folder where Access is installed.

PROJECT: You are Katherine Lamont, Theatre Arts Division instructor at Niagara Peninsula College. You want to work on your grades for your PRD112 class over the weekend and you do not have Access installed on your personal laptop. You decide to export your Access grading table to Excel.

STEPS

① Open Access and then open the **NPCClasses** database file. (Remove the read-only attribute.)

② Click the Tables button on the Objects bar and then click once on *PRD112Grades* in the list box.

③ Click the down-pointing arrow at the right side of the OfficeLinks button on the Database toolbar.

④ At the drop-down list that displays, click *Analyze It with Microsoft Office Excel.*

⑤ When the data displays on the screen in Excel as a worksheet, insert the following grades in the specified cells:

D2	=	B
D5	=	A
D13	=	D
D15	=	C
D16	=	D
D17	=	B

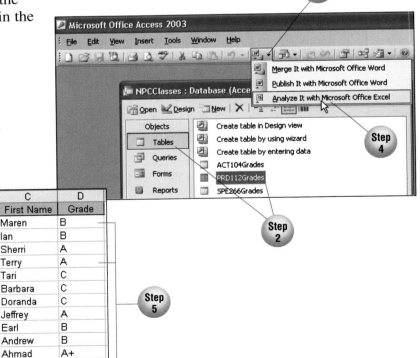

INTEGRATED 2

138

INTEGRATING WORD, EXCEL, AND ACCESS

6 Select cells A1 through D17.

7 Click Format and then AutoFormat.

8 At the AutoFormat dialog box, scroll down the list of autoformats until *List 1* is visible and then double-click *List 1*.

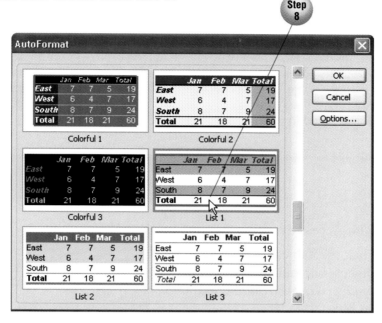

9 Deselect the cells by clicking outside the selected cells.

10 Save the worksheet with Save As and name it **IntE2-01**.

11 Print and then close **IntE2-01**.

12 Click the button on the Taskbar representing the Access database file **NPCClasses** and then close the database file.

In Addition

Exporting to Excel

Three methods are available for exporting Access data to an Excel worksheet. You can export data using the *Analyze It with Microsoft Office Excel* option from the OfficeLinks drop-down list as you did in this topic. You can save the output of a datasheet, form, or report directly as an Excel *(.xls)* worksheet or you can export the datasheet as unformatted data to Excel.

IN BRIEF

Export Access Table to Excel
1 Open database file.
2 Click Tables button on Objects bar and then click desired table.
3 Click down-pointing arrow at right side of OfficeLinks button.
4 Click *Analyze It with Microsoft Office Excel.*

I-2.2 Exporting Access Data to Word

Export data from Access to Word in the same manner as exporting to Excel. To export data to Word, open the database file, select the table, form, or report, and then click the OfficeLinks button on the Database toolbar. At the drop-down list, click *Publish It with Microsoft Office Word.* Word automatically opens and the data displays in a Word document that is automatically saved with the same name as the database table, form, or report. The difference is that the file extension *.rtf* is added to the name rather than the Word file extension *.doc.* An rtf file is saved in "rich-text format," which preserves formatting such as fonts and styles. You can export a document saved with the *.rtf* extension in Word and other Windows word processing or desktop publishing programs.

PROJECT: Roman Deptulski, the manager of overseas distribution for Worldwide Enterprises, has asked you to export an Access database table containing information on overseas distributors to a Word document. He needs some of the information for a distribution meeting.

STEPS

1. With Access the active program, open **WECompany**.

2. Click the Tables button on the Objects bar and then click once on *OverseasDistributors* in the list box.

3. Click the down-pointing arrow at the right side of the OfficeLinks button on the Database toolbar and then click *Publish It with Microsoft Office Word* at the drop-down list.

4. When the data displays on the screen in Word, select all of the cells in the two *Street* columns.

5. Delete the selected columns by clicking Table, pointing to Delete, and then clicking Columns.

6. Select all of the cells in the *Postal Code, Telephone,* and *Fax* columns, click Table, point to Delete, and then click Columns.

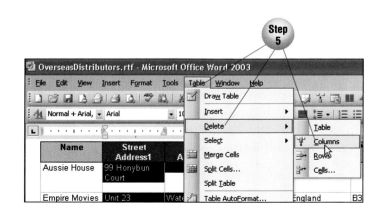

7 The Word Table feature has an autofit feature that will automatically adjust the column widths to the contents of the columns. Make sure the insertion point is positioned in a cell in the table and then use this feature by clicking Table, pointing to AutoFit, and then clicking AutoFit to Contents.

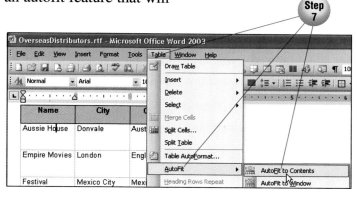

Step 7

8 With the insertion point positioned in any cell in the table, click Table and then Table AutoFormat.

9 At the Table AutoFormat dialog box, double-click *Table List 7* in the *Table styles* list box.

10 Click the Save button 🖫 to save the document with the same name (**OverseasDistributors**).

11 Print and then close **OverseasDistributors**.

12 Click the button on the Taskbar representing the **WECompany** Access database file and then close the database file.

Step 9

In Addition

Adjusting a Table

In this section, you adjusted the Word table to the cell contents. The Table AutoFit feature contains several options for adjusting table contents. These options are:

Option	Action
AutoFit to Contents	Adjusts table to accommodate the table text
AutoFit to Window	Resizes table to fit within the window or browser. If browser changes size, table size automatically adjusts to fit within window
Fixed Column Width	Adjusts each column to a fixed width using the current widths of the columns
Distribute Rows Evenly	Changes selected rows or cells to equal row height
Distribute Columns Evenly	Changes selected columns or cells to equal column width

In BRIEF

Export Access Table to Word
1 Open database file.
2 Click Tables button on Objects bar and then click desired table.
3 Click down-pointing arrow at right side of OfficeLinks button.
4 Click *Publish It with Microsoft Office Word.*

I-2.3 Exporting an Access Report to Word

An Access report, like an Access table, can be exported to a Word document. Export a report to Word by using the *Publish It with Microsoft Office Word* option from the OfficeLinks drop-down list. One of the advantages to exporting a report to Word is that formatting can be applied to the report using Word formatting features.

PROJECT: Sam Vestering, manager of North American distribution for Worldwide Enterprises, needs a list of Canadian distributors. He has asked you to export a report to Word and then apply specific formatting to the report. He needs some of the information for a contact list.

S T E P S

① With Access the active program, open **WECompany**.

② At the WECompany : Database window, click the Reports button on the Objects bar.

③ Click *CanadianDistributorsAddresses* in the list box.

④ Click the down-pointing arrow at the right side of the OfficeLinks button and then click *Publish It with Microsoft Office Word*.

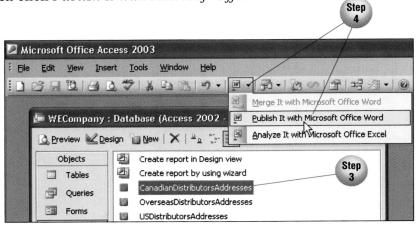

⑤ When the data displays on the screen in Word, press Ctrl + A to select the entire document.

⑥ Click the down-pointing arrow at the right side of the Font button on the Formatting toolbar and then click *Arial* at the drop-down list.

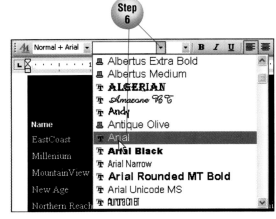

7 With the document still selected, click the down-pointing arrow at the right side of the Font Size button on the Formatting toolbar and then click *10* at the drop-down list.

8 Press Ctrl + Home to move the insertion point to the beginning of the document and then type **Worldwide Enterprises**.

Step 7

9 Press Enter and then type **Canadian Distributors**.

10 Select *Worldwide Enterprises* and then change the font to 22-point Arial bold.

11 Select *Canadian Distributors* and then change the font to 18-point Arial bold.

12 Click the Save button 🖫 to save the report with the default name **(CanadianDistributorsAddresses)**.

13 Print and then close **CanadianDistributorsAddresses**.

> The **CanadianDistributorsAddresses** document prints in landscape orientation and includes a footer at the bottom of the page that prints the current date.

14 Exit Word.

15 In Access, close the **WECompany** Access database file.

In Addition

Merging Access Data with a Word Document

Word includes a mail merge feature that you can use to create letters and envelopes and much more, with personalized information. Generally, a merge requires two documents—the *data source* and the *main document*. The data source contains the variable information that will be inserted in the main document. Create a data source document in Word or create a data source using data from an Access table. When merging Access data, you can either type the text in the main document or merge Access data with an existing Word document. To merge data in an Access table, open the database file, click the Tables button on the Objects bar, and then click the desired table. Click the OfficeLinks button on the Database toolbar and then click Merge It with Microsoft Office Word. Follow the steps presented in the Mail Merge task pane to complete the merge.

In Brief

Export Access Report to Word
1 Open database file.
2 Click Reports button on Objects bar and then click desired report.
3 Click down-pointing arrow at right side of OfficeLinks button.
4 Click *Publish It with Microsoft Office Word*.

I-2.4 Importing Data to a New Table

In the previous three topics, you exported Access data to Excel and Word. You can also import data from other programs into an Access table. For example, you can import data from an Excel worksheet and create a new table in a database file. Data in the original program is not connected to the data imported into an Access table. If you make changes to the data in the original program, those changes are not reflected in the Access table.

PROJECT: You are Gina Simmons, Theatre Arts instructor, and have recorded grades in an Excel worksheet for your students in the Beginning Theatre class. You want to import those grades into the NPCClasses database file.

STEPS

1. In Access, open the **NPCClasses** database file and then click the Tables button on the Objects bar.

2. Import an Excel worksheet by clicking File, pointing to Get External Data, and then clicking Import.

3. At the Import dialog box, change the *Files of type* option to *Microsoft Excel*, and then double-click **NPCBegThGrades** in the list box.

   Your list of documents may vary from what you see in the image below and at the right.

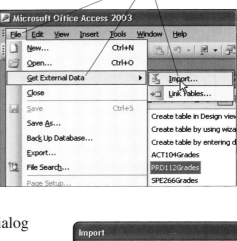

Step 2

PROBLEM? If *NPCBegThGrades* does not display in the list box, you may need to navigate to another folder. Check with your instructor.

4. At the first Import Spreadsheet Wizard dialog box, click the Next button.

5. At the second dialog box, insert a check mark in the *First Row Contains Column Headings* option and then click the Next button.

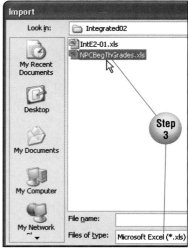

Step 3

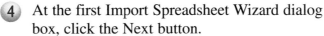
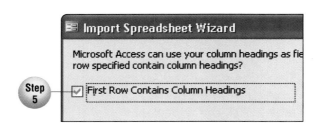

Step 5

6 At the third dialog box, make sure the *In a New Table* option is selected and then click the Next button.

7 At the fourth dialog box, click the Next button.

8 At the fifth dialog box, click the *Choose my own primary key* option (this inserts *Student No* in the text box located to the right of the option), and then click the Next button.

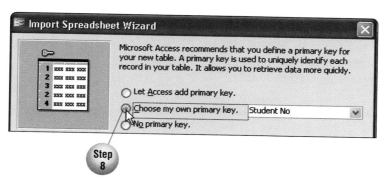

Step 8

9 At the sixth dialog box, type **BegThGrades** in the *Import to Table* text box and then click the Finish button.

10 At the message saying the data was imported, click OK.

11 Open the new table by double-clicking **BegThGrades** in the list box.

12 Print and then close **BegThGrades**.

13 Close the **NPCClasses** database file.

Step 9

In Addition

Importing or Linking a Table

You can import data from another program into an Access table or you can link the data. Choose the method depending on how you are going to use the data. Import data to a table if you are going to use the data only in Access. Access generally operates faster working with its own tables. Link data to an Access table if the data will be changed or updated in a program other than Access. Changes made to linked data are reflected in both the source and destination programs.

IN BRIEF

Import Data to a New Table
1 Open database file.
2 Click Tables button on Objects bar.
3 Click File, Get External Data, Import.
4 Follow the Import Wizard steps.

I-2.5 Linking Data to a New Table and Editing Linked Data

Imported data is not connected to the source program. If you know that you will use your data only in Access, import it. However, if you want to update data in a program other than Access, link the data. Changes made to linked data are reflected in both the source and destination programs. For example, you can link an Excel worksheet with an Access table and when you make changes in either the Excel worksheet or the Access table, the change is reflected in the other program. To link data to a new table, open the database file, click File, point to Get External Data, and then click Link Tables. At the Link dialog box, double-click the desired document name. This activates the link wizard that walks you through the steps to link the data.

PROJECT: You are Gina Simmons, Theatre Arts instructor at Niagara Peninsula College. You record students' grades in an Excel worksheet and also link the grades to an Access database file. With the data linked, changes you make to either the Excel table or the Access table will be reflected in the other table.

S T E P S

1. Open Excel and then open **NPCTRA220**.

2. Save the worksheet with Save As and name it **IntE2-02**.

3. Print and then close **IntE2-02**.

4. Make Access the active program, open the **NPCClasses** database file, and then click the Tables button on the Objects bar.

5. Link an Excel worksheet by clicking File, pointing to Get External Data, and then clicking Link Tables.

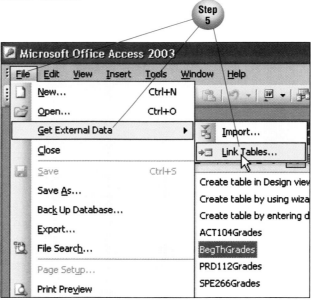

6. At the Link dialog box, change the *Files of type* option to *Microsoft Excel* and then double-click **IntE2-02** in the list box.

   Depending on your system configuration, you may need to navigate to the folder containing **IntE2-02**.

7. At the first Link Spreadsheet Wizard dialog box, make sure *Show Worksheets* is selected, and that *Sheet1* is selected in the list box, and then click the Next button.

8. At the second dialog box, make sure the *First Row Contains Column Headings* option contains a check mark and then click the Next button.

Step 7

Link Spreadsheet Wizard

Your spreadsheet file contains more than one would you like?

⦿ Show Worksheets
◯ Show Named Ranges

Sheet1
Sheet2
Sheet3

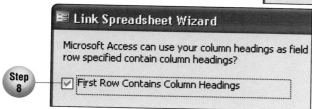

Link Spreadsheet Wizard

Microsoft Access can use your column headings as field row specified contain column headings?

Step 8

☑ First Row Contains Column Headings

9. At the third dialog box, type **LinkedGrades** in the *Linked Table Name* text box, and then click the Finish button.

10. At the message stating the link is finished, click OK.

> Access uses different icons to represent linked tables and tables that are stored in the current database. Notice the icon that displays before the LinkedGrades table.

Link Spreadsheet Wizard

That's all the information the wizard needs to

Linked Table Name:

LinkedGrades

Step 9

11. Open the new LinkedGrades table in Datasheet view.

12. As you look at the table, you realize that you need to add a student to the end of the list. Add the following new record in the specified fields (see image below):

Student No	Student	Midterm
138-456-749	Yui, T.	3.25

LinkedGrades : Table

Student No	Student	Midterm	Final
111-75-156	Bastow, M.	3.25	
359-845-475	Collyer, S.	1.50	
157-457-856	Dwyer, B.	3.50	
348-876-486	Ennis, A.	2.25	
378-159-746	Gagne, M.	3.00	
197-486-745	Koning, J.	2.75	
314-745-856	Morgan, B.	3.75	
349-874-658	Retieffe, S.	4.00	
138-456-749	Yui, T.	3.25	

Step 12

(continued)

⑬ Print and then close the LinkedGrades table.

The new record is automatically saved when the table is closed.

⑭ Make Excel the active program and then open **IntE2-02**.

Notice that the worksheet contains the student, Yui, T., you added to the Access table.

⑮ You have finished grading student finals and need to insert the grades in the worksheet. Insert the following grades in the specified cells:

D2	=	2.75
D3	=	1
D4	=	3.5
D5	=	2
D6	=	3.5
D7	=	2.5
D8	=	3
D9	=	3.5
D10	=	2.5

	A	B	C	D
1	Student No	Student	Midterm	Final
2	111-75-156	Bastow, M.	3.25	2.75
3	359-845-475	Collyer, S.	1.50	1.00
4	157-457-856	Dwyer, B.	3.50	3.50
5	348-876-486	Ennis, A.	2.25	2.00
6	378-159-746	Gagne, M.	3.00	3.50
7	197-486-745	Koning, J.	2.75	2.50
8	314-745-856	Morgan, B.	3.75	3.00
9	349-874-658	Retieffe, S.	4.00	3.50
10	138-456-749	Yui, T.	3.25	2.50

Step 15

⑯ Make cell E2 the active cell and then insert a formula to average scores by clicking the Insert Function button f_x on the Formula bar.

⑰ At the Insert Function dialog box, double-click *AVERAGE* in the *Select a function* list box.

PROBLEM ?

If AVERAGE is not visible in the *Select a function* list box, click the down-pointing arrow at the right side of the *Or select a category* option box, and then click *Most Recently Used* at the drop-down list.

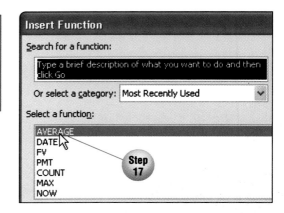

Insert Function

Search for a function:

Type a brief description of what you want to do and then click Go

Or select a category: Most Recently Used

Select a function:

AVERAGE
DATE
FV
PMT
COUNT
MAX
NOW

Step 17

18 At the formula palette, make sure *C2:D2* displays in the Number1 text box and then click OK.

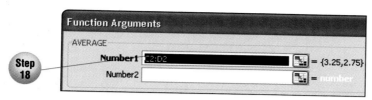

Step 18

Function Arguments
AVERAGE
Number1 C2:D2 = {3.25,2.75}
Number2 = number

19 Using the fill handle, copy the formula down to cell E10.

	A	B	C	D	E
1	Student No	Student	Midterm	Final	Average
2	111-75-156	Bastow, M.	3.25	2.75	3.00
3	359-845-475	Collyer, S.	1.50	1.00	1.25
4	157-457-856	Dwyer, B.	3.50	3.50	3.50
5	348-876-486	Ennis, A.	2.25	2.00	2.13
6	378-159-746	Gagne, M.	3.00	3.50	3.25
7	197-486-745	Koning, J.	2.75	2.50	2.63
8	314-745-856	Morgan, B.	3.75	3.00	3.38
9	349-874-658	Retieffe, S.	4.00	3.50	3.75
10	138-456-749	Yui, T.	3.25	2.50	2.88
11					

Step 19

20 Deselect the cells by clicking outside the selected cells.

21 Save and then print **IntE2-02**.

22 Click the button on the Taskbar representing the **NPCClasses** Access database file.

23 Open the LinkedGrades table.

Notice that this linked table contains the final grades and the average scores you inserted in the Excel **IntE2-02** worksheet.

24 Print and then close the LinkedGrades table.

25 Close the **NPCClasses** database file and then close Access.

26 With Excel the active program, close **IntE2-02** and then close Excel.

In Addition

Deleting the Link to a Linked Table

If you want to delete the link to a table, open the database file, and then click the Tables button on the Objects bar. Click the linked table in the list box and then click the Delete button on the Tables toolbar (or press the Delete key). At the Microsoft question asking if you want to remove the link to the table, click Yes. Access deletes the link and removes the table's name from the list box. When you delete a linked table, you are deleting the information Access uses to open the table, not the table itself. You can link to the same table again, if necessary.

In Brief

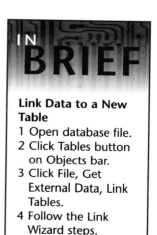

Link Data to a New Table
1 Open database file.
2 Click Tables button on Objects bar.
3 Click File, Get External Data, Link Tables.
4 Follow the Link Wizard steps.

SKILLS REVIEW

Activity 1: EXPORTING ACCESS DATA TO EXCEL

1. Open Access and then open the **PTCostumes** database file.
2. Click the Tables button on the Objects bar and then export the data in the CostumeInventory table to Excel.
3. When the data displays in Excel, make the following changes in the specified cells:

    C4 = Change *110.00* to *120.00*
    C5 = Change *110.00* to *125.00*
    C7 = Change *99.50* to *105.00*

4. Select cells A1 through E17 and then apply an autoformat of your choosing.
5. Save the worksheet with Save As and name it **IntE2-R1**.
6. Print and then close **IntE2-R1**.
7. Click the button on the Taskbar representing the Access database file **PTCostumes** and then close the database file.

Activity 2: EXPORTING ACCESS DATA TO WORD

1. With Access the active program, open **WBSupplies**.
2. Click the Tables button on the Objects bar and then export the data in the InventoryList table to Word.
3. When the data displays on the screen in Word, apply a table autoformat of your choosing to the table.
4. Move the insertion point to the beginning of the document, press Enter three times, and then move the insertion point back to the beginning of the document.
5. Type **The Waterfront Bistro** on the first line and type **Inventory List** on the second line.
6. Select *The Waterfront Bistro* and *Inventory List* and then change the font to 22-point Arial bold.
7. Save the Word document with the default name (**InventoryList**).
8. Print and then close **InventoryList**.
9. Click the button on the Taskbar representing the Access database file **WBSupplies** and then close the database file.

Activity 3: EXPORTING AN ACCESS REPORT TO WORD

1. With Access the active program, open **PTCostumes**.
2. At the PTCostumes Database window, click the Reports button on the Objects bar and then export the CostumeInventory report to a Word document.
3. When the data displays on the screen in Word, move the insertion point to the beginning of the document and then type **Performance Threads**.
4. Press the Enter key and then type **Costume Inventory**.
5. Increase the size and apply bolding to *Performance Threads* and *Costume Inventory*.
6. Save the Word document with the default name (**CostumeInventory**).
7. Print and then close **CostumeInventory**.
8. Exit Word.
9. With Access the active program, close the **PTCostumes** database file.

Activity 4: IMPORTING DATA TO A NEW TABLE

1 In Access, open the **PTCostumes** database file and then click the Tables button on the Objects bar.
2 Import the Excel worksheet named **PTCostumeHours**. (Make sure you change the *Files of type* option to *Microsoft Excel (*.xls),* and then double-click *PTCostumeHours* in the list box. Do not make any changes to the first Import Spreadsheet Wizard dialog box. At the second dialog box, make sure the *First Row Contains Column Headings* option contains a check mark. Make sure the *In a New Table* option is selected at the third dialog box. Do not make changes to the fourth dialog box and click the *No Primary key* option at the fifth dialog box. At the sixth dialog box, type DesignHours in the *Import to Table* text box, and then click the Finish button.)
3 Open the new DesignHours table.
4 Print and then close the DesignHours table.
5 Close the **PTCostumes** database file.

Activity 5: LINKING DATA TO A NEW TABLE AND EDITING LINKED DATA

1 Open Excel and then open **FCTBookings**.
2 Save the worksheet with Save As and name it **IntE2-R2**.
3 Make Access the active program, open the **FCTCommissions** database file, and then click the Tables button on the Objects bar.
4 Link the Excel worksheet **IntE2-R2** with the **FCTCommissions** database file. (At the Link dialog box, make sure you change the *Files of type* option to *Microsoft Excel.* At the third Link Spreadsheet Wizard dialog box, type LinkedCommissions in the *Linked Table Name* text box.)
5 Open, print, and then close the new LinkedCommissions table.
6 Click the button on the Taskbar representing the Excel worksheet **IntE2-R2**.
7 Make cell C2 active and then type the formula =B2*0.03 and then press Enter.
8 Make cell C2 active and then use the fill handle to copy the formula down to cell C13.
9 Save, print, and then close **IntE2-R2**.
10 Click the button on the Taskbar representing the **FCTCommissions** Access database file and then open the LinkedCommissions table.
11 Save, print, and then close the LinkedCommissions table.
12 Close the **FCTCommissions** database file.
13 Exit Access and then exit Excel.

INDEX

MARQUEE SERIES

MICROSOFT®
POWERPOINT
2003

EMCParadigm
PUBLISHING

NITA RUTKOSKY
Pierce College at Puyallup – Puyallup, Washington

DENISE SEGUIN
Fanshawe College – London, Ontario

CONTENTS

The Marquee Series Team: Desiree Faulkner, Developmental Editor; Leslie Anderson, Senior Designer; Jennifer Wreisner, Cover Designer; Leslie And~ Erica Tava, Desktop Production; Teri Linander, Tester; Sharon O'Donnell, Copyeditor; Lynn Reichel, Proofreader; and Nancy Fulton, Indexer.

Publishing Team: George Provol, Publisher; Janice Johnson, Director of Product Development; Tony Galvin, Acquisitions Editor; Lori Landwer, Marke~ Manager; Shelley Clubb, Electronic Design and Production Manager.

Acknowledgment: The authors and publisher wish to thank the following reviewer for her technical and academic assistance in testing exercises and ass~ instruction: Susan Lynn Bowen, Valdosta Technical College, Valdosta, GA.

Library of Congress Cataloging-in-Publication Data
> Rutkosky, Nita Hewitt.
> Microsoft PowerPoint 2003 / Nita Rutkosky, Denise Seguin.
>   p.cm. – (Marquee series)
> Includes index.
> ISBN 0-7638-2081-4 (text) – ISBN 0-7638-2080-6 (text & CD)
>   1. Computer graphics. 2. Microsoft PowerPoint (Computer file). 3. Business presentations–Graphic methods–Computer programs.
I. Seguin, Denise. II. Title. III. Series

Text + CD: 0-7638-2080-6
Order Number: 05631

© 2004 by Paradigm Publishing Inc.
Published by **EMC**Paradigm
875 Montreal Way
St. Paul, MN 55102

(800) 535-6865
E-mail: educate@emcp.com
Web site: www.emcp.com

Printed in the United States of America   10 9 8 7 6 5 4

Introducing
POWERPOINT® 2003

Create colorful and powerful presentations using PowerPoint, Microsoft's presentation program that is included in the Office suite. With PowerPoint, you can organize and present information and create visual aids for a presentation. PowerPoint is a full-featured presentation program that provides a wide variety of editing and formatting features as well as sophisticated visual elements such as clip art, WordArt, drawn objects, and diagrams. Make your presentation interactive by saving it as a Web page, view and run the presentation in the default browser, and insert hyperlinks in a slide linking to other slides, presentations, or sites on the Internet.

While working in PowerPoint, you will produce presentations for the following six companies:

 First Choice Travel is a travel center offering a full range of traveling services from booking flights, hotel reservations, and rental cars to offering traveling seminars.

 Marquee Productions is involved in all aspects of creating movies from script writing and development to filming.

 The Waterfront Bistro offers fine dining for lunch and dinner and also offers banquet facilities, a wine cellar, and catering services.

 Performance Threads maintains an inventory of rental costumes and also researches, designs, and sews special-order and custom-made costumes.

 Worldwide Enterprises is a national and international distributor of products for a variety of companies and is the exclusive movie distribution agent for Marquee Productions.

 The mission of the Niagara Peninsula College Theatre Arts Division is to offer a curriculum designed to provide students with a thorough exposure to all aspects of the theatre arts.

Preparing, Editing, and Formatting Presentations Using PowerPoint 2003

Use the AutoContent Wizard and slide design templates provided by PowerPoint to take most of the hard work out of preparing a presentation. The AutoContent Wizard walks you through the process of preparing a presentation and provides helpful hints and tips. Choose a slide design template and formatting is automatically applied to slides. Navigate in a presentation, enter text in slides, rearrange slides, and run a presentation using different views offered by PowerPoint. Edit slides and slide elements in a presentation to customize and personalize the presentation. Enhance the visual appeal of a presentation by adding and customizing elements such as clip art, WordArt, drawn objects, and diagrams and add interest to slides by adding transitions, sounds, or applying animation schemes. Use PowerPoint features in a workgroup setting to collaborate with others on preparing and editing a presentation and make a presentation available on a company intranet or on the Internet by publishing it to the Web. Interesting PowerPoint features and elements that you will learn in each section are described below.

Section 1
Preparing a Presentation

Prepare a presentation for Marquee Productions using the AutoContent Wizard and use a design template to prepare a presentation on a movie production project.

Presentation Prepared in Topic 1.1

Create this slide plus seven additional slides using the AutoContent Wizard.

Slide 1

Presentation Prepared and Edited in Topics 1.2 – 1.10

Use different slide layouts to easily change the appearance of slides.

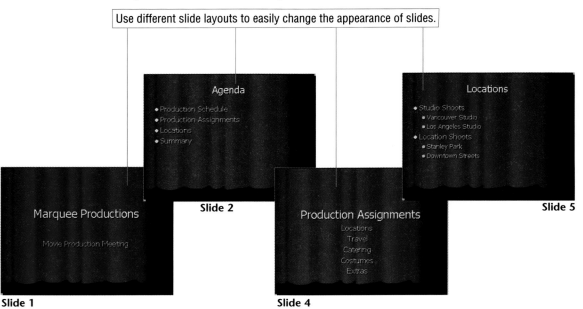

Slide 1

Slide 2

Slide 4

Slide 5

Section 2
Editing Slides and Slide Elements

Open an existing presentation for Marquee Productions on a documentary project, edit and format the presentation, and then insert a clip art image and logo.

Presentation Prepared, Edited, and Formatted in Topics 2.1 – 2.12

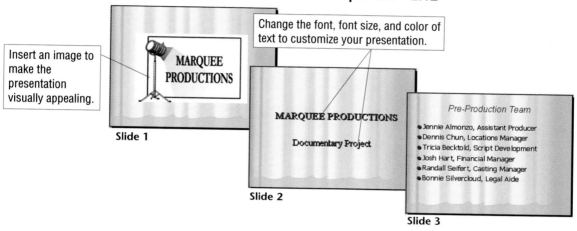

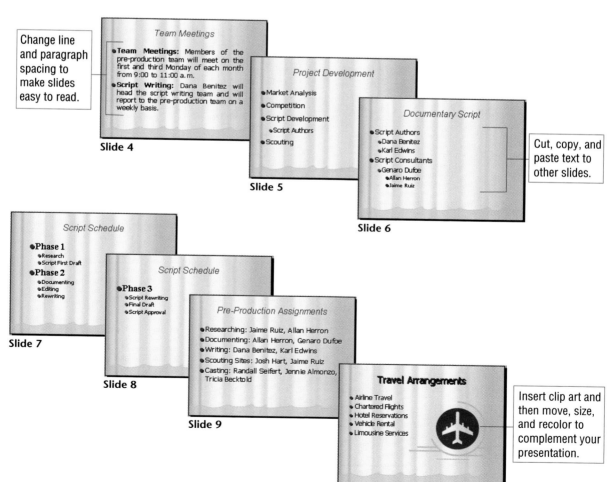

Section 3
Formatting and Enhancing a Presentation

Open an existing presentation on filming in the Toronto area, edit and format the presentation, and then add visual appeal to the presentation.

Presentation Prepared, Edited, and Formatted in Topics 3.1 – 3.12

Use WordArt to create, distort, modify, and/or conform text to a variety of shapes.

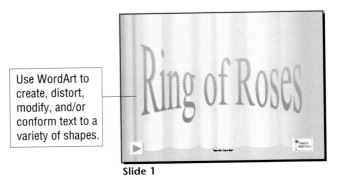

Slide 1

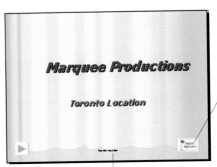

Slide 2

Insert images using the slide master and title master slide.

Create a footer on slides using the Header and Footer dialog box or the slide master.

Slide 3

Add visual appeal to a slide by including autoshapes and text boxes.

Organizational charts and diagrams add interest and impact to the information in your presentation.

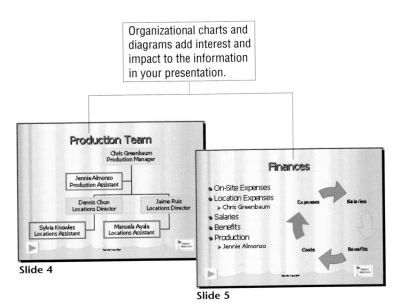

Slide 4

Slide 5

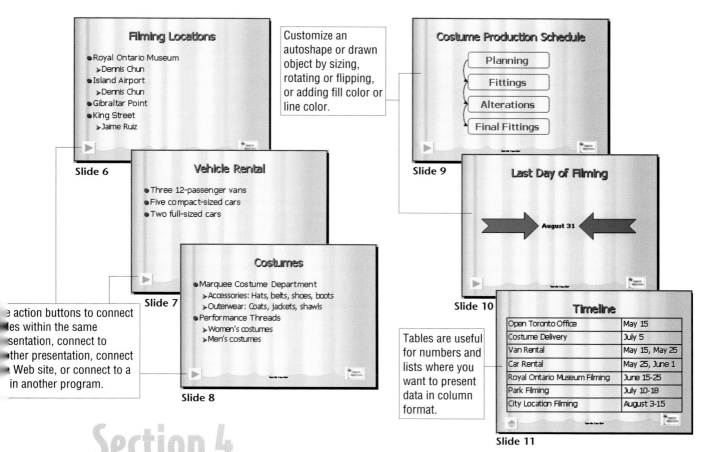

Filming Locations
- Royal Ontario Museum
  - Dennis Chun
- Island Airport
  - Dennis Chun
- Gibraltar Point
- King Street
  - Jaime Ruiz

Slide 6

Customize an autoshape or drawn object by sizing, rotating or flipping, or adding fill color or line color.

Vehicle Rental
- Three 12-passenger vans
- Five compact-sized cars
- Two full-sized cars

Slide 7

Costumes
- Marquee Costume Department
  - Accessories: Hats, belts, shoes, boots
  - Outerwear: Coats, jackets, shawls
- Performance Threads
  - Women's costumes
  - Men's costumes

Slide 8

e action buttons to connect les within the same sentation, connect to ther presentation, connect Web site, or connect to a in another program.

Costume Production Schedule
- Planning
- Fittings
- Alterations
- Final Fittings

Slide 9

Last Day of Filming
August 31

Slide 10

Tables are useful for numbers and lists where you want to present data in column format.

Timeline

Open Toronto Office	May 15
Costume Delivery	July 5
Van Rental	May 15, May 25
Car Rental	May 25, June 1
Royal Ontario Museum Filming	June 15-25
Park Filming	July 10-18
City Location Filming	August 3-15

Slide 11

Section 4

Customizing and Managing Presentations

Open a documentary project presentation, apply more than one design template, format using multiple slide masters, add interest with sound and video, send and edit a presentation for review, create a customized design template, and publish a presentation to the Web.

Presentation Prepared, Edited, Formatted, and Customized in Topics 4.1 – 4.11

Use multiple slide masters to apply formatting to slides in a presentation.

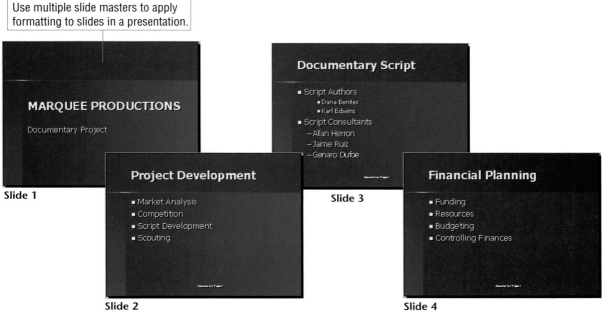

MARQUEE PRODUCTIONS
Documentary Project

Slide 1

Project Development
- Market Analysis
- Competition
- Script Development
- Scouting

Slide 2

Documentary Script
- Script Authors
  - Dana Benitez
  - Karl Edwins
- Script Consultants
  - Allan Herron
  - Jaime Ruiz
  - Genaro Dufoe

Slide 3

Financial Planning
- Funding
- Resources
- Budgeting
- Controlling Finances

Slide 4

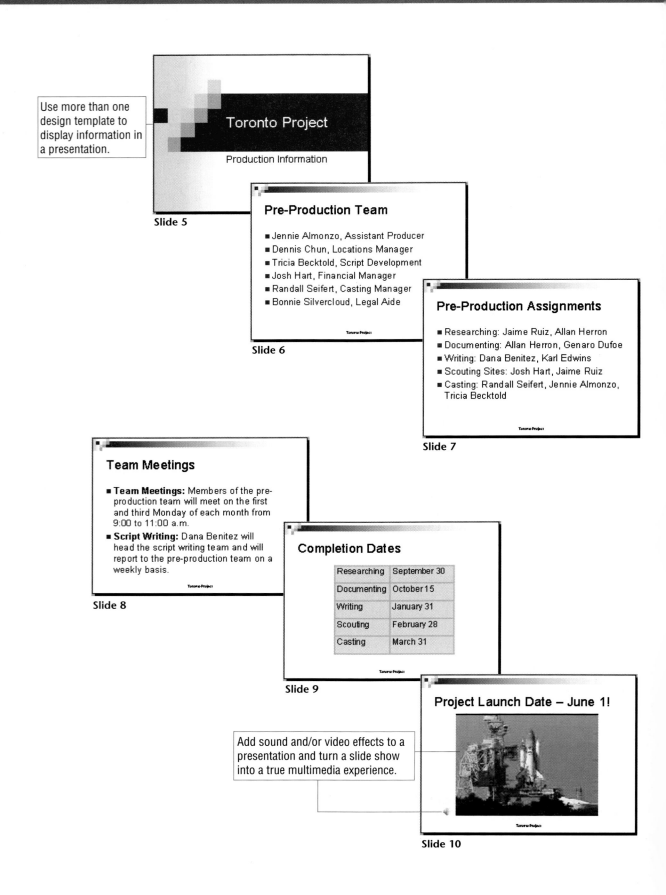

Use more than one design template to display information in a presentation.

Toronto Project

Production Information

Slide 5

Pre-Production Team

- Jennie Almonzo, Assistant Producer
- Dennis Chun, Locations Manager
- Tricia Becktold, Script Development
- Josh Hart, Financial Manager
- Randall Seifert, Casting Manager
- Bonnie Silvercloud, Legal Aide

Toronto Project

Slide 6

Pre-Production Assignments

- Researching: Jaime Ruiz, Allan Herron
- Documenting: Allan Herron, Genaro Dufoe
- Writing: Dana Benitez, Karl Edwins
- Scouting Sites: Josh Hart, Jaime Ruiz
- Casting: Randall Seifert, Jennie Almonzo, Tricia Becktold

Toronto Project

Slide 7

Team Meetings

- **Team Meetings:** Members of the pre-production team will meet on the first and third Monday of each month from 9:00 to 11:00 a.m.
- **Script Writing:** Dana Benitez will head the script writing team and will report to the pre-production team on a weekly basis.

Toronto Project

Slide 8

Completion Dates

Researching	September 30
Documenting	October 15
Writing	January 31
Scouting	February 28
Casting	March 31

Toronto Project

Slide 9

Add sound and/or video effects to a presentation and turn a slide show into a true multimedia experience.

Project Launch Date – June 1!

Toronto Project

Slide 10

POWERPOINT SECTION 1

Preparing a Presentation

Present data and information in a colorful and powerful format using Microsoft's presentation graphics program, PowerPoint. Use PowerPoint to organize and display information and create visual aids for a presentation. Run a PowerPoint presentation on a computer or prepare 35mm slides or transparencies with the slides in the presentation. Preparing a presentation consists of general steps such as creating and editing slides; adding enhancements to slides; and saving, running, previewing, printing and closing a presentation. In this section, you will learn the skills and complete the projects described here.

Note: Before beginning this section, copy to a disk or other location the PowerPointS1 subfolder from the PowerPoint folder on the CD that accompanies this textbook and then make PowerPointS1 the active folder. Steps on copying a folder, deleting a folder, and making a folder active are located on the inside back cover of this textbook.

Skills

- Complete the presentation cycle
- Choose a design template
- Create a new slide
- Navigate in a presentation
- Insert a slide in a presentation
- Change the presentation view
- Change the slide layout
- Use the Help feature
- Check spelling in a presentation
- Use Thesaurus to display synonyms for words
- Run a presentation and use the pen and highlighter during a presentation
- Add transition and sound to a presentation
- Print and preview a presentation

Projects

Use the AutoContent Wizard to prepare a strategy planning presentation and an employee orientation presentation for Marquee Productions; prepare a movie production meeting presentation and a location team meeting presentation.

Prepare an executive meeting presentation for Worldwide Enterprises.

Prepare a presentation containing information on the accommodations and services offered by The Waterfront Bistro.

Locate information on vacationing in Cancun using the Internet and then use that information to prepare a presentation for First Choice Travel.

1.1 Completing the Presentation Cycle

PowerPoint is a presentation graphics program that you can use to organize and present information. With PowerPoint, you can create visual aids for a presentation and then print copies of the aids as well as run the presentation. Several methods are available for creating a presentation such as using design templates, using the AutoContent Wizard, and creating a blank presentation. Preparing a presentation in PowerPoint generally follows a presentation cycle. The steps in the cycle vary but generally include: opening PowerPoint; creating and editing slides; saving, printing, running, and closing the presentation; and then closing PowerPoint.

PROJECT: In preparation for an upcoming seminar, you need to prepare a strategy planning presentation for Marquee Productions using the AutoContent Wizard.

S T E P S

1. Open PowerPoint by clicking the Start button **start** on the Windows Taskbar, pointing to All Programs, pointing to Microsoft Office, and then clicking Microsoft Office PowerPoint 2003.

   Depending on your system configuration, the steps you complete to open PowerPoint may vary.

   PROBLEM If these steps do not open PowerPoint, check with your instructor.

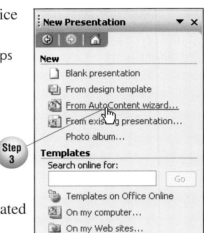

2. At the PowerPoint window, click File and then click New.

3. Click the From AutoContent wizard hyperlink located in the New Presentation task pane.

   The New Presentation task pane displays at the right side of the screen. If this task pane is not visible, display it by clicking View and then Task Pane.

4. At the AutoContent Wizard Start dialog box, click the Next button that displays toward the bottom right side of the dialog box.

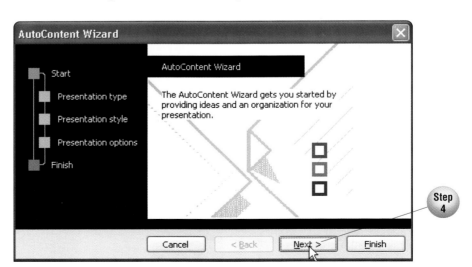

5. At the next dialog box, click *Recommending a Strategy* in the list box and then click the Next button.

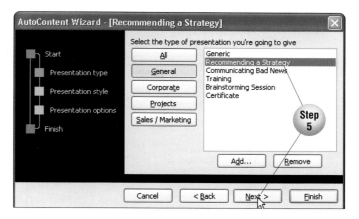

6. At the next dialog box, make sure the *On-screen presentation* option is selected and then click the Next button.

7. At the next dialog box, click inside the *Presentation title* text box and then type **Strategy Planning**.

8. Press the Tab key, type **Marquee Productions Strategy Planning**, and then click the Next button.

9. At the next dialog box, click the Finish button.

10. The presentation created by the AutoContent Wizard displays in the Normal view. What displays in the PowerPoint window will vary depending on what type of presentation you are creating. However, the PowerPoint window contains some consistent elements. Figure P1.1 contains callouts specifying the various elements.

Refer to Table P1.1 for a description of the window elements.

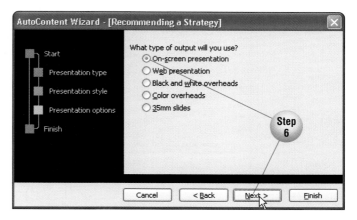

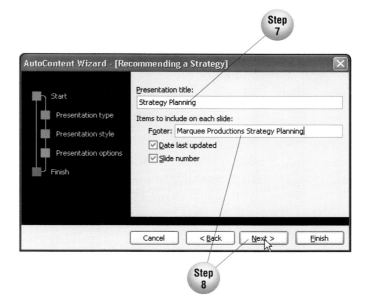

(continued)

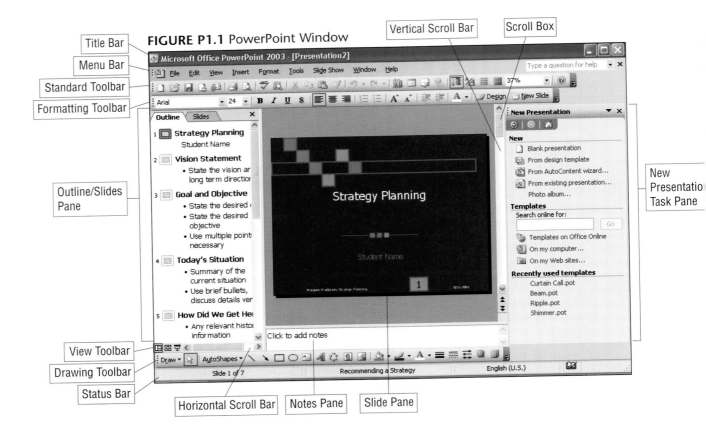

FIGURE P1.1 PowerPoint Window

Labels (clockwise): Vertical Scroll Bar · Scroll Box · Title Bar · Menu Bar · Standard Toolbar · Formatting Toolbar · Outline/Slides Pane · View Toolbar · Drawing Toolbar · Status Bar · Horizontal Scroll Bar · Notes Pane · Slide Pane · New Presentation Task Pane

11. Run the presentation by clicking the Slide Show button located on the View toolbar.

12. When the first slide fills the screen, read the information and then click the left mouse button.

13. Continue reading the information in each slide and clicking the left mouse button to advance to the next slide.

14. When all seven slides have run, a black screen displays with a message telling you to click to exit. At this black screen, click the left mouse button and the first slide displays in the Normal view.

15. Save the presentation by clicking the Save button on the Standard toolbar.

16. At the Save As dialog box, make sure the PowerPointS1 folder on your disk is the active folder, type **MPStrategyPlanning** in the *File name* text box, and then press Enter.

> The *Save in* option at the Save As dialog box displays the active folder. If you need to make the PowerPointS1 folder on your disk in drive A the active folder, click the down-pointing arrow at the right of the *Save in* option and then click *3½ Floppy (A:)*. Double-click *PowerPointS1* in the list box.

(17) At the PowerPoint window, print the presentation information in outline view by clicking File and then Print.

(18) At the Print dialog box, click the down-pointing arrow at the right of the *Print what* option and then click *Outline View*.

(19) Click OK to close the Print dialog box.

(20) Close the presentation by clicking File and then Close.

> If a message displays asking if you want to save the presentation, click Yes.

(21) Close PowerPoint by clicking File and then Exit.

Step 18

TABLE P1.1 PowerPoint Window Elements

Feature	Description
Title Bar	Displays program and presentation names.
Menu Bar	Contains a list of options to manage, format, and customize presentations.
Standard Toolbar	Contains buttons that are shortcuts for the most popular commands.
Formatting Toolbar	Contains buttons for applying formatting to text.
Drawing Toolbar	Contains buttons for drawing and customizing lines and shapes.
Outline/Slides Pane	Displays at left side of window with two tabs—Outline and Slides. With the Outline tab selected, contents of presentation display and with Slides tab selected, slide miniatures display in the pane.
Slide Pane	Displays the slide and slide contents.
Notes Pane	Add notes to a presentation in this pane.
Vertical Scroll Bar	Display specific slides using this scroll bar.
Horizontal Scroll Bar	Shifts text left or right in the Outline/Slides pane.
Task Pane	Presents features to help you easily identify and use more of the program. The name and options in the task pane vary depending on what function is being performed.
View Toolbar	Contains buttons for changing the presentation view.
Status Bar	Displays messages about PowerPoint features and also information about the view.

IN BRIEF

Open PowerPoint
1 Click Start button.
2 Point to All Programs.
3 Point to Microsoft Office.
4 Click Microsoft Office PowerPoint 2003.

Run a Presentation
1 Click Slide Show button.
2 Click left mouse button to advance slides.

Save a Presentation
1 Click Save button.
2 Type presentation name.
3 Click Save button or press Enter.

Print a Presentation
1 Click File, Print.
2 At Print dialog box, specify how you want presentation printed.
3 Click OK.

Close a Presentation
Click File, Close.

Exit PowerPoint
Click File, Exit.

1.2 Choosing a Design Template, Creating Slides, and Closing a Presentation

PowerPoint provides several methods for creating a presentation. In the previous section, you used the AutoContent Wizard to create a presentation. You can also create a presentation using predesigned templates, which provide formatting for slides. If you want to apply your own formatting to slides, choose a blank presentation. When you choose a design template or a blank presentation, you are presented with the PowerPoint screen in Normal view. In this view, three panes are available for entering text—the Outline/Slides pane, Slide pane,

and Notes pane. Use either the Slide pane or the Outline/Slides pane with the Outline tab selected to enter text in a slide. Use the Notes page to insert a note in a slide.

PROJECT: Chris Greenbaum, production manager for Marquee Productions, has asked you to prepare slides for a movie production meeting. You decide to prepare the presentation using a design template offered by PowerPoint.

S T E P S

1. Open PowerPoint.

2. At the PowerPoint window, click the Slide Design button ☐ Design on the Formatting toolbar.

   > If the Standard and Formatting toolbars are positioned on the same row, separate them by clicking Tools and then Customize. At the Tools dialog box with the Options tab selected, click the *Show Standard and Formatting toolbars on two rows* check box to insert a check mark, and then click OK. Clicking the Slide Design button on the Formatting toolbar displays the Slide Design task pane at the right side of the screen.

3. Click Curtain Call in the *Apply a design template* list box in the Slide Design task pane. (You will need to scroll down the list to display this design template.)

   > Position the mouse pointer on the slide design miniature and a box displays with the name of the design. By default, some design templates install on first use. Depending on the installation on your system, you may need to install some design templates.

   PROBLEM

   If this slide design is not available, it may need to be installed.

4. Click anywhere in the text *Click to add title* that displays in the slide in the Slide pane and then type **Marquee Productions**.

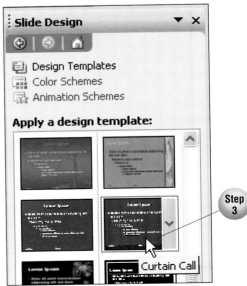

⑤ Click anywhere in the text *Click to add subtitle* that displays in the slide and then type **Movie Production Meeting**.

⑥ Click the New Slide button ⊟ New Slide located on the Formatting toolbar.

> Clicking the New Slide button displays a new slide in the Slide pane and also displays the Slide Layout task pane containing slide layouts. The Title and Text slide layout is automatically chosen for the slide in the Slide pane.

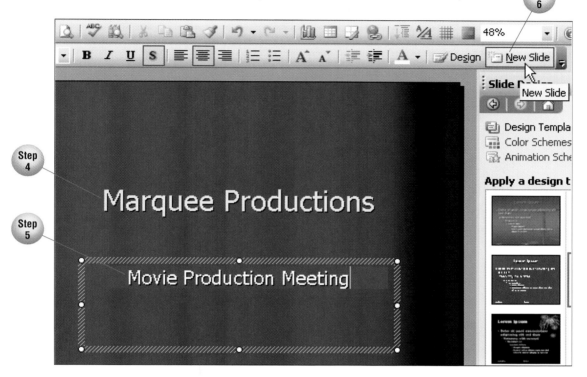

⑦ Click anywhere in the text *Click to add title* that displays in the slide and then type **Agenda**.

⑧ Click anywhere in the text *Click to add text* that displays in the slide and then type **Production Schedule**.

⑨ Press the Enter key and then type the following agenda items, pressing the Enter key after each item: **Production Assignments**, **Locations**, and **Summary**.

⑩ Click the New Slide button ⊟ New Slide on the Formatting toolbar.

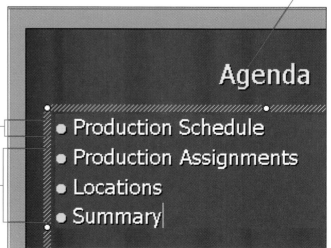

(continued)

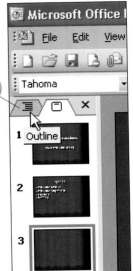

11 Click the Outline tab located toward the top of the Outline/Slides pane.

12 Click in the Outline/Slides pane immediately right of the slide icon after the number 3, type **Locations**, and then press Enter.

13 Press the Tab key, type **Studio Shoots**, and then press the Enter key.

> Pressing the Tab key demotes the insertion point to the next level, while pressing Shift + Tab promotes the insertion point to the previous level.

14 Press the Tab key, type **Vancouver Studio**, and then press Enter.

15 Type **Los Angeles Studio** and then press Enter.

16 Press Shift + Tab, type **Location Shoots**, and then press Enter.

17 Press the Tab key, type **Stanley Park**, and then press Enter.

18 Type **Downtown Streets**.

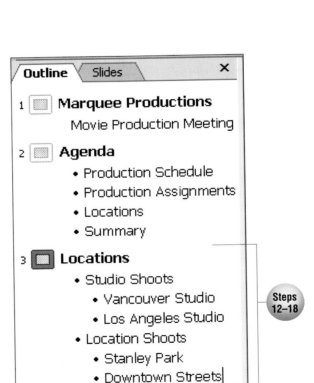

19 Click anywhere in the text *Click to add notes* in the Notes pane and then type **Camille Matsui will report on the park location.**

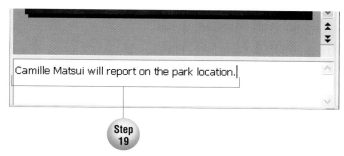

Camille Matsui will report on the park location.

Step 19

20 Click the Slides tab located toward the top of the Outline/Slides pane.

21 Click the Save button on the Standard toolbar.

22 At the Save As dialog box, make sure the PowerPointS1 folder on your disk is the active folder, type **PPS1-01** in the *File name* text box, and then press Enter.

23 Close the presentation by clicking File and then Close.

In Addition

Displaying and Maneuvering in Task Panes

As you use various PowerPoint features, a task pane may display at the right side of the screen. The name of the task pane varies depending on the feature. For example, when you click the Slide Design button on the Formatting toolbar the Slide Design task pane displays. If you click Format on the Menu bar and then click Slide Layout, the Slide Layout task pane displays. A task pane presents features to help you easily identify and use more of the program.

You can maneuver within various task panes by clicking the Back button (contains a left-pointing arrow) and/or the Forward button (contains a right-pointing arrow) that display at the top of the task pane. You can also maneuver within various task panes by clicking the Other Task Panes button (contains the name of the task pane and a down-pointing arrow) and then clicking the desired task pane at the drop-down list.

You can control whether the display of the task pane is on or off by clicking View and then Task Pane. You can also close the task pane by clicking the Close button (contains an X) located in the upper right corner of the task pane.

The task pane can be docked and undocked. By default, the task pane is docked at the right side of the screen. Move (undock) the task pane by positioning the mouse pointer on the task pane Title bar, holding down the left mouse button, and then dragging the task pane to the desired location. If you move the task pane (undock it), you can dock it back at the right side of the screen by double-clicking the task pane Title bar.

IN BRIEF

Choose a Design Template
1 Click Slide Design button on Formatting toolbar.
2 Click desired slide design in Slide Design task pane.

1.3 Opening, Navigating, and Inserting Slides in a Presentation

Open a saved presentation by clicking the Open button on the Standard toolbar and then double-clicking the desired presentation at the Open dialog box. Navigate through slides in a presentation with buttons on the vertical scroll bar by clicking text in the desired slide in the Outline/Slides pane, or using keys on the keyboard. Insert a new slide in a presentation by navigating to the slide that will precede the new slide and then clicking the New Slide button on the Formatting toolbar.

PROJECT: Chris Greenbaum has asked you to add more information to the movie production meeting presentation. You will insert a new slide between the second and third slides in the presentation and then add a slide at the end of the presentation.

S T E P S

① Click the Open button 📂 on the Standard toolbar.

② At the Open dialog box, make sure the PowerPointS1 folder on your disk is the active folder and then double-click *PPS1-01* in the list box.

PROBLEM ?
If **PPS1-01** does not display in the Open dialog box, you may need to change the folder. Check with your instructor.

③ With **PPS1-01** open, click the Next Slide button ⬇ located at the bottom of the vertical scroll bar.

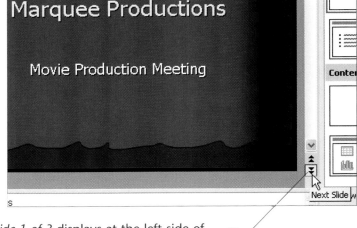

Clicking this button displays the next slide, Slide 2, in the presentation. Notice that *Slide 2 of 3* displays at the left side of the Status bar.

④ Click the Previous Slide button ⬆ located toward the bottom of the vertical scroll bar to display Slide 1.

When you click the Previous Slide button, *Slide 1 of 3* displays at the left side of the Status bar.

Step 3

⑤ Display Slide 2 in the Slide pane by clicking the Next Slide button ⬇ located at the bottom of the vertical scroll bar.

⑥ Insert a new slide between Slides 2 and 3 by clicking the New Slide button 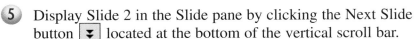 on the Formatting toolbar.

7 Click anywhere in the text *Click to add title* in the slide in the Slide pane and then type **Production Schedule**.

8 Click anywhere in the text *Click to add text* located in the slide and then type the bulleted text as shown in the slide at the right. Press the Enter key after each item *except* the last item.

Step 7

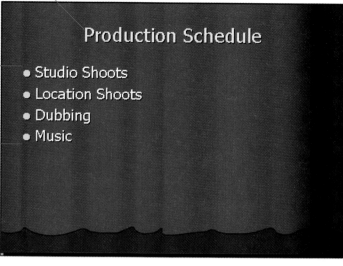

Step 8

Step 9

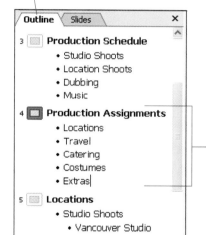

9 Click the Outline tab located toward the top of the Outline/Slides pane.

10 Click immediately right of the text *Music* located toward the middle of the pane, press the Enter key, and then press Shift + Tab.

> This moves the insertion point back a level and inserts the number 4 followed by a slide icon.

Steps 10–11

11 Type **Production Assignments**, press the Enter key, and then press the Tab key. Type the remaining text for Slide 4 as shown at the left. Do not press the Enter key after typing *Extras*.

> When you are finished typing the text, the presentation will contain five slides.

12 Click the Save button  on the Standard toolbar to save **PPS1-01**.

In Addition

Correcting Errors in PowerPoint

PowerPoint's AutoCorrect feature automatically corrects certain words as you type them. For example, type *teh* and press the spacebar, and AutoCorrect changes it to *the*. PowerPoint also contains a spelling feature that inserts a wavy red line below words that are not contained in the Spelling dictionary or not corrected by AutoCorrect. If the word containing a wavy red line is correct, you can leave it as written. The wavy red line does not print. If the word is incorrect, edit it.

In Brief

Open a Presentation
1 Click Open button.
2 Double-click desired presentation.

Create a New Slide
1 Click New Slide button.
2 Click desired slide layout in Slide Layout task pane.

1.4 Changing Views; Choosing a Slide Layout

PowerPoint provides viewing options for a presentation. Change the presentation view with buttons on the View toolbar that displays below the Outline/Slides pane or with options at the View drop-down list. The Normal view, also referred to as the *tri-pane view*, is the default view and displays three panes—Outline/Slides, Slide, and Notes. You can change from the Normal view to the Slide view, Slide Sorter view, or Notes Page view. Choose the view based on the type of activity you are performing in the presentation. Click the New Slide button on the Formatting toolbar and the Slide Layout task pane displays with slide layout choices. Click the desired layout in the *Apply slide layout* list box.

PROJECT: After reviewing the movie production presentation, Chris Greenbaum has asked you to edit a slide and create a new slide.

S T E P S

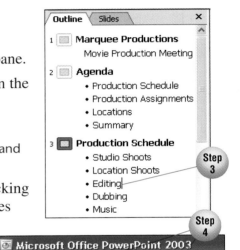

1. With **PPS1-01** open, check to make sure the Outline tab is selected in the Outline/Slides pane.

2. Click immediately right of *Location Shoots* in the third slide.

3. Press the Enter key and then type **Editing**.

    This inserts *Editing* between *Location Shoots* and *Dubbing*.

4. Display the slides in Notes Page view by clicking View on the Menu bar and then clicking Notes Page at the drop-down list.

    In Notes Page view, an individual slide displays on a page with any added notes displayed below the slide.

5. Click the Next Slide button on the vertical scroll bar until Slide 5 (the last slide) displays.

    Notice that the note you created to Camille Matsui displays below the slide in the page.

6. Increase the zoom by clicking the down-pointing arrow at the right side of the Zoom button on the Standard toolbar and then clicking *66%* at the drop-down list.

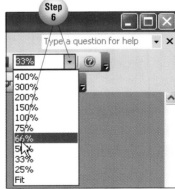

7. After viewing the larger slide and note text, click the down-pointing arrow at the right side of the Zoom button and then click *33%* at the drop-down list.

8. View all slides in the presentation in slide miniature by clicking the Slide Sorter View button 🔲 on the View toolbar.

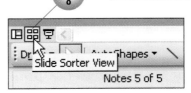

⑨ Click the Normal View button 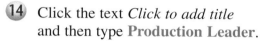 on the View toolbar.

⑩ Click the Slides tab in the Outline/Slides pane.

> With the Slides tab selected, slide miniatures display in the Outline/Slides pane.

⑪ Click below the Slide 5 miniature in the Outline/Slides pane.

> When you click below the slide miniatures, a blinking black line displays below Slide 5.

⑫ Click the New Slide button on the Formatting toolbar.

⑬ Click the Title Slide layout that displays in the *Apply slide layout* list box in the Slide Layout task pane.

> Position the mouse pointer on a slide layout and a box displays with the name of the layout.

⑭ Click the text *Click to add title* and then type **Production Leader**.

⑮ Click the text *Click to add subtitle* and then type **Chris Greenbaum**.

⑯ Click the Slide 1 miniature in the Outline/Slides pane to make it the active slide.

⑰ Save **PPS1-01**.

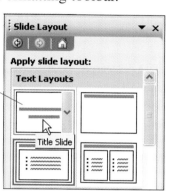

In Addition

Expanding Drop-Down Menus

When you open PowerPoint, the menus display a limited selection of basic commands called *first rank options*. At the bottom of each menu is a down-pointing double arrow. Click this double arrow to expand the drop-down menu and display additional options, known as *second rank options*. Or, allow the mouse pointer to rest on the menu option for approximately five seconds and the menu will expand to show all options. Second rank options display with a lighter gray background. As you create and edit presentations, the commands you use most often are stored as personalized options and display on the drop-down menus when you select them. To disable the personalized menu feature and display all menu options, click Tools and then Customize. At the Customize dialog box, click the Options tab. Click the *Always show full menus* option to insert a check mark in the check box and then click the Close button to close the dialog box.

1.5 Changing the Slide Layout; Selecting and Moving a Placeholder

The slides you have created have been based on a slide layout. You can change the slide layout by clicking a different slide layout option at the Slide Layout task pane. This task pane displays when you click the New Slide button. You can also display this task pane by clicking Format and then Slide Layout. Objects in a slide such as text, a chart, a table, or other graphic element are generally positioned in a placeholder. Click the object to select the placeholder. You can move, size, and/or delete a selected placeholder.

PROJECT: You have decided to make a few changes to the layout of slides in the movie production presentation.

S T E P S

1. With **PPS1-01** open, position the mouse pointer on the scroll box located on the vertical scroll bar. Hold down the left mouse button, drag the scroll box to the bottom of the scroll bar, and then release the mouse button.

    > This displays Slide 6 in the Slide pane. As you drag the scroll box on the vertical scroll bar, a box displays indicating the slide number.

2. Make sure the Slide Layout task pane displays. If it does not, click Format on the Menu bar and then click Slide Layout at the drop-down menu.

3. Click the Title and Text slide layout in the Slide Layout task pane.

    > Position the mouse pointer on a slide layout and the name of the layout displays in a box.

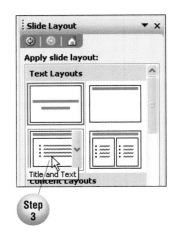

Step 3

4. Click immediately right of the *r* in *Leader* (this selects the placeholder), press the Backspace key until *Leader* is deleted, and then type **Team**.

    > White sizing handles display around the selected placeholder. Use these sizing handles to increase and/or decrease the size of the placeholder.

Step 4

5. Click immediately right of the *m* in *Greenbaum*.

6. Type a comma (,), press the spacebar, and then type **Production Manager**.

7. Press the Enter key and then type the remaining names and titles shown in the slide at the right. (Do not press the Enter key after typing *Josh Hart, Locations Director*.)

8. Click the Previous Slide button on the vertical scroll bar until Slide 4 displays.

Production Team

- Chris Greenbaum, Production Manager
- Camille Matsui, Production Assistant
- Jennie Almonzo, Assistant Producer
- Dennis Chun, Locations Director
- Josh Hart, Locations Director

Step 6

Step 7

9 Change the slide layout by clicking the Title Slide layout in the Slide Layout task pane.

10 If the text below the title decreases in size, click the AutoFit Options button ⊞ located at the left side of the placeholder and then click *Stop Fitting Text to This Placeholder* at the drop-down menu.

Step 9

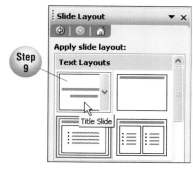

11 Click anywhere in the text *Locations*.

> This selects the placeholder containing the text.

12 Move the placeholder by positioning the mouse pointer on the border of the placeholder until the mouse pointer displays with a four-headed arrow attached. Hold down the left mouse button, drag up to the approximate location shown at the right, and then release the mouse button.

Step 12

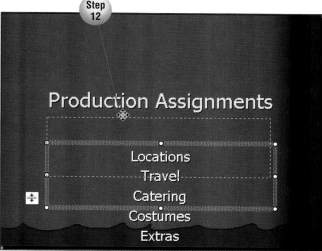

13 Click outside the placeholder to deselect it.

14 Save **PPS1-01**.

In Addition

Using the AutoFit Options Button

When you selected the placeholder in Slide 4, an AutoFit Options button displayed at the left side of the placeholder. Click the AutoFit Options button and a list of choices displays for positioning objects in the placeholder as shown below. Click the *AutoFit Text to Placeholder* option to fit text within the boundaries of the placeholder. The middle choice, *Stop Fitting Text to This Placeholder*, is selected by default and indicates that PowerPoint will not automatically fit the text or object within the placeholder. Choose the last option, *Control AutoCorrect Options,* to display the AutoCorrect dialog box with the AutoFormat As You Type tab selected.

IN BRIEF

Change Slide Layout
1 Click Format, Slide Layout.
2 Click desired slide layout in Slide Layout task pane.

Move Placeholder
1 Click inside placeholder.
2 Drag with mouse to desired position.

Size Placeholder
1 Click inside placeholder.
2 Drag sizing handles with mouse to increase/decrease size.

1.6 Using Help; Checking Spelling; Using Thesaurus

Use the PowerPoint Help feature to display information on PowerPoint features. One method for displaying Help information is to click in the Ask a Question box located at the right side of the Menu bar. Type a question in this text box and then press Enter. At the Search Results task pane that displays, click the desired topic and information will display in a Microsoft Office PowerPoint Help window. For example, you might search for information on checking the spelling of text in slides. Use the Thesaurus feature to find synonyms, antonyms, and related words for a particular word. To use the Thesaurus, click the word for which you want to display synonyms and antonyms, click Tools, and then click Thesaurus. This displays the Research task pane with information about the word where the insertion point is positioned.

PROJECT: You have decided to create a new slide in the movie production presentation. Because several changes have been made to the presentation, you know that checking the spelling of all of the slide text is important, but you are not sure how to do it. You will use the Help feature to learn how to complete a spelling check and then use the Thesaurus feature to replace a couple of words with synonyms.

STEPS

1. With **PPS1-01** open, display Slide 6 in the Slide pane, and then click the New Slide button on the Formatting toolbar.

   This inserts a new slide at the end of the presentation.

2. Click the text *Click to add title* and then type **Summary**.

3. Click the text *Click to add text* and then type the text shown in the slide below. After typing *Budgget*, click outside the placeholder to deselect it.

   Type the words exactly as shown. You will check the spelling in a later step.

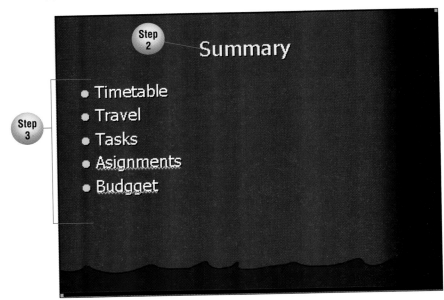

4. Learn how to complete a spelling check. To begin, click in the *Ask a Question* text box located at the right side of the Menu bar.

⑤ Type **How do I check spelling?** and then press Enter.

⑥ Click <u>Check spelling</u> in the Search Results task pane list box.

⑦ At the Microsoft Office PowerPoint Help window, click the <u>Check spelling in the whole presentation</u> hyperlink.

⑧ Read the information that displays about spell checking and then click the Close button (contains an *X*) located in the upper right corner of the Microsoft Office PowerPoint Help window.

⑨ Complete a spelling check by clicking the Spelling button 🔤 on the Standard toolbar.

⑩ When the spelling checker selects *Asignments* in Slide 7 and displays *Assignments* in the *Change to* text box in the Spelling dialog box, click the Change button.

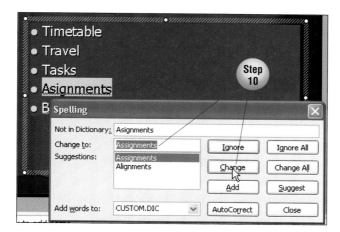

⑪ When the spelling checker selects *Budgget* in Slide 7 and displays *Budget* in the *Change to* text box in the Spelling dialog box, click the Change button.

(continued)

(12) When the spelling checker selects *Greenbaum* in Slide 6, click the Ignore button.

Greenbaum is a proper name and is spelled correctly. Clicking the Ignore button tells the spelling checker to leave the name as spelled.

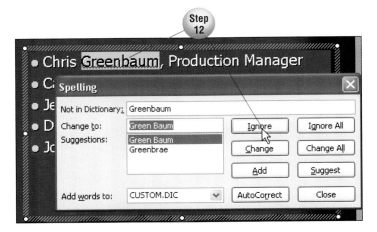

(13) When the spelling checker selects *Almonzo* in Slide 6, click the Ignore button.

(14) At the message telling you that the spelling check is complete, click the OK button.

(15) Display Slide 7 in the Slide pane and then click the word *Timetable*.

(16) Look up synonyms for *Timetable* by clicking Tools and then Thesaurus.

This displays the Research task pane containing lists of synonyms for *Timetable*. Depending on the word you are looking up, the words in the Research task pane list box may display followed by *(n.)* for *noun*, *(adj.)* for *adjective*, or *(adv.)* for *adverb*. Antonyms may display in the list of related synonyms, generally at the end of the list of related synonyms, and are followed by *(Antonym)*.

(17) Position the mouse pointer on the word *schedule* in the Research task pane, click the down-pointing arrow at the right of the word, and then click *Insert* at the drop-down list.

This replaces *Timetable* with *Schedule*.

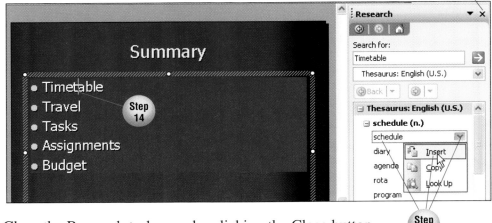

(18) Close the Research task pane by clicking the Close button located in the upper right corner of the task pane.

19 Right-click on the word *Tasks*, located in Slide 7, point to Synonyms, and then click *responsibilities*.

The shortcut menu offers another method for displaying synonyms for words.

20 Capitalize the *r* in *responsibilities*.

21 Save **PPS1-01**.

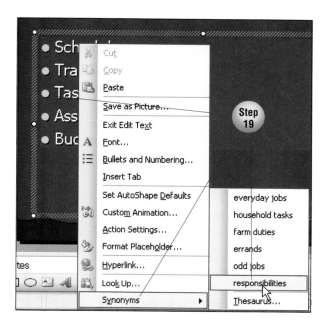

Step 19

In Addition

Turning On/Turning Off the Office Assistant

Microsoft Office includes an Office Assistant that automatically provides topics and tips on tasks you perform as you work. You can turn on the display of the Office Assistant by clicking Help and then Show the Office Assistant. Turn off the display of the assistant by clicking Help and then Hide the Office Assistant. If you turn on the display of the assistant and then decide to turn it off (rather than just hiding it), click the Office Assistant and then click the Options button that displays in the yellow box. At the Office Assistant dialog box, click the *Use the Office Assistant* option to remove the check mark, and then click OK.

IN BRIEF

Use Help
1 Click in the *Ask a Question* text box.
2 Type desired question and press Enter.
3 Click desired topic at drop-down list.

Complete a Spelling Check
1 Click Spelling button.
2 Change or ignore words highlighted.
3 When spelling check is completed, click OK.

Use Thesaurus
1 Click desired word.
2 Click Tools, Thesaurus.
3 Position mouse pointer on desired replacement word in Research task pane, click down-pointing arrow at right of word, and then click Insert.

1.7 Running a Presentation

Several methods can be used to run a slide show. Slides created in PowerPoint can be converted to 35mm slides or transparencies, or the computer screen can provide the output. An on-screen presentation saves the expense of producing slides, requires no projection equipment, and lets you use the computer's color capability. You can run a presentation in PowerPoint manually, advance the slides automatically, or set up a slide show to run continuously for demonstration purposes. To run a slide show manually, click the Slide Show button on the View toolbar and then use the mouse or keyboard to advance through the slides. You can also use buttons on the Slide Show toolbar. This toolbar displays when you move the mouse pointer while running a presentation.

PROJECT: You are now ready to run the movie production meeting presentation. You will use the mouse to perform various actions while running the presentation.

S T E P S

1. With **PPS1-01** open, click the Previous Slide button ⬆ located toward the bottom of the vertical scroll bar until Slide 1 displays in the Slide pane.

   When you click the Slide Show button on the View toolbar, the presentation begins on the active slide. If you want to run the presentation from the beginning, make sure the first slide is active.

2. Click the Slide Show button 🖳 on the View toolbar.

   Clicking this button begins the presentation and Slide 1 fills the entire screen.

3. After viewing Slide 1, click the left mouse button to advance to the next slide.

4. After viewing Slide 2, click the left mouse button to advance to the next slide.

5. At Slide 3, move the mouse pointer until the Slide Show toolbar displays and then click the left arrow button on the toolbar to display the previous slide (Slide 2).

   With buttons on the Slide Show toolbar you can display the next slide, the previous slide, display a specific slide, and use the pen and highlighter to emphasize text on the slide. You can also display the Slide Show Help window shown in Figure P1.2 that describes all of the navigating options when running a presentation. Display this window by clicking the slide icon button on the Slide Show toolbar and then clicking Help.

6. Click the right arrow button on the Slide Show toolbar to display the next slide (Slide 3).

7. Display the previous slide (Slide 2) by clicking the *right* mouse button and then clicking Previous at the pop-up menu.

   Clicking the *right* mouse button causes a pop-up menu to display with a variety of options including options to display the previous or next slide.

(8) Display the next slide by clicking the slide icon button on the Slide Show toolbar and then clicking the Next option.

(9) Display Slide 5 by typing **5** on the keyboard and then pressing Enter.

> Move to any slide in a presentation by typing the slide number and pressing Enter.

(10) Change to a black screen by typing **B** on the keyboard.

> When you type the letter *B*, the slide is removed from the screen and the screen displays black. This might be useful in a situation where you want to discuss something unrelated to the slide.

(11) Return to Slide 5 by typing **B** on the keyboard.

> Typing the letter *B* switches between the slide and a black screen. Type the letter *W* if you want to switch between the slide and a white screen.

(12) Click the left mouse button to display Slide 6. Continue clicking the left mouse button until a black screen displays. At the black screen, click the left mouse button again.

> This returns the presentation to the Normal view.

(13) Display Slide 2 by clicking the Next Slide button located at the bottom of the vertical scroll bar.

> Begin a presentation on any slide by making the desired slide active and then clicking the Slide Show button on the View toolbar.

(14) Click the Slide Show button on the View toolbar.

(15) Run the presentation by clicking the left mouse button at each slide. At the black screen, click the left mouse button again.

FIGURE P1.2 Slide Show Help Window

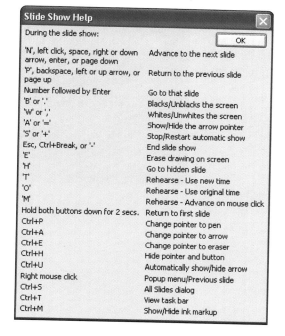

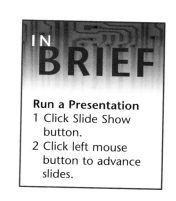

Run a Presentation
1 Click Slide Show button.
2 Click left mouse button to advance slides.

1.8 Using the Pen and Highlighter during a Presentation

Emphasize major points or draw the attention of the audience to specific items in a slide during a presentation using the pen or highlighter. To use the pen on a slide, run the presentation, and when the desired slide displays, move the mouse to display the Slide Show toolbar. Click the pen button on the toolbar and then click either Ballpoint Pen or Felt Tip Pen. The felt tip pen draws a thicker line than the ballpoint pen. Use the mouse to draw in the slide to emphasize a point or specific text. If you want to erase the marks you made with the pen, click the pen button and then click Eraser. This causes the mouse pointer to display as an eraser. Drag through an ink mark to remove it. To remove all ink marks at the same time, click the Erase All Ink on Slide option. When you are finished with the pen, click the Arrow option to return the mouse pointer to an arrow.

PROJECT: You will run the movie production meeting presentation again for another group of Marquee Production staff and use the pen and highlighter to emphasize points in slides.

STEPS

1. With **PPS1-01** open, display Slide 1 in the Slide pane.
2. Click the Slide Show button 🖵 on the View toolbar.
3. Run the presentation by clicking the left mouse button to advance slides until Slide 3 displays. (This is the slide with the title *Production Schedule*.)
4. Move the mouse to display the Slide Show toolbar, click the pen button, and then click Felt Tip Pen.

    This turns the mouse pointer into a small circle.

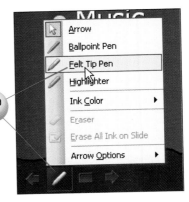

Step 4

5. Using the mouse, draw a circle around the text *Location Shoots*.
6. Using the mouse, draw a line below *Dubbing*.
7. Erase the pen markings by clicking the pen button on the Slide Show toolbar and then clicking Erase All Ink on Slide.

Step 5
Step 6

Step 7

8. Change the color of the ink by clicking the pen button, pointing to Ink Color, and then clicking the bright yellow color.

9. Draw a yellow line below the word *Music*.

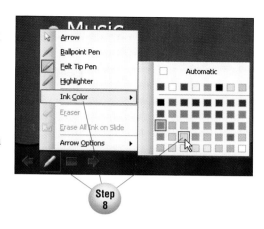

Step 8

10. Return the mouse pointer back to an arrow by clicking the pen button and then clicking Arrow at the pop-up menu.

11. Click the left mouse button to advance to Slide 4.

12. Click the pen button and then click Highlighter at the pop-up menu.

> This changes the mouse pointer to a light yellow rectangle.

13. Drag through the word *Locations* to highlight it.

14. Drag through the word *Costumes* to highlight it.

15. Return the mouse pointer back to an arrow by clicking the pen button and then clicking Arrow.

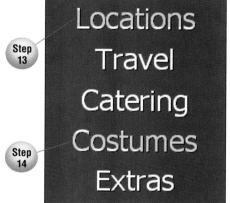

Step 13

Step 14

16. Press the Esc key on the keyboard to end the presentation without running the remaining slides. At the message asking if you want to keep your ink annotations, click the Discard button.

In Addition

Hiding/Displaying the Mouse Pointer

When running a presentation, the mouse pointer is set, by default, to be hidden automatically after three seconds of inactivity. The mouse pointer will appear again when you move the mouse. You can change this default setting by clicking the pen button on the Slide Show toolbar, pointing to Arrow Options, and then clicking Visible if you want the mouse pointer always visible or Hidden if you do not want the mouse to display at all as you run the presentation. The Automatic option is the default setting.

In BRIEF

Use the Pen/Highlighter When Running a Presentation

1 Click Slide Show button.
2 At desired slide, move mouse.
3 Click the pen button on the Slide Show toolbar and then click desired pen or highlighter option.
4 Draw with the pen/highlighter in the slide.

1.9 Adding Transition and Sound

You can apply interesting transitions and sounds to a presentation. A *transition* is how one slide is removed from the screen during a presentation and the next slide is displayed. Interesting transitions can be added such as blinds, boxes, checkerboards, covers, random bars, stripes, and wipes. Add a sound to a presentation and the sound is heard when a slide is displayed on the screen during a presentation. Add transitions and sounds with options at the Slide Transition task pane.

PROJECT: You have decided to enhance the movie production meeting presentation by adding transitions and sound to the slides.

S T E P S

1 With **PPS1-01** open, click the Slide Sorter View button ⊞ on the View toolbar.

> When you change to the Slide Sorter view, the Slide Sorter toolbar displays below the Standard toolbar.

2 Click the Slide Transition button ⊞ Transition that displays at the right side of the Slide Sorter toolbar.

> Clicking the Slide Transition button displays the Slide Transition task pane. You can also display this task pane by clicking Slide Show on the Menu bar and then clicking Slide Transition.

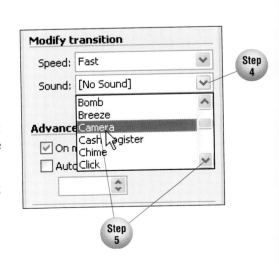

3 Click the *Checkerboard Across* option in the *Apply to selected slides* list box in the Slide Transition task pane.

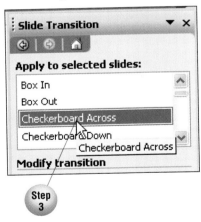

4 Click the down-pointing arrow at the right side of the *Sound* option box (contains the text *[No Sound]*) located in the *Modify transition* section of the Slide Transition task pane.

5 At the drop-down list that displays, click the down-pointing arrow until *Camera* displays and then click *Camera*.

6 Click the Apply to All Slides button located toward the bottom of the Slide Transition task pane.

> Notice that a transition icon displays below the lower left corner of each slide. Click one of these icons below a miniature slide and the transition displays in the miniature and the sound is played.

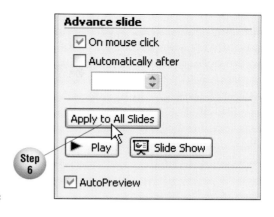

Step 6

7 Click Slide 1 to make it the active slide.

8 Click the Normal View button ⊞ on the View toolbar.

9 Run the presentation by clicking the Slide Show button 🖵 on the View toolbar.

10 Click the left mouse button to advance each slide.

11 At the black screen that displays after the last slide, click the left mouse button again to return the presentation to the Normal view.

12 Save **PPS1-01**.

In Addition

Running a Slide Show Automatically

Slides in a slide show can be advanced automatically after a specific number of seconds with options in the *Advance slide* section of the Slide Transition task pane. To automatically advance slides, click in the *Automatically after* check box and then insert the desired number of seconds in the text box. Change the time in the text box by clicking the up- or down-pointing arrow at the right side of the text box or by selecting any text in the text box and then typing the desired time. If you want the transition time to affect all slides in the presentation, click the Apply to All Slides button. In Slide Sorter view, the transition time displays below each effected slide. To automatically run the presentation, make sure the first slide is selected and then click the Slide Show button located toward the bottom of the task pane. (You can also click the Slide Show button on the View toolbar.) The first slide displays for the specified amount of time and then the next slide automatically displays.

IN BRIEF

Add Transition and Sound
1 Click Slide Sorter View button.
2 Click Slide Transition button on Slide Sorter toolbar.
3 Choose desired transition and sound in the Slide Transition task pane.
4 Click Apply to All Slides button.

You can print each slide on a separate piece of paper; print each slide at the top of the page, leaving the bottom of the page for notes; print up to nine slides or a specific number of slides on a single piece of paper; or print the slide titles and topics in outline form. Use the *Print what* option at the Print dialog box to specify what you want printed. Before printing a presentation, consider previewing the presentation. To do this, click the Print Preview button on the Standard toolbar. Use options on the Print Preview toolbar to display the next or previous slide, display the Print dialog box, specify how you want the presentation printed, change the zoom (percentage of display), choose an orientation (portrait or landscape), and close Print Preview. You can also change page orientation with options at the Page Setup dialog box as well as change page width and height.

PROJECT: Staff members need the movie production meeting slides printed as handouts and as an outline. You will preview and then print the presentation in various formats.

STEPS

1. With **PPS1-01** open, display Slide 1 in the Slide pane and then click Print Preview button on the Standard toolbar.

   This displays Slide 1 in the Print Preview window as it will appear when printed.

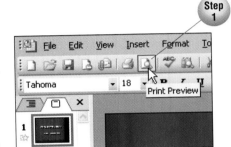

Step 1

2. Click the Next Page button on the Print Preview toolbar.

   This displays Slide 2 in the Print Preview window.

3. You decide to print all slides on one page and you want to preview how the slides will appear on the page. To do this, click the down-pointing arrow at the right of the *Print What* option box and then click *Handouts (9 slides per page)* at the drop-down list.

4. Click the Print button on the Print Preview toolbar.

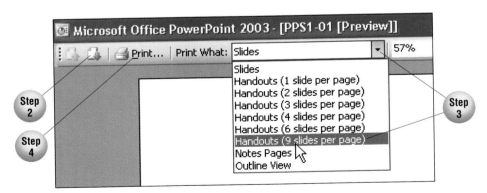

Step 2
Step 4
Step 3

5. At the Print dialog box, click OK.

6. Click the Close button to close Print Preview.

7. You want to print all slide text on one page and use the printing as a reference. To do this, click File and then Print to display the Print dialog box.

8 At the Print dialog box, click the down-pointing arrow at the right side of the *Print what* option and then click *Outline View* at the drop-down list.

9 Click OK.

> With the *Outline View* option selected, the presentation prints on one page with slide numbers, slide icons, and slide text in outline form.

10 Change the slide orientation from *Landscape* to *Portrait* by clicking File and then Page Setup.

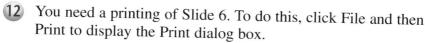
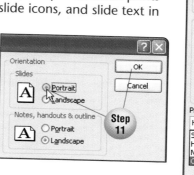

11 At the Page Setup dialog box, click the *Portrait* option in the *Slides* section and then click OK.

12 You need a printing of Slide 6. To do this, click File and then Print to display the Print dialog box.

13 At the Print dialog box, click the down-pointing arrow at the right side of the *Print what* option and then click *Slides* at the drop-down list.

14 Click the *Slides* option in the *Print range* section, type 6 in the text box, and then click OK.

15 Return the orientation for slides back to *Landscape*. To do this, click File and then Page Setup. At the Page Setup dialog box, click *Landscape* in the *Slides* section and then click OK.

16 Save **PPS1-01** and close the presentation by clicking File and then Close.

In Addition

Previewing with the Color/Grayscale Button

Along with Print Preview, you can view your presentation in color, grayscale, or black and white with options from the Color/Grayscale button on the Standard toolbar. Click the Color/Grayscale button and a drop-down list displays with three options—Color, Grayscale, and Pure Black and White. Click the Color option to display your presentation. Click the Grayscale option and the presentation displays in black and white and the Grayscale View shortcut menu displays. Click the Setting option on the Grayscale View shortcut menu and options display for changing the appearance of objects on the slides in the presentation. Click the Pure Black and White option and most objects in slides display in either black or white. The display of objects depends on the options you select with the Setting option on the Grayscale View shortcut menu.

IN BRIEF

Print a Presentation
1 Click File, Print.
2 At Print dialog box, specify how you want presentation printed.
3 Click OK.

Preview a Presentation
1 Click Print Preview button on Standard toolbar.
2 View presentation and then click Close button.

Display Page Setup Dialog Box
Click File, Page Setup.

FEATURES SUMMARY

Feature	Button	Menu	Keyboard
Close a presentation	×	File, Close	Ctrl + W
Normal view	⊞	View, Normal	
Notes Page view		View, Notes Page	
Open dialog box	📂	File, Open	Ctrl + O
Print dialog box		File, Print	Ctrl + P
Print Preview	🔍	File, Print Preview	
Run a presentation	🖥	View, Slide Show	F5
Save a presentation	💾	File, Save	Ctrl + S
Slide Design task pane	Design	Format, Slide Design	
Slide Layout task pane	New Slide	Format, Slide Layout	
Slide Sorter view	▦	View, Slide Sorter	
Slide Transition task pane	Transition	Slide Show, Slide Transition	
Spelling check	ABC	Tools, Spelling	F7
Thesaurus		Tools, Thesaurus	Shift + F7

PROCEDURES CHECK

Completion: In the space provided at the right, indicate the correct key, command, or option.

1. This toolbar contains buttons that are shortcuts for popular commands. _____
2. This pane contains two tabs and displays at the left side of the window in Normal view. _____
3. Display specific slides using this scroll bar. _____
4. Display the Slide Design task pane by clicking the Slide Design button on this toolbar. _____
5. Choose a layout for a slide with options at this task pane. _____
6. Use this box, located at the right side of the Menu bar, to access the Microsoft Office PowerPoint Help feature. _____
7. Click this button on the View toolbar and all slides in the presentation display in slide miniature. _____
8. Run a presentation by clicking this button on the View toolbar. _____
9. When running a presentation, move the mouse and this toolbar displays. _____
10. Press this key on the keyboard to end a presentation without running all of the slides. _____
11. Add a transition and/or sound to slides with options at this task pane. _____
12. Click this button on the Standard toolbar to display the active slide as it will appear when printed. _____

SKILLS REVIEW

Activity 1: CHOOSING A DESIGN AND CREATING SLIDES

1 With PowerPoint open, click the Slide Design button on the Formatting toolbar.
2 Click the Digital Dots slide design in the *Apply a design template* section of the Slide Design task pane.
3 Type the title and subtitle for Slide 1 as shown in Figure P1.3.
4 Click the New Slide button on the Formatting toolbar.
5 Type the text shown for Slide 2 in Figure P1.3.
6 Continue creating the slides for the presentation as shown in Figure P1.3.
7 Save the presentation and name it **PPS1-R1**.

FIGURE P1.3 Activity 1

Slide 1	Title	=	Marquee Productions
	Subtitle	=	Location Team Meeting
Slide 2	Title	=	Current Status
	Bullets	=	• Overview of Project
			• Tasks on Schedule
			• Tasks behind Schedule
Slide 3	Title	=	Filming Sites
	Bullets	=	• Gardiner Expressway
			• Kings Mill Park
			• Island Airport
			• Royal Ontario Museum
			• Black Creek Pioneer Village
			• Additional Sites
Slide 4	Title	=	Key Issues
	Bullets	=	• Equipment Rental
			• Budget Overruns
			• Transportation Concerns
			• Location Agreements

Activity 2: INSERTING A SLIDE; CHANGING LAYOUT; MOVING A PLACEHOLDER

1 With **PPS1-R1** open, insert a new Slide 3 between the current Slides 2 and 3 with the text shown in Figure P1.4.
2 Display Slide 2 in the Slide pane and then change the slide layout to Title Slide. (If the Slide Layout task pane is not visible, display it by clicking Format and then Slide Layout.)
3 Click the text *Current Status* to select the placeholder and then move the placeholder up about an inch.
4 Click the text *Overview of Project* to select the placeholder and then move the placeholder up about an inch. Make sure that the text is centered horizontally and vertically on the slide.
5 Save **PPS1-R1**.

Slide 3	Title	=	Resources
	Bullets	=	• Location Contacts
			• Movie Extras
			• Catering Company
			• Lodging
			• Transportation Rentals

Activity 3: ADDING TRANSITION AND SOUND; RUNNING AND PRINTING THE PRESENTATION

1 With **PPS1-R1** open, change to Slide Sorter view.
2 Click the Slide Transition button on the Slide Sorter toolbar.
3 At the Slide Transition task pane, choose a transition and sound (you determine the type of transition and sound) and apply them to all slides in the presentation.
4 Change to Normal view.
5 Make Slide 1 the active slide and then run the presentation.
6 Print the presentation in outline view.
7 Print the presentation with all five slides on one page.
8 Save and then close **PPS1-R1**.

PERFORMANCE PLUS

Assessment 1: PREPARING A PRESENTATION FOR WORLDWIDE ENTERPRISES

1 Prepare a presentation for Worldwide Enterprises with the information shown in Figure P1.5. (You determine the design template.)
2 Add a transition and sound of your choosing to all slides in the presentation.
3 Run the presentation.
4 Print the presentation with all five slides on one page.
5 Save the presentation and name it **PPS1-P1**.
6 Close **PPS1-P1**.

FIGURE P1.5 Assessment 1

Slide 1	Title	=	Worldwide Enterprises
	Subtitle	=	Executive Meeting
Slide 2	Title	=	Accounting Policies
	Bullets	=	• Cash Equivalents
			• Short-term Investments
			• Inventory Valuation
			• Property and Equipment
			• Foreign Currency Translation
Slide 3	Title	=	Financial Instruments
	Bullets	=	• Investments
			• Derivative Instruments
			• Credit Risks
			• Fair Value of Instruments

Slide 4	Title	=	Inventories
	Bullets	=	• Products
			• Raw Material
			• Equipment
			• Buildings
Slide 5	Title	=	Employee Plans
	Bullets	=	• Stock Options
			• Bonus Plan
			• Savings and Retirement Plan
			• Defined Benefits Plan
			• Foreign Subsidiaries

Assessment 2: PREPARING A PRESENTATION FOR THE WATERFRONT BISTRO

1 Prepare a presentation for The Waterfront Bistro with the information shown in Figure P1.5. (You determine the design template.)
2 Add a transition and sound of your choosing to all slides in the presentation.
3 Run the presentation.
4 Print the presentation with all five slides on one page.
5 Save the presentation and name it **PPS1-P2**.
6 Close **PPS1-P2**.

FIGURE P1.6 Assessment 2

Slide 1	Title	=	The Waterfront Bistro
	Subtitle	=	3104 Rivermist Drive
			Buffalo, NY 14280
			(716) 555-3166
Slide 2	Title	=	Accommodations
	Bullets	=	• Dining Area
			• Salon
			• Two Banquet Rooms
			• Wine Cellar
Slide 3	Title	=	Menus
	Bullets	=	• Lunch
			• Dinner
			• Wines
			• Desserts
Slide 4	Title	=	Catering Services
	Bullets	=	• Lunch
			- Continental
			- Deli
			- Hot
			• Dinner
			- Vegetarian
			- Meat
			- Seafood
Slide 5	Title	=	Resource
	Subtitle	=	Dana Hirsch, Manager

Assessment 3: FINDING INFORMATION ON THE UNDO BUTTON

1 Open **PPS1-P2**.
2 With **PPS1-P2** open, use the *Ask a Question* text box on the Menu bar to learn how to undo an action. (***Hint: Type the question*** How do I undo an action?)
3 After learning how to undo an action, make Slide 5 the active slide.
4 In the Slide pane, click immediately right of the text *Dana Hirsch, Manager*, and then press Enter.
5 Type the e-mail address HirschD@emcp.net and then press Enter. (PowerPoint converts the e-mail address to a hyperlink [changes color and underlines the text].)
6 Undo the action (converting the text to a hyperlink).
7 Type Web site: www.emcp.com/wfbistro.
8 Press the Enter key (this converts the Web site to a hyperlink).
9 Undo the action (converting the text to a hyperlink).
10 Print only Slide 5.
11 Save and then close **PPS1-P2**.

Assessment 4: FINDING INFORMATION ON SETTING SLIDE SHOW TIMINGS

1 Open **PPS1-P2**.
2 With **PPS1-P2** open, use the *Ask a Question* text box to find information on how to set slide show timings manually.
3 Set up the presentation so that, when running the presentation, each slide advances after three seconds.
4 Run the presentation.
5 Save and then close **PPS1-P2**.

Assessment 5: LOCATING INFORMATION AND PREPARING A PRESENTATION FOR FIRST CHOICE TRAVEL

1 You are Melissa Gehring, president of the Los Angeles branch of First Choice Travel. You are interested in arranging a vacation travel package to Cancun, Mexico. Connect to the Internet and search for information on Cancun. (One possible site for information is www.cancun.com.) Locate information on lodging (hotels), restaurants, activities, and transportation.
2 Using PowerPoint, create a presentation about Cancun that contains the following:
   • Title slide containing the company name, *First Choice Travel*, and the subtitle *Vacationing in Cancun*
   • Slide containing the names of at least three major airlines that travel to Cancun
   • Slide containing the names of at least four hotels or resorts in Cancun
   • Slide containing the names of at least four restaurants in Cancun
   • Slide containing at least four activities in Cancun
3 Run the presentation.
4 Print all of the slides on one page.
5 Save the presentation and name it **PPS1-P3**.
6 Close **PPS1-P3**.

POWERPOINT SECTION 2

Editing Slides and Slide Elements

Edit slides and slide elements in a presentation to customize and personalize the presentation. When editing a slide, use the presentation view that most efficiently accomplishes the editing task. Editing can include such functions as rearranging and deleting slides, cutting and pasting text, copying and pasting text, and changing the line and paragraph spacing of text in a slide. Change the appearance of slide text with buttons on the Formatting toolbar and with options at the Font dialog box. Automate the formatting of slide elements with the Format Painter feature and add visual appeal to a presentation by inserting pictures, images, and applying an animation scheme. In this section, you will learn the skills and complete the projects described here.

Note: Before beginning this section, delete the PowerPointS1 folder on your disk. Next, copy to your disk or other location the PowerPointS2 subfolder from the CD that accompanies this textbook and then make PowerPointS2 the active folder.

Skills

- Open a presentation and save it with a new name
- Rearrange and delete slides
- Increase and decrease the indent of text
- Select, cut, copy, and paste text
- Apply font and font effects using buttons on the Formatting toolbar and options at the Font dialog box
- Find and replace fonts
- Apply formatting with Format Painter
- Change alignment and line and paragraph spacing
- Change the slide design and color scheme
- Insert, size, and move images
- Insert and recolor clip art images
- Add an animation scheme to a presentation

Projects

MARQUEE PRODUCTIONS Open an existing project presentation for Marquee Productions, save the presentation with a new name, and then edit and format the presentation; open an existing annual meeting presentation for Marquee Productions and then save, edit, and format the presentation.

Niagara Peninsula COLLEGE Open an existing presentation for the Theatre Arts Division of Niagara Peninsula College and then save, edit, and format the presentation.

FIRST CHOICE Travel Open an existing presentation containing information on vacation specials offered by First Choice Travel and then save, edit, and format the presentation.

The Waterfront Bistro Locate information on the Internet on competing bistros in and around the Toronto area and then prepare a presentation to the owners of the bistro containing the information located.

2.1 Rearranging, Deleting, and Hiding Slides

If you open an existing presentation and make changes to it, you can then save it with the same name or a different name. Save an existing presentation with a new name at the Save As dialog box. PowerPoint provides various views for creating and managing a presentation. Use the view that most easily accomplishes the task. For example, consider using the Slide Sorter view to delete, rearrange, and hide slides in a presentation.

PROJECT: You want to create another version of an existing project presentation for Marquee Productions. The changes for the second version include deleting, rearranging, and hiding slides in the presentation.

S T E P S

1. With PowerPoint open, click the Open button 📂 on the Standard toolbar.

2. At the Open dialog box, make sure PowerPointS2 is the active folder and then double-click *MPProject* in the list box.

PROBLEM ?

If *MPProject* does not display in the Open dialog box list box, you may need to change the folder. Check with your instructor.

3. With **MPProject** open, click File and then Save As.

4. At the Save As dialog box, make sure PowerPointS2 is the active folder, type **PPS2-01** in the *File name* text box, and then press Enter.

5. Click the Slide Sorter View button 🔲 on the View toolbar.

6. Click Slide 5 to select it and click Edit and then Delete Slide.

> A slide selected in Slide Sorter view displays surrounded by a dark blue border. You can also delete a selected slide by pressing the Delete key on the keyboard.

7. Click Slide 5 to make it active.

8. Position the mouse pointer on Slide 5, hold down the left mouse button, drag the arrow pointer (with a square attached) to the left of Slide 2, and then release the mouse button.

Step 6

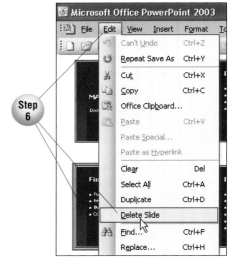

Step 8

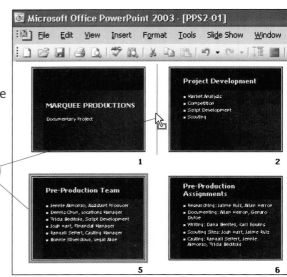

9. Click Slide 3 to make it active and hide the slide by clicking Slide Show and then Hide Slide.

> When a slide is hidden, a box containing a slash displays around the slide number.

10. Click the Normal view button ⊞ on the View toolbar.

11. Click the Slides tab in the Outline/Slides pane. (Skip this step if the Slides tab is already selected.)

12. Scroll down the Outline/Slides pane until Slide 7 displays. Position the mouse pointer on the Slide 7 miniature, hold down the left mouse button, drag up until a thin, horizontal line displays immediately below the Slide 2 miniature, and then release the mouse button.

13. Make Slide 1 the active slide and then run the presentation.

14. After running the presentation, you decide to redisplay the hidden slide. To do this, click Slide 4 in the Outline/Slides pane, click Slide Show on the Menu bar, and then click Hide Slide.

15. Save **PPS2-01** by clicking the Save button on the Standard toolbar.

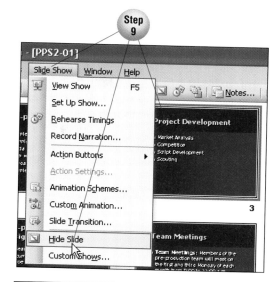

Step 9

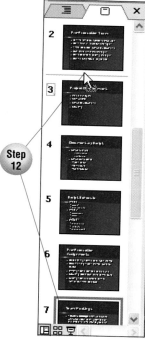

Step 12

In Addition

Copying Slides within a Presentation

Copying a slide within a presentation is similar to moving a slide. To copy a slide, first change to the Slide Sorter view. Position the arrow pointer on the desired slide and then hold down the Ctrl key and the left mouse button. Drag to the location where you want the slide copied and release the left mouse button and then the Ctrl key. When you drag with the mouse, the mouse pointer displays with a square and a plus symbol next to the pointer.

IN BRIEF

Save a Presentation with a New Name
1 Click File, Save As.
2 Type presentation name.
3 Click Save or press Enter.

Delete a Slide
1 Click Slide Sorter View button.
2 Click desired slide.
3 Click Edit, Delete Slide.

Move a Slide
1 Click Slide Sorter View button.
2 Click desired slide.
3 Drag slide to desired position.

2.2 Increasing and Decreasing Indents

In the Outline/Slides pane with the Outline tab selected, each slide title appears next to a number and a slide icon. In this pane, you can organize and develop the content of the presentation by rearranging points within a slide, moving slides, or increasing or decreasing the indent of text within slides. Click the Decrease Indent button on the Formatting toolbar or press Shift + Tab to promote text to the previous level. Click the Increase Indent button on the Formatting toolbar or press Tab to demote text to the next level. You can also increase and/or decrease the indent of text in the slide in the Slide pane.

PROJECT: As you edit the documentary project presentation, you will increase and/or decrease the indent of text in slides.

STEPS

1. With **PPS2-01** open, make sure the presentation displays in Normal view.

2. Display Slide 5 in the Slide pane.

3. Looking at the text in Slide 5, you decide that the names below *Script Authors* should be promoted to the previous tab stop. To do this, position the mouse pointer immediately left of the *D* in *Dana*, click the left mouse button, and then click the Decrease Indent button on the Formatting toolbar.

   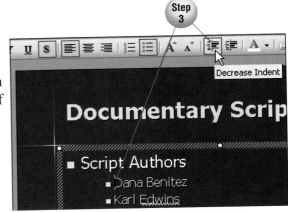

   You can also promote text by pressing Shift + Tab.

4. In Slide 5, position the insertion point immediately left of the *K* in *Karl*, and then promote the text to the previous level by pressing Shift + Tab.

5. You decide that two of the names below *Script Consultants* should be demoted. To do this, click immediately left of the *J* in *Jaime*, and then click the Increase Indent button on the Formatting toolbar.

   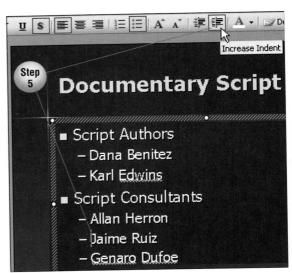

   You can also demote text by pressing the Tab key.

6. Position the insertion point immediately left of the *G* in *Genaro* and then press the Tab key.

7. Display Slide 6 in the Slide pane.

8. Click the Outline tab in the Outline/Slides pane.

⑨ Looking at Slide 6, you decide that the slide contains too much text and want to make a new slide with some of the text. To do this, click immediately left of the *P* in *Phase 3* in the text in the Outline/Slides pane and then press Shift + Tab.

Pressing Shift + Tab promotes the text to the previous level and creates a new slide with *Phase 3* as the title of the slide.

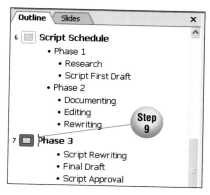

⑩ Change the title of the slide by typing **Script Schedule** and then pressing Enter.

As you type *Script Schedule*, the text *Phase 3* moves to the right. When you press Enter, *Phase 3* moves to the next line and begins a new slide.

⑪ Demote the text *Phase 3* by pressing the Tab key.

The new slide now contains the title *Script Schedule* with *Phase 3* as a bulleted item with three bulleted items below demoted to the next level.

⑫ Save **PPS2-01**.

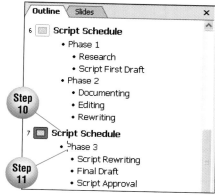

In Addition

Using Buttons on the Outlining Toolbar

The Outlining toolbar contains buttons for arranging and displaying text and slides. Turn on the Outlining toolbar by clicking View, pointing to Toolbars, and then clicking Outlining. The buttons on the Outlining toolbar are named below.

Button	Name	Function
⬅	Promote	Move insertion point to previous tab stop to left
➡	Demote	Move insertion point to next tab stop to right
⬆	Move Up	Move insertion point up to previous line
⬇	Move Down	Move insertion point down to next line
−	Collapse	Display only titles of slides
✚	Expand	Display all levels of slides
⬆☰	Collapse All	Display only titles of slides
⬇☰	Expand All	Display titles and body text for all slides
▦	Summary Slide	Create a summary slide of presentation based on titles of slides selected
ᴬ/ᴬ	Show Formatting	Display all character formatting

2.3 Selecting, Cutting, Copying, and Pasting Text

Text in a slide can be selected and then can be deleted from the slide, cut from one location and pasted into another, or copied and pasted. Select text using the mouse or the keyboard. Cut, copy, and paste text using buttons on the Standard toolbar or with options at the Edit drop-down menu. Select, cut, copy, and/or paste text in slides in the Outline/Slides pane.

PROJECT: As you review the documentary project presentation again, you decide to delete, move, and copy specific text items.

S T E P S

1. With **PPS2-01** open, make sure the presentation displays in Normal view and then display Slide 5 in the Slide pane.

2. Click anywhere in the bulleted text.

   Clicking in the bulleted text selects the placeholder containing the text.

3. Position the mouse pointer on the bullet that displays before *Genaro Dufoe* until the pointer turns into a four-headed arrow and then click the left mouse button.

   Refer to Table P2.1 for additional information on selecting text.

4. Click the Cut button on the Standard toolbar.

5. Position the mouse pointer immediately left of the *A* in *Allan Herron*, click the left mouse button, and then click the Paste button on the Standard toolbar.

6. With the insertion point positioned immediately left of the *A* in *Allan Herron*, press the Tab key to demote the name.

7. Position the insertion point immediately left of the *G* in *Genaro Dufoe* and then press Shift + Tab to promote the name.

8. Select the text *Script Authors*, and then click the Copy button on the Standard toolbar.

   When you select the text, make sure you select only the text *Script Authors* and not any space after the text.

9. Make Slide 4 the active slide and then position the insertion point immediately to the right of the text *Script Development*.

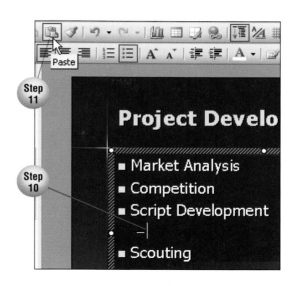

10 Press the Enter key and then press the Tab key.

Pressing the Enter key moves the insertion point down to the next line and pressing the Tab key demotes the insertion point to the next level.

11 Click the Paste button 📋 on the Standard toolbar.

Step 11

Step 10

Project Develo

- Market Analysis
- Competition
- Script Development
  —|
- Scouting

ROBLEM **?**

If a blank line occurs below *Script Authors* you probably selected the invisible paragraph symbol after the text. When selecting the text, make sure you select only *Script Authors* and not the space after the text.

12 Save **PPS2-01**.

TABLE P2.1 Selecting Text

To Do This	Perform This Action
Select text mouse pointer passes through	Click and drag with mouse
Select entire word	Double-click word
Select entire paragraph	Triple-click anywhere in paragraph
Select entire sentence	Ctrl + click anywhere in sentence
Select all text in selected object box	Click Edit, Select All; or press Ctrl + A

In Addition

Copying a Slide between Presentations

You can copy a slide or slides from one presentation into another. To do this, display the slide that will precede the copied slide, click Insert, and then click Slides from Files. At the Slide Finder dialog box, click the Browse button, locate the presentation containing the slide you want to copy, and then double-click the presentation. This displays the beginning slides in the presentation in the *Select slides* section of the Slide Finder dialog box. Click the desired slide in the *Select slides* section and then click the Insert button. If the desired slide is not visible, use the horizontal scroll bar along the bottom of the *Select slides* section to display the desired slide. After inserting the desired slide, click the Close button to close the Slide Finder dialog box.

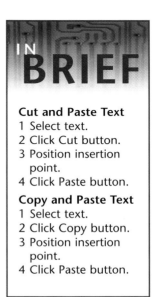

IN BRIEF

Cut and Paste Text
1 Select text.
2 Click Cut button.
3 Position insertion point.
4 Click Paste button.

Copy and Paste Text
1 Select text.
2 Click Copy button.
3 Position insertion point.
4 Click Paste button.

2.4 Applying Font Effects Using the Formatting Toolbar

The PowerPoint Formatting toolbar contains several buttons for applying font effects to text. Click the Bold button to apply bold formatting, the Italic button to apply italic formatting, the Underline button to underline selected text, and the Shadow button to apply shadow formatting. Each slide design template sets slide text in a specific font and font size. Click the Increase Font Size button on the Formatting toolbar to increase the point size of selected text by 4 points or click the Decrease Font Size button to decrease selected text by 4 points.

PROJECT: Certain text elements on slides in the documentary project presentation need to be highlighted to make them stand out. You will apply font effects to specific text and change the font size of selected text.

STEPS

1 With **PPS2-01** open, display Slide 1 in the Slide pane.

2 Select the title *MARQUEE PRODUCTIONS* and then click the Italic button I on the Formatting toolbar.

Make sure the Formatting toolbar displays on a row separate from the Standard toolbar. If the toolbars are on the same row, separate them by clicking Tools and then Customize. At the Customize dialog box, click the *Standard and Formatting toolbars share one row* check box to remove the check mark and then click the Close button.

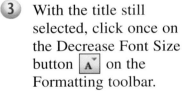

3 With the title still selected, click once on the Decrease Font Size button A on the Formatting toolbar.

4 Select the subtitle *Documentary Project* and then increase the font size by clicking once on the Increase Font Size button A on the Formatting toolbar.

PROBLEM? If the subtitle wraps in the placeholder, click the Decrease Font Size button until the subtitle displays on one line.

5 With the subtitle still selected, click the Bold button B and then click the Italic button I on the Formatting toolbar.

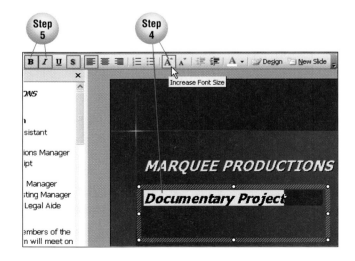

⑥ Make Slide 6 active in the Slide pane.

⑦ Select the text *Phase 1* and then click the Underline button **U** on the Formatting toolbar.

⑧ Select and then underline the text *Phase 2*.

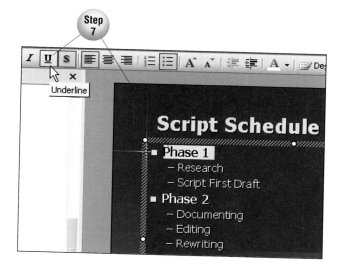

⑨ Make Slide 7 active in the Slide pane and then select and underline the text *Phase 3*.

⑩ Deselect the text.

⑪ Save **PPS2-01**.

In Addition

Changing Font Color

The design template generally determines text color in a presentation. Change text color by selecting text and then clicking the Font Color button on the Drawing toolbar. The color of the selected text changes to the color displayed below the *A* on the Font Color button. The Drawing toolbar displays between the View toolbar and the Status bar. If the toolbar is not visible, right-click any currently displayed toolbar, and then click *Drawing* at the pop-up list. If you want to choose another color, click the down-pointing arrow at the right side of the Font Color button on the Drawing toolbar and then click the desired color at the color palette shown above at the right. The colors on the color palette vary depending on the design template.

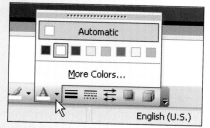

IN BRIEF

Apply Font Effects
1 Select text.
2 Click desired font effect button on Formatting toolbar.

2.5 Changing the Font Using Buttons on the Formatting Toolbar

Along with buttons for changing font effects, the Formatting toolbar also contains a Font button to change the font for selected text and a Font Size button for changing the point size of text. The slide design template generally determines the font and font size for text. Change this default with the Font button or the Font Size button. When you click the Font button, a drop-down list displays with the available fonts. This drop-down list displays the font name in the actual font. Use this visual display to help you select the appropriate font.

PROJECT: As you continue working to improve the appearance of slides in the documentary project, you decide to change the font and font size for specific headings and subheadings.

STEPS

1. With **PPS2-01** open, display Slide 1 in the Slide pane and then click the Slides tab in the Outline/Slides pane.

2. Select the title *MARQUEE PRODUCTIONS*.

3. Click the down-pointing arrow at the right side of the Font button on the Formatting toolbar.

4. Scroll toward the end of the list box (fonts display in alphabetical order) until *Times New Roman* is visible and then click *Times New Roman*.

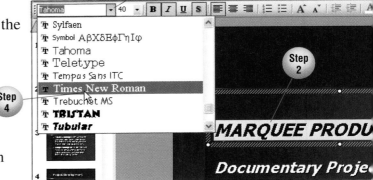

5. Select the subtitle *Documentary Project*, click the down-pointing arrow at the right side of the Font button on the Formatting toolbar, and then click *Times New Roman* at the drop-down list.

   > The Font drop-down list displays the most recently used fonts at the beginning of the list.

6. Make Slide 6 the active slide, select the text *Phase 1*, click the Underline button to remove underlining, and then click the Bold button (to apply bold formatting).

7. With *Phase 1* still selected, click the down-pointing arrow at the right side of the Font button and then click *Times New Roman* at the drop-down list.

8. With *Phase 1* still selected, click the down-pointing arrow at the right side of the Font Size button, scroll down the list until *40* displays, and then click *40*.

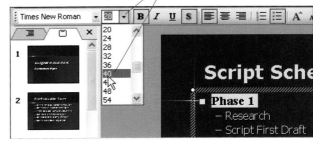

9. Select the text *Phase 2*, remove the underlining, turn on bold, change the font to Times New Roman, and change the font size to 40.

10. Make Slide 7 active.

11. Select the text *Phase 3*, remove underlining, turn on bold, change the font to Times New Roman, and change the font size to 40.

12. Print Slides 1, 6, and 7 by clicking File and then Print.

13. At the Print dialog box, click the *Slides* option in the *Print range* section and then type **1,6,7**.

14. Click the down-pointing arrow at the right side of the *Print what* text box and then click *Handouts* at the drop-down list.

15. Click OK to close the Print dialog box.

> The three slides print in miniature on the same page.

16. Save **PPS2-01**.

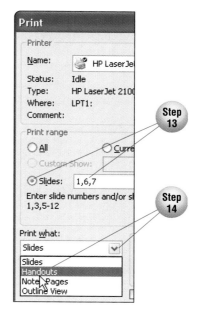

In Addition

Choosing Typefaces

A typeface is a set of characters with a common design and shape. PowerPoint refers to a typeface as a *font*. Typefaces can be decorative or plain and are either monospaced or proportional. A monospaced typeface allots the same amount of horizontal space for each character while a proportional typeface allots a varying amount of space for each character. Proportional typefaces are divided into two main categories: serif and sans serif. A serif is a small line at the end of a character stroke. Consider using a serif typeface for text-intensive slides because the serifs help move the reader's eyes across the text. Use a sans serif typeface for titles, subtitles, headings, and short text lines.

IN BRIEF

Change the Font Using the Font Button
1 Select text.
2 Click down-pointing arrow at right side of Font button.
3 Click desired font at the drop-down list.

Change the Font Size Using the Font Size Button
1 Select text.
2 Click down-pointing arrow at the right side of Font Size button.
3 Click desired font size at drop-down list.

2.6 Changing the Font at the Font Dialog Box; Replacing Fonts

In addition to buttons on the Formatting toolbar, you can apply font formatting with options at the Font dialog box. With options at this dialog box, you can change the font, font style, and size; change the font color; and apply formatting effects such as underline, shadow, emboss, superscript, and subscript. If you decide to change the font for all slides in a presentation, use the Replace Font dialog box to replace all occurrences of a specific font in the presentation.

PROJECT: Still not satisfied with the font choices in the documentary presentation, you decide to change the font for the title and subtitle and replace the Tahoma font on the remaining slides.

S T E P S

1. With **PPS2-01** open, make Slide 1 the active slide.

2. Select the title *MARQUEE PRODUCTIONS.*

3. Display the Font dialog box by clicking Format and then Font.

4. At the Font dialog box, click *Bold* in the *Font style* list box.

5. Click *44* in the *Size* list box.

   If *44* is not visible in the *Size* list box, click the down-pointing arrow at the bottom of the vertical scroll bar at the right side of the *Size* list box until *44* is visible.

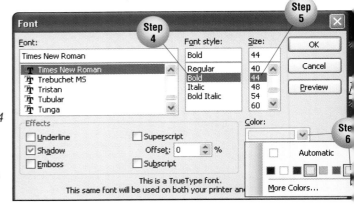

6. Click the down-pointing arrow at the right side of the *Color* option box and then click the light yellow color option that displays in the color palette.

7. Click OK to close the Font dialog box.

8. Select the subtitle *Documentary Project.*

9. Click Format and then Font to display the Font dialog box.

10. Click *Regular* in the *Font style* list box.

11. Click *40* in the *Size* list box.

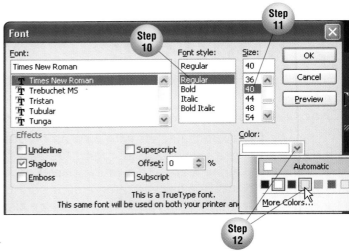

12. Click the down-pointing arrow at the right side of the *Color* option box and then click the light gray color option that displays in the color palette.

⑬ Click OK to close the Font dialog box and then deselect the text.

⑭ After looking at the other slides in the presentation, you decide to replace all occurrences of the Tahoma font with the Times New Roman font. To do this, click Format and then Replace Fonts. Make sure *Tahoma* displays in the *Replace* option box.

> If Tahoma does not display in the *Replace* option box, click the down-pointing arrow at the right side of the text box and then click *Tahoma* at the drop-down list.

⑮ Click the down-pointing arrow at the right side of the *With* option box and then click *Times New Roman* at the drop-down list. (You will need to scroll down the list box to display *Times New Roman*.)

⑯ Click the Replace button and then click the Close button.

⑰ Save **PPS2-01**.

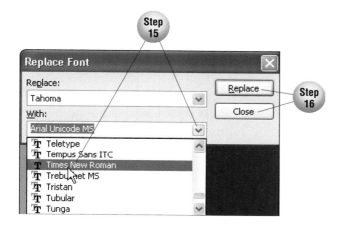

Choosing Presentation Typefaces

Choose a typeface for a presentation based on the tone and message you want the presentation to portray. For example, choose a more serious typeface such as Times New Roman for a conservative audience and choose a less formal font such as Comic Sans MS, Lucida Handwriting, or Mistral for a more informal or lighthearted audience. For text-intensive slides choose a serif typeface such as Times New Roman, Georgia, or Bookman Old Style. For titles, subtitles, headings, and short text items, consider a sans serif typeface such as Arial, Tahoma, or Univers. Use no more than two or three different fonts in each presentation. To ensure text readability in a slide, choose a font color that contrasts with the slide background.

IN BRIEF

Change the Font at the Font Dialog Box
1 Select text.
2 Click Format, Font.
3 At the Font dialog box, choose desired font, style, size, effects, and color.
4 Click OK.

Change All Occurrences of a Font
1 Click Format, Replace Fonts.
2 At Replace Font dialog box, make sure font to be changed displays in *Replace* text box.
3 Press the Tab key.
4 Select the desired replacement font.
5 Click Replace button.
6 Click Close button.

2.7 Formatting with Format Painter

Use the Format Painter feature to apply the same formatting in more than one location in a slide or slides. To use the Format Painter, apply the desired formatting to text, position the insertion point anywhere in the formatted text, and then double-click the Format Painter button on the Standard toolbar. Using the mouse, select the additional text to which you want the formatting applied. After applying the formatting in the desired locations, click the Format Painter button to deactivate it. If you need to apply formatting in only one other location, click the Format Painter button once. The first time you select text, the formatting is applied and the Format Painter is deactivated.

PROJECT: Improve the appearance of slides in the documentary project presentation by applying a font and then using the Format Painter to apply the formatting to other text.

STEPS

1. With **PPS2-01** open, make Slide 2 the active slide.

2. Select the title *Pre-Production Team*.

3. Display the Font dialog box by clicking Format and then Font.

4. At the Font dialog box, click *Arial* in the *Font* list box, *Bold Italic* in the *Font style* list box, and *40* in the *Size* list box. Click the *Shadow* option in the *Effects* section of the dialog box to remove the check mark.

   > Removing the check mark from the *Shadow* check box removes shadow formatting from the selected text.

5. Click OK to close the Font dialog box.

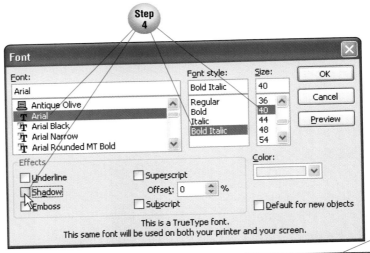

6. At the slide, deselect the text by clicking in the slide outside the selected text.

7. Click anywhere in the title *Pre-Production Team*.

8. Double-click the Format Painter button on the Standard toolbar.

9. Click the Next Slide button to display Slide 3.

(10) Using the mouse, select the title *Team Meetings*.

> The mouse pointer displays with a paintbrush attached. This indicates that the Format Painter feature is active. When you select the title, the formatting is applied to the title. You can also apply the formatting by clicking each word in the title rather than selecting the title.

(11) Click the Next Slide button to display Slide 4.

(12) Using the mouse, select the title *Project Development*.

PROBLEM?

> If the paintbrush is no longer attached to the mouse pointer, Format Painter has been turned off. Turn it back on by clicking in a slide title with the desired formatting and then double-clicking the Format Painter button.

(13) Apply formatting to the titles in the remaining four slides.

(14) When formatting has been applied to all slide titles, click the Format Painter button 🖌 on the Standard toolbar.

> Clicking the Format Painter button turns off the feature.

(15) Save **PPS2-01**.

In Addition

Choosing a Custom Color

Click the down-pointing arrow at the right side of the *Color* option at the Font dialog box, and a palette of color choices displays. Click the *More Colors* option and the Colors dialog box displays with a honeycomb of color options. Click the Custom tab and the dialog box displays as shown at the right. With options at this dialog box you can mix your own color. Click the desired color in the *Colors* palette or enter the values for the color in the *Hue*, *Sat*, *Lum*, *Red*, *Green*, and *Blue* text boxes. Adjust the luminosity of the current color by dragging the slider located at the right side of the color palette.

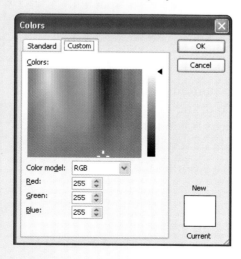

IN BRIEF

Format with Format Painter
1 Position insertion point on text containing desired formatting.
2 Double-click Format Painter button.
3 Select text to which you want to apply formatting.
4 Click Format Painter button.

2.8 Changing Alignment and Line and Paragraph Spacing

The slide design template generally determines the alignment of text in placeholders. Text may be left aligned, center aligned, or right aligned in a placeholder. You can change alignment for specific text with buttons on the Formatting toolbar or with options at the Format, Alignment side menu. To better space text in a placeholder, use options at the Line Spacing dialog box to change line and/or paragraph spacing. With options at this dialog box, you can adjust the amount of vertical space between lines of selected text and adjust the vertical space before or after paragraphs of text.

PROJECT: Change the alignment for specific text in slides and improve the appearance of text in slides by adjusting the vertical line and paragraph spacing of text.

STEPS

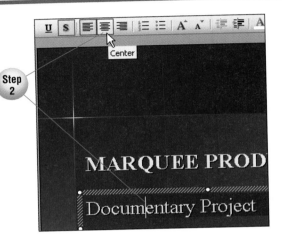

1. With **PPS2-01** open, make Slide 1 the active slide.

2. Click anywhere in the text *Documentary Project* and then click the Center button 📄 on the Formatting toolbar.

   > Text alignment can also be changed with the shortcut keys show in Table P2.2.

3. Make Slide 3 the active slide (this slide contains the heading *Team Meetings*), click once in the bulleted text, and then press Ctrl + A to select all of the bulleted text.

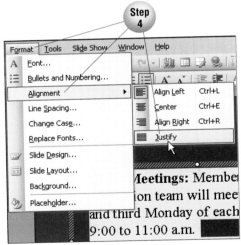

4. Justify the text by clicking Format, pointing to Alignment, and then clicking Justify.

5. With the bulleted text still selected, click Format and then Line Spacing.

6. Click the down-pointing arrow at the right side of the *Line spacing* text box until *0.9* displays in the text box.

7. Click the up-pointing arrow at the right side of the *Before paragraph* text box until *0.4* displays in the text box.

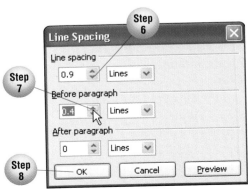

8. Click OK to close the dialog box.

9. Make Slide 4 the active slide (contains the title *Project Development*).

10. Click once in the bulleted text and select all of the bulleted text by clicking Edit and then Select All.

11. Increase the line spacing by clicking Format and then Line Spacing.

12. Click the up-pointing arrow at the right side of the *Line spacing* text box until *1.3* displays in the text box and then click OK.

13. Save **PPS2-01**.

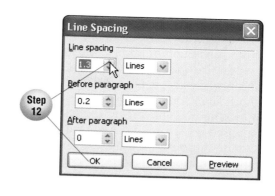

Step 12

TABLE P2.2 Alignment Shortcut Keys

Alignment	Shortcut Keys
Left align	Ctrl + L
Center align	Ctrl + E
Right align	Ctrl + R
Justify align	Ctrl + J

In Addition

Inserting a New Line

When creating bulleted text in a slide, pressing the Enter key causes the insertion point to move to the next line, inserting another bullet. Situations may occur where you want to create a blank line between bulleted items without creating another bullet. One method for doing this is to use the New Line command, Shift + Enter. Pressing Shift + Enter inserts a new line that is considered part of the previous paragraph.

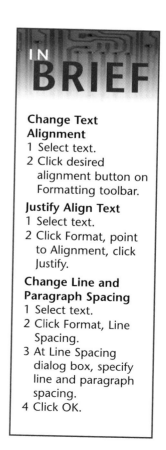

IN BRIEF

Change Text Alignment
1 Select text.
2 Click desired alignment button on Formatting toolbar.

Justify Align Text
1 Select text.
2 Click Format, point to Alignment, click Justify.

Change Line and Paragraph Spacing
1 Select text.
2 Click Format, Line Spacing.
3 At Line Spacing dialog box, specify line and paragraph spacing.
4 Click OK.

2.9 Changing the Slide Design and Color Scheme

Choose a slide design template before creating the slides for a presentation or apply a slide design to existing slides. Change the design template if you want to change the colors or tone of the presentation. To change the design, click the Slide Design button on the Formatting toolbar and then click the desired design at the Slide Design task pane. A design template includes a default color scheme consisting of eight colors. Colors are chosen for the background, accents, text, fills, shadows, title text, and hyperlinks. Additional color schemes are available for slide designs. To choose another color scheme, click the Color Schemes hyperlink located toward the top of the Slide Design task pane, and then click the desired scheme in the list box. Customize a design template by clicking the Edit Color Schemes hyperlink located at the bottom of the Slide Design task pane.

PROJECT: You are not pleased with the slide design for the documentary project presentation and decide to apply a different slide design and then change the color scheme for the design.

STEPS

1. With **PPS2-01** open, click the Slide Design button on the Formatting toolbar.

2. Click the *Curtain Call* slide design in the *Apply a design template* list box.

   The slide design used in the current presentation displays toward the top of the Slide Design task pane. All slide designs display in the list box in alphabetical order below the most recently used slide design.

3. Change the color scheme by clicking the Color Schemes hyperlink located toward the top of the Slide Design task pane.

4. Click the last color scheme option in the list box.

5. After looking at the presentation with the new color scheme applied, you decide you want to change some of the colors. To do this, click the Edit Color Schemes hyperlink located at the bottom of the Slide Design task pane.

6. At the Edit Color Scheme dialog box with the *Background* option selected in the *Scheme colors* section, click the Change Color button.

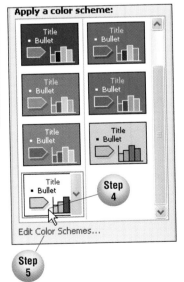

⑦ At the Background Color dialog box, click the Standard tab and then click the light yellow color shown at the right.

⑧ Click OK to close the Background Color dialog box.

⑨ At the Edit Color Scheme dialog box, click the box preceding *Accent and hyperlink* and then click the Change Color button.

⑩ At the Accent and Hyperlink Color dialog box, click the Standard tab and then click the dark blue color shown below at the right.

⑪ Click OK to close the Accent and Hyperlink Color dialog box.

⑫ Click the Apply button located in the upper right corner of the Edit Color Scheme dialog box.

⑬ Save **PPS2-01**.

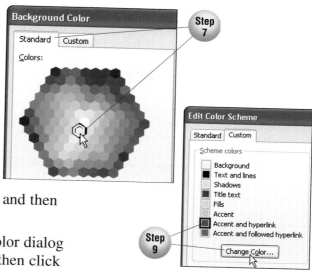

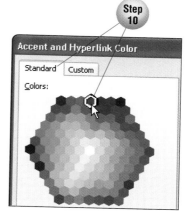

In Addition

Changing Background Color

Change background color with options at the Edit Color Scheme dialog box or at the Background dialog box shown below. Display this dialog box by clicking Format and then Background. At the Background dialog box, click the down-pointing arrow at the right of the *Background fill* option box and then click the desired color at the drop-down list. Click the Apply button to apply the background color to the active slide or click the Apply to All button to apply the background color to all slides.

IN BRIEF

Change Slide Design
1 Click Slide Design button on Formatting toolbar.
2 Click desired slide design in the Slide Design task pane.

Change Color Scheme
1 Display Slide Design task pane.
2 Click Color Schemes hyperlink.
3 Click desired color scheme in Slide Design task pane.

2.10 Inserting, Sizing, and Moving an Image

Add visual appeal to a presentation by inserting a graphic image such as a logo, picture, or clip art in a slide. To insert an image from a drive or folder, choose a slide layout containing a Content placeholder and then click the Insert Picture button in the placeholder. At the Insert Picture dialog box, navigate to the desired drive or folder and then double-click the image. Increase or decrease the size of an image using the sizing handles that display around a selected image. A selected image can also be moved within the slide.

PROJECT: Chris Greenbaum has asked you to insert a slide at the beginning of the document and insert the company logo on the new slide.

S T E P S

① With **PPS2-01** open, click the Slide Sorter View button on the View toolbar.

② Click immediately left of the first slide, click Insert on the Menu bar, and then click New Slide at the drop-down list.

> Clicking immediately before the first slide will insert a new slide at the beginning of the presentation.

Step 2
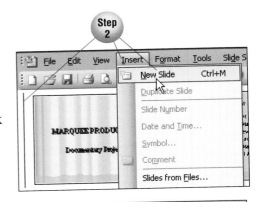

③ Double-click the new Slide 1.

> This changes the display to Normal view.

④ Insert the company logo in the new slide as shown in Figure P2.1. To begin, click the Content slide layout in the Slide Layout task pane.

⑤ Click the Insert Picture button 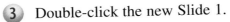 in the Content placeholder.

> You can also display the Insert Picture dialog box by clicking Insert, pointing to Picture, and then clicking From File.

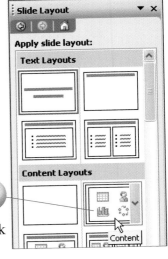
Step 4

⑥ At the Insert Picture dialog box, navigate to PowerPointS2 folder on your disk and then double-click the file named **M_Prod.tif**.

> The image is inserted in the slide, selection handles display around the image, and the Picture toolbar displays. Refer to Table P2.3 for information on the buttons.

Step 5

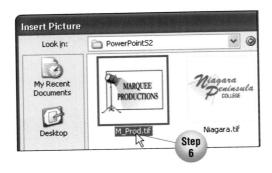
Step 6

7 Increase the size of the logo by positioning the mouse pointer on the bottom right sizing handle until the pointer turns into a two-headed diagonally pointing arrow. Hold down the left mouse button, drag down and to the right until the image is the approximate size shown in Figure P2.1, and then release the mouse button.

> Use the middle sizing handles to increase or decrease the width of an image. Use the top and bottom handles to increase or decrease the height, and use the corner sizing handles to increase or decrease both the width and height of the image at the same time.

8 Move the logo so it is positioned as shown in Figure P2.1. To do this, position the mouse pointer on the image until the pointer displays with a four-headed arrow attached, drag the image to the position shown in the figure, and then release the mouse button.

9 Click outside the logo to deselect it.

10 Save **PPS2-01**.

FIGURE P2.1 Slide 1

TABLE P2.3 Picture Toolbar Buttons

Button	Name	Function
	Insert Picture	Display the Insert Picture dialog box
	Color	Display a drop-down list with options for controlling how the image displays
	More Contrast	Increase contrast of the image
	Less Contrast	Decrease contrast of the image
	More Brightness	Increase brightness of the image
	Less Brightness	Decrease brightness of the image
	Crop	Crop image so only a specific portion of the image is visible
	Rotate Left 90°	Rotate selected object 90 degrees to the left
	Line Style	Insert a border around the image and specify the border-line style
	Compress Pictures	Display dialog box with options for reducing the picture's file size
	Recolor Picture	Display Recolor Picture dialog box with options for changing colors of image components
	Format Picture	Display Format Picture dialog box with options for formatting the color, lines, size, and position of the image
	Set Transparent Color	Change a solid color to transparent for some pictures and clip art
	Reset Picture	Reset picture to its original size, position, and color

2.11 Inserting and Recoloring Clip Art Images

Microsoft Office includes a gallery of clip art images you can insert in an Office program such as PowerPoint. Insert a clip art image by choosing a slide layout containing a Content placeholder. Click the Insert Clip Art button in the Content placeholder and the Select Picture dialog box displays. Type a category in the *Search text* box and then press Enter. From the list that displays, double-click the desired image. If you are connected to the Internet, Word will search for images at the Microsoft Design Gallery Live Web site matching

the topic. When a clip art image is selected, the Picture toolbar displays. Use buttons on this toolbar to customize the image. For example, customize the clip art image colors by clicking the Recolor Picture button on the Picture toolbar. This displays the Recolor Picture dialog box containing colors used for various components of the image.

PROJECT: Enhance the visual appeal of the documentary presentation by inserting and recoloring a clip art image.

STEPS

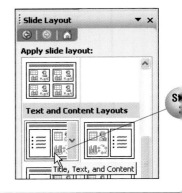

1. With **PPS2-01** open, create the new slide shown in Figure P2.2. Begin by making Slide 9 the active slide and then clicking the New Slide button.

2. Click the Title, Text, and Content slide layout in the Slide Layout task pane. (You will need to scroll down the list to display this layout.)

3. Click the text *Click to add title* and then type **Travel Arrangements**.

4. Click the text *Click to add text* and then type the bulleted text shown at the right and in the slide in Figure P2.2.

5. Click the Insert Clip Art button located in the Content placeholder.

6. At the Select Picture dialog box, type **transportation** in the *Search text* box and then press Enter.

7. When the list of clip art images displays, double-click the image shown in Figure P2.2.

> You can also insert clip art images at the Insert Clip Art task pane. Display this task pane by clicking the Insert Clip Art button on the Drawing toolbar or by clicking Insert, pointing to Picture, and then clicking Clip Art.

PROBLEM? If the jet image is not available, check with your instructor to determine which clip art image you should substitute.

8. Recolor the image so it complements the slide design color scheme. To do this, click the Recolor Picture button on the Picture toolbar.

(9) At the Recolor Picture dialog box, click the down-pointing arrow at the right side of the first option box below the *New* heading. At the color palette that displays, click the third color from the right (medium gray).

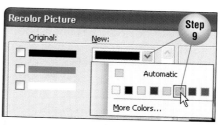

(10) At the Recolor Picture dialog box, click the down-pointing arrow at the right side of the second option box below the *New* heading. At the color palette that displays, click the second color from the right (dark blue).

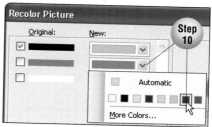

(11) Click OK to close the Recolor Picture dialog box.

(12) Increase the size of the image and move it so it is positioned as shown in Figure P2.2.

(13) Click outside the clip art image to deselect it.

(14) Save **PPS2-01**.

FIGURE P2.2 Slide 10

In Addition

Adding Bitmapped Graphics to a Slide

PowerPoint recognizes a variety of picture formats dependent on the graphic filters installed with your program. Basically, pictures fall into one of two file categories—bitmaps and metafiles. Most clip art images are saved in a metafile format (named with a *.wmf* extension). Metafiles can be edited in PowerPoint, while bitmap files cannot. However, bitmaps can be edited in Microsoft Paint, Microsoft Photo Editor, or the program in which they were created. Pictures created in bitmap format are made from a series of small dots that form shapes and lines. Many scanned pictures are bitmapped. Bitmaps cannot be converted to drawing objects, but they can be scaled, sized, and moved. Insert a bitmap image in a PowerPoint presentation by clicking the Insert Picture button on the Drawing toolbar or by clicking Insert, pointing to Picture, and then clicking From File. At the Insert Picture dialog box, change to the folder containing the bitmap image, and then double-click the desired image in the list box.

IN BRIEF

Insert a Clip Art Image
1 Click Insert Clip Art button in Content placeholder.
2 At Select Picture dialog box, type a category and then press Enter.
3 Double-click desired image.

Recolor Clip Art Image
1 Click image to select it.
2 Click Recolor Picture button on Picture toolbar.
3 Choose desired colors at Recolor Picture dialog box.
4 Click OK.

2.12 Applying an Animation Scheme

You can animate objects in a slide to add visual interest to your presentation as well as create focus on specific items. PowerPoint includes preset animation schemes you can apply to objects in a presentation. Display these preset animation schemes by clicking Slide Show and then Animation Schemes or clicking the <u>Animation Schemes</u> hyperlink located toward the top of the Slide Design task pane. When an animation scheme is applied to a slide, objects will appear on the slide in a specific order. When running the presentation, the slide will display on the screen followed by the slide title. To display any subtitles or bulleted text, click the mouse button. The animation scheme controls how much text displays when you click the mouse. If your slide contains bulleted text, clicking the left mouse button when running the presentation will cause the first bulleted item to display. Click the left mouse button again to display the next bulleted item, and so on.

PROJECT: As the final step in preparing the documentary presentation, you will apply an animation scheme to all slides in the presentation.

STEPS

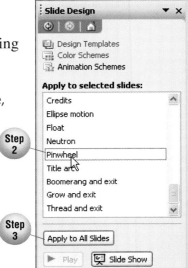

1 With **PPS2-01** open, display animation schemes by clicking Slide Show on the Menu bar and then clicking Animation Schemes.

> Animation schemes display in the Slide Design task pane and are grouped into three categories—Subtle, Moderate, and Exciting. When you click an animation effect, the effect displays in the slide in the Slide pane.

2 Scroll to the end of the *Apply to selected slides* list box and then click *Pinwheel*.

> When you click *Pinwheel*, the animation effect automatically plays in the active slide.

3 Click the Apply to All Slides button located toward the bottom of the task pane.

> By default, an animation scheme is applied only to the active slide. Clicking the Apply to All Slides button applies the scheme to all slides in the presentation.

4 Make sure the Slides tab is selected in the Outline/Slides pane and then notice the animation icon that displays below each slide in the Outline/Slides pane. Click the animation icon below the Slide 2 miniature.

> This displays the animation scheme in Slide 2 in the Slide pane.

5 Click the Slide 1 slide miniature in the Outline/Slides pane.

6 Run the presentation by clicking the Slide Show button located in the lower right corner of the Slide Design task pane. Click the left mouse button to display objects in the slides.

(7) After running the presentation, save **PPS2-01**.

(8) Print the presentation as handouts with six slides per page. To do this, display the Print dialog box by clicking File and then Print.

(9) At the Print dialog box, click the down-pointing arrow at the right side of the *Print what* option box and then click *Handouts* at the drop-down list. Make sure the *Slides per page* option displays as *6*.

(10) Click OK.

> Six slides print on the first page and four slides print on the second page.

(11) Close **PPS2-01**.

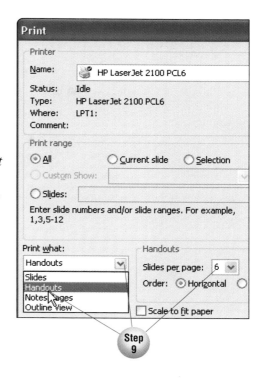

Step 9

In Addition

Applying a Custom Animation

To further control slide animation, use options at the Custom Animation task pane shown at the right. With options at this task pane, you can control the order in which objects appear on a slide, specify entrance emphasis, and apply more than one animation to an object. Objects in the active slide display in the Custom Animation task pane list box. Click an object and the buttons and options in the task pane become active. Click the Change button and then specify the entrance, emphasis, exit, or motion paths animation. Click the down-pointing arrow at the right side of the *Speed* option box and then choose an animation speed at the drop-down list. Rearrange the objects in the task pane list box in the order in which you want them to appear on the slide.

IN BRIEF

Apply Animation Scheme
1 Click Slide Show, Animation Schemes.
2 Click desired animation scheme in Slide Design task pane.

FEATURES SUMMARY

Feature	Button	Menu	Keyboard
Align text center	≡	Format, Alignment, Center	Ctrl + E
Align text justify		Format, Alignment, Justify	Ctrl + J
Align text left	≡	Format, Alignment, Align Left	Ctrl + L
Align text right	≡	Format, Alignment, Align Right	Ctrl + R
Animation schemes		Slide Show, Animation Schemes	
Apply font to text	Arial		Ctrl + Shift + F
Bold text	**B**		Ctrl + B
Change font size of text	10		Ctrl + Shift + P
Copy text or slide		Edit, Copy	Ctrl + C
Cut text or slide		Edit, Cut	Ctrl + X
Decrease font size of text	A˅		Ctrl + Shift + <
Decrease text indent			Shift + Tab
Font dialog box		Format, Font	Ctrl + T
Format Painter			
Increase font size of text	A˄		Ctrl + Shift + >
Increase text indent			Tab
Insert Picture dialog box		Insert, Picture, From File	
Italicize text	*I*		Ctrl + I
Line Spacing dialog box		Format, Line Spacing	
Paste text or slide		Edit, Paste	Ctrl + V
Replace Font dialog box		Format, Replace Fonts	
Save As dialog box		File, Save As	F12
Select Picture dialog box			
Shadow effect	S		
Underline text	U		Ctrl + U

PROCEDURES CHECK

Completion: In the space provided at the right, indicate the correct term, symbol, or command.

1. Display this dialog box to save a presentation with a new name. _____
2. Delete a slide by selecting the slide, clicking Edit on the Menu bar, and then clicking this option at the drop-down menu.
3. Press these keys on the keyboard to decrease the indent of text. _____
4. Press these keys on the keyboard to select all text in the placeholder.
5. Click this button on the Formatting toolbar to insert copied text in the slide at the location of the insertion point. _____
6. The Bold button is located on this toolbar. _____
7. Display a list of available fonts by clicking the down-pointing arrow at the right side of this button on the Formatting toolbar. _____
8. Use this feature to apply the same formatting in more than one location in a slide or slides.
9. Specify spacing before a paragraph with options at this dialog box. _____
10. Press these keys on the keyboard to change the text alignment to center. _____
11. Click the Color Schemes hyperlink located toward the top of this task pane and available color schemes display in a list box. _____
12. These display around a selected image. _____
13. Recolor a clip art image with options at this dialog box. _____
14. Display animation schemes in the Slide Design task pane by clicking this option on the Menu bar and then clicking Animation Schemes at the drop-down menu. _____

SKILLS REVIEW

Activity 1: REARRANGING AND DELETING SLIDES

1 With PowerPoint open, click the Open button on the Standard toolbar.
2 At the Open dialog box, double-click *MPAnnualMeeting*.
3 Click File and then Save As.
4 At the Save As dialog box, type **PPS2-R1** and then press Enter.
5 Click the Slide Sorter View button.
6 Select and then delete Slide 5 (contains the title *Financial*).
7 Move Slide 7 (*Expenses*) immediately after Slide 3 (*Review of Goals*).
8 Move Slide 6 (*Future Goals*) immediately after Slide 7 (*Technology*).
9 Save **PPS2-R1**.

Activity 2: DECREASING AND INCREASING INDENTS

1 With **PPS2-R1** open, click the Normal View button.
2 Make Slide 4 *(Expenses)* the active slide.
3 Decrease the indent of *Payroll* so it displays aligned at the left with *Administration*.
4 Decrease the indent of *Benefits* so it displays aligned at the left with *Payroll* and *Administration*.
5 Make Slide 6 *(Technology)* the active slide.
6 Increase the indent of *Hardware* to the next level.
7 Increase the indent of *Software* to the next level.
8 Increase the indent of *Technical Support* to the next level.
9 Save **PPS2-R1**.

Activity 3: COPYING AND PASTING TEXT

1 With **PPS2-R1** open, make Slide 7 *(Future Goals)* the active slide.
2 Select the name *Chris Greenbaum* and then click the Copy button. (Make sure you select only the name.)
3 Make Slide 3 *(Review of Goals)* the active slide.
4 Move the insertion point immediately to the right of *Overview of Goals*, press the Enter key, press the Tab key, and then click the Paste button.
5 Move the insertion point immediately to the right of *Completed Goals*, press the Enter key, press the Tab key, and then click the Paste button. (Clicking the Paste button inserts the name *Chris Greenbaum.*)
6 Make Slide 7 *(Future Goals)* the active slide.
7 Select the name *Shannon Grey* and then click the Copy button.
8 Make Slide 3 *(Review of Goals)* the active slide and then paste the name *Shannon Grey* below *Goals Remaining* at the same tab location as *Chris Greenbaum.*
9 Paste the name *Shannon Grey* below *Analysis/Discussion* at the same tab location as *Chris Greenbaum.*
10 Save **PPS2-R1**.

Activity 4: APPLYING FONTS AND USING FORMAT PAINTER

1 With **PPS2-R1** open, display the Replace Font dialog box and then replace the *Tahoma* font with the *Times New Roman* font.
2 Make Slide 1 the active slide.
3 Select the text *Marquee Productions*, change the font to *Arial* and turn on bold.
4 Select the text *Annual Meeting*, change the font to *Arial*, the font style to *Bold*, and the size to *44*.
5 Make Slide 2 *(Agenda)* the active slide.
6 Select the title *Agenda* and then change the font to *Arial*, the font style to *Bold*, and the size to *48*.
7 Using Format Painter, apply the same formatting to the title in each of the remaining slides.
8 Save **PPS2-R1**.

Activity 5: CHANGING ALIGNMENT AND LINE SPACING

1 With **PPS2-R1** open, make Slide 1 the active slide.
2 Click anywhere in the subtitle *Annual Meeting* and then click the Align Right button.
3 Make Slide 6 active, select all of the bulleted text, and then change the line spacing to 1.3.
4 Make Slide 8 active, select all of the bulleted text, and then change the spacing before paragraphs to 0.4.
5 Save **PPS2-R1**.

Activity 6: INSERTING A LOGO AND A CLIP ART IMAGE

1 With **PPS2-R1** open, insert a new Slide 1 at the beginning of the presentation, and choose the Content slide layout for the slide.
2 Click the Insert Picture button in the Content placeholder, navigate to the PowerPointS2 folder on your disk, and then double-click *M_Prod.tif*.
3 Size and move the logo so it is positioned attractively on the slide.
4 Make Slide 5 the active slide and then change the slide layout to Title, Text, and Content.
5 Click the Insert Clip Art button in the Content placeholder.
6 At the Select Picture dialog box, search for a clip art image related to *money* and then double-click a clip art image of your choosing related to money.
7 Recolor the image so the colors follow the slide design color scheme.
8 Size and move the image so it is positioned attractively on the slide.
9 Save **PPS2-R1**.

Activity 7: APPLYING AN ANIMATION SCHEME

1 With **PPS2-R1** open, click Slide Show and then Animation Schemes.
2 Click the *Elegant* animation scheme in the *Moderate* section of the *Apply to selected slides* list box.
3 Click the Apply to All Slides button.
4 Make Slide 1 the active slide and then run the presentation.
5 Print the presentation as handouts with all nine slides on one page.
6 Save and then close **PPS2-R1**.

PERFORMANCE PLUS

Assessment 1: FORMATTING A PRESENTATION FOR NIAGARA PENINSULA COLLEGE, THEATRE ARTS DIVISION

1 With PowerPoint open, open the presentation named **NPCTheatreArts**.
2 Save the presentation with Save As and name it **PPS2-P1**.
3 Move Slide 7 *(Associate Degrees)* immediately after Slide 2 *(Mission Statement)*.
4 Move Slide 6 *(Semester Costs)* immediately after Slide 7 *(Fall Semester Classes)*.
5 Make Slide 3 the active slide and then decrease the indent of *Acting* and *Set Design* to the previous level.
6 Make Slide 2 *(Mission Statement)* active, click in the paragraph below the title *Mission Statement*, and then change the alignment to justify.
7 Change the line spacing to 1.3 for the bulleted text in Slides 3, 4, 5, and 7.
8 Make Slide 5 the active slide, select the bulleted items, and then apply italics formatting.
9 Display color schemes for the slide design and then click the color scheme with a blue-gray background.
10 Insert a new Slide 1 at the beginning of the presentation and choose the Content slide layout for the slide.
11 Click the Insert Picture button in the Content placeholder, navigate to the PowerPointS2 folder on your disk, and then double-click *Niagara.tif*.
12 Size and move the logo so it is positioned attractively on the slide.
13 Make Slide 5 the active slide and then change the slide layout to Title, Text, and Content.
14 Insert a clip art image in the slide related to *teacher*.
15 Recolor the image so the colors follow the slide design color scheme.
16 Size and move the image so it is positioned attractively on the slide.
17 Apply an animation scheme of your choosing to all slides in the presentation.
18 Run the presentation.
19 Print the presentation as handouts with all nine slides on one page.
20 Save and then close **PPS2-P1**.

Assessment 2: FORMATTING A PRESENTATION FOR FIRST CHOICE TRAVEL

1 With PowerPoint open, open the presentation named **FCTVacations**.
2 Save the presentation with Save As and name it **PPS2-P2**.
3 Apply any formatting you feel is necessary to improve the appearance of each slide.
4 Apply an animation scheme of your choosing to all slides in the presentation.
5 Run the presentation.
6 Print the presentation as handouts with all six slides on one page.
7 Save and then close **PPS2-P2**.

Assessment 3: FINDING INFORMATION ON MOVING PLACEHOLDERS

1 Open **PPS2-P2**.
2 With **PPS2-P2** open, use the *Ask a Question* text box on the Menu bar to learn how to position a placeholder. (***Hint: Type the question*** How do I position a placeholder? ***in the*** **Ask a Question** ***text box.***)
3 After learning how to position a placeholder, make Slide 1 the active slide.
4 Move the placeholder containing the title closer to the subtitle (you determine how far to move the title). Make sure the *l* in *Travel* aligns at the right with the *s* in *Specials*.
5 Save **PPS2-P2**.

Assessment 4: FINDING INFORMATION ON SIZING PLACEHOLDERS

1 With **PPS2-P2** open, use the *Ask a Question* text box on the Menu bar to learn how to resize a placeholder. (***Hint: Type the question*** How do I resize a placeholder? ***in the*** **Ask a Question** ***text box.***)
2 After learning how to resize a placeholder, make Slide 4 the active slide.
3 Size the placeholder containing the bulleted text so the borders of the placeholder are close to the text.
4 Move the placeholder so the bulleted text is centered below the title *Cruise Prices*.
5 Run **PPS2-P2**.
6 Print the presentation as handouts with all six slides on one page.
7 Save and then close **PPS2-P2**.

Assessment 5: LOCATING INFORMATION AND PREPARING A PRESENTATION FOR THE WATERFRONT BISTRO

1 You are Dana Hirsch, Manager of The Waterfront Bistro. The owners of the bistro are interested in opening a bistro in Toronto and you need to prepare a presentation on currently open bistros in and around the Toronto area. Connect to the Internet and search for information on bistros in Toronto. (One possible site for information is the *Toronto Life Restaurant Guide* site.)
2 Using PowerPoint, create a presentation on competing bistros that contains a title slide with the name *The Waterfront Bistro* along with an appropriate subtitle. Include information on at least four bistros in and around Toronto. Create a slide for each bistro. You determine what information to put on the slide. (Consider information such as name, address, telephone number, Web site, type of food, hours, and so on.)
3 Apply an animation scheme of your choosing to all slides in the presentation.
4 Save the presentation and name it **PPS2-P3**.
5 Run the presentation.
6 Print the slides as handouts with six slides per page.
7 Save and then close **PPS2-P3**.

Assessment 6: LOCATING INFORMATION ON THEATRE ARTS UNDERGRADUATE PROGRAMS

1 Cal Rubine, chair of the Theatre Arts Division at Niagara Peninsula College, has prepared a presentation for an upcoming advising fair. After reviewing the presentation, he has asked you to make some changes. Open the presentation named **NPCTheatreArts** located in the PowerPointS2 folder on your disk. Save the presentation with Save As and name it **PPS2-P4**.

2 Display color schemes for the slide design and then click the color scheme with a blue-gray background.

3 Make Slide 7 the active slide and then insert a clip art image in the slide related to *theatre*. Recolor the image so the colors follow the slide design color scheme and size and move the image so it is positioned attractively on the slide.

4 Using a search engine of your choosing, search for undergraduate programs in theater (or theatre) or drama in New York City and Toronto. Find at least three universities in New York City and/or Toronto that offer undergraduate programs in theater arts or drama. Create a new Slide 8 that includes information on the three universities and title the slide *Transfer Universities*. You determine what information to include in the slide. If all of the information does not fit on Slide 8, create a new Slide 9.

5 Print the presentation as handouts with six slides per page.

6 Save and then close **PPS2-P4**.

POWERPOINT
SECTION 3
Formatting and Enhancing a Presentation

Use the PowerPoint Clipboard task pane to collect items and paste them in various locations in slides. Search for specific text and replace with other text with options at the Replace dialog box. Automate the formatting of slide elements using a slide master and a title master. Enhance the visual appeal of a presentation by adding and customizing elements such as WordArt, shapes, objects, tables, and organizational charts. Customize visual elements by changing element colors and rotating, flipping, and changing the fill color of objects. Make a presentation available on the Internet or a company intranet by publishing it to the Web, and create a hyperlink between a presentation and a location on the Internet. In this section, you will learn the skills and complete the projects described here.

Note: Before beginning this section, delete the PowerPointS2 folder on your disk. Next, copy to your disk or other location the PowerPointS3 subfolder from the CD that accompanies this textbook and then make PowerPointS3 the active folder.

Skills
- Copy and paste items using the Clipboard task pane
- Find and replace text
- Format slide elements with a slide master and a title master slide
- Insert, move, and size WordArt
- Draw and customize objects
- Create a table in a slide
- Add action buttons to slides
- Create and customize an organizational chart and diagram
- Insert headers and footers
- Insert a hyperlink in a slide
- Publish a presentation to the Web

Projects

MARQUEE PRODUCTIONS
Open an existing presentation on filming in Toronto, save the presentation with a new name, and then format and add visual appeal to the presentation; open an existing presentation on a documentary project, save the presentation with a new name, and then format and add visual appeal to the presentation.

Performance Threads
Theatrical Fabrics, Costumes and Supplies
Open an existing presentation on costume designs for Marquee Productions, save the presentation with a new name, and then format and add visual appeal to the presentation; locate sites on the Internet where employees can do costume research and then prepare a presentation containing the information.

FIRST CHOICE Travel
Open an existing presentation on a fine arts cruise offered by First Choice Travel in conjunction with Bluewater Galleries; save the presentation with a new name and then format and add visual appeal to the presentation.

3.1 Using the Clipboard Task Pane

Display the Clipboard task pane and you can collect up to 24 different items and then paste them in various locations. To display the Clipboard task pane, click Edit on the Menu bar and then click Office Clipboard. Select data or an object you want to copy and then click the Copy button on the Standard toolbar. Continue selecting text or items and clicking the Copy button. To insert an item, position the insertion point in the desired location and then click the item in the Clipboard task pane. If the copied item is text, the first 50 characters display. After inserting all desired items, click the Clear All button to remove any remaining items.

PROJECT: In preparation for a meeting on the Toronto location shoot, you will open the MPToronto presentation and then copy and paste multiple items in the appropriate slides.

S T E P S

1. With PowerPoint open, click the Open button 📂. Make sure the PowerPointS3 folder on your disk is active and then double-click *MPToronto*.

2. Click File and then Save As. At the Save As dialog box, type **PPS3-01** and then press Enter.

3. Display the Clipboard task pane by clicking Edit and then Office Clipboard. If items display in the Clipboard task pane, click the Clear All button located in the upper right corner of the task pane.

4. Make Slide 2 the active slide.

5. Select the name *Chris Greenbaum* and then click the Copy button 📋 on the Standard toolbar.

> When you click the Copy button, the name *Chris Greenbaum* is inserted as an item in the Clipboard task pane.

6. Select the name *Camille Matsui* and then click the Copy button.

7. Select the name *Dennis Chun* and then click the Copy button.

8. Select the name *Josh Hart* and then click the Copy button.

9. Make Slide 3 the active slide, position the insertion point immediately to the right of *Location Expenses*, press the Enter key, and then press the Tab key.

> Pressing the Enter key moves the insertion point down to the next line and pressing the Tab key demotes the insertion point to the next level.

10. Position the arrow pointer on the item in the Clipboard task pane representing *Chris Greenbaum* and then click the left mouse button.

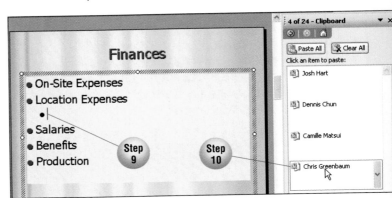

POWERPOINT

66

SECTION 3: FORMATTING AND ENHANCING A PRESENTATION

11. Position the insertion point immediately to the right of *Production*, press the Enter key, press the Tab key, and then click the item in the Clipboard task pane representing *Camille Matsui*.

12. Make Slide 4 the active slide, position the insertion point immediately to the right of *Royal Ontario Museum*, press the Enter key, press the Tab key, and then click the item in the Clipboard task pane representing *Dennis Chun*.

13. Position the insertion point immediately to the right of *Island Airport*, press the Enter key, press the Tab key, and then click the item in the Clipboard task pane representing *Dennis Chun*.

14. Position the insertion point immediately to the right of *King Street*, press the Enter key, press the Tab key, and then click the item in the Clipboard task pane representing *Josh Hart*.

15. Click the Clear All button located in the upper right corner of the Clipboard task pane to clear the task pane.

16. Close the Clipboard task pane by clicking the Close button located in the upper right corner of the task pane.

17. Save **PPS3-01**.

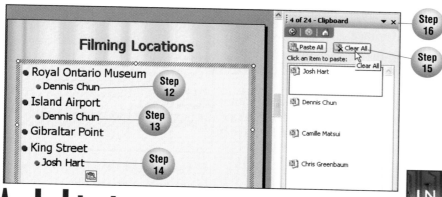

In Addition

Clipboard Task Pane Options

Click the Options button located toward the bottom of the Clipboard task pane and a pop-up menu displays with five options as shown below at the right. Insert a check mark before those options that you want active. For example, you can choose to display the Clipboard task pane automatically when you cut or copy text, cut and copy text without displaying the Clipboard task pane, display the *Office Clipboard* icon near the Taskbar when the clipboard is active, and display the item message when copying items to the Clipboard.

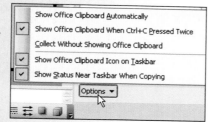

IN BRIEF

Use the Clipboard Task Pane
1. Click Edit, Office Clipboard.
2. Select text and click Copy button.
3. Continue selecting text and clicking Copy button.
4. Position insertion point.
5. Click desired item in Clipboard task pane.
6. Insert any additional items.
7. Click Clear All button.
8. Close Clipboard task pane.

3.2 Finding and Replacing Text

Use the find and replace feature to look for specific text or formatting in slides in a presentation and replace with other text or formatting. Display the Find dialog box if you want to find something specific in a presentation. Display the Replace dialog box if you want to find something in a presentation and replace it with another element.

PROJECT: A couple of people have been replaced on the Toronto location. Use the replace feature to find names and replace with new names in the Toronto location presentation.

STEPS

1 With **PPS3-01** open, make Slide 1 the active slide.

2 Camille Matsui has been replaced on the project by Jennie Almonzo. Begin the find and replace by clicking Edit and then Replace.

> This displays the Replace dialog box with the insertion point positioned in the *Find what* text box.

3 Type **Camille Matsui** in the *Find what* text box.

4 Press the Tab key and then type **Jennie Almonzo** in the *Replace with* text box.

5 Click the Replace All button.

> Clicking the Replace All button replaces all occurrences of the text in the presentation. If you want control over what is replaced in a document, click the Replace button to replace text or click the Find Next button to move to the next occurrence of the text.

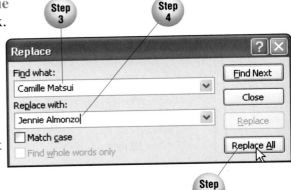

6 At the message telling you that two replacements were made, click OK.

> The Replace dialog box remains on the screen.

7 Josh Hart had to leave the project and is being replaced by Jaime Ruiz. At the Replace dialog box, type **Josh Hart** in the *Find what* text box.

> When you begin typing the name *Josh Hart* the previous name Camille Matsui is deleted.

8 Press the Tab key, type **Jaime Ruiz** in the *Replace with* text box, and then click the Replace All button.

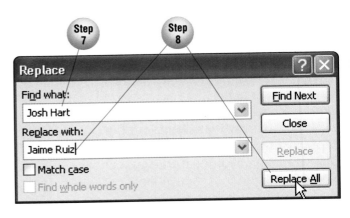

⑨ At the message telling you that two replacements were made, click OK.

The Replace dialog box remains on the screen.

⑩ The title *Manager* has been changed to *Director*. At the Replace dialog box, type **Manager** in the *Find what* text box.

⑪ Press the Tab key, type **Director** in the *Replace with* text box, and then click the Replace All button.

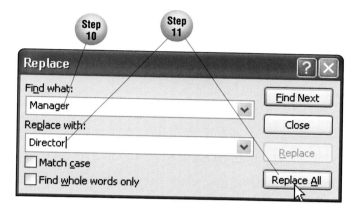

⑫ At the message telling you that one replacement was made, click OK.

⑬ Close the Replace dialog box by clicking the Close button located at the right side of the dialog box.

⑭ Save **PPS3-01**.

In Addition

Replace Dialog Box Options

The Replace dialog box shown below at the right contains two options for completing a find and replace. Choose the *Match case* option if you want to exactly match the case of the find text. For example, if you look for *Company*, PowerPoint will stop at *Company* but not *company* or *COMPANY*. Choose the *Find whole words only* option if you want to find a whole word, not a part of a word. For example, if you search for *his* and *did not* select *Find whole words only*, PowerPoint will stop at t*his*, *his*tory, c*his*el, and so on.

IN BRIEF

Find and Replace Text
1 Click Edit, Replace.
2 At Replace dialog box, type find text.
3 Press Tab and then type replace text.
4 Click Replace All button.
5 Click Close button.

3.3 Formatting with a Slide Master

If you use a PowerPoint design template, you may choose to use the formatting provided by the template, or you may want to customize the formatting. If you customize formatting in a presentation, PowerPoint's slide master can be very helpful in reducing the steps needed to format slides in a presentation. A slide master is added to a presentation when a design template is applied. Generally, a template contains a slide master as well as a title master. Changes made to a title master affect all slides with the Title Slide layout applied. Changes made to a slide master affect all other slides in a presentation. To format a slide master and/or title master, change to the Slide Master view. To do this, position the insertion point on the Normal View button on the View toolbar, hold down the Shift key (this causes the Normal View button to change to the Slide Master View button), and then click the left mouse button.

PROJECT: To save time formatting the presentation, you will use the slide master to improve the appearance of titles and bullets in Slides 2 through 6 and insert the company logo.

STEPS

1. With **PPS3-01** open, make Slide 2 the active slide.

2. Hold down the Shift key, click the Normal View button 🔲 on the View toolbar, and then release the Shift key.

   When you hold down the Shift key, the Normal View button changes to the Slide Master View button. When you click the Slide Master View button, a slide master displays in the Slide pane, a slide-title master pair display as slide miniatures at the left side of the window, and a Slide Master View toolbar displays. Position the mouse pointer on the slide miniature and the name of the miniature displays in a yellow box. Click the desired slide master miniature and then apply specific formatting to the slide master in the Slide pane.

   PROBLEM? If the slide master does not display, make sure you hold down the Shift key while clicking the left mouse button.

3. Click in the text *Click to edit Master title style*.

4. Click Format and then Font.

5. At the Font dialog box, click the down-pointing arrow at the right side of the *Color* text box, click the purple color that displays at the right side of the pop-up menu, and then click OK.

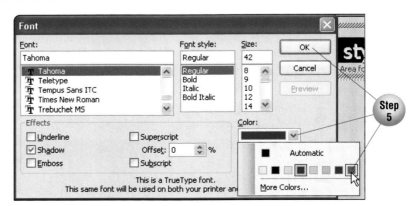

6. Click in the text *Second level* (located below the text *Click to edit Master text styles*).

(7) Change the bullet by clicking Format and then Bullets and Numbering.

> Customize bullets and numbering formatting with options at the Bullets and Numbering dialog box.

(8) At the Bullets and Numbering dialog box, click the arrow bullet shown at the right. (If this bullet is not available, choose another arrow bullet.)

(9) Click OK to close the Bullets and Numbering dialog box.

(10) Insert the company logo in the slide master. To do this click Insert, point to Picture, and then click From File.

(11) At the Insert Picture dialog box, navigate to the PowerPointS3 folder on your disk, and then double-click *M_Prod.tif* in the list box.

(12) Using the mouse, drag the logo to the lower right corner of the slide.

(13) Remove the slide master view by clicking the Normal View button ⊞ on the View toolbar.

(14) Save **PPS3-01**.

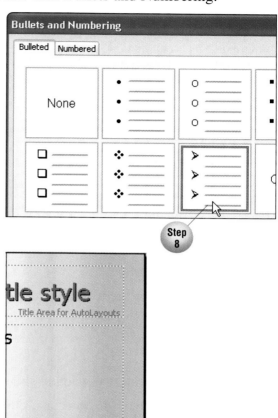

In Addition

Applying More than One Design Template to a Presentation

Each design template applies specific formatting to slides. You can apply more than one design template to slides in a presentation. To do this, select the specific slides and then choose the desired design template. The design template is applied only to the selected slides. If you apply more than one design template to a presentation, multiple slide masters will display in the Slide Master view. For example, if you apply two design templates to a presentation, two slide-title master pairs will display—one pair for each design template. Use these slide-title master pairs to specify the formatting for each design template.

In BRIEF

Display Slide Master
1 Hold down Shift key.
2 Click Slide Master View button (previously Normal View button).

3.4 Formatting with a Title Master Slide

Along with the slide master, you can also apply formatting to slides in a presentation with the title master slide. Formatting applied to the title master slide affects only those slides created using the Title Slide autolayout. Format a title slide in the same manner as the slide master.

PROJECT: Using a title master slide, you will improve the appearance of the two title slides.

STEPS

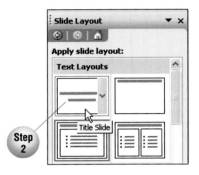

Step 2

1. With **PPS3-01** open, make Slide 1 the active slide and then click the New Slide button on the Formatting toolbar.

2. Click the Title Slide layout in the Slide Layout task pane.

3. Click the text *Click to add title* and then type **Location Timeline**.

4. Click the text *Click to add subtitle* and then type **May 15 – August 31**.

5. Make Slide 1 the active slide.

6. Hold down the Shift key, click the Normal View button (changes to the Slide Master View button) on the View toolbar, and then release the Shift key.

7. Click once in the text *Click to edit Master title style*.

8. Change the font style and color for the title text by clicking Format and then Font.

9. At the Font dialog box, click *Bold Italic* in the *Font style* list box.

10. Click the down-pointing arrow at the right side of the *Color* text box and then click the dark blue color (second color from the right).

11. Click OK to close the Font dialog box.

12. Click once in the text *Click to edit Master subtitle style*.

13. Change the font style and color for the title text by clicking Format and then Font.

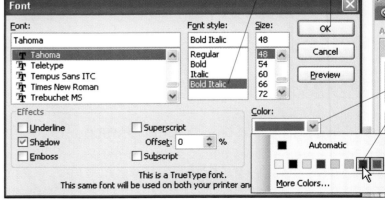

Step 9

Step 11

14 At the Font dialog box, click *Bold Italic* in the *Font style* list box.

15 Click the down-pointing arrow at the right side of the *Color* text box and then click the purple color (first color from the right).

16 Click OK to close the Font dialog box.

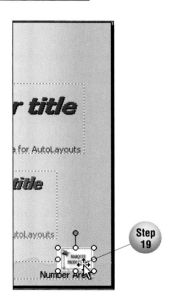

17 Insert the logo in the corner of the two title slides. To do this, click Insert, point to Picture, and then click From File.

18 At the Insert Picture dialog box, make sure the PowerPointS3 folder on your disk is the active folder, and then double-click *M_Prod.tif*.

19 Drag the logo to the lower right corner of the title master slide as shown at the right.

20 Remove the title master slide view by clicking the Normal View button on the View toolbar.

21 Save **PPS3-01**.

In Addition

Deleting a Presentation

Delete a presentation from a disk or folder on the hard drive at the Open dialog box. To delete a presentation, click File and then Open. At the Open dialog box, display the drive or folder containing the presentation. Click the presentation and then click the Delete button on the dialog box toolbar. At the message asking if you are sure you want to delete the presentation or send the contents to the Recycle Bin, click the Yes button. If you are deleting a presentation from a disk, PowerPoint will ask if you want to delete the presentation. If you are deleting a presentation from a hard drive, PowerPoint will ask if you want to send the presentation to the Recycle Bin.

3.5 Inserting and Formatting WordArt

Use the WordArt application to distort or modify text to conform to a variety of shapes. With WordArt, you can change the font, style, and alignment of text; use different fill patterns and colors; customize border lines; and add shadow and three-dimensional effects. Office provides the WordArt Gallery with predesigned and formatted WordArt choices. Display the WordArt Gallery by clicking the Insert WordArt button on the Drawing toolbar or by clicking Insert, pointing to Picture, and then clicking WordArt.

PROJECT: You decide to add a new slide to the Toronto site presentation that contains the title of the film as WordArt.

STEPS

1. With **PPS3-01** open, click the Slide Sorter View button 🔡 on the View toolbar.

2. Click immediately left of Slide 1, click Insert, and then click New Slide.

3. Click the Blank slide layout in the Slide Layout task pane.

4. Double-click Slide 1.

   This changes the view to Normal View and displays Slide 1 in the Slide pane.

5. Click the Insert WordArt button 🔳 on the Drawing toolbar.

   If the Drawing toolbar is not visible, right-click any currently displayed toolbar, and then click *Drawing* at the drop-down list.

6. At the WordArt Gallery, double-click the fifth option from the left in the third row.

7. At the Edit WordArt Text dialog box, type **Ring of Roses** and then click the OK button.

   The WordArt text *Ring of Roses* is inserted in the slide and the WordArt toolbar displays.

8. Change the shape of the WordArt by clicking the WordArt Shape button 🅰 on the WordArt toolbar and then clicking the second shape from the left in the fourth row (Deflate).

   Refer to Table P3.1 for a description of the WordArt toolbar buttons.

Step 3

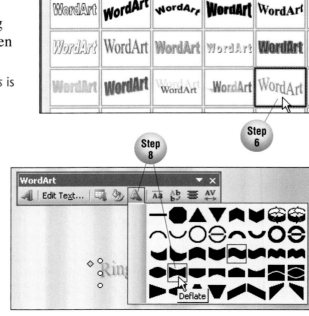

Step 6

Step 8

9 Drag the WordArt to the upper left corner of the slide (see figure at the right) by positioning the mouse pointer on the WordArt until the pointer displays with a four-headed arrow attached. Hold down the left mouse button, drag the outline of the WordArt so it is positioned in the upper left corner of the slide, and then release the mouse button.

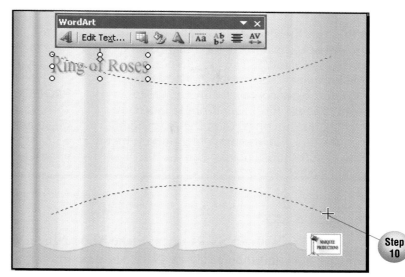

Step 10

10 Increase the size of the WordArt by positioning the mouse pointer on the bottom right sizing handle (white circle) until the pointer turns into a two-headed arrow pointing diagonally. Hold down the left mouse button, drag down and to the right, and then release the mouse button.

11 Drag the WordArt so it displays in the middle of the slide.

12 Click outside the WordArt to deselect it.

13 Save **PPS3-01**.

TABLE P3.1 WordArt Toolbar Buttons

Button	Name	Function
	Insert WordArt	Display WordArt Gallery
Edit Text...	**Edit Text**	Display Edit WordArt Text dialog box where you can edit text of the selected WordArt object
	WordArt Gallery	Display WordArt Gallery
	Format WordArt	Format the line, color, fill, pattern, size, position, and so on, of the selected WordArt object
	WordArt Shape	Display pop-up menu containing shapes
	WordArt Same Letter Heights	Make all letters in the current WordArt object the same height
	WordArt Vertical Text	Stack the text in the selected WordArt object vertically so it can be read from top to bottom
	WordArt Alignment	Specify the alignment of the WordArt text
	WordArt Character Spacing	Specify the spacing between WordArt text characters

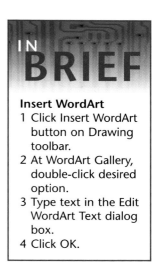

IN BRIEF

Insert WordArt
1 Click Insert WordArt button on Drawing toolbar.
2 At WordArt Gallery, double-click desired option.
3 Type text in the Edit WordArt Text dialog box.
4 Click OK.

3.6 Drawing and Customizing an AutoShape, Text Box, and Connector Line

With buttons on the Drawing toolbar, you can draw a variety of shapes such as circles, squares, rectangles, and ovals. You can also draw straight lines, free-form lines, and lines with arrowheads. The Drawing toolbar contains an AutoShapes button with options for drawing predesigned shapes and connector lines. Click the AutoShapes button on the Drawing toolbar and a pop-up menu displays with autoshape choices. Use the Text Box button on the Drawing toolbar to draw a box in a slide in which you can insert text. You can draw a text box inside a shape or an autoshape.

PROJECT: You will create a new slide for the Toronto site presentation that includes the Toronto office address inside a text box drawn inside an autoshape and also add connector lines to objects in a slide.

STEPS

① With **PPS3-01** open, make Slide 2 the active slide, and then click the New Slide button on the Formatting toolbar.

② Click the Blank slide layout in the Slide Layout task pane.

③ With the new slide displayed in the Slide pane, click the AutoShapes button on the Drawing toolbar, point to Stars and Banners, and then click the second autoshape from the left in the bottom row (Horizontal Scroll).

④ Position the mouse pointer in the slide, hold down the left mouse button, drag to create the shape as shown at the right, and then release the mouse button.

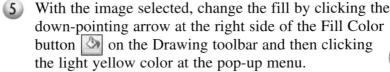

If you are not satisfied with the size and shape of the image, press the Delete key to remove the image, and then draw the image again.

⑤ With the image selected, change the fill by clicking the down-pointing arrow at the right side of the Fill Color button on the Drawing toolbar and then clicking the light yellow color at the pop-up menu.

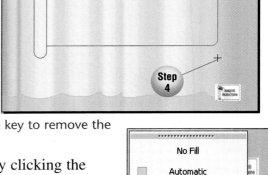

⑥ Draw a text box inside the shape by clicking the Text Box button on the Drawing toolbar and then dragging with the mouse to create the text box as shown at the right.

⑦ With the insertion point inside the text box, click the down-pointing arrow at the right side of the Font Size button and then click *24* at the drop-down list.

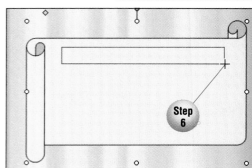

⑧ Click the Bold button **B** and the Center button ≣ on the Formatting toolbar, and then type the following text (the text will appear double spaced on the slide):

MARQUEE PRODUCTIONS
Toronto Office
905 Bathurst Street
Toronto, ON M4P 4E5

⑨ Make Slide 10 the active slide and then draw the connector line from the *Planning* box to the *Fittings* box as shown in Figure P3.1. To do this, click the AutoShapes button on the Drawing toolbar, point to Connectors, and then click Curved Arrow Connector. Click the left edge of the *Planning* box and then click the left edge of the *Fittings* box.

> After selecting the desired connector, passing the pointer over a connection site such as an object causes blue circles to display around the object and the mouse pointer to display as a connector pointer. You can connect an object to another object or an object to a specific location on the slide.

⑩ Draw a connector line from the *Fittings* box to the *Alterations* box by completing steps similar to those in Step 9.

⑪ Draw a connector line from the *Alterations* box to the *Final Fittings* box by completing steps similar to those in Step 9.

⑫ Save **PPS3-01**.

Figure P3.1 Slide 10

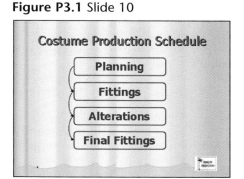

In Addition

Wrapping Text in an AutoShape

If you want to customize how text wraps within an autoshape, click the Text Box button, click inside an autoshape, click Format, and then click Text Box. At the Format Text Box dialog box, click the Text Box tab. This displays the dialog box as shown at the right. At the dialog box, choose the *Word wrap text in AutoShape* option if you want text to wrap within the autoshape. Choose the *Resize AutoShape to fit text* option if you want the size of the autoshape to conform to the text. Rotate text in a text box by choosing the *Rotate text within AutoShape by 90°* option.

IN BRIEF

Draw an Autoshape
1 Click AutoShapes button on Drawing toolbar, point to desired option, click desired autoshape.
2 Drag in slide to draw shape.

Create a Text Box
1 Click Text Box button on Drawing toolbar.
2 Drag in slide to draw text box.
3 Type text inside the text box.

3.7 Displaying Guide Lines and the Grid; Copying and Rotating Shapes

You can rotate and flip selected objects in a slide horizontally and vertically. To rotate or flip an object, select the object, click the Draw button on the Drawing toolbar, point to Rotate or Flip, and then click the desired rotation or flip option at the side menu. You can rotate a drawn object but not a text box. If you draw more than one object in a slide, you can select the objects as a unit so you can work with them as if they were a single object. You can format, size, move, flip, and/or rotate selected objects as a single unit. To help position elements such as shapes and images on a slide, consider displaying guide lines and/or gridlines. Guide lines are horizontal and vertical dashed lines that display on the slide in the Slide pane and the grid is a set of intersecting lines.

PROJECT: You need to create a new slide for the Toronto site presentation that displays the date for the last day of filming in Toronto. To highlight this important information, you will insert an arrow autoshape.

STEPS

① With **PPS3-01** open, make Slide 10 the active slide, click the New Slide button on the Formatting toolbar, and then click the Title Only slide layout in the Slide Layout task pane.

② At the new slide, click in the text *Click to add title* and then type **Last Day of Filming**.

③ Turn on the display of guide lines and the grid. To do this, click View and then Grid and Guides. At the Grid and Guides dialog box, click the *Display grid on screen* option to insert a check mark and then click the *Display drawing guides on screen* option to insert a check mark. Click OK to close the dialog box.

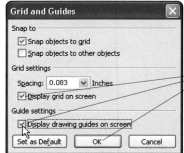

> You can click the Show/Hide Grid button on the Standard toolbar to turn on/off the display of the grid.

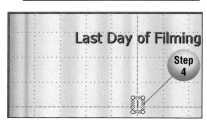

④ Click the Text Box button 📧 on the Drawing toolbar and then click once in the middle of the slide where the guide lines intersect (see image at the right).

> Clicking in the middle of the slide inserts a small text box with the insertion point positioned inside.

⑤ Change the font size to 24, turn on bold, change the alignment to center, and then type **August 31**.

> If a border displays around the text box, remove the border by clicking the down-pointing arrow at the right of the Line Color button on the Drawing toolbar and then clicking the *No Line* option.

⑥ Click the AutoShapes button on the Drawing toolbar, point to Block Arrows, and then click the second option from the left in the fifth row (Notched Right Arrow).

7. Position the mouse pointer at the left side of the slide, hold down the left mouse button drag to create the arrow shape as shown at the right, and then release the mouse button.

> Use the guide lines and the grid to help position the arrow.

Step 7

8. With the arrow selected, click the down-pointing arrow at the right side of the Fill Color button and then click the purple color.

9. With the arrow image selected, copy the arrow by positioning the mouse pointer inside the image until it displays with a four-headed arrow attached. Hold down the Ctrl key and then the left mouse button. Drag the arrow to the right side of the date, and then release the left mouse button and the Ctrl key.

10. Flip the copied arrow by clicking the Draw button on the Drawing toolbar, pointing to Rotate or Flip, and then clicking Flip Horizontal.

11. Using the mouse pointer, draw a border around the three objects.

12. Center align the three grouped objects by clicking the Draw button on the Drawing toolbar, pointing to Align or Distribute, and then clicking Align Middle.

Step 11

13. Click outside the objects to deselect them.

14. Turn off the display of the guide lines and the grid. To do this, click View and then Grid and Guides. At the Grid and Guides dialog box, click the *Display grid on screen* option to remove the check mark, click the *Display drawing guides on screen* option to remove the check mark, and then click OK to close the dialog box.

15. Save **PPS3-01**.

In Addition

Rotating Objects

Use the rotation handle that displays near a selected object to rotate the object. Position the mouse pointer on the rotation handle until the pointer displays as a circular arrow as shown at the right. Hold down the left mouse button, drag in the desired direction, and then release the mouse button.

3.8 Creating a Table in a Slide

The Content placeholder in a slide layout contains a number of buttons including an Insert Table button. Use this button to create a table in a slide. Click the Insert Table button and then specify the number of columns and rows at the Insert Table dialog box. Format a table in a slide with buttons on the Tables and Borders toolbar. Display this toolbar by clicking the Tables and Borders button on the Standard toolbar. After formatting the table, double-click inside the first cell, and then type the text. Move the insertion point to the next cell by pressing the Tab key or press Shift + Tab to move the insertion point to the previous cell.

PROJECT: After reviewing the slides, you decide to include additional information on the location timeline. To do this, you will delete a slide and then create a table with specific dates.

S T E P S

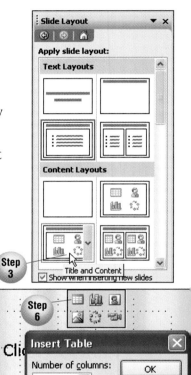

1. With **PPS3-01** open, delete Slide 4. (This is the slide containing the title *Location Timeline* and the subtitle *May 15 – August 31*.)

2. Make Slide 10 the active slide and then click the New Slide button on the Formatting toolbar.

3. Click the Title and Content layout in the Slide Layout task pane.

4. Turn on the display of the grid by clicking the Show/Hide Grid button ⊞ on the Standard toolbar.

5. Click the text *Click to add title* in the new slide and then type **Timeline**.

6. Click the Insert Table button that displays in the Content placeholder.

7. At the Insert Table dialog box, make sure *2* displays in the *Number of columns* text box.

8. Press the Tab key and then type *7* in the *Number of Rows* text box.

9. Click OK to close the Insert Table dialog box.

10. Column 1 needs to be widened to accommodate the project tasks. Move the vertical gridline in the table by positioning the mouse pointer on the gridline until it displays as a double-headed arrow with two short lines between. Hold down the left mouse button, drag to the right to the approximate position shown in the image above at the right, and then release the mouse button.

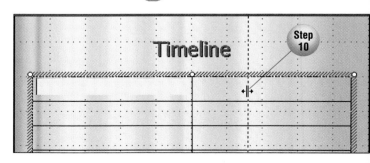

(11) With the insertion point positioned in the first cell, type the text shown in Figure P3.2. Press the Tab key to move the insertion point to the next cell. Press Shift + Enter to move the insertion point to the previous cell.

> If text wraps in either column, increase the size of the column so all text fits on one line.

OBLEM **?**

■ (12) With the table selected (short diagonal lines display around the table), use the mouse to drag the table up slightly so the bottom border of the table is positioned just above the Marquee Productions logo located in the lower right corner of the slide.

(13) Click the Show/Hide Grid button to turn off the display of the grid.

(14) Save **PPS3-01**.

FIGURE P3.2 Slide Table

Timeline	
Open Toronto Office	May 15
Costume Delivery	July 5
Van Rental	May 15, May 25
Car Rental	May 25, June 1
Royal Ontario Museum Filming	June 15-25
Park Filming	July 10-18
City Location Filming	August 3-15

In Addition

Using Buttons on the Tables and Borders Toolbar

Use buttons on the Tables and Borders toolbar shown below to customize a table in a PowerPoint slide. Display this toolbar by clicking the Tables and Borders button ▦ on the Standard toolbar.

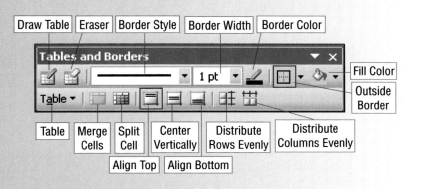

IN BRIEF

Create a Table in a Slide
1 Click Insert Table button in Content placeholder.
2 At Insert Table dialog box, specify desired number of columns and rows.
3 Click OK.
4 Customize table and then type text.

3.9 Adding Action Buttons

Action buttons are drawn objects on a slide that have a routine attached to them that is activated when the viewer or the speaker clicks the button. For example, you could include an action button that displays a specific Web page, a file in another program, or the next slide in the presentation. Creating an action button is a two-step process. The button is drawn using the AutoShapes button on the Drawing toolbar and then the action that will take place is defined in the Action Settings dialog box. Once an action button has been created it can be customized using the same techniques employed for customizing drawn objects. When the viewer or speaker moves the mouse over an action button during a presentation, the pointer changes to a hand with a finger pointing upward to indicate clicking will result in an action.

PROJECT: To automate the running of the presentation, you decide to insert an action button at the bottom of each slide that will link to the next slide or the first slide.

S T E P S

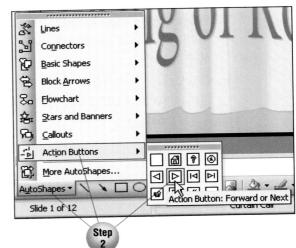

① With **PPS3-01** open, make Slide 1 the active slide.

② Insert an action button that, when clicked, will display the next slide. To begin, click the AutoShapes button on the Drawing toolbar, point to Action Buttons, and then click Action Button: Forward or Next (second button from the left in the second row).

Step 2

③ Position the crosshair pointer in the lower left corner of Slide 1 and then drag to create a button that is approximately 0.5 inch tall and wide.

④ At the Action Settings dialog box that displays, click OK. (The default setting is *Hyperlink to Next Slide*.)

⑤ With the button selected, click the down-pointing arrow at the right side of the Fill Color button and then click the light yellow color at the pop-up menu.

PROBLEM **?**

If you are not pleased with the size of the button, use the sizing handles to increase or decrease size. If you are not pleased with the location of the button, drag the selected button to the desired position.

Step 3

⑥ Instead of drawing the button on each slide, you decide to copy and then paste it in other slides. To do this, make sure the button is selected and then click the Copy button on the Standard toolbar.

⑦ Make Slide 2 the active slide and then click the Paste button.

⑧ Make Slide 3 the active slide and then click the Paste button.

⑨ Continue pasting the button in Slides 4 through 10. (Do not paste the button on the last slide, Slide 11.)

⑩ Make Slide 11 the active slide and then insert an action button that displays the first slide. To begin, click the AutoShapes button on the Drawing toolbar, point to Action Buttons, and then click Action Button: Home (second button from the left in the top row).

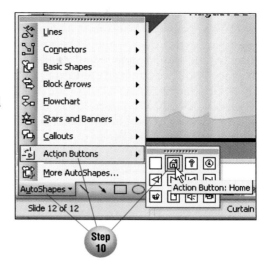

Step 10

⑪ Position the crosshair pointer in the lower left corner of Slide 1 and then drag to create a button that is approximately 0.5 inch tall and wide.

⑫ At the Action Settings dialog box that displays, click OK. (The default setting is *Hyperlink to First Slide*.)

⑬ With the button selected, click the Fill Color button on the Drawing toolbar.

> You changed the fill color to light yellow in an earlier step and that remains the fill color for the Fill Color button until you close the presentation.

⑭ Click outside the action button to deselect it.

⑮ Make Slide 1 the active slide, click the Slide Show button on the View toolbar, and then navigate through the slide show by clicking the action button. After viewing the presentation at least twice, press the Esc key to end the presentation.

⑯ Save **PPS3-01**.

In Addition

Linking with Action Buttons

You can specify that an action button links to a Web site during a presentation. To do this, draw an Action button. At the Action Settings dialog box, click the *Hyperlink to* option, click the down-pointing arrow at the right side of the *Hyperlink to* option box, and then click *URL* at the drop-down list. At the Hyperlink To URL dialog box, type the Web address in the *URL* text box, and then click OK. Click OK to close the Action Settings dialog box. Other actions you can link to using the *Hyperlink to* drop-down list include: Next Slide, Previous Slide, First Slide, Last Slide, Last Slide Viewed, End Show, Custom Show, Slide, URL, Other PowerPoint Presentation, and Other File. The Action Settings dialog box can also be used to run another program when the action button is selected, to run a macro, or to activate an embedded object.

IN BRIEF

Add an Action Button
1 Click AutoShapes button, point to Action Buttons, click desired button.
2 Drag in slide to create button.
3 At Action Settings dialog box, click OK.

3.10 Creating an Organizational Chart and Diagram

Use the Diagram Gallery to create organizational charts or other types of diagrams. Display the Diagram Gallery dialog box by clicking the Insert Diagram or Organization Chart button on the Drawing toolbar or by clicking Insert and then Diagram. You can also display the Diagram Gallery dialog box by choosing a slide layout containing a Content placeholder and then clicking the Insert Diagram or Organization Chart button in the Content placeholder. At the Diagram Gallery dialog box, click the desired option in the *Select a diagram type* list box and then click OK. If you choose the

organizational chart option, chart boxes appear in the slide and the Organization Chart toolbar displays. If you choose a diagram option, the Diagram toolbar displays. Use buttons on these toolbars to customize the organizational chart or diagram.

PROJECT: After viewing the presentation, you decide to add visual appeal to the presentation by inserting an organizational chart and diagram.

STEPS

1. With **PPS3-01** open, make Slide 4 the active slide and then select the placeholder by clicking anywhere in the bulleted text.

2. Press Ctrl + A to select all of the text in the placeholder and then press the Delete key.

3. Display slide layouts by clicking Format and then Slide Layout and then click the Title and Content slide layout in the Slide Layout task pane.

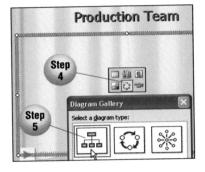

4. Create the organizational chart shown in Figure P3.3. To begin, click the Insert Diagram or Organization Chart button located in the Content placeholder.

5. At the Diagram Gallery dialog box, double-click the first option from the left in the top row.

6. Click the down-pointing arrow at the right side of the Insert Shape button on the Organization Chart toolbar and then click *Assistant* at the drop-down list.

7. Position the mouse pointer on the border of the lower right organization chart box until the pointer displays with a four-headed arrow, click the left mouse button, and then press the Delete key to remove the box.

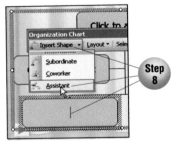

8. Click the lower left organization chart box, click the down-pointing arrow at the right of the Insert Shape button, and then click *Assistant* at the drop-down list.

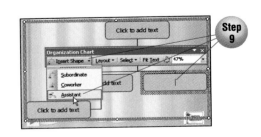

9. Click the lower right organization chart box, click the down-pointing arrow at the right of the Insert Shape button, and then click *Assistant* at the drop-down list.

10 Click the Autoformat button on the Organization Chart toolbar and then double-click *Thick Outline* at the Organization Chart Style Gallery.

11 Click in the top organization chart box and then type the name and title shown in Figure P3.3. Click in each of the remaining organization chart boxes and then type the names and titles shown in Figure P3.3.

FIGURE P3.3 Slide 4

12 Using the mouse, drag the organization chart border up in the slide so the chart is positioned in the slide as shown in Figure P3.3.

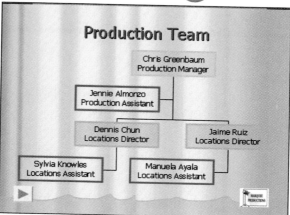

13 Click Slide 5 to make it the active slide and then insert the diagram shown in Figure P3.4. To begin, click Insert on the Menu bar and then click Diagram.

14 At the Diagram Gallery, double-click the Cycle Diagram (second option from the left in the top row).

FIGURE P3.4 Slide 5

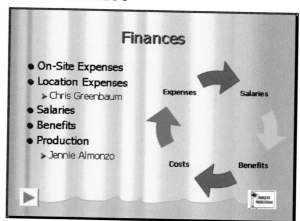

15 Click the Insert Shape button on the Diagram toolbar to insert an additional arrow shape.

16 Click the AutoFormat button and then double-click *Primary Colors* at the Diagram Style Gallery dialog box.

17 Click in each of the diagram text boxes and type the text shown in Figure P3.4.

18 Select the text in each diagram text box (individually) and then turn on Bold and change the font size to *18*.

19 Save **PPS3-01**.

Create an Organizational Chart or Diagram
1 Click Insert Diagram or Organization Chart button in Content placeholder.
2 At Diagram Gallery dialog box, double-click desired option.
3 Use buttons on Organization Chart toolbar to customize chart.

Inserting Headers and Footers

Insert information you want to appear at the top or bottom of each slide or on note and handout pages with options at the Header and Footer dialog box. If you want the information to appear on all slides, display the Header and Footer dialog box with the Slide tab selected. With options at this dialog box, you can insert the date and time, insert the slide number, and create a footer. To insert header or footer elements in notes or handouts, choose options at the Header and Footer dialog box with the Notes and Handouts tab selected.

PROJECT: You decide to insert the current date and slide number in the Toronto location presentation and create a header for notes pages.

S T E P S

1 With **PPS3-01** open, display Slide 1 in Normal view.

2 Click View and then Header and Footer.

3 At the Header and Footer dialog box with the Slide tab selected, click the *Date and time* check box to remove the check mark.

4 Click in the *Footer* text box and then type **Toronto Location**.

5 Click the Apply to All button.

6 Make Slide 3 the active slide.

7 Click in the Notes pane and then type **When the telephone is connected, include the number on this slide.**

8 Insert a header in notes and handouts by clicking View and then Header and Footer.

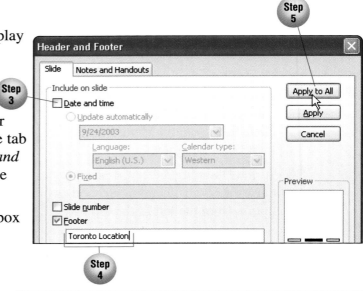

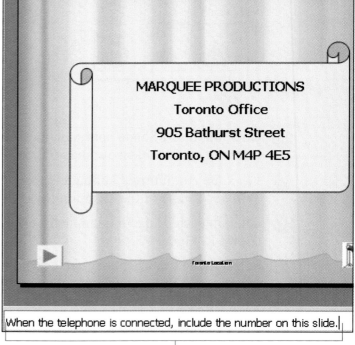

⑨ At the Header and Footer dialog box, click the Notes and Handouts tab, and then click the *Update automatically* option.

⑩ Click in the *Header* text box and then type **Marquee Productions**.

⑪ Click in the *Footer* text box and then type **Toronto Location**.

⑫ Click the Apply to All button.

⑬ Print the presentation as handouts with six slides per page.

⑭ Print Slide 3 as a notes page. To do this, click File and then Print. At the Print dialog box, click the down-pointing arrow at the right side of the *Print what* option and then click *Notes Pages*.

⑮ Click in the *Slides* text box, type 3, and then click OK.

⑯ Save **PPS3-01**.

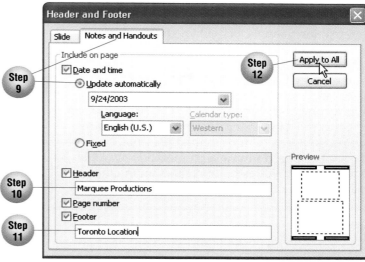

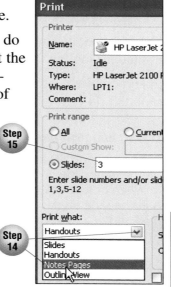

In Addition

Creating Notes while Running a Presentation

You can create and/or display speaker notes while a presentation is running. To do this, run the presentation, and then display the desired slide. Move the mouse to display the Slide Show toolbar. Click the slide icon button, point to Screen, and then click Speaker Notes. This displays the Speaker Notes dialog box shown at the right. View, type, or edit text at this dialog box and then click the Close button.

IN BRIEF

Insert Header/Footer on Slide
1 Click View, Header and Footer.
2 At Header and Footer dialog box with Slide tab selected, choose desired options.
3 Click Apply to All button.

Insert Header/Footer in Notes and Handouts
1 Click View, Header and Footer.
2 At Header and Footer dialog box, click Notes and Handouts tab.
3 Choose desired options.
4 Click the Apply to All button.

3.12 Creating a Hyperlink; Publishing a Presentation to the Web

A presentation can include a hyperlink that will connect to a specific Internet site while the presentation is running. Insert a hyperlink with options at the Insert Hyperlink dialog box. Save a presentation as a Web page and PowerPoint will place a copy of the presentation in HTML format on the Web. You can run a presentation published to the Web in PowerPoint or run the presentation with Internet Explorer. To make a presentation available on the Internet, you need to contact an Internet Service Provider that will allocate space for the Web presentation. If you want to publish a presentation to a company intranet, you must have access to a Web server.

PROJECT: Since one of Marquee Productions' filming sites is the Royal Ontario Museum, you will create a hyperlink to the museum's Web site, publish the Toronto location presentation to the Web, and then preview the presentation in the default browser.

STEPS

1. With **PPS3-01** open, make Slide 6 the active slide.

2. Select *Royal Ontario Museum* and then click the Insert Hyperlink button on the Standard toolbar.

3. At the Insert Hyperlink dialog box, make sure PowerPointS3 on your disk is the active folder, type **www.rom.on.ca** in the *Address* text box, and then press Enter.

    > PowerPoint automatically inserts *http://* at the beginning of the Web address. When a hyperlink is inserted, the text in the slide displays underlined and in a different color.

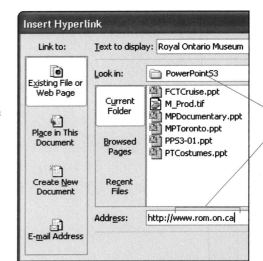

4. Make Slide 1 the active slide and then publish the presentation as a Web page by clicking File and then Save as Web Page.

5. At the Save As dialog box, type **TorontoPresentation** in the *File name* text box and then press Enter.

    > At the Save As dialog box, the *Save as type* option will default to *Single File Web Page* (which saves the presentation with a *.mht* file extension). You can change this default to *Web Page*, which will save the presentation with the file extension *.htm*.

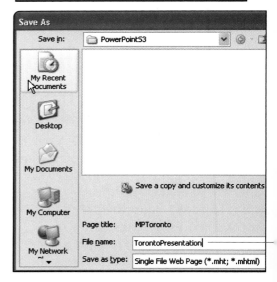

6. Preview the presentation in your Web browser by clicking File and then Web Page Preview.

    > Skip this step if the presentation automatically displays in your browser.

7. Display Slide 6 in the browser by clicking *Filming Locations* in the pane located at the left side of the browser window.

8. Jump to the Royal Ontario Museum Web site by clicking <u>Royal Ontario Museum</u> in the slide.

9. After viewing the museum Web site, close the browser window containing the museum Web site by clicking File and then Close.

In *Addition*

Using Options at the Publish as Web Page Dialog Box

At the Save As dialog box that displays when saving a presentation as a Web page, clicking the Publish button displays the Publish as Web Page dialog box shown at the right. If you do not want to convert all of the slides in the presentation, specify the starting slide number in the *Slide number* text box and the ending slide number in the *through* text box in the *Publish what?* section. You can convert to specific versions of Web browser software with the options in the *Browser support* section. Click the Web Options button to display the Web Options dialog box. This dialog box contains a variety of tabs with options such as customizing slide appearance, specifying the target browsers, and specifying file names and location.

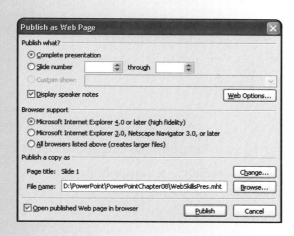

IN BRIEF

Create a Hyperlink
1. Select text in slide.
2. Click Insert Hyperlink button.
3. At Insert Hyperlink dialog box, type Web site address in *Address* text box.
4. Click OK.

Publish a Presentation to the Web
1. Click File, Save as Web Page.
2. At the Save As dialog box, type desired name in the *File name* text box.
3. Click Save button.

FEATURES SUMMARY

Feature	Button	Menu	Keyboard
Autoshape options	AutoShapes ▾		
Change selected object line color	🖌		
Clipboard task pane		Edit, Office Clipboard	Ctrl + C, Ctrl + C
Create a text box	🅰	Insert, Text Box	
Diagram Gallery	🔄	Insert, Diagram or Organization Chart	
Fill selected object	🪣		
Header and Footer dialog box		View, Header and Footer	
Insert a table	▦	Insert, Table	
Insert Hyperlink dialog box	🌐	Insert, Hyperlink	Ctrl + K
Preview presentation in Web browser		File, Web Page Preview	
Replace dialog box		Edit, Replace	Ctrl + H
Rotate selected object		Draw, Rotate or Flip	
Save presentation as a Web page		File, Save as Web Page	
Slide Master View	Shift + ▣	View, Master, Slide Master	
WordArt Gallery	🅰	Insert, Picture, WordArt	

PROCEDURES CHECK

Completion: In the space provided at the right, indicate the correct term, symbol, or command.

1. Display this task pane to collect and paste multiple items.
2. Display the Replace dialog box by clicking this option on the Menu bar and then clicking Replace.
3. To format a slide master and/or title master, change to this view.
4. Click the Insert WordArt button on the Drawing toolbar and this displays.
5. Click this button on the WordArt toolbar to display a pop-up menu containing shapes.
6. Click this button on the Drawing toolbar and a pop-up menu displays with predesigned shape categories.
7. Copy a selected object by holding down this key on the keyboard and then dragging the image to the desired location.

8. Flip a selected object by clicking the Draw button on the Drawing toolbar, pointing to this option, and then clicking the desired direction.

9. These buttons are drawn objects on a slide that have a routine attached to them. _____

10. Click this button in a Content placeholder to display the Diagram Gallery. _____

11. Create footer text that displays at the bottom of all slides with options at this dialog box. _____

12. To create a hyperlink, select text in a slide, and then click this button on the Standard toolbar. _____

13. Click File and then this option to display a presentation in your Web browser. _____

SKILLS REVIEW

Activity 1: USING THE CLIPBOARD TASK PANE AND FINDING AND REPLACING TEXT

1 With PowerPoint open, open the presentation named **MPDocumentary**.
2 Save the presentation with Save As and name it **PPS3-R1**.
3 Make Slide 3 the active slide.
4 Turn on the display of the Clipboard task pane and clear any contents in the task pane.
5 Select and then copy *Chris Greenbaum*.
6 Select and then copy *Camille Matsui*.
7 Select and then copy *Amy Eisman*.
8 Select and then copy *Tricia Becktold*.
9 Make Slide 4 the active slide.
10 Position the insertion point immediately to the right of *On-Site Expenses*, press the Enter key, press the Tab key, and then click *Camille Matsui* in the task pane.
11 Position the insertion point immediately to the right of *Benefits*, press the Enter key, press the Tab key, and then click *Chris Greenbaum* in the task pane.
12 Position the insertion point immediately to the right of *Production*, press the Enter key, press the Tab key, and then click *Amy Eisman*.
13 Press the Enter key and then click *Tricia Becktold*.
14 Clear the contents of the Clipboard task pane and then close the task pane.
15 Make Slide 1 active and then find all occurrences of *Camille Matsui* and replace with *Jennie Almonzo*.
16 Find all occurrences of *Tricia Becktold* and replace with *Nick Jaffe*.
17 Save **PPS3-R1**.

Activity 2: FORMATTING WITH THE SLIDE MASTER

1 With **PPS3-R1** open, make Slide 2 the active slide.
2 Select the title *MARQUEE PRODUCTIONS*, turn on bold, turn on italics, and change the font color to light purple.
3 Select the subtitle *Documentary Project*, turn on bold and turn on italics.
4 Make Slide 3 the active slide.
5 Hold down the Shift key and then click the Normal View button (Slide Master View button).
6 At the slide master, click the text *Click to edit Master title style*, turn on bold, turn on italics, and change the font color to light purple.
7 Click the Normal View button.
8 Save **PPS3-R1**.

Activity 3: INSERTING WORDART

1 With **PPS3-R1** open, make Slide 1 the active slide.
2 Insert the name of the documentary, *Red Skies,* as WordArt in Slide 1. You determine the formatting and shape of the WordArt.
3 Increase the size of the WordArt so it fills most of the slide and position the WordArt so it is centered in the slide.
4 Save **PPS3-R1**.

Activity 4: DRAWING AND CUSTOMIZING AN AUTOSHAPE

1 With **PPS3-R1** open, make Slide 6 the active slide.
2 Create the autoshape arrows shown in Figure P3.5 inserting the text in text boxes in the autoshapes as shown. Add a fill color of your choosing to the autoshapes.
3 Save **PPS3-R1**.

FIGURE P3.5 Activity 4

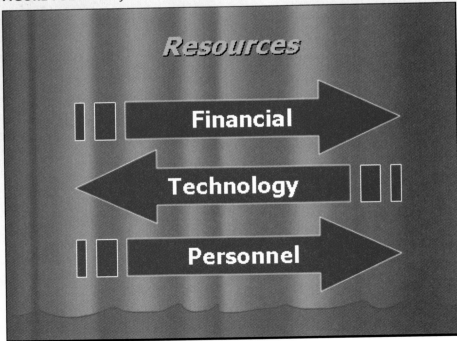

Activity 5: CREATING A TABLE IN A SLIDE

1 With **PPS3-R1** open, make Slide 5 the active slide.
2 Create the table shown in Figure P3.6.
3 Save **PPS3-R1**.

FIGURE P3.6 Activity 5

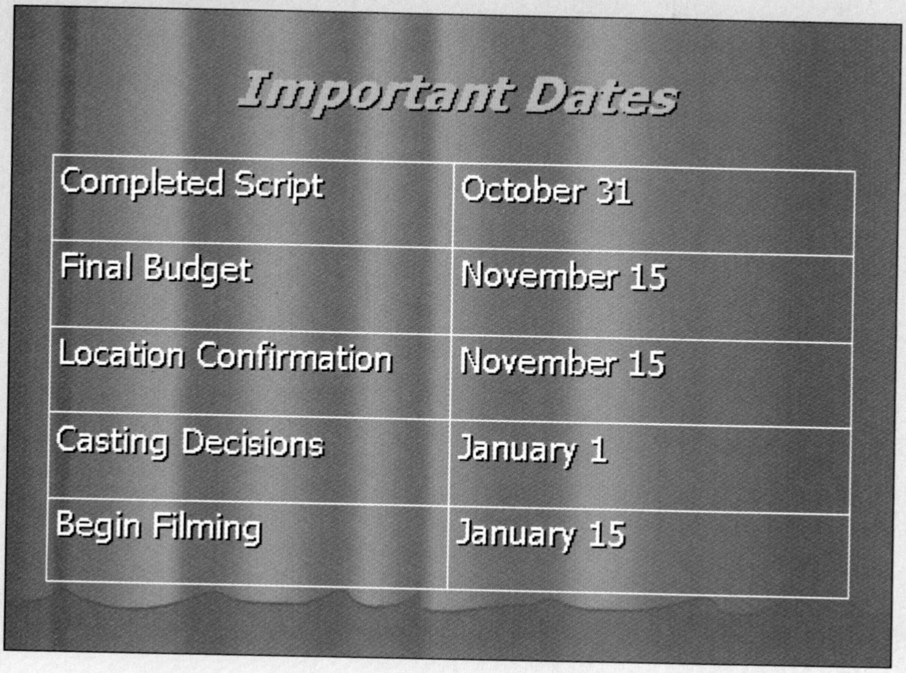

Activity 6: ADDING ACTION BUTTONS

1 With **PPS3-R1** open, make Slide 1 the active slide.
2 Draw an action button named Action Button: Forward or Next in the lower right corner of the slide. Fill the button with a color that complements the slide design.
3 Copy the button and paste it in Slides 2, 3, 4, and 5.
4 Save **PPS3-R1**.

Activity 7: CREATING AN ORGANIZATIONAL CHART AND INSERTING A FOOTER

1 With **PPS3-R1** open, make Slide 3 the active slide.
2 Select and then delete the bulleted text.
3 Display the Slide Layout task pane and then click the Title and Content layout.
4 Create the organizational chart shown in Figure P3.7. (Apply the *Square Shadows* autolayout to the organizational chart.)
5 Display the Header and Footer dialog box. Make sure the *Date and time* check box contains a check mark and then click the *Update automatically* option. (This inserts the current date in the lower left corner of each slide.)
6 Click in the *Footer* text box, type **Red Skies Documentary**, and then click the Apply to All button.
7 Save **PPS3-R1**.
8 Make Slide 1 the active slide and then run the presentation.

9 Print the presentation as handouts with all six slides on one page.
10 Close **PPS3-R1**.

FIGURE P3.7 Activity 7

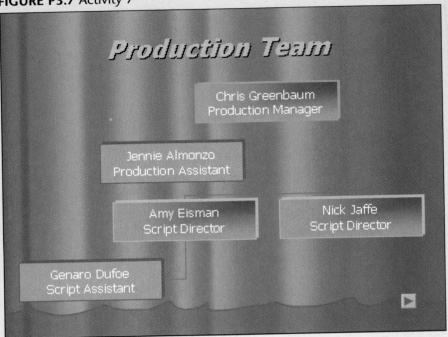

PERFORMANCE PLUS

Assessment 1: FORMATTING A PRESENTATION FOR PERFORMANCE THREADS

1 With PowerPoint open, open the presentation named **PTCostumes**.
2 Save the presentation with Save As and name it **PPS3-P1**.
3 Make Slide 1 the active slide and then insert the name of the company, *Performance Threads,* as WordArt. You determine the formatting, shape, size, and position of the WordArt in the slide.
4 Make Slide 3 the active slide and then display the slide master. Click the text *Click to edit Master title style*, turn on bold, turn on italics, and then change the font color to dark green. Change back to the Normal view.
5 Make Slide 4 the active slide, create an autoshape (you determine the autoshape), and then add an appropriate fill to the autoshape. Copy the autoshape two times (so the slide contains a total of three autoshapes) and then insert in the first autoshape the text *Research.* Insert in the second autoshape the text *Design* and insert in the third autoshape the text *Production.*
6 Make Slide 5 the active slide and then insert the following information in a table:

Designer	Date
Scott Bercini	June 21
Terri Cantrell	June 13
Paul Gottlieb	June 28
Tae Jeong	June 13
Rosa Levens	June 28

7   Display Slide 2 and then apply an animation scheme of your choosing to all slides in the presentation. (The animation scheme will not apply to Slide 1 because that slide contains only WordArt.)
8   Insert the footer *Performance Threads* on each slide.
9   Save **PPS3-P1**.
10   Run the presentation.
11   Print the presentation handouts with all six slides on one page.
12   Close **PPS3-P1**.

Assessment 2: FORMATTING A PRESENTATION FOR FIRST CHOICE TRAVEL

1   With PowerPoint open, open the presentation named **FCTCruise**.
2   Save the presentation with Save As and name it **PPS3-P2**.
3   Apply a slide design template of your choosing.
4   Make Slide 2 the active slide and then insert *Fine Arts Cruise* as WordArt. You determine the formatting, shape, size, and position of the WordArt in the slide.
5   Make Slide 7 the active slide and then create an autoshape of a sun and fill the shape with yellow fill. Insert inside the shape the text *Fun in the Sun!*
6   Make Slide 6 the active slide and then insert the following information in a table:

Artist	Day
Pablo Jimenez	May 15
Jocelyn Forrester	May 16
Caesar Benigni	May 18
Everett Shinn	May 19
Alberta Teune	May 21

7   Add an animation scheme of your choosing to all slides in the presentation. (The animation scheme will not apply to Slide 2 because that slide contains only WordArt.)
8   Insert the footer *Fine Arts Cruise* on each slide.
9   Save **PPS3-P2**.
10   Run the presentation.
11   Print the presentation as handouts with nine slides per page.
12   Close **PPS3-P2**.

Assessment 3: LEARNING ABOUT THE TABLES AND BORDERS TOOLBAR

1   Open **PPS3-R1** and then make Slide 5 the active slide.
2   Use the Help feature to learn how to change a table border.
3   After reading the information on changing a table border, display the Tables and Borders toolbar by clicking the Tables and Borders button on the Standard toolbar.
4   Hover the mouse pointer over each button on the toolbar to display the button name.
5   Make the following changes to the table:
   • Change the border width to *4½ pt*, make sure the Draw Table button is active, and then draw over the four outside lines of the table. (This changes the border lines to a 4½-point border line.)

- Select all of the cells in the table and then center the text vertically in each cell.
- With the cells still selected add a fill color of your choosing to the table. (Make sure the text in the table is readable.)

6 Save **PPS3-R1**.
7 Print only Slide 5 of the presentation.
8 Close **PPS3-R1**.

Assessment 4: LEARNING ABOUT SELF-RUNNING PRESENTATION

1 Open **PPS3-R1**.
2 Save the presentation with Save As and name it **PPS3-P3**.
3 Use the Help feature to learn about *self-running presentations*.
4 After learning how to prepare a self-running presentation, set up **PPS3-P3** to run automatically with each slide advancing after 4 seconds.
5 Make Slide 1 the active slide and then run the presentation. (If you have the presentation set up to run on a continuous loop, press the Esc key to end the presentation.)
6 Save and then close **PPS3-P3**.

Assessment 5: LOCATING INFORMATION AND PREPARING A PRESENTATION FOR PERFORMANCE THREADS

1 You are Sophie Yong, design manager for Performance Threads. You are responsible for preparing a presentation on resources for Performance Threads employees. You need to find Internet sites where employees can do costume research (such as museum sites), sites on costume design, and sites on costume supplies. Locate at least two sites in each category (research, design, supplies).

2 Using PowerPoint, create a presentation on the costume resources you have located on the Internet. You determine how to arrange the information and what information to include in the presentation. Create a hyperlink to the Internet sites you mention in the slides.

3 Apply an animation scheme to all slides in the presentation.
4 Save the presentation and name it **PPS3-P4**.
5 Run the presentation.
6 Print the presentation as handouts with six slides per page.
7 Save and then close **PPS3-P4**.

POWERPOINT
SECTION 4
Customizing and Managing Presentations

You can apply more than one slide design template to slides in a presentation and then display multiple slide-title master pairs to customize slides. PowerPoint contains additional features for customizing a presentation including creating a custom show, inserting and formatting a table, and adding sound and video to slides. If you are part of a workgroup in a company, you may want to share presentation files with coworkers. PowerPoint contains features you can use to send multiple copies of a presentation to others for review, merge the reviewed presentation with the original, and then accept or reject the suggested changes. Other options for managing a presentation include setting and rehearsing times for a presentation, creating a folder, creating and saving a customized design template, saving a presentation in Outline/RTF format, using the Package for CD feature, and publishing a presentation to the Web. In this section, you will learn the skills and complete the projects described here.

Note: Before beginning this section, delete the PowerPointS3 folder on your disk. Next, copy to your disk the PowerPointS4 subfolder from the CD that accompanies this textbook and then make PowerPointS4 the active folder.

Skills

- Apply more than one design template to a presentation
- Manage multiple slide masters
- Create and edit a custom show
- Customize and format a table
- Add sound and video to slides in a presentation
- Send a presentation for review
- Edit a presentation sent for review
- Accept and/or reject changes made by reviewers
- Set and rehearse timings for a presentation
- Insert and print comments
- Save a presentation in Outline/RTF format
- Use the Package for CD feature
- Create a folder
- Create and save a customized design template
- Publish a presentation to the Web

Projects

Open and customize a documentary project presentation; send the presentation to two other employees for review; use the Package for CD feature; publish the presentation as a Web page.

Open and customize a Theatre Arts Department presentation; copy slides for another presentation into the department presentation; send the presentation to two other employees for review.

Open and customize a presentation on vacation packages; use the Slide Finder feature to insert a slide from another presentation; download a sound clip from the Microsoft Office Online Web site.

Each design template applies specific formatting to slides and more than one design template can be applied to slides in a presentation. To do this, select the specific slides and then choose the desired design template. The design template is applied only to the selected slides. If you apply more than one design template to a presentation and you change to Slide Master view, slide-title master pairs display as slide miniatures at the left side of the window and a Slide Master View toolbar displays. Click the desired slide master miniature and then

apply specific formatting to the slide master in the Slide pane. Switch between the slide-title master pairs by clicking the desired miniature.

PROJECT: You are Chris Greenbaum, production manager for Marquee Productions. You are preparing for a production meeting and are reviewing a presentation you have prepared. You decide to add some visual interest to the presentation by applying a different design to slides particular to the Toronto project.

STEPS

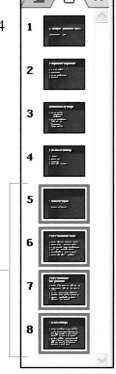

1. Open **MPProject**. Save the presentation into the PowerPointS4 folder on your disk and name the presentation **PPS4-01**.

2. Delete Slide 4 (contains the title *Script Schedule*).

3. Insert a new slide between the existing Slides 4 and 5 and choose the Title Slide layout in the Slide Layout task pane.

4. At the new Slide 5, type Toronto Project as the slide title and type Production Information as the subtitle.

5. Make sure the Normal view is selected and the Slides tab is selected in the Outline/Slides pane.

6. With Slide 5 selected in the Outline/Slides pane (dark border displays around the slide), hold down the Shift key, click Slide 8, and then release the Shift key.

   > Holding down the Shift key while clicking Slide 8 causes Slides 5, 6, 7, and 8 to be selected (each slide surrounded by a dark border).

   Step 6

7. Click the Slide Design button on the Formatting toolbar and then click the Pixel slide design in the *Apply a design template* section of the Slide Design task pane.

8. Display the slide-title master pairs by holding down the Shift key and then clicking the Normal View button on the View toolbar.

   > The slide-title master pairs display at the left side of the window. Position the mouse pointer on a slide-title miniature and the name of the miniature displays in a yellow box next to the miniature. Switch between the slide-title master pairs by clicking the desired miniature.

   Step 7

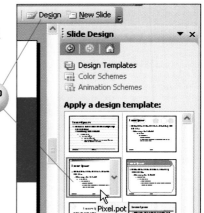

9. Click the Shimmer Slide Master slide miniature located at the left side of the window (the top slide miniature).

10. Click anywhere in the text *Click to edit Master title style*.

11. Click the down-pointing arrow at the right side of the Font Color button on the Formatting toolbar and then click the second color from the right (light yellow).

Step 9

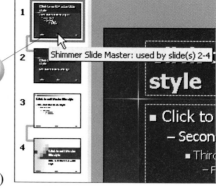

12. Click in the text *<footer>* that displays in the *Footer Area* located at the middle along the bottom of the slide master (this selects *<footer>*) and then type Documentary Project.

> This inserts the text *Documentary Project* as a footer that displays on all slides (except the first slide) containing the Shimmer slide design.

13. Click the Pixel Slide Master miniature located at the left side of the window (the third slide miniature from the top).

14. Click in the text *<footer>* that displays in the *Footer Area* located at the middle along the bottom of the slide master (this selects *<footer>*) and then type Toronto Project.

Step 13

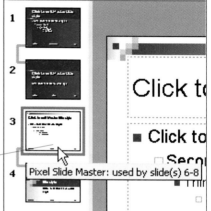

15. Click the Normal View button, make Slide 1 the active slide, and then run the **PPS4-01** presentation.

16. Save **PPS4-01**.

In Addition

Adding Animated GIFs

GIF files are graphic files saved in *Graphics Interchange Format*, which is a type of file format commonly used for graphics on Web pages. Animated GIFs are GIF files that have been programmed to display a series of images one on top of another that give the illusion of motion. If you surf the Internet you will see most Web sites have incorporated one or more animated GIFs on their pages to add interest and variety to their site. Animated GIFs do not display the motion until you display the slide in a slide show. To insert an animated GIF that you have stored as a file on disk, click the Insert Picture button on the Drawing toolbar or click Insert, point to Picture, and then click From File. Navigate to the folder containing the GIF file and then double-click the file name. Once the GIF image has been placed in the slide it can be resized and moved using the sizing handles.

4.2 Creating and Editing a Custom Show

You can select specific slides within a presentation to create a presentation within a presentation. This might be useful in situations where you want to show only a select number of slides to a particular audience. To create a custom show, open the presentation, click Slide Show, and then click Custom Shows. At the Custom Shows dialog box, click the New button and the Define Custom Show dialog box opens containing options to specify the custom show.

PROJECT: You are going to present the documentary project to a variety of groups and need to create a custom slide show that contains only the Toronto project slides.

STEPS

1. With **PPS4-01** open, create a custom show that contains Slides 5 through 8. To begin, click Slide Show and then Custom Shows.

2. At the Custom Shows dialog box, click the New button.

3. At the Define Custom Show dialog box, type **Toronto Project** in the *Slide show name* text box.

4. Click Slide 5 in the *Slides in presentation* list box, hold down the Shift key, and then click Slide 8.

5. Click the Add button and then click OK.

6. Click the Close button to close the Custom Shows dialog box.

7. Run the custom show by clicking Slide Show and then Custom Shows.

8. At the Custom Shows dialog box, make sure *Toronto Project* displays in the *Custom shows* list box and then click the Show button.

   A custom show is saved with the presentation.

9. Navigate through the custom show slides.

10. Print the custom show. To begin, click File and then Print.

11. At the Print dialog box, click the *Custom Show* option in the *Print range* section and make sure *Toronto Project* displays in the list box.

12. Change the *Print what* option to *Handouts*, make sure the *Slides per page* option is set at 6, and then click OK.

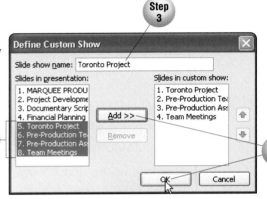

Step 3

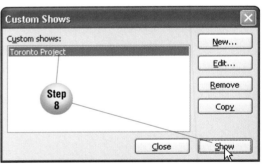

Step 4

Step 8

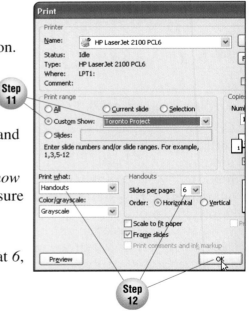

Step 11

Step 12

13) You decide to edit the Toronto Project custom show. To begin, click Slide Show and then Custom Shows.

14) At the Custom Shows dialog box, make sure *Toronto Project* is selected in the list box and then click the Edit button.

15) At the Define Custom Show dialog box, click Slide 4 in the *Slides in custom show* list box and then click the up arrow button two times.

> This moves Slide 4 in the custom show before Slide 2.

16) Click OK to close the Define Custom Show dialog box.

17) At the Custom Shows dialog box, click the Show button.

18) Navigate through the custom show slides.

19) Save **PPS4-01**.

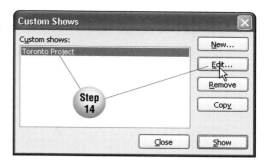

In Addition

Creating Multiple Custom Shows

You can create multiple custom shows in a presentation. Each custom show displays in the *Custom shows* list box at the Custom Shows dialog box. For example, if the PPS4-01 presentation contained two custom shows—*Toronto Project* and *Documentary Project*—the Custom Shows dialog box would display as shown at the right. To run a specific custom show, click the custom show name in the *Custom shows* list box and then click the Show button. To edit a custom show, click the desired custom show in the list box and then click the Edit button.

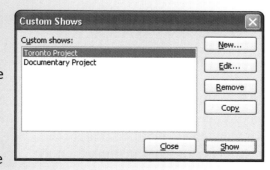

IN BRIEF

Create a Custom Show
1 Click Slide Show, Custom Shows.
2 Click New button.
3 Type custom show name in *Slide show name* text box.
4 Select desired slides in *Slides in presentation* list box.
5 Click Add button.
6 Click OK.
7 Click Close button.

Edit a Custom Show
1 Click Slide Show, Custom Shows.
2 Select desired custom show.
3 Click Edit button.
4 Make desired changes.
5 Click OK.
6 Click Close button.

4.3 Customizing and Formatting a Table

You can resize, move, format, and customize a table created in a PowerPoint slide. Click the table to select it and then use the sizing handles that display around the table to increase or decrease the size. To move the table, point to the border of the table until the mouse pointer displays with a four-headed arrow attached, and then drag the table to the desired position. Use buttons on the Tables and Borders toolbar to format a table. For example, you can insert and/or delete rows and columns from the table. You can also use buttons on the toolbar to change the border style, width, and color and add fill color or effects to the table. The Tables and Borders toolbar should appear automatically when you click inside a cell.

PROJECT: After reviewing the presentation, you have decided to include a slide containing a table listing completion dates.

S T E P S

1 With **PPS4-01** open, make sure the Slides tab is selected in the Outline/Slides pane and then click immediately below the last slide.

This causes a thin horizontal line to blink below Slide 8 in the Outline/Slides pane.

PROBLEM **?**

If Slide 8 is not visible in the Outline/Slides pane, you may need to scroll down the pane.

FIGURE P4.1 Slide 9

Completion Dates

Researching	September 30
Documenting	October 15
Writing	January 31
Scouting	February 28
Casting	March 31

Toronto Project

2 Click the New Slide button on the Formatting toolbar and then click the Title and Content slide layout in the Slide Layout task pane. Click the text *Click to add title* and then type Completion Dates.

3 Click the Insert Table button in the Content placeholder. At the Insert Table dialog box, press the Tab key, type 5, and then click OK.

This inserts a table with two columns and five rows in the slide.

4 Type the text in the slide as shown in Figure P4.1.

5 Turn on the display of the horizontal and vertical rulers by clicking View and then Ruler.

This displays a horizontal ruler above the slide and a vertical ruler at the left side of the slide.

6 Click anywhere in the first cell (contains the text *Researching*), position the mouse pointer on the middle gridline until the pointer turns into a double vertical bar with a left- and right-pointing arrow attached, and then drag to the left to approximately the 2.5-inch mark on the horizontal ruler.

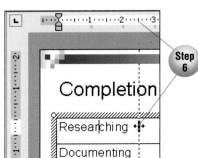

Step 6

7. Position the mouse pointer on the gridline at the right side of the table until the pointer turns into a double vertical bar with a left- and right-pointing arrow and then drag to the left to approximately the 5.5-inch mark on the horizontal ruler.

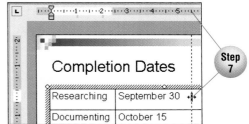

8. Position the arrow pointer along the border of the table until the pointer displays with a four-headed arrow attached, and then drag the table until it displays centered in the middle of the slide.

9. Turn off the display of the rulers by clicking View and then Ruler. If the Tables and Borders toolbar is not displayed, turn it on by clicking the Tables and Borders button [ ] on the Standard toolbar.

10. Select all cells in the table by clicking in any cell in the table, clicking Edit, and then clicking Select All.

11. Click the down-pointing arrow on the Border Width button on the Tables and Borders toolbar and then click *4½ pt* at the drop-down list.

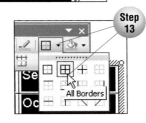

12. Click the Border Color button on the Tables and Borders toolbar and then click the sixth color (medium blue-gray) from the left.

13. Click the down-pointing arrow at the right of the Outside Borders button on the Tables and Borders toolbar and then click the All Borders button (second button from the left in the top row).

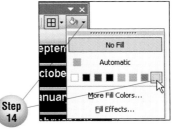

14. Click the down-pointing arrow to the right of the Fill Color button on the Tables and Borders toolbar and then click the last color from the left (light blue-gray).

15. Click outside the table to deselect it. Your slide should look like the slide shown in Figure P4.2.

16. Save **PPS4-01**.

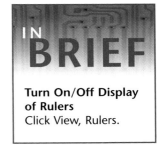

FIGURE P4.2 Modified Table in Slide 9

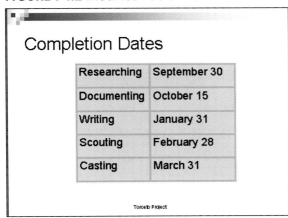

Completion Dates

Researching	September 30
Documenting	October 15
Writing	January 31
Scouting	February 28
Casting	March 31

Toronto Project

IN BRIEF

Turn On/Off Display of Rulers
Click View, Rulers.

4.4 Adding Sound and Video

Adding sound and/or video effects to a presentation will turn a slide show into a true multimedia experience for your audience. Including a variety of elements in a presentation will stimulate interest in your presentation and keep the audience motivated. To add a sound to your presentation, choose Insert, point to Movies and Sounds, and then click Sound from Clip Organizer or click Sound from File. Clicking Sound from Clip Organizer will display sound files in the Clip Art task pane. Click the desired sound to insert it in the active slide. If the sound you want to incorporate into your presentation is not part of the gallery but

stored in a file on disk, click Sound from File. This displays the Insert Sound dialog box where you can navigate to the file's location and then double-click the sound to insert it in the active slide. Adding a video clip is a similar process to adding sound. Click Insert, point to Movies and Sounds, and then click either Movie from Clip Organizer or Movie from File.

PROJECT: To add interest to the presentation, you decide to insert a new slide with a video clip and a sound clip.

STEPS

① With **PPS4-01** open, make sure the Slides tab is selected in the Outline/Slides pane and then click below the last slide in the presentation (Slide 9). You may need to scroll down the Outline/Slides pane to display the last slide.

② Click the New Slide button on the Formatting toolbar and then click the Title Only slide layout in the Slide Layout task pane.

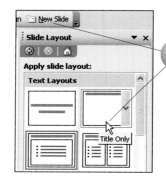

③ Click the text *Click to add title* and then type **Project Launch Date – June 1!**

④ Insert a video clip by clicking Insert, pointing to Movies and Sounds, and then clicking Movie from File.

⑤ At the Insert Movie dialog box, navigate to the SoundandVideo folder on the CD that accompanies this textbook, and then double-click the file named ***Launch.mpeg***.

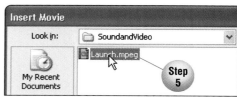

PROBLEM?
If the Launch.mpeg file does not display, make sure you navigated to the correct file folder on the CD.

⑥ At the message asking how you want the movie to start in the slide show, click the When Clicked button.

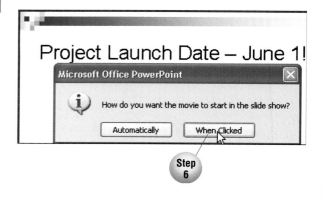

(7) Resize and position the movie on the slide as shown in Figure P4.3.

(8) Add a sound clip by clicking Insert, pointing to Movies and Sounds, and then clicking Sound from File.

(9) At the Insert Sound dialog box, navigate to the SoundandVideo folder on the CD that accompanies this textbook and then double-click the file named **Greatfire.mid**.

(10) At the message asking how you want the sound to start in the slide show, click the Automatically button.

(11) Resize and position the sound icon as shown in Figure P4.3.

(12) Make Slide 1 the active slide and then run the presentation. When the last slide (Slide 10) displays, as soon as you hear the music, click the video image to begin the video. After viewing the video and listening to the music for about 30 seconds, end the slide show.

(13) Print only Slide 10.

(14) Delete Slide 10 (this slide requires quite a bit of additional disk space).

(15) Save **PPS4-01**.

FIGURE P4.3 Slide 10

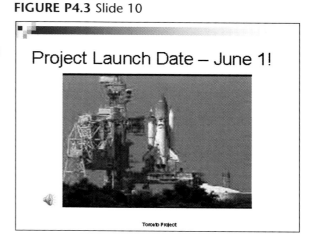

In Addition

Looping Sound and Video Continuously

You can set sounds and videos to loop continuously. The sound and/or video will continue playing over and over again until the slide show is ended. When the speaker has finished the presentation, he or she might choose to have the sound and video play for a few minutes until the audience has left the room. To change the video in Slide 10 to loop continuously you would right-click the video and then click Edit Movie Object at the shortcut menu. At the Movie Options dialog box, you would click *Loop until stopped* to insert a check mark, and then click OK. To change the sound in Slide 10 to loop continuously, you would right-click the sound icon and then click Edit Sound Object at the shortcut menu. At the Sound Options dialog box, you would click *Loop until stopped*, and then click OK.

IN BRIEF

Insert Video Clip
1 Click Insert, Movies and Sounds, Movie from File.
2 Navigate to desired folder.
3 Double-click desired video clip file.

Insert Sound Clip
1 Click Insert, Movies and Sounds, Sound from File.
2 Navigate to desired folder.
3 Double-click desired sound clip file.

4.5 Sending a Presentation for Review; Editing a Presentation Sent for Review

Some employees in a company may be part of a *workgroup*, which is a networked collection of computers sharing files, printers, and other resources. If you are part of a workgroup, you may want to send a copy of a PowerPoint presentation to other members of the workgroup for review. To do this, you would set up a review cycle for reviewing the presentation. If you are using Microsoft Outlook to send the presentation, click File, point to Send To, and then click Mail Recipient (for Review). Specify to whom you want the presentation sent and then click the Send button. If you are using an e-mail program other than Outlook, you would complete the steps similar to those on this page. When a presentation is saved as a presentation for review, PowerPoint inserts a link

in the copy of the presentation back to the original presentation. When you open the copy of the presentation, a message displays asking if you want to merge changes to the copy of the presentation back into the original presentation. Click Yes if you want changes you make to the copy of the presentation to apply to the original. Click No if you do not want the original presentation to reflect the changes you make to the copy. Make the desired changes to the presentation and then save it in the normal manner.

PROJECT: You need to send the presentation for review by Amy Eisman, script developer, and Josh Hart, locations director. You want their feedback on the presentation before the production meeting.

STEPS

1. With **PPS4-01** open, save the presentation for review by Amy Eisman. To do this, click File and then Save As.

2. At the Save As dialog box, type **PresentationEditedbyAE** in the *File name* text box.

   Make sure PowerPointS4 on your disk is the active folder.

3. Click the down-pointing arrow at the right of the *Save as type* option box, click *Presentation for Review* in the drop-down list, and then click the Save button.

PROBLEM **?**

If the *Presentation for Review* option is not visible, you may need to scroll down the list.

Step 3

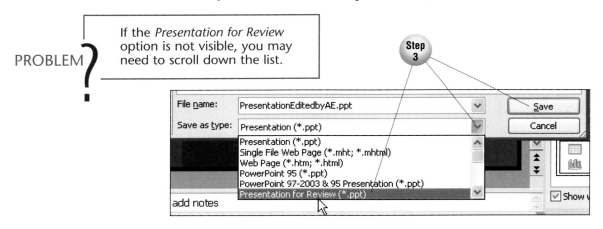

4. Save the presentation for review by Josh Hart by completing Steps 2 and 3 except save the presentation with the name **PresentationEditedbyJH**.

5. Close **PPS4-01**.

6. At the blank PowerPoint screen, change the user name and initials by clicking Tools and then Options.

7 At the Options dialog box, click the General tab. (Make a note of the current name and initials. You will reenter this information later in this exercise.)

8 Select the name in the *Name* text box and then type Amy Eisman. Select the initials in the *Initials* text box and then type AE. Click OK to close the dialog box.

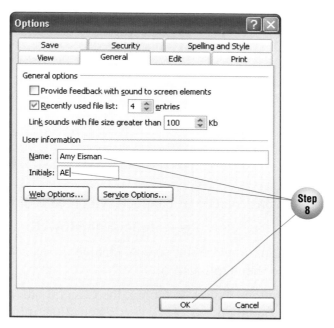

9 Open the presentation named **PresentationEditedbyAE** in the PowerPointS4 folder on your disk. At the message asking if you want to merge changes in **PresentationEditedbyAE** back into **PPS4-01**, click No.

10 Make Slide 1 the active slide, click anywhere in the title *MARQUEE PRODUCTIONS,* and then click the Center button on the Formatting toolbar.

11 Click anywhere in the subtitle *Documentary Project* and then click the Center button on the Formatting toolbar.

12 Make Slide 2 the active slide, click immediately right of the text *Competition*, press the Enter key, and then type Research Documentation.

(continued)

13. Make Slide 4 the active slide, click immediately right of the text *Budgeting*, press the Enter key, and then type Location Costs.

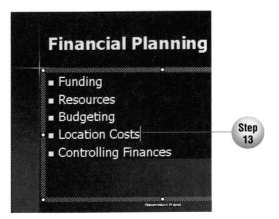

14. Print the presentation as handouts with nine slides per page.

15. Save and then close **PresentationEditedbyAE**.

16. At the blank PowerPoint screen, change the user name and initials by clicking Tools and then Options.

17. At the Options dialog box, click the General tab, select the name in the *Name* text box, and then type Josh Hart. Select the initials in the *Initials* text box, type JH, and then click OK.

    Changes made by other reviewers display in different colors.

18. Open **PresentationEditedbyJH** located in the PowerPointS4 folder on your disk. At the message asking if you want to merge changes in **PresentationEditedbyJH** back into **PPS4-01**, click No.

19. Make Slide 1 the active slide, select the text *Documentary Project*, and then type Project Phases.

    When you begin typing *Project Phases*, the selected text is automatically deleted.

20. Make Slide 3 the active slide, select the names *Dana Benitez* and *Karl Edwins*, and then click once on the Decrease Indent button on the Formatting toolbar.

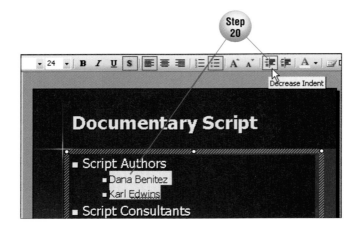

21 Make Slide 7 the active slide, click immediately left of the *D* in *Dana* (located after *Writing:*), type **Amy Eisman,** and then press the spacebar once.

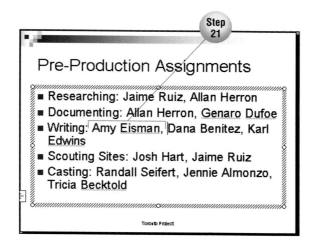

22 Print the presentation as handouts with nine slides per page.

23 Save and then close **PresentationEditedbyJH**.

24 Change the name and initials in the *User* information back to the original information by clicking Tools and then Options. At the Options dialog box with the General tab selected, type the original name in the *Name* text box. Press the Tab key and then type the original initials in the *Initials* text box. Click OK to close the dialog box.

In Addition

Setting Up a Review Cycle

If you are part of a workgroup, you may want to send a copy of a PowerPoint presentation to other members of the workgroup for review. To do this, you would set up a review cycle for reviewing the presentation. This cycle consists of the following general steps:

1. Send a separate copy of the presentation to each person who is to review the presentation using Microsoft Outlook or using other e-mail programs.
2. Each reviewer makes changes to his or her own copy of the presentation.
3. Each reviewer sends his or her own edited presentation back to you.
4. You compare each edited presentation with the original presentation and determine if you want to accept or reject changes.

Send Presentation for Review
1. Open presentation.
2. Click File, Save As.
3. Type new name for presentation.
4. Change *Save as type* option to *Presentation for Review*.
5. Click Save button.

4.6 Accepting/Rejecting Changes from Reviewers

If you used an e-mail program other than Outlook to distribute presentations for review, use PowerPoint's Compare and Merge Presentations feature to combine changes. To use this feature, open the original presentation, click Tools, and then click Compare and Merge Presentations. At the Choose Files to Merge with Current Presentation dialog box, click to select all reviewed presentations, and then click the Merge button. This displays the original presentation with change markers identifying changes made by each reviewer. The Revisions pane also displays at the right side of the PowerPoint screen along with the Reviewing toolbar, which displays immediately below the Formatting toolbar. Changes made by each reviewer display in a change marker in the original presentation. Change markers for each reviewer display in a different color. To accept a change to a slide, click the change marker, and then click the check box located in the change marker box to insert a check mark.

PROJECT: You need to review the revisions suggested by Amy and Josh and decide whether or not to accept the revision.

S T E P S

1. Open **PPS4-01**.

2. Compare this presentation with the two edited presentations by clicking Tools and then Compare and Merge Presentations.

3. At the Choose Files to Merge with Current Presentation dialog box, make sure the PowerPointS4 folder on your disk is the active folder, click ***PresentationEditedbyAE***, hold down the Ctrl key, and then click ***PresentationEditedbyJH***. (This selects both presentations.)

4. Click the Merge button located in the lower right corner of the dialog box.

   This displays Slide 1 in the Slide pane, displays the Reviewing toolbar below the Formatting toolbar, and also displays the Revisions pane at the right side of the screen. Notice the two change markers (in two different colors) that display in Slide 1.

5. Click the change marker located at the far right side of the Slide 1 title. (This displays a description of the change followed by the reviewer's name *Amy Eisman*.) You do not want to make this change, so click in the slide outside the change description box.

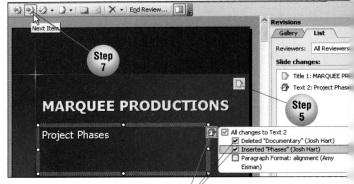

6. Click the change marker located at the right side of the Slide 1 subtitle. Accept the changes made by Josh Hart by clicking in each of the check boxes preceding changes made by Josh Hart.

7. Click the Next Item button on the Reviewing toolbar to display the next change (located on Slide 2).

⑧ Accept the change to Slide 2 by clicking the check box preceding the description of the change (this inserts a check mark and accepts the change).

⑨ Click the Next Item button on the Reviewing toolbar and then accept the change to Slide 3 by clicking the check box preceding *All changes to Text 2*.

⑩ Click the Next Item button. (This displays Slide 4.) Click the Next Item button to ignore the change and display the next change.

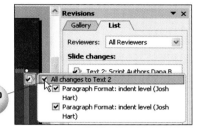

PROBLEM **?**

If you want to return to a previous change, click the Previous Item button on the Reviewing toolbar.

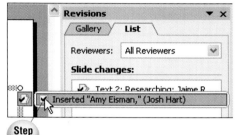

⑪ When Slide 7 displays, click the check box preceding the change.

⑫ Click the Next Item button. At the message asking if you want to continue at the beginning of the presentation, click the Cancel button.

⑬ Save the presentation with Save As and name it **MergedPPS4-01**.

⑭ Click the Show/Hide Markup button on the Reviewing toolbar (first button from the left), turn off the display of the Reviewing toolbar, and then turn off the display of the Revisions pane.

⑮ Print the presentation as handouts with nine slides per page.

In Addition

Accepting All Changes

To accept all changes made to a slide, click the down-pointing arrow at the right side of the Apply button on the Reviewing toolbar, and then click *Apply All Changes to the Current Slide* at the drop-down list. To accept all changes made by one reviewer on one slide, click the Gallery tab at the Revisions pane. Click the check box that displays for the specific reviewer above the slide miniature. You can also point to a slide miniature of the reviewer whose changes you want to accept, click the down-pointing arrow that displays at the right side of the miniature, and then click Apply Changes By This Reviewer at the drop-down list. To accept all changes made to the presentation, click the down-pointing arrow at the right side of the Apply button on the Reviewing toolbar, and then click *Apply All Changes to the Presentation*.

IN BRIEF

Compare Presentations
1 Open original presentation.
2 Click Tools, Compare and Merge Presentations.
3 Hold down Ctrl key and then click edited presentation file names.
4 Click Merge button.

4.7 Setting and Rehearsing Timings for a Presentation

If you want a presentation to run automatically and each slide to display a specific number of seconds, use the Rehearse Timings feature to help set the times for slides as you practice delivering the slide show. To set times for slides, click Slide Show and then click Rehearse Timings. The first slide displays in Slide Show view and the Rehearsal toolbar displays on the slide. Use buttons on this toolbar to specify times for each slide. Use options at the Set Up Show dialog box to control the slide show. Display this dialog box by clicking Slide Show and then Set Up Show. Use options in the *Show type* section to specify the type of slide show you want to display. If you want the presentation to be totally automatic and run continuously until you end the show, click the *Loop continuously until 'Esc'* check box to insert a check mark. In the *Advance slides* section, the *Using timings, if present* option should be selected by default. Select *Manually* if you want to advance the slides using the mouse during the slide show instead of the slides advancing using your preset times.

PROJECT: You decide to experiment with the Rehearse Timings feature to determine if you want to set up the presentation to run automatically while you are speaking at the meeting.

STEPS

① With **MergedPPS4-01** open, click Slide Show and then Rehearse Timings.

> The first slide displays in Slide Show view and the Rehearsal toolbar displays. Refer to Figure P4.4 for the names of the Rehearsal toolbar buttons.

② Wait until the time displayed for the current slide reaches 4 seconds and then click the Next button.

> If you miss the time, click the Repeat button to reset the clock back to zero for the current slide.

FIGURE P4.4 Rehearsal Toolbar Buttons

③ Set the following times for the remaining slides:

Slide 2	=	7 seconds
Slide 3	=	6 seconds
Slide 4	=	5 seconds
Slide 5	=	4 seconds
Slide 6	=	6 seconds
Slide 7	=	8 seconds
Slide 8	=	8 seconds
Slide 9	=	6 seconds

④ After the last slide has displayed, click Yes at the message asking if you want the new slide timings.

(5) Set up the slide show to run continuously by clicking Slide Show and then Set Up Show.

(6) At the Set Up Show dialog box, click the *Loop continuously until 'Esc'* check box.

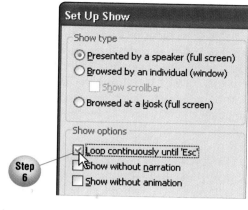

(7) Click OK to close the dialog box.

(8) Make Slide 1 the active slide and then click the Slide Show button on the View toolbar. The slide show will start and run continuously. Watch the presentation until it has started for the second time and then end the show by pressing the Esc key.

(9) After viewing the presentation with automatic timings, you decide you want to advance the slides manually. To make this change, click Slide Show and then click Set Up Show. At the Set Up Show dialog box, click the *Manually* option in the *Advance slides* section, click the *Loop continuously until 'Esc'* option to remove the check mark, and then click OK.

(10) Save **MergedPPS4-01**.

In Addition

Setting Times Manually

The time a slide remains on the screen during a slide show can be manually set using the *Automatically after* option at the Slide Transition task pane. Display this task pane by clicking Slide Show and then Slide Transition. At the Slide Transition task pane, type the number of seconds in the seconds text box and the time is applied to the current slide. If you want the time to apply to all slides in the presentation, click the Apply to All Slides button.

IN BRIEF

Set and Rehearse Timings
1 Click Slide Show, Rehearse Timings.
2 When desired time displays, click Next button.
3 Continue until times are set for each slide in presentation.
4 Click Yes at message asking if you want to record new timings.

Set Up Show to Run Continuously
1 Click Slide Show, Set Up Show.
2 Click *Loop continuously until 'Esc'* check box.
3 Click OK.

4.8 Inserting and Printing Comments

If you are sending out a presentation for review and want to ask reviewers specific questions or provide information about slides in a presentation, insert a comment. To insert a comment, display the desired slide and then position the insertion point where you want the comment to appear. Click Insert on the Menu bar and then click Comment. At the comment box that displays, type the desired comment and then click outside the comment box. A small box displays at the right side of the slide aligned horizontally with the position where the comment was inserted. The user's initials display in the box followed by a number. Comments by individual users are numbered sequentially beginning with 1. To delete a comment from a slide, right-click the box containing the initials and then click Delete at the shortcut menu. To print comments, display the Print dialog box, choose how you want slides printed with the *Print what* option, and then insert a check mark in the *Print comments and ink markup* check box. Comments print on a separate page after the presentation is printed.

PROJECT: You have asked Ron Sugiyama, vice president at Marquee Productions, to view the project presentation and make comments.

STEPS

1. With **MergedPPS4-01** open, click Tools and then Options. At the Options dialog box with the General tab selected, change the *Name* to *Ron Sugiyama* and the *Initials* to *RS*. Click OK to close the dialog box.

2. Click the Normal View button on the View toolbar.

3. Make Slide 3 the active slide and then click immediately right of *Script Authors*.

4. Insert a comment by clicking Insert on the Menu bar and then clicking Comment.

    This inserts a comment box in the slide in a color different than the colors used for Amy Eisman and Josh Hart.

5. Type **Please include Amy Eisman's name in this list. She has been assigned as the lead author.**

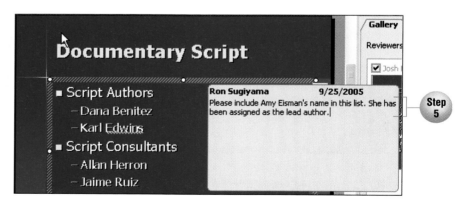

6. Click in the slide outside the comment box.

7. Make Slide 8 the active slide and then click immediately right of the name *Dana Benitez* (displays after *Script Writing:*).

8. Click Insert and then Comment.

⑨ Type **Amy Eisman will head the script writing team.** in the comment box.

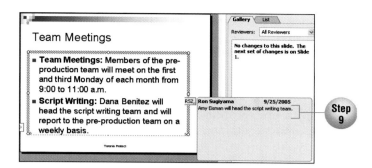

Step 9

⑩ Click in the slide outside the comment box.

⑪ Print the presentation and comments by clicking File and then Print.

⑫ At the Print dialog box, click the down-pointing arrow at the right side of *Print what* and then click *Handouts*. Click the down-pointing arrow at the right of the *Slides per page* option and then click *9* at the drop-down list.

⑬ Make sure the *Print comments and ink markup* check box contains a check mark and then click OK.

⑭ Run the presentation beginning with Slide 1.

⑮ Save and then close **MergedPPS4-01**.

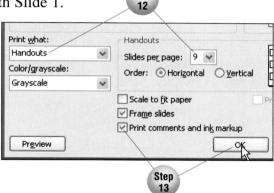

Step 12

Step 13

In Addition

Using the Reviewing Toolbar

The Reviewing toolbar contains buttons for working with comments including the Insert Comment, Delete Comment, and Edit Comment buttons. These buttons, along with the other buttons on the Reviewing toolbar, are named below.

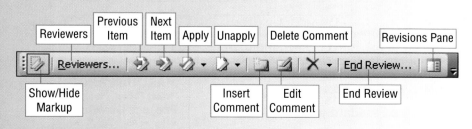

IN BRIEF

Insert Comment
1 Click in desired location in slide.
2 Click Insert, Comment.
3 Type comment in comment box.

Print Comments
1 Click File, Print.
2 Make sure *Print comments and ink markup* check box contains a check mark.
3 Click OK.

4.9 Saving a Presentation in Outline/RTF Format; Using the Package for CD Feature

With the *Save as type* option at the Save As dialog box, you can save a presentation in a different format such as a Web page, a previous version of PowerPoint, a design template, and as an outline in rich text format (Outline/RTF). The safest way to transport a PowerPoint presentation to another computer is to use the Package for CD feature. With this feature, you can copy a presentation including all of the linked files, fonts used, and PowerPoint Viewer program in case the destination computer does not have PowerPoint installed on it onto a CD or to a folder or network location.

PROJECT: You will be presenting the documentary project presentation in a variety of locations so you decide to save the presentation in Outline/RTF format and also using the Package for CD feature.

S T E P S

① Open **PPS4-01** and then save the presentation as a Word outline in rich text format. To begin, click File and then Save As.

② At the Save As dialog box, type **ProjectOutline** in the *File name* text box.

③ Click the down-pointing arrow at the right side of the *Save as type* option box and then click *Outline/RTF (*.rtf)* at the drop-down list. (You will need to scroll to the end of the list to display this option.)

> When you save a presentation using the *Outline/RTF* option, the presentation is saved in Word in the rich text format. In this format, the presentation loses graphical elements but retains the character formatting of the presentation.

④ Click the Save button.

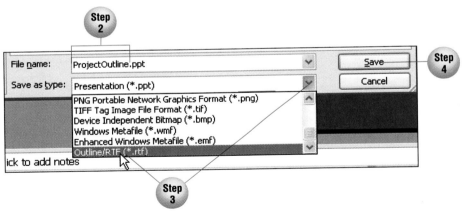

⑤ Open Microsoft Word and then click the Open button to display the Open dialog box.

⑥ Change the *Files of type* option to *All Files (*.*)* and then double-click the document named ***ProjectOutline.rtf*** located in the PowerPointS4 folder on your disk.

PROBLEM **?** If the **ProjectOutline.rtf** document does not display, make sure you navigated to the correct folder and that the *Files of type* option is changed to *All Files (*.*)*.

⑦ With the **ProjectOutline.rtf** document open, click the Print button on the Standard toolbar.

⑧ Close the **ProjectOutlinel.rtf** document and then exit Word.

⑨ With **PPS4-01** displayed, use the Package for CD feature. To begin click File and then Package for CD.

⑩ At the Package for CD dialog box, type **PackagedDocPres** in the *Name the CD* text box and then click the Options button.

⑪ At the Options dialog box, remove the check mark from the *PowerPoint Viewer* check box. Make sure the *Linked files* option contains a check mark. Insert a check mark in the *Embedded TrueType fonts* check box and then click OK to close the Options dialog box.

⑫ At the Package for CD dialog box, click the Copy to Folder button.

⑬ At the Copy to Folder dialog box, click the Browse button. Navigate to the PowerPointS4 folder on your disk in drive A, and then click the Select button.

⑭ At the Copy to Folder dialog box, click OK.

⑮ After the presentation is saved, close the Package for CD dialog box by clicking the Close button.

> The Package for CD feature saved the presentation in a folder named PackagedDocPres in the PowerPointS4 folder on your disk.

⑯ Close **PPS4-01**.

In Addition

Customizing the Package for CD Feature

Click the Options button at the Package for CD dialog box and the Options dialog box displays as shown below. Insert a check mark in the check box for those features you want to be included on the CD or in the folder or remove the check mark from those you do not want to include. If the computer you will be using does not contain the PowerPoint program, insert a check mark in the *PowerPoint Viewer* check box. The PowerPoint Viewer allows you to run a presentation on a computer that does not contain PowerPoint. If charts or other files are linked to the presentation, insert a check mark in the *Linked files* check box and, if the destination computer does not have the same fonts installed, insert a check mark in the *Embedded TrueType fonts* check box.

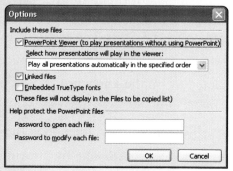

In BRIEF

Save Presentation in Outline/RTF Format
1. Display Save As dialog box.
2. Type name for file.
3. Change *Save as type* option to *Outline/RTF (*.rtf)*.
4. Click Save button.

Use Package for CD Feature
1. Click File, Package for CD.
2. Type name.
3. Click Options button.
4. Make desired changes at Options dialog box.
5. Click OK.
6. Click Copy to Folder button.
7. Click Browse button.
8. Navigate to desired folder.
9. Click Select button.
10. Click OK.

4.10 Creating a Folder; Customizing Templates

In PowerPoint, presentations can be grouped logically and stored in folders. A folder can be created within a folder (called a *subfolder*). For example, if you create presentations for a department by individual, each individual could have a subfolder name within the department folder. Each PowerPoint presentation is based on a template. The Slide Design task pane offers a number of design templates that apply specific formatting to slides in a presentation. If you customize a design template and then decide you want to use the customized template in the future, save it as a template. To save a customized design as a design template,

click File and then Save As. At the Save As dialog box, type a name for the template, click the down-pointing arrow at the right side of the *Save as type* option box, and then click *Design Template* at the drop-down list. Specify the location where you want the design template saved and then click the Save button.

PROJECT: Shannon Grey, the president of Marquee Productions, has requested that all company presentations contain the same formatting. You decide to create a template from an existing presentation that you can use to apply to other presentations and save the template in a new folder.

STEPS

1. At the blank PowerPoint screen, click the Open button on the Standard toolbar. Make sure that the PowerPointS4 folder on your disk is the active folder.

2. Create a new folder by clicking the Create New Folder button on the Open dialog box toolbar.

3. At the New Folder dialog box, type MarqueeTemplate and then click OK.

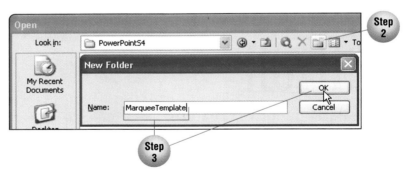

4. Click the Up One Level button on the Open dialog box toolbar to return to the PowerPointS4 folder and then click the Cancel button to close the Open dialog box.

5. Open the presentation **MPToronto** located in the PowerPointS4 folder on your disk.

6. Use the design template formatting to create a template document. To begin, make sure Slide 1 is selected in the Outline/Slides pane (with the Slides tab selected), hold down the Shift key, and then click Slide 7.

   This selects all of the slides in the presentation.

7. Press the Delete key on the keyboard.

   This deletes all of the slides in the presentation.

8. Click the New Slide button and then click the Blank slide layout.

9. Save the slide as a design template by clicking File and then Save As.

10 At the Save As dialog box, type MarqueeDesignTemplate in the *File name* text box. Click the down-pointing arrow at the right of the *Save as type* option and then click *Design Template (*.pot)*.

11 Change the *Save in* option to the MarqueeTemplate folder in the PowerPointS4 folder on your disk and then click the Save button.

12 Close the **MarqueeDesignTemplate** presentation.

13 Open the **MPProject** presentation located in the PowerPointS4 folder on your disk.

14 Apply the MarqueeDesignTemplate. To begin, click the Slide Design button.

15 At the Slide Design task pane, click the Browse hyperlink located at the bottom of the task pane.

16 At the Apply Design Template dialog box, navigate to the MarqueeTemplate folder in the PowerPointS4 folder on your disk and then double-click *MarqueeDesignTemplate* in the list box.

17 Save the presentation with Save As and name it **PPS4-02**.

18 Print the presentation as handouts with all eight slides on one page.

19 Close **PPS4-02**.

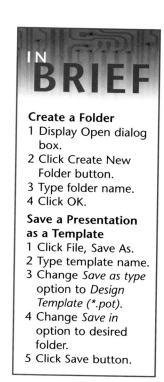

Step 10

| File name: | MarqueeDesignTemplate.ppt |
| Save as type: | Presentation (*.ppt) |

Presentation for Review (*.ppt)
Design Template (*.pot)
PowerPoint Show (*.pps)
PowerPoint Add-In (*.ppa)
GIF Graphics Interchange Format (*.gif)
JPEG File Interchange Format (*.jpg)

Design Templates on Microsoft Office Online

Browse...

Step 15

Apply Design Template

Look in: MarqueeTemplate

My Recent Documents

MarqueeDesignTemplate.pot

Step 16

In Addition

Maintaining Presentation Files

When you have been working with PowerPoint for a period of time, you will have accumulated a number of presentation files. These files should be organized into folders to facilitate fast retrieval of information. Occasionally you should perform file maintenance activities such as copying, moving, renaming, and deleting presentation files to ensure the presentations in your various folders are manageable. Many file management tasks can be completed at the Open dialog box (and some at the Save As dialog box). These tasks can include creating a new folder; copying, moving, printing, and renaming presentation files; and opening and closing multiple presentations.

IN BRIEF

Create a Folder
1 Display Open dialog box.
2 Click Create New Folder button.
3 Type folder name.
4 Click OK.

Save a Presentation as a Template
1 Click File, Save As.
2 Type template name.
3 Change *Save as type* option to *Design Template (*.pot)*.
4 Change *Save in* option to desired folder.
5 Click Save button.

4.11 Publishing a Presentation to the Web

In Section 3, you learned how to save a presentation as a Web page. If you click the Publish button at the Save As dialog box, the Publish as Web Page dialog box displays. At this dialog box, you can identify specific slides for publishing, specify the starting and ending slide numbers, and identify the browser support. Include a title for the Web page with options at the Change Title dialog box. Display this dialog box by clicking the Change Title button at the Save As dialog box.

PROJECT: You want to make the first four slides of the documentary project presentation available to others in the company so you decide to publish it to the Web.

S T E P S

1. Open **PPS4-01**.

2. Publish the presentation to the Web. To begin, click File and then Save As Web Page.

3. At the Save As dialog box, click the Change Title button.

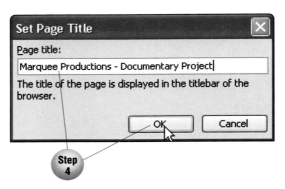

4. At the Set Page Title dialog box, type **Marquee Productions – Documentary Project** in the *Page title* text box and then click OK.

5. At the Save As dialog box, click the Publish button.

6. At the Publish as Web Page dialog box, choose the target browser in the *Browser support* section that applies to your school.

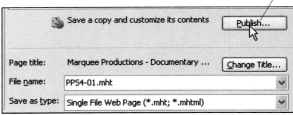

> Check with your instructor if you are not sure which target browser you should be using. The default selection is Microsoft Internet Explorer 4.0 or later.

7. Click the *Slide number* option and then click the down-pointing arrow at the right of the *Through* option box until *4* displays.

8 Click the Browse button next to the *File name* text box.

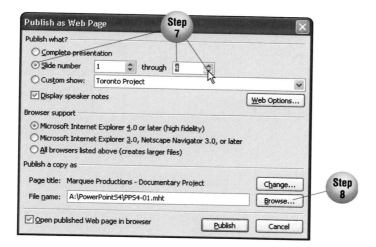

9 At the Publish As dialog box, make sure PowerPointS4 is the active folder, type WebPPS4-01 in the *File name* text box, and then click OK.

10 At the Publish as Web Page dialog box, click the *Open published Web page in browser* check box to insert a check mark and then click the Publish button.

In a few moments, the conversion will be complete and the Microsoft Internet Explorer or other default browser window will open with the opening page of the presentation displayed.

11 Navigate through the presentation by clicking the slide titles along the left frame, or using the Next Slide and Previous Slide navigation buttons along the bottom of the window. When you have finished viewing all of the slides, close the Internet Explorer or other browser window.

The title you typed for the Web page may not display in the browser title bar. To display the title, open your browser, and then open the **WebPPS4-01** file (see In Addition below).

12 Close **PPS4-01** without saving the changes.

In Addition

Opening a Presentation Using Internet Explorer

In Internet Explorer, you can open a presentation saved as a Web page. To do this, double-click the *Internet Explorer* icon on your desktop. When the Internet Explorer window opens, click File on the Menu bar and then click Open at the drop-down menu. At the Open dialog box, click the Browse button. At the Microsoft Internet Explorer dialog box, navigate to the folder containing the presentation you want to open, and then double-click the presentation in the list box.

FEATURES SUMMARY

Feature	Button	Menu
Choose Files to Merge with Current Presentation dialog box		Tools, Compare and Merge Presentations
Custom Shows dialog box		Slide Show, Custom Shows
Display rulers		View, Ruler
Insert comment		Insert, Comment
Insert Movie dialog box		Insert, Movies and Sounds, Movie from File
Insert Sound dialog box		Insert, Movies and Sounds, Sound from File
New Folder dialog box		
Options dialog box		Tools, Options
Package for CD dialog box		File, Package for CD
Publish presentation to the Web		File, Save as Web page
Rehearsal toolbar		Slide Show, Rehearse Timings
Save presentation as template		Display Save As dialog box, change *Save as type* option to *Design Template (*.pot)*, change *Save in* option to desired folder, click Save button
Save presentation for review		Display Save As dialog box, change *Save as type* option to *Presentation for Review*, click Save button.
Save presentation in Outline/RTF format		Display Save As dialog box, change *Save as type* option to *Outline/RTF*, click Save button
Set Up Show dialog box		Slide Show, Set Up Show
Tables and Borders toolbar		View, Toolbar, Tables and Borders

PROCEDURES CHECK

Completion: In the space provided at the right, indicate the correct term, symbol, or command.

1. If more than one slide design is applied to a presentation, holding down the Shift key and then clicking the Normal View button causes these pairs to display at the left side of the window. _____

2. Display the Custom Shows dialog box by clicking this option on the Menu bar and then clicking Custom Shows. _____

3. Run a custom show by clicking this button at the Custom Shows dialog box. _____

4. Customize a table in a slide using buttons on this toolbar. _____

5. Display the Insert Movie dialog box by clicking Insert, pointing to this option, and then clicking Movie from File. _____

6. Save a presentation for review by clicking the down-pointing arrow at the right side of the *Save as type* option in the Save As dialog box and then clicking this option. _____

7. Display the Choose Files to Merge with Current Presentation dialog box by clicking Tools and then clicking this option. _____

8. When the desired time displays on the Rehearsal toolbar, click this button on the Rehearsal toolbar to display the next slide. _____

9. Click this button on the Rehearsal toolbar to reset the clock back to zero for the current slide. _____

10. Use this feature to copy a presentation including all linked files, fonts, and the PowerPoint Viewer program in case the destination computer does not have PowerPoint installed. _____

11. Click this button on the Open dialog box toolbar to display the New Folder dialog box. _____

12. To save a presentation as a design template, change the *Save as type* option to this at the Save As dialog box. _____

SKILLS REVIEW

(Note: Before beginning the Skills Review activities, delete the following presentations from your disk: MergedPPS4-01, PPS4-01, PPS4-02, PresentationEditedbyAE, PresentationEditedbyJH, and WebPPS4-01.)

Activity 1: APPLYING SLIDE DESIGNS

1. Open **NPCTheatreArts** and then save the presentation with Save As and name it **PPS4-R1**.
2. Click the Slide Design button on the Formatting toolbar and then click the <u>Color Schemes</u> hyperlink that displays toward the top of the Slide Design task pane.

3   Click the color scheme with the blue-gray background in the *Apply a color scheme* section of the task pane.
4   Delete Slides 3 and 4.
5   Open **NPCPlacementServices** and make sure the presentation displays in Normal view with the Slides tab selected in the Outline/Slides pane.
6   With the first slide selected in the Outline/Slides pane, hold down the Shift key, and then click the last slide (Slide 4).
7   Click the Copy button on the Formatting toolbar.
8   Click the button on the Taskbar representing **PPS4-R1**.
9   Click below the last slide in the Outline/Slides pane with the Slides tab selected and then click the Paste button. (This pastes the four slides in the **PPS4-R1** presentation.)
10 Click the button on the Taskbar representing **NPCPlacementServices** and then close the presentation. (This displays the **PPS4-R1** presentation.)
11 Make sure Slides 7 through 10 are selected. (If they are not, click Slide 7, hold down the Shift key, and then click Slide 10.)
12 Click the Design Templates hyperlink located toward the top of the Slide Design task pane and then click the Curtain Call design in the *Apply a design template* section of the task pane.
13 Click the Color Schemes hyperlink and then click the color scheme with a white background.
14 Save **PPS4-R1**.

Activity 2: MANAGING SLIDE MASTERS

1   With **PPS4-R1** open, hold down the Shift key and then click the Normal View button on the View toolbar. (This displays the slide-title master pairs.)
2   Click the Romanesque Slide Master miniature (top miniature).
3   Click anywhere in the text *Click to edit Master title style* and then change the font color to light gray (the light gray color that follows the color scheme).
4   Click the Curtain Call Slide Master miniature (third from the top).
5   Click anywhere in the text *Click to edit Master title style* and then change the font to Times New Roman.
6   Select all of the bulleted text in the master slide and then change the font to Times New Roman.
7   Click the Normal View button on the View toolbar.
8   Save **PPS4-R1**.

Activity 3: CREATING A CUSTOM SHOW

1   With **PPS4-R1** open, click Slide Show and then Custom Shows.
2   At the Custom Shows dialog box, click the New button.
3   At the Define Custom Show dialog box, create a custom show named Placement Services that contains Slides 7 through 10.
4   Run the custom show.
5   Print the custom show.

Activity 4: CREATING AND CUSTOMIZING A TABLE

1 With **PPS4-R1** open, insert a new slide between Slides 5 and 6 using the Title and Content slide layout. (If necessary, change the color scheme to the blue-gray background.)
2 At the new slide (Slide 6), click the text *Click to add title* and then type Drama Productions.
3 Click the Insert Table button in the Content placeholder and then create a table with two columns and five rows.
4 Type the following text in the cells in the table:

Production	Dates
Extreme Velocity	October 16–25
Aidan's Requiem	December 8–17
Calling All Candidates	February 12–21
Esprit	April 18–27

5 Turn on the display of the horizontal and vertical rulers.
6 Click in the first cell.
7 Drag the right border of the table to approximately the 7-inch mark on the horizontal ruler.
8 Drag the table so it is centered on the slide.
9 Select all cells in the table.
10 Change the border width to *3 pt* and change the border color to gold.
11 Click the down-pointing arrow at the right side of the Outside Borders button on the Tables and Borders toolbar and then click the All Borders button.
12 Click outside the table to deselect it.
13 Turn off the display of the horizontal and vertical rulers.
14 Save **PPS4-R1**.

Activity 5: INSERTING A SOUND FILE

1 With **PPS4-R1** open, make Slide 11 the active slide (this is the last slide in the presentation).
2 Click Insert, point to Movies and Sounds, and then click Sound from File.
3 At the Insert Sound dialog box, navigate to the SoundandVideo folder on the CD that accompanies this textbook, and then double-click the sound file named *SoundClip.mid*. At the message asking how you want to play the sound, click the When Clicked button.
4 Move the sound icon to the lower left corner of the slide.
5 Make Slide 1 the active slide and then run the presentation. When the last slide displays (Slide 11), click the sound icon to play the sound. After listening to the sound for about 30 seconds, press the Esc key to end the presentation.
6 Print the presentation as handouts with six slides per page.
7 Save **PPS4-R1**.

Activity 6: SENDING A PRESENTATION FOR REVIEW; EDITING A PRESENTATION SENT FOR REVIEW

1 With **PPS4-R1** open, save the presentation for review by Rhonda Goldman and name the presentation **PresEditedbyRG**.
2 Save the presentation for review by Louis Michaud and name the presentation **PresEditedbyLM**.

3 Close **PPS4-R1**.
4 Display the Options dialog box with the General tab selected, change the *Name* to *Rhonda Goldman*, change the *Initials* to *RG*, and then close the dialog box.
5 Open **PresEditedbyRG** and then click No at the message that displays.
6 Make the following changes:
   • Make Slide 3 active and then change *$200* to *$250*.
   • Make Slide 7 active and then change the telephone number for the Academic Advising Department to *(905) 555-2280*.
7 Save and then close **PresEditedbyRG**.
8 Display the Options dialog box with the General tab selected, change the *Name* to *Louis Michaud*, change the *Initials* to *LM*, and then close the dialog box.
9 Open **PresEditedbyLM** and then click No at the message that displays.
10 Make the following changes:
   • Make Slide 9 active, select *Tutoring Position*, and then type **Cooperative Work Experience**.
   • Make Slide 10 active and then insert the new bulleted item *Film Editing Studio* at the end of the bulleted list.
11 Save and then close **PresEditedbyLM**.
12 Display the Options dialog box with the General tab selected, change the name and initials back to the original information, and then close the dialog box.

Activity 7: ACCEPTING/REJECTING CHANGES FROM REVIEWERS

1 Open **PPS4-R1**.
2 Click Tools and then Compare and Merge Presentations. At the Choose Files to Merge with Current Presentation dialog box, select ***PresEditedbyLM*** and ***PresEditedbyRG*** and then click the Merge button.
3 Accept or reject changes as follows:
   • Do not accept the change made to Slide 3.
   • Accept all of the changes made to Slide 7.
   • Accept all of the changes made to Slide 9.
   • Do not accept the change made to Slide 10.
4 Click the Markup button on the Reviewing toolbar and then turn off the display of the Reviewing toolbar and the Revisions pane.
5 Save the presentation with Save As and name it **MergedPPS4-R1**.
6 Print the presentation as handouts with six slides per page.

Activity 8: SETTING AND REHEARSING TIMINGS

1 With **MergedPPS4-R1** open, click Slide Show and then Rehearse Timings.
2 Record 5 seconds for each slide in the presentation.
3 After the last slide has displayed, click Yes at the message asking if you want to record the new slide timings.
4 Set up the slide show to run continuously.
5 Display the Slide Transition task pane and then apply a transition of your choosing to all slides in the presentation.
6 Make Slide 1 active and then run the presentation. After viewing the presentation at least once, press the Esc key.

7 Print the presentation as handouts with six slides per page.
8 Save and then close **MergedPPS4-R1**.

PERFORMANCE PLUS

(Note: Before completing the Performance Plus activities, delete the following presentations: MergedPPS4-R1, PresEditedbyLM, PresEditedbyRG, and PPS4-R1.)

Assessment 1: APPLYING DESIGNS

1 Open **FCTVacations**.
2 Save the presentation with Save As and name it **PPS4-P1**.
3 Create a new slide between Slides 5 and 6 (the new slide is Slide 6) and include the following information:

Title   =   **Snow Skiing Packages**

Bulleted items   =   • **Sun Valley – 3 days, 2 nights at the Alpine Village Lodge starting at $239**
                                • **Vail – 5 days, 4 nights at the Vail Ski Lodge starting at $399**
                                • **Whistler – 7 days, 6 nights at the Wilderness Ridge Lodge starting at $859**

4 Select Slides 5 through 7 and then apply the *Mountain Top* slide design and change to the color scheme with a white background.
5 Save **PPS4-P1**.

Assessment 2: MANAGING MULTIPLE SLIDE MASTERS

1 With **PPS4-P1** open, display the slide-title master pairs, and then click the Japanese Waves Slide Master (top miniature).
2 Click anywhere in the text *Click to edit Master title style* and then change the font to *Arial* and the font size to *48*.
3 Select all of the bulleted text in the slide master and then change the font to *Arial*.
4 Click the Japanese Waves Title Master (second miniature from the top).
5 Click anywhere in the text *Click to edit Master title style* and then change the font size to *54*.
6 Click anywhere in the text *Click to edit Master subtitle style* and then change the font size to *48*.
7 Click the Normal View button.
8 Save **PPS4-P1**.

Assessment 3: INSERTING A VIDEO CLIP

1 With **PPS4-P1** open, insert a new slide at the end of the presentation (Slide 8) and choose the Title Only slide layout. (If necessary, change the color scheme to the white background.)
2 Type **Let us plan a vacation for you that is out of this world!** as the slide title.

3 Insert the **Launch.mpeg** video clip that is located in the SoundandVideo folder on the CD that accompanies this textbook. Insert the video clip so it plays automatically when the slide displays.

4 Increase the size of the image and move the image so it is better centered on the slide.

5 Print the presentation as handouts with nine slides per page.

6 Make Slide 1 active and then run the presentation.

7 Save and then close **PPS4-P1**.

Assessment 4: INSERTING A SLIDE WITH THE SLIDE FINDER FEATURE

1 Use PowerPoint's Help feature to learn how to copy slides with the Slide Finder feature.

2 After reading the information, insert a slide from one presentation into another by completing these basic steps:

  • Open **PPS4-P1**.
  • Make Slide 4 active.
  • Using the information you learned in the Help files, insert Slide 4 from the **FCTCruise** presentation (located in the PowerPointS4 folder on your disk) into the current slide. (The inserted slide becomes Slide 5. Make sure you use the Slide Finder feature to do this.)
  • Check the inserted slide and make any necessary minor adjustments.

3 Make Slide 1 active and then run the presentation.

4 Print the presentation as handouts with nine slides per page.

5 Save and then close **PPS4-P1**.

Assessment 5: SEARCHING FOR SOUND CLIPS ONLINE

1 Open **PPS4-P1** and then make Slide 9 the active slide.

2 Click Insert, point to Movies and Sound, and then click Sound from Clip Organizer. (This displays the Clip Art task pane.)

3 Click the <u>Clip art on Office Online</u> hyperlink located toward the bottom of the Clip Art task pane.

4 At the Microsoft Office Online Web site, change the *Search* option to *Sounds*, type **songs**, and then press Enter. When a list of songs displays, download a song that interests you and then insert the song in Slide 9.

5 Make Slide 1 active and then run the presentation, playing the sound clip in Slide 9.

6 Save and then close **PPS4-P1**.

INTEGRATED 3
Integrating Word, Excel, and PowerPoint

Microsoft Office is popular with businesses because it allows data from one program to seamlessly integrate into another program. Integration is the process of completing a document by adding parts to it from other sources. Because of integration features offered by programs in the Office suite, duplication of data should rarely occur. For example, using the Send To option from the File drop-down menu, you can export data from a PowerPoint presentation to a Word document and from a Word outline document to a PowerPoint presentation. Integration also occurs when data is linked. Link data between programs if you want to update the data in either the source or the destination program. Changes made to the object in one program are reflected in the object in the other program. Embed an object if you want to edit the object in the destination program using tools from the source program. In this section, you will learn the following skills and complete the projects described here.

 Note: Before beginning this section, copy to a disk the Integrated03 subfolder from the Integrated folder on the CD that accompanies this textbook and then make Integrated03 the active folder.

Skills

- Export a PowerPoint presentation to a Word document
- Export a Word outline document to a PowerPoint presentation
- Link an Excel chart with a Word document and a PowerPoint presentation
- Edit a linked object
- Embed a Word table in a PowerPoint presentation
- Edit an embedded object

Projects

MARQUEE PRODUCTIONS — Create and format a Word document containing information on the annual meeting using data in a PowerPoint presentation.

 Prepare a presentation for the Distribution Department of Worldwide Enterprises using a Word outline; copy an Excel chart and link it to the Distribution Department meeting presentation and to a Word document and then edit the linked chart; copy a Word table containing data on preview distribution dates, embed it in a PowerPoint slide, and then update the table.

FIRST CHOICE Travel — Export a PowerPoint presentation containing information on vacation specials offered by First Choice Travel to a Word document.

Niagara Peninsula COLLEGE — Export a Word outline document containing information on the Theatre Arts Division to a PowerPoint presentation; link an Excel chart containing information on department enrollments to a PowerPoint slide and then update the chart in Excel; embed a Word table in a PowerPoint slide and then edit the table in the slide.

I-3.1 Exporting a PowerPoint Presentation to Word

You can send data in one program to another program. For example, you can send Word data to a PowerPoint presentation and data in a PowerPoint presentation to a Word document. To send presentation data to Word, open the presentation, click File, point to Send To, and then click Microsoft Office Word. At the Send To Microsoft Office Word dialog box that displays, specify the layout of the data in the Word document, and then click OK. One of the advantages of sending presentation data to a Word document is that you can have greater control over the formatting of the data in Word.

PROJECT: Create and format a Word document containing information on the annual meeting for Marquee Productions from data in a PowerPoint presentation.

STEPS

1. Make sure both Word and PowerPoint are open.

2. With PowerPoint the active program, open the presentation named **MPAnnualMeeting**.

3. Send the PowerPoint data to Word by clicking File, pointing to Send To, and then clicking Microsoft Office Word.

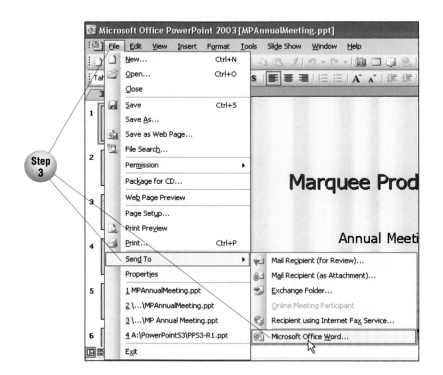

④ At the Send To Microsoft Office Word dialog box, click the *Outline only* option.

⑤ Click OK to close the dialog box.

> In a few moments, a Word document will display on the screen containing the presentation data.

⑥ Select the subtitle *Annual Meeting*, click the down-pointing arrow at the right side of the Font Size button on the Formatting toolbar, and then click *22* at the drop-down list.

⑦ The outline should flow to a second page. Check the page break in the document and, if the default page break is in an undesirable location, insert your own page break by pressing Ctrl + Enter.

PROBLEM ?
> If the default page break displays between a heading and text that follows the heading, insert your own page break at the beginning of the heading.

⑧ Save the Word document and name it **IntW3-01**.

> Make sure you save the document in the Integrated03 folder on your disk. Microsoft Office may create the Word document in a temporary folder. If this is the case, display the appropriate folder and then save the Word document.

⑨ Print and then close **IntW3-01**.

⑩ Click the button on the Taskbar representing the PowerPoint presentation **MPAnnualMeeting**.

⑪ Close the presentation.

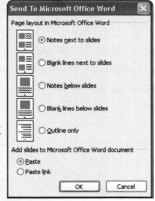

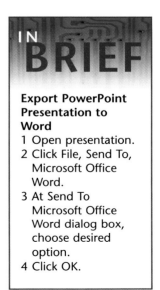

In Addition

Pasting and Linking Data

The *Paste* option at the Send To Microsoft Office Word dialog box shown at the right is selected by default and is available for all of the page layout options. With this option selected, the data inserted in Word is not connected or linked to the original data in the PowerPoint presentation. If you plan to update the data in the presentation and want the data updated in the Word document, select the *Paste link* option at the Send To Microsoft Office Word dialog box. This option is available for all of the page layout options except the *Outline only* option.

IN BRIEF

Export PowerPoint Presentation to Word
1 Open presentation.
2 Click File, Send To, Microsoft Office Word.
3 At Send To Microsoft Office Word dialog box, choose desired option.
4 Click OK.

I-3.2 Exporting a Word Outline to a PowerPoint Presentation

As you learned in the previous section, you can send data in one program to another program. For example, you can send Word data to a PowerPoint presentation and data in a PowerPoint presentation to a Word document. You can create text for slides in a Word outline and then export that outline to PowerPoint. PowerPoint creates new slides based on the heading styles used in the Word outline. Paragraphs formatted with a Heading 1 style become slide titles. Heading 2 text becomes first-level bulleted text, Heading 3 text becomes second-level bulleted text, and so on. If styles are not applied to outline text in Word, PowerPoint uses tabs or indents to place text on slides.

PROJECT: Prepare a presentation for the Distribution Department of Worldwide Enterprises using a Word outline.

STEPS

1. Make sure both Word and PowerPoint are open.

2. With Word the active program, open the document named **WEOutline**.

   Text in this document has been formatted with the Heading 1 and Heading 2 styles.

3. Export the outline to PowerPoint by clicking File, pointing to Send To, and then clicking Microsoft Office PowerPoint.

   PROBLEM? If the presentation does not display on the screen, click the button on the Taskbar representing PowerPoint.

4. When the presentation displays on the screen, make sure Normal view is selected, and Slide 1 is the active slide.

   The presentation is created with a blank design template.

5. Display the Slide Layout task pane by clicking Format and then Slide Layout.

6. Click the Title Slide layout in the Slide Layout task pane.

7. Make Slide 4 the active slide and then click the Title Only slide layout in the Slide Layout task pane.

8. Make Slide 5 the active slide and then click the Title Only slide layout.

9. Make Slide 6 the active slide and then click the Title Only slide layout.

10. Apply a slide design template by clicking the Slide Design button on the Formatting toolbar.

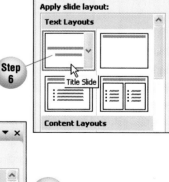

Step 6

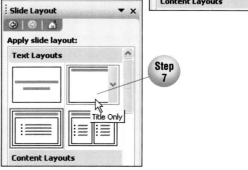

Step 7

⑪ Click the Globe slide design in the Slide Design task pane.

> You will need to scroll down the *Apply a design template* list box to display the Globe design.

⑫ Save the presentation and name it **IntP3-01**.

⑬ Close **IntP3-01**.

⑭ Click the button on the Taskbar representing the Word document WEOutline and then close **WEOutline**.

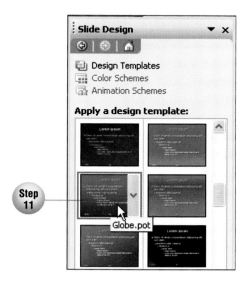

Step 11

In Addition

Applying a Style in Word

Heading styles were already applied to the text in the WEOutline Word document. If you create an outline in Word that you want to export to PowerPoint, apply styles using the Style button on the Formatting toolbar. To apply a heading style, select the desired text in the Word document and then click the down-pointing arrow at the right side of the Style button. This causes a drop-down menu to display as shown at the right that contains preformatted style headings. The drop-down list displays the names of the available styles and also applies the style formatting to the style name. Click the desired style at this drop-down list.

IN BRIEF

Export Word Outline to PowerPoint Presentation
1 Open Word outline document.
2 Click File, Send To, Microsoft Office PowerPoint.

I-3.3 Linking an Excel Chart with a Word Document and a PowerPoint Presentation

You can copy and link an object such as a table or chart to documents in other programs. For example, you can copy an Excel chart and link it to a Word document and/or a PowerPoint presentation. The advantage to copying and linking over just copying and pasting is that you can edit the object in the originating program, called the *source* program, and the object is updated in the linked documents in the *destination* programs. When an object is linked, the object exists in the source program but not as a separate object in the destination program. Since the object is located only in the source program, changes made to the object in the source program are reflected in the destination program.

PROJECT: Copy an Excel chart and link it to the Worldwide Enterprises Distribution Department meeting presentation and to a Word document.

STEPS

1. Make sure Word, Excel, and PowerPoint are open.

2. Make Word the active program and then open the document named **WERevDocument**. Save the document with Save As and name it **IntW3-02**.

3. Make PowerPoint the active program, open the presentation named **IntP3-01**, and then make Slide 6 the active slide.

4. Make Excel the active program and then open the worksheet named **WERevChart**. Save the worksheet with Save As and name it ***IntE3-01.***

5. Copy and link the chart to the Word document and the PowerPoint presentation by clicking once in the chart to select it.

   Make sure you select the chart and not a specific chart element. Try selecting the chart by clicking just inside the chart border.

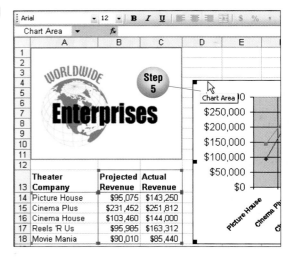

6. With the chart selected, click the Copy button on the Standard toolbar.

7. Click the button on the Taskbar representing the Word document **IntW3-02**.

8. Press Ctrl + End to move the insertion point to the end of the document, click Edit, and then click Paste Special.

9. At the Paste Special dialog box, click the *Paste link* option, make sure *Microsoft Office Excel Chart Object* is selected in the *As* list box, and then click OK.

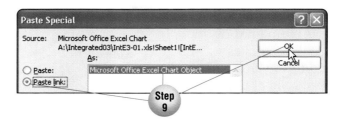

10. Make sure the chart is centered below the subtitle *Projected/Actual Revenues*.

11. Save, print, and then close **IntW3-02**.

12. Click the button on the Taskbar representing the PowerPoint presentation **IntP3-01**.

13. With Slide 6 the active slide, click Edit and then Paste Special.

14. At the Paste Special dialog box, click the *Paste link* option, make sure *Microsoft Office Excel Chart Object* is selected in the *As* list box, and then click OK.

15. Increase the size of the chart so it better fills the slide and then move the chart so it is centered on the slide.

16. Click outside the chart to deselect it.

17. Save the presentation with the same name (**IntP3-01**), print only Slide 6, and then close **IntP3-01**.

18. Click the button on the Taskbar representing the Excel worksheet **IntE3-01**. At the worksheet, click outside the chart to deselect it.

19. Save, print, and then close **IntE3-01**.

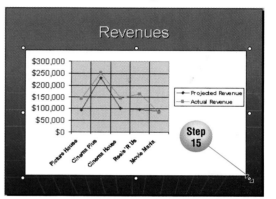

In Addition

Linking Data or an Object within a Program

In this section, you learned to link an object between programs using the Paste Special dialog box. You can also link an object using options at the Insert Object dialog box. To do this, click Insert and then Object. At the Insert Object dialog box, click the *Create from file* option. At the Insert Object dialog box with the *Create from file* option selected as shown below, type the desired file name in the *File* text box or click the Browse button and then select the desired file from the appropriate folder. At the Insert Object dialog box, click the *Link* check box to insert a check mark, and then click OK.

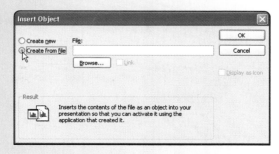

IN BRIEF

Link an Object between Programs
1 Open source program and open file containing object.
2 Select object and then click Copy button.
3 Open destination program and then open file into which object will be linked.
4 Click Edit, Paste Special.
5 At Paste Special dialog box, click *Paste link*, and then click OK.

I-3.4 Editing a Linked Object

The advantage of linking an object over copying data is that editing the object in the source program will automatically update the object in the destination program(s). To edit a linked object, open the document containing the object in the source program, make the desired edits, and then save the document. The next time you open the document, worksheet, or presentation in the destination program, the object is updated.

PROJECT: Edit the actual and projected revenue numbers in the Worldwide Enterprises Excel worksheet and then open and print the Word document and PowerPoint presentation containing the linked chart.

STEPS

1. Make sure the Word, Excel, and PowerPoint programs are open.

2. Make Excel the active program and then open the worksheet named **IntE3-01**.

3. You discover that one theater company was left out of the revenues chart. Add a row to the worksheet by clicking once in cell A15 to make it the active cell. Click Insert and then Rows.

4. Insert the following data in the specified cells:

    A15 = **Regal Theaters**
    B15 = 69,550
    C15 = 60,320

5. Click in cell A12.

6. Save, print, and then close **IntE3-01**.

7. Make Word the active program and then open **IntW3-02**. At the message asking if you want to update the linked file, click the Yes button.

8. Notice how the linked chart is automatically updated to reflect the changes you made to the chart in Excel.

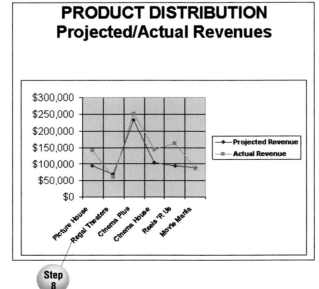

Step 8

9. Save, print, and then close **IntW3-02**.

10. Make PowerPoint the active program and then open **IntP3-01**.

11. At the message telling you that the presentation contains links, click the Update Links button.

12. Make Slide 6 the active slide and the notice how the linked chart is automatically updated to reflect the changes you made to the chart in Excel.

13. Save **IntP3-01**.

14. Print only Slide 6.

15. Close **IntP3-01**.

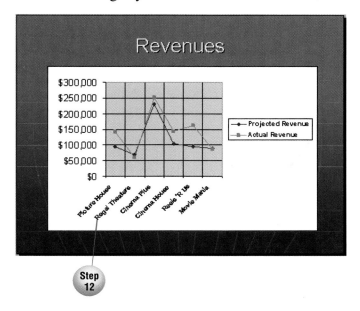

Step 12

In *Addition*

Updating a Link Manually

You can choose to update a link manually in the destination program. To do this, click Edit and then Links. This displays the Links dialog box shown at the right. Click the *Manual* option in the *Update* section located at the bottom of the dialog box and then click Close. When the Update setting is changed to *Manual*, a link is updated only when you display the Links dialog box, click the link in the *Links* list box, and then click the Update Now button.

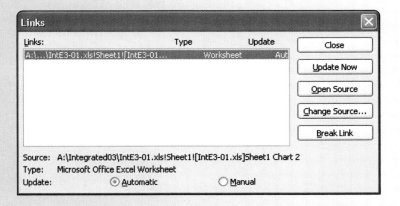

I-3.5 Embedding a Word Table in a PowerPoint Presentation

You can copy an object from one file and paste it into a file in another program or you can copy and link an object or copy and embed an object. A linked object resides in the source program but not as a separate object in the destination program. An embedded object resides in the document in the source program as well as the destination program. If you make a change to an embedded object at the source program, the change is not made to the object in the destination program. Since an embedded object is not automatically updated as is a linked object, the only advantage to embedding rather than simply copying and pasting is that you can edit an embedded object in the destination program using the tools of the source program.

PROJECT: Copy a Word table containing data on preview distribution dates for Worldwide Enterprises and then embed the table in a slide in a PowerPoint presentation.

S T E P S

1. Make sure the Word and PowerPoint programs are open.

2. Make PowerPoint the active program and then open **IntP3-01**.

3. At the message telling you the presentation contains links, click the Update Links button.

4. Make Slide 4 the active slide.

5. Make Word the active program and then open the document named **WETable01**.

6. Click inside the table, click Table, point to Select, and then click Table.

7. With the table selected, click the Copy button on the Standard toolbar.

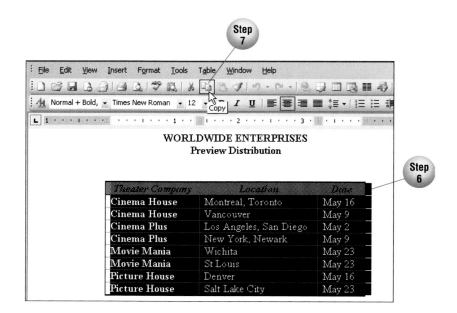

8. Click the button on the Taskbar representing the PowerPoint presentation **IntP3-01**.

9. With Slide 4 the active slide, click Edit and then Paste Special.

10. At the Paste Special dialog box, click *Microsoft Office Word Document Object* in the *As* list box and then click OK.

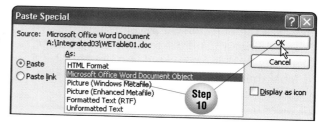

11. With the table selected in the slide, use the sizing handles to increase the size and change the position of the table as shown below.

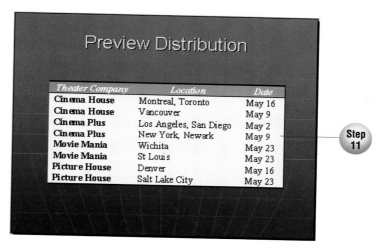

12. Click outside the table to deselect it.

13. Save **IntP3-01**.

14. Print Slide 4 of the presentation.

15. Click the button on the Taskbar representing the Word document **WETable01** and then close the document.

In Addition

Working with a Cropped Object

Some embedded or linked objects may appear cropped on the right or bottom side of the object even if enough room is available to fit the image on the page or slide. A large embedded or linked object may appear cropped because Word converts the object into a Windows metafile *(.wmf)*, which has a maximum height and width. If the embedded or linked object exceeds this maximum size, it appears cropped. To prevent an object from appearing cropped, consider reducing the size of the data by changing formatting such as reducing the font size, column size, line spacing, and so on.

IN BRIEF

Embed an Object
1. Open source program and open file containing object.
2. Select object and then click Copy button.
3. Open destination program and then open file into which object will be embedded.
4. Click Edit, Paste Special.
5. At Paste Special dialog box, make sure object is selected in *As* list box and then click OK.

Embedding and Editing a Word Table in a PowerPoint Presentation

You can edit an embedded object in the destination program using the tools of the source program. Double-click the object in the document in the destination program and the tools from the source program display. For example, if you double-click a Word table that is embedded in a PowerPoint slide, the Word Menu bar and Standard and Formatting toolbars display at the top of the screen.

PROJECT: Update the distribution dates for the two embedded tables in the Worldwide Enterprises Distribution Department meeting presentation.

STEPS

1. Make PowerPoint the active program and make sure the presentation named **IntP3-01** is open.

2. Make Slide 5 the active slide.

3. Make Word the active program and then open the document named **WETable02**.

4. Click once in the table, click Table, point to Select, and then click Table.

5. Click the Copy button on the Standard toolbar.

6. Click the button on the Taskbar representing the PowerPoint presentation **IntP3-01**.

7. With Slide 5 the active slide, click Edit and then Paste Special.

8. At the Paste Special dialog box, click *Microsoft Office Word Document Object* in the *As* list box, and then click OK.

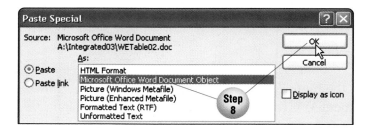

9. Increase the size and position of the table in the slide so it displays as shown below.

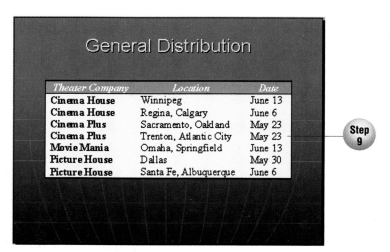

10 The distribution date to Cinema Plus in Sacramento and Oakland has been delayed until May 30. Edit the date by double-clicking the table in the slide.

> Double-clicking the table displays the Word Menu bar and Standard and Formatting toolbars at the top of the screen. A horizontal and vertical ruler also display around the table.

11 Using the mouse, select *23* after *May*, and then type *30*.

12 Click outside the table to deselect it.

> Clicking outside the table deselects it and also removes the Word Menu bar and Standard and Formatting toolbars.

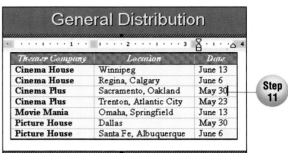

General Distribution

Theater Company	Location	Date
Cinema House	Winnipeg	June 13
Cinema House	Regina, Calgary	June 6
Cinema Plus	Sacramento, Oakland	May 30
Cinema Plus	Trenton, Atlantic City	May 23
Movie Mania	Omaha, Springfield	June 13
Picture House	Dallas	May 30
Picture House	Santa Fe, Albuquerque	June 6

Step 11

PROBLEM ? If the size of the table decreases, select the table and then use the sizing handles to increase the size.

13 Print Slide 5 of the presentation.

14 Apply an animation scheme of your choosing to all slides in the presentation.

15 Run the presentation.

16 Save and then close **IntP3-01**.

17 Click the button on the Taskbar representing the Word document **WETable02** and then close **WETable02**.

In Addition

Displaying an Embedded Object as an Icon

An embedded object displays in the destination program as it appears in the source program. You can embed an object as an icon in the destination program representing the object. Double-click the icon in the destination program and the object displays in the source program. After viewing the object, return to the destination program by clicking File and then Close and Return to *file name*.

In Brief

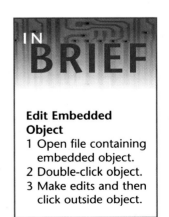

Edit Embedded Object
1 Open file containing embedded object.
2 Double-click object.
3 Make edits and then click outside object.

SKILLS REVIEW

Activity 1: EXPORTING A POWERPOINT PRESENTATION TO WORD

1. Make sure both Word and PowerPoint are open.
2. With PowerPoint the active program, open the presentation named **FCTVacations**.
3. Send the PowerPoint data to Word as an outline. (At the Send To Microsoft Office Word dialog box, click the *Outline only* option.)
4. At the Word document, select the entire document and then change the font to 12-point Times New Roman regular.
5. Select the title *First Choice Travel* and the subtitle *Vacation Specials* and then change the font to 18-point Times New Roman bold.
6. Select the heading *Ocean Vista Cruise Lines* and then change the font to 14-point Times New Roman bold.
7. Use Format Painter to paint the 14-point Times New Roman bold formatting onto the remaining headings: *Cruise Categories*, *Cruise Prices*, *Getaway Weekends*, and *First Choice Points*.
8. Move the insertion point immediately after the subtitle *Vacation Specials* and then press the Enter key. (This separates the subtitle from the first heading.)
9. Save the Word document in the appropriate folder and name it **IntW3-R1**. (You may need to change to the desired folder before saving the document.)
10. Print and then close **IntW3-R1**.
11. Click the button on the Taskbar representing the PowerPoint presentation **FCTVacations** and then close the presentation.

Activity 2: EXPORTING A WORD OUTLINE TO A POWERPOINT PRESENTATION

1. Make sure both Word and PowerPoint are open.
2. With Word the active program, open the document named **NPCOutline**.
3. Export the outline to PowerPoint.
4. In PowerPoint, make sure Normal view is selected and Slide 1 is the active slide.
5. Change the Slide 1 slide layout to Title Slide.
6. Make Slide 4 the active slide and then change the slide layout to Title Only.
7. Make Slide 5 the active slide and then change the slide layout to Title Only.
8. Apply the Edge slide design template. (If this template is not available, choose a different template.)
9. Save the presentation and name it **IntP3-R1**.
10. Click the button on the Taskbar representing the Word document **NPCOutline** and then close **NPCOutline**.

Activity 3: LINKING AND EDITING AN EXCEL CHART IN A POWERPOINT SLIDE

1. Make sure both Excel and PowerPoint are open.
2. Make PowerPoint the active program, make sure the presentation named **IntP3-R1** is open, and then make Slide 4 the active slide.

3   Make Excel the active program and then open the worksheet named **NPCChart01**. Save the worksheet with Save As and name it **IntE3-R1**.

4   Click the chart once to select it (make sure you select the entire chart and not a chart element) and then copy and link the chart to Slide 4 in the **IntP3-R1** PowerPoint presentation. (Be sure and use the Paste Special dialog box to link the chart.)

5   Increase the size of the chart so it better fills the slide and then move the chart so it is centered on the slide.

6   Click outside the chart to deselect it.

7   Save the presentation with the same name (**IntP3-R1**).

8   Print only Slide 4 of the presentation and then close **IntP3-R1**.

9   Click the button on the Taskbar representing the Excel worksheet **IntE3-R1**.

10 Click outside the chart to deselect it.

11 Save and then print **IntE3-R1**.

12 Insert another department in the worksheet (and chart) by making cell A7 active, clicking Insert, and then clicking Rows. (This creates a new row 7.) Type the following text in the specified cells:

    A7 = **Directing**
    B7 = **18**
    C7 = **32**
    D7 = **25**

13 Click in cell A4.

14 Save, print, and then close **IntE3-R1**.

15 Click the button on the Taskbar representing PowerPoint and then open **IntP3-R1**. At the message telling you that the presentation contains links, click the Update Links button. Display Slide 4 and then notice the change to the chart.

16 Save **IntP3-R1** and then print only Slide 4.

Activity 4: EMBEDDING AND EDITING A WORD TABLE IN A POWERPOINT SLIDE

1   Make sure Word and PowerPoint are open.

2   Make PowerPoint the active program, make sure **IntP3-R1** is open, and then make Slide 5 the active slide.

3   Make Word the active program and then open the document named **NPCContacts**.

4   Select the table and then copy and embed it in Slide 5 in the **IntP3-R1** presentation. (Make sure you use the Paste Special dialog box.)

5   With the table selected in the slide, use the sizing handles to increase the size and change the position of the table so it better fills the slide.

6   Click outside the table to deselect it and then save **IntP3-R1**.

7   Double-click the table, select *Editing* in the company name *Emerson Editing*, and then type **Edits**.

8   Click outside the table to deselect it.

9   Print Slide 5 of the presentation.

10 Apply an animation scheme of your choosing to all slides in the presentation.

11 Run the presentation.

12 Save and then close **IntP3-R1** and then exit PowerPoint.

13 Close the Word document **NPCContacts** and then exit Word.